MUSIC LESSONS

Pierre Boulez

MUSIC LESSONS

The Collège de France Lectures

Edited and translated by Jonathan Dunsby,
Jonathan Goldman and Arnold Whittall

FABER & FABER

First published in 2018
by Faber & Faber Limited
Bloomsbury House
74–77 Great Russell Street
London WC1B 3DA

Typeset by Ian Bahrami
Printed and bound by CPI Group (UK) Ltd, Croydon, CR0 4YY

Originally published in French as *Pierre Boulez, Leçons de musique (Points de repère, III): Deux décennies d'enseignement au Collège de France (1976–1995)*, edited by Jean-Jacques Nattiez and Jonathan Goldman, Christian Bourgois éditeur, Paris, 2005

Supported by the Irène Deliège Translation Fund, managed by the
King Baudouin Foundation, Brussels

King Baudouin
Foundation
Working together for a better society

A CIP record for this book
is available from the British Library

ISBN 978-0-571-33427-8

2 4 6 8 10 9 7 5 3 1

Contents

Preface by Jonathan Goldman   vii

Pierre Boulez, Lecturer   xxiii
by Jean-Jacques Nattiez

Part 1: Preliminaries
1 Invention, Technique and Language (1976)   3
2 Invention/Research (1976)   8

Part 2: From Work to Idea
3 Idea, Realisation, Craft (1977–78)   21
4 Language, Material and Structure (1978–79)   57

Part 3: The Composer's Gesture
5 Composition and Its Various Gestures (1979–80)   87
6 Automatism and Decision (1980–81)   119

Part 4: The Problem of Thematics
7 The Notion of Theme and Its Evolution (1982–83)   149
8 Theme, Variations and Form (1983–84)   182
9 Athematicism, Identity and Variation (1984–85)   222

Part 5: The Eye and the Ear
10 The System and the Idea (1985–86)   281
11 Between Order and Chaos (1987–88)   357

Part 6: Memory, Writing and Form
12 Memory and Creation (1988–90)   405

CONTENTS

13 The Concept of Writing (1990–91)   485

14 Notation, Transcription, Invention (1991–92)   526

15 Writing and Idea (1992–93)   560

16 The Work: Whole or Fragment? (1994–95)   592

Index   633

Preface
by Jonathan Goldman

With the passing of Pierre Boulez, it is impossible to avoid the impression of the end of an era: that of the 'heroic' age of post-war musical modernism and all its aesthetic and political struggles. The death of Boulez, perhaps the last prominent avatar of the European post-war avant-garde, closed another link in a chain of influential composers who predeceased him (such as Luigi Nono in 1990, John Cage in 1992, Karel Goeyvaerts in 1993, Iannis Xenakis in 2001, Luciano Berio in 2003, György Ligeti in 2006, Karlheinz Stockhausen in 2007, Henri Pousseur in 2009 and Elliott Carter in 2012), and his passing was followed by those of contemporaries as prominent as Peter Maxwell Davies and Pauline Oliveros, both in 2016. Inevitably, journalistic tributes to the famed composer and conductor announced 'a truly final full stop for the twentieth-century musical avant-garde which he had notably helped to shape',[1] no doubt owing to the fact that the successive phases of Boulez's artistic development mirrored those of the better part of a generation of composers, and took him from a 'parametric' post-Webernian phase to electroacoustic experiments, from 'mobile' aleatoric works to real-time electronic sound processing, from neo-expressionist miniatures to a return to large-scale form.

One of the characteristics of Boulez's cohort is their inclination towards theorising, their tendency to formulate overarching principles. While some might view this sceptically as the expression of an 'imperialistic' impulse – an attempt to set the boundaries within which art can take place, or a modernistic tendency to impose constraints on others' fields of activity – others may also be able to admire and learn from a generation's ability and will to *think* clearly about music, sometimes in a provocative, manifesto-like style. In fact, an expression used in the title of Boulez's first monograph, *Penser la musique aujourd'hui* (it reads oddly in English: 'To "Think" Music Today'), leaves out any mediating preposition between the thinking and the music. It is as if such a preposition would imply a distance that is barred from the aesthetic programme of Boulez and several of his contemporaries. Given this will to *think* music in all-encompassing terms, one is not surprised to find that there are seventeen (partly posthumous) volumes of Stockhausen's *Texte zur Musik* ('Texts about Music', still mostly untranslated), as well as slimmer but no less rich volumes of writings by Pousseur, Berio and Carter, not to mention the many thousands of pages of Boulez's writings collected in the *Points de repère* collection.[2] In the case of Boulez, the impulse to write was particularly intense and productive: one does not hesitate to call him a writer, in addition to his many other laurels (composer, conductor, founder of musical institutions). Nor is one surprised to discover that several of Boulez's earliest texts ('Current Investigations' (1954), 'Corruption in the Censors' (1956), 'Alea' (1957)) were published in a literary journal, *La Nouvelle revue française* (NRF).[3]

Boulez's theoretical project was particularly ambitious. He took his instinct for a 'zero-hour', post-apocalyptic *tabula rasa* to the extreme of seeking to reinvent music from the bottom up, with internally consistent foundations – at least according to a letter he wrote to Karlheinz Stockhausen, no doubt in the spirit of friendly artistic competition, in December 1959:

> As a matter of fact, I've been giving much thought in general
> to the foundations of today's music. It will be the theme of my
> course at Darmstadt: six lectures on a new musical methodology.
> In preparation, I'm rereading Descartes; and I'm struck by how
> much our musical reasoning is in general inconsistent and without
> peremptory logic. We have to try to give our thought an internal
> rigour which it is far from possessing.[4]

Even though a proposed multi-volume treatise on music never came to fruition, the tenor of the project can be sensed by imagining a combination of *Penser la musique aujourd'hui* and the 1963 lecture 'The Necessity of an Aesthetic Orientation'.[5] And yet, Boulez's theoretical writings seem to have temporarily run out of steam around that time,

1963 being the year in which, according to Jean-Jacques Nattiez, 'Pierre Boulez temporarily ceases to write texts pertaining to the elaboration of musical language.'[6] This is evident in the text 'Periform', which Boulez wrote as a talk for a 1965 conference on musical form, in which he sounds more Dada than Descartes: 'Is the virgin forest a form? No doubt.'[7] The shortage of theoretical writings during the decade following this essay was likely at least in part the result of Boulez's new role as an internationally renowned conductor: he conducted the *The Rite of Spring* at the Théâtre des Champs-Élysées on 18 June 1963 to great acclaim, which set him on a trajectory that culminated in his simultaneous appointment to the New York Philharmonic and the BBC Symphony Orchestra in 1971. However, his silence as a writer was perhaps also due to his disillusionment with theoretical considerations per se.

His impulse towards theorising was renewed when, following a proposal from Collège de France member and Boulez admirer Michel Foucault[8] and a formal invitation from the historian Emmanuel Le Roy Ladurie, Boulez was appointed to the chair of Invention, Technique and Language in Music at the Collège. This venerable French institution was founded in the sixteenth century and brings together scholars in all the major fields of the sciences and the arts. In addition to conducting their own research, scholars are required to give public lectures – or '*leçons*', in the Collège's time-honoured and somewhat archaic parlance – for a lay audience. Although Boulez was not the Collège's first chair in music – the musicologist Jules Combarieu gave a course in music history there between 1904 and 1910[9] – his appointment revealed the institution's desire to expand its scope to include creative activities. As is the Collège's custom, the precise naming of the chair is made to measure for each particular candidate. Boulez's appointment as Chair of Invention, Technique and Language in Music was tailor-made for a composer who had taken the metaphor of music as language to new heights in his writings. The appointment parallels Foucault's nomination as the Collège's Chair of the History of Systems of Thought in 1970, a chair that was, of course, designed precisely for him. Boulez would have been approached before the chair was created, and would have had a hand in crafting the text of nomination that Le Roy Ladurie submitted to the Collège's administration on 16 March 1975, a text containing many themes dear to Boulez himself. For example, in a critical appraisal of Schoenberg, Le Roy Ladurie writes that 'Schoenberg's approach focuses on each element of sound separately: pitch, intensivity [*sic*], duration, timbre. Twelve-tone technique is often portrayed as being too systematic. In fact, it is not, or else it is systematic only in the short term. It is not always capable, for example, of "thinking" form.'[10] That Boulez needed to continue the formal explorations left hanging by the 'Viennese master' is consistent with the aesthetic programme of the author of 'Schoenberg Is Dead' (1951). So it was that, once appointed to this new chair, Boulez gave nine one-hour lectures plus five two-hour seminars per year, beginning with the inaugural address on 10 December 1976 and continuing until the spring of 1995, with only a few exceptions, including two years in which no lectures took place. Boulez's very assiduity at the Collège is perhaps surprising given his heavy conducting schedule during this period, but understandable given the strict regulations of Collège professors, who are under no circumstances allowed to vary the number of *leçons* they give each year.

Boulez did not prepare written lectures for each of his *leçons* and seminars at the Collège. Instead, each academic year he would write a single essay of approximately twenty to thirty pages, each of which was devoted to a specific theme, and then he delivered all of the year's lectures and seminars by extemporising from the prepared text. As a result, when Jean-Jacques Nattiez prepared the original French version of this volume, he published one essay per academic session, following Boulez's own instructions rather than the established custom of publishing each of the nine lectures as a separate essay. Boulez subsequently revised each of the essays with a view to publication, and this current volume follows that form. In his revisions, Boulez removed some of the references to specific musical examples that were included during the lectures, heightening our sense that these essays are meditations on music in general rather than commentaries on specific works. Some of the works mentioned in Boulez's lecture notes but subsequently redacted from the final version shed a fascinating light on his appraisal of the works of his own time, including a good number composed after 1970. In the

1979–80 courses that became 'Automatism and Decision', for example, Boulez mentioned works that exhibit indeterminacy on different planes. Among works that include various degrees of chance and determination in their form or structure, one finds not only Cage's *Music of Changes*, Stockhausen's *Klavierstück XI* and Henri Pousseur's *Mobile*, but also Brian Ferneyhough's *Time and Motion Study II* (1973–6); among pieces that exhibit degrees of indeterminacy with regard to pitch and timbre, Boulez cites not only Varèse's *Ionisation*, as might have been expected, but also Heinz Holliger's *Psaume* (1971) and *Cardiophonie* (1971), as well as Berio's *Circles*. His discussion of indeterminacy in the form of 'found objects' includes references to Kagel's *Exotica* (1970–1) and *Acustica* (1968/1970), as well as Dieter Schnebel's *Maulwerke* (1968–74). In other categories of indeterminacy, Boulez cites graphic scores by Earle Brown and Sylvano Bussotti, and even Paul Méfano's *Périple(s) à 1* (1978) for solo saxophone, composed scarcely a year before the lecture. Not that there is anything surprising about Boulez being familiar with the most recent works by his contemporaries and the younger generation of composers – one has only to consider that he was programming many of these works in concerts by the Ensemble InterContemporain, just as he had decades earlier in his Domaine Musical seasons. These musical examples nevertheless illustrate that whatever his reasons for omitting reference to them in the essays' final versions, familiarity with and reflection on the works of the musical present shaped the ultimate form of these musical meditations. Boulez also decided not to publish the lecture notes he prepared for the seminars, many of which featured collaborations with researchers associated with IRCAM, his institute for acoustical and musical research, including David Wessel, Andrew Gerzso and Giuseppe di Giugno, perhaps because their interactive style did not lend itself to the essay format.

Boulez's procedure of writing a single essay for each academic year (or sometimes for several successive years – see below) is what accounts for the (relative) brevity of this volume, considering that it covers fifteen academic sessions. One need only compare it with the 2015 publication of Pierre Bourdieu's Collège de France lectures from only three sessions (1989–92), which spans some six hundred pages.[11] The essays here were collected by Nattiez, in collaboration with their author, and published first in the volume *Jalons (pour une décennie)* (1989), which includes ten years' worth of lectures, and then in *Leçons de musique: Points de repère III* (2005), which assembles the nearly complete essays, newly corrected and approved by Boulez, of which this volume is the translation.[12] In several cases, the titles of the essays were different from those used for the yearly lecture themes; these new titles were added either by Boulez or by Nattiez with the composer's approval. Indeed, one could imagine a future critical edition of Boulez's complete Collège de France lectures, transcribed from the audio recordings of the *leçons*, that would require several volumes, along the lines of Foucault's complete Collège lectures.[13]

Of the essays collected here, Chapter 1 is the *projet d'enseignement*, or 'teaching statement', that Boulez submitted as part of his official acceptance of the invitation to be appointed as chair; hence, its title here is taken from that of the chair itself, i.e. 'Invention, Technique and Language'. Chapter 2, here given the title 'Invention/Research', is the text of Boulez's inaugural address, the lecture that is traditionally 'delivered solemnly in the presence of colleagues to a large audience, [. . .] an opportunity to situate his or her writings and teaching in relation to predecessors and to the most recent research developments.'[14] This inaugural address was published by Boulez in the programme of a series of concerts and exhibitions that marked the opening of IRCAM in 1977, in which he collaborated with sound engineers and computer programmers at the forefront of innovations in sound-processing technology, rather than in a separate Collège de France publication, as is the custom.[15]

After this inaugural address, Boulez gave no lectures in the first academic session (1976–7). Chapter 3, 'Idea, Realisation, Craft', is derived from the lecture notes used in the 1977–8 academic year, whose title was announced as 'Musical Invention I: Origins and Antecedents'. Chapter 4, 'Language, Material and Structure', corresponds to the lectures given in the 1978–9 session, which were originally advertised as 'Musical Invention II: Dimensions and Codes'. Chapter 5, 'Composition and Its Various Gestures', formed the basis for the 1979–80 academic year, which received the same title, as did Chapter 6, 'Automatism and Decision', for 1980–1. The latter title is clearly an allusion to György

Ligeti's well-known 1958 analysis of the first piece of Boulez's *Structures* for two pianos (1951–2).[16] Apparently unsatisfied with the text from the 1981–2 session, 'Research and Creation', Boulez chose not to include it in either *Jalons* or *Leçons de musique*. Chapter 7, 'The Notion of Theme and Its Evolution', is the text used for the 1982–3 academic year, which was given the same title. Chapter 8, 'Theme, Variations and Form', and Chapter 9, 'Athematicism, Identity and Variation', were used in the 1983–4 and 1984–5 sessions respectively, both under the title of 'The Thematic Challenge'. Chapter 10, 'The System and the Idea', corresponds to the 1985–6 academic year, in which Boulez derived his lectures from a journal article that he had recently published.[17] Similarly, after not having given lectures in 1986–7, for the 1987–8 session, 'Between Order and Chaos' (Chapter 11), Boulez used a recently published journal article as the basis for his lectures.[18] Nevertheless, for these two articles, the texts that Boulez prepared for *Leçons de musique* are considerably altered from the versions originally published: in the case of 'The System and the Idea', the essay published here is fully twice as long. Chapter 12, 'Memory and Creation', formed the basis for the lectures given in both 1988–9 and 1989–90, which were announced under the same title. Chapter 13 (here titled 'The Concept of Writing'), Chapter 14 ('Notation, Transcription, Invention') and Chapter 15 ('Writing and Idea') formed the basis for the 1990–1, 1991–2 and 1992–3 series respectively, all of which were originally announced under the title 'The Concept of Writing'. There were no lectures in 1993–4, while in the final year of the appointment, 1994–5, Boulez gave lectures under the title 'The Work: Whole or Fragment?' The dates and titles of the original lectures, established from recordings, Collège de France records and Boulez's agenda entries, are listed below in the original French:

Lecture Dates and Annual Topics[19]

Inaugural address: 10 Dec. 1976

1977–8: *L'invention musicale – I: origines et antécédents*
11 Jan. 1978, 25 Jan., 1 Feb., 22 Feb., 1 Mar., 22 Mar., 29 Mar., 12 Apr., 19 Apr.

1978–9: *L'invention musicale – II: dimensions et codes*
6 Oct. 1978, 13 Oct., 20 Oct., 27 Oct., 3 Nov., 10 Nov., 17 Nov., 24 Nov., 1 Dec.

1979–80: *La composition et ses différents gestes*
18 Jan. 1980, 25 Jan., 1 Feb., 8 Feb., 15 Feb., 22 Feb., 29 Feb., 7 Mar., 14 Mar.

1980–1: *Automatisme et décision*
27 Feb. 1981, 6 Mar., 13 Mar., 20 Mar., 4 Apr., 24 Apr., 2 May, 12 Jun., 19 Jun.

1981–2: *Recherche et création*
15 Jan. 1982, 22 Jan., 29 Jan., 5 Feb., 19 Feb., 20 Feb., 12 Mar., 13 Mar., 19 Mar.

1982–3: *La notion de thème et son évolution*
14 Jan. 1983, 21 Jan., 29 Jan., 4 Feb., 18 Feb., 25 Feb., 4 Mar., 11 Mar., 25 Mar.

1983–4: *L'enjeu thématique – I*
13 Jan. 1984, 20 Jan., 27 Jan., 3 Feb., 2 Mar., 9 Mar., 16 Mar., 23 Mar., 30 Mar.

1984–5: *L'enjeu thématique – II*
11 Jan. 1985, 12 Jan., 18 Jan., 19 Jan., 1 Feb., 2 Feb., 8 Feb., 9 Feb., 15 Feb.

1985–6: no lectures

1986–7: *Le système et l'idée*
30 Jan. 1987, 20 Feb., 20 Mar., 27 Mar., 3 Apr., 10 Apr., 15 May, 22 May, 29 May

1987–8: *Entre ordre et chaos*
29 Jan. 1988, 5 Feb., 12 Feb., 19 Feb., 15 Apr., 22 Apr., 29 Apr., 6 May, 13 May

1988–9: *Mémoire et creation – I*
3 Feb. 1989, 4 Feb., 10 Feb., 11 Feb., 17 Feb., 18 Feb., 24 Feb.,
25 Feb., 3 Mar.

1989–90: *Mémoire et création – II*
26 Jan. 1990, 27 Jan., 2 Feb., 3 Feb., 16 Feb., 17 Feb., 9 Mar.,
10 Mar., 17 Mar.

1990–1: *Le concept d'écriture – I*
30 Nov. 1990, 1 Dec., 7 Dec., 8 Dec., 14 Dec., 15 Dec., 18 Jan. 1991,
19 Jan., 25 Jan.

1991–2: *Le concept d'écriture – II*
10 Jan. 1992, 11 Jan., 24 Jan., 25 Jan., 11 Apr., 16 Apr., 17 Apr.,
18 Apr., 19 Jun.

1992–3: *Le concept d'écriture – III*
30 Oct. 1992, 31 Oct., 6 Nov., 7 Nov., 13 Nov., 14 Nov., 8 Jan. 1993,
9 Jan., 12 Feb.

1993–4: no lectures

1994–5: *L'oeuvre: tout/fragment*
21 Oct. 1994, 22 Oct., 28 Oct., 29 Oct., 3 Feb. 1995, 4 Feb., 17 Feb.,
18 Feb., 8 Apr.

Boulez's Collège de France period coincided with a new phase in his own compositional career and a marked stylistic departure, as witnessed by such works as *Rituel* (1974–5), *Messagesquisse* (1976–7) and the magnum opus of this period, *Répons* (1981; 1984), as well as later large-scale works such as *Sur Incises* (1996–8) and *Dérive 2* (1988–2006/2009). We cannot really trace how theory and practice developed together in Boulez's mind, but it remains clear that this period was marked by a return to systematic thinking – to thinking music in all its generality. Far from bearing only on Boulez's own music or musical thought, the ideas elaborated in this volume apply in principle to any musical language and may well be of interest to composers, performers and music lovers of all kinds – 'no aesthetic orientation necessary', as it were. It might further be suggested that the two lectures that concern the central Boulezian concept of 'invention' (Chapters 1 and 2) could apply equally well to any creative endeavour and contribute to the current scholarly conversation about the nature of creativity.

This English edition complements the last English volume of Boulez's writings, *Orientations*, published in 1986.[20] All other volumes published in English since that time have been a retranslation of an existing volume,[21] a collection of letters[22] or a book-length series of conversations or interviews.[23] The texts contained here can at times be read as a kind of diary of the problems and discoveries Boulez encountered during the gestation of his compositions: the reflections presented here on idea, gesture, creativity, the musical object, the concept of writing, the status of the musical 'work' and the notions of deduction and envelope are inextricably linked to Boulez's development as a composer. For example, in the final year's course, 'The Work: Whole or Fragment?', Boulez makes no secret of the fact that in studying the status of the musical work, he is reflecting on a problem of particular personal interest. The relationship between fragment and whole is, of course, central to his reflections on form; his works *Dérive 1* (1984), *Mémoriale* (. . . *explosante-fixe . . . Originel*) (1985) and *Anthèmes 1* (1991–2) and 2 (1998), for example, are fragments, grafts or extensions of *Répons* and . . . *explosante-fixe . . .* (1971; 1991–3) respectively.

In these lectures, Boulez was still searching for solutions to musical problems after half a century of compositional experience. It is remarkable to find him still meditating in the 1980s and 1990s on the consequences of two of his most fundamentally important compositional experiments from the 1950s: total serialism, the iconic example being his *Structures* for two pianos, book 1 (1951–2); and open or mobile form, whose *locus classicus* is the Third Piano Sonata (1958–63). Indeed, with regard to open form, and more generally the cluster of concepts that include indeterminacy, aleatorics and chance, Chapter 6 contains a sustained reflection, replete with aesthetic detail, that at times recalls the now-classic correspondence in which Boulez and John Cage circled around these compositional issues.[24] But there are also abundant new areas of focus here, most significantly concerning the theme and thematic processes (Chapters 7–9), perceptual markers that he terms 'envelopes' and 'signals' (Chapters 9–11), the problem of 'authenticity' (Chapter 12) and large-scale form (Chapters 12–16), among many others.

Boulez's highly literary style, with its crisp and precise sentences, also reveals his affiliation to a French literary as well as musical tradition. In this respect, he follows in the footsteps of another literary titan, Hector Berlioz. Boulez also shows himself to be the product of a classical education: many of the concepts he uses to describe musical discourse are inspired by notions in classical rhetoric (tropes, schema, invention, etc.), so much so that one sometimes has the impression of reading a manual on musical rhetoric in the tradition of Johann Mattheson's *Das neu-eröffnete Orchestre* (1713). This should come as no surprise, given the classical elements of Boulez's musical discourse.[25] Moreover, as Patrick McCreless noted, 'What the later eighteenth century tended to call rhetoric gradually began to be subsumed under what the nineteenth century called structure, to the point that musical rhetoric disappeared altogether. It was left to twentieth-century musicology to recover, underneath the nineteenth-century concepts of expression, organicism, and structure, the rhetorical roots of the music and music theory of the preceding centuries.'[26] It is conceivable that modern composers like Boulez did the same in their writings and compositions. Indeed, some readers may be struck by the underlying organicism of Boulez's approach, as if his *leçons* were follow-ups to the lectures that formed Anton Webern's posthumous volume *The Path to the New Music*, a book that Boulez quotes repeatedly here. Boulez is at any rate unabashed about appealing to organic metaphors, such as when he notes, in Chapter 9, that 'The difficulty is in transmission: to create not only an *order* that can be perceived, but also a living, sensate organism that displays this order in a perceptible way.'[27] It may also be that the classical tropes of Boulez's thought in the Collège lectures are the flip side of his other major activity during those years: his directorship of IRCAM, from its beginnings in the early 1970s until 1993. As is stated in the official Collège document presenting Boulez's candidacy for the chair, signed by Le Roy Ladurie and presented on 29 June 1975: 'Boulez's teaching at the Collège de France will take place in parallel with his activity as director of IRCAM [. . .] The collaboration between musicians and scientists, research conducted at IRCAM and, in parallel, Pierre Boulez's teaching at the Collège de France, will form a kind of laboratory that is at once individual and collective, in which contemporary music and its science will be created; in which one will create and, at any rate, think the music of today.'[28] Indeed, as lectures in the hallowed halls of the Collège de France, Boulez's musical meditations take on a timeless character, one in which technology and what he terms the 'machine' play only supporting roles. This double identity – IRCAM technologist in the morning, Collège de France classicist in the afternoon – is, of course, the mirror image of the double (viz. *Dialogue de l'ombre double*) and indeed multiple (viz. *Éclat/Multiples*) nature of Boulez the musician.

Other readers will be struck by the affinity of many of these chapters with contemporaneous musicological writing. For example, when, in Chapter 5, Boulez states that 'For a long time, music did not address the problem of expression (and its sentimental caricature, "being expressive") as a distinct category', one feels that such a sentence might be found on a page of Carl Dahlhaus's writings. Elsewhere, Boulez writes in a mode that in English is usually understood as that of the critic. In Chapter 3, speaking of works that are 'geological cataclysms that have entirely changed musical thinking', he recalls T. S. Eliot's well-known theory of poetic genius in the poet's famous essay 'Tradition and the Individual Talent', an essay that Boulez quotes at length in Chapter 12.[29] Sometimes, his prose makes striking use of political or even martial metaphors, as when he discusses a musical idea that when 'conceived with enough power, it can eventually invade territories far removed from where it began.'[30] At other times, he clearly wants the politically charged connotations of words like 'hierarchy' to ring out: 'This is by no means a hierarchy setting out what is important and what is not – one of distinction versus contempt, noble versus ignoble – but rather a hierarchy distinguishing what is at the centre from what is peripheral, what is decisive from what is relative.'[31]

It has often been noted (by Célestin Deliège and Nattiez in particular) that the Collège de France lectures represented a decisive turn towards an exploration of the way music is perceived in practice, even if sensitivity to perceptual factors can hardly be underestimated in either

Boulez's earliest writings or indeed his compositions, and it is salutory, in an era when so much modernist musical production is dismissed out of hand as mere *Augenmusik* divorced from real musical experience, to read Boulez's claim that

> being conscious of the various forms of musical perception and knowing how to explore and exploit them enriches invention considerably. Perception through presence and perception through absence mark the limits within which lies an immense field of possibilities. Elements set in relief or hollowed out, reassured or thwarted memory – these are the two poles of the listener's relationship with the work.[32]

And yet it is instructive to consider to what extent the Collège de France lectures represent an aesthetic reversal of the position set out in the earlier writings. Perhaps, if one likes – and in a nod to the title of the earlier volume of Boulez's writings – these lectures could be considered as theoretical and methodological 'reorientations'? Rather than speaking of an aesthetic turn, it would probably be more accurate to focus on how this volume reminds us once again of the crucial role played by the listener in Boulez's conception of the musical experience.[33] The concern for the nature of sound perception evident in these writings is also a reflection of the kind of psychoacoustic research that was taking shape then at IRCAM, spearheaded by David Wessel and, later, Stephen McAdams. One senses in Boulez's comments about perception, memory and signals a sincere belief, shared by other IRCAM composers at the time, that new findings in psychoacoustics would soon transform the way music was composed.[34]

❊ ❊ ❊

This translation received financial support from the Irène Deliège Translation Fund managed by the King Baudouin Foundation, Brussels, and the translators wish to express their sincere gratitude to Professor Deliège, as well as to the president of the Fund's board, John Sloboda, for their generous support in bringing this project to fruition. We gratefully acknowledge Jean-Jacques Nattiez's help in answering our queries, and especially for having facilitated this edition immeasurably through the rigorous editing of *Leçons de musique*. We also heartily thank Belinda Matthews and the editorial team at Faber for their support at each stage of this volume's production. Finally, we wish to gratefully acknowledge the superb craft and attention to detail of Michael Downes (University of St Andrews), who painstakingly edited this translation with a keen eye for readability, concision, precision and fidelity to the French original. Boulez's original French text contained no references to sources. All footnotes in this volume are editorial. Where possible, we have identified the sources from which Boulez quoted and have reproduced an existing translation into English. In some cases, where Boulez was presumably quoting from memory, and no exact reference has been discoverable, we provide no footnoted information.

1 '. . . *un point véritablement final au XXᵉ siècle musical avant-gardiste qu'il avait notablement contribué à façonner*': Renaud Machart, 'Mort de Pierre Boulez, symbole d'un XXe siècle musical avant-gardiste', *Le Monde*, 6 January 2016, www.lemonde.fr/disparitions/article/2016/01/06/mort-du-compositeur-et-chef-d-orchestre-pierre-boulez_4842501_3382.html. Boulez's book contained no notes, and all the endnotes in this volume are editorial.
2 *Points de repère* (Paris, Bourgois, 1981, 1985), *Points de repères I. Imaginer* (Paris: Bourgois, 1995), *Regards sur autrui. Points de repère II* (Paris: Bourgois, 1995) and *Leçons de musique. Points de repère III* (Paris: Bourgois, 2005).
3 'Current Investigations' ['Recherches maintenant'](1954), 'Corruption in the Censors' ['La Corruption dans les encensoirs'] (1956), 'Alea' ['Aléa'] (1957), all published in Pierre Boulez, *Stocktakings from an Apprenticeship*, ed. Paule Thévenin, trans. Stephen Walsh, intro. Robert Piencikowski (Oxford: Oxford University Press, 1991), pp. 15–19, 20–5 and 26–38.
4 Quoted in Philippe Albèra, *Pli selon pli. Études et entretien* (Geneva: Contrechamps, 2003), p. 78.
5 The first part of this essay is translated as 'Putting the Phantoms to Flight', in *Orientations*, ed. Jean-Jacques Nattiez, trans. Martin Cooper (London: Faber, 1986), pp. 63–83.
6 '*Si l'année 1963 avait été retenue [. . .], c'est parce que, après cette date, Pierre Boulez cesse d'écrire, provisoirement, des textes relatifs à l'élaboration de son langage musical,*' in Jonathan Goldman, Jean-Jacques Nattiez and François Nicolas, eds., *La pensée de Pierre Boulez à travers ses écrits* (Sampzon: Delatour, 2009), p. 13.
7 '*Est-ce que la forêt vierge est une forme? Sans doute*': 'Périforme', in Boulez, *Points de repère 1. Imaginer*, ed. Jean-Jacques Nattiez (Paris, Bourgois, 1995), pp. 397–403.
8 Michel Foucault, 'Pierre Boulez, the Pierced Screen' (1982), in James

D. Faubion, ed., *Aesthetics, Method and Epistemology: Essential Works of Foucault 1954–1984*, trans. A. M. Sheridan (London, Penguin: 1998), pp. 241–4. This text was included in the French edition of this volume.

9 Rémy Campos, Nicolas Donin and Frédéric Keck, 'Musique, musicologie, sciences humaines: sociabilités intellectuelles, engagements esthétiques et malentendus disciplinaires (1870–1970)', *Revue d'histoire des sciences humaines*, no. 14 (2006/1), pp. 3–17; 6–7.

10 'L'effort de Schönberg porte séparément sur chaque élément du son: la hauteur, l'intensivité [sic], la durée, le timbre. La dodécaphonie est souvent présentée comme étant trop systématique. En fait, elle ne l'est pas, ou bien elle l'est à court terme. Elle ne se révèlera pas toujours capable, par exemple, de penser la forme': 'Proposition de création d'une chaire intitulée Invention, Technique et Langage en Musique, par M. Emmanuel LE ROY LADURIE', presented to the Cabinet de l'Administrateur of the Collège de France on 16 March 1975, pp. 44–8, 45. In the Boulez Archives, Université de Montréal.

11 Pierre Bourdieu, *De l'état. Cours au Collège de France (1989–1992)*, eds. Patrick Champagne, Remi Lenoir, Franck Poupeau and Marie-Christine Rivière (Paris: Raison d'agir/Seuil, 2012). English translation: *On the State: Lectures at the Collège de France, 1989–1992*, trans. David Fernbach (Cambridge: Polity Press, 2014).

12 Pierre Boulez, *Jalons (pour une décennie)*, ed. Jean-Jacques Nattiez, pref. Michel Foucault (Paris: Bourgois, 1989), and *Leçons de musique: Points de repère III*, pref. Jean-Jacques Nattiez, Michel Foucault and Jonathan Goldman (Paris: Bourgois, 2005).

13 The eight volumes in the series 'Lectures at the Collège de France', published between 2003 and 2016. For example, Michel Foucault, *Lectures on the Will to Know. Lectures at the Collège de France 1970–1971 and Oedipal Knowledge*, ed. Daniel Defert, gen. eds. François Ewald and Alessandro Fontana, series ed. Arnold I. Davidson, trans. Graham Burchell (New York: Palgrave Macmillan, 2013).

14 According to the official website of the Collège de France, '*Solennellement prononcée en présence de ses collègues et d'un large public, elle est pour lui l'occasion de situer ses travaux et son enseignement par rapport à ceux de ses prédécesseurs et aux développements les plus récents de la recherche,*' books. openedition.org/cdf/156.

15 Until 2003, these inaugural lectures were published as *Leçons inaugurales* (Edition Collège de France). Boulez's lecture was published as 'Invention/ Recherche' in *Passage du XXe siècle (1ère partie)*, January–June 1977 (IRCAM); an English translation of this essay was published as 'Technology and the Composer' in *The Times Literary Supplement*, 6 May 1977, and reprinted in *Orientations*, op. cit., pp. 486–94.

16 György Ligeti, 'Pierre Boulez: Decision and Automatism in Structure Ia', *Die Reihe*, no. 4 (1960), pp. 36–62.

17 'Le Système et l'idée', *InHarmonique*, no. 1 (December 1986), pp. 62–104.

18 'Entre ordre et chaos', *InHarmonique*, no. 3 (March 1988), pp. 104–36.

19 Dates assembled by Jean-Jacques Nattiez and deposited in the Pierre Boulez Fonds at the Université de Montréal; the years of the different lectures are also listed in Nattiez's original preface to the French edition, 'Pierre Boulez professeur', in *Leçons de musique*, op. cit., pp. 11–16.

20 Pierre Boulez, *Orientations*, op. cit.

21 *Stocktakings from an Apprenticeship*, trans. Stephen Walsh, intro. Robert
    T. Piencikowski (Oxford: Oxford University Press, 1991); first translation
    published as *Notes of an Apprenticeship* (London: Random House, 1968).
22 Pierre Boulez and John Cage, *The Boulez–Cage Correspondence*, ed. Jean-
    Jacques Nattiez, trans. Robert Samuels (Cambridge: Cambridge University
    Press, 1995).
23 Rocco Di Pietro, *Dialogues with Boulez* (Lanham, MD: Scarecrow Press,
    2001); *Conversations with Boulez: Thoughts on Conducting*, trans. Camille
    Naish (Portland, OR: Amadeus Press, 1996); *Boulez on Conducting:
    Conversation with Cécile Gilly* (London: Faber, 2003).
24 Pierre Boulez and John Cage, *The Boulez–Cage Correspondence*, op. cit.
25 Arnold Whittall, 'Boulez et le classicisme moderne (Schönberg, Berg)', in *La
    pensée de Pierre Boulez à travers ses écrits*, op. cit., pp. 195–208.
26 Patrick McCreless, 'Music and Rhetoric', *Cambridge History of Western Music
    Theory* (Cambridge: Cambridge University Press, 2006), pp. 847–79, 876.
27 See p. 244.
28 'L'enseignement de Pierre Boulez au Collège de France se déroulerait
    parallèlement avec son activité de Directeur de l'IRCAM [. . .] La collaboration
    entre musiciens et scientifiques, l'expérimentation musicale, les recherches
    menées à l'IRCAM, et parallèlement l'enseignement de Pierre Boulez au Collège
    de France formeront une sorte de laboratoire à la fois individuel et collectif où
    l'on créera aussi la musique contemporaine et sa science; où l'on créera et où
    en tout cas l'on pensera la musique aujourd'hui': excerpt from 'Proposition de
    création d'une chaire intitulée Invention, Technique et Langage en Musique,
    par M. Emmanuel LE ROY LADURIE', op.cit.
29 See p. 26; Eliot citation on pp. 480–3.
30 See p. 40.
31 See p. 72.
32 See p. 259.
33 Other recurring concepts are discussed in Chapter 4 of Jonathan Goldman, *The
    Musical Language of Pierre Boulez* (Cambridge: Cambridge University Press,
    2011), pp. 53–82; this chapter contains the better part of the author's preface to
    the original French version of the current volume.
34 I wish to thank Nicolas Donin for suggesting this point to me. This
    psychoacoustic research is highlighted in the seminal volume showcasing
    research at IRCAM and other similar laboratories in the 1980s: Jean-Baptiste
    Barrière, ed., *Le timbre, métaphore pour la composition* (Paris: Bourgois,
    1991). Significantly, the contributions by David Wessel and Stephen McAdams
    are both collaborations with composers, suggesting the extent to which
    composers in the IRCAM orbit had a stake in psychoacoustic research and
    the study of perception more generally: Jean-Claude Risset and David L.
    Wessel, 'Exploration du timbre par analyse et synthèse' and 'Qualités et
    fonctions du timbre musical', and Stephen McAdams and Kaija Saariaho,
    'Qualités et fonctions du timbre musical', both in *Le timbre, métaphore pour la
    composition*, op. cit., pp. 102–33 and 164–81.

Pierre Boulez, Lecturer
by Jean-Jacques Nattiez

This English version of Pierre Boulez's *Music Lessons*, published in French in 2005, under the title *Leçons de musique*, when he was eighty, provides all the texts on which he based his Collège de France teachings between 1976 and 1995. The French publication formed part of a larger collection of Boulez's writings, as described by Jonathan Goldman in the preceding Preface. This was a composer who cared deeply that his public should be aware of the evolution of his thinking, and of the new trends in his theoretical reflections since the original *Points de repère* (that is, the *Orientations* of 1986).

We should not expect Pierre Boulez's Collège de France lectures to claim to offer a pedagogical composition manual – Chapter 1: How to Sharpen Your Pencil; Chapter 2: How to Draw the Staves; Chapter 3: How to Construct a Series; Chapter 4: How to Transpose It . . . and so on! By entitling the first version of some of these writings 'Milestones' (*Jalons*), Boulez meant to emphasise that he was directly addressing the concrete issues with which he was dealing in his compositions at the time: *Notations* for orchestra (1978–84, 1997, 2004), the various versions of *Répons* (1981, 1982, 1984), *Dérive 1*, *Dérive 2* (1988–2006/2009), . . . *explosante-fixe* . . . and *Anthèmes* all inspired, explicitly or implicitly, this first-hand testimony of the creative craft.

One may wonder whether the profusion of ideas and images prompted by the creativity of a figure such as Boulez would spill over here into disorder, but each successive chapter consistently reveals concerns that we recognise from *Orientations*: the conflict between a composer's responsibility and the lure of chance; the illusions of neoclassicism; the stalemate of integral serialism; the dialectical interplay of strict and free composition. And yet, unlike the fiery younger Boulez, here he focuses continually on how the composer needs to respect perception. He analyses the role that thematicism and other procedures must play in listeners' orientation, and discusses the role of memory in composing and performing musical works, which leads him to extensive reflection on the much debated question of authenticity in interpretation.

These topics, though – one would almost like to call them leitmotivs – recur less like the refrains of a rondo than as the stages of an unfolding *spiral*. If you were to read this volume uninterruptedly over four or five days, you would be taken on a continuous *trajectory*: from the initial Idea to the deductions – a favourite term of Boulez's – that the creative gesture draws from it, through to the perception of the whole work. Here, in the music of the last century, analysis and the mysteries of writing are at stake, as is the link with notation. Does the work of a musician originate in the eye of the deaf? What remains of overly pure schemes and systems? And can we reconcile creativity and perception without becoming stuck in the rut of neo-romanticism, or simplistic repetitiveness, or the aporias of the postmodern? Taken up year upon year, but always from a different perspective, the threads of a veritable poetics of music, occasionally self-critical, weave a labyrinth of relatively simple ideas.

It has therefore been necessary in publishing this course of lectures to preserve its chronology. Although reading these pages continuously, like fast-forwarding a film, can allow us to encompass nearly twenty years of research and reflection in a short time, these musical lectures, like any journey through an urban maze, also offer alternative routes. If I may suggest several itineraries, Chapter 5, 'Composition and Its Various Gestures', is definitely the one that most synthesises the fundamental ideas elaborated in the rest of the book, and is undoubtedly a good place to start. If an idea familiar to the music-lover is the best vehicle for approaching Boulez's thinking, I suggest beginning with Part 3, devoted to 'The Composer's Gesture', as well as the fine Chapter 12, 'Memory and Creation', in which Boulez addresses the concept of authenticity that underlies new approaches to the interpretation of early and baroque music. On the other hand, for those who still think of Boulez as an esoteric composer, overlooking the actual effect of his works on the listener, there are surprises in store in Part 5: in 'The System and the Idea'

(Chapter 10), for example, where he is happy to maintain that system is a 'crutch' for the imagination; or in 'Between Order and Chaos' (Chapter 11), which covers what the composer needs to know about music perception. If we wish to know what Boulez has to say about the giants of the twentieth century – Mahler, Debussy, Stravinsky or Varèse – then 'Theme, Variations and Form' (Chapter 8) is the place to look. And the index can be consulted as a working guide.

Boulez deliberately excluded from his chapters as too specific a whole series of references to particular works and composers. He reread and took charge of his manuscript from first page to last, and wanted *Music Lessons* to be first of all a *book*, one that offers broad reflections, beyond personal and passing contingencies. Paradoxically, the more abstract the discussion, the easier it is for the non-musician to take it in.

Are these pages therefore somehow remote from music, and Boulez's own music in particular? I would like to offer some personal testimony, having worked on the first edition of this book – which appeared under the title *Jalons (pour une décennie)* in 1989 – at the same time as hearing and studying *Répons*. Just as *Répons* forgoes the harshness of *Éclat* (1965) and the Piano Sonata No. 2 (1947–8), so Boulez's way of writing at this period is no longer as pointed, polemical and provocative as it was in his youth, when the very construction of a language was at stake. It takes its time to unfold and to develop, permits extra thoughts and digressions, just like the 'tropes' that expanded the content of *Répons* from one version to the next and gradually gave it a new face.

❂ ❂ ❂

The French edition of *Music Lessons* would have been impossible without the careful work of Nancy Hartmann, on the first twelve chapters, and Klaus-Peter Altekruse, on Chapters 12–16, both of whom were responsible for typing out the manuscript; of Gaétan Martel, who helped me to finalise the first four parts; and of Astrid Schirmer, as an effective intermediary between Pierre Boulez and me. Yolande Martel processed all the chapters for the first edition. I express my gratitude to the Université de Montréal for the years of financial support that enabled me to complete this project. I can hardly thank Jonathan Goldman enough for his diligence and the quality of his extensive contributions to the initial preparation of this book, as well as today for this English version. I offer him here my deep gratitude.

Jean-Jacques Nattiez
October 2004; revised March 2017

PART 1: PRELIMINARIES

1

Invention, Technique and Language
(1976)

Since the beginning of the twentieth century, music has evolved so quickly that many time-honoured principles and rules that we once took for granted have been called into question. There have been periods during which musicians devoted themselves to investigating the rational foundations of musical language, systematically exploring the techniques through which they express themselves – but such periods are few and far between. The last attempt to provide such comprehensive explanation was during the eighteenth century, and the idea of tonality it established endured for nearly two hundred years. Since then, composers have charted much new ground and abandoned almost all previous constraints. But despite the publication of highly technical books that examine aspects of musical language or the implications of key works, music theory has not kept up with the progress composers have made.

Almost from the start, my own priority has been not so much to codify something that is constantly evolving as to grasp more precisely how today's music works. In my lectures at Darmstadt, some of which have been published,[1] I tried to put everyday compositional problems in context in order to see how we could build on the work of our immediate predecessors.

Those lectures were only snapshots taken during a period of transition. Since I gave them, new and even more radical questions have been raised, forcing us to reconsider not just the musical grammar that still exists, for better or worse, but also the very material with which we work. In short, musical creativity must now be examined afresh, taking into account both ends and means.

We should perhaps begin by acknowledging musicians' deep dissatisfaction with the current situation. This is caused first of all by the frequent inadequacy of the sound material, both old and new, that is at their

3

disposal. For all sorts of reasons, not least financial, the realm of instruments hardly ever varies – or if it does, it is only to make more money. The instrumental paradigms with which we work were bequeathed to us by previous centuries and are based on a musical language that is now completely obsolete. These paradigms, whose endurance is guaranteed by musical pedagogy, make composers impatient because they cannot supply them with the sonorous material they dream of. On the other hand, composers who use electronic or electroacoustic material often have to deal with equipment that is either rudimentary or extremely complex and yet to be fully understood. The potential is there, but it is difficult to see clearly how it can be exploited, and in particular how free and effective musical expression can be produced by mechanisms that even now remain intimidating.

Whatever the problems it presents, material is nonetheless an essential part of musical invention. Just as architects' choice of materials influences – and sometimes brutally dictates – the evolution and realisation of their ideas, for musicians, too, creativity and material are inextricably linked. In our own tradition we have seen instruments evolve towards their optimum form; once musical ideas go beyond what these instruments are capable of, those instruments fall into disfavour and are soon forgotten.

This coincidence is so striking that, just as one can reconstruct the evolution of certain civilisations through changes in their ceramics and pottery, one could almost establish a history of musical language through a history of the evolution of musical instruments. Similarly, when one observes different musical cultures, one sees that certain civilisations became attached to particular types of instrument because they expressed something about their manner of existence. Musical invention is thus directly linked to material and requires its renewal, while at the same time making unexpected demands of it. This reciprocity of invention and material is one of the most fundamental characteristics of any musical civilisation.

The way in which material is used is itself a question of technique. Sound exists in its own right, of course, but in order to become a valid element of musical language, it must be integrated into a project: once

4

again, technique and material are closely tied to one another, as we can easily demonstrate. Musical language in the European tradition increasingly aspired to neutralise sound, removing its immediate individuality in order to incorporate it more fully into an overall conception. Our tradition homogenised sonic space, and traditional music theory has supported it by bringing elements that inherently resist integration into a logical, abstract construction, whether willingly or under duress. If they offer too much resistance, we reject them. If we can accommodate their resistance – if we can make them part of a comprehensible pattern – we can include them in the system. In such a system, a note is above all an abstract symbol, reducible to, and interchangeable with, other abstract symbols. Peripheral phenomena are either minimised or annihilated. Musical language thus establishes hierarchies by force in order to dominate its material, giving it unity and homogeneity. These hierarchies are maintained by centralising laws that codify the form of the work and direct our perceptions of it.

Recent musical history attests to the struggle against this state of affairs. Increasingly anarchic procedures and choices have progressively undermined the highly organised musical hierarchy. Moreover, constantly renewed perceptions broke down the former symmetries and did away with classicism's cherished neutralisation of sound. Not only did elements of language regain an individuality of function that had long since been lost, but material became increasingly heterogeneous. Let us first consider the instrumental domain. To begin with, instruments were chosen for their individual character. We systematically explored the various playing techniques an instrument offered, and we used them in heterogeneous combinations to ensure the distinctiveness of the musical entity. When traditional methods of playing an instrument did not permit the individuality we sought, we used 'eccentric' means instead, defying the assumptions of the instrument's inventors. As for the electroacoustic realm, it is still too rich and unexplored to be codified hierarchically; it has a chaotic character that composers exploit as a means for liberation. In that realm, laws are made up from decisions made in the moment: when an instrument can be altered electroacoustically, it suggests that secular taboos have been cast aside or destroyed.

Unpredictability prevails, requiring today's musical language to evolve in two directions at the same time: that of global rigour and that of freedom in the moment.

These upheavals in technique led to a complete reassessment of musical language. Notions that were once believed to be eternal are now seen as transitory. In truth, the investigation of musical language has barely begun. By comparison with spoken or written language, music remains unexplored. Its current evolution obliges us to examine it, since even the signs that are used to transcribe music are increasingly called into question. The notation that evolved many centuries ago became a precise, nearly perfect tool for all of the 'neutral' phenomena that it purported to transcribe. But now, the complex – and often highly individual – nature of sound phenomena means that notation has become overloaded with symbols, and consequently nearly every score uses its own code. Until recently, notation was analytical, accounting for each component of sound phenomena and their context: pitch, dynamics, duration, timbre and absolute or relative speed. The intersection of these various fields of notation provided an extremely precise idea of the sonic result. But from the moment we sought to describe more individualised phenomena, or even events not intended for transcription in this form – as when electroacoustic music was notated – traditional notation failed to capture the music's essence, for reasons that are all too easy to imagine. Thus, a problem that at first appears to be purely one of transcription ends up highlighting a fundamental limitation of our present resources.

Today, these problems are bound together, making it interesting to study them simultaneously. The future of music is richer than it has ever been. But the period we are living through encourages us to examine problems that in other periods could have been resolved intuitively. In this respect, music is simply following language. Of course, a theoretical approach will never be enough on its own, and will never replace artistic creation. But composers are justified in feeling frustrated at seeing their ideas nullified by a musical practice that lags behind them, and that is itself not daring enough in its analysis of the current situation. I propose to move forward by exploring how invention, technique and language interact in the field of musical composition, and I believe that this exploration could be of great importance to contemporary music, helping it to enlarge its scope, develop its resources and place itself in the position it should occupy in today's world. Music should not be allowed simply to muddle through the process of its own evolution, trailing behind other art forms. It must be given a chance to become as integrated as possible into contemporary consciousness and to play its part in global endeavours.

1 Pierre Boulez, *Boulez on Music Today*, trans. Susan Bradshaw and Richard Rodney Bennett (London: Faber, 1971).

2

Invention / Research[1]

(1976)

Invention/research: a problem of constant concern that lies at the very heart of creative activity today.

Creative invention in music is often the object of prohibitions and taboos that we transgress at our peril. Creativity is seen as the private and exclusive property of genius, or at least of talent. Of course, it cannot be explained in strictly rational terms, since it eludes analysis by producing unpredictable results from nowhere. But is that 'nowhere' really like a conjuror's hat, a void from which objects magically appear? And is the context from which these 'unpredictable results' emerge really so unpredictable? Creativity does not come from nowhere but is nurtured by contact with music of the past (sometimes the recent past), and emerges through reflection on antecedents, immediate or remote. This reflection will naturally focus on the philosophical underpinnings, the mental mechanisms and the intellectual journey evident in works that have been chosen as models, but it nonetheless deals with sonic material itself, since music cannot exist without this medium. Musical material has evolved through the centuries, providing each era with a characteristic sonic profile that will constantly be renewed – slowly, perhaps, but inescapably.

Nevertheless, creativity today finds itself grappling with certain problems concerning the relationship between composers' conception or vision and the sonic realisation of their thoughts. For some time now, composers have indulged the opportunity for 'wild' invention, exploring ideas quite different from those that the physical medium – the sound material – can realise. The divergence of these paths has created obstacles to the creative process significant enough to threaten its natural character: when either material or thought is developed on its own, with no regard to the relationship between them, a profound imbalance sets in, to the detriment of the work, which is tugged between these distorted priorities. Of course, these obstacles originate from causes beyond the composer's own will, over which there is little control, but one should remain conscious of them in order to try to find a remedy.

Obstacles of a social nature are immediately apparent. At least since the beginning of the twentieth century, our culture has been oriented towards historicism and conservation. As if from a reflex for self-preservation, the more technology progresses and subjugates, the more culture feebly hides behind what it considers to be the immutable and imperishable values of the past. Meanwhile, the consumption of music increased considerably, since a larger (though still quite limited) section of society had the leisure time and purchasing power to access musical culture more easily, and since the means for its dissemination became more numerous and more affordable. Ongoing consumption generated boredom with music that was heard too often. Searches took place for a replacement repertoire, located in the same stylistic tradition as established works but providing a diversion from them, albeit short-lived and inadequate. Consumption all too rarely leads to a genuine extension of the repertoire, one that breathes new life into works that have become the exclusive property of libraries. Another strategy to avoid boredom, for those who throw themselves into it, is research into the historical particularities of earlier performances. Musical life thus assumes the character of a museum, with its almost obsessive concern with reconstructing the conditions of the past as faithfully as possible. This phenomenon of historicism reveals the dangers courted by a culture that so openly admits its weakness: it spends its time not creating models, or destroying them to allow new ones to grow out of them, but rather reconstructing and venerating them like totems, emblems of a long-gone golden age.

Among the consequences of this culture of historicism has been an almost complete cessation in the evolution of musical material. For both social and economic reasons, the development of instruments has suffered a fatal stall. The major channels of musical consumption almost exclusively promote works from the past, and therefore rely on outdated means of transmission, those that proved most effective at the time the pieces were composed. This state of mind is, of course, faithfully mirrored in musical pedagogy, which chooses works from a narrow period of history for study. This limits the techniques and sound materials available to musicians right from the start, which has the pernicious consequence of inspiring a narrow-minded outlook that considers what is learned in class as a definitive judgement. Musical-instrument manufacturers are not likely to commit financial suicide, so they merely respond to the demands made of them, fine-tuning commercially established models without any thought for innovation or transformation. Once market forces and economic demand come into play, such as in the realm of pop music, where the constraints of historicity do not exist, we see how manufacturers of instruments, like their colleagues who make cars or household appliances, have an incentive to develop prototypes, which they then adjust minimally in order to find new markets and hitherto unexploited opportunities. By comparison, the economic power of so-called serious music is, of course, feeble, offering slender potential for profit and therefore attracting little interest from manufacturers. Thus, two forces come together to paralyse the evolution of musical material, trapping it in a territory conquered and explored by other musical eras for needs that do not necessarily coincide with our own. A civilisation admires itself complacently in the mirror of history, no longer creating the demands that would make renewal an economic necessity.

In another sector of musical life, one with little connection to the 'historically informed' clan, musical material has in the last thirty years taken on a life of its own, almost independently from musical invention. As if in revenge for negligence and intransigence, this material has appeared like a gift that one sometimes wonders how to exploit. Its urgent importance is apparent even before it becomes integrated into thought, into strictly musical invention. In fact, technological research has often been the work of scientists who, while interested in music, stand outside the usual circles of musical education and culture. Of course, here too there are obvious points of contact with the economic processes of a society that depends on and ceaselessly demands technological evolution in order to store and preserve information: the secondary functions of this technology can sometimes be used to surprising ends, perhaps far removed from the initial research. The economic processes were driven by the goal of reproducing pre-existing music that was part of our cultural heritage; ever more advanced and accessible technology consolidated both the manufacturers' grip on the market and the rigid supremacy of this heritage. In time, however, the technologies of recording, reproduction and broadcasting – microphones, loudspeakers, amplifiers, magnetic tape – developed to the point where they became unfaithful to their initial goal, which was to reproduce without intervention. Over time, techniques of reproduction showed an increasingly irrepressible tendency towards autonomy, supplying their own image of pre-existing music rather than reproducing live listening conditions as faithfully as possible. It is easy to justify the rebellion against non-recorded reality: creating a *trompe l'œil* reproduction makes no sense when one considers the very different conditions and purposes of listening that motivate its manufacture, and the different perceptual criteria that are consequently applied. This is a musical version of a controversy that is already well worn in relation to books and films: why provide a false picture of reality by giving an exaggerated importance to detail, by using lighting in an unusual way, by introducing movement into a static universe? Regardless of this tendency towards technological autonomy in the world of sound reproduction, whatever its reasons, it is easy to see how unrelenting market pressures drive rapid change and development.

Sensitive to these areas of progress and research, and at the same time aware of the stagnation of the instrumental world, the most adventurous musical spirits dreamed of using technology to other ends. Through an intuition that was both certain about the direction and uncertain about its implications, they imagined that technology could be useful in the search for new material. The meaning and significance of this exploration were revealed only much later: irrational need preceded aesthetic reflection, the latter being considered superfluous even and liable to hinder the free expansion of unconstrained material. The musical creators proceeded by radically adapting, distorting or overturning the functions for which the technology was originally intended. Neither oscillators, nor amplifiers, nor computers were invented to make music, but their functions proved so generally applicable (especially in the case of the computer), so eminently transferable, that the desire to use the technology for a different purpose can be easily understood. Chance encounters resulted in mutation. The new sound material has a tendency – the result if not of chance, then of an extrapolation of unexpected possibilities – to proliferate on its own, without control, rich in possibilities that we do not yet have the mental capacity to exploit. For musicians accustomed to very precise boundaries, to a controlled hierarchy and to codes and conventions that solidified from century to century, the new material offered disorganised, disorienting solutions. It revealed immense potential without pointing us towards any specific methods.

So we are now at a crossroads. One of the diverging paths leads in the direction of conservative historicism, which restricts – or perhaps completely blocks – invention by failing to provide it with the new material it needs to express or renew itself. This creates obstructions in the circuit between composer and performer (or, more generally, between thought and material), preventing it from functioning productively and practically destroying the reciprocity of these two creative poles. On the other path, we find futurist technology whose powers of expression and evolution are harnessed to enable musical materials to proliferate, whether or not in accordance with musical thought. This naturally prioritises autonomy over the overall coherence of the sound world. (That said, long before current technology existed, the history of instruments was littered with the cadavers of superfluous or overly complex inventions that could not be incorporated within the musical thought of their era, and since a balance between originality and necessity could not be found, they fell into disuse.)

Thus, inventors, engineers and technicians, motivated by personal taste, began to research new methods, choosing almost on a whim which elements to emphasise. The interest they chose to take in any given phenomenon was the result of serendipity, or sometimes of their scientific concerns, rather than musical considerations. In contrast, musicians in general felt daunted by specifically technical or scientific issues, since their training and culture had done nothing to prepare them for understanding such discussions, let alone contributing to them. Their most immediate and basic reaction was to select samples, or to tinker at a straightforward technical level. Only rarely did anyone have the courage or opportunity directly to confront the forbidding challenges posed by current technology, and by its rapid evolution, which often had no immediate application. Rather than asking the fundamental questions – does the material fit the musical thought, and is this thought compatible with the material? – they yielded to the dangerous temptation of the superficial and simple one: is this material capable of meeting my immediate needs? Such spur-of-the-moment and frankly servile choices could not, of course, take us very far, because they excluded any real dialectic and assumed that invention could be detached from material, and that abstract schemes could exist in isolation from a sound medium. This assumption does not apply even to music from previous eras that was not explicitly written for specific instruments, because its very composition implied the notion of *some* musical instrument, albeit perhaps only a monophonic one with a limited register. When invention loses interest in the essential function of musical material, when it concerns itself only with fortuitously occurring phenomena of passing interest, it can no longer develop organically. It uses – literally uses up – the discoveries to hand, exhausting them without having truly explored them or exploited their potential. Creativity thereby condemns itself to die with the seasons.[2]

The requirement for collaboration between scientists and musicians (to use generic terms that, of course, encompass numerous more specialised categories) is therefore not obvious when viewed from the outside. One might well imagine that musical creativity has no need of technology. Many scientists do indeed think that way, justifying their view by claiming that artistic creation belongs specifically to the realm of intuition, of the irrational, and thereby questioning whether this utopian union of water and fire could ever produce anything worthwhile. If it is a mystery, then a mystery it must remain. Any investigation into combining the two could easily be considered sacrilegious.

The inability of many scientists to understand exactly what musicians want from them, and their failure to identify possible fields of co-operation, leads them to sense the absurdity of the situation. It's as if a sorcerer were forced to beg for the services of a plumber! The confusion is even greater if sorcerers come to believe that the plumber alone can provide everything they need. It is hard to see how technological and musical invention could ever find a common language.

In the end, musical creativity must somehow learn the vocabulary of technology, and even adopt it. Of course, musicians cannot be expected to conquer the entire technological arsenal, and much of what it contains goes well beyond any possible expertise they might have. Nonetheless, they can assimilate the fundamental mechanisms of technology, seeing how it works, understanding the mental patterns it requires, and then assessing whether or not it could interact with the mechanisms of musical composition, and whether it could underpin them. Genuine creativity should not be satisfied by a chance encounter of material, even if it uses and builds upon the opportunities that chance encounters provide. To return to the famous comparison, the encounter of an umbrella with a sewing machine does not in itself create an event; a dissection table is needed . . .[3] In other words, it is crucial that musical invention should encourage the creation of the musical material it feels it needs. Its initiatives will give technology the impetus to respond effectively to its imagination and desires. Its approach should be flexible enough to avoid the rigidity and impoverishment that excessive determinism causes, to embrace the unforeseen, and even to integrate it into a greater and richer conception. Not only should considered research and spontaneous discovery be dependent on each other, the reciprocity of their fields of action should be acknowledged.

We could draw a parallel with the familiar world of instruments. When composers study orchestration, they do not need to gain practical or technical knowledge of every instrument at their disposal. There is no need to learn to play them all, even if personal curiosity leads one to become familiar with, or even master, some of them. Nor does one need to learn how these instruments are made, how they reached their current stage of development, or how certain possibilities have been developed at the expense of others during the course of their evolution; though here, too, the composer can choose to become informed about points of particular interest – it is a matter of personal choice. Nor does a composer need to learn about the acoustic structure of the sounds produced by any given family of instruments, although curiosity or intellectual interest may inspire a desire to corroborate musical impressions with scientific analysis. This entire body of knowledge may remain untouched, yet none of the functions an instrument can serve, either practical or technical, need remain outside the composer's attention. Compositional training is, in some ways, virtual rather than concrete. One can know what an instrument is able to do and what it would be absurd to ask of it, what is easy to play and what is impossible, what comes naturally and what is cumbersome; one can understand how register and timbral qualities affect the difficulty of enunciating sounds, and how variety can be obtained through performing techniques or mechanical modifications such as a mute, and how the weight of each instrument's sound blends with others – all these insights can be confirmed through their practical application, when one's imagination indulges in the delights of extrapolation. Talent consists precisely of intuition applied to acquired knowledge. Virtual knowledge of the instrumental realm will enable composers to integrate the vast resources it offers into their musical invention even before they begin to compose; this knowledge is part of creativity.

In the same way, some knowledge of contemporary technology must be part of a musician's creativity. Without that, although scientists, technicians and musicians can certainly interact and assist one other, their activities will remain separate. Our grand plan for this era is to move towards this integration, to engage in fruitful dialogue, and to arrive at a common language that takes the requirements both of musical invention and of technology into account. This dialogue will take place on the levels both of material and concepts.

In terms of material, such a dialogue seems possible right now: it is of immediate interest and the difficulties it presents are far from insurmountable. Through education and our cultural inheritance, we have seen and experienced the ways in which instrumental models function and what they can produce. But in the realm of electronics and the computer, where instruments are directly involved no models exist, or if they do, they are incomplete and owe a lot to the imagination. With no sonic blueprints to grasp, this realm has seemed intimidatingly vast, chaotic and even inorganic, or at least disorganised. Naturally, we were tempted to explore this new realm using tried and tested methods, and to apply the parameters of known categories to unexplored material, ones that seemed to meet our needs and which we were therefore happy to use. Of course, the existing categories helped us at first to map this uncharted space, and also better to understand, through reconstruction and synthesis, the natural world we think we know so well but which seems to elude precise investigation the more we address it. It is not only the question 'What is a sound made of?' that demands a response, but also the tougher question 'How is a sound perceived with respect to its constituent elements?' Thus, by juxtaposing what is known and what is unknown, what is now possible and what will one day become so, we establish a geography of the world of sounds, identifying the continents in currently unknown landscapes.

Needless to say, the rational extrapolation of material will give rise to new modes of thought. Thought and material reflect each other in a complex game of mirrors, in which images are constantly sent back and forth. A robust system of thought will naturally seek to create its own material, and conversely, new material leads inevitably to new thinking. There is an analogy with architecture, in which structural constraints have been radically altered by the use of new materials such as concrete, glass and steel. Of course, stylistic development does not proceed continuously in a straight line. There have been many pauses and frequent recourse to historical references as a means of investing parvenu ideas with a sort of nobility. Novelty overtook imitation and thoroughly transformed architectural inventions and ideas, which came to rely on technology much more than previously. Technical calculation controlled even aesthetic decisions, and engineers and architects had to find a common language such as we currently seek in music.

Although the choice of material turns out to be decisive in the evolution of creative thought, this does not mean that thought must be left to its own devices, nor that a change of material leads automatically to concepts relevant to musical invention. As in architecture, there will certainly be unsuccessful attempts and delays, and an irrepressible desire to apply old concepts in a perhaps absurd bid to validate new material. But if we want to resist the temptation to achieve immediate results, we must think in terms of new categories, in order to change not only the processes but the very objects of composition. It might seem surprising that in the musical developments of the last sixty years, many stylistic attitudes have been so negative, their essential goal being to avoid any sort of reference; where there were references, they existed in a raw, unassimilated form, as if they were a parody, part of a collage, or even intended to be understood sarcastically. By trying to destroy or amalgamate, recourse to allusion in fact demonstrates an incapacity to absorb, and lays bare the weakness of a stylistic conception that is unable to 'ingest' what it holds in its grasp. Nonetheless, if we take stylistic integrity to be a fundamental criterion – and since material is rich in connotations acquired through previous use and suggests unconscious connections that could risk leading expression astray – then in practical terms one needs at the very least to take the material to the limit of its possibilities, if not subvert it completely. Coincidences no longer exist, or can exist only as a choice within a specialised domain – that is, as a rejection of many other domains that would bring excessively strong external references. An overly cautious attitude will no longer hold its own in the face of new material, which is why connotation is then shunned. The relationship between thought and material becomes highly positive, and stylistic integrity no longer risks being called into question.

From this point on, creative thought is able to consider the right course of action, to interrogate its own mechanisms. Whether through the development of formal structures, the use of determinism or the manipulation of chance, whether through a constructional scheme based on coherence or disruption, the field is vast and open for today's creativity. One could even go so far as to imagine virtual works in which material and thought would be made to coincide through a final, instantaneous act that gave them real but provisional existence: an act of the composer, the performer or even the audience. The finite categories we tend to use will surely be of less interest once the reality of this dizzying prospect dawns: the instantaneous creation of something new from gathered potential.

Before we get there, the effort must be collective if it is to be at all . . .[4] A single individual, however talented they may be, can never solve all the problems posed by the current stage of musical expression.

Individual/collective and research/invention: the vast potential of that double dialectic can generate an infinity of possibilities. That invention is more particularly marked by individuality is self-evident, but this must not entail exclusively ad hoc, isolated solutions that somehow remain the property of their author. What matters above all is the absolute necessity of global, generally applicable solutions. With respect both to material and to method, there must be a continual flow between modes of thought and types of action, a constant exchange between what is received and what is given. From this permanent dialogue, in all probability, will emerge our future experience. Will there be enough of us to make it happen?

1 Text originally published in *Passage du XXe siecle, 1^e partie*, January/July 1977 (Paris, IRCAM) under the title 'Invention/Recherche'. Published in English in *The Times Literary Supplement*, 6 May 1977, unnamed translator; reprinted in *Orientations, Collected Writings* (Cambridge: Harvard University Press, 1986), pp. 486–95; this chapter contains a new translation.

2 Boulez's phrase *'l'invention se condamne dès lors à mourir sur les saisons'* echoes the first line of the last poem, 'Adieu', from Arthur Rimbaud's *Une Saison en enfer* (*A Season in Hell*): *'L'automne, déjà! – Mais pourquoi regretter un éternel soleil, si nous sommes engagés à la découverte de la clarté divine, – loin des gens qui meurent sur les saisons*. The translation 'die with the seasons' is suggested by A. S. Kline's translation: www.poetryintranslation.com/PITBR/French/Rimbaud3.htm#anchor_Toc202003798.

3 A reference to the famous phrase found in the Comte de Lautréamont's *Les Chants de Maldoror* (*Œuvres complètes*, Lautréamont, ed. Guy Lévis Mano, 1938, chant VI, 1, p. 256), the 'chance encounter between an umbrella and a sewing machine on a dissection table' later taken up by André Breton as one of the tenets of surrealism.

4 Boulez's phrase *'l'effort sera collectif ou ne sera pas'* clearly recalls André Breton's famous line *'La beauté sera érotique-voilée, explosante-fixe, magique-circonstancielle ou ne sera pas'*, which also supplied Boulez with the title for one of his major works: *. . . explosante-fixe . . .*

PART 2: FROM WORK TO IDEA

3

Idea, Realisation, Craft
(1977–78)

An idea does not exist until we realise how it may be used. In musical terms, there is no such thing as an idea *in itself*; it is a reaction to our whole cultural environment. Before composers consider the relationship between idea and realisation on its own terms, they must first understand it in context – although they can never be sure of having grasped its precise significance. Once realised, the idea itself can never truly be uncovered. If we try to retrace the path from idea to realisation, we miss the underlying motivation, which will have been consumed by the realisation, burned away so that the work can be made. A real work annihilates the urge that produced it; it both transcends and negates the original idea.

If we start from the original idea, the work itself cannot be foreseen. When we compare sketches with their definitive realisations, the liberties that are taken at every stage amaze us. But how different nothingness is from an object, even if it is only in a provisional form!

All that we can do with a work is analyse it, proceeding backwards from realisation to idea, arriving through inspection at a kind of distorted reconstruction. What does analysis enable us to see? We describe the object, sometimes very precisely, and try to draw lessons and conclusions from it. Analysis can have a speculative goal: it can attempt to construct a theory about composition or form, and to extract general principles of structure from each particular case.

Quite often, though, analysis merely translates the musical notation of the work into a different vocabulary. While such translations can accurately account for even the smallest details of the work, they cannot explain why the object is the way it is. Criteria come into play that elude formal analysis because they are intuitive or irrational. This is why boring works can yield elaborate analyses that fail to account for their relative or complete lack of interest.

Analyses often, if not always, concentrate on formal criteria – on the creative framework. Their conclusions are therefore valid only because correspondences and equivalences have been assumed to exist even before the process began.

Scholars examine everything that is visibly structured – formal plans such as fugue, sonata or rondo – and discover in the work everything that relates to that formal preconception. Anomalies are noted, exceptions recorded to demonstrate accordance with the general plan. In this way, ingenious minds classify Bach's fugues according to the types that they most closely resemble.

More recently, analysis has become focused on things that can be precisely categorised – the twelve-tone row, for example, and the extent to which a composer adheres to its rules. In short, it seeks a representation that will allow the work – or what is left of it – to be embedded in the carcass of pre-existing knowledge. Yet behind these often impeccable analytical edifices the work, or at least its deeper meaning, disappears. The *how* has been regimented rather than explored.

Once one has had enough of regulation – seeing that in the end it falls short, overlooking the question of *why* – then we can indulge in a burst of *explanation*. This will supplement the regulation with varying degrees of success, sometimes using poetic analogies, sometimes sociological frameworks – all of which will only confirm the analysis as ill-suited to its goals.

Incidentally, it is odd how the most analysed, most *scrutinised* works are those that could be called 'didactic', in which the formal plans are the simplest to see – above all, the serial works of Webern. Count the notes, verify the rows, find a correspondence between the musical mechanisms and simple, classical, even scholarly forms, and you are done – or so it would seem. What is lacking is an understanding of *why* Webern so patently simplified his musical language and renounced more complex elements. What did he gain from this, and what did he lose? What does this language draw from his previous achievements? What within it is progress, and what retreat? Why did his thought crystallise around historical forms? These strike me as the more interesting questions. Everything else is merely the means through which he presented these problems to us.

The same is true of the serial Schoenberg, especially his Variations for Orchestra, whose principles are simple and easy to perceive. His development took place in a defined and narrow context: compositions were models to be followed and transformed. But when it comes to the Schoenberg of *Erwartung* or the Webern of opp. 13, 14 and 15, templates are more difficult to apply. We cannot see the music's form, in the sense of material that can be simplified and reduced. The language's rules are mutable, not explicitly defined, and the composer evades rather than follows them. All this is difficult for us to assimilate.

And the issue is not confined to Schoenberg and Webern. Debussy's late works elude us despite the simplicity of their outline. Try as we might, we risk missing the *why* of spontaneous invention. Why, at this very moment, is this particular motive transformed in that way? If we want to avoid a kind of accounting that is as crude as it is arbitrary, we will never answer that question. What is the point of quantifying a rhythmic gesture when that is certainly not what attracts us about it? Surely the codification of intervallic relationships is an endeavour that can only be vague and ambiguous, if not downright unrealistic – a mere prelude to what is *essential* in them. But what is this essential property?

It is buried in the work, and only the work can reveal it. One might as well find a reliable poetic analogy. Poetic analysis has a poor reputation – justifiably, as it usually attempts to conceal the work behind a veil, or wall, of subjective comparisons. Sometimes, of course, correspondences are so superficial, the symbolism they draw on so facile, as to be useless. Discovering the sense of a work, recovering its meaning, is an eminently praiseworthy goal in itself. But can one go about it that way? Symbolism is difficult to decipher if it is not explained by the artist and refers to no known codes. From this point of view, and this alone, music signifies *nothing*. It is not some sort of superior alphabet.[1]

Music's meanings can be uncovered through its formal methods, which will show either deep *contradiction* or deep *unity*. Although formal means alone do not define a work, analysis cannot afford to ignore them. They are the path from idea to realisation – a path that can easily become overgrown, never to be trodden again.

Wagner offered lengthy explanations of his intentions, but he never analysed his works. We have a wealth of documentation about his ideas, his vision, but his sketches provide the only traces of the path between his intentions and his works. As the works are the only reliable evidence of his intentions, he did not give us any easy answers. The complexity of his methods makes us lose sight of his initial intentions because it diverts, erases, multiplies or replaces them.

So analysis is the pursuit of the labyrinth that binds idea to realisation, a pursuit that is probably ultimately hopeless. Every important finished work is full of departures from the initial idea, accidents that make it more interesting than the idea itself. Mediocre or unsuccessful works, by contrast, are less interesting than their ideas, because no labyrinth was negotiated, no accidents took place.

In reality, analysis cannot hope to reconstruct the labyrinth, recreate the accidents, repeat the proliferation. This is why non-creative analysis mutilates: it reduces works through its finite, preconceived methods. It considers the work as the sum of forces held in balance with each other, in which invention is captured. It positions invention as belonging to those forces, unable to escape them. It does not admit that those forces can be centrifugal; it sends them back to the inside of a work, of a specific historical period. Its references are always to the past, to antecedents; its conclusions are predictable, since they fit within a smooth linear narrative about processes that in fact were often born of contradiction, caesura, error, vacillation – in short, of decisions that could not be foreseen. Analysis culminates in description, whereas it should display doubt and dissatisfaction.

The academic approach sometimes brings us knowledge about a work, or rather, a painstakingly exact description of it, but this is of no consequence either for ourselves or for others. Analysis is a closed circuit: knowledge that can be of no creative use is folded in on itself – rational, detailed knowledge whose apparent logic is seductive but which lacks intuitive potential. The satisfaction of these descriptions is that they suggest something beyond the accidental, offering the comfort of the immortality (*aere perennius*) so dear to scholarship.

Such distorted analysis is vital in establishing panoramas and overviews, but closer inspection suggests that it eviscerates much of the truth about composers and their works, and that all that it offers other than comfort is a crude, if effective, didacticism.

The greatest temptation is to create another labyrinth from the first, to superimpose one's own labyrinth upon the composer's. Rather than trying in vain to reconstruct the original approach, we create another from our uncertain image of the first. Such 'productive' analysis, in its freest form, is probably false analysis: it finds in the work not general truths, but particular, transitory insights, and grafts the analyst's imagination onto that of the composer. But such analytical encounters – such sudden detonations, subjective as they may be – are the only creative ones.

We do not need, however, to view analysis as an exercise in itself – long, fastidious, detailed and rational – for analysis does not necessarily require the global and comprehensive understanding to which it aspires. Analysis can be brief, quick and intuitive. It need not deal with the work as a whole; it can immediately latch onto an apparently secondary detail or emerge from an inspired, surprising encounter. It does not need to bother itself with the composer's intentions; it can even set itself against them, demonstrating their irrelevance by isolating them from their context.

We must nevertheless understand that a composer approaching the works of his predecessors cannot achieve such intuitive critical spontaneity immediately. Initially, when the composer's work is characterised more by doggedness than deep personal creativity, such insight occurs only rarely, since it is creativity that enables fragmentary and intuitive analysis. Inexperienced composers do not know what to find in the work: their preoccupations are too vague to suggest a precise path, a selective choice. Curiously, it is only when composers are developing, obliged to consider the work in its totality in order to apprehend it, that their analyses will be 'objective'.

An apprenticeship in this conceptual process is certainly advisable. We slowly and patiently learn to invent by following someone else's work. We thereby learn to see, to dissect, to follow the different components of the work. Whether it is overall form, elements of vocabulary, configuration of structures or characteristics of developmental passages, nothing can – or rather, should – be excluded from a systematic investigation. Every composer must undertake these analyses of works that seem closest and most important, since they force one to re-examine every expressive phase. Through this rational, systematic exploration, composers have to learn, in a sense, to intuit. The further they progress, the more detailed, rational investigation will strike them as superfluous, because having practised this kind of study on major works will allow them immediately to perceive global points of view elsewhere. A certain amount of formalism in the composer's language always exists and remains unchanged, whatever the happenstance of each work. I am not speaking here of forms as such, but rather of the formal concepts of a composer's language, the formal mannerisms that allow us almost without fail to recognise a particular stylistic profile.

If the composer's personality is strong enough, there will be progress to the following stage. Intuition will have solidified thanks to the rich experience provided by exhaustive and deep investigation of the work. During this analysis, exhaustively pursued and rationally conducted, the composer is likely to seek out and focus on those characteristics of the work that are of most direct concern. A selective approach leads to selective understanding. Intuitive selectivity is the only purposeful analytical tool, because it is the only one that permits conclusions that will inevitably be personal – to the analyst, not to mention the analysed.

Through such analysis, our understanding of ourselves deepens, and this is no less important than our understanding of history. In the beginning, though, comprehensive and rational analysis leads most obviously to an understanding of the importance and implications of historical antecedents. The goal is to get one's bearings in terrain whose coordinates are being plotted; more even than in a physical location, the need for engagement must be understood.

It is disconcerting to see how often even well-known composers and works remain ignored. For me, it is extremely important to recognise the air of inevitability that some works convey, to discover that in their wake it is impossible to compose as before; that not only do these works touch us personally, they are geological cataclysms that have entirely changed musical thinking. In such cases, we are far beyond narrowly formalist analysis, instead referring consistently to that which is *inescapable* in an important work. But this grasp of the inescapable appears only rarely, because it is the realm of only the sharpest intuition, sensing the profoundly irreversible nature of the flow of creativity.

We often believe that one creative invention can be added to another, that this sum of successive inventions sanctions eclectic choices of technique, and that this allows us to fuse heterogeneous elements together. Were this so, we would be able to pull samples from the drawers of history and shape them to our liking, according to our mood and expressive needs. This view of musical history as a linear path along which we can wander back and forth seems to me somewhat superficial. Every important work (not only individual works, but a composer's entire oeuvre) is a new achievement in which an individual drive has accomplished a hitherto unknown synthesis – one that need not be universal, but is particular, disregarding a certain number of elements. This synthesis is accomplished once and for all and excludes any other syntheses of the same order. These could be only reproductions, lacking in originality and, therefore, strictly speaking not syntheses at all; they merely borrow superficial, 'local' characteristics from the original synthesis and so achieve nothing but mannered repetition. Of course, part of the original synthesis may be forgotten or neglected for a time, because it was so rich and challenging that its future was temporarily occluded, but it waits for its iridescent power to be revealed and appreciated, sometimes in the most unexpected ways.

Finally, after those phases of rational analysis and intuitive analytical 'detonation', the composer needs to meet intuitive need with inner resources. At this point, memory rejects historical phenomena, or at least disregards them as no longer of direct interest; the fundamental elements of previous encounters now disappear almost completely to make room for inner experience.

It would be easy to take issue with the idea that composers go through three 'periods' or 'styles'. This familiar formulation, used for the first time in relation to Beethoven, can hardly be justified, since such compartmentalisation cannot apply rigidly to all composers. However, we can perhaps speak of composers going through three 'stages', which

correspond quite well to the three stages of memory and either formalised or non-formalised analysis.

The *first stage* is that of immediate memory, of complete, rational,
objective analysis. It gives the composer the impetus needed to forge
working methods. Even when a language is distinct from previous
models, the traits of the model are still recognisable and the new work
recognises its ancestry. These links are easy to establish, even if there is
already an essential irreducibility between antecedent and consequent.
The new work is replete with meanings that are impossible to find in the
model. The two works are as distinct as they are connected.

The *second stage* is that of sporadic memory, of analytical intuition
that is *partial* in both senses of the word. The composer is confident
enough to avoid needing to look at models. One may sometimes refer
to models, but in an imperious, predatory way that means that they can
no longer be recognised as such. These models, or portions thereof,
are chosen because they already seem to belong to us, as if the mere
fact of choosing them had shaped them into our own language. They
arise only as points of orientation, confirming a vision, supporting a
hypothesis.

The *third stage* is that of the latent, underlying memory of a permanent and autonomous analysis of one's own thought, as it shifts to
unknown, unforeseen dimensions. Strictly speaking, there is no longer
any source! Language becomes highly individualised. Even remote references are excluded, or if they exist at all, they refer back only to us.
The composer then mines the deepest reaches of intuition; every prospect plays itself out and is a measure of one's own accomplishment.

It is not only the working methods of musicians that should be analysed in this way, but those of any creative artist. Some of these are much
more imitable and revealing than others. Naturally, there is interaction
between these stages; they are not completely free-standing, but with
certain obsessive artists the working methods are clear. The trajectory between Beethoven's early sonatas and late quartets is similar to
Mallarmé's path from his early poems to 'Un coup de dés'. There are also
examples of minds that skip some of the steps with surprising speed, yet
even for a Mozart or a Rimbaud these stages of memory do exist, and a

significant random event – Mozart's discovery of Bach and Handel, for example – can, strangely enough, bring them back into play.

❊ ❊ ❊

There is more to say about the relationship between composition and models. Either tradition is accepted or there is rebellion. Secondary episodes graft themselves onto the three stages described above, sometimes contradicting them. The picture is rounded out – personalised – with a high degree of chance. The stages can vary in duration and significance for different artists. Nevertheless, this pathway from the reducible to the irreducible is fundamental.

In every early work, much of the creative process is reducible to models, or at least references to models remain apparent, although there is also a degree of irreducibility that reveals the composer's personality. Although the *gesture* of the composer is conditioned by more or less conscious imitation of a model chosen for its *relevance*, this gesture is already entirely personal. In this initial gesture lie enduring features that will become personal and irreducible. *Collective* style has given way to *individual* style.

We often speak of early works with a certain disdain, because we see them only in relation to models that are generally more successful and accomplished. We tend to characterise them as methodologically insecure, demonstrating weak or inchoate personality, and displaying individual traits only rarely. Such findings are too simplistic to be of interest. What is interesting about early works is to discover that part of them that is irreducible to their model. Curiously, one often finds greater virtuosity in early works, and I do not mean only virtuosic writing, but also virtuosity of conception: I am thinking of Stravinsky's *Firebird*, for example, of Webern's Passacaglia and Schoenberg's *Verklärte Nacht*.

The paradox is only apparent, and can be explained by closer inspection. In effect, by using a pre-existing model the composer adopts a creative process in which most, if not all, problems have been at least partially resolved. Creativity is grafted onto known, assimilated phenomena. Invention acts in a different way in the new work: whereas the predecessor had to solve a new problem with an original solution, which might be hard won, fragile or precarious, the successor takes this solution as an acquisition. It no longer has to be striven for; it can be taken as found, and enriched with new, individual potential, creating a kind of variation on an existing structure. While the predecessor's imagination was focused on the novelty of the solution, the successor's imagination perfects, refines and expands it. Hence, the virtuosity one often finds in early works with respect to their models. Whether in the use of musical language, laying out a form or orchestration, this *facility* with respect to material is striking.

Another phenomenon to be observed in early works is talent – or its absence, which no amount of acquired skills or analysis can remedy. An encounter with predecessors clearly reveals the qualities and deficiencies of a personality, as brilliant as it may be – the qualities that it has the potential to acquire and those that even the best and most predestined will never gain.

One might be tempted to believe that the experience of the predecessor will be conveyed and absorbed through studying a model; even that the model's strengths may be refined and magnified, and its weaknesses detected, analysed and rejected. However, this line of reasoning is a gross oversimplification. If deductions could be made with such insight, then reaching the summit would be child's play. Strangely, even for the most talented individuals, deductions drawn from models cannot eradicate every deficiency; there are some shortcomings that no external influence ever removes. Certain qualities in predecessors may be immediately grasped, amplified and cleverly and sensitively magnified, and yet other aspects of language may be completely overlooked and unused. Directed in a very personal way towards such specificities of language, talent acquires skill and virtuosity in one area, but seems incapable of manipulating and transforming the elements on offer in another.

It might seem surprising to see a composer proceed from youthful virtuosity and brilliance to inflexibility and general stiffness in later life. It is rare for a composer to maintain lifelong, consistent *skill* in handling musical material. There are many examples of composers who initially meet the challenges of language with increasing awareness. Later, as they shed the superficial and showy skilfulness of early works, they end up with an awkward kind of language, or at least with a certain *roughness*. They no longer try to disguise the difficulties they experience in handling recalcitrant elements that transgress the rules they once followed, and no longer respond to the prognoses offered by models from earlier eras.

Schoenberg provides us with the best example of this phenomenon, as do works from a certain period by his two Viennese contemporaries. The virtuosity of the post-Romantic *Verklärte Nacht* and *Gurrelieder* is really remarkable: virtuosic writing, with intertwined harmony and counterpoint; virtuosity of large-scale formal continuity and development; and virtuosity of instrumentation and, in *Gurrelieder*, of the use of timbre across a gigantic orchestra. Next to these, his later works seem much less elaborate, and even struggle to find a satisfactory language. The discipline of the series means that each element of the vocabulary is laboriously derived from a rule. These elements are not generated by spontaneous organisation within a known, well-practised code, and so the musical *figuration* is problematic, relying on features that cannot be extrapolated from other works. The constant obligation to follow a restrictive method leads Schoenberg, in his Variations, op. 31, towards academic techniques (collectively embraced) that justify and extend the original rule. The effects of constraint range from elementary procedures to large formal structures, and thus spontaneity gives way to constant self-reflection on vocabulary and technique. This happened for Webern, too, as is witnessed by the difference between the seductiveness of his early works and the ascetic rigour and calculated instrumentation of his later ones; and also for Berg – the musical proliferation found in *Wozzeck* is completely different from the pieces written under the constraint of the series. We can also see Stravinsky's attitude to inherited vocabularies, from classicism to Webern, as a superficial facility that disguises, if not clumsiness, then at least considerable ineptitude. In late Beethoven, meanwhile, thematic development pushes harmonic language beyond the realm of the possible, especially when applied to strict forms like the fugue, but also to freer forms such as variation. One thinks also of the *elliptical* vocabulary of the Debussy of the *Études*, where transition is reduced to a minimum and formal elements are distorted by being juxtaposed or disconnected.

✳ ✳ ✳

Everything that has just been described concerns the musician's craft. This is both acquired and not acquired from predecessors, given the divergence and the uniqueness of *gesture*; there are innate predispositions that produce the individual gesture and determine which features of language will be the focus of attention. The transmission of this craft is therefore extremely haphazard. It depends first and foremost on a latent, personal profile waiting to be revealed, slowly clarified, taking shape through significant interactions, dependent both on chance, in terms of what historical material is encountered, and *necessity*, in terms of how content is selected. René Char speaks of 'transmitted powers',[2] but transmission sometimes seems so anomalous and so unpredictable that it is difficult to tackle this question without speaking of the particular gesture of the composer.

How, in the early stages, does creativity relate to craft? Encounters with predecessors yield quite unpredictable results, which reflect the differences in gesture between observer and observed. Classical musicology has mostly been preoccupied with describing certain processes of imitation, in order to discover evidence of originality. What it generally misses – which it would be far more interesting to discuss – is the persistence of a given composer's *gesture*: how this gesture can be passed on to someone else; how it therefore changes another composer's gesture, adding to or subtracting from it; how the gesture coalesces, becomes aware of its own substance; how, finally, it is refined, magnified and becomes irreducible to any other sort of gesture.

This permanent, individual gesture, which links involuntary initial uncertainty to the great and purposeful uncertainty of maturity, is the very stuff of personality – or of genius, if you like; a gesture in which uncertainty is at first involuntary, as it encounters the more or less hesitant and incomplete gestures of predecessors; a gesture in which, through self-exploration, uncertainty turns up once again, because the territory is consciously selected as unknown. Gesture and craft interact, evolving over a composer's lifetime in a relationship that is difficult to account for.

It should not be thought, however, that experiences end with apprenticeship, and that *craft*, once learned, remains fixed for life. Inasmuch as *creativity* underpins all compositional activity, it is likely that experience will be replete with chance occurrences – not necessarily musical in nature – that can corroborate or destroy what had been foreseen, sending it in different directions.

I have already suggested that the composer's imagination is awakened by – even exists because of – contact with the imaginations of more or less distant precursors. This purely irrational, sentimental, confused relationship, however, cannot itself give birth to creativity without any technical inheritance. Any influence, however minor, must pass through the process of analysis, filtering and technical adaptation implied by musical composition. Whether in the field of vocabulary, stylistic features or formal structures, influence arises from knowledge. This perhaps implies that the greater the accuracy of the knowledge, the deeper the influence, but I have already stressed how far experiences can be selective and analysis subjective. Messiaen's biased analysis of *The Rite of Spring* comes to mind, as well as Stockhausen's analysis of Webern's String Quartet, and Ligeti's analysis of my own *Structures* for two pianos.[3] But even amid this partiality, there exists a certain objectivity when it comes to matters of technique. The search for knowledge means that there is no escape from that constraint.

Whether the approach is almost entirely intuitive, when a coincidence of personality allows this, or more rational, curiosity dispensing with initial excitement so that more detail can be assimilated later on, a work reveals itself gradually as it unfolds after making its initial impact. What one remembers, before coming to more general and important conclusions, is a set of procedures, located within a system that employs a precise code of compositional grammar – for example, in the construction of themes, their architecture, their assembly into phrases and decomposition into elementary cells. This is also how these cells multiply, grow, mutually influence each other or even destroy or dissolve one into another, as in Berg's *Lyric Suite* and *Wozzeck*. What one also notices are the hierarchical relationships in the structure of a work: which element controls the others at a given moment, and what deductions it draws from them, as in Bartók's quartets or Debussy's *Études*. We remember, too, the sense of proportion in the form of a work, and the roles that rhythm, density, timbre and register play within it. All these formal categories help us in giving a description that could otherwise rely only on comparison and analogy.

Every work will somehow demand that I be aware of every means of articulation it offers. This technical apparatus will let me forge the technique I need to realise my own thinking as closely as possible.

As a matter of fact, I was wrong to suggest that this thinking needs to be translated through techniques that can be adjusted. Of course, this is what we do in analysis, where we encounter a sensibility, a mode of expression, other than our own.

We can appropriate it for a while, as identification leads us towards knowledge, but as soon as we leave the composer's universe, these thoughts, this expression and this sensibility become foreign to us again – not in the way they were when still unknown to us, but because we have returned to being ourselves, and the line between our model and what we are seeking to express has reappeared.

Given the very specific nature of music, it is quite impossible to 'restate' an idea in a different way, to say something novel with vocabulary that is reused. Idea and expression are inextricably linked. Thought and expression imply stylistic characteristics that can only be adapted and justified to serve this *particular* thought and expression. There is practically no common vocabulary, only common primary *elements*, those that pre-date the composer's decisive stylistic unification. The history of music, perhaps more than that of any other art form, is defined by the evolution of its linguistic characteristics.

I remember Boris de Schloezer once remarking that the date of a civilisation could be deduced from the design on a piece of ceramic. This pure, graphic invention allows us to reconstruct the development of a culture through technical analysis. Similarly, it is the technical characteristics of a musical work that convey the thinking to which they

34

are inextricably linked. The development of musical expression in our Western tradition really can be transcribed in technical terms. The development from counterpoint to harmony, the enrichment of harmony through the contrapuntal dimension, the progressive abolition of longstanding hierarchical relationships, the suspension of a predetermined order to be replaced by a local one, the temporary renunciation of harmonic control in order to retrieve such control through different means – all this comprises the development of musical thought in the West. Music was at first the reflection of a certain immutable *order*, of divine or natural origin, and then tended to chart the inner world of the individual – that is to say, personal *disorder*, or at least an unstable order. Musical technique has reflected this evolution through successive rebellions for which composers thought themselves responsible.

These rebellions against current practice are thus inseparable from what we call 'craft'. This term is used as if it were a completely indispensable and universally accepted notion, and yet nothing is trickier to define. Today, as in the past, the word 'craft' inspires antipathy and anxiety, both justified and undeserved. It often carries connotations that are, if not pejorative, then certainly prosaic and trivial, as though 'craft' stands in opposition to the poetry of creativity, to the elevation of the idea. Most of the time, 'craft' is considered as a necessary evil at best, which often leads to a desire to forgo it in the name of a supposedly adventurous utopianism. The myth of Icarus continues to fascinate, even though we all know that his story did not end well. And, to be sure, craft – one's own craft – cannot be learned from another person. We can find in other composers only the principles of our craft. Our own craft itself cannot truly be found in another composer's work, because craft unites a composer's ideas and technique in a unique amalgam. To try to wrest one from the other is a sterile activity that can lead only to ghoulish epigonism or fantastical mannerism.

This is one of the general problems with education that I find absolutely insoluble. There is no valid, all-encompassing answer to questions of craft. Only an individual response will create the sort of provisional law that an individual needs. No educational system, however refined, can teach you *your own* craft. This may seem to imply that composers have nothing to learn from any educational system, but then one asks why it is that in even in the most adventurous – or most tentative – of works their craft can be made out, while its lack is apparent in conventional ones? Moreover, our concern is not only with music that is contained, however precariously, within an essentially *written* tradition of notation. In this tradition, notation inscribes all the codes of a work, even when it entails or implies a departure from its own conventions: for instance, when notation denotes not a single object but a family of musical objects, or when the shorthand may be interpreted in more than one way – in short, when notation becomes multivalent.

But what can be said about music created with new technology, in which invention may exceed the limits of transcription, in which we notate only actions intended to produce results in the form of varied, perhaps unpredictable sonorous objects? Could form depend on isolated actions, disconnected from the material? We have recently seen the development of a real antinomy between, on the one hand, notation that implies an action that generates the intended objects, and on the other, notation of actions that are almost unconnected with those objects, and that could generate different objects each time if the codes were changed. There is certainly a vampiric aspect to creativity, which clutches at opportunities for encounters in which it can extract the substances – the blood – it needs to survive. Of course, creativity *invents*, but it also pillages and absorbs while rendering the elements it has consumed unrecognisable. These elements do not necessarily arise from our own milieu: literary expression or visual art can provide them just as well, through a transubstantiation no less natural than what happens within a purely musical realm.

Craft is thus a protean concept that mediates the composer's gesture through the act of creativity. The portion of craft that can be learned relates first of all to foresight: to the anticipation of the process of writing, the shaping of form, the finding of pragmatic solutions. The process of writing can be learned insofar as it entails solving the multiple problems that arise as we relate one note, one line, one chord to another. *Responsibility* – stylistic responsibility – is the basis of all composition. If it vanishes, coherence and style immediately collapse. Responsibility is taken through general rules for deriving one note, or group of notes, from another. When we introduced aleatoric elements and then pure chance into our dealings with sound, so that material was no longer chosen but rather provided externally, we forgot this fundamental fact of musical language: that each element depends on every other one. The derivation of one motive or interval from another, or of the vertical dimension from the horizontal, are processes that seem to me indispensable if coherence is to be achieved – if language is to be *necessary*.

Responsibility does not necessarily entail a unique relationship between one element, one note, and another. For much of musical history, responsibility was indeed defined in this way. But even while retaining this property of uniqueness, responsibility can be taken with varying degrees of severity. It can be assured by rather free general rules that validate a set of relationships. The composer is then free to choose this or that solution, but stricter laws will impose additional conditions that restrict what is possible, limiting the options for a solution that satisfies them all. This is just the method by which we learn counterpoint. We can write free or strict counterpoint, and it is precisely that choice that creates different stylistic conditions, because it entails compositional consequences for the dependence of one note or line on another.

This law of specific responsibility applied throughout the development of musical language, from early organum through to Webern's canonical constructions. From the primacy of the *cantus firmus* to the most extreme extrapolations from canonical forms, freed from normal harmonic relationships, the principle of responsibility did not change, though the procedures themselves continually developed. It would be wrong to suppose that the principle of responsibility applies only to the strictest types of composition, those univalent structures in which a given phenomenon must correspond only to some other unique phenomenon. These extreme instances certainly provide the most obvious evidence of responsibility, but all composition is shaped by it, consciously or unconsciously, intentionally or not. Whatever the era in which it was composed, a melodic line unmistakably reveals this essential dependency. In classical music, with its rules of harmony, form and rhythmic patterning, melodic invention can happen only when one interval is responsible

37

for another within an elaborate formal structure; and there is also an underlying dependency among the structural notes in a melodic line, as well as a secondary dependency between the fundamental and any ornamentation. Phrase marks may indicate the boundaries between zones of interdependency, and one item in a phrase may develop overall responsibility for the others. The all-encompassing nature of this network of responsibility is what establishes the unity, the validity, the very meaning of the phrase.

This notion of responsibility applies to all the elements in a language and all the components of formal structures. For example, form can never be analysed, as has so often been attempted, in terms of balance, juxtaposition, aggregates, succession or alternation. Any part of the form depends both on the other parts and on the totality. This assumption of responsibility expresses its necessity in its relationship to particular aspects of the form, as well as to the form as a whole.

Responsibility does not depend on transitory laws of musical language, but exists as a result of the language itself, whatever its stylistic characteristics. Webern's phrases, from this point of view, are no different from Mozart's or Machaut's. No matter how completely vertical responsibility changes its meaning, however much its importance with respect to other elements varies, whether it obeys a pre-existing code or just adheres to transitory ones, it is nevertheless always present, acknowledged, organising the distribution of intervals according to the rules of the age. Now that form is no longer considered as pre-existing, it is created by individual instances, but the various moments and different elements of form are nonetheless linked by a responsibility that was previously specific and is now multiple. Even in the case of mobile forms, like my Third Piano Sonata, this responsibility still exists. Responsibility need not establish a unique, univalent relationship of one element with another, even though it was defined in this way for a long time. It can equally well organise multivalent relationships in which one element is responsible for a field of corresponding elements, or in which individual elements are maintained as a whole by a field of elements. Instead of a single solution, necessity will require a set of possible solutions. Form is the domain that immediately comes to mind, having been explored most recently. Instead of a linear form in which all elements, or moments, are built on a principle of unique, irreversible succession, the work is organised as a field of possibilities, with basic characteristics like register, rhythm, harmonic fields and global envelopes proceeding from each other according to the requirements of a higher-order necessity. Thus, instead of moving from one well-defined object to another equally well-defined object, we proceed from one family of objects to another family; the link between the two will be no less necessary, but the necessity will be of a multivalent type.

✿ ✿ ✿

Necessity, with respect to creativity, implies the art of *deduction*. What strikes me about the most influential composers and their most important works is the deep connection between necessity, responsibility and deduction. Thus, if we do not limit ourselves to the idea that composing is learned 'naturally', we could say that to acquire craft consists in large part of learning to make deductions – initially from history, and then from ourselves, at the point when we become exclusively devoted to our own creativity. Imagination is the intuition in this process of deduction, which can be a long and laborious process and which needs to be seen through. Of course, some laws of deduction can indeed be learned, though they change as musical language evolves. The laws of counterpoint, harmony and horizontal and vertical relationships are organised according to a code that allows the musician to make deductions with optimum efficiency and logic. But over and above these laws that provide the basis of composition, deduction has a personal character that applies both to the invention of the *idea* itself and to the consequences that can be deduced from this primordial idea. Deduction helps us to find the idea, then to make it proliferate.

Creativity is not some kind of vague and generous profusion; it is profusion *through deduction*. Craft, in this sense, is the counterpart and corollary of creativity. It is produced according to stylistic coordinates. The initial stage of creative invention remains wild, unexpected. Later, of course, it can be ascribed to some act of the will, some lineage, or

39

chance. But Breton's 'uncrackable kernel of night' remains nonetheless.[4] At first inexplicable, it remains unexplained to the end. It is the primordial *gesture* that can be elucidated only with that most banal and inevitable of words: personality.

Of course, there is no telling whether this original gesture will remain unaltered in the finished work. If it does, we realise that the purpose of our labour is not only to refine, to make more salient, more intentional, more exceptional or more *personal*; our work is there also to make *deduction* itself richer, more visible, more unpredictable. In effect, deduction exists along a spectrum. There are banal, superficial deductions that do not lead to any genuine or novel consequences; deductions that only repeat the initial idea, while robbing it of the content it could have had. On the other hand, there are unpredictable deductions that enrich the initial idea and bring its latent potential to fruition. This is probably why we remain interested in listening to works that we already know well: unpredictable deduction becomes necessary. What separates great works from the rest is precisely the power and the vision with which deductions are made from an *idea*. I include here the idea in all its forms, whether relating to duration, timbre or, of course, pitch. The idea can initially be very partial, but if it is conceived with enough power, it can eventually invade territories far removed from where it began.

Deduction, contrary to the restrictive definition of the term, is not only the rational application of an aptitude for drawing consequences from some given. It can be highly illogical or irrational, and its force can systematically short-circuit the chain of consequences. Deduction is implicit in the *idea*: the material perfection of the idea is subjected to the tyranny of deduction. In fact, in recent times the looser the codes and expected frameworks for invention, the less often a work used pre-existing formal structures, the more composers relied on deduction. In order to create formal structure, in order to generate coherence in the absence of a generally understood code, the more materials, forms and structures had to be derived from increasingly decisive initial ideas. This *vision* of the work as emerging from the initial gesture is what Schoenberg was trying to express, even if he self-servingly likened it to working miracles.

To summarise, it is deduction that helps a composer to find and develop an *idea*, and to know how to make it proliferate. The role of craft is to ensure the vitality and suitability of this deduction, to assert the responsibility of every element to every other. Craft must therefore be considered the counterpart and corollary of creativity.

Craft is both foresight and transgression. Familiarity with existing codes allows for foresight, for a network of possible deductions to be established, and it also helps us to settle on choices and conceive how an idea can move from imagination to reality. But craft is also the transgression of codes and the search for new ones, individual or collective, as well as the destruction, transformation or reconstruction of ancient codes in order to imbue them with a different meaning. Consequently, if foresight is grounded only in the reproduction or the imitation of models, craft becomes mere skill. But when knowledge produces transgression, craft can also be the fundamental pivot of creative invention, creating a responsibility yet to be explored, both in its forms and its implications.

From initial material to final transcription, craft is a means for continuous investigation of the possible. It knows when to initiate material and when to let it withdraw, how to revive, create and transform, how to reassemble and disperse. The *craft of the real* relates to the *craft of the imagined* in a perpetual dialogue. The work can exist only in this exchange between the known and the unknown. The unknown surfaces from the known in a sequence that is inescapable and irreversible.

It is clear that some elements of craft can be learned. Those that concern foresight are acquired only as a springboard or starting point. The rest requires faculties of deduction and the ability to *foresee* development and proliferation in certain material. To learn the technique to apply such deduction requires significant effort. However, anything that we cannot directly acquire from somebody else – that which can at most be transmitted to us in the form of an attitude – is transgression. Transgression remains individual: it is what will strongly or even exclusively determine the contours of a work, its methods, perhaps its very existence. The examples of other composers can teach us to transgress codes, but they can never teach us *how* to transgress them.

We therefore owe only the least substantial (though by no means negligible) part of our craft to others, to our direct and indirect forebears. We owe the rest to ourselves alone, since it is inextricably linked to our own compositional *gesture*. The two parts can exist only *together*, even if the ratio of inheritance to autonomy varies. Between the transubstantiation of what is transmitted and the irreducibility of what is invented there is a permanent osmosis of which we are not always conscious. The web that is constantly woven between the learned and the unknown is what we call craft. We cannot be certain that this delicate web will stay intact over the course of a composer's life. Craft can be corrupted by knowledge, or damaged by the unknown. Rupture or disaster can occur in the course of artistic creation, calling this fundamentally precarious balance into question.

✦ ✦ ✦

Today, more than ever, the question of craft is raised in relation to new means of sound production, means that not only fail to provide models, but also seem so disorganised, or even unorganisable, that one might question their legitimacy. Either these new means offer us no precedents, or else the precedents are so tenuous that they are usually matters of individual reaction or personal gesture. It is no longer a question of composing musical objects – of the responsibility of one musical object towards another, according to established codes – for not only is that reference forbidden, but reference to *any* given material becomes in a certain sense annulled. The most obvious reaction to this overturning of centuries-old norms would be to reject *any* inherited craft, to interpret the rejection of *notation* as a symbol of a comprehensive rejection of tradition. It is claimed, not without reason, that a new technique requires a new approach, and that this new approach is necessarily incompatible with older ones. Even supposing that to be the case, however, a certain amateurism can be discerned in many works that use electronic material. Amateurism is apparent not only in the structures of the composition, which are often very rudimentary, but also in the approach, in the discovery of the material itself and – most cripplingly of all – in the wholesale incompatibility between material and composition (or rather, lack of composition).

The sometimes superficial methods provided by electronics produce results that are rarely spectacular, and almost always narrowly circumscribed, precluding flexibility or pliability. This is what happens when we become fascinated by operational gesture and get drawn into superficial manipulation, rather than reflecting on means or method. In these cases, despite some skill in the execution, the result is amateurish or even incompetent when evaluated as a composition. It seems to me that this is why this domain has progressed so little, although we have been dabbling in it for years, and why it has so often given rise to dissatisfaction, frustration and a sense of its own inferiority to musical thought that is expressed instrumentally.

This anecdotal, illustrative tendency has persisted for years. In truth, this kind of electronic or para-electronic music is readily accessible and is constantly and abundantly used to evoke imagery that is all too easy to describe. This imagery involves a vaguely futuristic conception of space, of the mystery of 'interstellar worlds', of cosmic catastrophe, of the strangeness of science fiction. The whole panoply of tacky, pseudo-scientific images is now matched by well-established convention with a sound world in which association reigns supreme and from which all structural or properly musical thought has disappeared. It is a simplistic reflex that precludes the creation of masterpieces, through the use of material that is non-musical in the sense that it is isolated from musical history, but instead binds ignorance to entertaining visual fantasies. Amid this banal and facile exoticism, there is never any thought of integrating the superficial surprises of the material into the structure of the composition.

This applies not only to electronic material, but also to the instrumental material that accompanies it, which is often created beyond any structural hierarchy as an external means to reinforce certain points in the musical structure. Most percussion instruments were introduced into music in this way, participating in the structures of musical language merely as a peripheral group, with no need to specify their relationship to the musical language. As a result, crude, undifferentiated classes lingered in this domain, at best used for accentuation, and therefore primitive in the context of the musical language in which they were briefly insinuated. When the central hierarchy became less exclusive, when the supremacy of certain instrumental groups over others was called into question, when the priorities of material were radically revised, people began to mix percussion instruments – those with indefinite pitch – with other instruments; or else percussion was used as if a truly differentiated hierarchy could be applied to any sound source – as if, by the mere whim of extending this hierarchy, problems of categorising sound sources and of the compatibility between the sound structures they created had been resolved. But since that had not been worked out conceptually, no integration took place. At best, percussion was camouflaged by a profusion of material, a profusion that was intended, consciously or not, to disorient perception, or to blur it, by making it difficult to hear auditory markers that were deemed to be unnecessary or were present only in diffuse form.

A similar approach can be noted in most electroacoustic works. The few attempts at 'restraint' encountered problems of validity: given the state of technical research, this sound was perceived as somehow impoverished, and people quickly turned to elaborate manipulation. The problem appeared to have been solved by abundance of material, but because the problem had not truly been foreseen, too much of what was produced neglected the crucial relationship between material and *true* composition, and was hence consigned to irrelevance. The structure of material and the structure of a composition are two aspects of the same fundamental investigation: when one aspect is lacking, there can be no real creative invention. Ultimately, the structure of material can develop properly only if the compositional structures controlling it are rethought in the same way, according to the same dialectic.

When we speak about craft in these wide-open fields, or when we speak of amateurism, we are always referring to the same concepts, to the relationship that must exist between thought and material. No futile burst of percussion or unusual electroacoustic manipulation of material can hide conceptual weakness; on the contrary, they serve only to highlight such weaknesses, revealing either irresponsibility or lack of control.

In these realms where so much still needs to be accomplished, craft – in the sense of deduction – means establishing a bridge between known and unknown categories. Not that the latter need to be recognised and organised in the same way and on the same scale as the former; but we can introduce analogous methods that fully satisfy us in the world we are exploring, and that stand comparison with those used in older fields. Only in rare exceptions is the new domain comparable to the older one. All of us have the sense, whether consciously or not, that technical progress has no bearing on – contributes little, if anything, to – the conceptual development of composition. We experience technical progress as an illusion, an evasion, even an escape hatch. More fundamental development fails to happen, or happens very slowly through sporadic and isolated work. We could even say that technical progress can truly be described as *progress* only when it perfectly matches the development of musical concepts, allowing creative engagement that completely suits the nature of the new material.

This is where the ideas that I have mentioned several times before become relevant: the notions of foresight, deduction and, in particular, transgression. Nothing can be more valid and stimulating than to allow space in one's work for accidents of inspired discovery; but if repeated application makes this merely a procedure, if this free-for-all comes to be considered as the intangible heart of creativity, such wholesale adoption of chance could never truly and correctly express our new world.

Foresight applies first of all to the material itself. How can a coherent, rich sound world capable of supporting structures – the scaffolding of a composition – be organised from this chaos, or shall we say from these possibilities, in which we see both potential limitations and an absence of obvious boundaries? We would need to interpolate and extrapolate existing notions that we already know how to handle, and from which we can get our bearings. Between the solid, discrete realm of instruments and the potential of the unbounded world of electronics (a term used for convenience, though instrumental transformation or computer-generated organisation may not always be involved) is where we should probably place the foundations of perception, no matter whether through science or instinct – although I would lean towards instinct, a better arbiter in such cases. It is perception that will allow us to predict the evolution of timbre, the transformation of one timbre into another, the thresholds of perception with respect to resemblance and difference. In short, this perceptual groundwork will allow us to *order* existing material and to predict the order of unexplored material with varying degrees of accuracy. Not that this order must remain immutable, like a constraint. It is, on the contrary, linked to the compositional project: it uses timbral paths whose structure is a function of the organisation of the work. The work transgresses that foresight, showing a clear preference for some aspects over others, developing patterns and relationships in the moment.

Craft will appear in these very reciprocal functions of the work and material, establishing their inevitable interdependency. This craft largely has to be *invented*; the few serious attempts made in this direction were quickly abandoned in the name of a short-lived showmanship that has, of course, lost its sheen over the years. All composers, good or bad, inherit the unity and consistency of the instrumental world; but in an electronic work, they have to create their own consistency and coherence. That is why this part of craft, which with instruments is a kind of supplementary skill, is foregrounded nowadays. The use of 'found material' has negated many well-intentioned efforts. In my opinion, such efforts should have focused on an aspect that has traditionally been deeply neglected because it is self-evident. Here, I see one of the fundamental differences between instruments and electronics: a reversal in the hierarchy of concepts and the urgency with which they demand attention. With electronics, deduction and foresight should focus centrally on material, the original source of composition in this domain.

I will now digress in order to consider the general differences between the hierarchies of these two worlds. In the traditional world of instruments, pitches and their organisation are by far the greatest priority. The language of pitches has always been formalised to the highest degree. Musical language could never have existed without the formalisation of intervals, scales and various types of vertical and horizontal control. The important functions of pitch (tonality, for instance) strictly controlled musical form. Compared to pitch structures, durational or temporal structures, with rare exceptions, have generally been much more crude.

In our Western tradition, of course, there has been a regrettable lack of reflection on this front. 'Rhythm' is considered in many contexts to be a natural invention, with its references to popular music – a memory of a past that has remained alive through many transmutations and therefore lost its original distant identity. When students are learning to compose, 'rhythm' is not taught except inasmuch as they are expected to be inventive and to create variety within more or less restrictive models. As for timbre and dynamics, which provide rhythm with an immediate profile, this is barely mentioned beyond certain practical formulas. Musical instruments, our thousand-year-old experiment, are there only to provide the clothing without which composition would be like Noah's drunkenness. Composition, after all, has a duty to cover up nakedness; there has often been something faintly embarrassing about the instrumental finery that we need to strip off a composition if we want to be quite clear about its value. Sonic creativity was supposed to proceed in noble isolation, and instruments were treated with suspicion, their virtuosity a symbol of hedonism and destructive mischief. It is as if traditional musical knowledge could be divided into *noble* and *plebeian* categories, with counterpoint and the fugue belonging to the nobility and musical instruments to the necessary world of craft.

Such categories certainly could not apply to electronics; one might even say that in this field, the hierarchy of values has been overturned. Sound is not disconnected timbre, and identifying sonic material no longer starts with isolating it from pitch into detached, abstract components. Sound data are identified by characteristics that cannot be separated from pitch, or rather, from the frequencies from which pitch is made up. In other words, frequency and timbre can no longer be separated, but must rather be considered as integral to the identification of a work's sound material. No longer a subsidiary issue, material became the most fundamental category upon which the work depends.

As for concepts of time, they too have fundamentally changed key, so to speak. I commented long ago[5] that temporal structures in music that is not meant to be performed by a musician cannot be considered according to a pulsed relationship but only in relation to an unpulsed one. The temporal grid is established only at one level, since it is no longer modified by the irrational and unpredictable dimension of the performer. Thus, all the relationships must be calculated in order fully to account for a 'time' event.

The relationship between time and sound is, however, difficult to pin down. Complex material develops within itself a version of time that is not necessarily compatible with a time envelope that connects sounds in an organised way. Instrumental time refers to individual, isolated pitches, and the instruments that together make up complex amalgams of timbre and pitch *individually* obey these one-off durational structures. In electroacoustics, the creation of an object from timbre, frequency and duration fuses those three parameters together *within* the material. They are in a communal state that inclines them to resist higher-order hierarchies that contradict their internal hierarchy; this hierarchy takes precedence while the global hierarchy merely fixes the order in which different sound objects appear, their alternation and their temporal location. Electroacoustic music is often justly criticised for being 'arrhythmic'. Beyond its incompatibility with traditional schematisation, it could be said that temporal succession in this music is too complex to be subordinated to anything else, creating this arrhythmic impression, this lack of trajectory. This is true not only of slow, 'suspended' material; even restless and frenetic material is perceived as arrhythmic.

✳ ✳ ✳

In the development of the hierarchy of long-established values, which were called into question and then overturned, the idea of craft is certainly difficult to maintain, all the more so because the new environment offers different ways of working, of which the instrumental world gave at most only a foretaste. I would like to speak more specifically of the *intersection* between a structure that is bound, mechanical, typically deriving from a machine and its resources, and a free structure whose variety, irregularity and constant renewal are ensured by spontaneous decision-making.

I have always been struck by the possible relationship between fixed and mobile structures. The fixed structure cannot by itself focus our attention on what it produces. Such is the case with many mechanical procedures that apply one kind of action to every resulting event. This distinctive way of structuring objects infuses them with non-developmental properties. If we just apply such procedures directly, the structures produced will tend to be flattened, negated by the one-sidedness of the method. These non-developmental properties have to be coupled with material that evolves, and that does so in a different way. Whatever is interesting in this approach will arise precisely from the unpredictable encounter between fixed and mobile forces.

This phenomenon can be produced at all levels of the composition and of its operation. No dimension is excluded, be it global or specific: pitch, timbre, structure too – the generating structure, or something applied to an existing one. Examples will demonstrate that although the rule is widely applicable, it is particularly relevant to the mechanical.

Take, for example, the case of the *filter*. Suppose we have composed a musical structure, one that can be performed and perceived as such, all its components truly finished. We then apply to this structure, for some time at least, a rigorous set of filters that will eliminate or transform pitches that lie outside a well-defined zone. Any musical object passing through this grid will be shorn of frequencies in the prescribed band. It will therefore become fragmentary, or even be eliminated, and this will occur independently of the original structure, which is not controlling it. Here I am, of course, referring again to the foundational principle of responsibility. A structure is formed of elements that are mutually dependent on each other, thus forming a whole. Another structure not dependent on the first, but possessing its own intrinsic dependencies, will modify it not by establishing new dependencies, but by creating events that result only from one structure being immune to another. The new structure inflects the first *without* taking its own nature into account.

We can thereby bring together two types of structure: one flexible, mobile, dependent on the composer's variable criteria; the other amorphous, with no inner life other than its identity, which is either deterministic or aleatoric. The combination of a *form* and an amorphous structure yields results in which immediate, spontaneous unpredictability still operates within a completely predictable field. This is as true of pitch, duration and dynamics as of timbre. If the structural *formations* result from actual composition, the formless structures depend on a mechanical process that, once set in motion, applies itself to everything, everywhere. Whatever musical object is exposed to this, the formless procedure will transform it – assuming its field of operation is valid – through its particular prism, giving it a new profile.

Here, too, inherited and still-familiar methods of working can be completely upended. In the old world, the work's starting point was amorphous structure, though that never fully imbued it: this was a pre-liminary state rather than an active force. For pitch, atemporal structure (or rather, structure that had not yet been temporally organised) had only potential meaning. The notes of a scale constitute a space in which to inscribe a melodic line or a harmonic relationship; the amorphous structure of the scale could not be formative. At most, they played the role of acoustic filler for the actual sound object: arpeggios or scales that could sometimes form a coherent, supportive backdrop. With duration, the closest analogy to this use of the amorphous can be found in rhythmic ostinatos, such as Berg's *Monoritmica*, or Messiaen's rhythmic canons, especially when such ostinatos do not coincide with the melodic or har-monic structures of the objects they govern. But as we have seen, these cases were marginal, the last outposts of a system in which everything was subordinated to those structures I have already named as formants.

In the foreseeable future, on the other hand, it will be crucial to move forward from this reversal of values and give an increasingly predom-inant role to these amorphous structures, which range from the strictest determinism to the most aleatoric indeterminacy; to give them, above all, a generative role that is central to developing material, to the very activity of composing. We see clearly from this that, henceforth, learned craft can hardly serve only to extrapolate; it will first and foremost be a process of transgression.

❊ ❊ ❊

This lengthy discussion of the fundamental ideas of analysis and craft allows me to describe how idea and realisation function as a binary pair.

This relationship remains a fundamental dilemma for a composer, and the source of any achievement. Realisation obviously cannot exist without the idea, but the idea is also enriched by realisation. Realisation cannot merely embody, still less serve as, clothing for the idea, but idea and realisation are closely intertwined in a fluid, even precarious process. To repeat: for me, an idea does not truly exist until we become aware of how to realise it.

The question remains, however, of where an idea comes from. I have shown that dealing with everything around us – not just cultural phenomena, and certainly not just musical ones – reveals our own potential to us. At first, we refer to the past, and we might as well use this as keenly as possible for self-discovery: we can be sure of who we are only through the sense of identity that emerges from contact with the works we study. In this sense, analysis can play a fundamental, albeit circumscribed, role. I would go so far as to say that analysis teaches us nothing that we did not perhaps already know, but it shows it to us and forces us to become aware of it. Analysis can only be this description of ourselves, by ourselves, through models, since the original creative labyrinth closes in on itself and is in that sense *unusable* by anyone but ourselves. Nobody will ever be able to penetrate the depths of the mystery that is enshrined in the work that we hear, and even if they could, it would only be like solving the mystery of a crime novel. Analysis first of all reveals us to ourselves, then shows us the way towards realisation. Since the work exceeds or even negates the initial idea, the path from this idea to realisation is difficult, if not impossible, to retrace, but to work back from a realisation to the original idea will guide us on our own path. We thereby learn to make deductions and to take responsibility for what those deductions imply.

However, the reciprocity of idea and realisation, the vital, ongoing relationship they maintain and the connection that binds them to the mechanisms of creativity all lead us to question if not which category has primacy, then at least which comes logically prior to the other. Where does the idea come from, given that we have prepared the ground for it to bloom? Do we find primarily continuity or disruption? Does it depend on a recurrence of the same conditions in order to appear, or does it emerge irrationally? Does it have abstract or concrete sources – that is, a material origin and impulse? How does it come into being and stabilise, and how will it develop, blossom and proliferate? Or does realisation, on the other hand, appear somewhere on the path to transmission? What does it actually capture? In other words, is realisation an intermediary or, rather, the quintessential means of deepening the idea? Might it even be the source of the idea?

There is a frequent tendency to simplify the problem, to look at only one of the multiple aspects of the idea–realisation pair, representing it as a stable relationship with an established hierarchy. In fact, the more we explore the mysteries of creativity, the more we realise that it eludes a simple dualistic explanation of forces having their own fields of action – sometimes overlapping, obeying certain laws, following a recognisable timeline. Instead, idea and realisation intertwine in such a way as to give rise to countless different situations.

We can say first of all that, for the composer, a new idea arises from previous experience, from some past realisation. During apprenticeship that earlier realisation is not one's own but the work of someone else, but the more we command our own territory, the more we refer only to ourselves and our own past. It is likely that some idea that has played a secondary role in a previous realisation will now strike one as unfulfilled, demanding a deeper, more rigorous investigation. This journey from one work to another occurs gradually, an initially limited perspective being progressively expanded in order to become sustainable. Realisation, in this case, is a powerful aid in the development of the idea, since it provides new material in need of further reflection. The idea will endure through its stronger hold on a problem that realisation has only partially succeeded in resolving; and realisation will in turn widen its scope and influence. Thus, one work is deduced from another – not entirely, but in certain features whose kernel the first work contains.

This reliable method is obviously not the only possible solution, nor even the most frequent. In creativity there is often surprise, discontinuity, sudden changes in the direction of thought, a focus on problems whose latent importance has been neither foreseen nor suspected. I do not mean simply superficial changes of direction, or a reliance on previously unexploited references that is in fact evidence of muddled thinking and impoverished creativity. There have been ample instances of this 'back to the past' habit: tiresome parodies of real exploration, based not on authentic gesture but on gesticulations in search of temporary validity. No! To transform, to discover an unnoticed field of invention, to imagine new possibilities – this is how to illuminate the creative plains that become occluded when we are dealing with apparently more urgent problems. As surprising, abrupt and unforeseen as this transformation might seem, it is nevertheless part of any process that faithfully reflects the composer's gesture, however unexpected initially.

The birth of the idea and its rebirth through realisation are essential to compositional practice, yet in the specifics of that pathway – in the revelation of the idea to itself by means of its realisation – influence is evident at every moment. In order to create, to overcome the barriers that realisation sets up against it, the idea is forced to multiply, to re-invent itself, to find many local solutions that collectively become global. When the idea is confronted by the challenge of realisation, it proliferates in order to encompass realisation and force it towards completion. Thus, at the end of the process, an idea has expended so much energy through replication and proliferation that its initial energy has gone, and it looks completely different from what was originally intended. There is a gain in potential over the course of the realisation – but also a certain loss, in that the initial idea cannot multiply indefinitely, but is dissipated through the germination of ideas that begin as subordinate but end up more powerful and expansive than the original one. The initial potential has increased along the way, while its priorities have altered or transformed. These changes of intention – inflections and reversals – often appear when a secondary parameter becomes primary, partially or completely modifying the initial one or imbuing it with an initially unforeseen meaning. A continual reordering can take place when creativity comes into play, as idea meets realisation, a confrontation full of conflicts and detours. Once the journey is completed, the idea has acquired stronger potential and found adequate means for realisation; deliberately or not, the ground has been laid for the next interaction. These mechanisms maintain their potency. Whether they are rediscovered by the same person or stimulate another composer, the finished work remains a permanent source of unresolved conflict and inexhaustible contradiction. Through its expressive force and continued impact, the work remains an ideal meeting ground of the known and the unknown. It can reveal the future to anyone who sets out to find it.

How and in what form does the initial impact happen? Is it only born of the idea's interaction with itself? Is it born of pure speculation, or is the impact already more material – that is, directly related to the material that enables creativity? There is a very familiar cliché about the invention of a theme – whether a melody, rhythm or chord – after which everything else is progressively worked out in real time. There is also another equally familiar cliché about the god-like composer who creates a work through the power of thought alone, as if material transcription were only an ancillary process. The spirit breathes, the work comes into *existence*, the hand moves . . . The supposedly a posteriori nature of transcription corroborates the myth that idea and realisation perfectly fuse in a single explosive moment.

It is only necessary to examine the early sketches of previous composers, or to discuss the matter with composers of the day, or to reflect on one's own practice to realise that there is a much wider range of scenarios than these two clichés suggest. They vary not only because of composers' differing personalities, but also from work to work. Whether one wishes to call this process inspiration, intention or even ingenuity, it can sometimes be completely abstract in nature, producing a structure or a form; but it can also sometimes appear as the most immediate, the most 'concrete' sound material. Strangely, this intuition, this initial survey of the future work does not imply comprehensive knowledge. Intuition can go a long way in a particular domain, either in the abstract or concretely, ignoring competing forces until later, when they can be dealt with more efficiently in order to restore balance. An intuition, an invention, might well be solely concerned with the sound world it plans to use – a given group of instruments, with certain timbral characteristics, or certain electroacoustic transformations – without yet having the slightest idea about what musical material will best suit the chosen timbral field. Realisation involves assimilating the characteristics of these timbres, these instruments, this electroacoustic machinery in order to deduce either the specific content of the musical ideas that will best do them justice or the proliferation and development that will result from the use of this sound world and best match the formal configuration. The choice of a particular form of sonic expression demands a search for the ideas, structures and form that will make that choice clear and necessary. The materiality of sound will lead the composer to create forms and musical ideas that would probably not have been imagined so intensely without that first choice having been made – one might initially think this process the opposite of the normal pathway of composition.

Sometimes, though, a completely abstract concept – about density, for example, contrasting two objects, such as single sounds against blocks of variable density – will trigger many different creative processes and result in highly concrete musical ideas. Or sometimes ideas about the perception of time will lead to compositional expression, to *musical* identification of variables experienced at first only vaguely or partially: setting up temporal suspension in contrast to measured pulse; projecting different temporalities; unifying different kinds of subdivision.

From this account one might infer that conceiving a work is a matter only of calculation, but I want to emphasise the narrowness of most intuitions, however strong they may be. An idea rarely reveals itself in full, but is generally discovered only in fits and starts, through the resistance in its realisation, which is what allows it to become itself – often incompletely, leaving much room for future encounters. And when I mention the technique of conceptual development I am not implying a removal of all that is irrational and unexpected, all that is offered by the initial impact. This is precisely where the poetic comes in to musical genesis. When I speak of time, one might be led to believe that I mean only its demarcation, its measurement for a particular purpose. When I speak of form, one might imagine that I mean only the construction of sustainable formal plans. When I discuss timbre, it might seem as if my only interest is in organising it as a coherent whole. Those are indeed the consequences of the realisation that my poetic world reveals. But if I speak of time and its crucial importance in the thinking for a given work, it is because the work's poetic content hinges on a desire to extend my temporal intuition to a realisation that will help me to sense it more profoundly, more genuinely, more powerfully than anything else I can imagine. Intuition is huge, but it cannot be satiated: realisation is but a provisional step; it provides us with a written, living testimony of this intuition. Rather than exhausting intuition, realisation can only help to bring it into focus, to prepare it for the ever broader expression of its potential, of its qualities.

And so, well beyond issues of analysis and craft, the dual nature of idea and realisation – a duality whose poles must be embraced when we want invention, meaning and expression to combine – points us towards our deepest mysteries. The many paths that lead from idea to realisation, or that lead us to them, are the very pathways of creativity. They are what allows our creativity to take on concrete meaning and to reflect the expression of a poetic world that is our goal, our fulfilment. Neither can be ignored without negating the other.

1 Boulez's statement harks back to Igor Stravinsky's formalist credo: 'Music is, by its very nature, essentially powerless to express anything at all' (Igor Stravinsky, *An Autobiography* (New York: Simon and Schuster, 1936), pp. 53–4), and to his own earlier statement, 'Music is an art that has no meaning' ('Aesthetics and the Fetishists' (1961), in *Orientations*, ed. Jean-Jacques Nattiez, trans. Martin Cooper (Cambridge: Harvard University Press, 1986), p. 32).
2 From Char's poem 'Song of the Sorgue'.
3 Olivier Messiaen, *Traité de rythme, de couleur et d'ornithologie*, vol. II (Paris: Alphonse Leduc, 1995), pp. 124–47; Karlheinz Stockhausen, 'Struktur und Erlebniszeit' (1955), in *Texte zur elektronischen und instrumentalen Musik*, vol. I, pp. 86–98; György Ligeti, 'Pierre Boulez. Decision and automatism in *Structure 1a*', *Die Reihe* 4 (1959), pp. 36–62.
4 This characterisation, '*L'infraccasable noyau de nuit*', is used by André Breton to describe 'the sexual world' ('*le monde sexuel*') in his preface to *Contes bizarres d'Achim von Arnim, illustrés par Valentine Hugo*, in Breton, *Œuvres complètes*, vol. 2 (Paris: Gallimard Bibliothèque de la Pléiade, 1988–2008), p. 359.
5 Pierre Boulez, 'At the Edge of Fertile Land (Paul Klee)'(1955), in *Stocktakings from an Apprenticeship*, ed. Paule Thevenin, trans. Stephen Walsh, intr. Robert Piencikowski (Oxford University Press, 1991), pp. 164–9.

4

Language, Material and Structure
(1978–79)

It is difficult to reduce musical creativity to a simple inventory of techniques, to explain the construction of a musical language through a
description of a set of resources that composers have at their disposal.
Nevertheless, musical creativity exists in tangible form only because of
these means of transmission, without which thought never goes beyond
intention. Clearly, without some more or less explicit procedures, musical creativity will not happen. Clearly, too, no system, however valid, will
on its own enable creativity – a creativity that is clear and enduring – to
arise. This network of expressed or implied explanations linking intuition
to a work is both indispensable and also of no significance: indispensable
in that it is our only means to describe a work (before or after its death!);
insignificant in that the work's ultimate value lies beyond its reach.
Nevertheless, reflecting on the necessity of a work requires us to analyse
its various components, its various creative dimensions, but without forgetting that they are without precedence or hierarchy, that they always
refer to each other, that none of these dimensions could exist on its own,
in isolation from the rest, without undermining its own validity.

I will start with the very notion of language. What does that word
mean when applied to music? Does it even have any meaning? Does
musical communication have to be channelled through language? These
are questions that need to be asked, since the idea of musical language
has increasingly been called into question, and above all because there
are certain misunderstandings that we need to explain, if not dispel.

I will then turn to a critical description of the elements out of which
this language, if this is what it is, is built. This will lead me to consider
materials, time and space. By passing from elements to the way in which
they are used, I can study the problems of formal organisation and style.
Finally, and in order to relate these two perspectives to compositional

shaping, I will discuss the vital features of manipulation and accident, closely related phenomena in the precarious creative balance created by 'abolished chance'.[1]

I come now to the question of language, an idea that has taken a pounding, been called into question, even flatly denied. Why is this?

Musical language, in past centuries, was truly a common code. I refer here only to Western civilisation, but the case of non-European music is even clearer from this point of view. In both it was unthinkable to express oneself outside a common, acknowledged, agreed code. In that sense, communication could be said to operate through explicit conventions by which individuals could aim for perfection. Sometimes, especially in any oral tradition, individuality can even completely dissipate in favour of anonymity. What counts is the work as conveyed, with all the haphazard elements and transformations such transmission implies. This is collective expression, either universally respected or adapted by the individual, depending on whether the work is tied to religious or social taboos, or linked to labour and recreation.

In enduring, non-European traditions, this is the point of view that has prevailed: collective language gives pre-eminence to anonymity, or at least to the anonymity of the composer, if not always of the performer. But I am speaking of living, or at least surviving, traditions, given that this idea of language brings the danger of a tendency towards laborious development – in short, sclerosis. Language is agreed to be static, dating from a golden age that offered a unique and ultimate solution. Needless to say, a particularly rude shock can swiftly annihilate this kind of conservatism: witness the ravages of colonialism on populations we call 'indigenous'. Lately, many traditional cultures have disappeared rapidly as society has undergone rapid change, the new situations that have been created no longer corresponding at all with agreed ways forward.

There is something deeply artificial about prolonging linguistic edicts that no longer correspond to reality. This is the case for Latin in the church, and the corresponding preservation of plainchant, or at any rate what is *considered* to be plainchant, given the lack of agreement among musicologists about how plainchant was performed during the centuries that saw it appear and develop. We have the texts, naturally, but the *musical* interpretation of these texts – I do not, of course, mean intervals or figures, but rather the features that cannot be captured in precise notation – the *musical* performance practice is just as mystifying as the actual pronunciation of medieval Latin or French. A full knowledge of this language cannot be obtained by tracking down data as precisely as possible. It is a paradox: the inherited language has changed so little that we can easily trace the original, yet at the same time we are faced with a lost language, because key information is missing. This phantom language is at once here and gone, perennial and outdated.

With the sole exception of plainchant, linked to ritual liturgical stability, Western societies have followed a path very different from non-European traditions. Almost from the start, the language of cultivated music was the product or prey of the individuals who helped to shape it. Of course, for a long time the language adopted was shared. Individuals who expressed themselves through laws of their own making did not yet exist. That sort of individualism contradicted the concept of a musical work. In this respect our Western cultures were close to non-European ones. Divine language demanded submission, and communion with the truth left no place for individual states of mind. From today's perspective it looks as though it took a long time for individuality, in the sense that we understand it now, to break free from this 'impersonal' situation. In fact, it is hard for us accurately to gauge the role that individuality played in archaic forms of musical expression, and the further back we look, the less secure our judgement. Proust said that when examining photographic portraits from another era, it is difficult to reconstruct the social strata, to distinguish the elite from the bourgeois, or the bourgeois from the labourer dressed in Sunday best, because we are much more conscious of their shared origins in the same bygone era, defined by customs and fashions that were common to all. It is the same with music of the past: we are vastly more aware of the traits shared by works from the same era than of those that distinguish one work from another, since the distance of centuries has produced a remarkable levelling that extends to expression itself, expression that now eludes us. In the same way that we cannot identify an individual's distinctive traits, we are also totally unequipped to appreciate the diversity of expression within a given musical language. Be they expressions of pain or pleasure, we can understand or appreciate very little of this. Where the poetic texts that these works set have disappeared, we probably often misinterpret the music.

Historical perspective only increases the impression of an extremely rapid acceleration of phenomena produced by the development – even the overdevelopment – of the concept of individuality. Musical language evolves because individuals model it according to their personal desires and needs. But even taking into account what seems like an optical illusion, we must recognise that the evolution of Western music increasingly results in conflict between musical language and the individual, between collective means of communication and the individual's quest for self-description, between *expression* and *self-expression*. This was reflected at the beginning of the twentieth century in the abolition of a universal code – tonality – in favour of a code in which methods could still be generalised but results depended almost exclusively on individual choice. Even this method was soon contested, and Schoenberg's illusion of having found a new *permanence* in musical language soon dissipated, quickly and decisively. Who, today, would dream of working towards a collective language? Schoenberg and the Viennese School were probably the last to entertain that utopian vision.

✣ ✣ ✣

The desire for an individual idiom can, of course, be observed in musical language. Sometimes we seem to be reliving the story of the Tower of Babel. None of the scholarly meetings that tried to find a rational solution to this problem succeeded in producing any tangible results, having run up against notation as the symbol of individual originality.[2] As a result either of experience or the lack of it, or of the complexity of the musical events to be notated, or of the approach adopted, which can notate either action or output, there is complete confusion, in which a given sign can describe one thing in one score and a completely opposite thing in another. This problem of notation, so familiar to performers of contemporary music, is not an isolated phenomenon attributable to the insubordination of certain composers. It results specifically from the fact that musical language has reached a point where people need to create particular areas corresponding to their expressive needs. What once served to facilitate communication has become a basic obstacle. Notation is, in a sense, the most obvious symbol of the extreme individualisation of a musical language that shuns collective coding and stops just short of forgoing language's most fundamental virtue: its power to communicate – or at least to communicate directly, encrypted messages being more and more common.

With electroacoustics the problem is undoubtedly still more acute. In notated music, a composer seeks both a personal mode of expression and to enable performers to follow that path. Notation is therefore a minimum condition if a community, however small, is to speak the same language. But as soon as a work is 'irrevocably' transcribed and no longer needs to be targeted at performers, notation becomes completely superfluous. At most, it can serve as a visual description of acoustic phenomena, a sketch drawn with varying degrees of precision of a work already realised.[3] Or else processes that gave rise to sound are described symbolically, by numbers, and no one who has not heard the work would be able to imagine the sonic actuality to which the transcribed processes correspond. Transcription will remain a completely secret language, meaningful only to the composer and the composer's own memory, and to those already familiar with the processing and its output.

In various facets of their activity, composers challenge the notion of a musical language that is anything other than strictly individual. It can be of practical use only for themselves: a language that is a personal possession, patented, as it were, by the composer.

The composer does, however, admit notions of organisation, of choice, of selection. Although the language, personal as it is, rests on individually established frameworks, these frameworks are established as a function of a system of coordinates that need to be plotted in order to grasp the meaning of the work. Regarding only sound, even this is organised within a system, and sonic material cannot be envisioned outside the codes of individual musical language. Some pretext, though – an ideological or philosophical pretext is actually preferable – can lead us to feel that there is no necessary link between language and material, that something is *music* in itself. If so, all that is needed is to put this article of faith – to be more precise, this premise – into action, to put it to 'work'. Anything can be used that originates in, and belongs to, sonic vibration, be it the sounds of daily life, of nature, of culture or technology. This can obviously amount to the complete negation of an understanding of language as a consistent and organic whole.

In fact, there is no attempt to hide this through excuses or pretence: the idea of language is simply discarded as a matter of principle, because it contradicts the external world and offers structures that are of no interest at all. Our reluctance to accept the constraint of language stems from the simple fact that language *excludes*, whereas we want to allow anything to happen. At most, I would be willing to construct convenient structures that would be as generous and receptive as my desire to accommodate everything within them. Expecting a structure – assuming it deserves to be considered as such at all – to be as open as this is clearly the opposite of responsibility. Even when we impose on such phenomena an idea of *temporal succession* – this is all it is, when ordering the phenomena temporally is all one does – they still in no way relate to the nature of this succession; logically, they could have occurred in another order, no less out of place, or no less *in* place for that matter.

Can we, then, still speak of language? If so, this language has no control over its events. Yet there is another kind of language, equally liberal and grounded in style. What we need from language is a kind of universality – and I emphasise *kind*. The question remains open as to whether this is real universality or simply appropriateness, whose justification is essentially poetic or even ideological. In effect, the expressive possibilities of a vocabulary are found to be much too limiting, leading to the desire to enlarge them not by expanding potential outputs, but by recovering elements found further up the chain, by rediscovering and integrating an arsenal of techniques taken from bygone worlds that are in this way reinvigorated. On the one hand, this is an attempt to apply the notion of language to each and every possible sonic event; on the other, it relates only to those drawn from our own culture and history.

It is difficult to fault those two starting points, postulates or articles of faith by arguing on the grounds of faith or poetic conviction. This is a decision in which freedom of choice really reigns supreme, and the integration of external or historical events into today's language has already happened in literature – and by no means only recently, since the surrealists and Joyce could be cited as embodiments of the same attitudes. But does the specificity of musical expression admit a similar approach? Do not the criteria defining musical language forbid that kind of integration of raw or sophisticated material, or at any rate exclude such a casual use of material, or its incorporation through a wealth of means that skirt the real problems, in order to wallow in a swamp of artificial techniques?

What strikes me as the most obviously controversial aspect of the unlimited incorporation of raw or cultural phenomena is the absence of a true relationship between the object and the language. In the first case, in which any sonic object is included, the link between event and structure is deliberately severed; composers refuse to select material for its potential formal integration, the constraints of musical development are ignored, and what could be merely an accident in relation to a given structure is taken as the very stuff of permutation. This explains why 'composition' splits into two entirely distinct, independent parts. On the one hand, following principles that are nothing to do with the material – the choice of which is often left until later, or even to the last minute – something that could be called a diagram is devised: meticulous, detailed charts of timing, density, performance and envelopes are produced, each one completely unrelated. These diagrams have their own internal, separate, unreal logic. They could apply to anything, and therein lies their weakness, because at no stage is the necessity of their existence confirmed by the way in which the musical material actually works. These diagrams are external instructions for what they are supposed to be controlling, taking no account at all of necessary reciprocal functions between material and structure. And then, often with wilful indifference to the diagrams that have been drawn up, material is defined according to an arbitrary or predetermined process.

I say that 'material is defined', but I should have said that 'material is *circumscribed*'. Strictly speaking, it is not defined by characteristics dictated by the diagrams, but is rather circumscribed by a completely external description that relies only on some poetic idea: this could be harmonies that are devised or random, or familiar sounds that correspond to or contradict the diagram. The joy seems to lie in an accidental encounter between a detailed diagram that is applicable to anything at all and nothing in particular, and material that is ill suited not only to this diagram, but to any diagram or even the very notion of one. The consequence for temporality is obvious: at best, we have a succession of events that could have occurred in any different order. It's just like the arithmetic of children's games: three apples plus five knives equals eight frogs. This sort of poetics can be delightful, but it offers little scope and cannot create anything new . . .

I feel, moreover, that producing formal diagrams in advance of the work's actual material is inimical to the very idea of creativity, because it presumes – at best – a sort of filling in of the blanks with any disparate material not conceived for this purpose. Such a method – or rather, just a way of doing things – suggests a disturbing indifference to material; it suggests that any kind of material can suit any formal plan, that no intrinsic relationship is sought or wished for, that creativity can innocently cordon itself off, exist in abstract, immaterial form. In the most intelligent strains of this tendency, there are reflections, unilateral ones, of tradition. In these prefabricated diagrams of timing, density, dynamics and timbre, of recurrences and new material, you can easily find traces of the ancient *cantus firmus*, a technique that is no less artificial, although it did give rise to polyphony. For what can be said about a technique that effectively consists of taking a melodic line and stretching it in time to such an extent that it loses all affinity with its content, its articulations, and then uses this lost identity to graft one or more identities onto it? Is this not also a case of a pre-existing diagram, based on a dismantled real object, which then imposes its ghostly presence on musical events that go on to disregard its very presence? Creative minds have always invented rigid frameworks of activity that can then be subjected to the fantasy that order can be destroyed with impunity. All discipline exists in order to be abolished . . .

These divergent paths can be seen throughout the history of music, especially at important turning points in its development. There is a dialectic of order and disorder that has turned out to be very fruitful, especially in recent eras, but this dialectic is about the relationship between object and musical language, which is itself linked to the choice of sonic material. With respect to musical material and language, the relationship has without doubt always been about verification and relevance. Implicitly, the first question asked about musical material is, 'Is this material musical?' or, more specifically, 'Is this material musical with respect to my conception, to my creativity?' Either we construct material in order to use it within a given system, or we force found material to comply with the system, eliminating some of its characteristics and eradicating connotations that contradict the system. In both cases – pre-compositional operation and compositional adjustment – the relationship between material and musical language is vital. There can be struggle and contradiction in both directions. The pre-existing, prefabricated musical material, linked to a system of thought and organisation, can be subject to too many constraints that pre-date its deployment by the current user. Sometimes this material has to be altered, constraining the creativity in play, because it does not necessarily match the requirements of the conceptual environment – in its capacity to conceive of timbre or pitch, for example. The operational field formed by existing material is thus seen to be inadequate, or at least out of place, given the field of exploration. But even when this material is interesting in itself, it can also resist integration into an organisation that is rationally extended to the most limiting consequences. Material has a constant tendency to transcend its conceptual premises. The field of operation of the material is thus displaced from its field of exploration, when it reveals itself as so rich that it proliferates outside the latter field.

This relationship between object and language is thus subject to dangerous oscillations that can even cause it to burst. When the field of operation of the material and the conceptual field no longer coincide, the validity of the musical material is certainly in doubt, but the question of the validity of the work's construction is even more pressing. In essence, the object truly exists only with respect to a language, and to the purposes of this language in relation to the overall plan. Broadly or narrowly defined plans will result in lesser or greater constraint in the choice of objects, of material – unless, that is, we resolve this 'tug of war', this stifling opposition between object and language, in a radical way by concluding that the situation is *absurd*. Unfortunately, though the result may be absurd, intentions are not at all to blame; or else the absurdity is quite innocent of its potential, and it is not intentions that play these discrepancies off each other in a way that could almost produce an X-ray of object and language. Although there have been such attempts, they barely anticipated the consequences of such interrogation, but stuck to a fairly primitive, comic attitude, or a smiling acceptance, whether derisory or cynical, of the random encounters that were for a while so dear to the hearts of the Surrealists. We no longer speak of onirism, nor of automatic writing, but the comic situations they produced, or carefully elaborated, scarcely rose above the level of the trivially haphazard.

More generally, this relationship between language and material can be seen as a form of relationship between concept, diagram and realisation. When we are committed to a creative process that goes from initial plan to finished work, concept generally seems to compete with material, and the very act of composing means that what we are conceiving has to direct both the idea (the family of ideas) and the material (the types of material). There is therefore a double analysis, almost a double inventory of possibilities with respect to how things are ordered. Today, with forms and materials ever less predetermined, the craze for cataloguing and charting is suppressed. One often sees misunderstandings about the very facts of composing.

To define a scheme or hierarchy, however temporary, to prevent possibilities from dissipating in a group of elements that is difficult to grasp, to somehow control the proliferation of material, we use categories of two kinds. In the first, distribution of the material follows certain existential characteristics, so that the elements we need are controlled, ready to be engaged compositionally, assigned a symbol or a form of reference that becomes very useful in the context of different systems of variation and combination. In the second case, we create families of objects, depending on a given procedure; they are assigned a code so that they can be of general use. All this amounts to a *reduction* of the material into a series of symbols that can be used in a formal plan; and at the same time, to a *negation* of this material, because by categorising the material, then creating this inventory of numerical symbols, we have clearly removed its reality, which can in no way be reduced to a series of events or deductions. This approach is, therefore, false and artificial from the outset, because it removes the actual vitality of the proposed material by eliminating its power and purpose.

But misunderstanding goes even further, because the exact opposite of this inventory of lexical elements, and a case that proceeds from an identical error, is that in which a chart specifies and arranges concepts that are too vague and general to be represented in this way. A chart of the musical development is created to organise either large-scale form or the formal details of a work, its articulation and its temporal unfolding. This produces a perfectly constructed general scheme for controlling everything. Composition then consists of filling in the blanks of this formal template with the inventory's previously determined categories. As long as the original definitions are in agreement – the most basic precaution that needs to be taken – a perfect tautology is created, one that is as totally unsatisfactory as it is absurd, since it was generated by a musically artificial syllogism. The work is pre-planned, programmed, and all that is left to do is to complete it. It may well provide complete gratification to its author and to superficial music analysts, the sort of gratification we find in any self-defining object.

This kind of procedure would be admissible only if one wanted temporarily to negate the active participation of the composer and of compositional choice in order to arrive 'at the limit of the fertile land',[4] at the *unconstrained* exploration of these categories, to yield musical objects according to statistical criteria – and this approach can be valid as long as we remain acutely conscious of its limitations. Yet plans and inventories can represent only a borderline case of a concept, that of allowing non-goal-directed, automatic gestures. In any such composition – there were many in the 1950s, but there is no shortage of them now either – what is most striking is the lack of constraint, or what I would call an absence of necessity. The oddest result of this diagrammatic tyranny is aimlessness, lack of intention. One feels one is listening to a piece that is not properly delineated in time, which has no 'before' and 'after'.

Rather, one has a strong sense of having been served a slice of time, well defined if the plan is well executed, but a slice all the same: a fragment of a larger, *implicit* whole.

That impression is quite correct, since out of all the possible permutations and combinations consistent with the formal plan, the composer has made an arbitrary decision, such as choosing to present only a certain number of them, because they seem more interesting than the others, with more noteworthy properties, or because they have common properties that distinguish them from all the other elements in the group. Yet we will sometimes ask: Why choose these figures or groups of figures rather than others? What can seem to be the strictest determinism can lead to the deepest sense of uncertainty. As always, this need not call the validity of such a project into question, because to present an arbitrarily chosen slice of time, and to make the audience aware that the direction does not count, that limits as such are irrelevant, that any moment can replace any other, that each moment belongs to an infinity of moments never to be heard but which can be imagined at leisure – all that is a compositional plan, or partial place, which I for one find fascinating since it embodies composition, in Mallarmé's terms, as the abolition of chance; although in what we have been describing, chance is not abolished but rather suspended, while acknowledging the arbitrary nature of this suspension.

However, it cannot be said that this use (and even abuse) of charts and inventories is usually aware of its limitations. I would say that if the chart does not result from the work, it can at most provide a foresight, convenient for the global idea of the work, but one that is modified as the work takes shape and can even be abandoned when necessary. Both the inventory of material and the conceptual plan can be used as sketches – precise and even prescriptive – that prevent the work from losing its way in pointless and flimsy proliferation. But the chart must be fully receptive to the possibility of chance, which might be destructive. No predetermined, large-scale organisation can take into account the interaction that must occur between idea and material at the very moment of composition. In a way, it is absurd to conceive a plan in the absence of this response to the material that is integral to its existence.

It is quite difficult, if not impossible, to determine the priority between a conceptual chart and organisation of material. The compositional process, if it is to be a rich and dynamic experience, must concentrate on developments at the level of localised creativity. The global plan can be an unformulated, informal underpinning. It can be replaced by an instinct that espouses irrationality, the indispensable vagaries of the moment, which an entirely formalised diagram must by its very nature exclude. Attaining this instinctive planning is no easy process, because the composer loses the security of continual reference to a known form and to an inventory of details. The superficial comforts of rationality are erased in the face of doubt about establishing deep and true relationships between idea and material. The uncertainty of this constant re-evaluation triumphs over the reassuring but misleading concept of a template.

For me, the relationship of language to object, chart to material and concept to realised work can never exist by relying on simplified, predetermined norms, any more than it can be effaced simply by some 'poetic' decision. In addition, such a relationship cannot be transplanted from literary or visual spheres, which equally means derivation from a 'poetic' decision. This relationship has no autonomous existence. In its obsession with classifying everything possible, and even things that cannot be classified, a *total* inventory is as absurd as the total absence of classification or, rather, of characterisation. On the other hand, constructing a work without any *final* plan is no more or less ideal than deriving everything from an *initial* one: it is as valid to explore these two musical extremes as it is invalid to say that they are the most important things. So we need to imagine the ways in which material and diagram can be paired, how each creates and influences the other; how formal plan and inventory must give way to notions that are more *real*, more profound, and arise directly from the act of composing and from the individual nature of the material selected. Once work has begun and certain classifications are established, we shall not mistake them for anything other than merely convenient ways to define certain problems.

Here I have addressed only plans that engage with and deploy ideas directly related to musical vocabulary, objects tied to a well-defined grammar by their description and notation, whereas others have claimed to extend experimentation to procedures that use either generalised visual signs as unconnected as possible to what is normally meant by notation of musical parameters, or words that describe an action, the material of which is left to choice or chance. The more distinct the procedure is from the specialisation of its musical language, the more it will provoke unpredictable reactions (unpredictable because they are triggered at the last minute or channelled in an all-too-vague manner by ill-defined categories), and the less one is able to trace the results back to the plan, so much so that one could almost say that any diagram induces any result. This recalls the Delphic oracle, in the sense that an event can always be associated with a 'prediction', since the prediction is so vague and handily formulated that any result is easily seen as its outcome.

This leads to an enormous impoverishment of musical intelligence. The proposed channels of creativity are so crude that they provoke above all superficial performance gestures, often having nothing whatsoever to do with the formal plan itself. In order to remedy the uncertainty and lack of precision of the formal plan and its chart, the performer must either appeal to personal inclination, by internally seeking objects that could more or less match the instructions, or try to comply with the instructions and thereby suspend personal inclinations in order to produce rudimentary, crude objects that in some sense fit the plan better, while being of little or no interest. In reality, there is no dialectic between plan and material. While the plan can influence the material tactically, there is no reciprocity, because at this fundamental level material does not influence the 'embodiment' of the plan. This always happens when musicians use an inadequate and perfunctory plan as a basis for improvisation. It can never be more than perfunctory since the performers need to react so quickly to it. It is inadequate because it is incapable of defining anything other than this tactical dimension, and the grammatical dimension is completely sidelined. Training for improvisation from a plan would basically consist of filling in its fundamental omissions, superimposing a fictional plan worked out during the course of training and memorised to replace the original plan in performance. It is, therefore, no surprise that when these plans are used by different individuals or groups, one hears fundamentally different results. What one hears is something derived from the plan but worked out and memorised by the performer or performers, an imaginary plan that, unlike the original, empirically establishes the dialectic between diagram and material. Without acknowledging the fact, this practice re-establishes the formal template necessary for any work, no matter how spontaneous or fleeting.

Nevertheless, for this kind of intention – I am not referring to the actual realisation – the plan is an absurd residue of a logical methodology; it becomes a perfectly vain object in and of itself. No matter whether this chart, graphic, set of instructions or poetic or para-musical text is presented as a finished work or as a starting point for improvisation, vanity is its main feature.

❊ ❊ ❊

I have discussed at length the problems encountered by today's musicians with respect to musical language, and described a certain number of partial solutions that are more promising than others, in order to give a sense of the sheer number of individual responses available. I do not claim to offer a global response. As I said, the illusion of a 'universal' solution flourished for one last time with the Viennese School, and I do not think that it is reasonable to hope to unify contemporary musical thought. One could nevertheless ask why solutions that seemed at first glance appealing, new and promising quickly proved to be provisional expedients whose potential would soon be exhausted; and wonder why such a plethora of extra-musical explanations has been offered to explain individual attitudes towards musical language.

We always tend to believe that our own times are unique, on account of characteristics thought to be inimical to the past, even the recent past, but one must admit that recently there has been a profusion of non-musical commentaries, intended to justify or sometimes to conceal. It seems that pure musical introspection can no longer be invoked to justify choices and decisions, which are now supposed to depend on non-musical elements. There is no shortage of pretexts: political engagement, philosophical reflection, scientific idolatry, mystique, all sorts of cosmogonies, so to speak, allowing us to evade the real issues. As a result, despite even the most brilliant and appealing external considerations, the issues persist. We think that we have found universal solutions that are in fact not even temporary or partial. In my opinion, they are, at most, naive or cunning expedients, depending on the temperaments of those who use them, hence the need for the many explanations of different attitudes and their rationales. It is almost as if musical composition could disappear altogether when it is not needed in order to understand mere intentions. The musical *act* becomes a kind of demonstration, almost superfluous. Commentary on the reasoning behind a compositional attitude becomes in the end more important than the musical act itself.

This is why we still need to return to musical language, for after our disappointment with commentaries, and commentaries on commentaries, it alone can provide us with what pretext-seeking cannot achieve. The first constraint that I feel we should remember is the implicit existence of a hierarchy. I do not conceive of hierarchy in terms of subordination, but almost in statistical terms. This is by no means a hierarchy setting out what is important and what is not – one of distinction versus contempt, noble versus ignoble – but rather a hierarchy distinguishing what is at the centre from what is peripheral, what is decisive from what is relative.

As I have already stated, much of the *validity* of the possibilities in musical language lies in precisely locating their territory. To engage with possibilities beyond that territory would amount to invalidating them, and therefore to destroying their reality. Every domain contains central elements that are sufficiently flexible and malleable. These possibilities can be integrated into different types of situations; they can never be recognised as unique and will not exert centrifugal force on a given structure. They can be used in general, permutational forms and can participate in non-specialised configurations. This, incidentally, corresponds to psychoacoustic situations in which our perception functions with ease, in which it is not hampered by overly complex analysis nor exclusively focused on something unusual that monopolises attention at the expense of other categories.

In the first case, in which our perception experiences excessive analytical difficulty, it loses interest in the phenomenon, especially if we do not give it the time it needs to get its bearings. This occurs with excessive density, with relentlessly complex and undifferentiated textures, when micro-intervals are used over too brief a time span, and when music constantly exceeds an acceptable level of volume. In all those cases, perception loses interest in the facts and can no longer relate them to each other. If there is order here, it is one that cannot be grasped; if there is disorder, it fails to sort elements into categories, however provisional. Either way, perception escapes us.

In the second case, in which perception is exclusively focused on, and monopolised by, something unusual, it rejects the structure that includes this phenomenon, since it is too strong and independent in the context of that structure. Whether it is a rough-and-ready object used as it is, or a constructed object, our perception seizes above all on its originality, its unique and exceptional qualities. If the object has connotations in daily life, even our best intentions will fail in the face of the object's resistance to integration. Thinking of Varèse and his repeated use of sirens in his scores, we can clearly see that he wanted to incorporate the possibility of a sound continuum into the world of discrete intervals. Unfortunately, this was tied to a means of production too crude for genuine integration, and the siren remains a separate object that strikes us more by its strong connotations in real life – alarms, police cars – than by its abstract relationship to the world of musical instruments. I could give countless examples of this kind of instrumental material: it would be impossible to listen to a piece made up entirely of Bartók pizzicato, for example, or an entire piece for wind instruments that exclusively used key and valve sounds.

Of course, as music develops, an extension of, or rather, *shift* in perception occurs. We are certainly more receptive today to complex chords. They no longer seem to us to be *only* complex; now we are able to evaluate their degree of complexity within a chromatic language. We have probably acquired this ability at the expense of a greater sensitivity to natural intonation, not derived from equal temperament. Similarly, our perception of time has greatly expanded compared to classical metre,

73

yet such gains have doubtless been made at the expense of our perception of accentuation and rhythmic phrasing. A new exploration cannot be rejected out of hand, its provisional results rebuffed, on the mistaken grounds that we cannot perceive it, but perception has, as it were, a central kernel in which it circulates freely, and margins that it accesses more rarely, with greater difficulty and less readily. The notion of a central kernel of perception is crucial for assessing the lines of force connecting structure and material, by which I mean compositional material rather than sonic material as such. Structure must be fully capable of maintaining its power to attract material, even if there are exceptions, borderline cases in which the material is sufficiently strong as to make us temporarily forget the structure.

Thus, there is a direct correlation with hierarchy, a problem of internal consistency and a problem of balancing elements. The problem of consistency is basic: material refers to structure and is selected as a function of the structure, a statement that could be reversed by saying that structure has to select its material in order to come into being.

I have already sufficiently described the fundamental inconsistency that flows from plan and object being ill suited, but I would like to address this question in another way. Hierarchy and consistency point towards an inescapable enquiry whose banality hides its difficulty: What is musical, and what is not? How can we decide on a criterion that would *in itself* distinguish one from the other? This is, nevertheless, the most spontaneous kind of criticism found on the lips of professionals and non-professionals alike, so much so that everyone thinks this criterion is fundamental, while at the same time being altogether incapable of providing a definition, or even a description. Does this impression of the musical and the non-musical stem only from what we are used to? In that case, there would really be no other way forward than study intended to overturn the range of values to which an individual appeals when expressing a preference. But surely the difference between musical and non-musical derives more from the relationship in a work between raw material and organising structure? Is not the internal consistency of the content the main element of persuasion? A moment's reflection can convince us that disappointment and disenchantment often result from the suspicion that a plan is somehow being inconsistently or inadequately executed. The plan may well have all the elements of originality and novelty, but if the means are not the product of a discriminating mind, the project will seem to us to have failed in its execution. Above all, the musical and the non-musical are – or at least should be – categories pertaining to execution rather than prerequisites.

I stated in effect that if it were a question only of habit, the problem would be relatively simple to solve through sustained, ongoing study. But would this kind of ongoing learning really suffice to define more flexible perceptual categories as deeply musical, as acceptable tactically rather than being of strategic, and completely and fundamentally musical, value?

Of course, our education opens up many channels through musical figures considered to be very models of perfection; it defines a perceptual and epistemological network that determines how we read and listen to any new score. Deliberately or not, consciously or not, our criteria of judgement are set by those antecedents, or at any rate our orientation is. We may not analyse our own reflexes, but it appears to be in that realm that these categories of musical and non-musical are truly difficult to handle, because in reality they apply to two different phenomena and their interaction.

The first phenomenon is material, and this is the most immediate, since it appeals directly to the culturally familiar. Cultural tradition has familiarised us with certain material, not only in terms of its quality, but also its hierarchy. We have a prescriptive, defined concept of it associated with precise objectives, determined by history and, I would even say, oriented towards the past. Any new material that does not respond to the same demands, that is not tied to the same imperatives, tends not to fit with implicitly or explicitly authorised definitions.

Every type of material that is in a sense outside the law seems to be a grammatical mistake, perhaps in bad taste, but above all incongruous. This situation has been constantly repeated, and the history of musical instruments is strewn with its victims: every one that could not be incorporated was killed off because it could not reach beyond the level of incongruity. One might suggest that they were sometimes able to

75

be assimilated precisely because of their high degree of incongruity, but generally once the shock of an exhilarating encounter dissipated, these instruments were rejected because of their lack of fit, either with instrumental norms or with the deeper development of musical thought, beyond these accidents of circumstance. These instruments may be so closely associated with their stylistic characteristics that it is very difficult, if not impossible, to isolate them from their specific usage, other than by giving that usage the air of a quotation. The ondes Martenot, saxophone and vibraphone exemplify these types of rejection or acceptance within instrumental norms. Naturally, it is not overtly because of their belonging to the 'officially' musical or the non-musical that they are abandoned or embraced; but even when nothing is claimed or even noted in passing, these criteria continue to underlie their status. Collective decisions, as these more or less are, are relatively unpredictable, and such reactions put us in the position of the grammarian studying neologisms – how they flourish, decline and disappear. These decisions are indeed collective, and may be anonymous. They do not even take into account the durability of works. When works still included in the repertoire have made use of such abandoned or neglected instruments, we will use more contemporary and appropriate instruments that 'conform' both with the current era and the enduring instrumental forces. Schoenberg's and Webern's use of the harmonium in excellent works did not guarantee its survival in the concert hall. Usually, instead of using instruments so worn with age as to be nearly unplayable, one is innocently obliged to substitute an electric organ, which certainly does not have the instrumental properties Webern or Schoenberg wanted, but provides a reasonable approximation. The same is true of Ravel and his use of the luthéal.

The obsolescence of musical instruments is not only a matter of their technical capacity, nor is it solely tied to the works using them. These two phenomena do certainly play a role, but instrumental obsolescence obeys such complex laws that predictions about the evolution of instrumental resources are little more than wild guesses. Of course, the development of certain instruments has been harmed by their limited capacity and restricted usefulness, but other instruments with limited mechanical capabilities have survived happily enough despite their poor potential for improvement, the reason being that they meet some unique instrumental need. The attempt to define an instrument's necessary qualities would include such characteristics as a suitably broad dynamic range, sufficiently complex mechanical properties to yield well-differentiated results and being sufficiently simple to be playable with ease, among many others; but that said, we still have not identified the reasons why an instrument will survive. Indeed, we can see before our very eyes the way the most recent instrumental family, percussion, is gradually being transformed.

What is clear is that no composer is in a position to determine this development. Beyond some obvious economic determinants – standardised manufacture, streamlined implementation – certain instruments establish themselves quickly and form instrumental families, while others remain marginal and are used in only a few works, often because a handful of composers take their cue from a particular work that had a strong impact, before they completely disappear or become a mere curiosity. I feel that the percussion family, as anarchic as it might seem today, is starting to show some organisation: keyboard instruments are beginning to occupy the most pre-eminent position, though this certainly does not mean the disappearance of drums on the grounds of archaism. Raw instrumental material therefore tends towards congruence; it enters the instrumental corpus and goes on to feel no longer exceptional. It becomes absorbed, even neutralised, when it ceases to seem incongruous. Such is the case with the xylophone: its intrinsic qualities are what is acknowledged, not the unusualness that first distinguished it. Material goes from being non-musical or, better, para-musical to being musical. This development takes place over a period of time marked by the bridge between works that used it because of its marginality and those that did so because of its 'neutrality'.

Cases have already been mentioned in which a work survives even though its instrument does not, but this discrepancy obviously disappears when the sonic medium is no longer independent of the work's conception. The more we have turned to the independent use of electroacoustic techniques, the more the risk of obsolescence is tied to the work itself, which becomes outdated because its material has been supplanted by technical developments, by technological progress, by the relationship between musical innovation and the technical 'instrument' that it employs. If the work remains a graphic to be reinterpreted and thereby rejuvenated, the resulting music has the deadly characteristic of lasting 'for ever'. Rejuvenation never takes hold of it, except for some tinkering with the presentation, so that what was once exceptional or incongruous becomes normal through familiarisation, repetition and distance. The exceptional disappears not only for these reasons, but also because other, more 'exceptional' phenomena are discovered in the meantime. Familiarisation destroys the exceptional character of these sonic phenomena, but it does not incorporate them into a generally usable sonic repertoire. Their novelty evaporates without their becoming universal. It is clear, incidentally, that there are composers who decide to work in this permanently temporary zone, whereas others reject it, or accept it only reluctantly, because they are trying as far as possible to create a permanent vocabulary.

It is still too early to predict the future of sound production, but materials themselves certainly do not age well, not only because it is so challenging to preserve them and technology is constantly being improved, but particularly because their potential for creativity is limited both by this problem of the medium and also by the very development of technical devices. Creativity depends not only on a state-of-the-art medium or technical means, but even more on the state of the technological thinking that gave rise to the medium and its technical devices. At a certain level of this kind of thinking, musical creativity will be entirely subservient to technology, even if it temporarily benefits from it. The arc of musical culture will be defined in terms of the arc of technology, and these arcs will be irrevocably confined to the past.

It will be objected that this is the same in the visual arts, that there is no reason to be unduly worried, because instead of relating to music in a timeless fashion, as our culture has taught us to do, we should appreciate the musical object directly and as inseparable from its technology. And indeed, musical experiences of this kind are sufficiently established and compelling for us to be able to draw conclusions similar to those within visual art. Nevertheless, we can look back on the last thirty years or so in order to gain perspective and insight. The truth is that experience is not conclusive. Is this only because, in general, works have not displayed a high level of creativity? Is it because we can become aware of the level of musical creativity only when we ignore the means used to realise works that today we find far too basic? It nevertheless remains true that what might once have appeared to be extra-musical or even non-musical still seems extra-musical today. But whereas at the time we heard these works we could still hope that materials would evolve into being better integrated, such hope has now been completely abandoned. What remains is *evidence*, testimonies to the uneasy fit between musical vocabulary and new material, but material cannot be replaced. The work is condemned to remain what it is, its creativity and realisation having happened at the same time and being forever inseparable. No category switch has occurred, from the musical to the non-musical, from the unusual to the neutral. Works are destined to remain *documents* of past history rather than fertile ground for musical thought, in constant development, subject to constant re-examination. What electroacoustics perhaps needs is the introduction of highly determined elements through which technological thought will be able to respond to the needs of re-examination by way of musical thought. For the moment, this is only an aspiration, for it is not clear how this overdetermination would come into play.

With respect to material itself, we have seen that the non-musical can either become musical or not, that the salience of the work to this material plays a significant role but is nevertheless not a sufficient condition, and that despite their striking, if passing, qualities, some kinds of material will never be foundational for their musical language, and we are never sure why natural selection yields such-and-such an outcome. We see the results and we can follow the history of this evolution, but the underlying mechanisms are so complex that it is practically impossible for us to predict or even to explain it convincingly in retrospect.

Yet the question 'What is musical and what is not?' is not only about raw material. We need also to be concerned with the work itself, its design, its structures. We can still call a work non-musical even when regarding its material as potentially musical. When material is acknowledged to be traditional, it may be used in ways that will make it non-musical for some listeners. This produces the endless criticism that a work is, say, inconsistent, that it lacks continuity, or that its pitch collections are unattractive. In the most up-to-date language, we say that the composer *fails to hear* what is written. Such an expression would be difficult to apply, however, to some producers of electroacoustic music, in that they do indeed hear what they make, at the very moment that they make it; the supposed inconsistency, discontinuity and unattractiveness have deeper roots than simply hearing, mentally or actually. What we find non-musical in a work that uses traditional material is thus the *absence* of qualities that we consider, through education, tradition or inclination, to be indispensable for this material. It is above all the way the material is used that we object to, not the material itself, and it can be more sheer force of habit than a composer's methods that causes us brusquely to reject unusual ways of handling material. This covers all the 'musical' dimensions of the organisation of musical language with respect to material: articulation, phrasing, accentuation, horizontal versus vertical and their interrelationship, how they control each other, and also every aspect of this language as a comprehensible form of expression. But meaning is not always understood rationally: it is much more common to experience the necessity and the power of expression of this musical language irrationally, and we often call something 'musical' precisely when it seems to go beyond grammatical analysis and the correct use of elements of vocabulary, by transcending its many inevitable, even prosaic components in order to attain what we feel to be a true, possibly unique form of expression.

A vast terrain lies between this 'musical' absolute to which we aspire and the 'non-musical' that we categorically reject, and this terrain must essentially submit to subjective criteria that do not necessarily involve the material. What do we mean by saying that a phrase is unmusical, even subjectively speaking? What objective criteria, maybe inflected by individualism, are we invoking? Why does a melodic phrase from *Erwartung* strike me as fundamentally musical, whereas a phrase from *Von Heute auf Morgen* does the opposite, being pointless, sterile, lacking musicality?

The material of each is fundamentally the same: the twelve tones, and the instruments of a classical orchestra. Can my different opinions of these two works be explained by some problem in perceiving the phrase? On the contrary, symmetry in later Schoenberg is often more apparent, in the neoclassical vein, than in the shifting structures of the Schoenberg of *Erwartung*. Could it be that the twelve-tone row creates perceptual issues here? On the contrary, when listening to phrases from *Erwartung* or *Von Heute auf Morgen* in isolation I do not take into account the large-scale structure, one that is undetermined and indeterminate in *Erwartung* and strictly determined in *Von Heute auf Morgen*. In any case, the series is not a sufficiently powerful feature to ensure that a phrase is of greater or lesser musicality. When I sense that such a problem is in fact related to technique, and in this particular case to twelve-tone technique, then how does this work? Would it be enough to say that in *Erwartung* I perceive the freedom and in *Von Heute auf Morgen* the constraint? While that is in effect the starting point, it still needs to be ascertained whether freedom and constraint are solely responsible for what I judge to be musical or unmusical, or at any rate, less musical. Should I take the composer into account, hearing his freedom or constraint in the way that he composed these melodic phrases? This is certainly the beginning of the answer.

It is not some quality within itself that makes material musical. It may be pleasant, unpleasant, interesting, impoverished, rich, surprising, predictable – in short, any criterion that our reflexes, cultural or otherwise, attribute to it. It is above all acoustic qualities such as brilliance, strength, variety and texture that attract us, intrinsic qualities independent of any application. Obviously, in this sense one can well maintain that all sounds rightfully exist in and of themselves. But can we claim that from the perspective of composition, sound is nothing in and of itself? Versatility and internal consistency allow it to be incorporated in the processes of a work. There is irreducible material or, more precisely, material with a strong tendency to be irreducible, and there is, on the other hand, material whose versatility lends itself ideally to the dialectics of composition. The interaction of material and language is essentially due to the capacity for adaptation or the irreducibility that these two components display.

I now hope to extend this definition to elaborated material, not only to sound sources. If the constraint imposed on elaborated material is such that it results in composition encountering basic antagonisms, this is the same situation as when sound sources were so highly individualised as to stamp their irreducibility on a work.

Since composing is itself so variable, following as it does whatever functions it is given, it follows that it would be futile – though we have been far too ready to do this – to define the musical and the non-musical on the basis of model compositions that have themselves established balance, hierarchy and consistency in an apparently satisfying way.

So it is true that that material is exploited as a function of organisation, even if it was chosen *before* being organised. If it displays strongly irreducible traits, it will play only a marginal, peripheral role, while in the opposite case it will stand at the very centre of the work/material relationship. This relationship, depending on the variable function and structure of a work, can even reverse that provisional hierarchy. Incidentally, hierarchies are always provisional; they temporarily regulate the essential balance of all the forces in play, a relationship that nowadays develops unpredictably even during the course of the work itself.

The musical and the non-musical certainly exist; they can even exist independently, but they can exist only in a transitory manner. This explains why – and it is not necessarily a discouraging conclusion – we can but trust our instincts to pin down at any point a category as mobile as this one, and try as we might it will always remain a decidedly individual notion, as well as a decidedly contestable and contested one. No matter how careful we are to produce musical coherence, no matter how indifferent we may claim to be to this problem, no matter how hostile we may be even to identifying this phenomenon as a problem, the evaluation of a work will nevertheless always imply an underlying judgement about something that is not itself a value. This is not exactly the least paradoxical aspect of any aesthetic evaluation of a musical or non-musical work.

1 Boulez's expression *'le hasard aboli'* is derived from Stéphane Mallarmé's poem 'Un coup de dés jamais n'abolira le hasard' ('A Throw of the Dice Will Never Abolish Chance'), which had a decisive influence on Boulez's experiments with open or mobile works.

2 This may refer in part to a conference on 'Notation in New Music' held at Darmstadt in 1964, in which Boulez participated, as well as Carl Dahlhaus and Earle Brown, among others.

3 Boulez is referring to *Hörpartitur*, or listening scores of electroacoustic works, the most famous being the elaborate graphic score of György Ligeti's *Artikulation* (1958), prepared by Rainer Wehinger, which was published by Schott in 1970.

4 'À la limite du pays fertile', the title of an essay by Boulez that was first published in German ('An der Grenzen des Fruchtlandes', *Die Reihe* 1, 1955), and published in English as '"At the Edge of Fertile Land" (Paul Klee)', in *Stocktakings from an Apprenticeship*, ed. Paule Thévenin, trans. Stephen Walsh (Oxford: Clarendon Press, 1991), pp. 158–72. The title is inspired by a painting by Paul Klee, *Monument am Grenzen des Fruchtlands*.

PART 3: THE COMPOSER'S GESTURE

5

Composition and Its Various Gestures
(1979–80)

Why speak of gestures?

Musical composition, perhaps more than any other creative activity, is based on *speculation* of the most abstract kind about specific concepts. It is also based on the *manipulation* of material that will be transmitted in order to come into being. The different gestures of composition are born of this duality, this contradiction between speculation and reality, each of which must accommodate the other.

Composition *formalises* and it *mediates*.

No matter what the sources and the origins of musical organisation may be, there is an absolute need to formalise the musical *idea*. Although musical discourse can exist only through the creative process, the idea, once generated, can be supported only by formal devices (old or new) that determine its true dimensions and set it on a trajectory that is defined strongly enough to capture our attention. Musical discourse needs to be elaborated from predetermined starting points, using deductive methods to amplify, transform and proliferate, without necessarily resorting to narrative or mere linearity. The formalisation inherent in musical composition thus extends from creating initial ideas to the overarching deductions that produce the eventual work. Such deduction may well be *intuitive*, even though we have learned from academic practices how to 'develop' material.

The other function of composition is to *mediate*. A composition truly exists only when material destined for performance is set in motion. Creative thinking must therefore take into account the inherent limitations of its material, the instrumental arsenal, which results from the craft of instrument-building and the instruments' individual characteristics. The rise of electronics has not eliminated the need to consider such constraints; it creates constraints of a different kind. What is gained, and what is lost for ever? In truth, one needs to *create a practice* in which these new obstacles will no longer impede our progress.

Whether at the very concrete stage of real material or the more abstract stage of building up a musical language, our thinking is both impeded and aided by constraints. They certainly limit the actions we can take, but they also endow them with meaning by assigning clear objectives.

If we consider the goals of composition, we could say that a work is meant to be *understood* as much as *conveyed*.

Everyone who listens to a work is in this situation: we understand the work and understand ourselves through it. The work is the repository of expression that we experience, then assimilate, then identify with. This knowledge is, of course, intuitive and does not need to be understood in technical terms, but it is nevertheless genuine – that can be seen at its best in the commentaries of poets and novelists who are not musicians, such as Proust writing about Wagner.

On the other hand, to *convey* a work means to communicate an actual code. Do we really know what transfers from a work to a listener as it unfolds? This purely literal approach can yield surprisingly convincing results – especially for an orchestral musician, for whom the music is divided into its smallest elements – with respect to the kind of transmission generally needed for understanding.

In fact, although *knowledge* and *transmission* are closely linked, they are not exactly the same. Intuitive understanding of a work, however deep, does not presuppose an understanding of how it is conveyed. Similarly, a grasp of the most rudimentary and immediate technical means of transmission does not necessarily lead to conscious understanding.

A discussion of the phenomenon of composition needs to come to terms with these fundamental paradoxes. Composition consists of a series of gestures, whose synchronicity is obvious – and even when not simultaneous they continually affect each other. What are they?

(1) *Genesis of the idea.* What is the origin of the musical idea? How does it attain its definitive, familiar form? What network of influences determines it? What is habitual about it? From which constraints can

it free itself? Can an idea be born independently of any syntax, or is it exclusively dependent upon one?

(2) *Deduction from an initial idea.* The phenomenon of deduction intensifies or diminishes according to the historical period and individual choices, which results in a predilection either for strictly organised, large-scale form or for small-scale form with looser relationships. But the problem remains: How does deduction happen? What laws does it obey, or break? We can distinguish between conscious deductions and intuitive ones that can be explained – if at all – only after the fact.

(3) *Deductive constraint and freedom.* It is likely that lack of deduction means a waste of ideas, in that new ones have to be invented at every turn in order to maintain the interest of musical discourse. But some deduction strains the link between original idea and final result so much that it ends up severing all connections, so that anything can be deduced from anything else. Between these extremes of deducing anything from everything, and nothing from nothing, where does the field of action really lie?

(4) *Music and expression: formal and instantaneous.* It follows that we need to see how to preserve a lasting expressive impulse, while at the same time connecting it to a deeper force. Should the composer's gesture be concerned with the listener's understanding – indeed, recognition – of the formal or the instantaneous?

(5) *Technique revealing new gestures.* Our expressive gestures may be limited, or at least strongly conditioned, by cultural recycling. Can immersion in technique be liberating, and how can that help us to discover unexpected expressive gestures?

(6) *Interference of external forces* (poetic content, theatrical conception, listening conditions). As a form of communication, music is only an overall gesture, which is actually made up of subordinate gestures. It changes a great deal when it depends not only on other gestures, but also *competes* with them.

(7) *Gestural reciprocity between composer and performer; the integral or shared gesture.* Both instrumental virtuosity and technology can transform a composer's gestures in our media-infused era. Composers cannot ignore this – it must be either dealt with or resisted. But is the

composer's gesture integral or shared? This follows from the previous issue: What happens to this gesture when the performer is an improviser, or when tasks are automated by a machine?

1. Genesis of the Idea

It might be thought that the idea derives from a mysterious power, that it is given to us. Is it difficult to trace? The idea is certainly not born in the abstract, in that creativity, even when totally spontaneous, depends on historical circumstances. It crystallises the unforeseen, and yet can result only from a particular situation. An idea arises within a certain vocabulary. It is the instant synthesis of scattered but specific, *existing* facts.

For example, an idea cannot arise independently of the scales being used. Even if that were the intention, an original idea expressed in pitch will conform to a pitch *consensus* typical of its period among some sector of society. Pitch means a hierarchical relationship giving rise to embryonic functions that will produce a structure. Similarly, even the slightest creative idea is almost immediately codified in rhythmic language. Even if the code is initially rudimentary, it implies a recognised hierarchy that quantifies durational relationships. These two elements, pitch and duration, are basics without which the musical idea cannot exist, strictly speaking.

Even the vaguest attempts of improvisers who follow patterns suggested by their instrument, or use only its most rudimentary potential, imply a grammar, or at least a *presumption* of the current state of grammar.

There are, of course, much more restrictive situations. If the idea is conceived with some precise application in mind – which is, or *was*, the ultimate goal of the composer, to adopt existing compositional practice and its habitual procedures – the initial idea will inevitably be explored in terms of its adaptation to some form or model.

Thus, the idea will perhaps have been influenced by some dance genre, such as gigue or minuet; by a movement structure such as sonata form, with its specific characterisation of first and second themes; by tempo, fast or slow; by the way the material is going to be used, in that themes can be designed for development, variation or simple repetition; or by the instrument, the idea being suitable for particular instrumental capacities.

In vocal music or music for the theatre, the idea is also influenced by the representation of images, characters or situations, so that musical creativity surfaces as an *association of ideas*, a descriptive association whose codes must be general enough to be recognisable. An idea can also arise from esoteric associations related to numbers, letters or paramusical codes – for example, the series associated with the characters of *Lulu* or, in the *Lyric Suite*, the notes, rhythms and intervals that have meaning only in relation to Berg's private life.

Even when the musical idea seems independent of such constraining circumstances, even when it appears liberated from any connection to existing hierarchies, even when supposedly detached from predetermined formal structures, the idea is still born of a constraint that is all the stronger because it is the most illusory: the constraint of memory.

Memory builds up models in us, including models of our own devising. This forms a stable world of references from which it is very difficult to escape. Without being completely conscious of it, or without wanting to recognise it overtly, we thereby create a personal language of references, a network of creative gestures that we tend to summon, and to which we refer in an emergency.

There is a deceptive spontaneity, tiresome to denounce, and easy to analyse. It is tempting to say that the quicker an artist works, believing that this rapidity in expression, construction and gesture demonstrates independence from others, as well as self-liberation, the more this composer is in fact imprisoned by gestural formulas that supply the entire expressive *stock*. Thus, whether constraint is imposed by a comprehensive system or resides within the individual (and is therefore less methodical, more tenuous), the genesis of an idea is not free. A creative gesture relies on the accumulation of historical or individual precursors.

It is interesting to see to what extent a more or less spontaneous idea must sometimes struggle in order to break free and to acquire its own coordinates that will allow it to emerge. This explains the interest in studying composers' sketches, in which we may observe this journey from the impulsive act to the organised gesture.

The so-called spontaneous idea – even if it is forged from real or virtual prototypes – is not necessarily well suited in its *absolute* form to compositional goals. There is still a gap between whatever spontaneity draws from its reserves and what will become *useful*. This obviously depends on the composer and the goals pursued. When a musical conception is flexible, adaptation will be instantaneous, notwithstanding the later refinements that will be needed. When a musical conception is stricter, the idea goes through a series of transformations before attaining a *convincing* form – that is, a form that will convince its composer that it is perfect for its purpose. Finally, in the case of very strict composition, the idea undergoes a series of repercussions caused by the challenges its handling throws up. There is always a process of feedback between origin and transformations, so much so that one may question whether everything has been foreseen by the composer. Schoenberg thought so, when he implicitly compared the composer to the omniscient and ever-present God of the Old Testament: from the moment the theme is created, so is the work, since it is implicit in the theme; from this perspective, the composer's gesture, from the first idea, is the work of a sorcerer.

Thinking of Bach and *The Art of Fugue*, or Webern and his series with their multiple properties, we might ask whether those artists did in fact truly foresee their works from the outset. That question remains unanswered, but we can say that the initial idea harbours within it a field of properties whose detail, not precisely foreseen, the author can explore. The fact that these properties are subject to a field of possibilities means that only *general* predictions can be made.

Yet is the first idea quite as real as I have just described? It seems that completely virtual, hypothetical ideas can serve as a basis for composition. In such cases, composition will depend on how these hypotheses engage with the reality of the musical material as they are validated and adjusted by it. Memory does play a less important role with this type of initial idea, which is more deeply conceptual and is not limited by the contingencies of an existing language. In truth, first ideas as abstract as this can be generated from any code. They are gestures in pure form, gestures that could in fact arise out of some other mode of expression. This explains why a composer can be struck, when 'reading' a chart or reflecting on anything similar, by the notorious 'demon of analogy'.[1]

The idea is singular and multiple, recognisable and unrecognisable. When an idea is highly circumscribed – as in the scenes of the third act of *Wozzeck* that are constructed on *one* sound, *one* chord, *one* rhythm, *one* moto perpetuo – it must contain great potential for creative invention. Creativity, with respect to the idea, implies a balancing of forces, because while the idea centralises and turns everything towards itself, it also disperses, and disperses *itself*.

2. Deduction from the Initial Idea

This is one of the most decisive gestures a composer can make – perhaps the most decisive of all. Depending on the era and on individual choice, the phenomenon of deduction intensifies or diminishes, which results in a predilection either for strictly organised, large-scale form or for small-scale form with looser relationships. The choice depends on the degree of familiarity with the grammar employed, and on the *action zone* – and also on whether or not the *original* idea was conceived as a function of deduction.

The framework of action. Once an idea is conceived for a particular form, it then conforms to particular structures, and its development follows predetermined laws. This is a framework that can be convenient, in that it is ready to be implemented by the imagination. It can also be a handicap, because it can hamper imagination. The entire evolution of music has been the attempt to make idea and form coincide through appropriate deductions. When the elements of language no longer allow this, because of excessive diversity attributable to the evolution of harmonic language, among other things, the idea *destroys* form or, in a more radical guise, *perverts* it.

This is the case with the evolution of fugue, which involves a subject, one or more countersubjects, a fixed number of voices, a tonal plan based on the polarities of tonal hierarchy, close or remote sequences, duration (augmentation, diminution), a more or less strict compositional style depending on how the sequences are handled; an exposition, counter-exposition, episodes and stretti – in short, a very precise framework that brings about complete formalisation, or formulation.

Since harmonic creativity slowly broke this rigorous framework apart, fugue became an archaic option, in which artistic licence increasingly prevailed, until it was either completely discarded, its defunct scaffolding left to pedagogues, or reduced to simpler notions more easily accommodated into concepts that had evolved to another linguistic plane (such as the passacaglia, for example), or else treated as a sort of facade whose basic functions had disappeared, replaced by simulacra that maintained merely its outward characteristics.

The evolution of deduction from the initial idea is almost always situated in a framework of global formalisation that relates to local formalisation. The current state of vocabulary must therefore allow for it and must allow this concept of development.

This phenomenon can be studied much more explicitly during a *crisis*, historical or individual.

Historical crisis. This occurred at the beginning of the twentieth century, particularly when the expansion of chromatic vocabulary and a commitment to non-repetition led the very principle of deduction to be called into question. At such moments, nothing more can be offered than exemplifications, or sequences of them, each with similar characteristics, to preserve stylistic homogeneity.

When reading the improvised confession that is the lectures Webern published under the title *The Path to the New Music*, his attitude at this particular point in his life is striking. He states that 'Here I had the feeling, "When all twelve notes have gone by, the piece is over."'[2] Thus, the search for absolute consistency of presentation, combined with the absolute desire for non-repetition, leads to a complete impasse.

For Webern, and also for Schoenberg, the solution was not to consider the transposed series as a repetition, even though it used the same twelve tones. Furthermore, it was posited that the pitch classes in a series could be given a different perspective as pitches in different registers, thereby appearing both new and derived. Webern's crisis, in particular, therefore involved the annihilation of deductive processes at all levels of the musical language. This explains why his works from this period are extremely brief, even by his own standards. Moreover, he uses poetic texts to link the row-form 'exemplifications', one after the other, in order to wrest formal deduction from another source.

Schoenberg adopted the same approach in composing *Erwartung*, where the link is above all dramatic, and in which it would be futile to try to find any extension or dissipation of the notion of form. As a matter of fact, when he wanted to 'groom' the row through formal frameworks, he resorted to older formal plans, which he adjusted to his present needs. Thus, nostalgia for *large-scale* form is not only a reaction against brevity, it derives from a vital taste for recapturing deduction, and a desire to imbue it with its true scope, which unavoidably implies temporal extension. Variations are another possible resource, this being a form that is linked to deduction – whether of a stricter or looser kind, whether for structural or ornamental purposes.

With respect to the historical crisis, *apparent* deduction, as practised purely externally in neoclassicism, should also be mentioned. In this case, procedures are adopted not for their deeper meaning, but as a kind of prosthesis which may or may not fit well.

Individual crisis. In the nineteenth century, ideas were ill adapted to deduction because they were not conceived for it. This is the syndrome of post-Beethoven symphonists, as described somewhat maliciously by Wagner. In other cases, deduction can be difficult to apply because its consequences fail to convince, as with Berg and his symmetries. They 'work' in certain circumstances, when the idea is conceived in terms of deduction (continuous or, alternatively, directionless rhythm), but when the idea is a goal-directed melody, it is inadequate with respect to any deduced symmetry.

What, then, is the *relationship of the idea to deduction*? Each is a reflection of the other . . . At first, they are not necessarily conceived completely and jointly. Through deduction, implicit properties of the idea can be discovered, but it is an entire aspect of the composer's work to discover the unforeseen in the foreseen.

An idea can be conceived in and of itself. The composer analyses its elements and deduces its implications for development. The challenge is a very *real* one, but the idea can be *virtual*, preceding any thematic material, in which case it determines both the nature of real images and their developments. One gets a good sense of this difference by comparing Schoenberg's Variations, op. 31, and the *idea* of variation developed by Webern in the Variations for Piano, op. 27, as well as the Variations for Orchestra, op. 30: the form of all these works is defined by the degree of proximity or distance, symmetry or asymmetry, with respect to a latent prototype.

Thus, we have moved from a properly thematic conception to one that we initially called *athematic*. In fact, in my *Sonatine* for flute and piano, deductions are made from an abstract network of possibilities that controls their presentation.

In general, in order to free ourselves from academic definitions of theme or figure, and the connotations they imply, I prefer to say that a *finite* idea corresponds to a *finite* development, and a *non-finite* development can correspond to a *non-finite* idea.

This idea of finite development has become familiar to us through the history of the Western tradition. The gesture is delineated by completion and, of course, determination of a form. This form is what leads us from one point to another, across twists and turns that may either be cloaked in more specifically structural characteristics or, on the other hand, tend towards immediacy of expression. Actually, these characteristics of meaning matter little. Since the twists and turns indicate form, the listener has to master and become familiar with the elements of this journey or story. Such are the objectives of the *finite* work.

There are also non-finite works based on principles that are finite to varying degrees. Such is the case with improvisation on ragas in Indian music. Conversely, the elaboration of a work can be finite when born of a virtual idea, as with Webern: although the starting point is not the same, the goal does not vary.

But one can and *must* conceive of the non-finite development of a non-finite idea. Of course, I am not speaking about an unfinished development, but rather of a development in which the notion of completion no longer makes sense.

Especially in the current era, in which much has been said about chance – including much that is erroneous and irrelevant – it is, rather, the notion of the *statistical* that can play a very important role. Chance cannot imply stylistic criteria; it rejects them by permitting any choice at all. It can yield only a jumble of actions connected purely by a priori decisions that arose either simultaneously or in succession. The limitations of such an approach are evident, since the initial surprises it offers will wane and will not reappear – not with the intensity or degree of novelty that our perception needs in order to create that dialectic of the recognisable and the unexpected that is vital for creating and maintaining interest.

On the contrary, statistical development adopts stylistic and grammatical premises but shifts the emphasis onto foreseeing multiple solutions or fields of development, and it is then a matter of indifference whether any particular solution is employed. Some outputs might be subjectively more interesting than others, but in general they are on the same scale of interest as other solutions would be. When reconsidering my own approaches, I can understand that my use of 'automatic' structures without 'aesthetic' decisions, such as those found in the first book of my *Structures* for two pianos, and my use of aleatoric forms, as in my Third Piano Sonata or *Éclat*, are in reality statistical approaches to development. This had been a long-standing concern of mine, and today I understand it more clearly, especially when I think of the solutions that are currently possible with computers and the specificity they offer by comparison with the composer's task of 'choosing'.

Compared with the limited number of choices the composer supplies, the computer can offer an infinity of choice that renders the very idea obsolete, forcing us to find a new conception of development and deduction.

As opposed to a *directional* deduction, one could imagine an absolutely *non-directional* deduction. We need not listen in succession to all the solutions that the machine offers us en masse, nor choose them one by one; they are presented in a certain context and can *appear* and *come into focus* during another event that provides them with an envelope to delineate and determine them.

These automatic deductions can then submit to various restrictive critiques that yield families of solutions of various sizes. However, this entails blocking a certain number of constituent elements from the degree zero of language, as in *Structures 1*.

From there, we can imagine a language that evolves from amorphic states to, as it were, 'morphic' ones. We are among two types of attitude: either a precise solution can develop as conditions become more restrictive and choices operate in a very restricted field in which personal judgement becomes an essential factor; or we make a certain number of transformations that imply degradation of the initial idea towards a form that no longer has any individual meaning, and in which the criteria disintegrate to the point of no longer offering any interest to global perception – this amounts to an entropy of the initial idea.

Each of these two categories can be deduced from the other, and they can be placed in succession or in alternation. Either one of these categories may also be made to act upon the other. The determinate, chosen idea could be used as an envelope for an indeterminate process, or the indeterminate process could proliferate and multiply the determinate idea to such an extent that it loses its individuality. The computer is clearly the most appropriate tool for this approach, the best suited for the statistical extension of deduction. Form, and the conception of form, thus absorb the idea of chance, of probability, but at the same time ensure the validity of its many deductions.

The consequences of this seem to me to be many, not only with respect to the flexibility of a work of which some sections can be finally written only as they are realised (albeit with the greatest precision), but also with respect to the internal consistency of musical language. From a completely closed language with unique solutions, we can create an open, non-directional musical language that implies perception of the same order.

Music, whose goal I would describe as almost inevitably *undefined*, can achieve this dream of the indefinite when it has adequate tools and no longer resorts to the mere semblance of such an approach.

3. Deductive Constraints and Freedoms

Lack of deduction wastes ideas, because ideas have to be created at any price to sustain the interest of musical discourse. Since excessive deduction stretches the path between the original idea and the final result, it ends up severing the link between those extremes and produces a situation in which anything can be deduced from anything else. Between deducing anything from anything on the one hand, and deducing nothing from nothing on the other, where is the true field of operation? Or, to put it another way, where are the boundaries of recognition and discovery, which Gilles Deleuze expressed in terms of repetition and difference? And consequently, what are the necessary relationships between deduction and perception?

From a historical perspective, we can see that perception has been oriented towards framing the unknown with the known, a tendency prevalent ever since musical language itself was established. There is a standardisation of tonal functions, sonic objects (chords) and formal functions. When we take on the conventions of a particular musical language, these elements are already there, and we can recognise them however varied their appearance. We could describe these as abstract functions that materialise in a specific context. This universe is readily accepted, so that we experience merely the consistency of its elements, but no redundancy, as they are varied and combined in different ways.

If we take the case of the tonal harmonic system, the chord and its inversions are the same object, but their elements are differently arranged, meaning that they acquire a new function. A chord in root position, for example, functions differently from a second-inversion chord, even though they are two permutations of the same initial object. On the other hand, degree functions and inversions are the same in every transposition, and the functions that relate to harmonic regions are the same for all cases.

With form, this is no less obvious. No matter what theme it sets in motion, a fugue, for example, can be understood to follow a certain formal plan, and every section of this plan uses a given type of procedure, a given manner of expressing it. Although form may be conveyed with different degrees of rigour, the formal scheme will be recognisable in the development of the initial materials, chosen to confirm their formal plan.

When listening to an unfamiliar theme, and also to deductions that we have not previously experienced, we can progressively recognise – I would even say *confirm* – the formal plan. Once again, this is Schoenberg's approach in the Variations, op. 31, and yet one asks why in this case things can no longer function as before: it is because although the form adopts a recognisable plan, and despite the looseness of this sectionalised form, the functions that could support such a plan no longer appear. In ornamental variations, like those so frequently composed between the end of the eighteenth century and the middle of the nineteenth, the harmonic plan was sufficiently simple to be recognised. Since the melodic plan went through outward transformations without the structure itself being modified, the initial plan could be recognised and mentally compared to the variations in order to appreciate the distance or degree of enrichment between the two, and the emphasis that was placed on certain aspects. Moreover, because of the material's brevity, the initial model could be retained in the memory in complete form.

As soon as the initial model became more complex, elements of manipulation more numerous and manipulation began to affect elements crucial to the ability (or inability) to recognise the theme, deciphering variations and understanding their relationship to the model became difficult.

As early as Beethoven, some movements based on the variation principle are hard to follow, for various reasons. Firstly, and very obviously, he rejects the sectionalisation that makes 'classical' variations so easy to follow. (When one is lost in a variation, memory resets to zero in order to decipher the next one.) The second reason is a more complex original structure that can no longer be easily stored in our memory to use as a basis for comparison: voice-leading variegation, proportional asymmetry and the difficulty of grasping the main voice compared with its counterpoint (or the proximity of the main and secondary voices, to use Schoenberg's vocabulary) all play a part in this. The third reason concerns temporal extension and the non-proximity of a variation and the theme. It could even be said that the more distant the variation becomes in time and appearance from the original, the more formalistic Beethoven becomes, in that he very literally respects certain givens of the initial object. The fourth reason is the freedom taken with some elements of the original: the harmony might be retained as an element of variation, while the original melody is erased; new figures might appear that are more important than the original ones; changes can be made to the voicing, as well as modifications to the proportions of the constituent sections or their tonal relationships.

While 'classical' variations used the principle of recognition, sometimes to the point of being uninteresting, the truly Beethovenian variations, those of his final years, play more and more on the tension created by the distance or closeness of a variation to the theme, by altering segmentation, by the rigorous observance of deep formal pattern in contrast to deformation of the surface and its appearances.

Getting back to Schoenberg's plan for the Variations, op. 31, one senses that he wanted to revive the tradition and that he, too, wanted to play on the dialectic between the recognised and the unknown. But there are no longer any tonal functions, and although at first certain intervallic characteristics sometimes become the symbol of a variation, the deductions derived from the series are not strictly recognisable. Therefore, the piece's unity relies on its genre as variations, otherwise we would simply have a succession of 'character pieces' whose presiding characteristics would above all be orchestral texture (chamber or large orchestra), rhythmic type or expressive envelope. This is why Schoenberg needs to separate sections, to allow listeners to change 'register' and thus plot their way through the succession of variations until the final variation and its coda.

I have chosen variations as the main point here because that best reveals musicians' need to play with repetition and difference. It is not surprising that most composers, having completely mastered their craft – that is, at a fairly advanced period of their careers – have either explicitly used variation form or implicitly adopted variation procedure. In fact, the whole history of Western music can be grafted onto this dilemma of repetition versus variety, of the recognised versus the unknown.

This brings us to a more general subject: What is a technique worth when its rationale can no longer be perceived? In the case of 'integral serialism', there were many constraints to the way an object was formed, and the transposition of these various constraints yielded a different object, but to what extent could we perceive this as a transformation?

What features need to be conserved in order to bring one object closer to another? Are only basic features required, or envelopes also? And when the envelopes will do, why then does one need to use such complex basic features?

Today's musical language is no longer founded on objects that are standard, and recognisable through the fact of being standardised. It is difficult to create deep recognition out of musical language, which is why it is necessary to turn to envelopes, or to illuminate one characteristic through another.

Incidentally, historically or symbolically speaking, is a *cantus firmus* meant to be recognised? Grafting one object onto another yields a new object whose predominant characteristic is not necessarily the recognition of deduction. We are confronted by another object that has become alien.

This presents us with a curious paradox: the more unrecognisable the constituent elements become, the more the envelopes need to be recognisable. Working with the constituent elements, our main concern will be to animate objects whose origins or family resemblance are recognisable, emphasised by a fundamental similarity, and differentiated by provisional characteristics.

When a work accumulates, through deduction, other objects that have become alien with respect to their origin, it will present a profile ranging somewhere between order and chaos. It is the same for the fundamental structures of composition – pitch, rhythm, vertical and horizontal dimensions – and also when instrumental timbre is transformed electroacoustically. The source instrument can be reduced to *anonymity* through a series of transformations that slowly submerge its originality, and its role may be dispersed.

4. Music and Expression: Formal and Instantaneous

Composition relies more than ever on the dialectic of repetition and difference, but the laws that govern it are increasingly empirical and *local*, even if they obey a *general* impulse. As a result, we need to see how an expressive impulse can be preserved as it happens, while at the same time connecting it to a deeper undercurrent. In perceiving a work, what relationship needs to be maintained between the formal and the instantaneous? In other words, should composers be concerned with recognising the formal in their gestures?

The first problem, that of the relationship between expressive impulse and formal pattern – or, if we wish to avoid that binary, of the levels of instantaneous invention in relation to long-term consequences – has been raised gradually as music has become more 'deformalised'. For a long time, music did not address the problem of expression (and its sentimental caricature, 'being expressive') as a distinct category. It seemed normal for expression to be formalised in a coherent and well-laid-out discourse. There were markers of all kinds, both formal and symbolic. There was almost a code of expression that enjoyed a collective consensus. Music, as a real language, transmits its messages *clearly*, or at least as clearly as it can in order to avoid ambiguity, although the relationship between music and what it can express has long needed to be addressed with caution – especially in the case of religious music tied to textual dogma, where the question was not personal expression, but expressing a faith beyond individuality, in which everyone had the right to partake. This accounts somewhat for the exceptional suitability of codified language. In much non-European music, especially in the musics of Asia, codes operate almost absolutely: they completely govern communication between musician and listener.

In the Western tradition, the use of certain intervals for direct expressions of joy or pain goes back several centuries. The roots of this go back to ancient Greek music, at least according to theoretical writings that can still be read today. The falling or rising semitone, and chromaticism in general, have sufficiently precise connotations to be perceived by anybody with the benefit of a certain cultural background. Tonalities also have expressive connotations; melismas and motives have functioned as codes of expression. Pushing this principle to the extreme, the musicologist André Pirro was able to establish a list of symbols used by Bach, although admittedly this was in an era awash with intense Wagnerian fervour.

Each of these means could easily be integrated into musical language because they were codes, but the more individual expression enters the

scene, the more obsolete such general codes become, with the consequence that each composer tries – sometimes desperately – to find a
completely personal transcription of not only an individual expressive
world, but also an *emotional* one.

'Emotion' is nearly tantamount to a break, a multiple fracture, to the
instantaneous, the uniqueness of experience, the struggle against the
contemptuous formalisation of the accidental. Music becomes analogous to a psychological oscillogram. The problem therefore becomes
increasingly acute for the composer: How can one's various impulses
be reconciled with what could be called the general expression of form?

Duration is clearly the first obstacle. How can a coherent, formal
whole be constructed from piecemeal data, or even from contradictory
tensions? This is not a new problem; it essentially amounts to the very
history of Romanticism, and the Romantics found several ingenious
tricks to deal with it.

They adopted *short form*, a form in which 'development' as such
was not important, since the limits within which it was placed allowed
for deduction from element to element in a restricted zone. This short
form, particularly apparent in lieder, is based on a 'unifying' figure from
which either the thematic or harmonic texture of the accompaniment
is entirely derived, save for decorative variants. On the other hand, its
form in the strict sense is strophic (or else made up of strophe and anti-
strophe), which also keeps deduction to a minimum. Once free of those
two levels in the notion of development, what counts is capturing the
moment, condensed into *one* unique event, as well as any shock waves
it directly triggers.

The Romantics adopted the technique of the *hermit crab*: they settled into the empty shell of classical symphonic form in order to try to
prolong the moment by means of a tried and tested technique. The
sonatas and symphonies of the Romantic era are by turns fascinating or
scholarly demonstrations of this attempt at adaptation. Since the themes
were not generally invented with a view to development, nor implicitly
created for the hierarchy to which they are forced to yield, there is a
struggle between their own nature and the nature of the procedures
they undergo. One has only to notice how expressively incongruous

and incompatible the reprises and repeats inherent to classical form become in such works! Not until Mahler was the challenge of the symphony truly addressed, when expressive overload caused it to burst out of both the formal framework and procedures for the working out of material.

Composers made use of a *poetic or dramatic stimulus* in order to find a way out of this impossible dilemma. In music drama and symphonic poems – programme music in both cases, whether actual or implicit – another means was used to control musical elements and provide them with the formal consistency that musical hierarchy alone was not able to assure.

Since that time when 'old forms', pre-established formal plans, were abandoned, the problem has been partly dismissed. There was no longer any divergence between the instantaneous and the pre-existing plan, but we had to remember to establish, on a case-by-case basis, overall plans to lend coherence to what I would call initial instantaneousness, and the deductions that follow it.

I will not return here to the crisis of the beginning of the twentieth century, particularly concerning the Viennese School; Stravinsky, whose *Les Noces* is an especially interesting example, could equally well be included in this discussion. I want instead to approach this problem by referring to serial and post-serial explorations. After Schoenberg and his successors, there was a kind of obsession with totality. The work had to be governed by a unique, global organisation of its different parameters. The way these parameters were used principally determined the *phases* of a structure. Moreover, and still following Schoenberg's legacy, non-repetition was considered to be fundamental, inescapably born of historical necessity. Trapped in this carcass, the composer had the task of inventing ceaselessly, but always working in a particular way. Of course, since that way could not offer limitless resources, non-repetition, in such a narrow context, was at times insufficiently malleable. Thus, we arrived at a contradiction, between excessively centralising technique and a desire for expression in the moment. This is what caused such discipline to break apart. Within overly flexible general control, local means had to be found whose nature depended on one's orientation – favouring particular harmonic fields, using narrowly selected materials, preferring vertical construction over horizontal, and so on.

A whole technique thus developed to admit the *accidental*, an essential element of any development. Similarly, the field of *free* as opposed to *strict* composition was rediscovered; there was no longer one *single* solution, but rather several, so much so that in wishing to keep, if not exploit, them all, we resorted to forms in which the choice of certain elements was left to chance and made on the spot. This formal *indeterminacy* was one possible response, and probably the most fruitful, to this problem of free domains versus non-elective ones. *Indeterminacy*, incidentally, was transferred at some risk to several other elements of musical language that could accommodate it either well or not so well.

Because of this very fact, another difficulty arose: even if we can recognise the expressive gesture, can we still recognise the formal one through which it is supposed to be transmitted? Can this formal gesture make sense even when it is different each time?

This relationship between speculation and perception has always caused difficulty, especially in an expressive medium like music that engages two 'categories', whether simultaneously or not: the eye and the ear.

The listener obviously embodies the category of the ear, or perhaps the ear aided by the eye. But the composer who initially *reads* the score while creating and transcribing it is torn between the two. Visual speculation can be a focus, as can any symbolic speculation, such as the transcription of numbers and letters. The many allusions found in the 'learned' music of *ars nova*, the secret canons of Bach, the remarkable obsessive codes used by Berg, all testify to this. The case of Berg, with the secret codes in the *Lyric Suite* or the symbolism of the number 3 in the Chamber Concerto, is extraordinary and deserves to be singled out. Can the listener perceive any aspect of these codes? Are they not conveyed by means of envelopes that are in reality scarcely amenable to the imagination?

There are two attitudes, which can never be reconciled:

(1) The ear is all that matters, because the ear is a guide, be it lazy or alert. But this guide needs to be stimulated in order to exercise its

powers. A vital mirroring effect needs to be set up between speculation and perception.

(2) The ear matters, of course, but the eye needs to be able to rule or, at any rate, never be neglected. The composer is the eye imagining the ear. Why, after all, should speculation and technical investigation be excluded simply because our perception is not able to follow it? Since technical inventiveness can force us to break free from habit, is it not well positioned to stimulate our imagination and push back familiar perceptual limits?

To what extent can and should composers be concerned with the perception of their formal gestures? 'Some of it will stick . . .'[3] because perception operates differently on different levels (such as levels of 'reading' music!). Should we be thinking about only a single level then? Which should we choose? The most elementary one? Can a work not also be a pretext for reflection? Can it not be the occasion for a series of paraphrases and developments by someone *other* than the composer? And most of all, does speculation not force us towards enrichment, towards the unknown?

The line between perception and speculation will never be drawn, and one of the composer's duties is to reject it.

5. Technique Revealing New Gestures

Our expressive gestures are perhaps limited, or if not, they are strongly conditioned by the atavistic tendencies of our culture. In what respect can immersion in technique be liberating and help us to discover expressive gestures that we were not expecting? In other words, what part of our expressive means is used consciously, and what proportion, though premeditated, leads to unforeseen consequences? How much play is there between the will and the accidental?

While composing a work, we are both referencing and enquiring. Referencing reaches back not only to the 'historical' past, but also to ourselves, to our own past, to our past discoveries, to what we provisionally created in an earlier work or works. Some features there strike us either as yet to be fully exploited or richer in possibilities than we had previously noticed; it is these deficiencies and potentials that we have in mind when contemplating the immediate future.

We then go down some of the same paths, even pursue some of the same obsessions, and our sensibilities want to grasp something new, without knowing yet how to approach it. We need to amplify, redirect, refashion; we call certain material into question. Despite our desire to project into the future, it is the recent or distant past that comes into play, that is called into question. Even before the conscious expression of the new, there is a reflection on the present state and deduction from, and extrapolation of, this state.

We then find ourselves drawing new conclusions and viewing material from a new angle. This speculation is accompanied by investigation, which involves our sensibility, for better or for worse, not knowing the way forward or what it will find. It is not what we know – about ourselves and about others – that will bring us to a compositional solution, but rather that the search for a solution to a compositional problem will lead us to a different form of expression. We can then justly claim that we would never have arrived at this form of expression if the compositional problem had not forced us to discover it.

I am speaking not only of the kinds of constraints already mentioned: Michelangelo's block of marble, Mallarmé's sonnet form, external conditioning or internal constraints. I am thinking more of the results of technique – techniques such as Bach's invertible counterpoint or Beethoven's retrograde forms – on sensual perception. The perception of these techniques will be all the stranger in that their consequences contradict their compositional norms as well as what we are used to hearing in their sonic vocabulary.

When Schoenberg used twelve-tone technique in the fifth piece of his op. 23, the series' deployment in four voices led him unexpectedly to discover a kind of 'diagonal' dimension, in which the distribution of sounds was more important than their vertical and horizontal distribution. This discovery was fleeting, and it is not the main aspect the piece investigates, but it is immediately noticeable to the attentive listener because of its strangeness in a rather traditional context.

Similarly, listening to Messiaen's 'Mode de valeurs et d'intensités', we realise that the composer's speculation about duration in particular led him to an entirely new form of expression, radically different from his previous practice, and brought him to the *statistical* evaluation of duration.

From these few examples, and many more recent ones, it can be seen how far reflection on musical language, and the search for a new practice, has generated a new sensibility towards sound phenomena.

Naturally, there have been mistakes in the relationship between speculation and perception. Sometimes perception has seemed completely different from conception. Real gestalts are created that are at odds with the intended gestalt, resisting any direct affiliation. Between the gesture as conceived by the composer and the one realised, there is no common ground other than this path from conception to realisation. The two cannot be connected through our knowledge of the way one leads to the other. Sometimes these two gestalts intersect, sometimes they do not. This is what occurs, for example, in some of Webern's works, such as the Quartet with saxophone, op. 22, or the Variations, op. 30.

Finally, we will address the problem of transgressing existing laws that determine our sensibilities and options. A crude transgression is often visible in some straightforward, liberating gesture, the spontaneous expression of one's compositional response, particularly early in a career, but also when a composer's knowledge of the vocabulary is more advanced. Such deliberate, serious transgressions can have long-lasting results, but in other cases composers, frightened by their own audacity, recoil from their transgressions and return to the way things are normally done. There are also the very rare occasions on which acknowledged transgressions of perception can turn out either to be sterile or to promise long-term renewal. But the composer finds it difficult to judge the consequences of such transgression, because there are transgressions that go unheeded for a time, until someone comes along to discover where they can lead.

6. Interference of External Forces

We have assumed that the composer's gesture is self-sufficient and completely autonomous. But given the ambition to acquire new material, it can represent a reflection on the musical present or one's consciousness, and through deduction and transgression barriers that previously seemed insurmountable are overcome. The composer will have found the *raison d'être* only internally, having reflected on individual musical material, even if this material could benefit from the influence of other experiences in different or even adjacent domains. All artists can be sensitive to experiences that do not directly involve them, and over and above differences of appearance, they can be influenced by any point of view found in their own artistic language.

The influence of external forces can be expressed in two ways: indirectly, when this external contribution will not literally be incorporated in a work; and directly, when one deliberately seeks to amalgamate the music with another mode of expression – these other modes, such as poetry, theatre, or drama more generally, can themselves be autonomous.

It is difficult to describe the first case, that of *indirect* influence, since this kind appears through signs so deeply absorbed into the musical substance of a work that unless we were privy to personal statements by the composer to this effect, it would be nearly impossible to find correspondences between the two on our own. The correspondences that history suggests to us are not necessarily real.

It is tempting, for example, to draw parallels between certain creative periods of Webern and Mondrian: the same tendency towards *reduction* of material, simplification of timbre and colour, 'geometrical' form and aphorism. Yet it is unlikely that Webern was aware of Mondrian's artistic development, and even less likely that Mondrian knew about Webern's practices: although contemporaneous, the two practices did not intersect. We therefore have to accept that a fundamental gesture, dependent on its era, but unconnected to actual circumstances, could lead each artist to devise his expression using profoundly similar means. Similarly, it is unlikely that Debussy's parsimonious approach to his own musical language, with its concentrated use of elements, directly benefited from any sustained contact with the late works of Cézanne, in which similar reductiveness can be observed. Thus, there are equivalences that can be established after the fact, the protagonists working in isolation but with common reference to materials characteristic of their era.

It might be possible to establish typologies from families united by temperament or by ways of acting and responding to the characteristics of an era. We might propose a Webern–Mondrian typology, for example, or Léger–Varèse, Schoenberg–Kandinsky, Stravinsky–Picasso, Matisse–Ravel, and so on. Of course, if we started to delve into the details, these parallels would reveal their limitations all too quickly. That said, the fact that they come to mind so readily indicates the existence of different narrative strands in a single era, when viewed with the simplification necessary for this kind of perspective.

As for the influence of writers and visual artists on composers, we have only their own pronouncements to go by. We know that Schopenhauer influenced Wagner because Wagner spoke about it abundantly. We also know that he was fairly impervious to painting, and that his choices in that respect were merely utilitarian, a function of their use within sets, which means that however 'picturesque' his works may sometimes be, this owes nothing to the vision of painters, but much more to Shakespeare and Greek tragedy. This latter influence was not exerted at all in the purely 'utilitarian' sense one might suspect, but rather through the reflection that led him to the dramatic power of music and motive, to the importance of continuity and transition. His conception of the orchestra – I am referring to its polyphonic interweaving with the singer's voice – benefited from his reflection on the role of the chorus in Greek tragedy. We might work out this influence for ourselves, but thanks to his writings we can understand the effect it had on him.

Here again, we should not expect to find comparisons on the same level. How often have musicians complained about poets' and painters' taste for minor composers? How many times have we come across musicians who are audacious in their own field but cautious in others? Influence does not always act between equals, nor within the same historical period. To claim such a correspondence would be too easy and would reflect a naive vision of the relationship of individuals, in all their complexity, with the world around them. No matter what source is taken as an external reference, the composer who finds it helpful will continue to seek it out, because the external gesture being referenced is attractive not necessarily through its intrinsic value, but rather through what it represents in the individual, concealed from other people, which the composer alone is able to uncover.

For myself, I would cite two examples of the influence of such external gestures that had a particular impact. Their effect was more to confirm some of my preoccupations than to produce new discoveries.

Having read the book in which Klee summarises what he taught at the Bauhaus,[4] I was struck by the overlap between my ideas on the organic development of pitch and rhythmic cells and Klee's visual use of similar ideas: the way one idea can *structurally* influence another (a line intersects a circle, modifies it and is modified by it, in a system of opposing forces acting reciprocally); the way an object or location can be viewed simultaneously from different perspectives, and can be the *viewpoint* of these various perspectives; the way space can be smooth and unmeasured, or striated and measured, which he calls dividual/individual. All these reflections corroborated my own, while enriching them from the specifically visual perspective; they suggested extensions and outcomes that I had not noticed, because the habit of handling musical objects led to certain reflexes (acquired through education) that made it difficult for me to keep the distance necessary to ask questions about the validity of what was customary.

Having long reflected on coordinated chance or, more precisely, plurality of choice, I discovered Mallarmé's *Livre* through the sketches that Jacques Scherer had by then published.[5] They corroborated ideas I had developed on multiple form, on the subordination of ideas to this type of form, on multiple readings of a group of structures whose meaning is revitalised in each verbal dimension, an example being the textural denseness, or complexity, that accrues the further one trawls through the *Livre*. Since the *Livre* is *circular*, this denseness unfolds as readers begin at some chosen point, until they have taken in the whole.

I cite Mallarmé because he loomed in the background of my structural concerns. But there was more impact on my concerns when it came to transcribing poems into music.

For composers, the most important external medium is the poem or the dramatic text. With poems, composers react above all to the poetic content, the imagery and the strophic structure. In my case, in the

'Deuxième improvisation sur Mallarmé' and *Cummings ist der Dichter* I sought to graft musical time onto the temporality of the poem, to organise musical structure as an equivalent to the structure of the poem regarding its versification, syllabic quantities and grammatical organisation. Musical writing is linked to every detailed quality of poetic writing.

Historically, in opera the libretto was made to measure in order to be moulded into musical forms. The challenge was to make the dramatic and musical events interact, given the differences of timing and enunciation. Schoenberg's solutions in *Erwartung* and *Die glückliche Hand* are the opposite of those he found for *Moses und Aron*. In *Lulu*, Berg expands, dilutes and dissolves the frameworks for action used in *Wozzeck*.

External forces have the effect of profoundly altering our view of what musical structures mean, their validity and the fundamental relationship between musical and other languages. Direct transcription is impossible. The elements must be transformed and adapted to the specific characteristics of musical language. Otherwise, false equivalences are created that cannot satisfy the particular rules of structural, idiomatic correspondence.

Three types of relationship are possible between external media: (1) concomitance and parallelism (one being the reflection of the other); (2) subordination and domination (one being the envelope of the other); and (3) confrontation and competition, in which conflict and antiphony reign between the media.

In discussing the influence of external media on the composer's gesture, I have not discussed an almost taboo domain that nevertheless both fascinates and deters today's composer: the domain of the sciences or, more specifically, of scientific language, invoked as the hallmark of modernity.

Sometimes this clearly amounts only to an empty shell, an external envelope, a vocabulary wrested from its proximate meaning to become nothing more than 'poetic' inspiration. Varèse's titles – only his titles – were coined in this spirit. The composer becomes possessed by the idea of finding a musical truth that transcends artistic instability, that rests on values apparently less contentious, though not more profound. Hence the titles *Intégrales* or *Hyperprisme*, evoking a solidity or truth beyond the human, beyond the transitory. Over and above the desire – which, incidentally, is itself totally irrational – to ground musical creativity on laws of nature, to transfer their inevitability onto the absolute necessity of a work similarly conceived, to thereby stamp it with a label of quality that transcends any aesthetic criteria based on judgements too vaguely formulated to be taken seriously, there is no truly decisive scientific influence or thought to be discerned in this mindset. The most that can be said is that it displays nostalgia for the absolute, a thirst for the indisputable, an expression of poetic aspiration par excellence.

It seems to me that basically this same desire for the absolute and the indisputable can be seen in most artistic appeals to science and scientific vocabulary. Mathematical tools appear to have an irrefutable foundation; if we leave aside constant reference to the laws of nature to which we are supposed to be subject, there nevertheless remains the idea of models containing truth that aesthetic judgement is too precarious to detect. Why not accept this illusion as a poetic stimulus? What does it matter if the imagination has been fired by a landscape, a psychological state or an intellectual idea, so long as this stimulus, turned into action, results in a properly musical work strictly following its own criteria? After all, clouds can inspire Debussyan nostalgia; or, in their statistical structure, expansion and contraction, the constructivism of a Xenakis or the excitement of a Ligeti. Legitimacy does not come from how the phenomenon of 'clouds' becomes a procedure, but from how the phenomenon gives a work its explicit quality.

What strikes me as harder to accept, and even sometimes invalid, is a lack of correspondence with the object of reflection. The direct transcription of one world into another can only be disappointing, because it does not take the particular laws of each into account. Most of the time, direct correspondences between the visual and the aural, in particular, are glaringly 'irrelevant'. A curve (the transcription of some function) will yield meaningless melodic results, because a glissando is the quintessentially annihilating, reductive element, an amorphous phenomenon that does not take into account what the ear finds most important – segmentation and intervals. Similarly, to believe that a timbre will be interesting because its profile on the oscilloscope is visually striking is an illusion quickly dismissed by the ear. More generally speaking, certain forms of thought in modern science have to be adequately transposed if they are to remain valid. A scientific or technical device may be used as a tool for the development of current technology to broaden musical activity, and that genuine *transmutation* from one language to another strikes me as the only justifiable option in such situations.

7. Gestural Reciprocity Between Composer and Performer; the Integral or Shared Gesture

The different types of media through which the composer passes, including both individual and collective instrumental virtuosity and technology, can transform compositional gesture. This is a factor that cannot be ignored, whether it is assimilated or rejected.

Part of the composer's gesture is to assign the form and function of the performers' gestures. These behaviours lie at opposite extremes: either the gesture of transmission is merely a necessity of no intrinsic value; or, on the contrary, the quality or level of this gesture determines what we want to see transmitted, and is responsible for the message.

These behaviours are not restricted to 'living' performers whose virtuosity may or may not be taken into account, but also apply to the recent realm of technology: either this technology is used as the optimal channel to achieve a 'controlling' concept, or else one is interested in technological properties or accidents in and of themselves – as *inspiration*, as springboards from the predictable to the unpredictable.

This problem of the reciprocity between compositional gestures and performance or realisation brings us to the question of the displacements of the composer, whose gestures trigger processes that become out of control, or in which control is no longer desired. The composer may simply proceed to author instructions through which other individuals inscribe themselves by improvisation, or set off automatic processes that machines, once programmed, will propagate. In both cases, there is an initial flick of the wrist, but after this minimal gesture the composer will be displaced, so to speak, from taking any initiative, tending to believe that a higher level of creativity has been attained: a stage where the authoritarian and tyrannical decision of one person no longer counts, but in which a process transcending the individual is put into play, whose validity will be situated beyond individual accident, although it consists entirely of a collection of individual accidents. This seems to me to mark a return to that utopia of the musician who wants to force the universe to speak through an individual's gesture, like a 'scientific' hypothesis, who thinks that it must be dispersed into the great unknown truth of the universe, to which, by these feeble means, we give absolute priority.

But what exactly is this utopia? Taken to the extreme, it is but a pious illusion, a flight from the challenges of language, because issues of gesture are thereby suppressed to a *lower* level. And I do mean a *lower* level. Since the composer does not commit to any personal gesture, and since by offering a gesture that is at most a caricature, unencumbered by any deep meaning, responsibility for the work is transferred to other, supposedly spontaneous and liberated gestures, which in reality are much more the prisoners of learned reflexes than the personal gesture would have been. The performer's gesture reflects memory most of all, instrumental habit. Memory reflects works performed previously, stored consciously or unconsciously in the performer's mind, and even when superficially deformed or manipulated their underlying pattern never varies. Performers thereby display cultural literacy and assimilation, and in that sense, rather than inventing they disassemble original gestures and drop them onto an assembly line, which is the extreme opposite of their supposed freedom. Psychologically, the manipulator perhaps feels free here, but in point of fact they are completely manipulated by memory, the plaything of individual culture. Similarly, the performer is dependent on instrumental habits, since contact with the instruments is how the musical culture on display was acquired. Performers remain prisoners of their raw reflexes, like it or not, and these reflexes inescapably mean avoiding fundamental questions of creativity – that is, the relationship between structure and material.

This relationship of structure and material is what conditions the reciprocity of gestures between the composer and the performer, or between the composer and the technology of production. But it must above all be an act born of reflection. One can have the illusion of inventing in the moment, but invention is only possible through reflection. I do not mean to define these categories of immediacy and reflection through duration or notation. Immediacy is not necessarily improvisation; the immediate can just as well be a work directly modelled on another in order to deduce the real consequences of the model. Conversely, reflection is not necessarily a product of notation and of the time spent writing music down; it can be instantaneous and found in improvisation.

But reflection does require what I might call a critical trance, whereas immediacy is only the appearance of a trance, in which the critical aspect is strangely absent. The gesture of the composer is thus irreplaceable, and any displacement of it results only in trivialisation: what we hear is not the sound of the universe but, on the contrary, a strange and disconcerting absence of any *idea* at all.

It is in compositional gesture that the relationship of structure to material is inscribed, and I distinguish three behaviours. (1) The gesture of the composer *negates* the gesture of the performer as such, which it allows only as a means of transmission (or does not directly take into consideration, as in my own *Structures 1*). (2) The gesture of the composer *absorbs* the gesture of the performer by analysing it on two fronts: interaction with the instrument, and interaction in individual or collective performance. (3) The gesture of the composer is *dominated* by the gesture of the performer, deferring to virtuosity, if not as the substance of the work, then at least as an obligatory and privileged intermediary. The same three attitudes can also be found in the relationship with technology.

In fact, although virtuosity or technology can be inspirational, the composer's gesture runs the risk of being destroyed or diminished when they are given priority. In the case of *absorption*, there is a dialectic between what the technological or instrumental gesture is able to provide and the requirements to which the composer submits this data. As far as *negating* it or forgetting it completely goes, this appears to be impossible. One can set aside the importance of transmission and make arrangements for it to cause as few problems as possible in relation to other, more important problems, but whether one wants it or not, these two intermediary gestures do exist, countering the force of inertia.

1 'Le démon de l'analogie', the title of a poem by Mallarmé.
2 Anton Webern, *The Path to the New Music*, ed. Willi Reich (London: Universal Edition, 1975; originally published in German in 1960), p. 51.
3 The phrase *'Calomniez, calomniez, il en restera toujours quelque chose'* ('Throw dirt enough and some of it will stick') is often attributed to Francis Bacon or Beaumarchais.
4 Paul Klee's 1925 *Pädagogisches Skizzenbuch*, published in English as *Pedagogical Sketchbooks* (New York: Praeger, 1953).
5 Jacques Scherer, *Le 'Livre' de Mallarmé. Premières recherches sur des documents inédits* (Paris: Gallimard, 1957; rev. 1978).

6

Automatism and Decision
(1980–81)

The theme of 'automatism and decision' in composition might seem very narrow, or at any rate exclusively related to recent techniques such as those that computers offer. But although the computer, more than any other type of equipment, symbolises the urgency of this question, it did not create the problem. The question of the relationship between *chance* and *determination* in composers' intentions, and the means used to realise those intentions in actual works, is already familiar.

This dilemma of automatism and decision is only an extreme aspect of a more general network of relationships that is as relevant to the genesis of the work as it is to its realisation, and which justifies portraying the work as the intersection between the selected and the found, between what is sought and what is accepted.

Is the work not just a series of *accidents*, a series of *choices* that in different circumstances might have produced completely different results? In the chaos of intentions that preceded it, what was the decisive phenomenon that crystallised the result? Is it a composer's goal to show this chaos, embrace it or annihilate it? And if the last, is it possible wholly to eliminate chance? And in turn, if chance is used as a guide, can the composer categorically reject any of its outcomes? Do we not rely on *method* to capture chance and give the outcome the appearance of being a work? So many questions, so much to put to work – literally.

There have been many debates about what chance or determination mean for the art form. There have been many statements of intent about the validity of starting points, intentions, materials and formal components. Many experiments have been made using chance, free of any interference, and also intuition, with spontaneous reactions and improvisation. There have also been many experiments based on total determinacy, in which the will of the composer was limited to triggering procedures that did the composing, in which every relationship was calculated, in which form was the result of how the procedures evolved. In every case, there is a kind of belief in a higher order of reality, with which we cannot interfere without making it lose its underlying meaning, which is something stronger than any individual action. In every case, it is all or nothing: I trust the all-powerful determinacy that transcends me and which I do not seek to understand; I put together an organism that will replace my own will and therefore will not submit to the accidents that I would otherwise encounter, which would undermine the objective truth of structural phenomena. In every case, I am the medium, either of irrational or rational forces – understanding, of course, that what seems to be irrationality is part of a rationality that eludes us, and literal rationality is the limited expression of a transcendent order, graspable only within these limits.

Highlighting these beliefs reveals the methods involved at the opposite extremes of total indeterminacy and strict determinacy as being oddly similar. We make rules of behaviour for ourselves, and the result is not supposed to involve anything that might alter these rules. The rule is totally divorced from contingency. The process stops once it has exhausted a number of operations of the same type – this is the bottom line. Unsurprisingly, when we listen to works that have truly adhered to those self-imposed standards, we think we are hearing a slice of time no more inevitable than any other, with no reason to begin in one place or finish in another. Similarly, the journey from first moment to last leaves us with no sense of direction. After a while, imaginary journeys on the one we actually hear are superimposed in our minds and become equally valid; the reality of the journey we hear is no more compelling than those we simultaneously create in our imagination from the same elements. The most we can do is assign a particular meaning to an accidental object, but since nothing justifies it, and it fails to remind us of anything else, we forget it until some accident of a different kind attracts our attention. These accidents remain strangely disconnected from the phenomena that gave rise to them and are unrelated to the procedures that generated them. They simply appear, fruit of the chance encounter, not corresponding to anything that previously or subsequently exists.

When composers become aware of this effect of suspension and of the *inescapable* character of what is presented, they either reinforce it, to make it clear that this was their deliberate intention or even to provoke, or else they decide to end it with a supplementary gesture, a terminal clause that will purposefully and artificially close off the slice of time that has just been presented.

But surely dealing with chance and determinacy requires us to address the very general problem of the meaning of a work? We referred to closed and open works, but only in a rather restricted sense: that of a completed, finished form consisting of a single journey from beginning to end; or a form suggesting multiple pathways between a beginning and an end which are not necessarily fixed points, although we can choose to fix them. Even when restricted to problems of form, such a notion was, of course, shown to be rich in possibilities. In fact, defining form in this way has implications on many other levels, and the multiple pathways through the open work require a different approach to musical material, one that is different from the creativity demanded by the unique pathway of a closed work. I shall return to this later when I deal with much less general problems, reflecting on formal determinacy or indeterminacy, and the directionality of the latter, which in its single or multiple networks must undergo the elementary stages of musical creativity.

✿ ✿ ✿

Chance or determinacy is really a choice to be made at our first point of contact with the simplest elements of musical language – or rather, with those elements that characterise composition's most rudimentary stage, since they are not so simple even here. This fundamental dilemma is inherent in the very material that one selects or rejects, and not merely because it is being selected or rejected. But when one chooses, there can be ambiguities that render the choice fragile and subject to partly foreseeable variations. When no choice is made, the instructions are already sufficient to impose decisive constraints.

Pitch and timbre are categories that can be much more malleable and ambiguous than is generally realised. While the history of Western instruments has tended towards complete standardisation, towards constraints that unite the abstract definition of musical material (as a constituent of musical language) with the concrete reality of sound, one particular category – percussion – has nevertheless always included numerous sources of indeterminacy. Of course, there are pitched instruments, such as timpani, keyboards and bells; although the latter may seem relatively unorthodox, the way they are played minimises the slippage between the reality of their sound and their abstract, hierarchical singularity. But then there are all those instruments that for convenience we call unpitched percussion. That characterisation is correct, strictly speaking, only for those few instruments whose sound is so complex as to be impossible to sum up. With the rest, one only has to hear them to realise that they do in fact have a distinct pitch. Whether or not this pitch belongs to the family of pitches used by standard instruments can be simply a question of adaptation or their capacity for adjustment: all instruments with a skin membrane are easily adjustable, while those made of metal or wood generally are not. What I find most striking in the expression 'unpitched percussion' is the implication it carries of non-participation in the hierarchy, of their mobile, intricate profile. Their construction cannot provide specific, interchangeable values. The hierarchy among percussion instruments will therefore be variable; executing the composer's plan will be predictable from every point of view *except* that of pitch, perhaps even timbre.

Consider the best-known example of percussion music, already several decades old: Varèse's *Ionisation*, in which everything is fixed. Nothing – not the instrumental families, nor the relative pitch ranges (high, medium or low), playing styles or types of mallets used, nor, obviously, anything included in the notation – will admit any variability in rhythm, dynamics, tempo and performance indications. Thus, no *deviation* is possible. And yet, notice how vague an instruction such as 'high, medium or low' is in relation to familiar pitch criteria. What we have is 'envelope' categories, sanctioning an enormous range of different interpretations at any given point. For instruments that produce complex sounds, such as the tam-tam, such a definition may suffice, but when dealing with two snare drums one has to ask what the interval between them should be – a fourth, a minor third, or some approximate, untempered interval? Listening to two different performances of the work – two recordings for example – makes clear the implicit pliability of material within the fixed plan. In the realm of pitch, nothing is ever exactly the same: all comparisons are parallels, but no two instances will have the same quantities. Yet we have no trouble recognising this material as a whole, which is something that we would be quite incapable of doing if – taking Varèse again as the example – we were dealing with, say, his writing for wind instruments.

Another example is the use of the voice in Schoenberg's *Ode to Napoleon*. It uses a reduced, or rather symbolic, notation. The accidentals – natural, flat, sharp – are the same as in standard notation, but they are applied to signs that appear to be pitches but in reality are not, because the crucial reference to a stave has been omitted. When the reciter intones this text, he does it in a way that parallels what another reciter has done, but never in an identical manner, whereas the strings and piano do come close to that ideal. Yet this does not distort the work, for it retains its overall identity, which shows that this indeterminacy in the vocal material was incorporated.

A network of precise and strictly determined relations can coexist with a network in which several identical codes function, at least when one of them concerns relationships resistant to unequivocal interpretation, as with *Sprechgesang* in a melodrama like *Pierrot lunaire*.

Similarly, in Berio's vocal writing, first in *Circles* then in other vocal works, the vocal transcription is different from the instrumental. The vocal material is by turns 'absolute', the entire pitch realm exactly specified, and relative, with relationships that, rather than being truly quantitative, are reduced to an approximation.

So the word 'approximation' matters. As a relief from determinacy, we effectively rely on the performers' ability to approximate the material to be interpreted, and on the method they choose. Any notation must contain both quantitative and qualitative concepts. The latter have always been quite vague, influenced more by performers' own psyches than by their ability to apprehend exactly. Quantitative concepts, on the other hand, have gradually been more precisely described and, thus, executed. We have gone from descriptive, suggestive notation directly connected to what it represents (I am thinking of Gregorian neumes) to more abstract, generalised concepts of the reality of the sounds to which they refer. The use of a number or a symbol is further from reality but allows us to control it better. This approximation, using the eye only as a physical intermediary, relies above all on the *quantity*, which is specified as closely as possible through numbers and symbols. This notation is, by the way, analytical, since it captures in different ways a whole that we can immediately reconstruct, by integrating the different components we read within a single phenomenon – symbols referring to pitch, duration, dynamics, speed, sonic profile, and so on. Since this notation is, in a sense, *too* precise, too analytical, when one is dealing with phenomena that do not need to be completely determined, it is abandoned in favour of a notation founded on different criteria of legibility, at once more richly suggestive yet poorer in terms of control.

Our initial definition, generally omitted, is that of the *stave*. When it is absent, pitch space is specified only by position, which the eye is responsible for measuring without reference to quantifying symbols. The original grid space becomes smooth. There are no more point-by-point definitions, but rather an absolute continuum in which we are free to choose according to our impression of distance from one point to another, or to the shape of a curve. This amounts then to a relative space, in terms of how it is specified and deciphered. Since our eye is a most imperfect instrument for judging distances, such notation necessarily includes a margin of error, sometimes as large as the distance represented. One can instead proceed as composers since Schoenberg have done, keeping one or two horizontal lines as a kind of visual guide to indicate registers. The approximation is then more limited with respect to register and range, but is no more precise in itself. Precision was eschewed along with the symbol, and fragments of symbols will never recapture this precision, even with respect to more general concepts.

In most cases, though, the traditional coordinates of pitch and space remain. Pitch is read from bottom to top (in the sense of moving from low to high frequencies), and time is represented as proceeding from left to right, with simultaneity recorded as vertical. Here again, the symbol is missing – in this case, anything numerical: the approximation of time now depends solely on visual relationships. Sometimes an initial unit is specified, as with the scale in a geographical map: a given length, say one centimetre, is made to correspond to a given unit such as one second. Armed with this index the eye estimates time-distances. These distances could have been written precisely by the composer, but the idea is *to include the error* of approximation in the interpretation. The unit may, though, be much larger, extending, for example, to an entire page whose approximate value is indicated. In principle, every event on that page has to happen within its overall duration. The overall approximation will thus depend on individual choice. Even though practice can improve the quality of the result, there will undoubtedly be enormous variation in the interpretation of instructions as 'qualitative' as those. One might well question the necessity of a notation whose margin of error could result from graphic representation, or at any rate from the transcription of certain kinds of graphic. But even when the desire to eliminate determinacy also led to the elimination of a graphic's purpose, the point nevertheless is that the shell of determinacy could be broken only by tackling the notation, rejecting the unidirectional and unequivocal aspects of the codes. In fact, when dealing with objects that forgo the hierarchy of pitch, for example, how could they be transcribed if not by avoiding, or even eliminating, the symbols created for that hierarchy?

Pitch and duration are genuinely quantified values, so one might suppose that with other sorts of value, radical alteration is less of a challenge. There is, however, a tendency with these other categories to portray sound in a global manner, in a kind of notation that I call an ideogram. Instead of writing the symbol for a given pitch, to which a symbol for dynamics is added, the two are fused by drawing noteheads of different sizes to represent the amplitude. The more complex the phenomenon, and the more parameters are incorporated with each other, the less decipherable the notation becomes, and the more haphazard interpretation of the notated symbol tends to be. Instead of instantly synthesising the various parameters, the eye must analyse the entire phenomenon with which it is faced. Curiously, this takes longer, and given that the quantities corresponding to these parameters are represented graphically, it yields results whose fluctuations are difficult to predict.

The gap between this stage and the final one, which means freeing oneself completely from the conventions of transcription, however residual, is crossed quite easily. The more we trust our eye to estimate the plan, the more trust we place in the graphics themselves and their value. Since the system of time–pitch coordinates could be taken as a reference for deciphering any graphic symbol, and since other criteria such as the thickness of the line or the brightness of the image could be made to correspond to dynamics or to density, why not try to make use of all possible coordinates? The truth is that we never really explored the significance – the relational validity – of these graphic representations as an interpretive network. Notation is worthwhile only when it suits the structures it is meant to convey. This is why the most recent computer-generated examples of graphic transcription are just as meaningless as their artisanal precursors made with ink or pencil.

❊ ❊ ❊

I have addressed developments in notation extensively because, contrary to what might be thought, notation is not the concluding stage of the compositional process but rather a central one. Notation associates the nature of material with the nature of how it is used. Of course, notation specifies the material, but it also indicates the responsibility the composer takes for its existence and elaboration. Since the nature of material is revealed through notation, and since the quality of the relationships in this material is changed creatively, notation must necessarily not only reflect but also express those profound changes. This accounts for notation's need to leave room for varying degrees of indeterminacy.

If we look at this from the point of view of conventional notation, it is clear that, on the one hand, some descriptive parameters are abandoned because they impose hierarchies that cannot apply in such cases; on the other, we use adjacent, flexible parameters that enrich sound with categories previously ignored or left aside. When sonic phenomena become so complex that their acoustic notation is awkward and impractical, we then have to turn to notating actions rather than outputs. I may then establish a table of correspondences between action and output as a kind of lexical transcription of a work, but the problem, if we want to deal with it, is that this type of notation lacks universality: if you have never *heard* the result, you cannot predict it from the notation alone. The more one moves towards idiomatic transcription, the less decipherable the work's reality becomes. It is a strange paradox that concrete perception of the work is obtained through abstract notation, whereas with concrete notation a work becomes decipherable only as abstract structures. In the first case, the universality of the notation allows us to imagine the reality of the work; in the second, we can refer only to a plan of the actions, because the sonic reality is inaccessible to us without the intermediary of a table of concordances, as it were.

Going back to the first examples of subversion that I cited – Varèse, Schoenberg, then Berio – it can be seen that indeterminacy of material was introduced into the Western tradition mainly through two particularly anarchic means: percussion and voice.

Percussion comes first, in that most of these instruments originated in other civilisations or were used to underscore only the broadest articulations of musical discourse. Thus, timpani were long used exclusively to support tonic–dominant relations: parts were always notated in C rather than being transposed, reflecting their status as a rudimentary, all-purpose element that could be detached from its context. The cymbals were a by-product of *alla turca* style. One could continue with this inventory and show how little these elements were integrated. They were initially introduced for non-musical, descriptive reasons, exotic or otherwise. Percussion, besides its musical function, can also be tasked with transmitting signals: instruments or actions that make *noise* are, in effect, fundamentally separate from musical language. A handclap can be incorporated into a rhythmic structure in the same way as knocking on a piece of wood. But the handclaps might simply signify an instruction, a call for assembly; as for knocks on wood, they can only be a functional behaviour. The rhythm born of these functional behaviours will in a way be a rhythm of labour when it displays characteristics of repetition and symmetry, which can prompt the incorporation of other categories.

Labour songs emerged by becoming embedded in bodily rhythms, to which they confer greater fluidity, most often in the case of collective labour that requires some degree of synchronisation.

Thus, we see an entirely haphazard material, closely related to everyday life, selected sometimes for its utility, sometimes for its rhythmic power. It can be incorporated into a musical or proto-musical language, or it can return to its simple purpose as a *utensil*. This explains why we see containers, pots and pans, oil barrels and brake drums comfortably transfer from one world to the other. From one point of view, this subverts the 'educated' hierarchy, but from another it constructs a different language – not to mention its role in transmitting secret messages or news. One world may even adopt and adapt the other. This is the case with those steel pans that turned to using traditional Western scales as the basis for their construction. When grouped into orchestras, steel bands are well suited to transcriptions of popular and classical music.[1] They have moved from their role as utilitarian objects of rhythmic accompaniment in traditional chants and dances to the 'enemy camp', conquering and being conquered by classical music, to the point where they are built for this purpose and even distorted by it, at least if one compares it with their original use. Anything capable of providing us with sonic signals within the familiar utilitarian universe can therefore potentially be incorporated into music as generally understood. But this material always tends to lie outside any given language, due to the many connotations that it can suddenly awaken, intentionally or otherwise. 'Cultivated' musicians took advantage of this natural phenomenon acquired from spontaneous culture. They introduced this ambiguity into their work quite intentionally, with no great spontaneity, in order to try to form a new poetic or critical dimension in their musical discourse: it is a poetic dimension when it delights in the humorous potential of the incongruous and the absurd; a critical dimension when it tends towards sarcasm and cultural negativity. I will return to this later, because there is a considerable temptation to subvert a cultural product while marketing it like any other consumer product, which strikes me as betraying a certain contradiction or even hypocrisy.

I cited the voice as the second destabilising element in a deterministic hierarchy. It seems paradoxical to introduce this here, considering that over the centuries the voice has been the main element through which musicality is represented. But, of course, not everything concerning the voice is purely *musical*. Music's associations with religious or secular ceremony and with drama have much to do with this. There have been ideas and feelings that only the voice can express, using words that define content with great precision. Whether singing of divine glory or that of a sovereign, the voice could convey a message of deference, and could also express rebellion. The voice was also used to coordinate rhythm in a work through words of description or protest, and also through onomatopoeia, reflecting and illustrating the reality of labour. There is no need to elaborate on the voice's crucial role in drama – it even serves to develop style – nor to recall the affinity between the instrumental and the vocal, so close that through mutual influence they could create a profound unity between drama and music. And yet, the more instruments were divorced from their individual potential in favour of a pure, even purist, approach, the more the voice was also emancipated from the tendency to make it an instrument capable of articulating words. As with percussion, folk music also played a role, and the imitative onomatopoeia of certain labour songs or mystical incantations has shown that the voice is capable of running the whole gamut of expressive possibilities that hierarchical orthodoxy tended to force it to renounce. Naturally, there were moments in this story when the voice would take advantage of its imitative powers, always at the risk of affectation: all the imitations of birds and battles that the sixteenth century bequeathed to us reveal a drive for emancipation, a thirst for independence, however disguised.

Through its expressive power, its continued survival in an instrumental environment, its ability to assimilate a text and its capacity to produce sounds that lie outside both linguistic and musical grammars, the voice can choose to submit to musical hierarchy, be incorporated in it or free itself completely. As a direct medium, not necessarily subject to the need to communicate or express anything, the voice can be cultivated as an instrument, a 'wild', indomitable resource.

The voice does, after all, have many ways to sabotage the hierarchies imposed on it. The vocal sphere is infinitely complex and irreducible to overly restrictive standards. It can colour timbre with its vowels and articulate with its consonants.

When these possibilities of articulation or exclusively vocal coloration are developed, the determinacy and standardisation of the instrumental sphere are kept at bay. Complex spectra and anarchical universes are common to the voice and percussion compared with the traditional components of our musical universe. They demand a different kind of relationship to compositional 'order' if we want to protect them from artificial and inadequate constraints and exploit their abundance of resources.

This leads us to distinguish between means that are generally natural and those that are specifically cultural, between the spontaneous (inasmuch as spontaneity is possible, given the conditioning effect of environment) and the acquired (or rather, the various degrees of acquisition). Even more specifically, we need to establish the difference between *found object* and *created object*. *Found objects* are those used for a musically defined purpose different from that for which they were constructed. They are then made to deviate from their original functions either by imbuing them with a temporary function that allows them to be used for musical expression – even if only rhythmic – or by the transmission and aural transcription of physiological rhythms (sleigh bells, bracelets and other accessories worn to temporarily produce sound). I call them 'found' objects in relation to the music in which they are engaged because such objects can be perfectly functional and manufactured with a very precise purpose in mind. The *created object*, on the contrary, is one that could not exist outside music, to which it owes its function and characteristics. It is created in order to produce a defined universe. Its 'untamed' potential is obviated or deliberately limited. It must follow established rules of construction and use. The *created object* is generally one that has been derived from a found object as the needs of a culture have become more demanding and have required more specific means of transmission. Experiencing the limits of the found object with respect to the creation of a musical language meant having to organise the object's potential into something that could truly be called an instrument. Sometimes, what is lost in richness is gained in rigour: it is impossible to curb the inherent potential of found features without introducing rejections and constraints that denude the original object of some of its potential, which thereby remains unexplored or marginal.

Within the instrument, a *centre* is found that has the potential for maximally rigorous determinacy, and a *periphery* in which the sounds produced are, if not completely indeterminate, then at least highly unstable. Compared to the rigour of the central hierarchy, musicians, especially those strongly influenced by instrumental practice, tend to want to explore those unstable regions that elude categorisation and often refer more to an action whose content and result are limited than to a global practice.

Many recent works have revealed the desire to organise the *centre–periphery* binary into a genuine compositional project, to make this instrument-specific schema interact with other schemas. It is not only a matter of variations of timbre, of changes in the instrumental arsenal, but more the use of a dimension that is *free* ('exceptional' sounds) rather than obligatory ('conventional' sounds). This variability of instrumental hierarchy parallels the variability of other hierarchies, not specifically instrumental, particularly that of time, and more generally that of formal structure. Unlike manufactured material that is claimed to be totally unadulterated and free of interference, chance (or a cluster of chances) is identified and incorporated as much as possible into a less restrictive universe. Thus, antagonistic forces whose coexistence is never straightforward are at work. In fact, sounds 'rationalised' by the manufacturer benefit from all the care taken in producing the instrument, not to mention the hierarchical universe to which they belong. In addition to being, if not unclassifiable, then at least tending towards anarchy, peripheral 'accidents' present difficulties of production or exact reproduction whenever they have interesting and complex particularities; or else these 'accidents' are of a trivial kind whose repetition becomes wholly intolerable, because their potential is quickly exhausted and comes to seem excessively anecdotal. Moreover, like any elements that are organised only superficially and do not truly belong to the structures of a musical language, they are not work-friendly, but intrude between one work and another as fixed, rigid invariants, like some kind of offstage hiss, to borrow a derogatory term from the theatre.

The further we travel, as it were, from the centre to the periphery of the instrument, the warier we need to be of the autonomy of accidents, of superficial integration, of anecdotal vacuity. Nothing is more destructive to creativity than 'effects', because they easily become an alibi behind which their poverty of structure and lack of organic definition are apparent all too soon. As a result, there is often nothing but organisational templates with no connection between what is organised and the way it is organised. These are templates applied to, or filled with – I would even say stuffed with – sonic events. The same template could be applied indifferently to other objects, because the means of generation are not specifically related: there is no function, only *arrangement*.

We cannot therefore let ourselves be guided by accidents, whether in the instrumental or electronic sphere, yet we should also not fail to take them into account. When we move away from strongly hierarchical events, it strikes me that we can give meaning to accidental ones in two ways: through direct linkage, or as a means of articulation.

I would compare direct linkage to what is known in classical harmony as an appoggiatura, or a passing note. Every determinate event in the realm of pitch can be surrounded by a zone of events with a variable function of greater or lesser complexity. The more we depart from the neutrality of the purposeful event within a hierarchy, the more we move towards particularising phenomena for which the hierarchy plays an increasingly minor role, until it becomes completely irrelevant. The extension of the hierarchy leads to its suspension. This is the case, for example, with multiphonic sounds that can be used according to their complexity, instability, dynamic range and timbral variety. They are like complex appoggiaturas of a single sound.

'Accidental' phenomena can be used equally well as a means of articulation. These events change categories when they are viewed not in terms of pitch, but rather rhythm, for example, or as formal signals. Thus, when Bartók uses the pizzicati named after him, it is precisely in this manner, whether in the *Music for Strings, Percussion and Celesta* or in the quartets. The sound produced belongs to a more indistinct, if not cruder, category, and he uses it for more general ends for which the distinction between sound and noise is not as critical. On the other hand, this twin affiliation to sound and to noise is used to signal notable structural landmarks, emphasising them more effectively than could dynamics, for example. When a category is insufficient, properties of another category are invoked, though that is the exception. Indeterminacy of a sound event as such – sound and noise combined in proportions difficult or even impossible to gauge – has the advantage, compared with strictly determined sounds, of forming an envelope category. Whether col legno on a bowed instrument, key clicks or unpitched breathing noises on wind instruments, their use entails the same requirements and results. A failure to assess these problems impoverishes a musical discourse based on categories too broad to be generally viable. Even the musical instrument as created object possesses significant features of the found object, ones that cannot be exploited without a true feeling for the requirements of this sonic phenomenon, if it is to participate in musical discourse.

✳ ✳ ✳

When considering *created* and *found* objects, however, we have to go beyond the material to see what these categories mean at another level: that of language itself. This problem is not exactly recent, although musical works addressed it much later than their equivalents in painting and literature. I am referring to the use of objects that are in a certain sense manufactured and do not depend directly on the language of the work, but are incorporated through a purposeful poetic decision, explicit or not. One could object that we are digressing from the subject of chance and determinacy, and that these relationships or stylistic diversions should rather be considered from the point of view of their expressive value, their power to convey meaning. Obviously, these conceptual fusions and overlaps are being introduced principally to represent styles, emotions, historical references, jaded clichés sometimes. But just as we are familiar in the visual sphere, for instance, with collages incorporating heterogeneous materials, uniting them despite themselves, or playing with this heterogeneous quality and approaching the manipulation of material in a spirit of provocation, so can those two tendencies be seen in music, too: either juxtaposing cultural objects detached from their context, or aiming to integrate them through a kind of over-determination.

Without wanting to write the complete history of stylistic reminiscence, it must nevertheless be recalled that neoclassicism tried to solve this problem of parody when, after several brilliant examples from Stravinsky, a whole generation tried its hand at incorporating the commonplace, the found object of the 'old song with naive chorus' kind. Since so-called learned music distanced itself from the popular kind, and since over the course of history learned music had moreover become distanced from itself, there was a strong temptation to reintegrate all of those spheres into a larger whole. Whether the tension is emphasised and exaggerated, or ironed out and concealed, in both cases one musical discourse is being corroborated or contradicted by another. At the level of grammar, the intersections will thus be left to the coincidence of the moment, or they can be prepared in advance by an infrastructure that tries to coordinate the different states of language involved. Chance or premeditation – can both be valid?

Whether in the form of a game, a *divertissement*, or from a deeper historical motivation, the final product seems to address our faculty of recognition; that is to say, when we are not in *the know*, a good part of its interest is missing. In the case of collage, quotation, one event superimposed on another, recognition applies in several ways. We are already familiar with the fragment and able to recognise it. We recognise it because it is presented over a sufficient length of time and with sufficient autonomy, and because none of its components has been substantially altered. If none of these conditions is present, the precise allusion escapes us, and consequently a large part of the intention. We are in a position to appreciate only stylistic divergence or convergence; that is to say, the greater or lesser degree of luck involved in the inclusion of one style within another. To try to determine the conditions of this combination is a considerably more ambitious goal: to imperceptibly alter this or that characteristic, which is so appropriately called 'stylising'. Some traits of the model are left recognisable, but others are transformed in the name of integration. Inclusion thus means ambiguity, and is apparent without destroying the unity of the language that conveys it.

It is noteworthy that it is above all works destined for the theatre that were preoccupied by the problem of integration and disintegration. Whether intended for a real or imaginary theatre, these works seem to have an extra-musical motivation that would on its own justify tearing musical language apart, in the context of contemporaneous norms. I speak of language being torn apart, not expanded, because whether chance or determinacy is used in these stylistic confrontations, in my opinion they never give the impression of unity, or even internal consistency. There is a dislocation between different stylistic profiles, especially when they are extended in time, but overall these divergences are simplistic, hence the recourse to external factors to explain or justify them.

I spoke of *found objects* incorporated more or less as they are into a real or imaginary theatrical context. The use of these kinds of textual quotation and selections of sound materials seems to me almost always to call (not without irony) for all the explanations, justifications and reminders that narcissistic cultural play requires.

Leaving aside the naivety or trickery of the material, one can observe the laborious effort of integration or the nonchalant attitude of the manipulator. From this borrowed material, one seeks to create a determinate structure within an organised system, or else we allow it to evolve as a fragment, with its own logic, its capacity for chance encounters. Incidentally, trickery or naivety are not always found where we expect them: much naivety can be revealed by a desire to organise, and there can be considerable cleverness behind nonchalance. Since the second attitude implies above all fortuitous combination, one cannot but notice the success or the failure of the experiment, and check whether such success resists repetition, once the element of surprise has faded. More curious are the attempts at integration, because they reveal a contradiction between intention and method: taking a musical example, such as a chorale, and then randomly distorting it by deleting, altering or twisting some of its components; making systematic distortions and presenting them as if they were in the original source; using a cliché or series of clichés organised according to a certain combinatorial logic; or progressively slipping from one style to another – those are samples, among others, of *parody* as it has been practised quite recently. And yet, no matter what the intentions might be – gentle or severe, sarcastic, vindictive or nostalgic – as with all parody the reference is always apparent. I do not believe that reference can ever take us very far, because it often, if not always, implies a dubious attachment to the past, and creative *invention* will always radically transform the reference to the point of making it unrecognisable and, in that sense, ineffective. Perhaps in my own case this comes from a deep aversion to the *game* that involves using chance as casual entertainment. The objects used have lost their deeper meaning without having acquired anything more than a fairly pointless decorative quality. We rapidly *seize* the intentions, and beyond these the methods turn out to be predictable. At best, this can amount to an episodic, circumstantial approach.

❊　❊　❊

If the intrusion of chance cannot be reduced to a superficial game, what can be done with this category that comes into conflict with everything, and that forces us to question the robustness and validity of the work concept? This was a very relevant question several decades ago. Is it just as relevant today? Do we still consider it as crucially important? Did not the call for chance derive above all from an excess of determinism? Since today this excess has diminished, loosened its grip, is the need to appeal to such an explosive force as strong?

Western tradition rallied around the unique perfection of the work, around the masterpiece that required a closed path, 'absolute' notation, and the concept of a model text; so much so that performance was reduced to the state of pure transmission, in which perfection was equated with neutrality. Recall the completely 'objective' performances demanded by composers like Ravel and Stravinsky. Even more restrictive than this notion of an absolute work with its closed-off, unique truth was the arrival, shortly thereafter, of a linguistic determinism in which every relationship depended on a hierarchy, which was defined both very precisely and also very vaguely.

'Very precisely' means that every intervallic relationship must depend on a close specification set out at the beginning of the work. The main figures, the chord structures, and the formal articulation are determined by a set of initial and derived relationships.

'Very vaguely' means that nothing about the initial choice or the deductions implies more general organisation of, say, harmonic relationships, chord types or intervallic relationships. There is only one prescription: to avoid doublings, which is very rudimentary. Thus, this new disciplined approach would still include many older hierarchies, adapted for better or worse to the newly created situation.

This brings us to the ambiguous situation in which a certain part of musical language is severely codified and rigidly applied, while another is forced to seek a foothold in laws that no longer have any rationale. It grew out of the empiricism of everyday practice and was then provisionally altered through the attempt at total codification in which, despite the requirements of logic apparently being satisfied, relationality issues were still not resolved, or resolved only through the very general proscription of doublings. It could be said that at that time, determinism reigned supreme over one part of the operation, and that indeterminacy, still intuitive, took charge of what could be called the big picture. To put it simply, the notes followed very precise laws, while their fields of action roamed in the arbitrary. Given this state of affairs, the uneasiness experienced in applying strict discipline within a fragmentary environment can well be imagined.

And yet one thing had been gained: in part, the rejection of any hierarchies other than local ones and, as a corollary, the rejection of pre-compositional formal plans. Despite all the contradictions and lacunae, one thing was certain: the work itself must generate its own determination. The dilemma remained: fixed composition or free-form?

We must not forget that the relationship to the performer became more and more controlling and, thus, less and less productive. Although objectivity may be required, and can be obtained through musical texts with controllable components, the same can hardly be said of scores so complex as to offer only a small chance of precision. When the determination of sound objects was brought to its most extreme conclusion, this resulted in performances that could be at best approximate. Here again, there was, if not a chasm, at least a real gap between the extreme detail of the object as contemplated and its approximation when performed. Objectivity and precision could be nothing but a diversion. And even if, looking for some justification, we thought that performers' abilities would become more acute in time and allow them to become comfortable through familiarity, there are limits beyond which only controlled approximation can reign. In truth, the potential of the performer would be more effectively aimed at a different target. This last consideration, one that re-engages with the need to solve the challenges of musical language and composition, resulted in attempts to imagine other solutions in order to *relativise* problems, to overcome an obstacle or difficulty, to widen the field of action, and to consider the work as something that can essentially be remodelled each time it is performed.

From what amounts to a different point of view, we dreamed of calling into question the notion of a unique work – a work inscribed in a single temporal path – that stems from individual choice on a particular occasion. The work could be conceived as the product of an anonymous force. In some ways, total determinacy as compositional technique ensured such a degree of anonymity. Once the prototype was selected, one could say, the outcomes were deduced without a composer intervening at all, beyond the formal arrangement of procedures for which the composer did not want to be responsible. Some composers placed their faith in numbers in order to efface their will with a more universal, inescapable determinacy that was less dependent on the moment and derived from an underlying, immutable rule. Others, finding that this governing rule could not be specified through restrictive frameworks, entrusted themselves once again to chance and refused to intervene even with regard to the starting point. But, at first, they did not entirely avoid a minimal degree of determinacy, in that chance operations were organising sound materials that had themselves been intentionally organised. Later, this contradiction was eliminated when they began using the laws of chance to arrange randomly generated material. The tendency to seek the suppression of the composer as a conscious organising agent was clear in its extreme consequence: the disavowal of any work characterised by personal will. The composer, if indeed that term is still relevant, seeks in that case simply to be a means of transmitting forces liberated from any individual impediment. Moreover, chance operations produce a situation where a segment of time is simply filled, nothing more; a similar phenomenon could be observed, by the way, when extreme determinacy delineated the trajectory of a work through the number of combinations used, by exhausting certain methods – in short, by the natural limits of operations in which the composer was not supposed to intervene.

Given some non-fixed elements, it naturally came to everything being non-fixed, for why should elements be organised in one respect if not in any other? Why not return what had become the obligatory temporal succession of possibilities to its original, genuine state – that is, one in which all these possibilities are envisioned not only without any hierarchical priority, but literally without any predetermined order? Instead of choosing one line of action, a field of action would be established in which it is not essential for one event to arrive before any other since, hierarchically speaking, they are on the same level. The path will therefore be set at the moment that the score is being realised, and with just as much validity. Performers regain fulfilment, since the frustration of imponderable challenges is eliminated by the goal-directedness they bring to the musical text, by the provisional determinacy with which they imbue it.

In this enlargement, however, it was soon noticed that several features were merely illusory, compared with the previous situation. This was noticed first and foremost with respect to the performer, who could not sustain a relationship to the work that consisted of instantaneous actions with no preconceived ideas. Once the work began to be studied, the pathway chosen was no longer innocent: even if the choices differed from performer to performer, preference would nevertheless be given to particular pathways, for reasons that are difficult to fathom. Had they been determined to apply the rules of this game, performers would be struggling against their working habits, and their spontaneous selections would become a negative in the context of their acquired skills.

Similarly, contemplating the results, the work's composer could not help but reflect more deeply on why one pathway through a work was more satisfying than another, since in these cases things are never equal and, as the saying goes, some results are more equal than others! Moreover, for fairly obvious reasons, a partial structure cannot connect effectively with all the other partial structures available, for they would need to have nothing in common in order to produce a contrast, or have a sufficient number of common features in order to link up. One is riven between ultimate singularity and total neutrality. Since one cannot permanently remain in such a paradoxical state, the different particles will seem to offer a number of elements that are of varying suitability for organic development. In order for these elements to connect with others, rather than being merely juxtaposed, their components must have something in common, which can be found only within certain limitations, i.e. the limitations of what can be conveyed by recognition and affinity. I would also mention more concrete problems, since the fragments must set up pitch fields, common or complementary configurations that allow them to be connected with a certain variety but also logic. In short, many potential relationships must be anticipated in this respect, from which a number of actual relationships are chosen in performance.

When performed in part or in full, does the work resolve into nothing but a demonstration of its own mobility? There may be a harmfully pedagogical side to this desire to demonstrate the different aspects that the work can take on. And how many demonstrations need there be? Should they be included in the work, or produced over the course of different performances? How will the work's mobility actually be perceived? Is it even necessary that it be perceived in such an emphatic way? Is this our final goal, to become aware of mobility by comparing several real cases, and to ascertain whether this writing could have been produced in a fixed universe? Many solutions, both invisible and overt, have been proposed, of which the least convincing is obviously the repetition of a work in a 'different' version. Another solution, more astute and intrinsic to the structure itself, would be to perform certain fragments several times, so that the different ways of linking them together can be noticed; but since the exact repetition of each cell is forbidden, this means slightly different criteria, which, if there are to be repetitions, must necessarily be very crude envelopes: playing the passage an octave higher, or with a different kind of articulation, or with relative dynamics altered – in short, a necessary but superficial kind of variation, in conflict with the complexity of the written relationships.

Since the original texture was not a premise but rather an effect, some spontaneous addition to it could only make for modification too superficial to be regarded as genuine variation.

If the goal of mobility is not demonstration, how should it be considered? The elements of the form must be inscribed in the formal path, and this pathway, whatever it is, must exhibit its fundamental characteristics. This intention cannot be left to pure chance, but must have recourse to multiple determinations. This is to say that the form must include the possibility of choice as a basic principle, by providing elements that can be placed in various locations, but which have totally predetermined characteristics of a certain order. Whatever the literal placement of elements may be, the use of registration, dynamics or rhythmic densities, for example, will serve as a global envelope for all of the events. Reading this pathway in such or such a way will mean that the envelope will be modified according to a different sequential order, but it will nevertheless be present just as strongly no matter what reading is adopted. Of course, the envelope can change its nature depending on the elements it controls. A registral characteristic can bind a certain number of elements together, while other elements are linked through dynamics or rhythmic figuration. With this kind of approach, there can be very broad flexibility, since this envelope can be created as one goes along, according to one's needs, through constraints that are imposed at the very moment the elements are linked together. The texts of the cells to be joined can be definitive, so that the sequence is dictated in one permanent (albeit multiple) fashion. At the end of each cell, there will therefore be merely an indication of which cell or cells can be connected, although characteristics of the subsequent cell can be indicated at the end of the one just performed. At the end of the fragment there could be, for instance, an indication of 'staccato, forte' that would apply to the next. In this way, the envelope is created from one element to the next, with each cell imposing characteristics on its successor, whichever element that may be.

These different types of envelope, constructed in advance or as a piece unfolds, imply a rigorous positioning of all the elements that are supposed to interact. If the musical text remains fixed while the order of succession is mobile, the difficulty resides only in the starting and finishing joints between elements. Even this comes with its share of problems. It implies registral nodes and antinodes, to borrow acoustic terminology. If the register widens over the course of the fragment, it should narrow down to a certain number of common or complementary notes both at the beginning and at the end. Since the fragments can be linked for similarity or contrast, either common ground or a sharply distinct tessitura needs to be envisaged. The other factors are, in a certain sense, easier to achieve, since they are not as constraining as pitch hierarchy.

But if the musical text is itself also subject to changes – in dynamics, playing style, speed – imposed by the order of succession, it thereby becomes correspondingly more complicated to predict subsequent developments. For if something is playable at a given speed, with a certain type of articulation, within a narrow dynamic range, it soon becomes unplayable once it goes beyond those limits. The musical text then runs the risk of being too neutral if it is to be subjected to fairly large variations of parameters, if the figures are to be excessively simplified. Thus, at a fast tempo, successions of regularly spaced notes and the articulation of large units are completely valid, but they become doubtful at a moderate tempo and quite unacceptable at a slow one. One needs to know when to discard certain elements and when to add others. Similarly, a wide variety of accentuation and dynamics will be possible at a slow tempo, but will lose all their meaning at a fast one, because they become unplayable. When one requires significant tempo variation, the extreme cases that cannot support such changes must therefore be *avoided*. Although one begins by intending to enrich the musical text with more potential for new versions, one ends up impoverishing it in order for this potential still to seem meaningful.

The mobility of structures thus imposes huge constraints on texture, which is no surprise given the organisational plurality it implies. Instead of being founded on unique relationships from element to element, such composition is founded on multiple relationships that require a number of selective choices if they are to be carried out without absurdity. Here, we once again encounter, not unexpectedly, the problem of 'freedom'! We wanted to explore mobile forms out of a desire to escape the empty shell of teleological form, and to offer the performer the power to select from several pathways, several solutions. Yet the freedom given with one hand was taken away with the other, through the severe – possibly excessive – constraints that composition required.

Of course, very few composers worried about this 'hyperlogic', contenting themselves with the delights of mobile form. Were they wrong? Shouldn't the danger of 'bad graphics', which reduce many elements of this logic to randomness, also be considered? The more complex the rules of the game become, the more difficult they are to respect. Even if it were not spontaneity that was sought first and foremost, we must recognise that beyond a certain limit, there will be a rate of error or failure of attention that will progressively destroy the superb machinery so carefully installed. This is particularly true for collective performance, in which the risk of inaccuracy increases in proportion to the number of performers.

And so, beyond pointless demonstrations, we need to see how the use in musical language of dimensions that are not strictly controllable can be justified. We can find its origins in the search for freedom, given the surfeit of control imposed on composition, which ruled out initiative, let alone spontaneity, since absolute obedience to the plan was seen as performers' primary obligation to the composer. We can also understand composers' reactions: at the risk of destroying their own language, they give performers the most radical opportunities to make their presence felt. And yet at the centre of this phenomenon, the contradiction between stasis and movement remains. By this I mean that the work must be set in a determinate way if it is to be heard at all: one can listen to a work only in the state in which it exists, however provisional this is. How, then, can the requirement of mobility and non-determination be inscribed not only into the formal results, but also into musical language itself? How can the contradictions this situation suggests be resolved without trammelling the 'freedom' on offer through an excessively cumbersome and restrictive set of rules?

We should note – as a constant, and even a dilemma that is part and parcel of our tradition – the persistent presence of two dimensions that tend, if not to clash, then at least to stand in opposition to each other: those of free and strict composition.

Free composition obeys laws from which constraint is certainly not absent, but adheres most of all to principles of internal consistency and of succession, leaving the door open to a great number of solutions. Harmonic writing was the form in which this free dimension could express itself most adequately, whereas polyphonic writing and counterpoint were usually a sign, the very hallmark, of strict composition. It is here that the dependence of one note, one group on another arises in a unique way, through an imperative law of deduction. Strictly canonical composition is the finest example of this model, since every figure inscribed in musical time generates one or more figures inscribed in the same time or in a version of it, while this network of horizontal relationships is controlled by vertical laws that are no less strict and whose exceptions (passing note, parallel consonances) all belong to very specific classes. These compositional characteristics are projected all the way up to the level of form. The prelude and fugue are archetypal examples of this juxtaposition of free and strict forms.

These fundamental oppositions were slowly eroded and the categories fused. But even in the least academically classical pieces, and even in the most spontaneous effusions of Romanticism, we see the alternation of free (I would even say stock) passages in relation to the themes explored, with passages where, in contrast, the composer used those themes as the core of deductions. The metamorphosis of the theme, ornamental variations, the isolation of various elements, the superimposition of certain figures on others, the transformation of figures by others – such are the strict procedures that composers have applied ever since the rigorous rules that were too closely associated with a particular style fell into disfavour. Nostalgia still remains for the order that guided music's progress through the discovery of deduction; nostalgia for canonical and fugal writing reappears regularly in more and more elaborate guises, far removed from its origins, whose academic degeneration was sealed once and for all by neoclassical caricature, and whose original components were dissolved in Webernian transcendence in order that they could infuse new compositional principles, calling the very materials of composition into question.

But over the course of a work there is always a desire to be able to change the *procedures* of deduction from a model. To move from this compositional variability to a variability of the elements themselves and of form is more complex than it might at first appear, because not all these kinds of variability correspond. As we have seen, variability of material, for example, does not automatically imply compositional variability. On the other hand, to let a structure generate itself automatically, through the evolution of the parameters that govern it, by no means implies lack of rigour – far from it. Finally, in the realm of form, open or closed options do not directly imply free or strict compositional procedures.

Among the multiple components of writing music, let us ask which element, if any, will decisively distinguish free from strict. Will there not be large areas of uncertainty, of ambiguity? Consider a rhythmic example, where the constraints are fewer and less obvious than with pitch. Say we hear irregular figures, with unequal durations that cannot be notated in regular metre. There are two ways to achieve this sensation of suspended, non-directional time. The durations can contradict a metrical definition by using artifices such as syncopation and accent displacement. In this way, the rhythmic figure will contradict, or at the very least weaken, the metre. But these durations can also be inscribed, beyond any metrical pulse, into an approximate chronometric time, either in time units or linked to another variable such as resonance. In the first case, the writing is entirely determined, its parameters fixed without any ambiguity. In the second, no parameter is quantified. This might be a question purely of evaluating a notated difference; whether this is strict or free composition, the result strikes the ear as distinctly similar.

I will provide another example of a rhythmic procedure. Some works use highly complex tempo relationships, executed either by performers or by mechanical means. Within these tempi, figures can be inscribed that are themselves rather elaborate. We wanted to play two games at once: complex tempo relationships between two textures, and internal complexity of each of these textures. The result is that we do perceive overall complexity, but unrelated to the relationship between the tempi. The complexity of the two textures could be reduced to a common metrical unit within a single tempo, since the margins of error of this reduction will lie well outside the threshold of perceptibility. Moreover, since no accentuation, no law of repetition or harmonic reprise can provide us with any indication of these different metrical pulses, we would have no reason to take one or the other as referential, but would have the impression of floating in a non-tempo that probably could have been achieved by other, simpler means. Thus, an impression of speed or slowness predominates, or irregularity or regularity, scarcely subject to any more precise category of perception. In order for the relationship between the two constant speeds to have been perceived, we would have needed to hear the metre of each one, to associate them, moreover, with periodic features of pitch and density; in short, with a sonic phenomenon that would have established the metrical state of each. Only when those states are concretely specified and assimilated does this confrontation become fully effective.

In fact, in the absence of 'specification', many events based on an opposition between free and strict composition do not have a strong enough profile to be perceived, or even for us to discern the category to which they belong or at least tend. This is due either to excessive complexity in one dimension without compensatory clarifying phenomena, or an underestimation of the relative importance of decisive parameters.

1 Boulez used a steel pan to impressive effect in *Sur Incises* (1996–8) for three pianos, three harps and three percussionists.

PART 4: THE PROBLEM OF THEMATICS

7

The Notion of Theme and Its Evolution
(1982–83)

In order to describe musical language, we focus first and foremost on describing consistent systems of organisation, including modal, tonal and non-tonal systems, or any other configuration of a pre-existing hierarchy that is expressed in a work, according to which it must behave.

We cannot conceive of a work that was not composed according to a consistent system – for example, of pitch – even when we do not see this consistency in use, but only its by-products. (A few major or minor chords can be used as residues of a system, like abandoned artefacts, without actually exploiting the system.) In the same way, we can compose using a consistent rhythmic system without this resulting in particularly unified music. To use relationships between values is to use the residue of proportional notation.

Thus, intentionally or not, consciously or not, music always originates from concepts that are in fact imposed on us by the instruments with which we try to convey musical discourse, as elementary as that discourse may be. There is a network embracing all of the materials, and except for the (barely imaginable) case of complete anarchy, something is presupposed thanks to predetermined models of realisation and the means of transmission.

And yet this is not enough to give musical composition cohesion. A musical work can be followed only when we sense deduction from rudimentary premises.

The more a work extends in time, the more complex its expression, the more we need to latch on to temporal markers that are easily recognised and that allow our memory to select and act.

The notion of unity that seems to have gained ground over all others is that of theme, a term that matters as much to the professional musician as to the amateur.

In analytical terminology, the word 'theme' and the concepts it implies are used all the time. It is intrinsically linked to ideas of variation, development and form. For themes in sonata form, theme and variations, two-theme form and rondo form there is a familiar specification in each case, and particular implications. Without this fundamental notion, it is difficult to imagine years and years of instruction, whether academic or not.

But the word 'theme' is also synonymous with illustration. Thus, in the theatre, stage directors wanting to characterise the incidental music may refer to a theme of anguish, joy, pride. In the tradition of the Wagnerian leitmotiv, we find the word 'theme' linked to a description of a character, type or concept, which is not a structural notion indicating that the theme will generate a number of corollaries in a certain order, but is about creating a musical figure that can be related to a psychological state, according to codes familiar from previous musical literature. This is an emotional code of which the basics are all too familiar: deep tremolos, glittering brass, solo violin, and so on. Meanings degenerate into slogans.

Yet however extreme these two notions may seem, they unite in an underlying expressive logic. It was in the nineteenth century that expressively charged symbols became weighed down by excessive baggage.

We do, of course, find descriptive – even naive – music before the nineteenth century, and on a higher level the integration of symbols (intervallic, numerical and formal) in musical language. But this symbolic treatment of the musical idea underlies, and remains subordinate to, order and to ordering.

In the theme, there is initially a generic notion, a combination of intervals developed in agreement with a system of coordinates.

The theme tended primarily to formalise developmental procedures, hence its brevity, to allow for a systematic exploitation of its resources.

Thematic organisation, and its interdependencies, may be very briefly described:

– it tended to organise the type of discourse, such as fugue or two-theme sonata;

– it guided the expressive urge and represented the symbolism of a text (Berlioz's *idée fixe*, Wagner's leitmotiv);

– it encapsulated the moment, thereby resisting the typical rhetoric of development (Debussy);

– it dominated both the structures of language and the formal structures of development (Schoenberg, Webern); and

– it ended up effacing the very idea from which it was born, when eventually everything became thematic while nothing was, in a fundamental *relativity* of thematic components.

The theme is therefore dependent on the evolution of language, so that it is impossible to analyse a Monteverdi madrigal or a Debussy sonata in the same way. Moreover, the theme is not the only factor contributing to unity.

In a recitative (*recitativo secco*), there are clearly no themes as such. At most, in *recitativo arioso*, a repetitive motive will permeate the harmonic texture and may sometimes anticipate the more formalised piece that follows. At both extremes of recitative, its harmonic progression connects the two items surrounding it. Within the recitative, however, there are harmonic progressions enabling both expression and articulation, to the extent that one could almost literally specify the content of a recitative: modulation means a new phrase or phrase element, the cadence means the end of a phrase with certain indicative melodic flourishes, and so on. Here, the composer uses the direct emotional power of a chord or interval. Nevertheless, recitatives have a unity of their own, even when there is no thematic process or even motivic working.

The musical Idea depends on a combination of features, and this has changed over the course of music history. It cannot be said that the Idea depends entirely on the circumstances in which it appeared, because the Idea also in turn affects musical language. This process of transformation is reciprocal: the evolution of the Idea will affect how a language is organised, and the status of musical language will affect the conception or profile of the Idea. Thus, a balancing act is set up between the codes of language and the significance of the Idea as function.

From the initial Idea to the completed discourse, an immense task of enlargement, structuration and construction occurs. This enlargement takes place according to codes, possibly conventions. These codes serve to *establish* the Idea, to *develop* it (by working with the melody, harmony, counterpoint, timbre and dynamics). They also serve to extend form. What do we find in Western culture regarding musical language? To put it very briefly, and to recall well-known aspects of pitch organisation, there was a development from modes to keys, then to total chromaticism, then to the comprehensive integration of all the elements of noise and sound. In rhythm, we moved from neumes to proportional notation, then to the incorporation of different types of hierarchies and temporal functions. Timbre and intensity played an increasingly functional role: they were incorporated into the compositional process more and more.

This is, of course, a superficial view of stylistic evolution. For example, Wagner's melodic invention is fundamentally inscribed in the dialectic of, and opposition between, diatonic and chromatic. Gesualdo and the madrigalists could also be assigned to that dialectic, since they follow nearly the same expressive codes, with chromaticism reserved for pain and the plaintive, while diatonicism is associated with affirmation, joy and serenity. Nevertheless, we know that Gesualdo's diatonicism and chromaticism are different from Wagner's. Something fundamental separates them, and this is due to the consolidation of a harmonic dimension of musical language (progressions, families of chords, specified harmonic relationships), but also the very conception of the musical Idea: strict imitative style, homophony, rhythmic resources, not to mention tessitura and vocal writing.

Although they use the same types of (chromatic or diatonic) intervallic relationships, all the other elements of musical language are fundamentally different. Why? Because coherence stems from a different logic of implementation.

Not only is there the difference between vocal and instrumental music (tessitura, texture), but there is, too, a difference in the nature of the chords used (chord families, progressions). There is also phrase construction, periodicity, the type of articulation used, the kinds of deduction, depending on whether the style is homophonic or uses overt imitation.

Can we find universal laws applying to different musical discourses, no matter what the basic materials or individual characteristics of any era? Since music is an art inscribed in time, it requires memory, immediate as well as more long-term. Memory establishes comparisons between objects supplied by the ear. There is no discourse unless it can be given coherence and intelligibility. It seems that the more language was founded in laws, codes, convention even, the *less* musical discourse needed the sovereign Idea. The omnipotence of the (new or predetermined) Idea appears at the moment at which the codes become weak and are no longer followed. Idea has tended to replace code.

Can unity be established only through thematicism in the strict sense? No, for it can have freer dimensions, especially with musical text-setting. Recitative makes use of stock signals. An *incomplete* musical language is forced to rely on the functions of another language, just as when Schoenberg, Webern and Berg, seeking the laws of a new musical language, relied frequently on texts in order to secure the form of their works.

Having eliminated tonality as a means of formal articulation, the three Viennese composers often sought that articulatory force in literary texts. During this arduous period, Webern in particular composed only vocal works. Here, the case is quite different from that of the recitative.

First of all, the way a text was transcribed no longer aimed to give pride of place to its immediate meaning, to convey it directly. It is no longer a matter of reducing the musical component to a coded substrate; on the contrary, creativity had to be organised according to the literary text that underpinned the sequence of musical events, providing the infrastructure of its ordering. Composition itself, in its elaboration, implies work that does not obey the usual conventions of thematic deduction, but makes ongoing connections of a different sort. This ambiguous relationship of text to music can be seen particularly clearly in *Erwartung*. Although there are a few very short passages in which the music becomes independent from the text – when the text is reduced to a word, a cry, and is even silent for a moment – for most of the piece the musical motive, focused on illustration of the text, is as ephemeral and volatile as the state of mind it represents. Therein lies the profound difference between *Pierrot lunaire* and *Erwartung*.

Pierrot lunaire is composed of a series of small rondeaux with verse repetitions: closed forms, enclosing a single moment or state. This accounts for the presence of a unique theme for each item, or else a binary type with two contrasting themes. The evolution of the form through contrast or variation follows the text exactly, although Schoenberg diverges significantly from the poem in one respect by not repeating the music when the verses repeat, choosing to vary the presentation each time. He pits the spirit of variation against the archaic form, while at the same time respecting the formal articulation imposed by textual repetition. In this sense he is following the tradition of the art song, as exemplified by Schubert, Mahler and Debussy.

Erwartung has other antecedents: Mussorgsky's *Zhenitba* and Debussy's *Pelléas et Mélisande*. It is characterised by continuous dramatic development, and there is even ambiguity concerning the status of the events, since everything could be a figment of the imagination of the woman who waits. The division into scenes does not really indicate formal division, in comparison with Berlioz's and Stravinsky's 'number cantatas'. The musical discourse is transformed from one state to the next, while only very rarely remaining static. In practical terms, this explains the absence of themes based on significant *reprise* of important figures. The harmonic functions have a resolute tendency *not* to provide emphasis. The motifs are so short, so strongly associated with the ongoing meaning of the text, that they do not take hold in the memory. Memory cannot really stop and take note of any figure, because it will be so short-lived, so similar in character to other, equally important figures. A figure tends to adhere to the moment, a *single* moment. These different figures are bound by a common syntax – chord types, harmonic progressions, melodic configurations, horizontal and vertical relationships – but these are only the common traits of a particular specification, rather than being in more formalised relationships. All of these figures are derived from the same common source, none of them truly individual. Here, in Schoenberg's thinking, but also in the musical thought of this period, one finds the extreme of thematic atomisation borne along by the meaning of the text and its dramatic force.

The same perspective, but in a different context, can be observed in *Die glückliche Hand*. From the thematic point of view, this and *Erwartung* are Schoenberg's two most adventurous works. It is very likely that such thematic suppression could not have taken place without the support, the *alibi* of the text. For a time, he broke with the thematic convention of the recognisable figure, its development and metamorphosis. The power of the text allowed him to discover possible alternative means of development.

I found a passage about Wagner in Cosima's diary that could apply particularly well to the relationship between musical language and dramatic expression in both these Schoenberg works: 'What is the written thing in the face of inspiration, what is the notated thing in the face of imagination? The former submits to certain conventional laws, the latter is free, limitless (and what is astounding about Beethoven is that in his late quartets he managed to contain his imagination, something he could attain only at his artistic peak). For me it is drama that unceasingly breaks conventions and brings new possibilities.' Wagner forces the evolution of one creative dimension through a different one, whereas Schoenberg deduces one thing from the next, achieving a balance achieved through, and structured by, the text, rather than through conventional coded correspondences, as in recitative.

However, to truly *consolidate* a musical language, to re-establish the foundations of large-scale form, this compromise, this sharing of musical power with the expressive and dramatic power of the text, would ultimately not satisfy him. And in *Moses und Aron*, he re-establishes the traditional duality or, more precisely, the relativity between formal coherence in the music itself and subordination to the text – to the meaning of the text that needs, first of all, to be conveyed.

✧ ✧ ✧

For Berg, the thematic conception of music in relation to dramatic content is fully explicit, as early as the *Altenberglieder*. He changes the terminology, preferring to speak of an *Erinnerungsmotiv* rather than a leitmotiv. But the function of each with respect to memory is very obviously the same. Motive is linked to character, emotion or situation. Thus, in *Wozzeck* we have Wozzeck's and Marie's motives, the motive of 'Wir arme Leute', or of the knife, and so on. The motives are of varying scope: some are universal and circulate throughout the work, some local, connected only with a particular situation. Some are developmental, others contribute only to the establishment of signals. We could call them 'variants', if they resemble the themes of sonatas, rondos and adagios, or 'invariants', when they can be cited in context or separately.

This approach to motive is taken fairly directly from Wagner, with perhaps a more deliberate consistency in Wagner, for one simple reason: he rejected the conventions of symphonic form – in fact, he rebuked Mozart for adopting conventions. Berg, in contrast, wanted to reconcile the immediate expression of the text with formal development. He wanted to combine dramatic evolution with formal rigour; that is to say, a structure *without repetition* with a structure based on the principle of *reprise* and, possibly, varied repetition. He took deliberate *non-reprise* from Wagner and Strauss: whenever the motives did not evolve themselves, they were located in contexts undergoing continual change, in which the formal and tonal references were in large part determined by the setting, by dramatic requirements. Musical form was not, strictly speaking, the outcome of motivic development. It is dramatic form that is decisive, using the theme as its material. The ability to *organise* musical texture lies, of course, in motives, but that organisation can be subordinate to another kind.

Berg seeks to combine two structures, the dramatic and the purely musical, but in such a way that each is autonomous, maintaining its meaning independently. We find, for example, human conflict, character development, evolving scenarios, crises and catastrophes, but the musical form expressing these conflicts or personages is valid independent of the context, according to exclusively musical criteria. Thus, one finds in Berg a *stylisation* of form, a *code* that connects drama and music. This code can seem arbitrary because it is predetermined. He uses generic forms such as the sonata, rondo, variations or scherzo, and strict forms like passacaglia and fugue. In short, he has recourse both to flexible forms that are adaptable despite being predetermined, and rigid forms with strict rules, barely amenable to dramatic development, whose formal structures are of a different kind. Combining the two may seem artificial – procedural artifice. For fear of failing to control the form, and by adhering to the dramatic development of the motivic configuration, Berg sets himself a formal framework from the beginning, and he forces this, rather unnaturally, to suit his dramatic purpose. We might also see a conservative attitude in this, in the sense that he reinstates conventional structures within a dramatic form, resisting the historical evolution whereby composers focused precisely on freeing themselves from these a priori formal plans.

A constant desire for formal comfort can certainly be sensed in Berg's endeavour. In all his works, even the non-dramatic ones, we find this same relationship between thematicism and form, this eminently *classical* need to devise vivid thematic figures grounded in a patent and explicit formal framework by means of strongly characterised articulation, and also this need to work within a predetermined formal convention. He composes variations – or rather, his creativity is shaped by the idea of variations, sonata, rondo. Form is not something he discovers while composing, but is *decided*, and therefore requires appropriate thematic working. He decides not only on the individual form, incidentally, but also on an envelope for these forms, which is then a macro-structure for introducing components into the overall plan. This is the case in the *Lyric Suite* and the Chamber Concerto, but also in *Wozzeck*: three times five scenes, with not only specific thematic writing and form pre-imposed, but also specific techniques. What, then, is the connection between thematic processes and musical structure on the one hand, and thematic and dramatic structure on the other? He clarifies the situation by means of form, symbolises it in a procedure.

Take the simplest case of the inventions in the third act of *Wozzeck*. With the exception of the first scene, which is a set of variations and a fugue, called 'inventions on a theme', control is reduced to a nevertheless decisive means of configuring the motives and cells, providing complete freedom in the formal planning. If you define control as 'invention on a note' and choose the note B, or if you limit the harmonic material to one chord, or the rhythmic figures to a single sequence – that is to say, to a single type of relationship ordered in only one way; or elsewhere, if you apply the principle of moto perpetuo – all of that leaves you free to follow the drama without having to adapt any pre-existing musical form to the events in the libretto. These points can be pursued with formal independence, in terms of their intrinsic meaning, without external reference, because the sole unifying procedure is going to be a procedure in the vocabulary. What does this sole procedure represent? Obsession and constriction, obligation and constraint. The action is focused on *one* obsessive psychological state conveyed to us by an obsessive musical state. The single note corresponds to the murder, the rhythm to the reveal, the chord to the suicide and the moto perpetuo to indifference about these two deaths. Although Berg is to be admired for characterising these obsessive moments sub-thematically, one could very well imagine these procedures being applied in another way, or being interchangeable. There is a certain arbitrariness about the choice itself: in *Lulu*, he used the – rapid – ostinato to describe flight and return via the comprehensive rhythmic reversibility of the figures. But although arbitrariness may be the starting point, it transforms into necessity in the act of applying the code to a scenario, especially if the code is loose enough to be able to respond to the dramatic flow and its stages. It seems that Berg used sub-thematic procedures in these scenes because of their infinite malleability.

And what of forms defined by wider contingencies? It should be remembered that in many scenes, Berg used forms that allow for enormous freedom. Act I, Scene 2 is a rhapsody. And what is a rhapsody? Something that can be assigned to any formal development and use barely functional thematic processes; function in this thematic approach is completely different from strict deduction. It is the same in the 'Quasi Rondo', where text and music are coordinated to produce a scene in which the rondo refrains are, of course, provided, but without that forcing other episodes to become their couplets. Berg also turns to *genres* such as the military march and lullaby (Act I, Scene 3), in which forms and thematic processes can be taken directly from the story, which is the most traditional way of crafting operatic form.

The passacaglia in Scene 4 of the first act is also a decision taken on principle, as a symbolic gesture. The theme of this passacaglia returns in each variation and is identified with the doctor's *idée fixe*. But once this symbolic decision has been made, the text is moulded to the musical form, and every one of its twists and turns is embraced by this shell, even after the murder, when all the words sung by the chorus and Wozzeck are incorporated into the rhythmic scaffolding. There are different degrees to which the text can be absorbed in its formal and thematic relationship with music, different levels of constraint. Although the passacaglia is a strict form, it is a kind of *non-evolving* form. The ever-present theme does not evolve: there is no development in the strict sense, but variation; there is no return to a previous situation, as in sonata form. But when Berg uses directional, evolving forms – exposition, development, recapitulation – is he able to maintain anything other than a very precarious relationship with the dramatic text? Under what conditions can he connect the themes with the characters? How can he convince us of the need for recapitulation? Of course, he uses a healthy dose of variation rather than literal repetition. And yet he applies the similarities, the phases of articulation of the literary text, to the musical one. As for thematic treatment, it is supremely symbolic: masculine theme – Wozzeck; feminine theme – Marie; transitional theme – the child. Using symbolism as extreme, as simple, as embedded as this, he is able to work in a more complex manner. In this case, form functions through two threads. The premises are identical and co-extensive, and then, as developmental complexity comes to the fore, the two threads (dramatic and musical form) become independent of each other, out of phase, with a separate sense of development. In the last section, the recapitulation – its longest part – is used as an interlude. Only the musical thread remains to make an impression on memory, in imaginary reconnection with the drama.

It hardly needs reiterating that Berg manipulates these concepts of theme and form with great mastery, and that he enriches our perception considerably in terms of both thematic symbolism and formal codification. But why was he so haunted by this preoccupation? Personal temperament, of course, since, as mentioned, elements of this approach can be found in his instrumental music, to such an extent that Adorno could describe it as opera without the voices. Nevertheless, the use of such resolute formalism in a drama raises questions about musical language. The symbolic codes of musical language up to and including Strauss were based on elements that were instinctively grasped, unmistakably imprinted by centuries of history. Major and minor chords, conscious or unconscious key symbolism, close or remote modulation – composers had an arsenal of procedures at their disposal in which neither thematicism nor form played any role at all, but this symbolism changed from work to work. Tonal relationships became increasingly distinct from the evolution of form, whereas during the classical period, tonic/dominant and close/remote tonal relationships had formal significance. The meaning, or rather effect, of these relationships had become progressively independent of their formal location. Relationships had become autonomous, hence the danger of formal chaos when relying on perceptual surprises rather than more solid underlying structural connections.

When composing *Wozzeck*, Berg no longer made use – or wanted to make use – of tonality to impart quasi-encoded meanings to his themes. The entire arsenal of tonality was thus no longer available as a way of expressing the meaning of the text. Of course, he used many other, equally indispensable parameters – speed, density, dynamics and texture – but they are neutral, interchangeable, risky parameters because they can characterise anything and nothing. So he had to find a stronger means of connection to replace the wealth of 'traditional' means he had abandoned. This is why he turned to a device that binds structure tightly to thematicism through strongly coherent formal development. It allowed him to use a vocabulary and musical language in which connotations no longer seem so direct. Like Wagner and Strauss, by the way, he *signals* key situations whenever necessary. *Lulu* provides even more strongly formalised examples of these a priori decisions that were normal for him, including some that the listener will find really esoteric – even the 'cultivated' listener, let alone the 'average' one. His way of deducing series for forging the themes that characterise Schön, Alwa, etc., from the primary series associated with Lulu herself is absolutely indecipherable to the ear. It is founded in calculations and numerical deductions that are immune to any kind of perception and can be understood only as symbolic. He buried a secret, like someone who hides a message in the foundations of a building while the first stone is being laid. We are in on this secret, and we empathise with its intentions, but our perception depends on different, tangible criteria – that is, the themes themselves, deduced from permutations of a twelve-tone row. I will not elaborate on his use of symbolism or the encoded choices of formal plans in this second opera. They result from the same thought processes and use similar thematic treatment and characterisation.

In itself, the way Berg fashions themes is extremely classical – I would even say 'academic', if this word had no pejorative connotation. But a firm tradition links his themes to Mahler and no less to Brahms – and further back, to Beethoven, much more than to Wagner and Strauss. I believe that the reason for this is obvious. In order to develop the formal plans through which he conveys the text on a higher level, not only through affective coordination, he needs to use highly elaborate thematic treatment in the structures themselves. He needs not only pliable leitmotivs adaptable to any situation (and based therefore on intervals and rhythms that are easily traced back to the original versions), but also the potential for development in his thematic writing. We therefore see a melodic differentiation as rigorous as in his instrumental music, founded on the viability and autonomy of musical structures alone.

✿   ✿   ✿

From the outset, the challenge of thematicism presented itself to Webern in completely different terms. For him, thematicism is directly related to every role that intervallic structure can take on in musical language, and from this point of view, his very first work is almost a manifesto: a passacaglia, a form that we also saw Berg use in the *Altenberglieder* and *Wozzeck*. But whereas for Berg the form of the passacaglia is a way to bring together diverse and sometimes heterogeneous musical ideas, through an organising principle tasked with providing unity, for Webern all the other ideas emerge from the passacaglia's principal idea and are strongly related to it through their very structure. Increasingly in his first period, without using particularly strict and restrictive compositional forms, Webern harnesses his thematicism to intervallic structure. This is how he gives pride of place to those intervals that he will later organise more comprehensively, as more *universally* rational: groups of major and minor thirds and sixths, perfect and augmented fourths, and semitones (or sevenths or ninths) are systematic features.

The figures are generally organised around these tensions, and whether in principal figures or secondary ones we find the same characteristic intervals or their complements. In a sequence of works Webern respected the normal concepts of melody and harmony, and his melodic, thematic figures are accompanied traditionally, by chord sequences. Most of his works are written in this way – for example, opp. 5, 6, 9 and 10. The composing is free, but the interconnections between the elements of musical language are very strong; emphasis is placed on unity between what frequently recurs as thematic material and what we hear as secondary. Moreover, it is not the brevity of Webern's forms that stimulates a particular kind of thematic writing; on the contrary, it is his take on thematic writing that explains why the form must inevitably be short. In op. 5, with the exception of the first piece, constructed as it is on classical thematic contrast, the pieces are all built out of a single thematic unit. Melodic, harmonic and contrapuntal development are elaborated from a basic idea – a *single* idea – that spreads out in one direction and another. A melody becomes a chord, or vice versa, or else an intervallic pattern is used to multiply it into counterpoint. What is striking, despite so many kinds of differentiation, is the tendency towards uniqueness in the way figures are deduced.

His unique deductive method would soon lead Webern to reduce and then eradicate the distinction between main figures, secondary figures and simple accompaniment. In the Bagatelles, op. 9, there is *no* theme in the accepted meaning of the term, while at the same time everything has become thematic. He formed a complex out of previously divergent concepts: complexes of sound, rhythm and dynamics become absolutely indissoluble in the formation of figures.

In the most radical of these Bagatelles, development happens more from a constant application of a principle than from processing motivic intervals. The role of time in this kind of work is already in evidence. Time either coagulates vertically or expands horizontally. In the fifth Bagatelle, to be specific, what principally unites the successive figures? It is the principle of chromatic complementarity, and thus of maximal unity, since the mode of generation of the figures remains tied to a single mode of deduction. What gets in the way of this unity? The fact that this single principle is overly general. It does not generate memorable figures, and thus suggests a neutrality that is inimical to perception and comprehension. Moreover, another obstacle, hardly the least serious, is Webern's self-imposed requirement for non-repetition. Nothing ever returns exactly. Even when the intrinsic relationships are very similar or even identical, the configuration or presentation differs – in register, naturally, but also through constantly reworked rhythmic shifts. This is true to such an extent that one no longer knows in what direction one is supposed to listen: the vertical merges with the horizontal and perception is sent to ambiguous, volatile ground, which renders it indecisive. Where does the arpeggiated chord begin, and where does the melody assigned to different timbres end? How is the articulation of motives perceived when the articulatory permutations cannot be distinguished from motivic ones? At this point in his output, Webern had clearly reached a limit: maximal unity equals maximal perceptual insecurity.

In a later period, Webern would react to this state of affairs by increasingly introducing strict deduction, albeit applied linearly and following a consistent rule. While deduction in the earlier period was local and varied, despite drawing on a unitary principle, he would later compensate for the absence of harmonic laws through precise intervallic relationships applying to a group or a phrase. At that moment he sacrificed free composition, which had reached a very dangerous point in terms of perception and unity, and reintroduced the principle of exact repetition; and he would go on to rely on strict canonical forms in which lines would be continuously connected, and recognising their family resemblance would become much easier. Although harmonic laws in the strict sense were not reintroduced, notions such as melody and counterpoint were reinstated and were once again very obviously distinguishable. This was not invariably the case. One senses during this period entirely devoted to lieder that Webern wavered between strict organisation, relying on traditional concepts, and a much more flexible, innovative type of organisation in which deduction was not predetermined. One sees an oscillation from light to darkness, from the unequivocal to the ambiguous. I have not placed any special emphasis on the poetic texts of these lieder because, although Webern obviously cares about their meaning and structure, it is equally obvious that they did not affect his musical evolution. The literary texts did perhaps help him in terms of formal organisation by locking him into an existing form, but without changing his technique: analysing the texts provides no additional reasons beyond the musical ones for why he chose strict composition for one piece and a much freer kind for another.

The voice, however, needs to be discussed, since it became ever more distinct from instrumental writing as he progressed. There were various reasons for this, of which the unity of the text is the least important. We might suggest that the words themselves provided him with the timbral articulation that elsewhere he was seeking instrumentally. And yet this argument is specious: the fact that the voice is made of pitches and phonemes itself makes for a kind of *Klangfarbenmelodie*, albeit one whose articulation is much freer and more mobile than instrumental *Klangfarbenmelodie*. Moreover, although Webern uses very jagged vocal intervals and maximal vocal range, he was always concerned, probably for practical reasons, with the continuity of the vocal line, with seamless vocal emission. In the late cantatas, vocal continuity contrasts with fragmentation of instrumental discourse to such an extent that this could be seen as a source of strong stylistic divergence. The unity to which he so strongly aspires is assured through synthesis on the one hand and analysis on the other: the voice synthesises a phrase through its streamlined timbre, but it also dictates the articulation; the instruments analyse the phrase by timbral highlighting of its articulation. In one case, the continuity is perceived more clearly; in the other, the components are more noticeable.

These cantatas belong to a period in which not only Webern's thematic processes, but also the genesis of his themes and motives depend on a higher-order principle: the row. He emphasises that the row is not selected innocently, any more than it can be chosen arbitrarily. He describes his choice and justifies it through the wealth of structural relationships that the row contains, which are inherently developmental, even though they could not really be called thematic, because they only plant the *germ*. This concept of the 'germinal' takes on increasing significance towards the end of his life and he continually evokes Goethe's *Metamorphosis of Plants*: 'The root is in fact no different from the stalk, the stalk no different from the leaf, and the leaf no different from the flower: variation of the same idea.'[1] In selecting his rows, Webern is very careful to include internal correspondences such as symmetry, combinatoriality and segmentation, which he considers to be the most obvious manifestations of unity. It can also be said that he reduces the row to a minimum of reproducible elements, and therefore to a minimum of perceptual references. These reductions are definitely more easily perceived through symmetry, because of the intelligibility of their deduction. Schoenberg's rows can only rarely be decomposed into such simple elements. As for Berg, as we have seen, he uses numerical properties so imperceptible that he is impelled to transform the row into themes, to provide them with more mnemonic potential. And while he uses a row that contains every interval in the *Lyric Suite*, he does not employ that structural property at all, but turns to the different, derived property of contrast between two diatonic scales – and even this trivial property is used only occasionally. (He would later use this white-key/black-key diatonicism more emphatically and persistently to characterise the athlete in *Lulu*.) Thus, compared with Berg in this period, Webern pays more attention to the inherent intervallic structure, which offers him the total organisation of a work via as narrow and constitutive a relationship as possible.

✲ ✲ ✲

The relationships between row and theme became the object of composers' attention. There were grounds to wonder what a sequence of registrally neutral tones, with no fixed relationship, and rhythmically unconnected, might represent. These twelve tones did, of course, have structural significance, but they could not have musical significance. Apart from its structural meaning, a scale or gamut has no other meaning either, though it imposes constraints of a different kind. The implications of scale degrees – for example, their melodic and harmonic function – is one aspect of this constraint, but the order of the notes is of no significance. In that respect a scale has no bearing on formal arrangement. Conversely, as practised by the Second Viennese School, the row has no consequences from the point of view of scale degrees and functions. All notes are equal, but their order is inflexible, even if this rule can be sidestepped by dividing the row into segments whose rhythmic profiles can be made to overlap. Schoenberg is well aware of both the structural constraint and its formal vacuum. He writes: 'A row is at the same time *more* and *less* than the theme of a set of variations.' 'More' in that the entirety of the work is more closely linked to the row; 'less' in that a row offers more limited possibilities of variation than a theme. The constraint is certainly literal and limiting, but it is relevant only to *one* dimension, and has a bearing on all the grammatical elements implied by a theme. This is only a matter of basic morphology. Even if, for Webern, the implications of morphology related to deduction, the gulf between the row and the theme can never be crossed. He says so himself: 'The twelve-note row is, as a rule, not a "theme". But I can also work without thematicism, that's to say much more freely, because of the unity that's now been achieved in another way; the row ensures unity.'[2]

I had not read that phrase, published long after Webern's scores became available, but from studying his works I was able to deduce very early on, in my *Sonatine* for flute and piano of 1946, that, in effect, once the functions of the initial material were defined, there was no absolute need to resort to the use of themes in the strict sense: over the course of a work, one thematic development could be linked to another through 'athematic' transitions. I was not completely sure at the time of the precise connotation of the term 'athematicism', but retrospectively I can say that athematicism means a rejection of the *absolute* form of a theme in order to arrive at a notion of a virtual theme in which, most of all, the elements are not initially and permanently fixed. Furthermore, no definitive priority is given to any interval as the source of musical development, but other elements, especially duration, can play a more important role, one to which pitches are subordinate. I will return to this, because it was the starting point for a process of evolution in which the notion of theme, and even thematic writing itself, was completely transformed, while progressively abandoning certain, initially very strict means.

＊ ＊ ＊

Why did Webern feel the need to 'compose' his row before composing his themes, and to compose it in such a way that through symmetry, combinatoriality or segmentation it could even be reduced to a *single* element? It was due to his desire for unity and for this unity to be *per-ceived*: 'No greater unity can be imagined than that which is obtained when, from one end of the work to the other, all of the parts express the same Idea.' This obviously runs the risk of creating a contradiction between this unity sought at any price and the urge for continual vari-ation in musical discourse. For while we can vary the presentation of a cell rhythmically or through changes of articulation, nevertheless per-ception is based fundamentally on *repetition*, and the invariant element – intervals – is stronger than the varied parameters. Particularly when the cell is short (two or three notes), the potential for registering the quan-tity of those elements in immediate perception may perhaps enhance the impression of unity, but it also increases the impression of stasis, of non-development in the handling of material. Because the musical figure is reduced to such short dimensions, it tends to undermine the specificity of its component intervals. Unity – uniqueness – destroys itself through the very act of being asserted. Despite this unity of Idea, in Webern one also finds figures that are generic in the sense of being so minimal that they can be related to any Idea (the major seventh and minor ninth). Alongside very specific elaborations, one encounters these 'anonymous' ones, just as one does, as a matter of fact, in classical music, in which, compared with strongly characterised elaborations, one finds transitions based on non-specific elements. Examining the thematic hierarchy of classical vocabulary more closely, we find that this use of the specific and the generic arose from a different line of thought, but the perceptual result is the same: in one case, we have a theme and transitional formulas encoded to varying degrees; in the other, a theme and extracts from this theme which are micro-formal elements with no particular affiliation.

This brings me back to the danger that the reduction of the Idea leads to repetition, which contradicts the concept of variation underlying all Webern's thought. He offers his own response: that the absence of repetition 'destroys comprehensibility'.[3] At the same time, he seeks in musical discourse 'the establishment of the utmost relatedness between all component parts'.[4] The Bagatelles, op. 9, his most radical work in terms of non-repetition, had revealed him to be on the edge of the incoherence to which that leads. Gradually, he began to establish repetition at the centre of his musical language – not literal repetition, naturally, but the principle of deduction of all voices from one and the same model. To that end, he used strict canons in an increasingly systematic manner in order to unify the various polyphonic elements. Free forms of composition would be abandoned in favour of the exclusive use of direct, formal dependence. For him, incidentally, this relates not only to a justification of his compositional methods, but also to a much more profound need for faith, for a belief that the work of art translates the Law of the Universe: 'All of the forms are similar and yet none *resembles any other*; and thus the choir alludes to a secret law, a sacred enigma.'

And what of the relationship of form to thematic processes and developmental means? It is curious to read Webern's analyses of his own music nowadays – specifically from a formal point of view, and particularly in his correspondence. He constantly refers to forms from the past. He thinks and expresses himself in terms of the sonata, overture and rondo, while his thematic content, strict composition and developmental means seem incompatible with the formal plans familiar to us from the works that gave rise to their classification; so much so that on initial contact with his Variations for Piano, op. 27, we have the innocent reaction of hearing variations without a theme. This impression takes us to the very meaning of the kind of renewal that Webern brings to thematic writing and its relationship to the row. Ahead of any composing, there are principles of generation: symmetries, groupings, densities, repetitions. This can be called a thematic virtuality. Webern describes it as the Idea, bringing him curiously close to Mallarmé's terminology. From this Idea, he generates Images. The Images do not refer explicitly to the Idea (in the way that variations can reference their theme), but they are nothing other than the manifold manifestations of the Idea. The Idea does not exist as a perceptible object but is revealed through specific actualisation in works. Thus, in his Variations, op. 27, symmetry – of figures, register, duration – is the fundamental, figural Idea. The intervallic series is a powerful mediator of this Idea, but it is not the only one. The Idea can be perceived only through its metamorphoses. The title 'Variations' is therefore not overturned, but it must be understood in a less 'realistic' sense.

In my view, Webern's central achievement remains the way he moved from the concept of real theme to virtual theme. Canon, row content, formal plans matching compositional method – those all seem secondary to me compared to the alternative meaning that he found for the very substance of musical composition. Over and above the determinism of his individual approach, elements can be reactivated in the state in which he left them, rather than being interpreted merely as harbingers of some final solution. But as with many important composers, it can easily be claimed that his trajectory led him to discard along the way possibilities that were just as ripe for potential elaboration. For example, the fact that he was so enthralled with canonical writing, that he wanted to reduce the principle of his virtual theme to one single Idea, that he often reduced his musical cells to completely symmetrical forms – all this diminished some of his previous discoveries, which had been conducted in a spirit of exuberance and freedom, with more flexible interrelationships and less rigid specifications. It should perhaps be said that order, or at least as overt an order as this, is not necessarily the best solution; and even if a certain transcription of nature is taken as one's goal, nature does not forgo any capacity for the aleatoric. Of course, an excess of order can seem naive and less fecund than it at first appears. Nevertheless, Webern's works, more than those of his contemporaries, lead us to a new definition of the components of musical language, and as he said himself, thematicism in particular is fundamentally reconceived. Compared with his music, other experiments in this area seem relatively timid, lacking in profound or radical implications.

* * *

I have lingered on the solutions offered by the Second Viennese School because they undeniably represent a fundamental development of the-maticism and all it implies. This is no surprise, and is part and parcel of the Germanic tradition: previous composers had similar concerns. But the Vienna composers' superiority lies in their conception of something universal. Musical expression cannot rely on only a single dimension, or a few of them; in order to be truly 'impressive' in both senses of that word, this form of expression must be rooted in the necessary connections between different levels and even different phases of musical language. The vocabulary of commentaries on certain works and composers gives pride of place to formulations such as sound mass, the grain of the sound and tensions in the material, as if these were intrinsic qualities of musical discourse, but that remains at the level of external description of music rather than the internal phenomena that gave rise to it, and fails to address the essential quality: development, or unity. If that is not at the centre of compositional activity, we risk not only lack of unity, but also scattering partially experienced elements, leaving fundamental gaps in the way compositional specifics are brought together.

In fact, this is a twin danger. On the one hand, one may neglect how music is assembled, and a kind of displacement of the compositional vector sets in, based on mood, lack of interest or lack of perseverance. I know that Debussy said something about deciding to go on to the next section when he had had enough of the preceding one, but that quip is a lapalissade, an amusing truism: it is true that the composer's arbitrary choices play a role at one point or another, but they are not as arbitrary as often implied, and they emerge from a real situation – exhaustion, an impasse or an unexpected discovery. A composer's reactions are con-ditioned at the very moment of making a personal decision. Be it an abrupt cut, a transition or an inflection, what is important is the delib-erate, considered or unconscious deduction made on the spot, based on a judgement at any given moment. Even if 'systematic thinking' is rejected, arbitrariness is still more or less its prisoner and, through instinct, avoids the inconsequential.

The parallel danger is of 'systematic thinking' being adopted regard-less of one's instinct. When has musical material truly been exhausted? Is it when apparent logic dictates it is so, or when after certain deductions the rest can be easily anticipated and is therefore of no interest? Musical material, until it has *truly* been exhausted, offers a certain number of possibilities of exchange, transformation and metamorphosis that it can be tempting to exploit systematically and fully. Whether the possibilities consist of combinations of themes, rhythmic elaboration or formal permutation, the danger is to confuse form with an inventory, even if the confusion is not quite that crude and conceals the inventory within a certain formal envelope. In fact, it is not difficult to sort certain types of transformation or families of permutation into categories, and then to divide form into different blocks that depend on those categories. But this is not an organic development of possible transformations, providing the succession from one state to another without formal implications. The form was intended to entail these different states, rather than those states having generated the formal elaboration. An even deeper danger lies in believing that a composition has been produced when a system, or at any rate a network of coordinates and variables, has in a sense been invented, and that all that is needed is to operate these variables through the coordinates, revealing all or part of their potential, exhausting the resources within a certain field. Although material is indispensable as a basis for a vocabulary, it still has to be made explicit through the invention of ideas and outputs, invention taking place at a different level, making musical ideas irreducible to the material that gave rise to them.

To return one last time to the Viennese School, I would like to consider the misunderstandings that arose. Confusion took root *post mortem*, as it were, in analyses of their works by pedagogues of the immediate post-war period who were both defensive and mistaken: there was a polemical defensiveness about music that was rejected and under attack; and a misunderstanding of the mechanisms and the underlying basis of invention. Strict twelve-tone works were addressed almost exclusively in terms of numerical analysis. Once numerical correspondences were found between the music and the rows from which it was derived, the analysts' work was effectively done, and thematic processes as well as formal organisation appeared only secondarily – as an envelope or mere packaging for the actual elaboration. At most, the musical text was taken as confirmation of the hierarchical properties of the row, whereas what is interesting about the double or quadruple canons in the first movement of Webern's Symphony, op. 21, is not to uncover, identify and numerically label different canonic voices, but to see how canon is used to suggest the ambiguity or ambivalence of some of its intervallic transpositions. What is interesting is to see how Webern comes closer to, or goes further from, a faithful reproduction of the initial image, through fixed registration in the exposition, voice-crossings and the concentration or fragmentation of the themes.

What calls for analysis is the relationship between a preparatory stage of invention – the intervallic array organised by specific vectors of unity – and invention itself. What are the functions of these intervallic relationships in relation to other 'vectors' of musical language? To what degree and in what respect is the reprise transformed with respect to the exposition? What is implied by variation within this reprise, and what is its goal? If this had been observed more clearly from the beginning, the relationship between a certain 'theoretical' substrate and the act of composition would have become that much more concrete, since it would have been based on elements that were not merely brought forward, but brought together.

I will return to this fundamental compositional relationship, but first I want to look at the attitudes of Ives, Stravinsky and Varèse, three composers of differing importance for whom thematicism played very different roles. All of them were opposed, however, to the 'organic' approach that characterised the Germanic tradition, whether this opposition was intentional or not.

❄   ❄   ❄

I will begin with Ives, who presents the problem in raw form. Of course, Ives has all the trappings of an amateur musician, with all the advantages and disadvantages this brings. The advantage of being an amateur is freedom from the burden of tradition, while the disadvantage lies in stumbling over problems that craft could have solved quickly and easily. Ives's musical language embodies the very essence of incoherence, and

I mean that in the deepest sense of the word rather than in any superficially polemical one. Not only did he not seek unity, he even rejected the systematic development of ideas. The only unity that can be ascribed to him is his attachment to sources inescapably associated with one region – New England – and with a period in the history of that region.

Alongside this, he displays a high degree of creativity, but without coherence, discipline, continuity, deduction. All this seems negative, which is undeniably the case, yet his fundamental incoherence saved him from the type of academicism into which he might easily have fallen, judging from certain aspects of his imagination: an academicism without craft, or rather only the appearance of academicism. What, then, accounts for Ives being fascinating *despite everything*, even though potential was left unexploited and his works leave only a virtual and imaginary legacy – too virtual and imaginary to have directly influenced the history of music? I believe that Ives's dilemma lay in the preponderance of *discovery* in his musical language, of *found* rather than *reformulated* thematicism, and in the end in a confused, even non-existent connection between discovery and thematic composition. The problems remain interesting, even though he resolved them episodically, even anecdotally, and even if most of the time they remained in a raw state, precariously realised. Mahler's music was also often inspired by a region, at a particular point in its history, with his *Ländler*, marches and folksong of a certain kind; but beyond that he uses a formidable technical arsenal to integrate external material and enable it not only to penetrate his formal innovations, but also to be rooted in his personal vocabulary.

The incorporation of 'found' thematic material from other sources was one of Stravinsky's many preoccupations, as well as Berg's. Both of them offered 'learned', if contrasting, responses, whereas Ives stuck to candour and innocence. Stravinsky manipulates, caricatures, amplifies or reduces characteristic traits of a style and vocabulary. Thus, *L'Histoire du soldat* and *Ragtime* play with elementary rhetoric through unusual configurations of it. This plays on complicity, with a knowing wink, presuming familiarity with models and archetypes. Stylistic distortion implies certain compositional consequences. He uses cadences, but with non-cadential chord types; regular rhythms become lame through unexpected, irregular expansion and contraction; he emphasises the facile nature of melodic formulas by sharpening their profiles. The original vocabulary remains the basis for the work, but doctored. In Berg (*Wozzeck*, *Lulu*, but also his instrumental 'absolute' music), the attachment to folk sources, quoted in the context of his individual style, is sentimental. Although there is caricature, there is also an emotional connection; his reaction, as with Mahler, is to absorb this universe into his personal vocabulary, while at the same time maintaining its status as quotation. There is no critical implication here, as there is with Stravinsky, but rather the attempt to dissipate distance, even though humour and a certain kind of detachment do come out in the thematic approach. Ives, on the other hand, adopts but does not adapt. His vocabulary is neither strong nor unifying enough to be able to absorb or to encompass; on the other hand, though, his intentions are not critical, but instead display, like Berg, a rather sentimental attachment. What remains are discoveries and thematicism, with an irrepressible tendency to separate like oil and water. The thematic approach remains tied to a particular kind of presentation, and the found objects remain isolated as microsystems with extremely short lifespans.

But I would also like to mention Varèse, whose most creative side lay in his attraction to the most palpable aspects of sonic material in itself: to its reality as an object, to those aspects of sound that are also most resistant to compositional discipline. Any system, or systematic thinking, seemed to him an unacceptable violation of his individual compositional rights and freedoms. What was for him a state of almost physical rebellion manifested itself in the rejection of any palpable formal constraint. And yet nobody could have asserted and defended exact calculation more than he did, if I may summarise his thinking in that way. Although he embraced calculations in respect of the density and tension in musical material, they needed to be personal and, indeed, secret. In effect, his work shows one central concern: to fashion a musical object with material of which pitch is only one element among many, and in which timbre, register and dynamics play a major role.

But was he able to dispense entirely with thematicism, motivic relationships and deduction in compositional construction? I do not use the word 'motivic' here in the conventional sense, which generally associates it with a melodic line or cell. But it does seem as if Varèse had a phobia with respect to those notions, precisely because they were tied to the academic definitions of which he had such a horror. Still, in rejecting them he became their victim, in the sense that compared with the other elements of his musical language, the thematic material was always primitive, deliberately ignored and neglected. This is less sensitive in his relatively short chamber works, in which these notions have less importance for the development of ideas. But in works of broader scope, like his major orchestral pieces *Amériques* and *Arcana*, developmental processes stumble and falter precisely because of his inability to evaluate thematic significance, whether in rhythmic, harmonic or melodic respects. Different types of object are set up, but there is no development as such, let alone transition. It can be maintained that one function of development is to rely on repetition. Varèse does repeat his themes and chords effectively, with certain variations in presentation, but one does not sense a deliberate intention to develop material, just a fleeting inclination. These traits are similar to some of Stravinsky's, but do not permeate the discourse as a whole as they do in Stravinsky.

In Stravinsky's music, at least in certain periods, there is a remarkable originality of musical discourse in which form is grounded in repetition and permutation. This is a singular aspect that has in general been observed only quite superficially. It is strange that at one time in Stravinsky's life he resorted to academic models of traditional, Germanic, organic development, when he had already found a different form of organic development that was highly original and had no equivalent in that tradition. We are not here to delve into his fears and doubts, but it is interesting to see how much he transformed the principle of the litany and verse–response pairing in two works in particular: *Les Noces* and the Symphonies of Wind Instruments. These principles are used to elaborate a very new concept of form, founded on the paradox that immobility generates movement – in other words, that the principle of repetition can generate formal development.

In *Les Noces*, what is the strongest thematic principle, the one that immediately attracts our attention? It is the permanent presence of a single pulse, metre or tempo. The underlying thematic unity is in the simple and overt relationship between generating pulse and derivations: the proportional relationship goes from simple to double, two to three, three to four. Large-scale thematic unity does not (or not only) arise therefore from melodic, harmonic or even rhythmic figures (by which I mean rhythmic configurations created on the basic pulse), but essentially from the conjunction of different tempi that characterise the developmental sections and thus function as formal markers. The figures themselves, of whatever kind, depend on the primary – primordial – order of a common tempo, which remains the main thematic reference point: the figures are inscribed in this tempo and connected to it without any possible deviation.

To measure the strength of such thematic connection, as applied in Stravinsky's *Les Noces*, we have only to compare this work with Webern's Second Cantata, in which, in addition to the row, Webern also applies tempo as a universal thematic unit. His tempo, in reality, clearly has to be modulated in order to correspond to the musical texture: the tempo common to the Cantata's six movements appears to be something 'superimposed', with which the composer was not *literally* concerned at the moment of composition. The tempo is specified and delineates a range of speeds, but it does not impose pulse. Webern contradicts this pulse by emphasising formal articulations, by expressive changes (rallentandos and accelerandos) that Stravinsky categorically rejects. The unity of tempo is 'ideal' in Webern, since it admits a flexibility that negates its very definition. Stravinsky, by contrast, makes figure and pulse intersect as closely as possible, with no exceptions: it is as if the rhythmic language itself is encoding the exceptions, its flexibility, through irregular metre. In this rhythmic plan, cells are shortened or lengthened by means of irregular values. This is what could be called Stravinsky's rubato: a measured and inexorable rubato, paradoxical as those terms might seem.

I mentioned the way tempi in *Les Noces* are generated from primary definitions: metronome markings of 60, 80, 120 and 160. There are but two exceptions: 104 and 112 for the 'Lamentation of the Two Mothers' and the following transition. The writing clearly highlights these numerical values by articulating and maintaining rhythmic continuity. It

executes the principle unwaveringly and is designed to make it perceptible by embodying it as noticeably as possible. The formal principle of
master tempi, which becomes a strong thematic component, was later
developed considerably by Elliott Carter, inspired certainly by Stravinsky
but also by a lesser-known composer, Conlon Nancarrow, who, although
he was eventually 'discovered', remained very little known because
of his chosen vehicle for expression (the player piano). Carter called
this principle 'metrical modulation', by analogy with harmonic modulation. The word 'modulation' should not be taken in the strict sense,
but rather denotes a change of speed or pulse at a given point, applied
in a systematic way rather than as an instinctive, expressive impulse.
The relationship two-to-three has a long history; the relationship of 2/4
to 6/8, and more generally of the duplet to the triplet, is a classic feature in the evolution of variation form. It is even the basis for a certain
number of thematic relationships in *Parsifal*, strongly expressed right
from the prelude to the first act. This rhythmic relationship, however,
is only one envelope among others, and it is not necessarily the most
prominent. In Carter's music, it becomes systematic, even the central
source of articulation. And just as with Stravinsky, in order to make the
articulation completely explicit, the figures used in transitions are deliberately constructed according to the proportional relationship that they
are designed to bridge. If a quintuplet quaver in one tempo needs to
become a quaver in the next one, the transition makes the whole quintuplet figure explicit, in that it turns into a complete figure containing five
quavers. This is helpful for the performer, but it also guides the listener's
perception. Rhythmic modulation, however, is not limited to codifying
tempo fluctuation, as it were. It also informs the invention of themes
and the way figures are adapted to a given speed. Thus, in the fifth of
the timpani pieces[5] there is an identifiable scale of tempi, similar to a
scale of pitches, with intervallic definitions (5/4, 4/3, 3/2, etc.), including intervals of fifths, fourths, thirds, and so on. This correspondence
between intervals and tempi also appears in Stockhausen's *Gruppen*, in
a more universally structural way: more 'abstract' in the sense that the
complexity of the notation in each tempo, the irregularity of the figures
and the avoidance of any perceptible pulse disguises the proportional

relationships. In fact, as soon as internal relationships in this kind of metrical approach become highly complex and irregular, they can express different pulses; it may even be that no pulse is necessary to apprehend them as a statistical gestalt.

The same happens in certain complex works by Carter, like the Third String Quartet. In order to compare two pulses, markers of the underlying regular specification have to be perceived, even when this regularity is not continuously explicit. This can be accomplished through dynamics, timbre, harmonic and melodic specifics – in short, through any envelopes facilitating the relative recognisability of irregular figures through underlying regularity. To use 'everything, everywhere' does not work because it robs perception of the only *fixed* criteria of judgement on which it can rely in order to appreciate a *mobile* reality. There is a substantial opportunity here. When rhythms are exaggeratedly repetitive and predictable, monotony sets in, and complexity can no longer be processed through instant comparisons, but is rather jammed in an unanalysable system: the monotony is the result of excess. The optimal zone is not really definable, because too many aspects compete for perception of a rhythmic figure against a basic pulse. But it surely exists, for reasons that are obvious and easy to describe.

After this rather lengthy excursion into the relationships between thematic processes and tempo, I now return to other characteristics of Stravinsky's style, not least because the experiments of American minimalists probably provide indications of what should and should not be done when it comes to rhythmic development. This is another type of rhythmic development, far removed from Carter's choice of non-repetition, of continually new figures and structures.

In *Les Noces* and the Symphonies of Wind Instruments, Stravinsky polarised different speeds around successive, related pulses. Phrases develop by means of a technique in which the repetition of fixed melodic figures predominates, though they can be minimally varied – if at all – through closely related ornamentation within fixed initial and final clauses. Stravinsky's concept of melodic development could be seen as based on psalmody or litany, in which deviations are infinitesimal with respect to the original model, though figures are lengthened or shortened, or accents displaced. This developmental approach works cumulatively, drawing on its inner strength: it is the accumulation of similar, only slightly differently presented figures that comprises the very essence of this kind of development. In that respect, this music distances itself from 'learned' music in order to embrace folk musics of a kind that used to be found in eastern Europe and still exist in sub-Saharan Africa. Musical development consists of tiny deviations from the exact repetition of a model, and also of an alternation – antiphony – of these accumulations. Repetition and alternation, each modulated by varying their presentation, are fundamental elements of a developmental procedure in which movement and stasis combine on assumptions that developmental techniques in our culture forgot, or rejected as unsuited to an 'evolved' mode of thought. This explains why unfavourable, mixed and enthusiastic responses to the intrusion of this kind of developmental process into learned music all agree on at least one point: they all refer to 'primitivism'. Stravinsky is praised for having summoned 'primitive' forces that had been numbed in a world of hyper-cultivation. Debussy would happily generalise about 'savage' music. As for the fearful, they saw it as an unacceptable attempt to destroy our culture through the primitivism of music worthy of cannibals. These reactions all demonstrate, no matter which side they are on, the *reductive* power of Stravinsky's thematic development (from which he would later try to escape in order to seek a more cultivated pedigree) in the models of a tradition that was fundamentally foreign to him. Cumulative development (I prefer this term to 'repetitive') excluded form based on other parameters of evolution and deduction.

It is hard to understand this need to embrace conventional form, when *Les Noces* and the Symphonies of Wind Instruments had shown the way towards new formal plans that were wholly appropriate to his type of developmental process. I would like to speak of kaleidoscopic form, in which an alternation of cumulative thematic development creates the form, at the same time as it builds the components of large-scale form from particular tempi, densities and timbres. In the Symphonies of Wind Instruments in particular, it could be said that several superimposed trajectories overlap, and that their alternation displays different developmental sections at various stages in their evolution. Thus, when a developing section is made *explicit*, becomes *manifest* through the existence of one of its phases, the other *underlying* developing sections wait their turn to surface, at some stage of their own evolution. There is undoubtedly a relationship between these developmental layers, but at no time are they merged or superimposed. We observe rather the perfect assembly of a network of trajectories whose intersections are determined by their own articulation. One of them is dropped in order for another to be taken up, and they are made to intersect at characteristic stages of their evolution.

More could be said about rhythmic thematicism, in particular about the use of heterophony, used by American minimalists in the form of 'phasing' extremely simplified structures. In fact, heterophony provides more interesting and varied resources than simple phasing or superimposing different periodicities, of which one quickly wearies as soon as one senses how they function. Here, too, there is an optimal zone of opportunity, outside which both extreme simplicity and excessive complexity discourage perception and interest. Superimposing periodicities presupposes regular meeting points between which different numbers of pulses occur. Phasing implies the displacement of one periodicity with respect to another, either by making the derived periodicity slightly faster or slower than the reference periodicity, or by progressively stretching or compressing the derived periodicity through a rallentando or an accelerando. Heterophony consists of parallel structures that do not follow the same internal specification. These procedures are modular, and each can truly be separated out from the other only through strict specification – and even then, more in theory than in practice. If we examine this problem more broadly, this amounts to saying that the trajectories I discussed above, which are brought to the fore by observing their points of articulation, can operate simultaneously and concurrently. Just as Carter's metrical modulation implies gradations, so this concept of superimposition can involve the continuous evolution either of speed or gradations. Carter used continuous evolution by having tempo evolve according to degrees that are sufficiently close to give the impression of an acceleration or a deceleration, just as a curve can be described via sufficiently small straight-line segments.

The extent to which thematic processes relating to tempo play an important role both in formal structure and in establishing basic figures can easily be seen. This may be the field in which contemporary musical thought has been most advanced, but it is also the most hindered in its progress, perhaps because rhythmic thought in Western music long ago stagnated by comparison with discoveries in other areas. It is sometimes in places where 'spontaneity' is most prevalent that speculation has a concomitant tendency to disappear, as discoveries tend not to be encouraged: musical vocabulary regresses rather than being enriched, and formulas set in and become pervasive. Perhaps the unruly intrusion of a different tradition is necessary, then, to create a jolt that inspires reflection and speculation, and the creation of works from given material other than that which was previously relied upon to govern that aspect of musical language.

1 *The Path to the New Music*, trans. Leo Black, ed. Willi Reich (Bryn Mawr, PA: Theodore Presser Company, 1963), p. 53.
2 Ibid., p. 55.
3 Ibid.
4 Ibid., p. 42.
5 The fifth piece of Elliott Carter's *Eight Pieces for Four Timpani* (1950; 1966), 'Improvisation'.

8

Theme, Variations and Form
(1983–84)

In a surprising sentence from *Jean Santeuil*, Proust speaks unexpectedly about 'that double sense of difference and likeness which can so profoundly affect the human spirit'.[1] I could not have found a better way to define what I have been calling the challenge of thematicism. I would go so far as to emphasise the *urgency* of the thematic challenge. Any work, but especially any musical work, displays the double condition of analogy and difference. Without these, and because music is inscribed in (irreversible) time, our perception would not be able to apprehend it. It is through analogy that perception can grasp a work's progression, and through difference that this progression can be brought to fruition. Any musical form depends completely on the dialectical relationship between analogy and difference, in whose characteristics formal articulation is based.

The challenge of thematicism implies above all the logic of musical discourse, and thereby its comprehensibility. It is the challenge of meaning itself, of a work's validity. When we speak of 'logic', we are thinking mainly about a principle of economy: an economy of means, naturally. How can a work be constructed without having perpetually to create *ex nihilo*? In anything presented as a work, amateurism can be immediately identified through the presence of the non sequitur: the fact that deduction is practically absent or exists in only a rudimentary state. I believe that craft can be recognised in a work when the economy of means is taken to the highest level. This does not mean that the ideas themselves have fundamental value. There can, as a matter of fact, be an illusory economy that uses stock ideas implying lack of economy, predictable deduction, something profoundly *unoriginal*. They imply a prefabricated economy that is used both to secure thematicism and what results from it. In this particular case, there is nothing at stake, just a posthumous exploitation of an economy that proved itself when it was established but which can function only as an empty shell when deprived of the context that gave rise to it.

This economy of means may be linked, in a trivial or not so trivial way, to another economy – that of creativity. Should artists recognise that their capacity for *creativity* is limited, and that their individual make-up imposes limits on their creative capacity; that the characteristics of their musical language – even if they expand, even if they are continually, if not spectacularly, refreshed – always display the characteristics of their personality; that the revitalisation of their creativity is therefore circumscribed within borders laid down by many circumstances, some of which they control, some of which they serve? Thus, a work's thematicism owes its existence to creative economy. Valéry spoke of the first verse just happening, while those that follow rely on persistence. Some have spoken, too, of inspiration and perspiration in varying percentages. These are different ways of expressing a common, central point: that thematicism is the result of inspiration, of crystallisation of a singular, irrational, anticipatory moment that comes to us by chance, one we need to be ever ready to accept, whose flowering can be fostered through our disposition towards it, though it is not the result of any decision we make. We therefore need to learn how to exploit these special, rare moments. The challenge of thematicism essentially consists of taking advantage of the exception, of being able to stretch the special moment of a revelation to workable temporal dimensions. And yet, when we look curiously at great composers' sketches, particularly those for whom thematicism is most at stake, we can see how much needed to be worked out sometimes to achieve the final shape of the theme, the thematic principle. Occasionally it can even be developmental economy that has forced the theme to be reworked. Consequently, the idea that an elaborated intuition can become a work is only a myth. Yet it is one that led Schoenberg himself astray, or so his writings lead us to believe, at any rate: he stated that in inventing a theme he knew all its deductions and developmental features in advance, and that the act of creation, from the embryonic stage onwards, was a divine, omniscient act.

The irrational aspects of creativity should certainly not be downplayed. Many short-circuits operate without our knowledge when we invent figures or assemble sounds for development. Indeed, we become somewhat fixated on our own ideas: even before they have been thoroughly exploited, we have already endowed them with our personality – that is, our characteristics – and also our limitations. This 'omniscience', this prescience, quite often runs the risk, then, of being nothing more than a personal routine, applying to a novel object a more or less conscious network of parameters that we have used before and is the fruit of our experience. Of course, as Proust generalised about love, we might feel that we are eternally condemned to have the same musical experience over and over again, and that our personalities force us to follow the same path each time, even if we are not aware of having trodden it before. This applies, in effect, to musical *gesture*, without which we would not be able to recognise a composer's particular signature. But the same gesture might operate in very different trajectories. It is not the gesture, strictly speaking, that characterises a work's trajectory. Trajectory must be found in the thematic object itself and in the outcomes of its formulation.

The thematic challenge of a work is thus not necessarily the result of creative economy. An involuntary, special moment or a stroke of inspiration can make possible the labour, the elaboration that will infuse longer stretches, ones that are more dependent on our preferences and vastly less significant. For should we not view the search for thematicism as the same kind of work, in reduced form, as the development of ideas? In other words, can the theme exist or arise for the composer without its potential elaborations? In composers' works and sketches we find themes that were abandoned, even though they do not strike us as any less rich than the ones used. In certain cases, is it not because of their lack of malleability, their inappropriateness for the object under construction? It seems as if a theme does not exist *in itself*, only as a function of a *guaranteed* development. Development does not necessarily mean length and stretching out in time. Thematic elaboration is certainly strongly linked to the relative dimensions of development, but before fastening on the structural link between potential richness and developmental dimensions, I stress that the *gift* of theme does not necessarily inter-sect with the developmental form that one means to construct. There may be mismatches – of characteristics and articulation, of potential, of individualisation or neutrality.

In this respect, Wagner is a unique object of study, because he not only provides us with a sketchbook to examine (as with Beethoven or Webern), but also an oeuvre in which the way themes are exploited reveals how he selected the objects most suitable for development from everything that he generated over a period of twenty years. Sometimes he did not select the most characteristic ones, but he always retained the most pliable – at least, this is how it seems to me. But here again, we must beware the reactions we have today and the causal relationships we believe we find; we cannot experience a thematic figure in isolation, abstracted from sub-sequent elaboration, in the way that the composer at least once knew it, despite Schoenberg's claims. We are biased: we do not judge thematic fig-ures in and of themselves, but only alongside their 'posterity' (or absence of it), and we evaluate on that basis. But perhaps in other circumstances, if the composer had needed a different kind of development, an envi-able posterity might have been provided for a figure that would otherwise have remained without heir. Despite the existence of a finished work, our judgement is based on conjecture and circumstance.

A theme is already a developmental passage in reduced form: it con-tains the potential for development within itself. The way we read the theme is strongly influenced by the relationship between the actual devel-opment and the potential that we identify in the thematic kernel. When we contemplate a theme in order to study its consequences, we bring this principle of uncertainty to it, because our approach can be neither naive nor objective. The *actual* consequences are the only ones that we can know; moreover, they are the only ones that we relate directly to the thematic figure, the only ones that we can specify as potential realised. We limit deduction to what is before our eyes. *In principle!* Because when any creative composer studies a work, the deductions that are not present in it will be invented and developed elsewhere, in that com-poser's own work. From the visible deductions are imagined the possible deductions yet to be exploited, or that were exploited only in a secondary or inchoate way. From the actual life of a work, an imagined life develops in which the composer invents other models and other deductions out of existing ones. There will be a creative analysis involving the composer's own lack of innocence: the composer knows that objectivity is of no use and rediscovers a different kind of innocence in order to imagine those different deductions. Only such a detour will allow thematic challenge faced by a precursor to become a new and individual thematic process; unlike a listener trying to determine the original itinerary, the composer invents imaginary ones by accepting that determination, which cannot be rejected but can be transgressed by refusing to accept its inevitability. Our thematic listening is a function of development. When we listen to a theme, and only to this theme, we are familiar with its 'history'; we can no longer experience it as 'initial' material. The task of the musical creator is to recover this sense of the material as a basis for composition, to adopt its 'history' and make another one for it. This is no doubt a part of what we call tradition, in which thematicism is one of the main things at stake.

✳   ✳   ✳

When we analyse a work in terms of its thematicism, we become conscious of the *actual* network of relationships developed by the composer between one or more thematic figures and the elaborations deduced from them. We cannot view a theme *innocently*. We judge a theme according to its consequences and its *history*. The theme's ingenuity has disappeared, even if we try to isolate it. Our memory cannot forget the field of activity in which it developed, even if we remember it only vaguely and in little detail. When analysis and memory have taken possession of the work, the network implied by the thematic figures remains all the more inseparable from them. But fruitful analysis does not content itself with a reconstruction, however faithful, of all the consequences and repercussions of the real thematic network. It creates an imaginary network extracted from the composer's gesture, once it has been reduced to something 'generic'. Out of this particular gesture, we work our way up to the family that the gesture might make manifest, from which consequences of a different order can be deduced. In the same way, we might prefer to take a scrap of fabric or a shard of pottery in order to discover the aesthetics of a culture. A real itinerary has been replaced by an imaginary, fundamentally intuitive one in which direct reference to the original is absent. The more electrifying or fleeting this encounter turns out to be, the further apart the two itineraries – real and imagined – will grow from each other, through intermediary distortions imposed by differences of character, and also by historical context, musical language, evolutionary stage and reflection through the lens of the composer–analyst's personality.

Incidentally, by 'analysis' I do not mean a deductive method methodically applied to all the consequences, from initial thematic gambit through to formal outcome, but rather a series of short-circuits and intuitions that never claim to 'exhaust' a work, but which embrace some of its aspects as key moments resulting only from a vision, a richness of perspective; it is not really about explaining the composer's material, since this is first and foremost being displaced from its particular 'scenario' into a bigger picture.

There are, however, cases – previously frequent, but now less so – in which thematic material is reviewed in itself and used without alterations that would make it suitable for generating new figures and forms. It is significant that appropriating the material of others happens most often in a form that might not really be one at all, i.e. variation form. Some variations amount to a series of compartmentalised forms in which the theme is subjected to superficial, more or less florid ornamentation. Rather than being rich, what generally connects them is an expansion of this ornamentation. Variations can also be much more than this, when multiple compartmentalised elements become corresponding components of large-scale formal organisation. Whatever the logic of permutation, what matters is the way it plays with the *identity* of the theme. Various procedures enrich the melodic material, distorting it, if not making it unrecognisable. The harmonic structure may be treated variationally or idiomatically, and unique rhythmic characteristics introduced, but the immediate reference is always *identity* with the underlying structure and formal distribution: the whole process is about playing with the *identity* and the *identification* of a unique musical entity that has been identified as material for variation.

It is obvious that this *material* need not be personal and that a borrowed thematic entity might lend itself to the play of *reconsideration* that is variation form. Instead of the imaginary itinerary, a *real* itinerary replaces that of the original composer. The composer's materials are taken up again and reconsidered, their appearance changed, and the identity thus appropriated. Themes used in variation sets are often borrowed from forms that are either undeveloped or somewhat restrained. Sometimes this thematic identity is even borrowed from a musical joke, challenge, or quotation. The two most extreme cases are Beethoven's Diabelli Variations and Berg's variations on Wedekind's lied in the third act of *Lulu*. In these cases, one cannot even speak of reconsideration of the original approach, because this was much too perfunctory and trivial to be relevant; if entailed in the intense elaboration of a complex discourse by these two 'transformers', it would be only a handicap. The richness of the result stems from the initial structures being so general, applicable to any figure in the language, allowing the composer to be much more concerned with the fundamental thematic archetype than with how the theme actually stood; at a pinch you could almost replace the theme with a completely different initial unit and produce the same result. In the Diabelli Variations in particular, some variations can be reduced to harmonic progressions whose initial pattern is purely generic, their only virtue being their neutrality. As for Berg, he plays with misappropriating the very trivial, even maladroit harmonic functions of the original, adding contexts that amplify these characteristics by loaning them a particular style or cancelling them out by relegating them to the background. Incidentally, Schoenberg dealt with the same problem, without any directly dramatic reference, in the variations from the Suite, op. 29.

Borrowed themes do not always draw on extremely simple material using a kind of pot luck, where everybody brings their own variations. History offers numerous examples of composers borrowing material from each other, especially in eras in which the variation genre was thriving. Leaving aside what Bach supposedly borrowed from his royal contact for *The Musical Offering* (we will never know if the King really wrote that theme), more than a century later we find a composer who avidly sought out such interactions: in his variations on themes by Paganini, Handel and Haydn, Brahms provided models of the genre – and probably the very last examples of it. If there is such a thing as genius in *high-yield* deduction of figures, it lies in these works, especially the Handel and Haydn variations. This could probably happen only because there was no structural difference between the language of the models and that of the composer, even though there was a substantial difference in the way the structure was exploited. The developmental elements, their exploitation and preparation, all drew on the same rules, allowing for maximum expansion in a way that maximised stylistic certainty and preservation. In these works by Brahms and Beethoven, as well as the Berg and Schoenberg variations, we see one fundamental thematic unit supporting many ancillary and secondary themes, episodic figures and transplanted ideas. Thematicism is considerably enlarged in these works, in the sense that a theme is not only preserved in its transformations, but can be seen as a structural *support* in its various different states. If only ornamentation is called for, the theme is intact in its full identity – enriched, but not to the point of being occluded or suffocated. But if we want to use its infrastructure to support new thematic figures, it can be shorn of its most external, most visible characteristics, with only internal relationships preserved. Being less overt does not make its presence less strong, but rather changes its meaning in such a way that it reconnects in the deepest way with the early role of the *cantus firmus*, of which immediate comprehension may be suppressed, although its function in articulation remains essential. When a *theme* is used in that way, its role is understood on a different level, ranging from immediate to subconscious apprehension, and has to be achieved by grafting other ideas onto it. The theme moves from the commonly accepted notion of *figure* to that of *structure*.

This happens, incidentally, in Webern, in whose music it is difficult to distinguish between the passacaglia and the variation set. They do not express a thematic idea in the same way, but the formal conception remains identical. Berg sometimes comes close to this outlook, and in *Wozzeck* it would be quite difficult to establish a basic difference between the Passacaglia from Act I (Wozzeck and the doctor) and the Variations from Act III (Marie reading from the Bible). In Webern's works, however, the ambiguity between *figure* and *structure* grows as he progressively masters twelve-tone technique. In the Passacaglia, op. 1, the theme is heard in isolation, conspicuously, like a figure. Out of this figure whose harmony is not made explicit – it is clearly discernible for certain degrees, but other degrees use various equally valid solutions – a series of derived figures develops that reduces the original figure to a structural function as the harmonic basis of the chords that will be treated polyphonically. As the work progresses, this underlying thematic figure hovers between functional states, our attention drawn to how far it is derived or not, compared with other figures. The terms 'primary' and 'secondary' are inappropriate here, because 'primary' suggests audibility and 'secondary' the opposite, yet it is when we are not able to 'hear' it that it is securing ultimate overall coherence.

In a work like the Variations, op. 27, there is no longer such ambiguity and immediate lushness, for the underlying structure is no longer exhaustively exposed, as was the case with the Passacaglia, op. 1. Here, that underlying structure is a preliminary and will not be heard in its most overt form. The first appearance will already be a 'figurative' combination, uncharacterised and neutral. All the successive ideas refer in various ways to the underlying structure, but this structure is never exposed, either during the work or introducing it. It is really factors other than such derivations from an underlying figure that organise the work. The formal framework, in its strict and limited sense, is not an adequate trajectory for Webern, which explains why he also chose variations as a segment of a form organised by the principle of sonata and overture (Variations, op. 30). At that time, whatever he lost from the point of view of the *figure/structure* dialectic was compensated for by reprising similar figures, and through the hierarchy of strong figures (exposition and development sections) as opposed to weak ones (introduction, transition). What was important in this transformed conception of variation was the reference to latent structural thematicism, where formally functional figures were derived from some prominent characteristic.

This was my reference point in composing my own *Structures* for two pianos, using material taken literally from Messiaen's 'Mode de valeurs et d'intensités'. Independently of all of the personal reasons that led to my borrowing that thematic element – and it was indeed a case of thematic borrowing – I would stress that the Messiaen material was not taken from finished material – that is, as an extract of the composed, performed piece – but rather from raw material, from Messiaen's own starting points, to which he provided the 'key', which is in fact easy to deduce from the score. Moreover, this material was altered fundamentally, from the start, not only in how it was handled, but also in the way that treatment was conceived. The point was not so much to liberate the materials from the model, but rather to allow the materials that are assembled and combined from point to point to be used independently of each other. The first challenge was simple: to make each of the parameters (pitch, duration, dynamics, profile) independent, which meant that I needed to specify fields rather than moments. This borrowed thematic material, seen in a new light, could lead to results far removed from the original, which had provided only a *single* solution. For me, the use of parameters had to be *generalised*, while at the same time I individualised them, made them fluid, gave them the capacity to generate form.

This brings us to the question of thematic significance: certainly in relation to form and its intended goals in terms of a work's dimensions; but equally in relation to its symbolic and dramatic functions. No kind of thematicism can suit every situation. This explains why, in the borrowings I have cited as sources of the variation form, we have a very explicit, borderline case in which thematicism changes its function without changing its appearance.

❀　❀　❀

With respect to the relationship between theme and form, there is a question of priority, not within the final hierarchy of a work, but in the generation of material. To put it another way, is it setting our sights on some goal that dominates the search for suitable thematicism, or does a thematically implied structure lead to one form rather than another?

We saw in variations that themes invented for a precise purpose, used as a function of one kind of 'output', would be made to deviate from their original function in order to adopt others. Thus, the thematicism may be directly, unilaterally associated with precise ends, but with the potential to widen this original field of activity, sometimes a great deal. That being said, despite frequent flexibility, style and the state of a musical language depend on clearly focused thematicism. I have already noted that thematicism evolved over the centuries – for expressive purposes, very obviously, but also because musical language required it, as did the formal elaboration of musical discourse.

To return to the example of the *cantus firmus*, formal elaboration was grafted onto precise thematicism, with the intentional distortion of the original melodic line. *Cantus firmus* technique is necessarily bound up with a kind of thematicism that could never suit different purposes. Incidentally, the evolution of polyphony demonstrates the metamorphosis of the *cantus firmus* concept. The addition of other parts, the concept of independence and voice leading all made it necessary progressively to abandon such a unitary, tyrannical function in favour of more adaptable, flexible and renewable thematic types.

We have seen this evolution culminate in that masterpiece of formal construction that is the fugue, in the foundational role of subjects and countersubjects. But is a fugue subject left to the vagaries of inspiration, and can we imagine a fugue subject invented without reference to its precise codes of use? At most, these laws can be so well assimilated, and handled with such compositional virtuosity, that imagination works to strict constraints taken into account without conscious (or indeed conscientious) control. The fugue subject obeys underlying harmonic rules: it must provide material for strict contrapuntal combination, with a view to stretto, and its figures must have unified to some extent. The countersubjects will necessarily be derived from this subject, while also requiring different, contrasting rhythmic figuration in order to be distinct from it. Thus, from the moment of conception these thematic features point to specific applications. Some trivial detail follows from this, such as the length of the subject: a fugue subject cannot exceed a certain length, if only because it will be repeated many times within the overall duration.

Proportion must be respected here – as essential as it is obvious. Moreover, regarding formal interest, since the fugal development will be based on increasing complexity and rigour in the relationships between different polyphonic lines, and since peak complexity and rigour are reached when all of the parts derive directly from the main thematic content, the most productive fugue subjects are those that can provide the greatest number of formal combinations and that can be repeated through voice exchanges – in other words, those that can contribute to the development of polyphonic combinations without distorting them. This accounts for many clever turns of invertible counterpoint and canonical imitation. It is obvious that not only the handling of this technique, but even more the creation of suitable objects, calls for creativity placed in the service of exact formal elaboration. When this became obsolete, mainly because of how musical language evolved, such thematicism also had to evolve, to enable it to cope with this new context.

Did that evolution occur out of necessity, or fatigue? The perfection of a given technique forces composers who follow in the wake of this to find other forms of development, to lose interest in previous ones or to transform them in such a way that they can be used in a different context. It could be said that the development of harmonic functions as form-bearing elements and the increasing complexity of increasingly transitional harmonic progressions made it impossible to use the fugue subject in its most optimal configuration. But equally, the strict constraints on the evolution of fugue subjects prevented their musical language from evolving beyond a certain limit, since the most complex polyphonic combinations permitted only relatively simplified harmonic functions. When these constraints came to be judged as inadequate, and were thus abandoned, thematic technique developed into a state where relationships were more flexible and contained a different kind of energy.

Two-theme form became one of the most fruitful kinds of generative relationship between figure and form. It brought into play elements that were more contrasting, more dramatic and more appropriate to how expressive means were developing. Above all, it was the notion of *conflict* that emerged, the evolutionarily radical factor. Within a field of thematic working, a specific configuration, figures could be deployed according to a more liberating, spontaneous grammar that allowed motives to be developed in more remote tonal regions. But besides the thematic contrast of sonata form, a different thematic potential was explored in the adagio and the rondo. Moreover, the fugue itself was never abandoned but was often 'rediscovered' and developed as enlargement and exception – those *licenze* so dear to Beethoven.

This evolution meant reciprocal influences: thematicism, in symbiosis with musical language, joined in defining form; at the same time, form to some extent defined thematicism, which was never so rigid as to be unsuited to a formal type. In fact, in the Viennese tradition, from Mozart and Beethoven to Berg, Schoenberg and Webern, there is a persistent tendency to associate one formal type with another. Far from this being rigid or compartmentalised, there is, on the contrary, permeability that allows one form to be enriched by the ambiguity of another. Thus, the refrains of a rondo can show traits of variations, an adagio can be an interweaving of two sets of variations, or fugue can appear in a sonata form as a development section. Countless examples of these hybrids can be found, transforming formal types to the extent that they lose their meaning. Thematicism and its formal specifications have evolved so far that theme and form are no longer related in the same way. When comparing the interaction of theme and form in the first movement of Beethoven's Piano Sonata, op. 106, or the first movement of Webern's Symphony, op. 21, it is hard to see them as similar. They share the constants of exposition, development, recapitulation and coda, yet apart from that domain which is so indifferent to the elements involved, their thematic materials have little in common.

Besides this, as the sonata developed, thematic specifics, for example, underwent such transformation and became so variable that labels such as principal, transitional or subordinate theme proliferated so much that analysts would often disagree on how to use them. Inappropriate deductions made a posteriori can just add to the confusion, such as when trying to show how some themes deduced from others support the underlying unity of a work. But when speaking at this level one could say anything at all, considering that one always ends up with definitions of basic intervals that can be found anywhere, in any circumstance. This obviously proves that although thematic creativity is inseparable from a theme's formal purpose, figure, theme and motive have wider and richer potential than their necessarily limited use in a particular work. Firstly, this potential is not readily *exhausted*; secondly, it is ambiguous and can suit different kinds of development or articulation; thirdly, there is no single method for the deployment and deduction of themes, but only the use of this potential to a greater or lesser extent. Nevertheless, thematicism and form have to be equated, leading one to ask whether some kinds of thematic work exclude some formal frameworks, and if so, why.

The works of most of Beethoven's Romantic successors are often cited as dangerously encumbered by this powerful inheritance, making them overly respectful and inconsequential. Wagner and Brahms stretched this dilemma to its furthest point. It has often been said that Schubert and Schumann, like Chopin, Liszt and Berlioz, failed to construct large-scale form, that they were always hampered by the formal framework of sonata and symphony and did not know what to do with it. It is claimed that their mechanical and artificial developmental techniques flagged through repetition or harmonic sequencing. In short, the framework was filled, but the form did not come to life. Despite the ingenious and brilliant qualities to be found in their musical ideas, it is generally claimed that this framework suited them poorly, that the essence of their poetics and creative power was found in shorter, freer, less restrictive formal frameworks, where they did not need to align their spontaneous creativity with rigorous practice. To be precise, thematicism was not appropriate to its given formal frameworks. But one asks: In what way? Above all, these Romantics captured the moment in a more volatile manner than their predecessors, and their formal procedures profoundly contradicted this feeling for the moment, for the unique event. Thus, without the use of overt and therefore 'artificial' techniques, it is impossible to enlarge form with an architecture of reprises, of moments re-experienced and transformed through development. We can say that as regards configuration, their themes cannot be 'disassembled', but are bound up in a whole through their expressive power. To dissociate the elements, to put each of them to 'work' in context, violates their expressive power in the quest to obtain an 'output' for which they were not designed. The very way that these figures were invented, the commonalities of their constituent elements, mean that they cannot be safely *disassembled*.

It is therefore impossible to manipulate them in a manner that is not inherently, deeply alien. This was the central contradiction of the Romantics. Brahms escaped it by employing a thematicism tied less to the moment than to development, whose consequences he drew most adroitly from classical tradition. It has been said that thematic creativity faded somewhere between the Romanticism of Schumann and Brahms, but that the latter knew how to develop material, whereas the former did not – or, at any rate, had little know-how relevant to this inherited kind of architecture. It is less that Romantic thematicism faded, however, than that in order to exist within its favoured formal configuration, Brahms's thematicism could not share the spontaneity of Schumann's: deduction and dependency were embedded in it from the beginning, and these could not help but affect its expressive potential.

How is it that Wagner, the polar opposite of Brahms, found thematicism suited to his work as a dramatist? Since he was composing for the stage, he had the benefit of being *personally* unencumbered by the burdens and constraints of symphonic tradition. His thematicism could adapt to two functions with no direct precedent: firstly, to symbolise a character, situation, object, feeling or idea; secondly, to represent action. In the context of temporal inexorability, the type of thematicism that was intended for reversible time no longer applied, and a thematicism suited above all to the evolution of characters and situations therefore had to be discovered. In Wagner's drama, form on the exposition/development/ recapitulation model is no longer conceivable, or on any model rooted in the reprise – whether periodic or not – of musical ideas. His dramatic perspective gradually forced him to transform the function of his thematicism, and consequently the very form of his themes. Their basic structure is amenable to a different type of development, of 'disassembly', of manipulation. Classical themes appeared in a particular context and were inconceivable *in isolation*; they are functional as soon as they are heard. Since Wagner's themes are designed to be symbolic, in any context, they are fundamentally *detachable* and extendable. This allows them to be differently configured in terms of speed, combination, preponderance or subordination; in full or divided up; in a strong presentation or as subsidiary; as vehicles for a radical development or a secondary episode; or they can simply be quoted. These thematic figures therefore lend themselves to multiple formal functions that are not predetermined from their first entrance. What they look like will depend on the interaction of drama and symbol: their identity emerges at the moment of this encounter. *Theme* and *form* are thus guaranteed to be independent.

* * *

Dramatic expression and the structural change it implies caused the construction of themes and motives to veer towards other uses or functions. Accordingly, musical language itself changed to accommodate these new functions. The relationship between language and theme took on different features. Themes were increasingly the fundamental source of textual elaboration. Predetermined form, for all its typical, sometimes excessive ambiguities, remained a field of constants. The notion of *reprise* was structurally crucial, based on underlying rules that were even independent of thematic requirements. Structural archetypes used formulas designed to function through themes supposed to determine their articulation. When drama – real or imaginary, whether in works for the stage or those based on programmes or even texts – controls formal structure, principles of *reprise* are redundant because they completely contradict the *narrative*. When a development separates exposition from recapitulation, for instance, that point in the work is characterised not so much by narration as by temporary conflict, confusion even, which needs to be dissipated so that the previous elements can reappear in their original hierarchy. This opposition between *conflict resolution* and *narrative* created problems for programme music, whose thematicism reflected the former notion and formal development the latter. Verbal descriptions of this programme music provide a *reductio ad absurdum* that comically highlights the combat in which themes settle down peacefully, only then to wage war on each other. Such descriptions literally embody the nonsensical nature of this procedure.

The notion of *narrative* emerged with Wagner and was developed in Mahler's symphonies. Mahler's thematicism is by nature *diffuse*, and each recurrence of a given thematic unit happens on its own terms, possibly varied so much that the very notion of recurrence, in the strict sense, yields to that of transformation. The narrative is constructed from varying degrees of either radical, thematic transformation or themes that respond to contextual requirements that may more or less monopolise them. Wagner's words to Liszt, as reported by Cosima, are prophetic: 'When we write symphonies, we should not set themes in opposition, since that genre was exhausted by Beethoven; we should weave a melodic thread right to the end, and most of all, nothing dramatic.' Even if we discern a thinly veiled hostility to Brahms here, and recognise that the use of the word 'dramatic' is too narrow for the word's true scope, it remains true that the *conflict* at the heart of classical form, symbolised to perfection by Beethoven, no longer functioned. New thematicism required a new type of development, and even if weaving a melodic thread oversimplifies the problem, *narrative* is what shines through the folding of this thread.

It could hardly be said of Mahler's symphonies that they merely 'weave a melodic thread' and exclude the dramatic, but dramatic content has taken the form of a narrative. Mahlerian form has often been compared to that of the novel, and its main historical significance has certainly been to resolve, in effect, the contradiction between repetitive and progressive form. If the word 'novel' connotes too much to embrace it musically, we can speak of the *epic*, in which Mahler's contributions are not all of the same strength or persistence. There are movements in the symphonies – those that are the most striking in their expression and their references, the scherzos, for example – in which both thematic creativity and formal structure revisit an enlarged, tried and tested tradition, adopting it wholesale and using literal archetypes. Thematicism as restrictive and characteristic as in the *Ländler* cannot but entail a kind of predetermined formal development. There is also a contrast between short vocal works, based on a single motive or figuration, and bigger works such as the Eighth Symphony or *Das Lied von der Erde*. Often, it is the slow movements that break free from formal constraint through the use of variations, in the full sense of that term. In fact, in the later works, thematic elements supply not only development in itself, but also the way the polyphonic texture is laid out. The Fifth Symphony marks a turning point in that respect: think only of the finale of the Ninth Symphony, in which a single motive generates broad development, and the writing is unified by an ornamental cell – a thoroughly traditional turn motive – borrowed directly, by the way, from the death of Isolde.

It is interesting to compare what Wagner and Mahler did with such similar, almost literally identical elements, to see the extent to which the thematic concept evolved in musical languages with similar foundations. Mahler's musical language is based, in this movement, on highly unstable harmonic development exploring remote regions. The motive becomes a strongly unifying element for this harmonic dissolution, albeit continually varied rhythmically or, more precisely, made subject to diminutions and augmentations that avoid the prosaic quality of literal repetition. This manipulation of motivic temporality does not seek to undermine textural or transitional coherence, but rather to heighten and relax tension coherently, in a symbiosis of durational tension and varying degrees of harmonic intensity. The only parallel for such motivic manipulation of time is found in Debussy, in whose *Prélude à l'après-midi d'un faune* elements are condensed and stretched, without having quite the same significance or meaning as in Mahler's late works. For Debussy, this is a linear rather than polyphonic phenomenon, but it affects motivic meaning, hierarchy and prominence – and also, of course, expressive force, which is not to be overlooked.

To return to Mahler's approach to duration and motive, its principle cannot be considered as unprecedented, but the way he applies it in music that may have led him down this path is radical. Based on imitative counterpoint, polyphonic writing would use various techniques to bind the different voices together in the interests of coherence. To heighten tension and enrich perception, the various voices were traditionally assigned to different proportional ratios: double, in general, or quadruple – canon by augmentation or double augmentation, and diminution or double diminution, marked the limits of internally consistent temporal dissociation, but this was practised by all the superimposed layers at once, so that the temporal basis of the entire texture could always be perceived. In some of Bach's large-scale choral works, and in one of the pieces from Schoenberg's *Pierrot lunaire*, this principle of doubling was widened to encompass the entire form. In the Mahler example, the Adagio from the Ninth Symphony, the ornamental turn motive covers different durations, albeit without defining a temporal layer, since the transformation applies to only a single motive, so that its logic is not pervasive, nor does the transformation belie its provenance. Our perception is disrupted at the same time as becoming focused, the proof being that if the performers fail to pay attention, they can mistakenly confuse one speed with another, which never happens when the figures are inscribed within a different actual tempo.

Mahler's slow movements are an excellent example of development through continuous variation, in which the 'theme' changes from one state to another by virtue of internal work on the very material of which it is composed, and also through the addition of new figures and registral placement to establish different listening hierarchies. Nevertheless, the large-scale outer movements are certainly the ones that most clearly illustrate the intrusion of *narrative* into a conflict-based form, in which the dramatic element retains all its power. Contrary to the way it is anticipated in Wagner, here narrative is formed by the succession of conflicts. In order to describe these forms, the vocabulary used until then – that is, exposition, repeat, development and recapitulation – loses a good part of its meaning, since in order to be precise it needs to be overburdened with incidences, insertions and exceptions that end up undermining the validity of the description. The themes are no longer destined to reappear like milestones or signposts along a well-charted route. They mark out the phases of formal development through how they change, and when repeated literally they are used only to get things going, for they very soon lose their original form. They deviate and drift towards another persona, a different texture. In this very particular approach to texture, it seems that Mahler plays above all on the figures' ambiguity, their ability to adapt by being infused with a new role, hierarchy and significance. This results in our losing touch with the thematic figures, because the figures we might have considered subsidiary begin to win our attention, or maintain an unstable equilibrium in which attention oscillates from one emphasis to another, assigning primacy to different elements of the polyphony in turn. These elements remain symbiotic, interdependent with the other, so we can perceive them.

Another aspect that Mahler developed to the utmost was the intrusion of thematicism that is fundamentally foreign or even irreducible within a given context. Although able to promote unity and consistency, he also developed the heterogeneous side of his compositional elements. Sometimes he would imaginatively repeat a theme in such different contexts that we have trouble recognising the first form in the second. Even when the deduction is clear, that does not expunge the heterogeneity of their appearances. I am thinking in particular of the theme shared by the Adagietto and Finale of the Fifth Symphony, in which the durational transformation – from slow to fast – overturns not only the perception of time, but also the theme's meaning. Is this one of the major features of a narrative – to transform our understanding of characters by changing the circumstances of their appearance, by revealing something new about known personages?

Many aspects of Mahler's writing are bound up with the enlargement of symphonic form, and this enlargement is so significant that it perhaps marks the abolition of form as a deterministic plan. Dismembering formal plans certainly played a part in Mahler's aesthetic project: from his earliest works, his thinking led him towards continuous development, which was a direct result of the influence of Wagner's approach to dramatic development, and yet the actual content has nothing to do with Wagnerian drama, any more than it represents any detailed programme. In his first symphonies, Mahler did yield to the temptation of a written programme, but he soon became aware that verbally expressed narrative is not suited to musical form. After that, it was above all his commentators who felt it necessary to identify feelings or mental states supposedly *represented* in or *translated* through these large-scale musical constructions; and yet that kind of synopsis is more or less alien to the inner substance of a work and trivially expresses a diffuse, obvious atmosphere that has little to do with the *narrative* of which I have been speaking. In this type of narrative, it is a matter of recounting not a series of logically

successive events, but rather derived prolongations of thematic figures – not referentially determined, nor subject to any developmental
hierarchy. These prolongations no doubt reference the formal goal-
directedness that Mahler inherited from a fairly distant tradition, though
sometimes they do so only very vaguely, and they part company from the
tradition in their open, liberated character.

What was off-putting to Mahler's early critics was the apparent
mismatch between the nature of the ideas and the quality of their elaboration, between the poverty or even vulgarity of certain aspects of his
thematicism and the disproportionate complexity and expansion of his
deductions. In line with the 'noble' tradition of the symphony, maintained up to Brahms and Bruckner, strict *thematic economy* was one of
the most intangible inherited values. Themes – main, transitional and
secondary – point to formal function from the moment they appear; they
are conceived in terms of this function and must possess the characteristics vital to their structural position. Of course, thematic functions
are not rigid to the point of excluding exceptions, but when they are
perceived as exceptional, the absolute power that formal principles hold
over thematic ideas is reinforced, and from his earliest works Mahler
subverted that hierarchy profoundly and irreversibly. He immediately
focused on the expressive profile of his themes, freighting them with
an emotional content that excluded standard symphonic planning. Of
course, there were precursors, close and remote, in Berlioz and Strauss.
But Berlioz's symphonic planning had turned out to be remarkably
similar to Beethoven's, except for the fact that his musical themes were
derived from the symbolic, or rather from imagery, without this affecting his actual forms; and Strauss, like Liszt, was interested above all in
conveying a series of circumstances, even anecdotes, thus excluding
'economy' in principle.

On the other hand, what irritated Mahler's hostile contemporaries was
the way he let elements seep into the symphony that should have been
kept out. This amounts to denouncing the exterior appearance of his
themes: the anecdotal connotations, the triviality, their source in folklore,
the absence of *invention* in the creation of figures. In short, from the
point of view of tradition, their character was condemned as unsuitable,

which is to say that ultimately they were formally incompatible. And in fact, through the nature of the expansions that they generated, through the ambiguity of their meaning, such thematic figures would slowly go on to bankrupt the formal economy of the symphony. Exposition, development and recapitulation lost their meanings as concepts, as well as the functions that had been attributed to them. Of course, not every movement in Mahler's symphonies is as radical as this, but the most innovative symphonies or movements are the most disturbing sites of Mahler's creativity to this day, not only because it is more difficult to absorb their temporal excesses and developmental complexity, but because by being based on transformation and dissolution they fundamentally unsettle our need for order founded on reprise and recovery. This is especially clear in the Sixth Symphony and the outer movements of the Seventh, which cannot be *summarised* but only *narrated*. The formal plan is not reducible to filled-out blocks that can be apprehended in a moment of synthesis and abstracted from their content; in a way, it is the *unfolding* that is crucial for understanding form and content alike.

Within the limits of a harmonic language that he both expanded and respected – and Adorno thought that in a certain way Mahler's musical language, in this precise area at any rate, was less adventurous than Wagner's – the richness and even heterogeneity of the thematic material are the result, in his symphonies, of a narrative form that creates the formal articulations necessary to proceed decisively. Once again, we observe that this transformation of form itself demands a different and essential concept of thematic creativity. This explains why Mahler's power of invention – progressive but also conservative, at a pivotal moment in the evolution of musical language – draws on such diverse material, material that is as heterogeneous as it is necessary. He dissolves the pre-established notion of genre as well as form. In a way that not even he could predict, he anticipated both Berg's composite aesthetic and the puritanical revival of material undertaken by Webern. In this subversion of form, Mahler worked in the same direction, if not according to the same meaning, as his exact contemporary Debussy.

❊ ❊ ❊

The word 'subversion' is often taken to imply violence and destruction, and it would be difficult to characterise Debussy's works in this way; and yet to the extent that Debussy shuns traditional thematic and formal economy, albeit in a suave rather than overbearing way, his oeuvre is definitely subversive. It is even more radically and definitively subversive than Mahler's in immediately breaking free from the symphonic, which had taken hold as much in France as everywhere else. The César Franck inheritance was obsessively fixated on the continuation of old forms, and in order to breathe new life into them they were overloaded with rules and purposes that, on the contrary, rendered them totally outdated, even caricatures. Faced with this tiresome academicism, Debussy guarded his freedom and arrived at the implausible marriage of the 'character piece', of the 'album leaf', with symphonic form.

Our admiration of Debussy's oeuvre and sensibilities is not lessened by acknowledging that the chief characteristic of most of his output is that it is made up of albums, or *collections*. Large-scale form that connects different movements organically – the symphony in particular – seemed to him to be an exhausted option. After his String Quartet, he would not use large-scale form until the three final sonatas, and it can hardly be said that the latter obey the economy of contrast that is typical between movements, not to mention within the form of those movements. Whether in the piano repertoire, the vocal works or the orchestral works before *La Mer*, whether in *Images*, *Estampes* or *Nocturnes*, Debussy adopts the preferred perspective of the Romantics: that of *moments* assembled not into a suite in which the logic of succession, although flexible, is fixed by a hierarchy that organises the contrasts – with the exception of the *Suite bergamasque* and *Pour le piano* – but more often assembled in a formally unconstrained order. In general, the last piece is the quickest, the one with the most contrasts, the most brilliant, finishing the set with panache. Besides this purely gestural choice, it could change places within the collection – at least, this is my impression – without fundamentally changing the meaning of the work. There is no sense of dependency from one piece to the next. In the sets of *Préludes* and *Études*, *order* is no less absent – or, at least, it is present arbitrarily. Succession no longer even obeys any apparent tonal logic, since we could imagine it otherwise. One thinks of the distinction Mallarmé made between Book and Album.

A closed compositional universe certainly does not call for thematicism analogous to what was required by a composer seeking expansion and coherence. In Debussy, and in the Romantics on whom he drew, there is in fact a conflict between the instantaneous and the formal plan. In many compositions, the individual *piece*'s formal plan is much more perfunctory than the overall sequence of ideas. There are many triptychs in which the two panels are laid out nearly symmetrically around a central panel, a plan which is the most immediately convincing easy option. Even in the *Études*, where the journey turns out to be more complex, a sense of *reprise* often marks the closing section. When the logic of development is based fundamentally on instinct, rather than on explicit phases of construction, it becomes almost unavoidable to *signal* – even in a cursory way – the onset, the launch, of the final phase. It almost goes without saying that a more or less obvious reprise represents an equal force compared with what has intervened, and signifies a return to the initial *order*. The final phase of the work returns to the initial state, possibly in varied form, for reasons of formal balance: starting from a static state, we went through a dynamic one, or a series of them, to return to that static state. Sonata form was similar but used a more formal, unyielding and developed code. In certain of Debussy's habitual forms, in the lineage of the Romantics, the dialectic on which sonata form had depended – of order/disorder/order – is present in evolved or corrupted guise, even to the extent of having the two themes return in the same key in the reprise: *evolved* in that the thematic material is more flexible, more pliable, less *predestined* to perform specific but constraining tasks; *corrupted* in that the sonata as it had evolved presented a less cursory succession and offered more ambiguity and richer possibilities than the simple contrast between repose and movement.

As Debussy was working out his personal 'chemistry', as he liked to call it, a dissolution of tradition was taking place, involving both the demise of practices that, for all their advantages, had become out of step with musical language, and an appeal to techniques that were more crude but also more immediate, and whose very perfunctoriness made them more appropriate as tools for transition. In that broad context, 'perfunctory' is certainly one word to characterise Debussy's thematic approach, but on the other hand it is that subtlety that escaped his contemporaries, attached as they were to an outdated formalism that made them find this music spineless and short-winded. It was surely not only expressive caution, even tenuousness sometimes, that caused these accusations to spread. Compared with this, praise for his moderation and clarity, qualities with which his genius was also weighed down, was no compensation. It is true that Debussy's themes and developmental material rarely exude affirmation and exuberance, yet many of his predecessors had also tended towards intimacy of expression. What was unsettling, and what strikes us even today as surprisingly modern, is the cut of the themes, their profile and the way they are used. One could still find *narrative* here, but it would be a highly condensed one by comparison with Mahler, and also of a different kind – in essence, elliptical. Moreover, to analyse a Debussy work according to its thematicism is to be condemned to describing non-formal development: one finds a succession of events whose logic is extremely convincing but profoundly inexplicable. *La Mer* is a particularly brilliant example of formal development that is both necessary and unpredictable. As beautiful and inventive as they otherwise are, neither the *Prélude à l'après-midi d'un faune* nor the *Nocturnes* linked thematic invention and the development of musical ideas in as surprising a way. *Jeux*, especially the first part, would revive this miracle, which was slightly lacking in *Images*.

What, then, is the thematic quality that allows Debussy to develop his creativity in such an original direction? The intrinsic aspects of these themes, motives, figures – whatever name we give them – need to be decisive. We note, *a contrario*, that whenever he wanted to borrow folk themes – that is, borrowing from a thematicism that he had not devised himself – Debussy almost always became bogged down in academic or repetitive procedures with which we sense he is as ill at ease as we are. The 'Rondes de printemps' is the most blatant case, unless its intention is to caricature, to poke fun through music rather than words at those who wrap unsuspecting folk melodies in overloaded layers of gaudy material. This quite artificially reclaimed 'folklore' was, incidentally, much more successful when it was cloaked in the exoticism of imaginary journeys. Whether in his fairly frequent incursions into Spain or his rarer escapades into Asia, Debussy seemed to display more mastery; he was more imaginative and spontaneous with material created from clichés neutral enough to be highly malleable. He recreates Spanish or Asian colour; he takes an isolated element, such as the pentatonic scale, but with little care for any irrelevant stylistic authenticity. A reminiscence filtered by his creativity, his individual language, helps him avoid the lure of the picturesque, while still retaining an aura (rather than the reality) of local colour. It seems that with French elements, Debussy was not able to distance himself as much: he felt overly constrained by their existence as musical vocabulary, and so could neither smooth over nor highlight their heterogeneity. Since exoticism could not be a factor, no familiarity or absorption was present to compensate – in the way that they do, say, in Mahler's contemporaneous use of that folkloric 'tone', which can also be found in some of Stravinsky's pieces, such as *Les Noces*. In Mahler and Stravinsky, each in his own way, there was an identification with this thematic material, which was less borrowed than appropriated. In Debussy, one senses, on the contrary, that he holds in his hands a foreign object that is both touching and absurd, like the gawky peasant girl he himself evoked with so much irony when speaking about some of his contemporaries. It is hard now to see what drove him to work with thematicism to which he was so clearly unsuited. The zeitgeist, of course! This was the heyday of all those nationalisms. But what is justified by context in some cases, when the folk environment is lively, maintained by a strong regional tradition – and even then, only when the composer is Stravinsky or Bartók – is no longer possible as a phenomenon of transmission or osmosis when traditions have become so weak that to exploit them is artificial; it is an act bereft of spontaneity, a spurious search for so-called national traditions that have long since waned or even vanished.

Debussy's creativity – to prove the point in negative terms – could develop only through one particular kind of thematicism. What was specific about it? The fact that it was tied to his musical language, which was essentially harmonic? Although Debussy's musical language uses a traditional harmonic vocabulary that is usually 'enriched', but also sometimes 'impoverished', compared with that of his immediate predecessors, it rejected above all the hierarchy of degrees, intervals and functions. The progressions are based on affinity, not universal rules, but one that results from a provisional decision that is no more valid than others would have been. Thus, the famous chords in parallel motion, and other consecutive fifths, that reject chordal and intervallic functions but establish any chord or interval as a sonic object; this approach is functionally different from the hitherto honoured rules of harmonic *progression* based on tonal scale degrees. Debussy seems to point, if not to anarchy, then at least to disorder – or, at any rate, as far as *progressions* are concerned, to doing whatever he pleased. There is no longer any *single* law, but only regulation in the moment. However wilful and determined it is, the subversion of harmonic progression is not radical in the sense of wanting to topple everything that existed before and replace it with a new law. From this perspective, Debussy was little concerned with organisation in a formal sense; he puts his faith in an instinct that he considers to be superior to any excessively rationalised choice. This has a few drawbacks, but also boundless advantages. The disadvantage is that, contrary to popular belief, instinct needs time to develop. It does not necessarily dictate a solution right away; it can make a decision quickly, but can also leave you in the lurch for some time, or even entirely empty-handed. As soon as Debussy is pressed for time, whenever he dips into one of his pentatonic, whole-tone or major/minor resources to satisfy the most urgent needs of the moment, the weaknesses of his vocabulary are apparent. A more rational organisation would probably have spared him from taking those emergency measures, but it would not have permitted him the spontaneous, unique side of his musical language, its most irreplaceable quality: besides his use of important, perhaps foundational articulations such as cadence, caesura, phrase ending and reprise, his creativity rejects any hierarchy other than that of the living development of form. Does this imply that his musical language comprises a succession of unique choices, at the great risk of incoherence? Certainly not. Preferences, if not laws, are articulated through his choices. Although the connections between objects are not narrowly circumscribed by outdated constraints, neither are they the fruit of chance or of 'doing as he pleases'. There is logic present, albeit more flexible and ambiguous, able to form relationships that are no longer unilateral and therefore by definition not completely predictable. In this sense, he draws on Wagner – or at least, a certain part of Wagner – in a much more subtle way than Wagner's more direct descendants.

There remains the question of thematicism, which does not particularly form part of this inheritance, although in *Pelléas* we do find traces of Wagnerian thematic usage and even literal borrowings (Golaud's theme bears a striking resemblance to Parsifal's). But the few correspondences of this sort would in the end reveal only a limited, superficial influence, because Debussy's thematic approach, as soon as it became apparent, was one of the most personal of its kind. Does the first theme of the *Prélude à l'après-midi d'un faune* refer to anything other than its own irreducible self? This theme is totally characteristic of the composer's approach to opening material. Whether in this *Prélude*, in the first of the *Nocturnes*, in *La Mer* or in *Jeux*, one has the impression that the motive is merely outlined, unable to head anywhere, that it can only repeat itself in different harmonic settings. Our initial feeling is that no real elaboration is possible, that the phrase is too short, destined to run out of steam, lacking the necessary breadth; that it condemns us to the incessant variation of relatively light figures. In short, however charming or original we may find these thematic figures to be, we intuit that they can generate nothing but miniatures. Debussy seems at first glance to provide 'lazy' material – tailored, of course, but in such a way that it leaves us uncertain as to its possible outcomes.

I do not mean to imply that *all* of Debussy's themes present or preserve this 'vague' character. Some are fleshed out from the start and immediately have the character of a definitive statement – for example, the theme that ends the first and third movements of *La Mer*. There is no doubt about the closed and conclusive character of this theme, but it is one of those very rare examples in Debussy's symphonic output of a coda that concludes through affirmation. Most of the other pieces or movements fade away, the motives disintegrating into the uncertainty from which they were born.

What is implied by this uncertainty of goal? Where does it come from? First of all, from the repulsion and horror with which Debussy experienced contemporaneous symphonic works. He could not bear to see a composition presented as a demonstration of thematic technique. The machinery is exhibited, dissected, taken apart and put back together. Nothing was further from his dream of a supreme conception than this rhetoric of disassembly and reassembly, like an appliance demonstrated by a travelling salesperson, and of which he had many examples around him in the 'deep' and 'serious' musical literature. His ideal goal in the realms both of composition and instrumentation was to preserve the illusion, so that the listener did not know 'how it was made', so that everything seemed to be organised according to permanently secret laws. Just as he refused to accept a hierarchy of received harmonic relationships, so he shunned procedures that made symphonic academicism feel safe and contented. Terms like main, secondary and transitional theme had no meaning for him; he regarded motives rather as having varying significance depending on their context. There are themes that are unstable because of their use of stock motives, there are completely static themes that recur as markers in different harmonic 'settings', and there are also those capable of being developed. Hence the extreme diversity of his conception of a theme, which can be anything from a four-note figure, a kind of transferrable call, to a completely well-formed and stable group. More than this, Debussy delights in changing the perspectives in which these figures are set. A secondary figure can become a main one, and vice versa. Here again, the hierarchy is mobile and transforms the material it controls. Debussy is, to borrow the expression that Wagner applied to himself, the composer of the transition. Given his goal – to create a form free of constraining contours, in which everything is meaningful, everything will be transformed, in which the trajectory is essential to grasping the whole and its coherence – Debussy was creating a thematicism that would allow him to produce that perpetual 'transition', that was flexible enough, sufficiently 'disoriented' for it. From the *Prélude à l'après-midi d'un faune* to *Jeux*, his entire symphonic output follows this trend. Even with some regrets and setbacks (as I noted with regard to *Images*), it shows inexorable progress in the osmosis of thematicism and form.

I have mentioned figures, motives and themes, but there is something even more radical when, in the *Études*, his thematic units are taken from intervals (fourths, sixths, thirds, octaves) or from one figure (ornamentations, compound arpeggios, opposed sonorities). Of course, one could react by pointing out that since these are études, their aim, as with all such pieces, is to present the performer with a specific challenge, and consequently they call on the composer to orient a work exclusively around this technical aspect, be it of an entirely elementary kind (an interval) or a combinatorial nature (a figure). That was the problem faced by Liszt and Chopin, not to mention many other less illustrious composers, and rarely have there been notable outcomes. Thirds and sixths are the targets of many études. The use of fourths – the most subversive interval in tonal aggregates – would not have made much difference, had Debussy not taken as his very starting point the determinate or indeterminate relationships that bind the pure interval in itself with a hierarchy that either adapts *to*, or withdraws *from*, it. One of the strongest and most productive tensions of tonal language has always been the relationship between interval and harmonic hierarchy. Should the hierarchy soften in order to absorb the interval, or must the interval yield to the discipline of harmonic control and thus adapt to a vertical context? Strict counterpoint rejects that kind of negotiation and correspondingly downgrades harmonic relationships; free composition favours flexibility in vertical writing, to the detriment of intervallic integrity.

Debussy consciously or unconsciously grapples with the fundamental dilemma of musical language, which lies in prioritising one compositional dimension over another, and it matters little whether this emerges from a purely pianistic starting point or not. He exploits this dilemma optimally, making an entire dialectic of development out of this one *element*, the interval. There are, of course, themes, thematic figures in the familiar sense of the term, but the underlying *theme* is the chosen interval. In the *Étude* 'Pour les quartes', the universe embracing Debussy's musical language is tonal, but this is an enlarged tonality, one of polarisation: functions can emerge as fundamental, while others are passed over or even ignored. The *Étude* will thus play on the bizarre, unstable relationships that hold between the invariant interval and tonal relationships. This, then, is the overall setting. He establishes an oscillation or contrast between diatonicism and chromaticism: in this particular case, between the perfect and altered (diminished or augmented) fourth. In turn, the fourth either completely dominates the texture or adapts to it and allows itself to be tamed, to the point of becoming indistinguishable within it, absorbed into 'standard' relationships. This creates a fundamental opposition, with non-standard chords as extensions of diatonic relationships that are *suspended* within a language foreign to their principle. These chords possess a value in and of themselves, unrelated to the hierarchy around them, and they do not need to be 'resolved' in order to be incorporated into the system. In the way it is used, this fourth therefore oscillates between being a *decorative* and a *determining* interval. In its thematic capacity, it is responsible for the overall invention.

I could also take the example of the *Étude* 'Pour les arpèges composés', in which the speed, the compression of the figures, makes this 'theme' turn from being a crucial melodic flourish into strictly secondary ornamentation. This thematic figure informs practically every compositional component. Thus, the *Étude* 'Pour les accords' invites the question of whether we hear the chord in itself, as an object, or as an element within a hierarchy?

As we have seen, Debussy's thematicism developed radically, but the subversion was not ostentatious. His concept of musical language, and of the hierarchical relationships needed in composition, generated a thematic concept that worked, imbued with a new and different profile. Can the results be understood independently of the constraint imposed by the 'pedagogical' goal of the piano étude? Remember how, in a different context, it was said that in *Jeux* the plot of the ballet was the driving force behind its formal innovations. Clearly, these different motivations for the idea of a 'composition' are related, and in both the *Études* and *Jeux* the 'anecdotal' constraint was deliberately selected and used to enhance an investigation that was felt to be inescapable.

❊ ❊ ❊

Stravinsky's thematicism, and sporadically Bartók's as well, suggests a different problem from those discussed above, in that both composers stood, deliberately or not, on the border between two sometimes antagonistic, often mutually indifferent cultural worlds. On the one hand, there was the 'erudite' world of learned culture, imbued with more or less international values and based on highly individualised works; on the other, a traditional world of oral tradition, anonymous and preserved as part of specific social functions. It is vital to inquire into social references. Everything traditional, hardy enough to have survived the industrial upheavals of the nineteenth century, or sufficiently distant to have been left practically untouched by them, indicates a sociology of delay, of non-evolution, or at least slow evolution. This corresponds to a stylistic manner that could be called 'unspoiled' or 'retrograde' – a fairly superficial description indicating a seemingly crude compositional technique that ignores numerous fields of application and uses a narrow range of vocal or instrumental techniques. And yet, far from being primitive, its specificity of scales, modes, rhythmic patterns and formal characteristics, as well as its subtlety with regard to intervals, inflections and rhythmic phrasing, are so far-reaching – and so embedded in musical language – that they thoroughly elude literal notation. The scrupulous transcriptions made by Bartók on his field trips display an over-abundance of detail that nearly obscures the legibility of the primary text. While Bartók took on this heritage in a politically inspired 'campaign', it infused Stravinsky in a more 'casual' way. He was, of course, aware of the poetic and musical value of this heritage, but he accepted it without asking the questions of an *activist*. On the contrary, part of his life was spent, if not in renunciation, then at least in flight from the grip of this environment, in favour of other allegiances that were perhaps more conscious, and certainly much less productive.

Bartók sometimes captured the reality of this traditional world in literal adaptations that are not among his best works, because a traditional form cannot be directly inserted into a composed piece with the same degree of immediacy. Moreover, one is always left with the impression of a visit, a vacation. The original text becomes a hybrid that does not truly belong to one world or the other; it has lost its necessity, its underlying function, without having found a new one to replace it. This realm of adaptation is less than convincing, for it brings out profound incompatibilities, from technique itself to the mode of expression.

A simple example will suffice to show what I mean by incompatibility. Consider the transcription of a vocal melody for piano and violin. The first – and crucial – difference is that the words have disappeared, and with them the entire melodic articulation. Secondly, the intervals were evened out when the vocality of the model was adapted to the requirements of the available violin technique. Thirdly, the melody had no accompaniment; at most, handclaps emphasised some of its rhythmic aspects. In the transcription, the melody is *harmonised*, provided with a scaffolding of unnecessary chords. Moreover, the composer *inflates* it with new harmonic apparatus that is mismatched with the melody's interval content. Fourthly, if it is a song about work, or ceremonial, only an excerpt will be presented, three or four verses at the most, to avoid the monotony of literal repetition and fit it into the conventional framework – duration and form – of a piano and violin 'piece'. Work songs, associated with crafts, are used to help and accompany gestures through repetition, and are in fact designed to be supportive, or narcotic, or distracting: repetition becomes an active agent of work. Listening to repetition that has lost its purpose becomes tedious: one is obliged to abridge it, and the strophic form thereby loses all its meaning.

Since direct transcription is so unconvincing – its value is, at best, documentary – questions are raised about its place in a 'learned' cultural world, its historical evolution, identity, *progressivity*, and its various social functions. There was a similar, less serious problem for classical composers who used dances of various kinds. But even in the symphonic tradition, and even in the baroque era, dances remained somewhat marginal, reserved for specific items such as the minuet or scherzo and similar. Large-scale baroque overtures, like symphonic movements, do not make use of that kind of thematicism. However, the rise of musical nationalism would make these problems ever more urgent and unsettling.

As far as Stravinsky is concerned, we can consider four works in which the problem appeared and was resolved, in different ways in each case. I will consider them in chronological order, even though we would not necessarily place them in that order if we were unaware of their dates of composition. They are: *The Rite of Spring* (1913), *L'Histoire du soldat* (1918), Symphonies of Wind Instruments (1920) and *Les Noces* (1914/1917–23). There are in fact contemporaneous compositions by Stravinsky in which this problem is completely eluded, the most typical being *Zvezdoliki* (*The King of the Stars*, 1912) and the *Three Japanese Lyrics* (1913), probably the two least 'Russian' of the works from the 'Russian' period.

As for *The Rite of Spring*, Debussy's quip about 'primitive music with all the modern conveniences' describes with precise humour the confluence of trends that lent the work its basic power.[2] From the rhythmic point of view alone, the work could not have existed without being infused with this folk tradition that is non-existent in Western art music. And when I speak of rhythm, I am thinking not only about the rhythmic thematicism locked into repeated chords whose accents are the only developmental elements, but more about the phrasing – in other words, the melodic segmentation that is inseparable from the rhythmic conception. Stravinsky has been criticised for his melodic invention, for having ideas that are unduly short, for not developing them, for doing little other than repeat them over and over again. In fact, the conception of melodic phrasing in *The Rite*, for instance, is based on limited scales with simple elements that are ideal for rhythmic variation. A phrase will acquire a quality of respiration through its prolonged or foreshortened repetition, through extension and abbreviation, or else by being interpolated with other elements. The static quality of the intervallic configuration contrasts with a rhythmic instability that is nevertheless very carefully grounded in distorted symmetry. The repetitive formal framework implies a certain symmetry of reprise, response and logic, but when these repetitions occur, they are made to deviate from their original profile through rhythmic alteration that adds, removes or interpolates one or several notes, so that symmetry is perceived in surface dissimilarity.

One of the chief characteristics of Stravinsky's melodic development, to be found from the very beginning of *The Rite*, is the deepening of the dialectical, simultaneous opposition of immobility and variance. He sets up different, completely static rhythmic strata, each occurring in cycles of different length, so that their common periodicity is the result of the multiplication of their individual periodicities. Superimposed on this is a variable periodicity made up of contractions, extensions and interpolations. The 'Procession of the Sage', the 'Dance of the Earth' and the 'Sacrificial Dance' all adhere to this plan. Stravinsky's thematicism is actually *conceived* as a function of repetition.

Moving on to *Les Noces*, written immediately after *The Rite*, this technique is brought to its peak of effectiveness. For while the themes of *The Rite* are tied to a single segment of the work – some could even pass as signals from one segment to the next – those of *Les Noces* are conceived in global fashion, infusing the whole work. And beyond that, their most important quality, and also the one that is most striking within the Western tradition, is that each theme is in a simple proportional relationship with all the others. The different tempi that govern the entire work, in a basic relationship of 2:3:4, control the thematicism. Theme and speed – or if you prefer, theme and temporal density – are connected by a formally decisive arithmetic relationship. In *Les Noces*, incidentally, one finds the beginnings of a form of development that would go on to be exploited in greater depth, through the use of more divergent material, in the Symphonies of Wind Instruments. It is a sectional form in which each thematic group preserves its identity and develops internally, isolated from the development elsewhere that is equally autonomous. This autonomy is brought out very clearly because these segments recur in the same general register, with the same instrumental forces. This results in interlocking developments conducted independently, in and of themselves. The form reflects the conception of how the theme itself is elaborated and taken to its ultimate conclusions: form and theme have exactly the same laws of formalisation.

In the Symphonies of Wind Instruments, a great distance separates the *origin* of the themes from the thematicism itself. The instrumentation – classical orchestra with strings, timpani and percussion omitted – matches the 'abstraction' of the ideas. The reference point here is above all learned cultural tradition: the choice is unambiguous, yet *Les Noces* reveals Stravinsky's dilemma of being caught between two cultures, even in instrumentation. We know how much he hesitated before finding the right instrumental forces to give the work its definitive form. Naturally, not only cultural considerations were in play here, but also Stravinsky's reflection on the ensemble of sounds, and above all the crucial *respiration* of the choral and solo voices. To support the latter, Stravinsky imagined a relatively conventional 'European' orchestra, supplemented by percussion. He then thought to embrace the technology of the day, as well as a folk instrument – thus considering a player piano and two cimbaloms, not to mention a harmonium and several percussion instruments. These doubts reveal the antinomy of *origin* and *abstraction*. Since the origin of his thematicism was apparent, yet he created forms and formal complexes of a kind that extended this thematicism independently of those origins, a definitive choice of instrumentation was still required to resolve the contradictions in his musical thinking. In the end, the solution leaned towards 'abstraction': the piano, that black-and-white,[3] one-dimensional instrument reflecting a whole cultural tradition, but here used for its percussive value, its 'austere' timbre, and therefore historically displaced. The implications of this use of the piano are underscored by different types of percussion: chromatic instruments (xylophone, crotales, timpani) and those that are unconstrained by pitch (cymbals, snare drum, bass drum, etc.). This is no longer some picturesque reference, but an enlargement of the concept of sound. *Les Noces* marks a temporary equipoise between the two cultures that formed Stravinsky's reference points. One has only to compare this work with *Renard*, for example, in which everything from the thematicism to the instrumentation leans in favour of a direct, folkloric influence, to see how much, despite all the allusions, references and interferences, Stravinsky's thinking was directed towards making global and generalisable categories from highly connotative elements.

After that culmination, he would go on to find very differently oriented references. Beginning with *L'Histoire du soldat*, 'abstraction' is drawn from disparate sources that encompass Russian folklore, Protestant chorales, 'modern' dances such as ragtime and the more traditional military march. Based on these models, interpreted as compositional archetypes, themes are forged in such a way as to be able to respond to their creator's manipulations. It is often said that Stravinsky recomposes or elaborates his themes from pre-existing models while preserving his own originality, lending his 'borrowings' an inescapably Stravinskian profile, but the reason for this has never really been explained. Perhaps the deepest reason is their suitability for the particular structure of his thematicism. It suffices to study the March that opens *L'Histoire du soldat* to understand this. No march has ever had a rhythmic profile like this one, because each of its elements obeys a unique rhythmic pattern: a periodicity of groups of four measures, a construction based on rudimentary tonal functions. If we turn to the military march in the first act of *Wozzeck*, we see that Berg respected all of those elements, including the march/trio/march form. He enriched the harmonic relationships, emphasising and exaggerating them to the point of a kind of caricature, but the characteristics were preserved. Stravinsky's use of this archetype takes the elements one by one; he isolates and then recomposes them according to his own logic. Of course, he takes the same basic pattern of *one, two, one, two*, but this no longer determines the rhythmic structure. The pattern constitutes *one* element, an *ostinato*, a fixed layer that perception will not necessarily take as a guide. From the beginning, the ostinato is clearly presented as extracted from the thematic element, while coinciding with it in the simplest relationship of tonic–dominant. This tonic–dominant relationship is incidentally characterised by its status as a quotation, and its independence from the melodic phrases. The ostinato is written as a *connotation* of the tonic–dominant relationship, not a real one. Effectively, it has only distant affinities and no constant harmonic or rhythmic relationship with the melodic phrases, nor does it have any sustained affinity with their formal organisation. It remains inert, invariant, detached from its context, providing its primitive pulse to the whole, separating, returning, animated by its elements rather than any functionality. Above this ostinato, the melodic phrases live their own individual rhythmic life and assume their own periodicities based on irregular metre, on the expansion, contraction and interpolation of rhythmic cells – in short, on the things we have already seen crystallised in *The Rite of Spring*. The *fixed* rhythm of the ostinato is sometimes in phase with this *mobile* rhythmic language, sometimes displaced: the two rhythmic features are therefore

sometimes in a consistent relationship, sometimes unrelated and sometimes contradictory. The principle of the march is set in quotation marks,
or parentheses. The techniques are dissociated, and the separate components live a life of their own. While Berg's military march is a *real* one that
could be used for a parade, Stravinsky's is a *virtual* march in which the
regularity of the steps is undermined by the formal mobility of the cells
and periods. Berg adapted himself to the archetype; Stravinsky adapted
the archetype to his musical language.

The various archetypes were adapted to a different extent, and with
various degrees of success – or, I would say, various degrees of perver-
sion! I will not spend time describing the extent of this success. Suffice
to say that the Waltz remains more anecdotal and superficial than the
'Triumphal March of the Devil', for example, and that the beginning and
ending of the Ragtime are less interesting than its central section. The
musical result is more interesting when its thematicism has truly been
transformed – that is, strongly diverted or, rather, made to drift away
from its profile and original functions.

In my opinion, the reason for Stravinsky's 'neoclassical' weakness is
that he was not able to master elements that stylistically outshone his
use of them, because, contrary to what people thought, he had not
'abused' them *enough*. The incompatibility between his own thematic
concept and these models is obvious. Such incompatibility was possibly
intentional, but we cannot be sure. We can view it as a desire to correct uncertainty and gain historical credibility. Whatever the motivation,
here again there was an attempt to isolate elements. As long as one was
turning to a different kind of culture – so-called folk culture – or as long
as one used relatively crude archetypes such as marches and dances,
this could be achieved relatively simply, since these elements did not
offer any *formal* resistance or stylistic incompatibility. When Stravinsky
turned to classical literature, an individual cultural phenomenon, the
task was much more difficult. With respect to the *Dumbarton Oaks* concerto, I can easily call it the seventh Brandenburg Concerto because
the composer took not merely some archetype as his model, but a work
from a particular, well-defined musico-historical period, at a specific
point in its stylistic evolution; a work whose compositional language may

belong to the baroque era, but whose composer had distinct individuality. Stravinsky's own thematicism had too weak a hold on it; there is simply no appropriation. The model does not hover in the background; rather, it is more powerful than its adaptation and remains the reference for what amounts to an arrangement. In this sense, *Pulcinella* expresses such a relationship more clearly, in the way that a stage director can enlighten us about a work by introducing unlikely parallels, by causing a kind of short-circuit. In every other case of 'neoclassicism', the results are hindered by a lack of profile compared with the cultural model; it is an unequal contest on a sloped playing field. In order truly to harness the power of the classics, you have to dig deeper, reach down to what made them behave in a particular way, to understand and to analyse their approach. It is not enough to observe the results and to *dispossess* them; creativity does not have sufficiently powerful thematicism at its disposal, but becomes spent, though referencing and distorting, no longer able to forge material only for itself. 'Ironic' readings are tiresome. They presuppose a cultural complicity, of course, one that offers a kind of class solidarity, or the solidarity of a cult with its arcane knowledge; but very often this ironic pleasure amounts to this complicity, or privilege, which is surely very impoverished compared with the creation of new values.

Bartók did not have to deal with these problems, probably because his geographical position kept him at a distance from the 'everyday' concerns of musical fashion. Of course, in the first movement of the Piano Concerto No. 2 there are indications of the back-to-Bach trend, but these amount more to traces or fleeting echoes than to deep, stylistic markers. And yet he too experienced tensions on his own ground. What is most striking to me is that the dichotomy exists within one and the same work, and that he adopted it as an organising principle, a little like Berg and the twelve-tone row. We are reminded of the organisation of the *Lyric Suite*, with its alternation, both within movements and from one movement to the next, of free and strict techniques. Similarly, we can note Bartók's alternation between absolutely original and borrowed thematicism, or perhaps thematicism that has transcended its original source of inspiration. Take the *Music for Strings, Percussion and Celesta*: the basis of the first movement, a fugue, is individual and *abstract*, using almost entirely chromatic relationships. In contrast, the finale is a mostly folkloric movement, directly inspired by dance rhythm. The second movement is inspired by certain 'folk' sources, though in this case strongly filtered and based principally on distinct elements that are nevertheless sufficiently distant from their origin to be suitable for advanced compositional techniques from the learned tradition. The third movement returns to individual thematicism, to a very personal vocabulary, in which local touches are suggested by a few rhythmic figures and characteristic melodies. Each movement is modelled at a certain distance from its original source, which locates it within the overall form of the work. Of course, since there are thematic connections between one movement and the next, rather than heterogeneous contrasts, this creates motion towards or away from a point of equilibrium. This can be seen, for example, when the chromatic fugue from the first movement is quoted at the end of the fourth: it is transformed according to a 'local' mode – 'disabstracted', as it were, by taking on a coloration that melds with the rest of the movement – whereas when quotations of this same fugue subject are used at joins in the third movement, they remain, on the contrary, chromatic, in their 'abstract' version. The same is true of the Sonata for Two Pianos and Percussion, between the different sections of the *Miraculous Mandarin*, and so on. In short, Bartók's output describes a scale of influence that supports thematicism according to its distance from, or proximity to, its cultural origins and sources.

1 Marcel Proust, *Jean Santeuil*, trans. Gerard Hopkins (London: Weidenfeld and Nicolson, 1955), p. 132.
2 In a 29 May 1913 letter to André Caplet: 'Le Sacre du Printemps *est une chose extraordinairement farouche . . . Si vous voulez: c'est de la musique sauvage avec tout le confort moderne!*' In Claude Debussy, *Correspondance 1872–1918*, ed. François Lesure and Denis Herlin (Paris: Gallimard, 2005), p. 1,609.
3 The French original is '*en blanc et noir*' rather than the more idiomatic '*en noir et blanc*', referencing Debussy's work of the same name for two pianos, a work that Boulez performed with Yvonne Loriod at, among other places, the Donaueschingen Music Days in 1956. *Les Noces'* ultimate instrumentation also included four pianos.

9

Athematicism, Identity and Variation
(1984–85)

It was the nineteenth century that passed down to us the notion of *theme* as we now generally understand it: not only as source of musical discourse and development, but also as bearer of symbolic, anecdotal, metaphysical or any other kind of meaning. But even within this widely accepted idea of theme, there is strong disagreement about its formal integration into the elaboration of a work.

Although *absolute music* in a way marked the triumph of the subordination of different formal components to the structural whole, anything that interfered with the specifically musical substance – especially theatre (opera, ballet) or poetry – tended towards the emancipation of the formal framework from its thematics. In this sense, influences external to music have come powerfully to composers' aid to free them from a pre-established path, to liberate them from the very visible constraints of strict reprise and repetition, and to illuminate a notion of form that is more emancipated in the moment. And yet, what can give coherence to musical discourse? Clearly, the idea of *theme*.

As the concept of form evolved, the notion of theme also had to change, since there is a complete interdependency between the way the theme is organised, the way it unfolds, and its function of breathing life into the necessary formal framework; all the more so since these two notions are linked by the evolution of musical language. Thus, from the moment that musical language diverts from its traditional field of action, theme plays a crucial role by spreading out in two opposite directions that go on to generate a conflict of choice, of options, but also of applications and techniques.

The dilemma is as follows: we find hyperthematicism in the lowest level of relationship, infrathematicism in the highest. How can that be? The theme can be both a hypertheme and an infratheme. Hypertheme means that all figures are directly deduced only from the intervals of a given underlying figure, and from *nothing* else. Infratheme means that the given underlying figure will have no thematic characteristics other than its intervals: neither rhythms, nor even durations, much less progressions, or accentual or dynamic emphasis. Everything therefore happens solely at the level of the interval, isolated from any concrete context; theme is reduced to pure, disembodied intervals ready for manipulation and transformation. The composition is deduced entirely from a series of such intervals – one could say the series is arbitrary, but its cardinality is determined by how many tones are implicit in the relevant intervallic space. Whether constructed from semitones or quarter-tones, this intervallic series excludes, in principle, any repetition. Its application to other domains is simple, and the principle of non-repetition is its only rule, given that rhythms, figures and associations are free from any other restriction. The notion of strict counterpoint is thus devoid of any challenge, or else is reduced to the most fundamental, if partial, level of a certain form of *cantus firmus*.

The way in which Schoenberg originally established this rule did not permit any exceptions and – in order to respect a notion of unity that, it must be admitted, was rather superficial – all the material of a work had to be deduced from a single series. This is to say that ultrathematisation was brought to a point of extreme rigour, just as infrathematisation had been. The original series had no profile other than its 'abstract' intervals.

Such an absolute conception, one so far removed from musical *reality* and from material and its capacity for development, could not have held up for long. One cannot set about developing a musical idea without having means other than intervallic relationships at one's disposal. These relationships are at once too restrictive, in the literal choices that they impose at every moment, and not restrictive enough, because they ignore all other categories of sound material. At every moment, rhythmic formulas, harmonic relationships and formal connections then need to be invented, and these have nothing to do with the intervallic hierarchy in any coherent and continuous way. They are superimposed on this hierarchy and sometimes corroborate it, but more often they conceal or destroy it. The series in raw form solves no problems, not even the problem of intervals, strictly speaking, unless functions that can order them at a higher level are discovered and applied.

Thus, alongside the series – both infrathematised and hyperthematised – the concept of theme can develop in either direction, and also simultaneously in both. Given the musical tradition that serialists fully and consciously adopted, they tended to re-establish rules of deduction that were less crude and more perceptible. An interval stripped of any connection to any other dimension possesses nothing with which to generate unity. It can belong to a unified whole, but it is powerless even to indicate unity in and of itself. Moreover, it fails to initiate any other level of perceptual activity. The ear easily gets lost, since no ordering principle can be deduced from the collections of sound it takes in, nor is there any rule governing such assemblages, in the literal sense of that word.

The first *'infra'* concern is therefore to segment this amorphous set of intervals to create subsets, particularly 'noteworthy' ones so that they can be recognised by family. One uses primary transpositions to reduce the field of action and suggest correspondences between fields with the potential to be enlarged into formal correspondences. This struggle occurs above all in the areas of identity and identification. In an amorphous set of intervals, perception has nothing to latch on to, and no such set can be distinguished from any other. The underlying need is therefore to create potential shapes within this amorphous set. Accomplishing that means an early stage of recognition even *before* it is used. This is an extension of infrathematisation. The elements are already linked by a connection ready to be highlighted at the moment of potential use. This is a long way from rules of harmony letting us immediately identify objects and their functions within a given hierarchy (but is there any reason literally to return to that?). And yet we get closer to identifiable objects as we endow them with identificatory function. Very often, an amorphous series of twelve tones is reduced to three- or four-note segments, which seems to be the ideal number for identification. Two notes form only a single interval, which is much too general to be identified as anything other than a basic combinatorial element. With two or three intervals, that is to say three or four notes, perception can get its bearings – more so with three than four – and recognise the families. Fields of interaction, of connection, are thereby defined independently of any figuration as such, but are able very strongly to condition it. Recognition relies on subsets specified by a series of determinants. This is still only an infrathematisation, but of a particular kind. It is an intermediary step between the completely amorphous world of the series and a strict morphology.

That is the way in which composers can play with such virtual objects, initially by remaining within the limitation of pitch and not touching on other domains. Take the case of three notes. These three notes could appear in temporal succession (without duration, if we restrict this discussion to succession). Thus, the perception of the order of appearance will be important: it will become the fundamental element for variation in the characterisation of any horizontal version. Similarly, depending on the families, one of the three notes used could be exchanged for a different pitch, establishing different degrees of similarity and difference. In opposition to succession stands simultaneity, which creates particular sonic entities through superimposition. It is in this domain above all that the opposition between virtual and real intervals can be explored. Similar objects will be connected when identical real intervals are applied to different pitches; or in a symmetrical case, objects can be organised according to the same absolute pitches and the same virtual intervals! They will be objects of the same family, with the same origin, but with a different appearance. It can be seen that from very simple, infrathematic notions, we can organise a universe of objects that depends on variations of a hierarchy and that is ready to take on multiple functions in the composition itself. In other words, from a purely amorphous state, we have in a way arrived at 'pre-compositional' material.

And yet this 'pre-compositional' material has been prepared only on a single plane, that of pitch. It has formal potential, but characteristics from other domains would need to be added to transform it into a real object – into musical material in the strict sense, usable for composition. I must emphasise the distance that separates this preparatory set of harmonic or melodic potentialities from sound objects that will become actual thematic entities, with a sufficiently defined profile to be, on the one hand, irreplaceable and unique and, on the other, susceptible to the derivation, variation and proliferation indispensable for musical development. One therefore searches for identity and identification at the same time as seeking the resources that are appropriate for exploiting it. It is here that contradictions cast doubt on the soundness of the infrathematic method.

Totally amorphous material can thus be transformed into precompositional material through selective procedures, but solely with respect to pitch. The definitive profile of this basic material will arise from its organisation into themes, motives and other thematic figures. But on what criteria? Quite simply, the same criteria as before (at least for Berg and Schoenberg; the case of Webern is more complex and exemplary, as we shall see). Starting from infrathematic material, themes are created through 'spontaneously' added rhythmic figures; by organising, with varying degrees of 'spontaneity', phrases that will classically comprise antecedents and consequents through melodic and harmonic contrast – in short, by taking up the ingredients and attitudes that characterised an earlier stage of musical language. A completely traditional thematic conception survived the vagaries of the very facts of musical language. I spoke of the 'spontaneity' of the control of more or less 'predetermined' pitch material by other criteria, be they rhythm, phrasing or harmony. The spontaneity of this way of superimposing methods is in fact only apparent, since it assumes that composers have historical memory at their disposal: they use methods provided by manifold cultural references in order definitively to shape material that, on genetic characteristics alone, would not have had sufficient power to organise a work.

The weakness, or even contradiction, between this fairly rigid and incomplete, or rather insufficient, first stage and the level required by composition is easy to discern. But a mode or, more generally speaking, a scale has no characteristics that are more specifically compositional either. Ultimately, this, too, is a series of amorphous intervals that require, indeed demand other criteria in order to be transformed into material suitable for composition. The difference between a scale and a series is that a scale implies functions organised within a hierarchy that not only yields identifiable objects, but also confers on these objects the potential to interact, to be interrelated. The series also contains identifiable objects, but they have no common function other than complementarity within chromatic space. One uses a semblance of functionality in order to organise the objects among themselves, but this pseudo-functionality is carried over from an alien universe. Whether a consequence or a cause of this derivation of functions, musical forms are also borrowed from the 'classical' world to provide a formal framework developed by analogy with generative techniques. Methods of composition that use *parody*, in the literal sense of the term, can be observed. The more the recourse to pre-existing forms is obvious, the stronger the divergence will be.

It is apparent, and logical, that Schoenberg's more 'informal' period – that of *Erwartung* – was a time when the basic hyperthematisation offered by the series had not yet been codified. The elements of vocabulary are specified by criteria sufficiently vague and flexible to adapt to the instant discoveries of his ever-changing thematic creativity. One therefore does not find important figures or groups of figures that, through deduction, would provide a way of developing and articulating musical discourse. There are families of chords, so to speak, constructed on intervallic similarity. The relationship between melody and harmony is rooted in direct chromatic complementarity. In short, development from one element to the next is directly modelled on dramatic expression. Could this formal creativity, in constant renewal, be preserved without the support and protection of control from outside musical vocabulary? This is the question that Schoenberg urgently confronted, and he resolved it by turning away from what no doubt seemed to him an anarchic situation, intolerable except in a period of transition, or when working with content more dramatic than musical. Schoenberg then used the material suggested by the series by superimposing it with a formal thematic grid that corresponded to the material only in certain basic elements; sectionalisation dissipated the absence of morphology and helped construct the elements of a vocabulary.

But there was also a more adequate and subtle means of using the series as a process of thematic generation. It has often seemed surprising that Webern focused so intensely on rigorous composition and strict counterpoint. After all, each of his serial works – the late ones even more than the earliest – makes use of all kinds of canonical techniques and keeps strictly within its extremely narrow limits. He understood – consciously or not, it matters little, though I think that this intuition slowly solidified in the rationality of practice – that the whole serial system is based on the coincidence between thematisation and the preparatory stages that provide the framework for it. Since all the material had to be deduced from the prime form, the only way to use this method was to enlarge it, from its basic state to the most advanced stages of elaboration. Everything and nothing in his works is a theme. There are no longer figures whose origins can be located in a succession of amorphous intervals to which external characteristics are added. The thematic figure is the amplification of characteristics 'found' in the row, highlighted by other parameters that directly corroborate it.

I just said 'found' in the row, but it is obvious that these characteristics were not 'found', but can be systematically exploited because they were already available, because the structure of the row is what makes all its applications possible, and this structure was devised to spawn these applications as well as entail them. Hence the importance for Webern of intervallic structure in the twelve-tone row. He was minutely obsessed with the conception of sets that can be divided into characteristic subsets displaying a number of symmetries. For him, composition begins with the composition of an intervallic universe. In other words, he avoids any amorphous aspect of the series in order to confer upon it, on the contrary, strong structural components that can *immediately* generate coherent thematic figures, without needing to impose other criteria. Dimensions other than pitch – such as duration, timbre and articulation – are already implicit in the initial stage of the creation of material. When he gives pride of place to three- or four-note figures that reduce the origin of the series to a single thematic object, highlighting the figure implies the following:

(1) A durational cell that corresponds to it.

(2) A specific timbre that provides it with perceptual coherence.

(3) A type of articulation that characterises or typifies it.

(4) A dynamic level, or profile, that particularises it within the scale of intensities.

Other characteristics could be added, of course, such as registral density, intervallic similarity, symmetry, etc. These various dimensions are linked to the direct expression of the structural content of the series. Thematics then consists of exposing, and highlighting for perception, the functional characteristics of basic material. There is no contradiction here with the other levels. On the contrary, everything is explication: each dimension is explained by another. In the thematic *exposition*, the dimensions corroborate and mutually confirm each other.

Development will be founded rather on the contradictions that the system can be made to take on: instead of having one dimension confirmed by another, they can be made to conflict with each other. Take as an example the partition of the row into four cells of three notes. If this partition exclusively highlights symmetry, this will be abolished or concealed during the developmental stage. This can happen in two ways. One option is to create different partitions of the set, even losing sight of numerical symmetry, since subsets of four, five or seven notes are used, in systematically irregular fashion; these asymmetrical segments also reduce the number of timbres, creating additional ambiguity. Alternatively, the original partition into three-note cells can be displaced in such a way that the intervals are altered and symmetry disappears, although an outline of the figure remains. Many methods are available to the composer for confirming the structure of the basic material or straying away from it. Thematic creativity thus means directly exploiting the resources implied by the basic material, established precisely as a function of the potentialities that one wishes to find in it.

But why the persistence and pervasiveness of canonical writing? Here again, it must be seen as the consequence of rigorous reflection on ways to elaborate material that is at once amorphous and yet conveys structure. As long as there were harmonic functions – controlling functions – a free dimension was possible. But when these disappeared, the only resource available was strictly maintaining the original intervallic specification. No part can be more or less strict than another, but all components of the polyphony must have the same origin and adopt the same generative processes. What Webern considered to be the logical consequence of the hyperthematisation of his basic material was the hyperthematisation of *all* his compositional material. The system therefore has no breaches: everything is composed *in relation* to the basic system.

But the one fundamental function that is missing, at least in the organisational logic, is harmonic control. This often exists in latent form, but it is imposed externally – and it fundamentally depends on obeying the rule of complementarity of chromatic space, which means avoiding octave doublings.

One of the methods of external control is to fix the entire system of pitches. Within a certain time frame, all pitches will be produced on a strictly invariable grid. Their distribution will be decided empirically and will preserve the unity of the figures suggested by the row and the most significant transpositions that reflect it directly. Another method is to preserve a fixed intervallic relationship between the different series of which the polyphony is comprised. This interval is not perceived as such when there is a canonical dimension in which horizontal dominates vertical perception. But when two lines are directly superimposed, and coincide rhythmically, their intervallic separation is perceived as an essential dimension. The harmonic relationship will therefore be whatever connects the different lines and subordinates them to the upper line.

This concern for deductive unity explains the originality of Webern's reflection on the new hierarchy. It is significant that a double analysis can be applied to these works, a characteristic that implies a certain ambiguity. For he composed and explained his own works according to classical formal criteria, such as sonatas, rondos and overtures . . . At the same time, another explanation is superimposed that can do perfectly well without the first one, except for the fact that it divides the form into sections, running counter to the historical tendency to develop non-recurrent, ever-expanding forms. Works based on less strict codes for the development of material were certainly freer formally, more flexible, more 'evolving'. The rigidity of the code in the use of material necessarily generated a formal rigidity that does not strike us today as the most necessary or desirable quality. And yet what remains extremely satisfying – even within a narrowly defined range – is the organic correlation of the generation of material, its exploitation and its shaping, not to mention its

expressive power. This correlation does not bring any historical handicap, and no model is implied in any of the direct references conjured
up by memory. The logical use of material suggests original thematic
expression. Any references were implicit, or sufficiently general to constrain neither the composer's nor the listener's memory, as was the case
with Schoenberg or Berg. In fact, this has little to do with expressive
power in general, since it can very well be based on something other
than the purity of the relationship between language and expression:
this can just as well result, unstably, from the variability of function and
relatedness between form, language and vocabulary. But this happens at
a different expressive level and is based on referents, rather than on the
value of creativity alone.

¤ ¤ ¤

From the models and favoured forms of reference mentioned above,
it would seem that laws arose that were capable of helping us organise
a wholly new sound world. There was no tinkering or tampering with
functions, but rather a fundamental stocktaking. We could not stop mid-
stream; we had to continue investigating and extend this to what we
then called 'all the components of language', not just pitch alone. What
accounts for this urge to amplify and extend ultrathematisation's field
of application? It is a desire for methodological unification, for it seems
contradictory to be so rigorous in one aspect of thematic construction,
pitch, and to leave the others to intuition or close analogy.

When we look at, for example, rhythmic organisation in the Second
Viennese School, it follows rules (of varying degrees of rigour) only when
figures are directly connected canonically. Rhythmic figures then follow
rules of repetition, diminution and augmentation, adopted from a much
earlier stage of musical language. They were not created to produce
anything new. When Berg developed the principle of *Hauptrhythmus*,
of *Monoritmica*, he was applying the principle of the passacaglia to
duration, creating durational ostinatos but dissociating them from pitch
figures. A rhythmic figure can reveal rhythmic and contrapuntal structures, but can also ignore them, or even conflict with them by creating a

fundamental contradiction between pitch and duration. However, even at a very elaborate, rationally organised level, a profound difference can be observed. The rhythmic means of organisation used by Berg or Webern is not amorphous material but figures or cells. When Webern uses durations in the Variations, op. 30, as a way to inscribe the pitch series into time, he is giving the four-note cell a profile. Through these durations, the cell becomes a thematic figure. The sequence of these four durations does not exist 'in and of itself', but purely as a function of its role in thematic coordination. Incidentally, this cell will be manipulated in order to evolve within the limits of total metrical recognition and the loss of perceptibility caused by the displacement of accents, by contractions and expansions, by the introduction of breaks – in short, by all the manipulations that are part and parcel of thematic development.

Two conclusions can be drawn at this point:

(1) The theme is fundamentally malleable material that can range from the most explicit characterisation to the reduction of amorphous components, thereby losing the advantages of having its own profile but gaining flexibility that permits infinitely more varied applications. The state is no longer provisional transition, but rather permanent variability, the consequence of which is the inscription of a work within a universe of perpetual becoming.

(2) The overall organisation cannot let the components of language develop in a state of isolation and mutual passivity. Optimally, the divergence between extreme rationality and free intuition creates a conflict, while in the worst case it creates a lack of unity that is unhelpful for our overall understanding.

Seen from the distance of some decades, these consequences can be summarised in all their generality. At the time, this was not exactly the case. The Viennese composers' rhythmic practice seemed simply to have lagged behind that of Stravinsky or Bartók, in which the metric conception, the development of rhythmic cells, was much more than a few additions imposed on an 'outdated' system. In Stravinsky's thematicism, for example, since melodic and harmonic entities are frozen onto a fixed grid, rhythmic development assumes the most important (and sometimes the exclusive) role. Rhythmic thematicism takes on great importance, almost acquiring autonomy from other thematic aspects, but always based on cells whose variability or invariance would animate musical discourse. Whether alternating or superimposing ostinatos, Stravinsky's rhythmic approach is by itself capable of polarising development, other dimensions being reduced to supporting roles.

✴ ✴ ✴

By observing what seem at first glance to be fundamentally contradictory modes of thought – which are, however, complementary in an important way – I began to explore the potential for common ground. In what way? In quite naively contradictory terms, I aspired at that time to a confrontation between thematicism and athematicism. It is an opposition that strikes me today, in less crude terms, as fundamental to the very idea of development.

I will explain what I mean through a concrete example, and I am able to do it more clearly today than I would have at the time. I would like to consider my *Sonatine* for flute and piano of 1946. The goal was to adopt the formal plan of Schoenberg's First Chamber Symphony; with other stylistic means, obviously, but also with other ways of organising form. As in the Schoenberg, there are the four traditional movements: an initial Allegro, preceded by an introduction; slow movement; repeated Scherzo with Trio; and finally a Presto finale, with a coda. The plan so far was as orthodox as could be, in relation both to the classical sonata and to Schoenberg's use of it. But since serialism had appeared between the model of the Chamber Symphony and my own work, it was no longer possible to think in the same thematic categories. At that time, my serial procedure was by no means strict. It was a safeguard, a compositional practice allowing me to organise melodic lines and chords with at least a basic degree of logic. Here, the series served mainly to invent a theme, in the most classical sense of that word – that is, a succession of figures and phrases making a unified whole from which more detailed elements can be derived. Thus, each movement of the sonatina had its main theme, but all were deduced from the initial theme of the first movement. The series was forgotten during these thematic manipulations; it

233

did not really have much to do with them. They were about variation of a principal theme through entirely classical procedures such as segmentation, fusion, expansion and overlap of the original elements.

In order to connect the four movements, I needed some transitions that did not have a precise thematic profile, but on the contrary offered contrast to the strongly characterised context by means of their 'vagueness'. I therefore juxtaposed thematicism and athematicism. How was this done? By reversing the priorities of musical language. Even in a complex development, the derivations of a theme preserve sufficient elements to prevent us losing sight of the unity of the thematic figures. Even when these derivations are isolated from the overall discursive context in which they originally appeared, they are fully recognisable, in isolation, as having belonged to this context. They are destined to return to the original group; their autonomy is only provisional. In the composition itself, this implies that pitch figures are identical or similar – or in any case recognisable as sharing the same profile, the same gestalt. Rhythms and intervals are connected thematically. While development can stretch this connection to the limits of perception, it is nevertheless always founded on this marriage of components. In the transitional passages which I intended to be athematic, I had to break this organic link, or at any rate not let it be perceived as such. How was this done? First, by giving priority to one of the components. Then, by selecting elements that were sufficiently neutral, sufficiently unique to be dissociated from any *collection* at all.

In this sonatina, transition was based on two *restrictions*. On the one hand, rhythm had to be the main source of organisation – the only one, in fact – through the repetition of a single, all-pervading cell: the envelope of all the other components, conveying perceptible logic. The cell was extracted from the main theme, but out of context it acquired complete neutrality. It was a *short–long* cell, as well as its opposite, *long–short*. Since this element conveyed no direction in itself, it could organise rather than stand alone. On the other hand, composing the pitches meant turning from the theme to the amorphous row. Instead of using notes from the theme, which had polarised the row and endowed it with meaning, I assigned the selection of pitches to the completely automatic application of a rhythmic grid. While the thematic intervals were dictated by the rhythmic cells, as well as organisation into phrases, here, in the name of contrast, I had reverted to atomised material, to a neutral rhythmic cell, potently non-directional, and 'amorphous', subordinate intervals.

What at the time I called athematicism is therefore based on the potential of the theme to break apart, to dissolve into undifferentiated material. But how, then, can direction or form be given to these transitions, if it is not founded exclusively on a statistical use of pitch and duration? By imposing on them what I much later called *envelopes*. Whatever organising elements of form are not structurally internal must be formally external, hence the word 'envelope'. These elements are no longer characteristic, constituent items from the vocabulary itself, such as a rhythmic cell or intervals drawn from an intervallic set, but rather features of application, placement and implementation. Thus, in the longest transition in this sonatina, both register and density serve as envelopes – not temporal density, that is, the relative speed of the cells or degree of entanglement, but rather the piano sounding thicker or thinner. At first, the rhythmic cells are 'materialised' at a rate of one note per duration. As the transition evolves, each duration is 'materialised' by a chord of two or more notes. Since the flute obviously sticks to a rate of one note per duration, the variance between flute and piano will accrue as it proceeds, due to differing densities.

From this example, we see how far thematic perception can change not only as to method, but also meaning. The characteristics of a development can migrate from within the material to the outside, from the actual substance to the envelope. This amounts to a hierarchical reversal, since it goes without saying that the envelope is nevertheless present when the thematic process employs *figurative* methods, though remaining in the background as a secondary function. When *non-figurative* methods are used, the envelope becomes, conversely, a fundamental element of construction and perception. (Those familiar with Beethoven's 'Hammerklavier' sonata are aware of the early stages of such a mode of thought: when the fugal answers and stretti are constructed exclusively from the interval of a tenth, which is itself the head of the fugue subject, the weight of this interval tends to dominate the musical discourse that it permeates and polarises.)

These were only the extreme forms of thematicism and athematicism. In the Scherzo, everything is based on a single rhythmic cell, made up of several notes, that completely reduces the material but because of its ever-recognisable profile can never become neutral and amorphous; it always remains thematic. In contrast, in the introduction, themes in the strict sense have yet to appear; instead, there are quite loosely related figures whose melody and harmony are derived from the series generating the theme, although these 'vague' figures could have been derived from any other series. It is undifferentiated material, in a state of instability, a kind of pre-material; the details still remain untouched by any precise potential.

The thematic practice in this sonatina can therefore be summarised very roughly as embodying one of four states: global thematics, exclusive thematics reduced to one cell, athematicism based on the neutrality of component elements and on the strength of the envelope, and pre-compositional athematicism.

I stress once again that these types of application are not formally decisive with regard to their thematic strictness or looseness: it is thematic procedure that specifies the formal sections. Of course, the form existed before the work; it rehearsed a particular model or class of historically validated models. Each of the components of this model corresponds to some kind of writing and, therefore, mode of expression, for expression itself is strengthened by the perceptual multiplicity generated by such means, which can be described roughly as the juxtaposition of strict and free writing.

◦ ◦ ◦

Compositional mode linked to form, musical expression linked to the variety of these compositional modes – that is the *Sonatine* for flute and piano in a nutshell, even if at the time I did not see the conclusions as clearly and schematically as I do now, especially since I did not immediately see their possible extensions and future consequences. These notions of thematicism and athematicism were paired with another compositional opposition – that between free and strict composition.

This rather ancient binary, one that is formalised even in the prelude/fugue relationship, presupposes techniques and procedures that, on the one hand, assume certain compositional *obligations*, and on the other, give free rein to compositional choice. Thematic manipulations, especially techniques that are strictly canonical rather than imitative, imply obligation. Athematic techniques offer more freedom as to both choice of components and ways of combining them. There is a continuity between the two states: for example, one of the dimensions can be strict, while another is not. In the transition between the third and the fourth parts of the sonatina, the pitch dimension is free of any strict intervallic control – its intervals are drawn from the series in an intentionally anarchic manner, the series serving in this case, as I said, as a convenient safeguard of chromatic coherence. But the rhythmic dimension is entirely subordinated to a single organic cell: the extremes of constraint or restriction combine with the most complete freedom. Compositional constraint and freedom can therefore characterise both thematic procedures and athematic ones.

In the works following the sonatina, my concerns went ever further in this direction and led me – in order to obtain richer combinations and realise the unforeseen – to a greater separation of pitch from duration, to a freer interaction between them, to using very general categories as opposed to more specific ones, to favouring one dimension over another. Thus, in my First Piano Sonata, which is in two movements, the relationship between the two amounted to a reversal of the relationship between interval and rhythm. Each movement is based on some duality: a rhythm with no perceptible pulse in slow or moderate tempo; or one made entirely from a fast pulse in irregular metre. The duality in the intervals is displayed through groups of intervals organised into thematic cells, set against intervals freely chosen from chromatic space. In the first movement, the thematic cells were to be governed by a rhythm not based on pulse, while a fast rhythmic pulse is brought out in the non-systematic pitches. In the second movement, conversely, the fast pulse was to be linked to groupings of characteristic intervals, while non-pulsed rhythm would apply to the free choice of intervals. Explained briefly, the contrast might appear rather abstract, removed from musical reality, but analysis of the score would show that (1) the procedures are in themselves more complex and less crude, and (2) the expressive personality of the parts of the sonata that follow those principles draws on many other features that cannot be described so succinctly. What I have just described should be viewed therefore only as a summary of a few compositional principles, which become specifically effective only when they cease to be merely principles – when they are modelled and modulated by musical invention working on material.

Nevertheless, in the process of searching and finding there is undoubtedly a tendency towards theorisation that is sometimes stronger than the composition itself needs. One wants to know why such-and-such a criterion or method has been chosen. Questions are asked about the techniques used. Inherited – memorised – techniques are the object of doubt and interrogation; without turning against history, one nevertheless seeks to go further than what is there at present. One of the most fundamental traits of musical evolution – if not *the* characteristic par excellence – is the urge to vary, as highlighted by Schoenberg: to avoid literal repetition, to let forms evolve towards a state of constant flux. In order to achieve this result, the thematic elements have to respond to a much stronger power of variation and wider variational field than previously. Thematic elements that are too inward-looking, where the initial figures are too strongly formulated, stand in the way of the power of variation, because they tend to impose an exclusive, inflexible hierarchy. A musical language had to be found in which the principle of variation would be embedded from the beginning. The twelve-tone row provided one of the elements of the variation principle, but the concept had to be enlarged, and in particular needed to be realistically deployed.

❀   ❀   ❀

The use of thematic elements according to a principle of variation, of renewal, implied that the components of language would be invoked independently: that they would combine with each other only after having been isolated and, in a sense, become autonomous. The divergence between rhythms and intervals helped us understand the scope of this terrain more clearly. A thematic figure itself presented an amalgam of intervals and rhythmic cells connected in several segments in order to form a phrase. The thematic figure could thus become the initial combination, the one that would be heard first, but which would not necessarily be stronger or more dominant than the rest: it would be an individual instance, naturally including 'fundamental' elements, but without imposing them as definitive. Pitch and rhythm were the components conceived separately from the start, in order to obtain greater independence in deduction and richer combinations. Exposing these two procedural areas soon meant that other categories should follow the same type of organisation. Dynamics and timbre were therefore added, at first in an entirely subsidiary way, for clarification or emphasis. And then, when an apparent logic pervaded everything and ensured coherence, the series had to be extended to all four components. We therefore arrived at a provisional specification of all the parameters, even those that to some extent did not lend themselves to this. But, in practice, it allowed for a convenient and streamlined application of dimensions that were admittedly problematic.

Even with the hindsight that gives us some perspective on the stages of these developments of the thematic concept, and their consequences for musical language, one cannot help noticing that there was at one time something of a disconnection between thematic techniques, advanced as they were, and the adoption of integral serialism; or rather, we notice the way a system that already existed for pitch was adapted to other primary parameters. The twelve-tone row and thematic creativity do not necessarily intersect. The series accommodated thematic construction – playing only a coordinating role – but conceived more rigorously, it entailed thematic development in its own structure. However, rhythms – I use that word advisedly – definitely do not respond to organisation of that type. They are already organised in cells, however short, implying a ratio of values. A rhythmic cell is not sub-material, unlike the twelve-tone row. It is pre-constituted material, albeit in embryonic form. As for dynamics and timbre, they belong to the category of the envelope, and apply to material that has already been worked out. No matter how far you may be able to take this kind of organisation, there are differences in level and quality between its various components.

In the hope of unifying these components of musical language, everything had to be made neutral, and quantities and relativities had to be established everywhere. This is why, without in fact intending it, we hit upon a concept of duration that no longer had anything to do with pulse – that is, with rhythm as such. This idea of duration was initially unconnected with any real-time meaning, paradoxical as that might seem; it was duration that no longer referred to any actual unit of time, but was calculated by a single constant.

In effect, by marshalling units of one to twelve we created twelve entities that directly related to the twelve pitches, but whose elements were unrelated except arithmetically. Even if these premises were naive, fortunately the consequences would allow for a deviation towards something concrete, which I later called smooth and striated time. Thanks to the disconnectedness of integral serialism, the concept of theme was radically transformed. One may deplore the rigidity of this potent form of organisation, and criticise the absurdity of its principles and number fetishism, but nevertheless this extreme form of control helped us to rethink thematic procedures from the bottom up, because it forced us completely to overturn our way of thinking and the very mechanisms of creativity. Not only were the elements of musical language tested anew, but ways of envisioning the formation of thematic units, the construction of developmental passages and the creation of formal structures were all radically probed.

The example of the first book of my *Structures* for two pianos can provide an idea of the work done at this time on materials taken from Messiaen's 'Mode de valeurs et d'intensités'. Here, it was not a matter, as with my *Sonatine*, of borrowing a formal idea from another composer, then organising it on completely different criteria. The material was provided intact; moreover, a work composed on this material already existed. This material gave me components of the following type: pitch, duration, dynamics and playing style – an already completely hierarchical universe. But it was used in a completely static fashion: established in one way at the beginning, it stayed the same for the entire work. In short, we did not have distinct categories but objects permanently bound to categories. Since the different hierarchies of the components had combined to form the received objects, those hierarchies were in a sense consigned to the work's prehistory, and they no longer needed to intervene. What was interesting was the statistical notion of development, which took place solely through permutations of these categories of objects.

I maintained two objectives based on that starting point:

(1) To breathe life into the generative hierarchies, to have each of them move around in relation to the others.

(2) To find formal criteria that were developmental rather than based only on a combinatorial process.

The first objective was straightforward, the second much less so.

In order to create mobility in the hierarchies, and therefore a multiplicity of objects, it sufficed to develop each of the hierarchies according to its own logic. The pitches, durations, timbral profiles and dynamics – the four specific characteristics that I had taken literally from the model provided by Messiaen – were each defined according to their own distinct networks, but each was fashioned according to the same 'transpositional' procedure. In order to obtain an object, the encounter between these four networks had to be organised. If a point belonging to a given dimension returned in a different context, it would be connected with different points in the three other dimensions. When applied to points in this way, these connections resulted in constant, 'absolute' variation. A given pitch belonging to a given series would be assigned a certain duration, a certain dynamic level and a certain profile. When belonging to a different series, this same pitch would be assigned another duration, another dynamic level and another profile. The infrathematic level, in the way it can be seen in Schoenberg's rows, was neutral with respect to the proposed object. Since it was based only on pitch, it did not include sufficient characteristics to determine a real object. This object was determined at the very moment of its composition, when rhythms, dynamics and articulations took charge of an amorphous object in order to make it into a compositional element. In the case of what we called integral serialism, the infrathematic level offered objects that were almost entirely prepared. The register could change and contribute to the definitive aspect of the created object; the duration was determined proportionately, fixed in chronometric time through the chosen speed, that is, the tempo; finally, the dynamics, defined through a relative scale, were fixed by the chosen instrument, which determined the real dynamic range. These conceptual networks therefore provided virtual relative material, and this virtual material was transformed into real objects by assigning tempo, space and timbre.

The most radical experiment involved exploiting to the maximum extent this principle of absolute variation, in which the composer intervened only in the process of fixing the real objects. Come to that, we should have defined different modes – of generation, relationships, succession and connection – and then let the networks develop on their own until their possibilities were exhausted; that is to say, until the – omitted – return of the starting point. Although in that era we could not have employed the vocabulary of computer science – which was totally unknown to musicians like us – this was nonetheless an attempt at programming, with the goal that structures would be automatically elaborated with no intervention from the composer once the programs were defined. Had this operation been successful, it would have been the ideal meeting point of the non-theme and the all-theme. 'Composition', if any was involved, would have been the strict ordering within an overall organisation of the various infrathematic elements. Perhaps this undertaking would have been 'radical', but even if we had not lacked the tools necessary to create such a program, would such an undertaking have been interesting as anything other than an exercise in testing the boundaries, by comparison with methods that are more empirical and artisanal, but at the same time more intelligent and sensitive?

It is here, in effect, that the compositional stakes lie. To let structures act upon themselves, so to speak, amounts to placing oneself in a field that is at once over- and under-defined. One can well appreciate that working exclusively with the material that I have just described, whether absolute or relative, the work of composition itself has, strictly speaking, not yet begun. If only through the density of events, through the importance of the chosen criteria with respect to others, and through the absence, deliberate omission or reduction of certain components, compositional activity demands that elements provided as raw material should be managed through methods, procedures and modes of thought that originate at a higher level of manipulation and integration. The choice of the initial material is, of course, arbitrary, but it is an arbitrariness that establishes a rational network of relationships. Once the original choice of hierarchy is made – the choice of a series, for example – the consequences of this choice will follow without any other arbitrary intervention. The material is developed according to its own internal logic. To superimpose several hierarchies – ones that apply, for example, to different categories of sounds – already presupposes a choice, but a choice that is not *the* choice: it is a preference of one choice over another, whose only necessity is the fit between the different categories. In fact, had the initial choice of connection not been exactly this one, the resulting material would, of course, be factually different, but not at all in terms of its principle. Arbitrariness is the initial click that gets all the connections working without any other form of intervention. This always remains within the sphere of the infratheme, but the more one adds other categories, the more distinctive the material becomes, the less malleable and more difficult it becomes to manipulate the material and move up to a higher level. In effect, composition's goal is a finished product that observes a trajectory. Musical form depends precisely on a guided, unique use of initial material, even though this material is generated through processes that are very close to being random, ones that tend towards infinite renewal. There is a tension, if not a contradiction, between material in a constant state of variation and form that congeals its use. Incidentally, from this stems the later appeal to *open* form that translated the need for complementarity between material that was unfinished in principle and form that only became materialised in a provisional, temporary manner, through the performer's choice, i.e. free will.

Integral serialism implied *open* infrathematic material, which was both completely inert because certain of its crucial specifications had not yet been attributed and extremely constraining because of the number of characteristics that presided over its construction. In the first book of my *Structures* for two pianos – at a moment in my own evolution when I had not yet had the idea of using open forms, of inventing a frame of action that takes the very construction of the material on which it is founded into account – I tried to resolve this contradiction between open material and closed form through recourse to globalising elements that would in a certain sense *constrain* the initial material. This is a very primitive form of thematic development, one that is incidentally independent of the literal components, and allows for certain criteria of the whole to be fixed. The play of elementary material is, in effect, completely insufficient to create a musical object, to create musical *life*, in the strict sense. Elementary objects are too undifferentiated because they result from the same type of combinations and are incapable of being perceptually striking. One needs most of all to fight against sound relationships that are undifferentiated throughout. The difficulty is in transmission: to create not only an *order* that can be perceived, but also a living, sensate organism that displays this order in a perceptible way.

I refer back to the first piece of the first book of *Structures* because it shows – in a way that could not be more visible, with no digressions – an approach that was followed in order to throw one's lot in with material, while at the same time submitting to formal constraint. Give material a chance? In a certain sense, yes, completely. The twelve-tone row is played without any alterations, always horizontally, connected with a row of twelve durations. Each segment therefore has a single durational constant. This came from a deliberate desire not to intervene at that stage. The pitch series, even if it was made more complex by its fusion with a durational one, was nonetheless used in raw form, with no segmentations, no inner characterisations: it was just played from beginning to end in the most basic way possible. But certain favoured series were used that were not left to perfectly random choice. These series elaborated on the initial one by favouring the sections and points along it that constituted points of articulation. But this is a choice that cannot be discovered in the resulting sound: it is a purely conceptual choice that is discovered through study of the score, that is in no way underscored or highlighted by any external characteristic.

The further I went, the more listening experience I had, the more I would give these substructures their own sonic *raisons d'être*, a perceptual emphasis. If the ear and one's sensations are not 'caught', spellbound by these sorts of sound signals, any conceptual effort remains futile. There is a divergence or divorce between the eye and the ear, which means that even the best intentions are in vain.

But I return to questions of formal organisation. Once the pitch and duration series are chosen, they still need to be inserted into a network that can give them the power of *development*. The first envelope was density: not density applied within the series (through which instead of a succession of points, one obtains a succession of chords or sound blocks), but density applied simply to the number of superimposed transpositions, without changing their length. When two or more transpositions are superimposed, they are placed exactly one on top of the other, so that they strictly obey the same norm. Thus, the piece has a global envelope of density that goes from a minimum of one to a maximum of six. Since this curve of densities is designed in such a way that it does not obey a regular increase or decrease, its evolution is flexible, arbitrary and unpredictable. This density of superimposed lines, combined with the pitch organisation of each series, guides the composition, if one wants to avoid octave relationships. When close together, the intersections will occur at the unison. If one pitch changes register, it has to be cancelled out by an intermediary semitone. This simple compositional rule implies that these pitches will be placed in a register according to certain constraints, but it leaves room for a sufficient amount of arbitrariness so as not to paralyse the compositional act entirely. The register becomes the relatively free result of an encounter between the chosen series and the density of superimposed layers. In order to give each series its definitive profile, and once again following Messiaen's model, dynamics and profile (or playing style) remained to be used. Recall that in Messiaen's 'Mode de valeurs et d'intensités', each note was assigned a dynamic level and a profile individually and for the entire length of the piece. Had I preserved Messiaen's usage with these superimposed layers – a usage that was valid for him, given the fixed way it was employed – it would have been impossible to recognise one series from another, one section from another, given that as close to a statistical distribution as is possible would have obtained in this realm. Thus, instead of assigning dynamics and timbral profiles note by note, I assigned them to entire series. In a given section, each series would be recognisable by this unique timbral profile and dynamic level, which would also further distinguish it from all the other ones. Each section would be recognisable through the uniqueness of its material or by superimposing the material. Each global change would signal the appearance of a new section. Finally, since these sections depended in a certain sense on having the same durational unit, I changed the chronometric dimension through the use of various tempi, which amounted to modulating the compositional density through the density of events in time.

In 'automatic' composition, a large amount of data and programs are demonstrably necessary to the organisation of a piece even as elementary as this one. In order to organise the development, I appealed to notions, not all of which were inherent to the initial material, nor derived from them, but which were invented rather over the top of the initial material that they 'constrained' and formed. These notions are sufficiently strong to be able to organise amorphous material, while at the same time being much too general to merit being called thematics. They guide form, orient perception, but they can also be described as anonymous. They can organise the composition at a certain level, but they do not focus perception and memory sufficiently because they are too general and not individualising enough.

The further I went in my work on the first book of *Structures*, the more I imposed a variety of procedures and the more I would invent different profiles to take charge of the initial material, so that it would be dominated through strong formal imperatives. Individualising characteristics are indispensable as a way to qualify this or that part of the form: the particularity of use, of compositional technique and of vocabulary. This clearly contradicts an infrathematic form that is as fixed as the integral series, being in a certain way a pre-material that is already too worked-out, compared to the applications that can be made of it. On the other hand, composition obviously cannot limit itself to superimposing horizontal segments. As I have said many times, in this type of writing the inevitable victim is the vertical – harmonic – control of all of these encounters between horizontal structures. It was therefore necessary to make progress on three fronts: to find material that was broader, more flexible and more immediately malleable than the rigorous way in which we had come to establish it; to find compositional modes that were more diversified, in which no dimension would be neglected; and finally, to find a form that could obey a defined trajectory, or else one that could make adjustments according to the various availabilities of material. In short, we had to find a discipline that would solidly establish composition within a fundamental necessity, but which guaranteed freedom of choice at every moment. We therefore had to retrieve the fundamental distinction between strict and free composition and make this technique perceptible through discernible sound events, allowing means and perception to meet in sensory identity.

❋ ❋ ❋

In the approach that I have just described, it can be seen that the notion of theme that was very strong at the beginning, since it permeated the musical text at every level, gave way to the notion of an interaction of structures according to which the sound bodies could be analysed. We went from a theme reality to virtual thematics, which explains the profound difficulty of making it perceptible, for two reasons: first of all – this is only too obvious – the tyranny of the basic organisation, or the luxury of details and excess of components that it presupposes; secondly – and not as paradoxically as it seems – the lack, in this set of initial data, of information suitable for creating a perceptible musical object. Before beginning compositional work as such, extremely onerous and rigid hierarchies hampered manoeuvrability, because instantaneous invention ceaselessly had to refer back to these totalising templates that – by virtue of their own nature – tended to impose a certain lack of differentiation in the sound relationships. Moreover, with respect to form, these onerous forms of organisation had an almost imposed tendency to obey their mode of generation – that is to say, to consider a development not as a *unique* thing with all the accidents and irregularities that this implies, but rather as an inescapable series of consequences deduced from first principles, with form being either a segment of all of the possibilities or a constraint brought in from the outside in order to circumscribe the proliferation of networks and impose a profile on them, giving a direction that they could not have had on their own. A more satisfactory resolution to the conflict between determinism and arbitrariness should have been possible by conceptualising the starting points as objects that are at once less undifferentiated and less circumscribed, because an excess of details in the initial definition led to too many difficulties in the subsequent individualisation.

The first 'reform' – and also the most urgent at the time – seemed to me, therefore, to be a revision of the very notion of the series, which had become a serious handicap to creative freedom because of the enrichment and expansion of its functions. The notion of *reference*, even of *momentary* reference, had to be fundamentally preserved from this series that organised all the functions right from the beginning. On the other hand, the notion of the series had to be made more flexible, it had to stop being that succession of points of equal importance; instead, *inequality*, so to speak, had to be re-established between the sound objects of which it was comprised, to introduce the possibility of choice, of free will in every instant, to find a possibility at last of controlled harmonic writing that does not only depend on the vagaries of the writing itself. One of the main things that bothered me about classical serial principles was in effect the weakness of its harmonic potential, and the fact that it aligned objects of constant density, made up of points of which none was truly more important than any other. The total anonymity of the notes struck me as a weakness of conception. To be obliged to obey the succession of the series from one point to the next turned out to be, for me, not an enrichment, but rather a fairly sterile constraint. Incidentally, the origins of the series were to be found in this law of succession – that is, in the extreme and radically reduced codification of a melodic line. Moreover, the succession without repeats from one point to another was not particularly varied, because it constantly engaged the entire chromatic continuum, and because the absence of variation dovetailed with total variation. But although this material had the advantage of neutrality, it did not yet have individuality. A certain neutrality therefore had to be preserved initially, while avoiding the reference to an obligatory melodic line. *Inequalities* of weight, of importance in the way objects were read had to be established, to allow for repetitions in order to prevent the elementary level of discourse from being obliged to obey rudimentary directivity.

To achieve this goal, I first established what was less a series than a collection of reference objects. This definition might not seem to be very hierarchical, and might suggest most of all a kind of willy-nilly heterogeneous collection of sound objects. In the manner that I would like to employ it now, 'object' has the much simpler sense of a *chord*, but a chord without harmonic functions defined within a given set. It is a layering of points that, in order to avoid confusion with the many notions implied by the word 'chord', I termed a *sound block*. These sound blocks were not created anarchically. At first, they were even quite strictly located within the chromatic continuum, and they were mutually complementary, although not necessarily of equal density. My series could thus be comprised of one block of two notes, one single sound, one block of three notes, etc. So much so that, as with Webern, I selected harmonic fields, but instead of presenting their notes successively, I presented them simultaneously.

You might ask what difference this makes. The differences were of two types, and these were crucial for me: in the establishment of reference series, and in the use of the objects with which they supplied me. With transpositions of linear series, density obviously never varies, and although special figures, regions and segments can be found, either in identical or permuted form, or containing a certain number of common notes and other different ones, these figures are inescapably used in the order of presentation of the series. The only way to break this linear order is to cheat – that is, to present two sounds simultaneously, for example, so that the resulting melodic line will skip a note in its horizontal presentation. (As I have already mentioned, in all of this one discerns the conflict between the purely melodic origin of the notion of the series and its application, which tends to find *all* compositional dimensions in it.)

In the deductions from these series of sound blocks, the density varied according to the sound block in which the deduction originated. If the sound block that ordered the deduction was small (something like two notes, for example), the pitch *multiplications* yielded quite thin objects, while deductions made from denser sound blocks naturally yielded very thick sound complexes, with as many as six or eight tones. The lower the density of the sound blocks, the more differentiated they were from each other. The higher their density, the more similar the sound blocks were to each other in terms of their components, along with the fact that they had more points in common than differences. A global harmonic reality was already inscribed in the material at my disposal: chords that could be grouped together by intervallic family, by similarities in their voicings and, more generally, by properties of various kinds. Between the original model and the deductions, the density evolved. Each deduction was different with respect to the model. It therefore offered a less rigid pitch substructure, one that was richer and less constraining in terms of its application. Needless to say, I felt in no way obliged to use the notes of these sound blocks simultaneously – that is, as real chords; rather I ran through the notes one at a time, making a sweep in any direction and any order. I would almost go so far as to consider each block as a simultaneous event, but one whose components time could penetrate and analyse at will. Thus, instead of having an obligatory succession, an unlimited sequence of decomposable units became available to me, whose order could be decided according to the circumstances and quality of its linkages. Moreover, given the multiplication of sound blocks with themselves, the same pitches could be found in several sound blocks, which yielded – when they were deployed horizontally – completely free and irregular repetitions and intervallic recurrences that could be used at will.

In these sound blocks that could be played vertically or deployed horizontally, I am reminded of Mallarmé's image of the fan that unfolds and then folds back up again: a musical reality that remains the same while changing its mechanism. The *accident* of the instant is preserved in the very use of its objects, the line that can be deduced finds itself enriched by overlaps and shared points, and the deep logic of succession gets all the more embedded in the reality of the musical object. Moreover, through the richness and variability of the possibilities contained within these objects, their sensory application is infinitely facilitated. The effort does not consist of forcing an excessively hierarchical material to express itself, but rather of deciphering and exploiting the full wealth of expression that it contains.

It is not surprising that the first application that I made of this device was in the third piece of Le Marteau sans maître, 'L'Artisanat furieux', an exclusively melodic piece for voice and flute: two monodies in counterpoint. There is therefore no visible harmonic association materialised by chords. Nevertheless, the whole piece is subtended by harmonic relationships both within each melodic line and between them. These blocks were 'exploited', if I can use this expression, or 'explored' by a set of rhythms that also allowed for great flexibility. There was no point-wise value as in Structures for two pianos, but rather a global definition that allowed for linking relationships without imposing any constraints within the sound block. The monody that closes the work was constructed in the same way. What became of the notion of theme in this adventure? It runs through it, but nowhere is it visibly present. The rigour and necessity of the succession continue to underlie it. What is visible, on the contrary, is the freedom of application, the flexibility of the outline, the possibility of one voice responding to another without having to submit to strict imitation. There are no literal thematics, but the sound objects can be described in similar ways. For it is precisely in the description of the objects that composition occurs, so that the underlying qualities become a reality.

Imagine an object made up of five notes, and another of three. If I describe this object with perfect regularity, I will obtain a quintuplet and a triplet. This figure will be able to provide me with a rhythmic localisation in addition to an intervallic profile. I would encounter this descriptive quality every time I used it; it would be immediately recognisable, even though it applied to different quantities each time. It is a generic property that I am able to recognise in every particular case; each one that I encounter can lead me to use this methodology. If, in another case, I divide the figure according to the principle of a group of grace notes followed by a main note, all the blocks analysed and expressed in this way will first be recognisable in this distribution and in the figure that it produces. It does not matter that in this figure the number of grace notes varies, that the direction of the intervals differs. The essential thing is that all of these types of figures are recognisable as having a similar use. A certain number of applications can be found and used, others may be discovered as you go along, and then some of them can be eliminated. It is this musical reality that circulates throughout the organisation, that creates a recognisable and perceptible wealth of material. It is a type of thematics, but of a multiple and virtual kind.

What does this approach consist of, more generally speaking? It highlights the internal relationships of material by establishing types of similarity (in the cited example, regular figures and ornamental ones), while at the same time moving away from an obviousness that is too quickly absorbed through a variation of quantity (quintuplet, triplet, many or few grace notes). *Identity and variation: this is the inescapable encounter that invention must provide.* Not real but virtual identity; the identity of principle of a family of musical objects conceived according to the same type of derivation, the same model of description. The variation of quantity with respect to the material will produce real objects that are different, even though they were derived from identical ideal objects. This use of material corresponds precisely to the notion of the matrix. The thematic components are no longer extracted from a finite object – the theme – by detaching some of its melodic, harmonic, rhythmic or dynamic properties; they are expressed in the form of principles and can be perceived only through the various 'materialisations' that they are able to carry out.

❊ ❊ ❊

In order to compose, there need to be identical methods both within and without the structural phenomenon as such. Besides thematic matrices, compositional highlighting is also founded in the notions that I have called *signals* and *envelopes*, signals being of a punctual nature and envelopes of a global one.

While the matrices determine the figures and give them 'character', signals are used to mark the points of articulation of a development, of a form. A signal can be considered above all as a mnemonic tool. The label might seem new in a musical context, but the procedure is not – far from it – and it can be found in music that is familiar to us. When Wagner has a leitmotiv return in isolation, not included in the polyphony, it is quite obvious that it functions as a signal of this type. When Bach returns to the unison after a multi-voiced polyphony, it is also a signal: one's memory immediately registers the change in the writing, its reduction to a single component. Before absorbing the thematic relationship, the most cursory perception signals a change of cycle (as is said of a motor) to the listener and alerts him to its formal evolution.

It is Berg most of all, and to a lesser extent Webern, who showed me the way to this notion of the signal. Since Berg was very fond of symbols and allegories, he felt the need to signal certain crucial points of a movement. I will mention only one example, one of the most striking, from the second movement of the Chamber Concerto. This movement is written for violin and wind instruments, and its form, roughly described, is in two parts, of which the second is the mirror image of the first. In order to signal the centre of the piece, the point of symmetry where everything turns around, the piano intervenes in what is its only intervention, playing a C sharp struck twelve times in a low register (midnight in *Igitur . . .*[1]). I would also cite the third movement of Bartók's *Music for Strings, Percussion and Celesta*, in which the different sections are separated by the sub-phrases of the fugue subject from the first movement, which is not organically blended in any other way into this development section.

A signal can encompass many phenomena, the simplest being, first of all, the isolated, single note detached from its context by a fermata, or held longer than the notes of the rhythmic environment that preceded it. It is a crude but effective alert, a tear in the continuity, a break in the temporal flow. When this break occurs in a complex context, for example, on the same note every time, then no matter how complex the environment, perception can apprehend this articulatory note without difficulty, since it almost triggers a reflex in our attention. This note can be considered as a break. If the temporal flow is less complex, or if one does not wish to stop it completely but rather to imbue it with the impression of a pivot point and, at the same time, a feeling of continuity, the presentation of this suspension can be varied by describing a curve of suspension, with varied durations and pitches that describe something like a trajectory within this suspension. Memory registers a kind of pointillistic continuity in the suspension. The thickness of this suspension can be varied, ranging from a very thin and porous partition to a thick, impervious wall – for example, a single note with no internal life, or a chord full of internal movement, or else the absence of any sound phenomena in a suspension that is totally silent. These various articulatory signals will be easily recognised as such, even – especially – when we are not very conscious (during a first hearing, for example) of what they articulate.

A signal can also take the form of a type of compositional texture. When we move from polyphonic writing to monody, this amounts to a signal. When we go from an ornamental style to strict composition, that is also a signal. In short, whether in the details of the composition or in the very principle of the compositional procedures, there is an infinite variety of signals, from the isolated, solitary signal to a family of them. In this family of signals, thematics can be developed as you go along, and what was at first a secondary signal of the pivots between types of events can become the main structure, the audible thematic unit, the previous main one being reduced to a secondary role, as in a passage from *Éclat/Multiples*. A signal is, in a sense, a reduction of thematics to a stronger element that absorbs all the others. Whether it is a fixed or variable signal, it *indicates* in a particularly strong way that it is capable of acquiring meaning on its own. A pivot thus becomes a theme; what was at first destined to alert us to significant points in the structure itself becomes structure and means of expression. As an explication of a complex structure through a reduced and more obvious phenomenon, it simultaneously displays and conceals.

While signals are punctual phenomena that mark articulations or discontinuity, *envelopes*, on the other hand, have a global character. They mark the prevalence for a time of one thematic dimension in relation to the others. This thematic element may be of a very precise nature – an interval, duration or any other completely quantitative parameter – but it can also be of a very general nature, such as register, speed, dynamics, timbre, or even texture, density, continuity, directionality – that is, parameters, or rather criteria, that are fundamentally qualitative. Thus, the theme, the thematic entity, cannot be conceived only in the form of precise figures, attached to given intervals or rhythms, but rather must be understood as more generalisable phenomena. A texture, a compositional direction, already functions as a thematic component. The texture forces creativity in a certain direction. Composition that is predominantly horizontal – contrapuntal – places emphasis on the interdependence of the different lines of which it is composed, and also on their autonomy: each line must be able to signify by itself, while its autonomous meaning must at the same time contribute to the global sense. The thematic elements – figures, cells – that comprise each of these lines must be hierarchically strong in order to contribute to the unity of the whole. In writing that is predominantly vertical – harmonic – in which the components coincide in time, the hierarchy that will take effect is one that relates the structure of the chords or sound blocks that are linked in a certain order of succession. The thematic emphasis will be placed above all on these relations of synthesis, and not on the independence of each individual element. Texture and developmental form are thus inseparable.

Among the other, less general criteria of envelopes, I would select the example of register. Register has no thematic quality in itself. It is a criterion of placement within the pitch scale; it is not, strictly speaking, linked to any invention. It is the most amorphous criterion imaginable, and yet it can be decisive in the envelope of a passage. It is, in effect, one of the broadest parameters, and because of that, one of the most immediately perceived. There is no shortage of specific qualities to describe it: indefinite components – narrow register, broad register or a register with a specific bandwidth (as with a filter); definite components – low, medium or high registers; precise components – the specific register of the notes used, the limits of the register and its evolution, etc. With this, you have defined nothing with respect to the content, but you have inscribed it within an envelope that will allow it to develop particular characteristics. It is obvious that inscribing figures or chords in a high register cannot be done in the same way as in a low register. One is required to take a certain number of natural laws into account that regulate the sound body: the chords can be more tightly voiced in the high register than in the low; a thick and fast polyphony will have no chance of being perceived in a low register; micro-intervals will not have much of a chance of being perceived in a high one, etc. The envelope of register is therefore not independent of the content; it conditions it considerably.

Other forms of envelopes are more directly bound up with the thematic concept and appeal to a dimension that is given pride of place: a rhythmic cell, for example. With respect to my own work, there are examples of this in both my oldest work (the *Sonatine* for flute and piano) and my most recent one (*Répons*). In these, it amounts to a developmental passage in which everything is subordinated to a single rhythmic cell: short–long. This figure dominates all the other hierarchies. In the case of the *Sonatine*, it is three-voiced counterpoint; in the case of *Répons*, it is an aleatoric layering of harmonic strata that depends on a global ordering. When the rhythmic cell disappears, the thematic envelope of this development disappears with it, and one is free to advance to other terrain.

The effectiveness of this way of working lies in the fact that it ensures developmental continuity while changing along with the envelope of this developmental passage. Transitions become possible by changing the importance of one envelope with respect to another. This also allows for directional moments to be set in opposition to suspended ones; for ordered, reduced moments fashioned with the help of a narrow choice of parameters to be contrasted with moments that become chaotic because of the excessive number of parameters involved.

✿ ✿ ✿

In large-scale form, in effect, order and disorder must be set in opposition; or, if the extreme limits of these two states do not confront each other, moments in which perception experiences a certain number of ambiguities before being able to get its bearings must at least be set in opposition with ones in which perception finds its way instantaneously, with no possible ambiguity. In order to move from one state to another, a change of hierarchy must be put into place – for example, by making a secondary characteristic a primary one, and vice versa. I will cite an example of this in *Éclat/Multiples*: specifically, the developmental passage that ends the work. Instrumentally speaking, it puts the group of violas in opposition to the group of resonant instruments. In the passage that immediately preceded it, the violas played a secondary role compared with the resonant instruments, which assumed the principal role, the violas being in a sense their reduction, their shadow. The last section begins with the violas spinning out multiple contrapuntal lines in order to arrive at a great antiphony, while the simple, linear writing gets supplemented along the way through grace notes to the point of becoming very ornamental, which forces the tempo to go from fast and regular to slow and irregular. Over the course of this evolution, the group of violas, which was an undifferentiated and fast-moving mass, becomes a collection of individuals, each with its own strongly highlighted personality. The groups of resonant instruments increasingly gain in importance until they become preponderant. They do not change their role over the course of this evolution; they signal the starting point of each horizontal segment that forms the texture of the violas. Since this texture at first changes rapidly via relatively short segments, although the resonant instruments do not maintain the dominance they had in the preceding section, they nevertheless remain very present through the frequency of their statements and through their sonic weight, which tends to obliterate the texture of the violas. As the contrapuntal segments become so long that they need to be organised antiphonally, their statements become more widely spaced, and although their function is unchanged, their appearance diminishes in importance, to such an extent that they retreat into the background. Therefore, through only the use of a specific thematic function, the foreground and background get reversed while moving progressively from one state to the other.

I could also note the negative components of a developmental passage, achieved through the elimination or hollowing-out of components that materialise only when they appear over the course of the text. With regard to the latter use, I will cite the piano cadenza at the beginning of *Éclat*, the piano with three pedals being the most ideally simple instrument to achieve this. One has only to depress a chord silently and to keep it held through the use of the middle pedal; it is then ready to turn up as soon as one of its constituent notes is sounded. Since this chord is the harmonic foundation of this short cadenza, it is evoked through its resonance each time the score encounters it. There will be an immediate 'revelation' when the piano is played staccato, because then the chord's notes will be the only ones left to resonate; but in a legato passage, or while using the pedal, as soon as you lift the pedal the only resonance left will be this 'hollowed-out' chord. The main thematic element – a harmonic one in this case – is never outlined as such, but it is always the consequence of more complex actions that reveal it as the underlying element.

One can also use figures that are at first inscribed in hollowed-out form and then clarified, becoming perceptible only through the retrospective action of memory. I used this method in the percussion part of the second piece of the *Notations*. It is a very simple cell of two or three single values. In the first stage, only the beginning of each sequence is indicated (by means of a highly perceptible element, a change of timbre, since each sequence begins with a different percussion instrument); in the second stage, and while still changing the timbre with each sequence, we hear the beginning of each cell; in the third stage, finally, the cells are heard in full. To the ear, the isolated points of the first phrase do not seem to be related to anything tangible or logical. One might imagine that they were random punctuations in the absence of any pulsation, in a void. The second phrase indicates to perception that there are irregular pulsations, but their distribution is not yet understood. The third phrase is totally explicit and so, retrospectively, the journey taken can be understood – like a text that is gradually decoded as you are given more and more elements with which to understand it.

I also did this when working on intervallic figures built upon absolutely fixed pitches. By omitting all of the pitches except for one, you obtain the repetition of a note that seems purely random. When you reinstate the text that had remained virtual and give it all its reality, everything gets progressively re-established into a satisfying unity. Naturally, if these perceptual labyrinths were exploited in such a rational and continuous fashion, one could not speak of artistic invention. While it is sometimes interesting to manipulate these means systematically in one's sketches, they must be used in a context that not only justifies them, but magnifies them: they need to be taken from the state of raw material to that of an elaborated work. Nevertheless, being conscious of the various forms of musical perception and knowing how to explore and exploit them enriches invention considerably. Perception through presence and perception through absence mark the limits within which lies an immense field of possibilities. Elements set in relief or hollowed out, reassured or thwarted memory – these are the poles of the listener's relationship with the work.

* * *

Our conception of form in general, and large-scale form in particular, is in effect based on reassured memory and thwarted memory – that is, on the notion of repetition and variation. On this topic, I would like to present a conception of form to which I am increasingly drawn, one that includes repetition and variation in the same impulse.

With respect to thematic material, form is one of the concepts that is most difficult to define. For a long time, form was conceived as a framework for action that is both necessary and constraining, and it is still perceived that way. We saw the reaction of a whole generation, such as that of the Second Viennese School, Stravinsky and Bartók. Over the course of their artistic existence, and despite their different vocabularies and points of view, they all, without exception, became increasingly committed to forms handed down to them by tradition. Having overhauled most musical elements, form remained the prestigious historical reference that was difficult to avoid. They appealed to it as a fetish object, an obstacle, a model. But it seems that after a period of effervescence, the different archetypes provided by history could be dispensed with. What interests us most now is not so much the period of reliance on them, but rather the moment when all these composers partly freed themselves as a result of the pressure that composition itself exerted. The non-musical circumstances that 'forced' these works to become what they are have often been mentioned: ballet plot lines (Bartók, Stravinsky); dramatic or literary source material (for Schoenberg's theatrical works and Berg's and Webern's lieder). It remains no less the case that these works rejected the formal plans of tradition, and that these plans were later recovered, for better or for worse, as part of a dubious restoration. What often puts us ill at ease when listening to these works is that their guiding plan has little in common with the tendencies of their vocabulary. How, then, can one resolve this problem of ensuring that creative invention itself, the source of any thematic entity, is in keeping with formal consequences?

One might say that form has 'naturally' evolved in such a way that revered categories have progressively vanished and been erased, because 'neoclassicism', in any form, has proved its vanity, or at any rate its fragility and its unsuitability. This is certainly true, but also insufficient. It is increasingly clear with the benefit of hindsight that the notion of form changed *as a result of*, and *thanks to*, the radicalisation of vocabulary itself. This radicalisation, this degree zero that we needed to experience, forced the composer to reconsider the notions that followed from it from the bottom up, starting with the notion of theme or, more generally, of the thematic entity. Since vocabulary itself was based on set parameters, form could truly be generated only through the evolution of these parameters with respect to one another. The different stages of this evolution could also then establish the elements of a form, elements that are totally incompatible with inherited forms, and considerably more compatible, paradoxically, with forms such as the ancient forms of polyphony that are less 'evolved' (so to speak) and, consequently, more open to being reworked and to changing their definitions. Concepts like *antiphony, responsory*[2] or *sequence* are vaguer and less defined from our point of view today. They can therefore lend themselves to more extensive interpretation, although they are meant, in truth, only to serve as comparisons, because if we refer to the historical examples that are designated by these words, we find that their conceptual affinities are far removed from each other. It is not a matter of exact replication but of allusion. Unavoidably, one or several adequate solutions for each particular case needed to be found. There existed a danger, as I have already noted, of a kind of mechanisation of form. This danger is all too real and is reflected in certain works from the era in which parameters interfere with one another to create a certain number of layers of activity without truly creating a form that could incorporate these different types of interference. In order to find a credible form for each work, a need, direction and justification for the evolution of material had to be created.

* * *

Did form then become such a specific characteristic of each individual work that it lost any general characteristics? Could no constants be identified? And how, in particular, could a living fusion of the constituent elements of a developmental passage be accomplished?

I would like to speak first of all about a notion arising from the recent evolution of music that was once much discussed: the notion of open rather than closed form.

To what does open form refer? To the necessity of having a formal principle coincide with a precise stage of vocabulary, of language regulated above all by lack of choice, or rather by multiple choice. I will examine this principle first, because it precisely demonstrates the relationship that gets established between form and thematic invention, and the fact that the evolution of the latter brought about the evolution of the former. The concept of open form, which had pervaded everything to the point of excluding any closed form at all, has since that time had its field of action limited, no doubt because it was noticed that multiple choice and freely selected paths are elements of construction just as much as fixed paths, and that they cannot be absolutely all-pervasive. Perhaps, incidentally, there are also other forms of instantaneous choices that have not yet been explored, which can be explored now or in the future only through the use of machines. But I return for the moment to the idea of open form that was developed and put into practice at the end of the 1950s.

In truth, this concept was based on two contradictory principles: first, the multiple choices offered to the performer – that is, a network of systematically organised possibilities, of which none is stronger than any other, since all are of equal value; on the other hand, this choice that the performer is supposed to make in the very instant of performance will either have been planned in advance or else will be made through a totally arbitrary act, one that is planned as little as possible. Faced with a complex network that was prepared with care, the act of making a choice therefore obeys a sort of rudimentary impulse, or else an intention that is itself also developed through deep study of the proposed network. While the first attitude – the 'spontaneous' choice – can only correspond to categories of relatively little importance, the second corresponds, on the contrary, to a reflection on the proposed concept. In my view, a 'spontaneous' choice can in no way go further than selecting between similar solutions, determining a running order, a permutation or a choice of dynamics – in short, choosing categories that effectively arise out of an impulse: surface categories, external descriptions that always felt stifled by an excessively rigid fixation on the score and which could free themselves from it in any performance. This choice is only a focalisation, an enlargement of a freedom that was put into practice for a long time or which may always have existed. But an absolute spontaneity that reigns over path selection, that calls into question the fundamental relationships that must obtain among the chosen elements, could obviously not exist, because the chosen material is too complex, too difficult to play, to be capable of being chosen without forethought. Familiarity with the score through practice is so strong, so charged, that it is impossible to let go of it as if it were encountered for the first time, when one would effectively have no reason to gravitate towards one element more than any other. While familiarity eliminates spontaneous choice at this deep level of structure, the notion remains of a deliberately chosen path, one that favours a given possible relationship over any other. Open form remains perfectly justified, and probably more truly so, by this informed choice that follows from study and is unencumbered by the expectation of 'spontaneity'. Just as spontaneity was a trap when choosing the form's trajectory because it went against the nature of the score, which we needed to understand deeply before being able to assimilate it, so does the choice of a trajectory coincide, on the contrary, with familiarity with the score, the search for multiple possibilities, the discovery of favoured directions, of connections that are stronger than others or, at any rate, stronger with respect to personal choices. The open form that refers first of all to the instant, left to the haphazardness of choices, corresponds to a quite different reality. The instant can apply only to minor, secondary, external and truly spontaneous categories, but it cannot encompass more fundamental categories of form. This probably explains why these open forms were abandoned as a panacea, and had to be relocated to a more modest playing field presiding over minor categories.

But where did the possibility of them come from? It came from the ambivalence of the material that was set in motion, its multiple derivations and, more generally speaking, the principle of permutation. Musical vocabulary is effectively composed of transposable elements that provide a certain number of derived elements with respect to the original. These derived elements can be sorted into families according to the characteristics to which they conform, or rather those that are made visible in them. In order to avoid having to deal with undifferentiated material, it is given a certain profile that restricts the field of possibilities. But to speak of a field of possibilities is to imply a certain number of favoured relationships between the figures that belong to it. Therefore, at this stage of the process, the question can be asked: Within a field of given possibilities, why should all of the others be excluded in favour of a single one? Why should I make *this* choice, considering that each of the figures is just as suitable as any other for the compositional activity? I do not make this choice. I compose all of the possibilities – working, of course, from a limited number of figures – and I leave it to the performer to choose *the* possibility at the very moment of performance. In a linear score, one that is destined to be read by a soloist in a single direction, this principle is particularly simple to apply.

This is what I came up with in my 'Troisième improvisation sur Mallarmé'.[3] The vocal line consisted of a series of successive segments, but the *variability* of these segments evolved from the *obligation* of a single solution to a possible *choice* between two or more solutions. Thus, the path itself remained unchanged, moving from segment A to segment B and on to segment C, etc. But segment A only offered one solution, segment B offered five, segment C three, etc. These solutions were linked to favoured transpositions that allowed for similar figures to arise. Whatever figure was adopted in a given segment, the trajectory passed through the same series of characteristics.

As a matter of fact, this was a major problem with open form: that the work had to make sense regardless of the direction in which it was read. The envelope that governed the characteristics of each element of form therefore needed to be chosen with care, to be sufficiently general to be able to link up with different elements, and also sufficiently particularising to avoid elements becoming anonymous and interchangeable because of their lack of individualisation. Extremely strong envelopes like register and dynamics thus became necessary. They were vague enough not to hinder internal thematic processes, while still influencing them. They were characteristic enough to singularise an element within its context. The difficulty of an open form is in imagining components of a permutable trajectory, but one that acquires the character of necessity in each of its incarnations. We have seen that the notion of a permutable trajectory is linked to the internal permutability of its component elements, in the consequent absence of an absolute hierarchy. Refusal of an absolute in the definition of form corresponded to refusal of an absolute in the very elements of vocabulary. This is far removed from the instant, from chance and spontaneity, external phenomena that perhaps provided the initial shock but were not the true root causes of this evolution.

The root cause must no doubt be sought in a reaction to the absolute determinism that preceded it, and the realisation that total determinism and chance were categories that were not so different from each other. During the period of absolute serialisation, everything was effectively determined by a manipulation of parameters that were founded in the outcomes of deductions made from the original set-up. Of course, we delineated the field of application, because if we hadn't, we would have been faced with billions of possibilities. Certain directions of application were also defined – for example, having components move in the direction of reduction or expansion. In short, we modified the playing rules as a function of what we wanted to obtain. In a sense, form was the placement of different rules into a general order, whether this order was evolving or not. Once the possibilities of a chosen field of application were exhausted, the form was *finished*, it became closed and completed. I am certainly simplifying my description of the procedures employed at the time, but while they were not as guilelessly simple as this might suggest, it does capture their principle. When confronted with these fields of application, the composer may well have many questions to ask, the first and most important naturally being: 'Why choose this narrow field of application rather than another?' And the second question: 'Since this field of application is only one among many others, could it not be replaced with another one?' These questions were asked with all the more urgency as results were produced from ever newer combinations of multiple permutations, without any notable difference from those obtained from entirely different permutations. As I said, the most tyrannical determinism resulted in a statistical operation, a slice of chance delineated in time – but every time segment based on the same principles was strictly equivalent to every other one. Why not make use of chance? But chance totally denies the creative act. The creative act, as Mallarmé said, is chance abolished. How were we temporarily to come to grips with this dilemma, if not by having the performer abolish chance, albeit using chance of a limited sort, but chance all the same? It can be observed that the evolution of form followed that of elements of musical vocabulary very precisely. These elements obeyed laws that made it impossible for them to submit to older formal designs. The question of the revival of older forms, which musicians from the first half of the twentieth century asked themselves with such force, had lost its entire *raison d'être*. Historical reference was not only useless, but also completely foreign to the very concepts that governed the elaboration of musical language.

The experience of open form was supposed profoundly to influence any later work, even though this notion would not maintain the supremacy that it in any case only apparently possessed, because of its limitations. Certain elements of choice could immediately be incorporated – those very elements which, as I have already stated, effectively pertained to the freedom and imagination of the performer: choices made in the instant about categories that are minor in terms of construction but major in terms of direct expression. Thus, the choices of melodic figures and rhythmic contours, and the order of these figures and contours, are products of a type of improvisation within a given framework: nothing fundamental, only a certain freedom of articulation with respect to the score. Besides these elements that are, of course, important – especially for the performer who is not enslaved by fanatical precision and an absolute obedience to rigid parameters – but secondary with respect to more global formal concepts, we started to reflect on the very notion of development that would go on to amplify the notions that I had much earlier separated intuitively into thematic and athematic development. One could speak at that point of directed development and non-directional development, which would correspond to elements of closed and open form.

Directed development corresponds to a required thematics that gives a precise trajectory to a developmental passage through its gesture. This gesture is unique and irreplaceable: it defines a beginning and an end; it is closed and makes reference only to its constituent elements. Non-directional, open development does not really presuppose any thematics. It makes do with structural elements in constant evolution whose characteristics have not been fixed. It is a non-gesture, an amorphous structure that does not, strictly speaking, have anything other than an arbitrary beginning or ending, like slits cut into the fabric of continuous time at places that have not been intentionally chosen. This dialectic of closed and open can enrich the concept of form and validly incorporate *incompleteness* into a finished form. Complementing the notion of form as thus described, there exist different strengths of the thematic entity that indicate the different levels at which the formal gesture is defined. And in one case, we could speak of a finished, real score that emerges from fixed and favoured thematic material; in the other, of a potential, virtual score that materialises in the instant from reworked material in constant evolution. We could also speak of circumscribed, determined form and of statistical, indeterminate form.

❊   ❊   ❊

From our Western perspective, the concept of work, and also of musical work, evolved towards an increasingly restrictive definition of the finished and the complete, while at the same time also making restriction felt with respect to the notion of individuality. The elements of language accepted as collective became increasingly sparse, and even when they had a real existence, their application passed through a highly individual filter, so much so that even performance was also affected by this obsession for restriction and was no longer supposed to be limited to a strict observance of the notation, an absolute respect for what was written. This goes to show how much any gesture that was appended to a work's statement was rejected; curiously, they call this 'fidelity to the text' . . .

Constraints of this type led inescapably to sterility. The impossibility of exactly rendering a world calculated in an exaggeratedly precise way by the composer probably led to reflection on performance itself, the conditions of its existence, but also on the relationship between the composer's designs and their embodiment in sound. This reflection would go on to be nourished by work in electroacoustic music that presented the negative image of this problem: music without performers.

In music written for performers, the formal design is presented via material that ranges from the most precise to the most vague. Thematic material as such, developmental manipulations and articulations of the form present different compositional levels that are far from obeying the same types of characteristic. Of course, the pitches themselves are without doubt the most inescapably precise part. But outside pitch, everything progressively deteriorates with respect to a certain ideal of precision. Rhythmic values are already to be treated with caution, given that they are influenced by a relatively mechanical phenomenon – speed – and by a network of much more subtle relationships with other components of the text, such as phrasing, articulation and density of texture. It follows that a rhythmic value is in reality a compromise or, to put it more positively, a fusion of various influences. As far as dynamics are concerned, since their starting point is extremely unquantitative they depend far too much on internal and external contingencies (the very structure of the work, the acoustics of the environment, physical 'geographic' distance, individual registers of the sounding bodies present) to make it feasible to strive for an absolute ideal of exactitude. As for the play of global interferences between different developmental passages of the form, and the influence of global perception on local events, they relativise any concept of objectivity to the point of rendering it unrecognisable, futile or even harmful.

No matter how far we were able to go with composition conceived as a play of parameters, there was an incredibly wide gap between the formal design and its realisation. The more unrealistic the requirements became, the more this gap widened. When the parameters varied incessantly, and in a strictly point-wise manner, it was overwhelmingly difficult for the performer to 'envelope' all of these points within a kind of curve or *gesture*. Conceptually at first, but also physically, registral leaps, extreme dynamics and rhythmic durations that were unconnected to pulsation rendered precision illusory. There was much information that was difficult to absorb in the mind and muscles; the results were thereby severely diminished. Performers' efforts were mostly focused on processing multiple, complex data that could not be absorbed by the faculty of memory, despite preparation; the text became a simple reference of something already known. Knowledge became impossible, or at least extremely arduous. And even if knowledge was produced, whether or not it was transmitted through the gestures of the performer became truly a matter of chance.

In the best case, we knew that we would provide the performer with an extremely complex network and that the performer's effort with respect to deciphering and transmitting this network would create the tension of the performance, the quality of the execution. By placing the bar too high, we knew that there would be deformations – tending towards simplification, deletion, erosion – but we thought that the musical reality that resulted from it would not have been possible without the excessive complexity of the musical statement provided. The element of relativity made its reappearance in a slightly shameful way, albeit one that was secretly deliberate. But is it logical – and, to be more prosaic, profitable – to leave the degree to which the formal design is embodied up to the muscular or mental capacities of the moment? Is there not an outrageous loss of energy between the formal design that was so painstakingly and so judiciously calculated and the diminished, deformed and elementary image that we risk being presented? Beyond the loss of energy, is there not also a loss, or even an alteration or annihilation, of meaning?

In any case, the imperfections had at least one advantage, which was to breathe life into the text through this constantly variable margin of error. And we could still label as 'rubato' the avatars of such strictly conceived scores, and not entirely in jest. But what is the status of music in which the performer as such no longer participates? All electroacoustic music, electronic music and the like, whose entirely finished objects contained certain relatively superficial aspects that were adjustable and easily modulated through external manipulations (dynamics, spatial projection), had to confront the greatest constraint of all: the inertia of material. It could be objected that the role of the performer gets folded into that of the composer, who chooses sound objects or manipulates their evolution in the creative moment. The first works of electronic music or of musique concrète aptly demonstrate the discomfort experienced with respect to this inertia of material.

In these examples of purely electronic music constructed according to a strict compositional formal design, we may note the lack of a flexible dimension, one that 'envelopes' all the material and gives it the vitality of a musical gesture. All the precision you could ever want is there, but none of those qualities that are difficult to grasp, through which density, articulation and texture take on meaning. They are objects that are perfect in a certain sense, but at the same time fairly lifeless. What is lacking is that deformation of the formal design that gives it its real hold over the material's expressive dimension. It is all too obvious that the design, when it is not overseen by enveloping phenomena, remains a prosaic tool for placement and has trouble attaining organic unity. As for musique concrète, it compensated for the deficiencies of design through the use of sequences in which the life of the sounds was already assured, often through anecdotal means, by taking samples that had already been elaborated. But this runs a no less formidable risk: that of heterogeneity and lack of unity. The design was so weak and superficial, and so unrelated to the material used, that one immediately became aware of 'intuitive' editing based on linkages that were much too elementary to be effective.

Thus, the problem of the exactitude of the plan and its organic unity became acute, and this was a problem that could not be resolved with a *reductio ad absurdum*. The reaction therefore was to rehabilitate the re-creative gesture of the performer by leaving them a certain number of freedoms with respect to the plan. On the one hand, composition itself took into account to a much greater degree the relationship between the score and its performers – their capacity to absorb, the possibilities of their resulting yield, their ability to synthesise the multiplicity of data that makes up musical language into the moment of musical expression. Composition would be altered in the sense that the notorious 'parameters' would once again simply become tools that obey a less visible but more inspired logic; they would disappear as tyrannical dispensers of a constraining and sterile order. Since the elements of language were radically reconceptualised, language had to be reinstated in less primitive forms: global, directly perceivable functions were reintroduced; data processing was allowed to operate on objects in the manner of a synthesis, rather than letting these objects be the random result of an implacably analytical approach.

It was not a matter of restoration, in the conservative sense of the term, because these factors of synthesis, reintroduced into a language that lay in tatters, had literally nothing to do with the organisation of elements from the past that were responsible for an earlier state of language. It was much more a matter of understanding the living relationship needed between the leading formal design and organic, real form, through experiments made during production and performance. Since composition was being transformed, the concept of form itself had no choice but to evolve, in the direction of the disappearance of absolute constraints. From a formal point of view, the possible multiplicity of performed versions corresponded in the most obvious way to this liberation from the absolute. Since there was relativity in the material itself, there would also be relativity in the form, and performers' power to choose, or even distort, would be liberated through the possibility of variable elements being modified – in the realm of sound objects, in their multiple possibilities of linking with other elements, or in the ordering of the constituent parts of the form.

Through an excess of enthusiasm for this struggle for liberation, we sometimes confronted the performer with new difficulties that were just as daunting as the older ones, or nearly so. The breadth of possibilities and the flexibility of the choice were restricted by so many rules that the music ran the risk of becoming a parlour game, a kind of Monopoly, in which the audience was sometimes asked to participate. Going from asceticism to permissiveness, the constraint had not varied, and although it assumed forms that were more pleasant and more socially engaging, in the end it was no more productive.

Logically speaking, this open choice should have led to improvisation, in which the material was not even literally provided, but depended rather on verbal instructions, or simply the pure complicity of the different performers in a group. It is here, as one can easily imagine, that thematic development fell to its lowest level, from two points of view: that of invention and that of exploitation. I will not elaborate on this because besides its power of emotional release, or its ability to compensate for pent-up frustrations, such a phenomenon was too primitive to bring about any sort of renewal. Musical language had regressed to such a degree that it had become founded only on impulsive elements in a pre-grammatical stage: it was literally infantile. Invention, if this word could still be used, consisted of taking up wisps of elements gleaned here and there, memorised and taken out of context. The descriptive envelope was more or less retained, as an external gesture, without the substance that relied on a grammar – even an exclusive and purely individual one. As far as manipulations go, they were more or less governed by a simplistic rule of contrast between states of activity and repose – that was simply repeated indefinitely. Improvisation was therefore able to liberate a few impulses, let out a few frustrations and give the impression of freedom. In reality, there was a submission to primitive forms of expression that called on a type of reductive memory, to the point of rendering the validity of the points of reference obsolete. The only interesting aspect – in the end, a rather tenuous one – was to give the performer the chance to concentrate on unusual modes of production of sound material. As for the 'polyphonic' relationship between the various personalities of a group, they fell into the category of either invitation or refusal – which, one must admit, are not particularly captivating states, quickly exhausting their capacity to influence.

o   o   o

A return to musical language itself, to composition, to reflection about form therefore became necessary – these were the conditions required for deep and durable renewal. What, then, became of the constituent techniques of musical language, the basis for all thematic invention, the precondition for any development, or even any formal conception? To recap briefly: we deduced an order from the thematic statement; then, from the pre-established order, we deduced the different thematic statements. We have seen that the order deduced from a thematic state-ment ran the risk of leading to a unilateral conception, one that is too sealed-off, too dependent on certain notions. We have also seen that the pre-existing order could not truly be conceived as an effective tool if it were not already directed, pre-constrained with respect to its future use. Otherwise, an order that is too general, one that is established with-out concern for anything other than fundamental hierarchy, will quickly prove incapable of organising anything at all. In order to be effective, it must be supplemented with numerous conditions of application in order to be capable of generating particular cases.

When using these very general structures, ones that were mutilated with respect to their operational domains, we might well have won-dered if it was necessary to invent them if they were only to be used in such a partial manner. The myth of the unity of basic organisation, so dear to Schoenberg when he defined the twelve-tone row, could cer-tainly no longer be sustained. Why not? Because the reference to this basic organisation, to this fundamental order, became increasingly weak the more we employed the characteristic specificities of a section of a work. Unity then becomes a chimera, a purely abstract reference whose perception is of absolutely no use in judging the internal relationships of the work, its cohesion and its trajectory. Had we wanted to keep this single reference in mind, we would always have had to use the same range of characteristics, through which we could immediately and directly work our way back to the origin. One quickly becomes aware of the dangers of uniformity and stasis that this implies. What would be valid for a work of relatively limited duration would not be bearable in a longer work. Over and above the exhaustion of possibilities, there would be an impression of rehashing.

In truth, one might well ask why the profound unity of a work should not be preserved by the unity of the order it obeys, and whether this would even be the *only* way to preserve such unity? Is it vital for the unity to be directly and consciously perceived? Is it not perceived unconsciously, and is such perception not sufficient? In my opinion, this reasoning emerges much more from the taboo of unity than from a real phenomenon of form and language. I would even say that among the most recent attempts to assure developmental unity through a fundamental Idea, I view them above all as ways of filling in a framework for action. I consider them to be a kind of developmental determinism, which seems to me the very opposite of the idea of development. Once the original order exists, it is verified each instant in predictable – and only in predictable – ways, whereas this order must be verified through the prism of the unpredictable. In my view, a pre-existing unitary hierarchy can function only as a constraint that places a series of events one after the other, without the time in which they are inserted or the relationship of succession through which they are ordered having anything to do with their reality. There is a divergence between the context and the realities that it successively presents. Reality cannot influence the context, thus it cannot be a living reality. It is forced to obey: there is no communication between form and reality, between the design and the object.

Therefore, if all global hierarchies are rejected, to what can we appeal in order to organise a work? I think that a chain of relative hierarchies, linked to each other through common points that allow for transitions, would be much more able to take charge of events, accidents and the reality of objects efficiently, at the same time inscribing them into a global context. What needs to be preserved when composing? I would say that even if this seems paradoxical, it is the possibility of the accident, of deviation.

Composition is certainly made up of deductions from fundamental ideas, and these deductions are linked through a singular logic that, incidentally, can just as well take the form of a transition as a discontinuity. But deduction does not necessarily imply a line inescapably spun out from initial elements, the inevitable consequence of the given premises. Deduction can, and even *must*, take its cue from the accident, the gesture. Form must be able to deviate from its planned trajectory in order to discover terrain that was not 'on the itinerary'. When resistance is encountered in the material or, on the contrary, its ductility is revealed, the developmental passage must be able to modulate over these accidents it encounters in the terrain. In order to avoid absurd relationships or unproductive encounters, in order to get one's material *in phase* with itself, in order to enable the necessities of local development to coincide with a limited hierarchy, it seems to me indispensable that we can invent this order as needed as we go along. But in that case, if the work constantly references the accident, if a local hierarchy has little authority over the contours of its environment, if we move from one hierarchy to the next only because we do not know what else to do with it, if we cannot find anything else to deduce from it, the work runs the risk of being chaotic. After having quickly exhausted a series of possibilities, one goes on to the next, and so on and so forth, until a sufficient number of them have been placed end to end to fill up a block of time long enough to seem like a work. If the accident were nothing more than this desperate search for continuity in discontinuity, composition would too obviously be reduced to a continual search for lifebuoys. In the way that I conceive of it, the accident consists in being able to incorporate the unpredictable into the predictable, to model deduction on the basis of the object, to follow a series of deductions with another one for reasons that are not to do with the need to fill in a pre-established formal framework, but stem from an internal necessity of transition.

But as for this extremely intentional form, I do not reject form without gesture – far from it. I embed them into two very different playing fields. Intentional, gestural form relies on local hierarchies that link together on the basis of their common characteristics. Sometimes a single displaced or modified characteristic is enough to entail a new order of deductions. Of course, this characteristic must not remain latent in the conditions of the hierarchy; it must be made manifest in the embodied sound. It must determine, for example, the function of an envelope, or it can function as a signal. In this way, we can move from one fragment to the next in a formal development by constantly changing the references, whether progressively or not. The advantage of this for the composer is that he need only invent hierarchies that are immediately necessary for the composition at hand, without becoming encumbered with global charts that need to be constantly reduced and mutilated in order to participate in a reality. This also has the advantage of creating a better fit between the order and the accident, because each depends heavily on the other in every instant.

Could this lead to consequences for the conception of gestural form, and in particular large-scale form? From the vantage point of the current stage in my own evolution, I think that there are in principle only two formal categories that correspond to such modes of generation and development, only two formal categories that correspond to the discontinuous and continuous and are general and neutral enough to allow for a vast variety of fields of application. I would place *permutation-form* in the category of the discontinuous, and *spiral-form* in the category of the continuous. By continuous and discontinuous, I am not implying formal categories that feature temporal continuity or discontinuity; I am thinking rather of the continuity or discontinuity of the hierarchies and of the orderings that come out in moments of transition and caesura.

Permutation is also not to be taken literally; it is an image in the same way as the spiral. By permutation, I am thinking of a certain number of formal categories, each with its own capacity for transformation, and yet highly polarised around a strong principle. The global play of form operates on the return of these formal categories, which are varied each time in a different order, or in combinations of several of them. Form will be fundamentally founded on the principle of caesura, of renewal through caesura, since the internal variation is independent of the context of its return, or of the frequency of this return. As for the principle of the spiral, it highlights, on the contrary, the transition that will always occur in the same direction from one formal category to another. Every time that we move to a higher level of the spiral, a given development is enriched by experiences gained over the course of the previous developmental passages on the same idea – always in the same direction. During this process, incidentally, certain elements might disappear and others can make their first appearance. This dialectic of transition and caesura, which is founded either in 'summarising', i.e. the condensation of the preceding developmental passage(s), or in a progressive change of characteristics, seems to me to correspond to the necessity of a general order that guarantees global unity, while at the same time ensuring the exercise of creative freedom at the local level.

I have spoken of form without gesture. I could also speak of a virtual, non-directional score. This type of score dispenses with the performer and could be considered as the logical conclusion of structural generation from basic material, without any need for intervention by any gesture other than the initial one setting out how events occur. I say 'virtual' because we could well imagine a network of connections between all of the parameters that we wish to bring out, giving them the freedom to develop according to a programme that we apply to them, one that takes their content into account. This is possible, of course, only because at the opposite end of the spectrum from composition as an intentional act, a machine can legitimately provide us with a form of composition in which elements proliferate on their own, once the initial impulse is given and provided that there is a program to control events.

Of course, the short-circuiting of decision-making that is implied by gestural composition stands in total opposition to absolute indifferentiation with respect to the gesture. But both these forms have a place in our perception. It is interesting to set them against each other, to contrast or superimpose them. The thematic material thereby covers extremes of the forms it can take, from local determinism to global aleatoricism. The paradox that seemed at the beginning to be an impossible obstacle can thereby be resolved. Informal and formal music – the apparently irreconcilable is reunited through mobility, flexibility and the ductility of thematic material in the strict sense. Because it is directly linked to local hierarchies and is determined as a function of them, it provokes the gesture, the succession of gestures needed to absorb chance, the accident. On the contrary, since thematic material is linked to global hierarchies and depends only on a general decision, it generates structures in which chance is present without being absorbed, ones to which the accident is completely foreign. These structures are undifferentiated and can only provoke sporadic listening, unconnected to any idea of beginning, of end, of continuity, even though in their essential features they display maximal continuity. On the contrary, intentional structures deduced from local hierarchies, ones that are unconnected to a characteristic of continuity in the work's progression, provoke continuity in listening, require completion, presuppose a beginning and an end, are delineated in their configuration.

Here one finds again, but on the level of form, considerations that I presented concerning different types of time: smooth time that is non-intentional and suspended, and striated time that is intentional and pulsed. In the end, the thematic entity unifies the composer's many actions, from the choice of material to decisions regarding form. Perception and musical expression are truly enriched by an entirely new realm, one that has only just begun to be explored, freed from any need for reference and, thanks to that very fact, freed from any negative attitude, from an obsession with avoiding or redoing.

Because it was preceded by a generation that – no matter with what type of adventure their allegiances lay – needed to verify its conquests by relying on formal plans as guardians, by using 'returns' of varying degrees of showiness, whether spectacular or camouflaged, my own generation was tempted above all by *non-return*. But reference cannot ceaselessly be *avoided*, nor can it constantly be reintroduced in the form of a quotation, a borrowing or even a parody. Musical language had therefore to be reduced to its most fundamental elements, its most reduced components, to *unity*, so to speak, in order to be able to head off once again in search of other irreducible definitions, ones capable of generating different categories in an *absolute* manner and of producing consequences of another kind. This is why, if truth be told, I remain sceptical about attempts at resuscitation that are detached from the context that gave rise to stylistic approaches of a certain type, whether classical, romantic, baroque or whatever term one wishes to use. Certainly, perceptible dimensions had to be discovered for the new materials of musical language, but not rediscovered.

I think that the most essential requirement for musical language is unity. It is only this profound unity that can generate diversity within internal consistency. Otherwise, one has only temporary solutions at one's disposal, ones that change with the seasons. This is what I once characterised as a cross between Descartes and haute couture.[4] I believe that the fundamental liberty of composition can be found only by *breaking out* – through the accident that is constantly absorbed by the law, and at the same time through the constantly renewed destruction of the law by the accident.

1 A reference to Stéphane Mallarmé's unfinished story *Igitur ou la folie d'Elbehnon* (1869), whose title character, Elbehnon Igitur, tries while lying on the ashes of his ancestors to abolish chance by throwing dice at the stroke of midnight.
2 The French word for responsory, '*répons*', is, of course, the title of Boulez's most expansive work from the 1980s. 'Séquence' and 'Antiphonie' are both titles of 'formants', i.e. movements, of Boulez's Third Piano Sonata (1955–7, rev. 1963).
3 Fourth movement of Boulez's *Pli selon pli* (1958–63).
4 A reference to Boulez's 1952 essay 'Éventuellement' ('Possibly'; in *Stocktakings from an Apprenticeship*, ed. Paule Thévenin, trans. Stephen Walsh (Oxford: Oxford University Press, 1991), pp. 111–40; 112): 'They will try to persuade you that the discoveries of serialism are old hat, that in 1920 it was all already known. Today one must create *anew*; and, in support of this brilliant theory, they will present bad imitations of Gounod and Chabrier, those champions of clarity, elegance, refinement: such eminently *French* qualities. (They love mixing Descartes with *haute couture*.)'

PART 5: THE EYE AND THE EAR

10

The System and the Idea[1]
(1985–86)

I have already addressed what is at stake in the matter of themes. But if we want to look further into the relationship between the thematic entity and that which helps it to instigate, develop and nourish the field of composition, we are inevitably led to consider the complex relationships that link any musical idea to the system from which it originated. Every musical language is based on the intersections of different systems – of pitch (ranges, modes, scales), of duration (rhythmic values, metres), of timbres (orchestral, synthesised), etc. – and these systems can be relatively strict (pitch, duration) or unconstrained (timbre), and relatively old or new. Those systems determine every flow of ideas, even if this is purely unconsciously, even if the ideas seem to be generated completely spontaneously.

In fact, the way in which idea and system are linked presents a fundamental challenge to the composer – whether wanting to take account of it or deny its existence by emphasising the inspiration of the moment. The idea will seem spontaneous if the system is completely absorbed as natural and inevitable, which implies habit and acquiescence, and yet in reality it will suffer from every conventional restriction and will risk not only unoriginality, but also excessive constraint, to the point of sterility. If the system is evolving, in the process of being defined, then logic will predominate, and the idea will risk being presented insubstantially or ephemerally, failing to be embodied or incarnated; and then not only is spontaneity in danger, but also, when it is too consciously controlled, the very lifeblood of creativity.

Between system and idea lies the process of *elaboration*, and we must reflect on what this represents, gauge how much separates system from worked idea and ask ourselves some very ambiguous questions: whether one must, even can, recognise the system via the idea; whether the idea can or should conceal the system. The development of twentieth-century music laid a strong emphasis, to the point of disruption, on this interplay between system and idea, a relationship hovering between the dogmatic and the liberal. Once the tonal system was no longer the main common factor among different techniques and aesthetics, that debate became ever more apparent. This system, in its various guises, brought some consensus on the elements of musical language that composers used, even as it crumbled away under the pressure of additions and exceptions. Once the system was rejected – perhaps restored, disman-tled again, even cannibalised – composers were attracted by autonomy, inventing (or thinking they were inventing) their own systems. In this way, everyone devised something that met an individual need, while paradoxically presenting it as universal. Some systems discussed in theory articles have been little more than individual working methods, sometimes strictly temporary. Is that not true of Debussy's whole-tone scale, which he chose to use less and less, and which is in any case closely associated with his musical language?

In essence, this is nearly always a matter of recovering something, such as integrating tonality into chromatic pitch space; or creating spe-cial harmonic fields, which means reverting to functions of the kind that organise tonality; and so on. Systems are applied above all to define pitch space, sometimes using acoustics, as with Rameau, to provide a physical and natural justification for the discourse and to keep in step with more recent practices, such as inharmonic sounds and spectral analysis. That certainly produces pieces of music, but the systems remain highly un-stable, and we see not only that they are temporary, but that they do not stimulate creativity, which exhausts itself through a lack of possibilities.

To consider the interaction between system and idea therefore takes us into some most challenging terrain, littered with every conceivable ambiguity, in which the composer's intentions, the personality factor and the shifting relationship between creativity and musical language are inextricably intertwined. It is a place where everything is relative. In the endless debate between dogmatists who view thought as total control and partisans of the spontaneous who regard inspiration as total disruption, I can see only a badly framed question engendering lame and inadequate responses. And so I will proceed to examine the *uncertainties* that bind system to idea.

✵ ✵ ✵

In the field of music there is a precarious balance – true of many cultures – between phenomena that are free and relatively spontaneous and activity that is more considered and self-aware. 'Popular' music has developed on its own terms, with the oral tradition taking charge of pedagogy, preservation and dissemination, resulting in very slow evolution or stasis leading to decline. Such a tradition risks rapid submersion and permanent disappearance through unexpected events, and the brutal incursion of a more vigorous and expanding world. Because of their sociological state traditional civilisations can experience real *sickness*. 'Learned' music often courts the same dangers of sclerosis and paralysis, fixed and frozen in a chosen historical moment that it believes renders it permanently motionless, though in fact proves to be increasingly artificial, no longer able to resist unforeseen jolts from outside. As for the West, think only of what happened to the Gregorian tradition.

And yet there is one kind of 'learned' music particularly enshrined in our Western tradition that came to rely on individual imagination making a personal style, on the value of the unique and irreplaceable, and this musical tradition, unlike others, yielded increasingly to evolutionary pressure, because excellence was no longer judged using criteria of preservation and consolidation, but of the will, indeed of destruction. The more individualism is asserted, the less consensus there is within the collective system, or the collection of systems designed to secure the coherence of the language in which musicians express themselves, to ensure the audience's too-immediate understanding of the musical works on offer. In the nineteenth century, music always developed in that way: I know the rules, you know the same rules, so we agree and understand each other. This is what everyday language enables: there is no ambiguity in meaning and no difficulty in communicating; and misunderstandings can be obviated with additional explanation. Once the poet intervenes, things are not so idyllically simple. Basic rules of language clearly remain, but everyday parlance is replaced by heightened expression that is not limited by rules that are concise and efficient, but also restrictive. Usage is more extensive, and can be problematic, depending on readers' cultural and educational level. Yet poets rarely *invent* rules or linguistic systems; where they do, it is intermittent and it remains a quasi-language, quickly and effectively explained as 'typical'. Even if the syntactic and morphological system is disturbed minimally, or not at all, it is nevertheless harder to work out the meaning than in everyday parlance. There may be rules that dictate quantity and sound, the number of syllables and their phonetic content. Mallarmé exploited this difficulty virtuosically in some sonnets, and certainly not to make them simpler to read or literally more musical. But many ensuing poems – and we find this even in Mallarmé – fail to respect such restrictions and have a meaning (or, I would say, meanings) that is difficult to interpret. Understanding does not directly derive from an acknowledged grammatical system or morphology.

In music, this problem is both simpler and more complex, given that rules are never related to actual meaning, to an immediate means of exchange, and given that, as a result, the only consensus is about the work itself and the particular style to which it refers. This is true even though the specifics of a work or repertoire can be understood in a wider context, and linked to cultural history and development. This autonomy of musical language is by no means completely disengaged from a notion of shared meaning, although those meanings rely above all on codes of general signification that refer through inherited authority. The codes change, though, more quickly than the laws of a grammatical system. A few centuries on, it is only by learning them that we have any hope of recovering the 'precise' meaning of certain music – always assuming that precision is a notion that can be applied to a musical universal that is very difficult to identify or define, although the codes are known and even familiar. We might describe some music of the past as like a dead language, but 'translation' is not enough to revive such pieces, even when adapted to modern instruments and techniques. There are many reasons why accurate reconstruction is a problem, of which the most unpalatable, indeed destructive, is the concept of authenticity. The more we try to get to the real model (mainly conceived after studying theoretical texts about a musical practice from a particular period or a specific subsection of it), the more we distance ourselves from immediate understanding, by making ourselves physically experience the music's historical – and thus remote – aspect. The whole compositional system binds music to a particular set of circumstances from which nothing can release it. Beyond faithful realisation, it can be modernised, or rather *modified*, and techniques or characteristics from today's musical language can be imposed upon it, but then the public is made aware in a different way of historical distance – by the unexpected, by time collapsing. Thus, in Stravinsky's *Pulcinella* there is no genuine stylistic grafting, even if that's all we perceive in it, when new colours or decorative additions lend piquancy to music in which we would otherwise lose interest. This is not really the equivalent of a painter copying a famous picture. It is not like Picasso paying tribute to Manet, Delacroix or Velázquez, people who are less easy to forget than the more modest Cimarosa, who belongs with the muted, the lowly, the entertaining. And yet the origin of the clash is the same, the stripping-out being more thorough in one case than the other, *reflection* being at an obviously more revealing level. It is the system into which the model is inserted that is warped. Its functions remain. They may be diverted, and not genuine, but stylistic awareness, if the memory is precise enough, judges the distance, or deformation, between the model and the new object. The system functions on two levels in relation to the ideas in play: referring, and also diverting. With painting, distance from the model brings the imitation/deformation relationship to 'nature'. Painters, if we leave their strictly pictorial qualities aside, focus on reproducing, that is, imitating the depicted object, and there is no difference in actual knowledge between what is in nature and what is in the picture – the transposition is more subtle than that and will be lost on a superficial, amateur observer. If the transposition is more radical and abrasive, producing a strongly individual vision compared with how things normally look, the systems will be derivative of each other, much more so than with musical arrangements, given that using the customary musical codes – at its simplest, tonal logic – cannot be equated with our visual perception of the external world. Listening to music, however simple, we enter the world of artifice, and direct reference to the natural world becomes meaningless. Whether we know it or not, we enter a system whose coordinates we know – perhaps unconsciously, but they nevertheless determine our hearing. Looking at a flower or fruit, on the other hand, does not oblige us to make reference to a pictorial gesture – a still life. The phenomenon of culture is allowed to be completely absent from that action, whereas it is inevitably present, I repeat, in music, however rudimentary or embryonic.

❋ ❋ ❋

The musical idea does not exist as a vague absolute, outside any system. It is completely determined by it, in its contour, functions, and in how it is prolonged. Its initial manifestation, before it is consolidated by the codes of a musical language, may relate to other sources, concrete, or visual and auditory, or abstract or conceptual. It will display some spontaneity, the result of the preliminary idea being nowhere near its final form; and having been *seized*, what is then needed is a process of elaboration, defining coordinates that allow the idea to be consolidated and conveyed. Equally, one needs to deduce from this first idea consequences that are varied enough to yield coherence and renewal in a dynamic process, giving birth to a form whose structure is entirely determined by the potential for development teased out of the first idea. The story of ideas and musical forms cannot be separated from the story of musical language, given the permanent interaction of system and idea, which come into conflict in an era of transformation. There is no point in asking whether the idea itself is what makes the system evolve, or whether it is the progressive transformation of a system that renders ideas inevitably different. System and idea live in strict symbiosis, with an entirely reciprocal history. In a firmly codified system the particular idea is deduced, so to speak, from a generic idea, along with a given form – so a fugue subject, for instance, cannot be just any kind of theme, but is invented in the light of a precise set of possible developments, susceptible to more or less strictly regulated rules of composition, following harmonic and contrapuntal laws that dictate both formal hierarchy and formal elements.

Fugue provides the best examples of ideas that are created to suit a system and are completely determined by it, although that restricts how varied they can be. Some conditions are restrictive, but there are sufficient others to enable a wealth of shapes in which intervals, rhythms, phrasing and articulation combine to generate a literally inexhaustible world, with the proviso that form, which is equally susceptible to endless possible variations, will obey certain principles that make it recognisable – fugal entries, expositional procedure, strict and free stretti. Thus, the tonal system, compositional codes and form stamp an individual profile on the musical idea – a profile of thematic invention with specific characteristics – related exclusively to one system, one type of composition, one form.

Classical sonata form provides a more flexible example of how the idea is tailored to the system. Here, too, themes are devised according to very precise functions: the abstract laws of the tonal universe, including the hierarchy of scale steps; and the more concrete laws of expression and contrast necessary in a form based on material opposition. These two kinds of law appear together, and the schemes imposed are open enough to enable them to appear in practically limitless ways, more than in a fairly strict form such as fugue. For all the variety on offer, we are immediately able to identify a sonata not only by recognising its form, how it unfolds, but also by the nature of the themes that are designed in order to construct that form. As the sonata and symphony developed and became thematically richer, more ambiguous, less of a binary contrast, less constrained, less grammatically controlled, their form was deeply affected. Architecturally, it became a narrative, admitted less deterministic conceptions, offered greater flexibility, richness and variety, at the expense – if such it was – of immediate recognisability. To some degree, creativity corrupted the system, its ideas needing to be followed in different ways, needing a different sort of development, a different kind of discourse.

Idea and system corroborated each other, struggled, transformed each other – showing history revealed by an individual, and evidence of the individual deliberately carving a niche in history, rebelling against what came before. The individual is so conditioned and exposed by the controlling circumstances that heritage is not completely mastered, cannot be adequately expressed in a vision of the world. Today, our vision is certainly more combative and antagonistic about relations between system and idea than that of musicians from before the start of the nineteenth century, when conflicts began that resulted from composers wanting to be solitary individuals, omnipotently resolute and decisive, rebels against society and the constraints of their heritage. Even more acute than the rebellion conducted by the most inventive and bold minds of the nineteenth century was that of the beginning of the twentieth century, by the Second Viennese School in particular, which severed some secular bonds, sparking resistance and recantation, which one can still sense in works that appeared many years ago. This idea shattered the system that had already been fractured by many transgressions, at first tolerated and then becoming commonplace! Yet must we believe that fundamental laws had thus been broken, that works lying beyond the law were doomed to failure, tainted by defects making them unfit to listen to – unfit for consumption, crudely put? Had the struggle between system and idea already found its definitive conclusion, expressing itself by a goal of categorical non-expression? From which, after some more or less hazardous experimental phases, there was some regression to Romanticism – to the origin of the problem, that is, to rejection of system in favour of idea – compared with previous returns to classicism, to rules, to a perfect unity of system and idea?

This paradox suggests that a generation that had been radical before the First World War felt the need in the interwar period for a return to order, to classicism. This generation had destroyed a great deal, and sensed the danger of anarchy and sterility if there were no return to rules. Unfortunately, as a collective it did not return to rules but to a project, or rather, a collection of projects that were no longer aligned with the evolution of musical language. The outcome was what is called neoclassicism, and its derivatives and 'distancings' (this *Verfremdung* having nothing to do with Brecht, at least in the hands of a Schoenberg or a Stravinsky).

In the one case, there was the attempt to reacclimatise tradition by incorporating morphologically, syntactically and formally whatever was available pedagogically. In the other, it was a matter rather of playing with objects chosen not through what might be called an evolutionarily sustained tradition, but by chance, cruising the bazaar of history. The former was a historical mission; the latter was pleasurable dabbling. Yet whatever the degree of emotional investment, the historical reference serves as a template – literally, an act of parody. Nowadays, we can see where system and idea were still linked: there was no stimulating exchange; the project that stemmed from a dead system steered composers more and more into dead ideas. One may observe only one, fairly sterile consequence of this: that the emptiness of the system forced people to be inventive.

As for the return to Romanticism, it was even less productive. At its most discerning moments neoclassicism tried to expose a confrontation, indeed to provide a shift in values. The new script was not just completely reduced to the project it had spawned; there was a kind of distortion that developed sometimes as caricature or humour, and sometimes like a history lesson. Neo-Romanticism, meanwhile, was no longer concerned with self-regard, but doggedly settled for isolated, bulimic medleys, without any kind of critical distancing. Paradoxically, to compensate for the perceived error of disordered ideas, composers updated precisely that which had initiated the disintegration, pushing this to its conclusion by destroying it. We should not attribute more importance to things done on a whim than they deserve. There was clearly deep disarray, incoherent thinking about the contemporaneous situation – this is worth noting in order to show how the credibility of creativity is seriously impaired, if not destroyed, when system and idea are no longer aligned.

Let us return, though, to the distant origins of the ever more precarious situation that has been developing, particularly since the beginning of the twentieth century.

❀ ❀ ❀

The system stayed mostly firm, at least in its most essential, simplest elements, despite evolving right through the nineteenth century, and despite individual forces that tended to push collective evolution, like it or not, into replacing the aesthetic of consent with that of domination. Even though becoming overloaded and very much more complex, the main elements of musical language meant the same in relation to its objects and the interaction of objects. As to those objects, the idea of their being identified with a generic model remained largely absolute, although there was no longer such a literal concept of *triadic chords*, instantly recognised and understood objects of highly limited types, or rather, contexts. Many ambiguous objects arose, which could belong to different categories and progressions, making them not really predictable, though very strongly connected. Moreover, although rich acoustically, their music-analytical status was less obvious, so that categorising them in families became increasingly complex.

The radical chromatic development of harmonic language has long been traced back to *Tristan*. Everyone remembers the harmonic progressions of the Prelude to Act 1. They have generated reams of commentary proving everything and nothing. In fact, we can speak of ambiguous chords that, in isolation, can resolve in very different ways. When they last long enough to establish their ambiguity and to be perceived as such, the surprise lies in the resolution, given the hesitancy we experienced. Other analysts, though, have wanted to show how these ambiguous chords are in reality only modifications of simple and functionally unequivocal chords, so that the ambiguous relationships are those acknowledged, classified and briefly disguised through alteration. The simple, straightforward relationship is easily grasped when you hear their resolution. Unfortunately, between these inaudible structures and what actually happens come the actual, multiple ambiguities of both the objects and their progression. Even if the structure is considered reasonably valid, that is not what we hear, nor is that something we can refer to. In the Prelude to Act 1 of *Tristan*, dominant seventh chords that support every element never lead to the key in which, theoretically, they lie and function. The first chord, the most ambiguous and least identifiable, with the most fluid possible function, resolves straight on to the dominant seventh that comes second. The function of the first chord is multiple and not nameable according to any conventional system, and its resolution tells us what its function was, whereas the second chord clearly functions according to a known system, but without completing that function. This dominant chord moves to a transposition of the first chord, initiating a harmonic progression that is normal due to there being two common notes – in other words, due to a feature unrelated to their actual functions.

It might be objected that that is not a normal harmonic analysis, and that it disregards the language of the period. Yet surely what matters is not the academic approach, but to observe how we nowadays perceive a language to be working.

*　*　*

I mentioned above that the objects used by composers had become richer and richer acoustically. That is particularly so in the orchestral repertoire. This repertoire was based originally on identity, on the identification of timbre. Especially when the orchestra had only just emerged from the domain of chamber music, combinations were limited, timbre serving to enhance the compositional conception and its components. In the baroque period, the instrumental ensemble was noticeably confined to being a grouping of individuals.

That said, the proliferation of these objects, and the variety in their organisation, is not such that they cannot be embraced by human memory. Their identity is the same wherever they are situated in the array of sounds. Their functions and relationships are of a general kind, not depending on particular cases, so that they would not alter from one work to the next, and even less so within a work. Hearing a work, and helped by memory if some command of culture has been acquired, the listener is able to refer to systematic schemes and codes so that the hierarchy of the work's objects can be evaluated, perhaps immediately. Moreover, novelty for composers until the beginning of the twentieth century did not generally lie in innovations in the sound objects themselves. It certainly lay in richer chords, and more complex relationships, for the underlying correspondences are practically unchanging. Evolution appeared more radically in two domains that are strongly linked to each other: on the one hand, functions – that is, the hierarchies to which objects are linked will be ever more personal, the composer's individual choice, detached from any global system; on the other, form, generated by the musical idea and deductions from it, will be completely impossible to reduce to a pre-existing scheme, with its precise functions and known hierarchy. If we can really use the word 'revolution', it would at first arrive much more from the combination of objects than from their intrinsic nature.

It is always the evolution of language towards total chromaticism that is emphasised, and within the Viennese School, which most experienced this continuity of evolution, the Wagner–Mahler–Schoenberg line emerges as a symbol of renewal. It should not be forgotten, however, that the renewal was of a certain kind, in which the goal-oriented functions of harmonic language more or less dissolved thanks to a constant resort to what one may call *roving* harmony, though more accurately they would be called 'multi-directional' chords.[2] The contrapuntal relationship between lines, on the other hand, is controlled by chromatic complementarity, but there is another strand guiding renewal, begun by Mussorgsky and pursued by Debussy and Stravinsky, in which objects are no longer endowed with continual ambiguity. In fact, fully identifiable objects are retained, but set in a particular acoustic position, so that their capacity to progress is removed. Debussy's parallel chord progressions are a model of this category. The triad enveloped in a seventh or ninth chord no longer functions as a triad. It is, as it were, the amplification of just one note. In Stravinsky, this phenomenon is enriched – especially in *The Rite of Spring* – by neighbouring notes that make a simple object complex, but which are not there for their original function, no longer having anything to do with a 'functional' chord, but rather are there for their acoustic properties. Varèse will do the same. In this 'defunctionalised' context, it can be claimed that chromaticism has no principal role here. Far from it: one can observe the opposite, which is reinforced diatonicism, or the use of all kinds of modes, whether originating from before the establishment of tonality or from other cultures, and adapted a lot or a little to the well-tempered scale that evolved in Western music. The underlying rationale for these borrowings, however, is neither archaism nor exoticism; rather, they are a different way to desecrate tonal functions, to put diatonicism in perspective. It cannot be denied that the aesthetic connotations of such archaism or exoticism, in a more general artistic context, often spring from the same cause: some nineteenth-century painters turned to the Japanese world, for example, and some painters of the twentieth to what has been called traditional African arts. In some cases, these influences can amount to a new definition of space and perspective; in others, to a redefinition of 'volume' with respect to shape and space.

Whereas in Debussy the harmonic universe engages diatonicism as much as chromaticism – Wagner, too, avails himself of that dialectic in *Parsifal*, and certainly not in *Tristan* – the Stravinsky of *The Rite of Spring*, like Varèse, uses what are essentially chromatic aggregates, of doubtful functionality to start with, given the tension within the very harmonic object itself.

The evolution of these two lines, however separate they may appear to be, is based on the same phenomenon: the rejection of functions that had become the consistent, coherent foundation of musical language.

✧ ✧ ✧

Until the beginning of the twentieth century, compositional innovation did not really lie in the renewal of sonic objects in themselves. This evolution happened more radically in two, strongly linked domains: function, the hierarchy in which these objects are embedded, which became the composer's individual choice, more and more disconnected from a universal system; and form, generated by the musical idea and deductions from it, which became irreducible to a pre-existing scheme.

Form, developing into narrative, would rely less and less on precise symmetry or reprises, becoming literally a non-repetition of previous events and deductions. This is not only about a broadening concept of variation, the superficial or structural reshuffling of musical material already used. It is also very much about presenting things differently: a change in the lighting, a flux in how important musical elements are regarded as being, a novel confrontation, the abrupt or surreptitious introduction of new elements.

We can make a distinction between the evolution of purely musical form, such as in symphonic or chamber music, and theatrical form. The latter was a little quicker to show a marked propensity for withdrawing from restrictive schemes to engage dramatic truth. Naturally, formal episodes, moments of reflection, halts in the dramatic flow still endured, and conformed to models of construction without losing much identity, given that musical intensity is stronger than stage action – the formal significance of the aria, the duet and the ensemble kept its autonomy basically through contrast to the recitative's narrative. When the border between action and reflection became more fluid, the form used by composers, above all Wagner, relied for dramatic truth on the *transition*; quotation become the only possible kind of reprise, and ongoing thematic material would have to respond continually to new contexts.

Literary influence, corruption even, was the first cause of symphonic formal renewal, initially with Berlioz. He tried to find the uncertain balance between forms in the repertoire and the story he wanted to tell, resulting in a difficult confrontation between strict form and anecdote, sometimes coming together happily (as in the *Symphonie fantastique*, *Roméo et Juliette* and *Lélio*), but elsewhere not. Liszt deliberately infringed the symphonic concept, parading a storyline no less than Berlioz. Both wrote for an imaginary theatre that let them shatter ideas that had become too rigid, drained of their original expressive powers. (In Berlioz's case, the imaginary theatre works better than the real one, which trapped him with rather sterile formal conventions.) The symphony itself stayed under the yoke of Beethoven, until Mahler found an effective way to combine formalism and narration. Movements may still be generic (e.g. scherzo, or slow movement), but the material tends towards proliferation, towards continuous development that mostly creates a specific form, remote from its prototype.

Chamber music is the musical domain that was for a long time the least 'contaminated' by *anarchy*! As I see it, the final works of Debussy – the *Études* for piano in particular, but also the sonatas – offer the most striking examples of remarkable liberation and autonomy, features that he had already displayed in symphonic works such as *La Mer* and *Jeux*. In the former, there is no narrative content as such; the movement titles are, rather, poetic indications, which do not imply any particular order or symbolic equivalence. In the latter, the storyline of the ballet is probably what inspired narrative continuity, and yet the subtlety of Debussy's formal procedure and the thematic effectiveness mean that there is no need to know it in order to follow the music: while expressing the storyline's course of development, the music clearly transcends it. The beginning and end, the only moments of nearly exact symmetry, are like a visible frame for the story, signs of opening and closure.

Theatrical form, like symphonic form, developed in the second half of the nineteenth century and the first quarter of the twentieth into a concept that increasingly rejected textural return, reprises or literal repetitions. Form could not rely on a general system once it had given up referring to the past, so that each work had to trigger its own system of formal referencing. Perception having been disoriented, initially, by ever-changing innovation, its path was strongly supported by being able to depend on a 'living' vocabulary: at least something – something essential – continued to convey an agreed, recognisable meaning. The simplest remaining elements of a system helped to clarify what was different, tending to destroy or annihilate. Considering all the bold compositions that followed *Tristan*, one can generalise that after a difficult period of adjustment, they were acknowledged because of this fixed, referential element supporting their vocabulary: the ambiguous turned into the stable, and uncertain, non-functional relationships gave way to clearly defined ones. The variety of, and difference between, these perceptual options nourished a work's meaning and often gave it its aesthetic characteristics. Paradoxically, what remained of the system was taken to be the most spontaneous and immediate, while infringements seemed the most artificial, the most arbitrarily *systematic*.

The precariousness of this situation became gradually clearer as infringement led to the disappearance of the system's functionality. As an expression of diversity, of plurality in aesthetic intention, the components of musical vocabulary quickly dispersed, if not into disorder, at least into freedom of individual judgement, so that the original system appeared to be only a phantom, a kind of lightning conductor against complete anarchy, a trick for decoding crucial moments and indispensable points of articulation. The idea of a system as such was then rejected, and all that remained of the consensus was a succession of lifebelts thrown to listeners. It was at this point – with the famous rift between the public and new works, marked by irredeemable incomprehension – that two attitudes began to appear, in very different ways. The basic object, the chord in itself, or vertical control of horizontal components, loses all reference to a matrix: it is fruit just of the moment, a fleeting encounter. This is the result of the tension in its chromatic make-up being pushed as far as possible, which is nothing if not logical: since form was already avoiding literal repetition and pre-established functions, it was natural that vocabulary, too, would begin to avoid regular schemes, foreseeable rules, identical deductions. Different composers had different solutions, but they all reflected individual ways of organising the sound world – instinctively, or based on systematic thinking, albeit rarely codified.

Apart from differences in intention and realisation, what was common to the various tendencies was the preponderance of chromaticism and chromatic relations. Relationships from note to note, voice to voice, chord to chord would be entirely dominated by chromatic complementarity, whether or not chromaticism was the entire constitutive element of the vocabulary, as it was with the Viennese School. There would be no doublings or repetitions, and the octave is banned whether as an intrinsic relationship within chords or an extrinsic, direct relationship between contrapuntal voices. In Stravinsky and Bartók, diatonic elements generally belonging to the modal universe are placed under the greatest possible tension, with the addition of chromaticism contradicting the logic of each individual element, or else chords are so overloaded with ambiguities that they have no general functionality but just exist in themselves – static, even unalterable, waiting, as it were, for some other entity to replace them. This vocabulary implies very strong polarisations orienting the objects used, providing direction and logic to the musical discourse, and thanks to these sturdy signposts the listener's perception is easily guided into acceptance once initial reticence is overcome. Order is readily restored, governing what may at first appear to be, if not anarchic, then nevertheless spinning out of control.

Things were different with the Viennese School – and I claim that there was a communal intention, despite very distinct aesthetics making for works that were more or less complex, more or less easy to grasp

– which introduced radical changes, sometimes so extreme that we still wonder how well founded they were. One single principle lay at the heart of the step they took, positively or negatively depending on how it is described, which one can call the principle of variation, or non-repetition. In fact, the result of constant variety was the avoidance of many previously acknowledged concepts that had passed into common practice and thus were considered natural. Harmonically, this translated most conspicuously into avoidance of the octave, triads being systematically excluded, especially in root position, by continual shunning of stable intervals such as the fifth, which could create a temporary polarity. Contrapuntally, integral variation was approached more cautiously for the very simple reason that such counterpoint would make the deduction of figures unrecognisable, though a certain strict academicism survived, sometimes rather contradicting the relentless harmonic variety. Perhaps a yearning for recognisability prevailed? Perhaps it was the allure of a compositional practice that was so difficult to pursue and control in a strictly tonal context, but which blended conceptual unity and diverse relationships fairly easily in the more relaxed context of chromaticism? In point of fact, the three Viennese composers made plentiful use, if very differently in each case, of canonic techniques, strict imitation and forms such as the passacaglia, with its relatively tight rules. Highly restrictive regulation seemed necessary in the face of harmonic anarchy, to avoid perception being completely thwarted. But aside from this contrapuntal discipline, which seemed to occur often, there was a paroxysm of individualism. The system shattered and seemed to have lost its rationale to the point of an almost absolute logic of continuity: no reduplication in the elements of an object, non-repetition of objects, no literal restatement of ideas, no reprise of formal sections. It was as if what constituted the basis of Western music – identity and recognition, codes and schemes, functions and formal relationships – had to be avoided at all cost. Thus, we can better explain the ten-year 'rift', which is still perceived as such today: the impression of drifting into a world that only repetition and familiarity would help one to understand.

Normal reality was challenged by Schoenberg, by the first abstract canvases of Kandinsky, as well as by Picasso and Stravinsky. One could no longer speak of a system. The idea is omnipotent, self-sufficient, setting up its own hierarchies, making up its own vocabulary, even when that followed general norms, albeit norms that were too general to establish genuine laws of continuity. In tonal harmonic practice, perception did not need to classify objects analytically because the system was so strong and coherent that objects could be effortlessly and instinctively assigned to one class or another, along with the resulting functions and progressions. The stronger, the more tyrannical a system is, the more spontaneous is the listener's response, to the point of being predictable, which may or may not be welcome. The less systematic things are, the more there is free will, then the more perception is mediated by thought, by the desire to assimilate, the need to rehear in order to be able to understand. Freedom of compositional practice inevitably leads to active listening, the kind that can analyse and find relationships. For instance, when each chord is constructed in a unique way, we initially perceive only its most external and crude characteristics, such as registral positioning, intervallic tension and timbral relationships. We will not immediately grasp its intervallic construction. If it is extended temporally, then we will be better placed to analyse and thus absorb it, but if it appears in passing, among similar but differently disposed chords, in practice it will be impossible to account for it.

It should not be thought that I am speaking here only about expert perception of such chords and sonic objects, that I regard hearing a work as like a long series of musical dictations – although the issues musical dictation raises may entail the same level of internal complexity, the same ability to discern and analyse the objects that then have to be transcribed, dictation being an acute, conscious phase of the relationship between the heard and the perceived object. We find those levels in the evaluation of perception in non-professional listeners accustomed to attentive listening by regular concert-going, as well as in listeners whose musical hearing is relatively poor and unrefined, due to a lack of interest or familiarisation. And yet we find the same among professionals, who will, for example, play a chord up or down on the piano to be sure of what they are listening to, quickly analysing its elements to reconstruct what they had initially missed. The more numerous, different and complex objects are, the more memory plays a role in perceiving them, comparing one object with another, gauging its similarity or difference and thus its potential to be linked to, and coherent with, various perceived objects. Our memory takes note of things, makes predictions, retrospectively validates, and relates events to each other. Parallel chords are assimilated very quickly, even complex ones, since they are only elaborations of a line. In chords that are almost parallel, a few divergences do not prevent us from perceiving their common identity; or if they correspond to a regular process of enlargement or contraction, then we follow the changes by interpreting that process. If we cannot read the *envelope*, then we perceive objects as different. The problem is always the relationship between contour and interval. Intervals can dominate and destroy contour. This is the struggle between perception of the particular and perception of the whole.

When what is perceived is too rich for memory to be able to play its coordinating role, the work seems incoherent, memory storing only isolated events, or strings of events that are too short or too isolated to form a continuous, temporal whole. We therefore often rely upon expressivity to compensate for this basic lack, perception being grounded in a psychological state or series of states in order to create more easily grasped and formulated chains of understanding. The Viennese trio used poetic or dramatic texts to construct their compositions, at the time when their language had become most atomised. This helped them as composers – they made up for a lack of immediacy in their language with expressive continuity – and was no less helpful to audiences, who were given an overt poetic or dramatic thread to hold on to. It ameliorated the problem of understanding the musical thread, whose components it was difficult to take in, both functionally and as regards temporal continuity.

✿ ✿ ✿

It seemed that any idea of system had had its day, at this stage of historical development; that hierarchies would never return, that intense individualism had reached a point beyond which would lie only communication failure. The obsession with constant innovation in whatever was selected meant the loss of the message; it became as difficult to utter as to understand. It would therefore be necessary to organise the sound world in another way, to seek different norms, if possible to establish new rules – without which compositional practice is no longer viable since it risks losing all its long-term coherence. In this period, composers tried with varying success to discover or revive musical laws, as best they could within their own sphere and circumstances. Insofar as it was expression that had in the preceding century propelled the evolution of language, with form as a necessary consequence, it was this historical stage that encouraged a tendency towards law and order, the establishment of rules to which individuality must submit in order to express and be intelligible. There was a powerful return to system – any system, new or copied – and one has to ask whether that was through fear of chaos, the desire to write oneself into history or exhaustion at the effort of finding a new pathway, of finding every step along the way. It is difficult to separate aesthetic need from the desire to console the intellect, or even the hands!

Law through imitation clearly means neoclassicism: a law that is in fact not a law, the semblance of hierarchy, norms mixed with chaos, just what is needed to satisfy our desire for novelty. We do not want to hear the same progressions, the same objects again, so we take those objects and add an ingredient not taken from any system, an ornament that adds something a little unforeseen to this known object, like spice on a dish that is too bland. It is the same with progressions: if a progression would be too trivial, too predictable, then it can be forced to divert, its components dislocated and made to go in a different direction. The entire compositional practice becomes like this: I know what the initial ideas are and the way in which they are faked, and I am comfortable in this new reality because it relates to my culture, to all the schemes I know, but it entertains me because the way things are diverted makes them 'piquant', unusual. It is a culture for the jaded palette, like an antiquarian making a bedside lamp out of an old trumpet. There is certainly some virtuosity, conjuring even, in this handling of styles and objects, but we always hear the references, and the original is so obviously present that it corrupts the imitation, like rising damp on a wall. Disenchantment will set in; the illusory edifice will be revealed, stripped of its value. Rules that are thinly disguised as free will cannot guarantee that a language will endure. Whether we speak of neoclassicism, neo-Romanticism or other artificial, naive revivals, we can be sure that they are decorative screens, basically originating in the question of how to express oneself in a language that is universal and universally understood. This type of badly conceived, badly understood question is about as useful and entertaining, I would say, as a masked ball; and after Shrove Tuesday comes Ash Wednesday, as night follows day.

Does this mean that rules should be more serious and austere, or indeed unpleasant? Theorising has frankly never been a source of much enlightenment: we prefer to concentrate on what we think creators are expressing, rather than focusing in detail on the tools they work with. You might say, quite rightly, that a tool is only the best means for conveying expression, that composers are thinking about the best possible tool, as they must, while listeners are interested only in the result. Composers' reflections on their work, if there are any, are there to provide reassurance about a route that has been taken but not yet fully understood, and these writings are studied to provide a clearer picture. The Viennese trio are depicted as theory-saturated composers, and indeed each of them wrote analyses, but those are explanations of their work rather than components of a theoretical framework – they are what would properly be called scattered fragments, *disjecta membra*, in classical studies. Even though there were no genuinely theoretical texts, the impression remains that *system* was at the heart of their thinking in the second part of their creative life, though incidentally with very different methods. Berg and Webern always felt themselves to be more or less under the tutelage of, and ready to bow to, their master, Schoenberg. However, their methods, seemingly systematic, remained far apart, which certainly had something to do with the composers' individual temperaments, reflecting divergent behaviours which it will be interesting to study chronologically, since they will give us perspective on a more general, longer-term process. Each of the three processes can be described as emblematic of a basic stance, exhibited by every creator, towards the dialectical relationship between system and idea.

It will be interesting to study this behaviour in relating system to idea in detail in order to apply it to a more general process.

First, is the system really a system? With the benefit of hindsight, it is striking how little is implied by the establishment of the twelve-note row in Schoenberg's formulation. It is at most a practical way to control chromatic complementarity, continuously and rationally. Apart from that there is really nothing to govern the different dimensions of compositional practice, nothing about harmonic laws, no new contrapuntal rules, or about procedures that stay the same as before, resurrected, at most, in their strictest form; equally, there is no prescribed rhythmic practice other than replicas of old rules, such as augmentation and diminution. Furthermore, harmonic control of counterpoint totally disappears, as it were, or rather, it is left to the composer's instinct to judge whether the interaction of different voices results in something harmonically satisfying. Rules more or less artificially derived from acoustics, stretched to breaking point by ambiguous and remote relationships, have disappeared in favour of instinct. The gaps in a system essentially retained as a simple means of coordination are huge and obvious. The systematic organisation of pitch stems from development of the thematic idea. This ever-growing concept, which takes precedence over all other elements of musical language, ended up completely dominating them, becoming both sub-theme and super-theme: sub-theme, in that it consists of pitch alone, completely neutral as to shape, register and durations, not to mention dynamics and timbre, all inessential to establishing a basic shape; and super-theme in the sense that the whole work will completely depend on this series, that the entire idea, and the actual themes, are derived from it, and the very basis of the work is the principle of uniqueness, of total reference. Thus, the two foundations of this concept are: strict intervallic *class* regardless of register – so that the third, for instance, may be regarded as identical to the tenth or the sixth, the most important thing being that it remains identifiable, however it appears; and *unity*, sustained in a work by obligatory reference to one matrix, despite the variety among the ideas deduced from it and the necessary formal contrast. Aside from the gaps already mentioned, today we can easily see how far the principles represent a formalist utopia, and how they have no *direct* consequences. An interval takes on a different identity when it is manipulated, when it belongs in another context. Other characteristics are needed to create sufficiently strong similarity, such as a rhythmic relationship or a series of intervals able to form a harmonic region. As part of a hierarchically higher order, an interval has no chance of being recognised in itself; it is not strong enough compared with characteristics that are more pertinent and conducive to perception.

It seems odd that Schoenberg, having codified his twelve-note method, would apparently lose interest in any truly systematic harmony. The end of his *Theory of Harmony* is devoted to the chromatic expansion of chordal relationships, an expansion that would suspend tonality. It considers at some length the potential of the whole-tone scale, and of a system of chords built on fourths. At that time, harmonic relationships were still a basic part of his thinking, and intervals were considered in relation to their context, function and arrangement. At a certain point, one preoccupation, thematic unity, would apparently dominate all the others, and harmony as such would be addressed only as a result of it. This is just as true in the output of Berg and Webern. All three composers seemed to be highly aware, in the first phase of their work, of the power of harmonic language. It was not about laws, strictly speaking, but we observe their meticulous choices regarding how harmonic networks are elaborated. This is a particularly notable aspect of Schoenberg's *Das Buch der hängenden Gärten*, all Berg's works up to and including *Wozzeck*, and Webern up to op. 13.

In all likelihood, that is inherited from Romanticism, the supreme era of harmony, even if such harmony, as in Wagner, is enlivened by the rich life of the voices that comprise it. Those voices may seem to be autonomous, but are in essence harmony in motion, not true counterpoint. They defer to the coherence of the whole before existing in themselves.

This inheritance from Wagner is clearly adopted in an ever-freer way, harmonic relationships coming under pressure from lines that risk dislocation through their increasingly autonomous tendency. Yet thematic deduction seems increasingly to have become the main agent of coherence; harmonic vocabulary was thus less important, becoming, as it were, a secondary result, no longer the composer's main concern. The stricter the thematic process becomes, the more random will be the harmonic outcome, tending to become a secondary phenomenon inaccessible to perception. You only have to listen to Webern's Five Movements for String Quartet, op. 5, and his String Trio, op. 20, side by side in order to hear this. Just like comparing Schoenberg's Five Pieces for Orchestra, op. 16, with his *Pierrot lunaire*, it reveals a change in compositional focus. Even Berg, who of the three held most strongly to the importance and stability of harmonic vocabulary, reveals increasing difficulty in controlling harmonic elements and techniques. It was difficult not to tip into incoherence, or at least not to cling to superficial coherence, by means that were anything other than local or slender, given that intervallic combination, particularly horizontal, had become the predominant device.

As these three composers developed, the preoccupation with harmony recurred, above all with Berg, who tried to recover some characteristics of tonal harmony. This is what he did in the Violin Concerto, in which the keys, if not the actual functions, of G minor and B major surface at significant points of the form. In the *Ode to Napoleon*, Schoenberg, too, devised quasi-tonal combinations in order to end in E flat major – but without exaggerating the importance of this allusion to Beethoven's *Eroica* symphony, it is easy to identify how the harmonic vocabulary has been simplified in certain ways. Even Webern increasingly organised his music for harmonic orientation, though he was the least close to these more or less nostalgic concerns. There are definitely linear invariants, polarities and, as it were, modulations, registrally determined, be it in the Cantata no. 2, op. 31, or the Variations, op. 30. In his case, this preoccupation appears sporadically after the Symphony, op. 21, which followed immediately after the String Trio, op. 20, the most anarchic work in this respect.

Thus, the problem of the relationship between the horizontal and the vertical resurfaced from composers who were clearly aware that musical expression needed a convincing solution, albeit only an empirical one.

As for a work's unity stemming from the unity of a matrix, the utopian nature of such an enterprise needs to be acknowledged, because what is *derived* from such a unique and sustained system has to be varied by textual non-repetition. And do the various deductions truly reflect their starting point, or do they become more or less autonomous, thanks to the characteristics they are required to adopt for reasons of development and form; and do they abandon the original matrix, unable to relate to that source except through visual gymnastics that have little to do with perception? The more that different versions of the idea take on an individual profile – in a way that is indispensable for the constitution of a work, or a part of it – the more they abandon particular referencing; conscious referencing can happen only by means that have no context, so that one hardly experiences any necessity in this completely artificial link.

Returning to what I stated earlier about the value of contour with respect to intervals: an interval in itself exists only *contextually*, and the series was meant to give it an *absolute* generative function. A minor third, say, in the abstract, is going to be transposable to any pitch level, and can be subject to all permutations, such as octave transposition, inversion or retrogression, regardless of whether it appears linearly or as a simultaneity. Now all these intervallic *contextualisations* are in conflict with the very notion of recognisable identity. The intervallic identity of a major sixth as such is stronger than the identity it has as an inverted minor third, at least if there is no other element in play to give it a different identity. Some rhythm, for instance – that is, the contour of a similar figure applied to the minor third as well as to the major sixth – will reduce these two intervals to a common element; but that rhythm may just as well introduce a different interval – a fourth, say. Moreover, although I have referred to 'an' interval, the moment there are several collections of intervals, perception needs to be directed by very strong kinds of relations for the intervals to be intact. On their own, there is not much they can do in isolation. In context, they control all our perception. The theoretical versus the real nature of the interval – this is the problem that Schoenberg's method came up against, and which weakened it.

Both micro- and macro-structurally, the very principle of the series is ineffective unless corroborated by other elements giving form and a sense of direction to the weak, literally informal element of the interval. It is interesting to analyse the response of the three Viennese composers to the shortcomings, deficiencies and weaknesses of the compositional principle they had established and espoused. Their work undoubtedly provides ample testimony to their awareness of these problems, even though they never formulated a critique during the period in which they placed their faith in the series. Composers of their calibre could certainly not avoid them, and each came up with a solution derived from his temperament, the demands of his language and expression, and his position, whether conscious or otherwise, in relation to his predecessors. Further, it can be said that although their use of the system sheds more light on their behaviour, it does not at all mean that it changed how they proceeded or inflected their motivation. Their concerns patently remained the same, and their aesthetic and stylistic evolution remained what one expects of consistently lively, developing and self-aware personalities. At most, there was some resistance, an instinct against strict discipline. They did not disown this historical phase, understood as the inevitable progress of polyphony, but exploited it, turned explicit rules to their advantage, tried to nurture some spontaneity within a domain that hardly seemed ready for it. For sure, it helped that free will was not in total command, that discipline remained a kind of safety barrier against evil temptations and sterile mistakes. And yet frugality cannot fuel the imagination. Particularly for those who grew up surrounded by post-Romantic flamboyance – Strauss and Mahler were their heroes and beacons – it was difficult to give in to numbers and calculation.

✿　✿　✿

'Mine is no system but only a method,' Schoenberg wrote; also, 'the basic set functions in the manner of a motive'; 'nothing is given by this method; but much is taken away'; and finally, 'one has to follow the basic set; but, nevertheless, one composes as freely as before'.[3] From Schoenberg's explanatory writings it is clear that the evolution of his language is based on the desire to unify a composition as strongly, as inevitably as possible, using a stringent system of themes and motives that saturates the musical texture, seizes it, provides its rationale, coherence and diversity. His thinking relies basically on deduction, and so not surprisingly, given his implacable wish to combine unity and diversity, he wants themes and motives to be derived from one core cell. But since this unique cell – that is, the series – was not susceptible to providing him with sufficiently varied raw material, he grafts onto it the old system, at that time virtually abandoned in practice, of various kinds of presentation used in strict counterpoint. On that basis, he thought he was able to create themes, motives and developments that were limitless, given the combinatorial richness of the matrix he used. Moreover, he thought there was no major problem with creating harmonic logic – of chords themselves, and their interrelationships – since there was no longer any difference between the vertical and the horizontal: the world is perceived to be free of gravity, as it were, and he cites Swedenborg and the Balzac of *Séraphîta* as supporting evidence (and later he evokes the cubist painters' take on objects). In this way, chords will be another way to perceive the motive, meaning that what works horizontally will work just as well vertically, and for the same reasons. Given that thematic and motivic structure rely on the basic principle of chromatic complementarity, the relationship between melody and harmony can equally be based on that principle.

Schoenberg, moreover, was so seized by having changed his methods without having changed their fundamental reference points that he used the same vocabulary for them, by analogy. For example, when speaking about the various transpositions of the series, he speaks of their resulting usage, compared with the original series, as modulations in relation to the main key. He has to make allowances, of course, for wanting to be understood and showing that his language is not a complete break with existing principles, that tradition and revolution go hand in hand here. Yet clearly his practice implies that overall reference, as he tries to draw together the old system and the new as closely as possible, to the point where the musical ideas he has created in the face of increasing anarchy and the need for a new system are going to change completely; they will somehow be under the yoke of the old procedures in order to support this new system and prove that it is no less valid. The hold of the old system over the new will, as its fundamental justification, force musical ideas to appear and to grow within a framework of restrictions that will make them seem to be prefabricated. Ideas are generated in the light of the conjunction of both systems, and there will no longer be just analogy, but wholesale retrieval. The new system will adopt by extension the functions of certain rules – mainly harmonic – that have disappeared, and so such functions must, it follows, be developed from the principal theme – which is what the series can be called.

On the basis of that unique feature, and its primary derivations, real themes will be generated and, by deduction, a variety of motives, and thus, as Schoenberg said, 'One composes as freely as before' – except that it was not his own 'before' that he referred to, but that of his fairly remote predecessors. He himself normally composed differently, writing works in which the form is created by the events, in which themes and motives follow each other, repeat and combine in a flexible hierarchy meeting the needs of the moment. In short, language and form were liberated, sometimes frantically. I stress that it is the idea that generates the system, however fragile and provisional it may seem, and it generates the form, too, a temporary capacity unique to the particular idea. Henceforth – if I may look at the bigger, radical perspective – ideas will be created and formulated in order to verify; they are constrained, even preconceived, through their intended use in a 'classical' framework. There are even textual reminders of the old system, left in like the fossil of a dead language. In the Wind Quintet, op. 25, the favoured transposition of the original series that will allow it to appear in related regions is the basic interval of tonality, the fifth. There can be no question of a return to the exact tonal functions of the fifth, and moreover, we do not take this transposition to be connected with that particular interval; but nevertheless, the phantom fifth is the perfect symbol of a state of mind, or rather, of the soul: it is sentimental, for sure, but it is no abdication.

There is hardly a need to pursue that matter given that it is the basis of reference throughout, from the language itself right up to the formal aspects, and in this way the work is perfectly coherent – at a deep level, it is its most convincing aspect. Every previous resource is going to be employed, perhaps revitalised, as a demonstration or a justification, be it the form of the classical sonata, or the pre-classical suite, or the successive blocks of variation form. Undoubtedly, the constraints of the new way of writing do not make the job of the composer any easier: the permanent imposition of what we may call motivic order fixes certain aspects of the language, inflicts a certain stiffness, prevents it from using certain kinds of ornament that are very necessary to vary the writing and make it flexible and fluid. In the history of music there has always been much room for manoeuvre between so-called 'strict' and 'free' composition: in the former, depending on how tight the rules are, going as far as the total and only solution, you are forced to write completely predetermined relationships between the notes; in the latter, on the other hand, the rules, which are of a more general kind, allow infinite progressions and figures, where freedom, the composer's choice, is always likely to break out. The margin of creativity between the total and only solution and unfettered choice is wide open; composers' use of, or hold over, the material will differ in kind as well as in scope. Validating the new system through the old one excludes some basic options, and this is barely outweighed by the richness of the recently gained territory, which leads to Schoenberg's own conclusion: that 'nothing is given by this method; but much is taken away'. What is more, validation means overturning the link between system and idea, it sets up a hierarchy that contradicts the past, imposes a kind of servitude on composers' creativity, shuts them into an unintended world, traps them in historicism – which ultimately means sterility.

✳   ✳   ✳

To digress: there is a certain stance among the three Viennese composers towards the spirit of the system – this despite Schoenberg using the word 'method' to imply a constrained, willingly limited outlook. It is highly symptomatic of what may be thought of as the *generic* mindset. These three, more than anyone else at the time, had a deep sense of historical continuity, of tradition, certainly in the most lively and fecund meaning of that word, but, equally, of tradition at its most restrictive and dutiful. Having worked out the consequences of what they found to be central to their creative approach, they found themselves at the heart of a way of writing created by their own concerns, confronted by an invented, agreed discipline, by the validation in certain compositional variables. It is crucial to observe and study their personal responses, because beyond the historical contingencies that led them to a method of writing lies a fundamental relationship between system, compositional practice and aesthetics.

This method of writing has always been regarded as far too formalist. Works, when understood at all, were understood to be valid, even while the soundness of the method and system was in dispute, and it was ironic, too, that a system designed to be stable had such a short life. And of course there were answers to those questions – for example, that stability is not about stasis but about how an idea can be transformed; and this Viennese idea was indeed transformed, dispersed through the passage of time, split into different ways of doing things. Whereas the initial system had a very short life in practice, its legacy was prolific, and sometimes found where it was least expected. As for the relationship between a work and the method, it seems to me difficult to rely on an absurd contradiction, for if a work does derive from the method, and the work is valid, then the method cannot be entirely false and must have some absolute validity. That is confirmed when we see the *principles* of writing coincide with the *reality* of writing, whereas when there is conflict with, or absence of, validation, writing is seriously weakened, losing coherence and meaning. The charge of formalism is too narrow when formulated in such a vague way that it refers only to the omnipotence and infallibility of instinct: only mindlessness falls to that charge, or it would lead to the rejection of many works which use forms of strict writing, rules of deduction requiring a science of implementation and of internal relationships. The only formalist works would be those using well-tested relationships, and anti-formalism would be only the visible evidence provided by memory. The real problem in this far too vague charge of formalism is when compositional constraint is more or less visible, when rigour is more or less obvious.

Much more could be said about the visibility of constraint. The rules of strict counterpoint are quite explicit in this respect, forcing us to consider the precise relationships between the various original and resulting objects of direct deduction. Because a relationship prevails so strongly, it is impossible not to be aware of what is obligatory. Beyond figures, it is perceived as such, or as a rule, or an acknowledged constraint defined by existing rules and strict codes. These rules and codes somehow define a mode of writing, indeed a whole form. The visibility of the constraints provides a framework for creativity, and will be perceived in exactly that way. However, when the constraint is hidden, deliberately or otherwise, by the whims of writing, it will seem difficult or impossible to detect it, other than perhaps in a certain resistance, as I mentioned with regard to Schoenberg, a lack of ease and flexibility. Also, a constraint may be transformed, free itself from the code, assume great variety in the application of rules that are adopted, changed or avoided. When Debussy adopts constraints in some of his piano *Études* that are as narrow but also malleable as the *interval* of a fourth, third, sixth or octave – and he was preceded in this by Chopin, among others – or as vague and flexible as *chord, compound arpeggio* or *eight fingers*, he is certainly not adopting a formal framework, a codified starting point or initial basis. In the *Étude* 'Pour les quartes' he lets this interval invade his vocabulary, but not exclusively. The fourth may be a determining element or only a kind of colouring, but what the formal conception of this *Étude* keeps of this initial constraint is only the more or less visible use of the interval, and this is the same with the other *Études*, where the constraint fades away, reappears only to depart, invading everywhere, but very subtly and changeably.

In the same spirit, one could also cite the third act of *Wozzeck*, with its various inventions on a *theme*, a *rhythm*, a *key*, a *moto perpetuo*, a *chord* and a *note*. Of those six constraints, apart from the first – which implies a set of variations on the given theme – none of the others can determine a form; and the constraint on the elements of vocabulary yields much less 'formalism', in the strictest sense, than the scene names of the second act (Sonata, Fugue, Lied, Scherzo, Rondo), in which the vocabulary does not, however, have to conform so strongly to external, enveloping obligations. The constraints in the third act spread into diverse formalisations that are sometimes unifying, gathering, but equally sometimes dissociating, through using components of a rhythm or, for instance, a chord.

This kind of constraint, such as that just discussed with respect to Debussy and Berg, has the advantage of adaptation, movement, transformation, but from a strict point of view it is a constraint all the same, particularly in Berg. It is a common denominator, for a certain time, of all the items in a particular vocabulary, whether of pitch or duration.

✿ ✿ ✿

That detour was needed in order to understand fully that I am not talking solely about the historical aspects of Schoenberg's, Berg's and Webern's choices, as if they were still current, and that I am focusing on the characteristics of their individual approaches, which, for me, exemplify the sense in which they typify how creativity responds to system.

Let us return to my conclusions about Schoenberg's approach. Schoenberg never stopped validating his own method through pre-existing categories. Previously, he had written works in which the form was created by the event, and themes and motifs were connected, repeated and combined in a subtle hierarchy born of the necessity of the moment. The idea generated the system, as fragile and provisional as it might seem. It also generated form that was unique to the particular idea. But afterwards ideas were created, formulated, for validation; constrained, indeed *pre-constrained*, by their future 'classical' use. Certain basic capacities were lost due to the validation of the new system by the old one, and this was barely outweighed by the richness of the recently gained territory. Validation means overturning the link between system and idea, it sets up a hierarchy that contradicts the past, it imposes a kind of servitude on the composers' creativity, shuts them into an unintended world, traps them in historicism, which in the long run means sterility.

I will not go over again the connection there may be between the historicism to which Schoenberg eventually turned and that found in Stravinsky. I have already explained the superficial similarities and fundamental differences in these historical obsessions of both composers during the same period. In Schoenberg's case, it was a search for authenticity by drawing directly from a revered tradition, and in Stravinsky's, it was playing with found objects, or rather, objects recovered from the storehouse of history: the first was a case of historical continuity at any price, and the second was one of reassembling history as a kind of puzzle. Truth or playing, all the same the common factor is reference, and the categorical distinction Adorno wanted to make between Schoenberg the progressive and Stravinsky the restorer seems nowadays ever more porous. It seems that, in fact, Stravinsky's project of restoration was impertinent, whereas Schoenberg's progressive attitude was moulded by respect, indeed devotion. Probably, Stravinsky, much more than Schoenberg, made the use of history impossible with his determined parodying, whereas Schoenberg's historicism – I would say more latent, more contained – maintains the illusion through nostalgia, even charm.

❁ ❁ ❁

The first characteristic in Schoenberg, then, is a decidedly unconfident dogmatism, uncertainty, the need for reassurance in the endurance of some criteria in a development that would otherwise spin out of control into randomness. How is Berg going to behave in relation to his master?

This relationship of master and disciple seems to me to play an important role in Berg's adoption of the principle of the twelve-note series at least. It is certainly not that he did this more from obedience than conviction, but his path and the choices he made did not predispose him at all to strict adherence. From his earliest works, Berg is no less particular about working with themes and motives than Schoenberg, having learned it from him. In some cases, he does use rigorously organised total chromaticism. But more than Schoenberg he feels the need for direct historical referencing, for tonal episodes. His aesthetic amalgamates more than it excludes. He feels the need to connect the world he has left with the one he has found, this meeting sometimes becoming eminently symbolic, as in the Bible-reading scene in the third act of *Wozzeck*, where tonality becomes the nostalgic citation of a bygone world.

In his very writing, Berg likes to deviate from a model. When he varies a melisma, or manipulates a motive, it is in relation as much to contour as to intervals. Organisation is not achieved by manipulating a fixed entity and changing how it is present, but much more by affinity, resemblance, gesture, to which the literal is inimical. Berg's genius lies in his ever-pliant technique, which makes it a better tool, preserving an unforeseen interaction with confluence and context, with no risk of incoherence or disorientation. Further, he had what one may call mysticism, or a number fetish, so that there are cases where he imposes numerical constraints on the number of bars, metronome marks or durations, or on compositional procedure. Those familiar with his work learn to spot these external constraints, which are not really supposed to be perceived – how would that be possible with a metronome mark? – but seize the composer's imagination in a strict framework that obliges him to find solutions, colluding with the score-reader who discovers the secret proportion or meaning hidden in the numbers. This presence of number in Berg's work is not entirely about obeying a rule, but is symbolic, a Pythagorean trace, a reliance on an absolute, higher order, whereas the expressive, fluid, even febrile musical expression continually deflects our attention from any abstract idea that controls it.

Moreover, Berg procrastinates when he adopts the serial system. He touches it and pulls back; he needs the conflict between free and strict composition; he sticks to gesture and contour rather than being captive to literal intervals. Some freely composed movements or parts of movements from the *Lyric Suite* contrast with other movements or parts which rely on strict compositional technique. Even there, he shuns the single series as the whole model for a work. He deduces from the series, each time, a specific series by reordering a few notes, by which he produces certain characteristics that he uses as the profile in the movement to which it applies. He goes even further, in what one may call decimating the system, in *Lulu*, where he abandons the initial material virtually to contradict it or show it – unconsciously? – to be void. The development of different series connected with characters in the opera linked to number ciphers, a hidden symbolism, is entirely casual in relation to the model, once the deduction has happened. It looks as if he were paying tribute to the series, out of respect and devotion, but once he has been through that ceremony he no longer feels bound to any kind of literal obedience. You have only to look a little more closely at his procedure to be persuaded, and the quotation I already offered from Schoenberg applies particularly well to this case: 'nevertheless, one composes as freely as before', from which I omit the first clause, 'one has to follow the basic set', as irrelevant.

What does he actually do? We have the original series, which is supposed to guarantee the unity of the whole work. He systematically takes
one note out of two, out of three, four, five, seven, to make a total each
time of twelve. He applies to the original series more complex procedures, taking every second note, every third, every fourth, every third,
every second, and so on, up to a total of twelve. He now has a collection in
which the structural relationships are both highly explicit as to procedure
and completely inaudible if they are not specifically expressed musically.
What does Berg do? He takes a theme from each of these deductions
– melodic or harmonic, or a combination of the two – and associates it
through its expressive character with one of the protagonists. By methods
that are no less complex, he takes a set of special intervals from the series,
such as fourths, or the white keys followed by the black keys, collections
which with a little artifice can be deduced from any series, considering
their basically generalised and amorphous nature. You could easily say
that from thematic content that he has already invented he goes back
to an initial matrix by means of tortuous processes, which is proof, were
it needed, that what he is most interested in is not deductions but the
thematic quality he can derive from them. You might in fact think that
given the interactions of the protagonists in the work, the musical language would convey this through the numerical derivation, but far from
it: derivations are withdrawn, forgotten, purely at the service of traditional thematic construction. Nothing is musically perceptible to point
you towards the sources: the sequence of deductions remains the exclusive property of the creator, and even the most acutely observant and
well-informed creator cannot trace it at all in the eventual text.

It is reasonable to ask, why resort to such rigorous and hidden methods of deduction, only to forget them once they have served their
purpose? Why rely on them when obviously the goal was already known
and did not require them in order to be achieved? It was paying tribute
to the system under the watchful eye of the master, extricating ideas
of one's own that would immediately reveal their independence. That
could have been Berg's psychology, showing his respect for a combinatorial discipline, which in his case equated to numerical mysticism, while
simultaneously recognising that on their own such operations cannot

engender musical creativity. It was an inextricable mix of obedience and irreverence, strict discipline and misbehaviour.

That is pretty clear, or even clearer, when he inscribes nostalgia into the very order of the row. The row was destined to be non-tonal, but Berg needs tonality, or rather, some elements of tonality, in order to express himself in the two idioms without transgressing principle or procedure. Such is the case in the Violin Concerto, where the notes of the row are arranged in a way that will yield triads. In this work, more visibly than in any other, the row is a kind of a posteriori justification for ideas that could have been found without it, especially as some serial manipulation corresponds to each idea and motive for exactly that reason. Thus, the system remains an *ideal* starting point, but since it is used for invention, for ideas, it is not impalpable, but continuously accommodates the goal of bringing an idea to life, in a kind of symbiosis with the system.

Schoenberg's comment, made in 1946, is particularly relevant to the use of tonal 'relics' so dear to Berg's heart, which let him bathe nostalgically in a lost world, resorting to citation and combining heterogeneous elements willy-nilly through conjuring tricks and combinatorial acrobatics: 'Though he was right as a composer, he was wrong theoretically.'[4] Meaning that to be a composer you have to disobey your watchful inner theorist? That theory exists only to stimulate the disobedience needed to create? But if theory is a pain you have to get used to and deal with, is it valid? In this way, Berg openly poses a fundamental dilemma: he cunningly poaches ideas that could have arisen independently of a system that – whether from deference, perhaps, or conviction – he feels he has to alter. I do not think he emerged unscathed from the constraints of compositional practice imposed upon him by *rules*. For sure, he can use strict composition to maximum effect, and the permutational idea that infuses the Allegro misterioso of the *Lyric Suite* is masterfully done. The composing is less flexible in some passages of *Lulu* and *Der Wein*, where there is less creative richness in the detail compared with what we find in the 'free' works. Can this greater rigidity, this lack of spontaneous creativity, perhaps be ascribed solely to compositional problems arising from a presumed antagonism towards the system? It is very difficult to claim that, to maintain only that hypothesis, given the period's tendency towards classicism, which was reflected in Berg no less than in all his contemporaries. All we can say is that when he is maximally *casual* about the system, as in the Violin Concerto, he finds the compositional virtuosity and expressive ease that are sometimes missing from work weighed down by constraints, rendered neutral and stiff by undue obedience. Berg's working methods show as clearly as possible the duality of system and idea that is the basis of all his later works, posing the question: Will the rule and the given be compatible?

*　*　*

After the Father and Son comes the Holy Ghost! For he, too, had something to say on the subject at this important time. He said it with habitual discretion, but so strongly, so radically, with such instinctive intelligence about his situation! He was certainly more obsessed than his two contemporaries with order and rigour. His attachment to Flemish music is just a symptom, as is the time he spent on musicology as a student. Moreover, this rigour was no ascetic exercise reflected in, and by, his writing. The most common word coming from Webern's pen when he comments on his working methods and compositional characteristics is 'coherence'. There are others that could also express his deep need, of which 'duty' is the first that comes to mind.

For Webern, in effect, it is not a question of a note or line taking full responsibility for another note or line, but one of a whole made up of consolidated elements, particularly through deduction that leads from a model to its derivatives, but also through precise calculation of its distribution. It is no surprise that strict canon fascinated him, to the point of monopolising his creative resources; no surprise how satisfying and safe he found this way of writing. Once this principle was established there could be no other solution. This solution was difficult, maybe, tough to find, but once it was in place any doubts about it completely disappeared. He wrote according to the Law, thus obeying the demands of Nature, in capital letters. The composer becomes the transcriber of the Truth that is revealed to him in this way. He transcribes himself, of course, but in doing so he goes far beyond his own self towards absolute proof: through him, immanent Order is revealed. Beside this basic preoccupation aimed at deductive unity, total coherence, lay another characterised by a radical revision of discourse through strict non-repetition, and these preoccupations are so contradictory that Webern soon found himself in the position of Malevich's *White on White*. The series of short lectures entitled *The Path to the New Music*, delivered in 1932, provides a retrospective description of the acute disarray in this decade: 'I had the feeling, "When all twelve notes have gone by, the piece is over."'[5] He shows himself struggling with the absurdity of this situation, which we can understand from this longer quotation from Webern's own text: 'In my sketchbook I wrote out the chromatic scale and crossed off the individual notes. Why? Because I had convinced myself, "This note has been there already." It sounds grotesque, incomprehensible, and it was incredibly difficult. The inner ear decided quite rightly that the man who wrote out the chromatic scale and crossed off individual notes *was no fool.*'[6]

Deduction reduced to the skeletal state of the notes in a chromatic scale cannot really create a whole universe. But then the twelve-note serial method, before he had observed, judged and appreciated all its rules, seemed to him a deliverance. From this tiny patch, in which he felt he was trapped, he saw some gateways opening towards a wider realm and could imagine air that was easier to breathe, less rarefied! But he came out of this descent into the abyss with some unshakeable principles: 'All twelve notes have equal rights,' and 'Twelve-note composition is not a "substitute for tonality" but leads much further.'[7] He speaks repeatedly about the 'urge to create unity' and 'variations on a theme', concepts that he never abandoned even after his radical experience of reduction. Admittedly, he hesitated and had doubts that reflected Schoenberg's influence, expressed in his master's own terms, for example, in a sentence that partly contradicts his own practice: 'For the rest, one composes as before, but on the basis of the row; on the basis of this fixed series one will have to invent.'[8]

That is not entirely wrong. Strict canon had always been favoured by Webern, and it remained in an incontestably special position compared with any other kind of control and deduction; to which is added the fact that every harmonic and contrapuntal relationship will refer to the same original model. Schoenberg maintained that in this respect it was no easy task, to which Webern had the perfect answer: 'Adherence is strict, often burdensome, but it's *salvation!*' He cagily added: 'This compulsion, adherence, is so powerful that one has to consider very carefully before finally committing oneself to it for a prolonged period.'[9]

What do those thoughts really mean? It is obvious that his first serial attempts show some confusion. System and idea are still widely separated, as we see, for example, in the Two Songs, op. 19, and again in the String Trio, op. 20. The row zigzags between the voices without creating truly recognisable entities, for two reasons: the row is, strictly speaking, uncharacterised, at least in the sense that its characteristics do not appear directly in the musical texture; and the row ensures only amorphously, so to speak, the chromatic complementation in its segments. These works, the first especially, could almost have been written using a different row. He draws on the total chromatic without attaching any functions, any structural relationships. The organisation generating the intervals has no influence at all on how the work is disposed, to the extent that we cannot perceive any relationship between them. He could always reassure himself by regarding that aspect of the question as negligible, honestly admitting when something was missing: 'If an untutored ear can't always follow the course of the row, there's no harm done . . . Something will stick in even the naivest soul.'[10]

Some consolation, but what does it solve? Webern could not be happy with the casual way, which is why he says, 'one aims at as many different intervals as possible' – which is relevant to Berg and the all-interval row he used in the first movement of the *Lyric Suite* – 'or certain correspondences within the row – symmetry, analogy, grouping (thrice four or four times three notes, for instance)'[11] – which applied directly to his own work, starting with the Symphony, op. 21, and even more so the Concerto, op. 24. 'Considerations of symmetry, regularity are now to the fore, as against the emphasis formerly laid on the principal intervals – dominant, subdominant, mediant, etc. For this reason, the middle of the octave – the diminished fifth – is now most important':[12] that is how he justifies all the considerations prior to fixing the row, which is itself prior to composing. A reminder immediately follows, like a denial: 'For the rest, one works as before', which means, as I have said, that canon remains the practical basis, as it had been in most of his earlier works. Berg and Schoenberg, too, and Berg in particular, made a fetish of this thinking about the row, but they were far from being taken in the same direction as Webern. When he refers to previous tonal schemes, he speaks of 'analogy' to establish very general functions, that is, characteristics such as tension–release, order–chaos, knowing–recognising, applicable to any kind of syntax. Thus, there is a contradiction between, on the one hand, his wish to refresh his language continually, his radical urge for non-repetition of any sort of element; and on the other, his wish to sustain strict links between the different elements of his composing, using procedures, especially strict canon, that tend to make a rule of exact imitation. There is a fundamental contradiction between perpetual variation and repetition, which led Webern to cover his tracks, as it were. He could write completely classical canons where one hears one voice reproducing another, but others where one would be completely at a loss to perceive them as such because other more important and 'striking' phenomena occupy our hearing.

How did he manage to do this? And first of all, was it deliberate, or the result of vocabulary and devices little suited to discriminating between lines? Certainly, a conjunct, continuous line – to use the word 'line' again – is infinitely easier to perceive than a disjunct, discontinuous one. Separating pitches in space and time lends them a certain autonomy, all the more strongly if we add timbral quality to the separation. It will take effort to identify those elements, which we tend to perceive in isolation, as a whole, and even if we are aware of the identity of this whole, our perception hardly helps us to take it in, favouring as it does the isolation of elements. An extra difficulty is the crossing of voices, for to the extent that registral homogeneity helps us follow a line, so does leaving a register, and the interpenetration of registers leads to confusion, when we no longer know which element to attach to which global entity; in extreme cases, perception fails completely.

There is a remarkable example of this state of affairs in the *exposition* of the first movement of the Symphony, op. 21. Without going into analytical detail, suffice it to say that this exposition is written in four voices, more or less virtual entities belonging more to the concept of voices than the reality familiar in, for instance, baroque counterpoint. These four voices are grouped in pairs in a double canon. The first two voices are segmented in a fairly visible way using a timbral structure that is rather overt. The other two voices are highly fragmentary, with a more ambiguous timbral structure. Thus, there is an intended contrast between a tangible reality in the individual voices and a reality that is difficult to perceive, almost virtual. Register adds to the ambiguity by making each pitch firmly fixed so that all the voices share this static collection which does not really characterise any of them. Register is therefore strongly inclined to overrule the individuality of each voice, and without close attention we perceive this exposition as a kind of registral animation, like a map where the notable locations light up in turn. Any given pitch, being firmly fixed as to register, is therefore itself more than it is part of some pitch complex or a particular voice. At worst, we will hear a collection of individual notes, the logic of their appearance escaping us.

Webern deliberately does not go that far in the struggle between individual element and global entity, and the majority of his writing remains dominated by classical concepts in which the details still stick closely to historical codes. He pulls every resolution possible from this conflict and uses them carefully, but to perfection. Yet there are plenty of other cases in his work where, on the contrary, one is aware of his difficulty in getting away from classical detail, when centrifugal forces such as large intervals, long silences, voice-crossing and registral confusion would exert less control. The exposition in the third movement of the Concerto, op. 24, with its repeated cells and fairly straight rhythm, shows the limits of renewal when these elements converge on a more traditional kind of writing.

An example of that kind is a strong reminder of Webern's sentence quoted above: 'For the rest, one composes as before, but on the basis of the row; on the basis of this fixed series one will have to invent.' On the contrary, he is at his highest level of invention, radicality and conceptual renovation when the centrifugal forces he uses stop him from writing as before. His starting point may be weighed down by traditional concepts, but these concepts burst out of the pressure from schemes of writing and lead to new concepts that perhaps Webern did not conceive directly, but which his imagination forced him to discover. Considering the narrow path he had to take to get there, we can say that he escaped brilliantly, remembering his practically degree-zero obsession with renewal when he crossed off the twelve notes one by one, and when he thought he could go no further for fear of literal repetition. From the desert of those isolated notes to the reconstitution of segments to rediscovery of form was certainly a difficult, painful path, particularly for someone as conscious as he was every day of the masterpieces of music history.

When Webern was struggling with the most basic tenets of his language, he thought of a solution that would be convincing at the structural level of *incorporation*. More precisely, this is what he said: 'The twelve-note row is, as a rule, not a "theme". But I can also work without thematicism, that is to say much more freely, because of the unity that has now been achieved in another way; the row ensures unity.'[13] The theme and the structure of the row are one and the same to him. I like to use the term 'incorporation' to describe that technique, and can explain it first by its opposite.

There are, or rather, have been (it is a kind of dabbling that tends to run out of steam), many music analyses purely of twelve-note structure. These often restrict themselves to showing that the various rows unfold accurately in terms of order. Each note is numbered, and it is confirmed that in various sections of the piece this or that row form is used in preference to another. Slightly more thorough analysis of row forms unearths all the symmetries, and potential symmetries, in a row, and what common features are found between a row segment and some other segment of some other row. The study of form was addressed as a supplementary envelope, related to some classical scheme and asserting, in different hands, some different property or analogy. Yet in these studies there is not even a hint of reference to the aesthetic potential of such structures, symmetries and fields. It is precisely there that I locate *incorporation*.

It makes complete sense to take structural elements as the premise for deduction and derivation, but how are those procedures of derivation and deduction reified, and what legitimacy will we give them? Berg's answer was clear: he deduced *themes* from entities extracted from each other by more or less numerical and mechanical processes. After that, he put those processes aside because he considered them to have been incorporated in the various themes. Future deductions and variations would start from this second stage, never returning to the original one. It is clear to see, therefore, where incorporation lay for him. For Schoenberg, incorporation lay just as much in the invention of a theme, but it does not ignore the other structural forms that have given him the row – for instance, the incorporation of harmonic rules. Those harmonic laws, which are more flexible than the theme proper, do not need a return to the original matrix once they have been created, like certain types of chord. They offer relationships and fields that are thus made perceptible.

In Webern, this incorporation is subtler in that it is highly variable. The first movement alone of the Variations, op. 27, shows how there is, in his words, 'work without thematicism'.[14] Incorporation is done through the tendency of a chosen harmony linked to the rhythm continuum, producing definitely not *a* figure, but a *type* of figure. The theme determines an *optimal* link between different elements, to make from them a strong figure, self-contained, an entity that can be stored in the memory. From that are deduced developments based on dismantling and reconstruction, ornamentation and thinning, but the reference point always remains the initial fusion of elements strongly presented to us when the theme appeared. Actually, Webern's conception of the relationships between the row and the work itself enables there to be many figures, but never realisation in a primordial one. Instead of being *deduced*, as in the case of the theme, successive incorporations are *induced* from an initial, virtual idea. The risk, very obvious in the subsequent period of development and excess, was that he would be working with virtual ideas, elaborated through various systems, based on permutation, symmetry and many numerical devices, without concern for other means of incorporation. Virtual systems would proliferate in their potential, providing raw material in a seemingly indiscriminate way, but not bringing with them any required incorporation. The more or less literal realisations one can make of the materials provided by the system are certainly real, but it is a kind of pre-reality preceding what can be called music. Relationships are perceived because of incorporation; it creates discernible phenomena that can be distinguished from one another. One will certainly not be aware of the phenomenon of incorporation itself – that is, the move from virtual to real – but one will perceive the main structures as discernible phenomena. This is how Webern, as a reminder, put it more directly: 'If an untutored ear can't always follow the course of the row, there's no harm done . . . Something will stick in even the naivest soul.'[15] He was talking about a case of relatively simple figures, but when there are more sources and combinations, even the naive soul will not have retained much, because in practice there will have been nothing more to retain. Imagine Berg with all his numerical deductions, as in *Lulu*, but no intermediate themes – what would one be able to grasp?

So should one precisely specify all the generative relationships, all the internal structures of the language? If so, does the work risk becoming nothing but a demonstration of the possibilities in the raw material that was used as a starting point? Without doubt, a discussion of the distance between system and the elaborated idea cannot be held in such simplistic terms. The elaboration of idea from system is an utterly complex, variable process that does not always take the same path. Does the incorporation always need to be recognisable? Definitely not, and I have already cited the case of the first movement of Webern's Concerto, op. 24, which hovers continuously between confession and denial, so to speak. Sometimes the symmetries on which its basic row is founded are highlighted, but sometimes it is segmented irregularly, so that we lose sight of its original intervallic symmetry. Incorporation, then, can make us sense the precision, the literalness in a realisation, but elaboration that is more extensive, and more misleading, can distance us from the original material. The two procedures are both sound, and the one very often borrows its validity from the other. Every sufficiently substantial work puts us through an alternation of evidence and doubt, of clarity and ambiguity. We see this asset in the forms of old, whose structure and articulation is nearly always based in this necessary contrast. Sonata form offers us exposition, development and recapitulation; fugue, different kinds of exposition and episodes; rondo, refrain and couplets. It is better to view these forms in such a way nowadays, so that we can still draw important lessons from them, rather than considering those forms on their own terms historically.

I will return to the different degrees of incorporation and to the kinds of identification it allows or disallows, but first I want to return to looking more closely at Webern and his individual technique. To establish his initial material – that is, the original row – he creates it by segmentation, creating symmetries, analogies, reconfigurations. As a result, the whole work will be governed by a favoured organisation of the intervals. Thus, he considerably reduces the scope of the row by dividing it into minimal figures that are perceptible; at the same time as perceiving the musical figures we grasp the underlying structure from which they were born. Obviously, here I am describing the most extreme case of extreme clarity. There are many other more complex ones, since perfect visibility quickly risks becoming more of an exegesis, boring and predictable. However, it has become inconceivable to separate figure from structure unless there is a temporary deviation, a derogation from the procedure – a temporary asymmetry in the notes, for instance – to be rectified at a later important point in the work, as a kind of recapitulation. In Webern's work, unlike in Berg, who builds up numerical operations meant to remain hidden in themselves, operations on the row are reductive, as simplifying as possible, to yield immediate identification, to reveal the evidence unambiguously. The composer's approach in the series of works beginning with op. 21 could not be more patent: idea and the organisation of the system totally coincide. Despite this almost forensic rigour, however, vertical relations remain very uncertain, dependent almost entirely on what the rhythm produces by chance and on what the horizontal voices produce vertically. To avoid clashes, to enhance the horizontal dimension by vertical meaning, Webern freezes registers – thus op. 21 begins, and thus op. 24 ends. Each item of the twelve-note row is given a fixed register, constituting a sort of harmonic justification (in the typographical sense). All the voices move according to this registral grid, creating mobile progression through static position. Given such constraints on the voices, at that point of polyphonic writing one would think of a similar dynamic element operating in a static context, particularly when the number of voices goes beyond a certain norm, so that the resulting harmony is completely static. Nevertheless, the harmonic structure overall cannot lie in a series of static states of that kind, especially if each voice is to have registral autonomy, and when vocal music restricts the range and possible flexibility within that range. If the writing is careful and controlled, vertical collections will avoid intervals, such as the octave, that would contradict the individual horizontal organisation, but this polyphony brings about doubtful relationships, the vertical result being at the mercy of concurrences in a *field* of pitches, and not obeying any note-to-note law. As strong as the system is in one domain, coinciding perfectly with the idea, in this other domain the system cannot really function except in extreme stasis, or in chance outcomes that approximate to that.

Note that in his later works in particular Webern is concerned to connect the two dimensions of writing, surely noticing how the law dominates one sector, while more or less controlled chance reigns in the other. He returned in some ways to the kinds of writing to be found in his earliest works, such as the Five Movements for String Quartet, op. 5, for example. There, one dimension often refers to the other, and sometimes the melodic line takes the form of a harmonic unfolding. But that connection happens essentially by instinct, step by step; there is no rule other than local judgement. Even recognising that this concern is not the predominant one, one cannot help but notice it here and there as a strong, unifying force relating the horizontal and vertical dimensions. In the late works, such as the Cantatas nos 1 and 2, he returns to this aim of connection in a more rational and organised way. But the idea remains of the horizontal as a deployment of the vertical, and the vertical of the horizontal, to use Mallarmé's terms about the fan and the absolute book. The harmony thus happens when the lines coincide on the downbeat, and the counterpoint happens on the second, third and fourth beats of the derived lines. (Note how attached he remains to the idea of harmony and counterpoint in *four* voices, a hangover from the world where the fourth voice could only double one of the other three, given that triads are the basis of harmony; this idea of four voices persists despite the evolution of the language to a stage very distant from its initial basis.)

So it is the harmony that indicates how one may, and must, understand the derivation of the voices. Yet despite that general perception, it is no less true that the diagonal relationships will not dominate the directly vertical relationships, which are always stronger, the verticalities being concretely, immediately perceived, much more strongly than in a virtual relationship, which implies a kind of mental reconstruction that is more elaborate, less instinctive – and often quite incapable of picking up such virtual relationships.

Did vocal writing, rather than instrumental, lead Webern to think of this temporal unfolding and folding? Perhaps, but probably that was only the trigger for his procedure. In these two cantatas there is in fact a contrast between a vocal, conjunct style and an instrumental, disjunct style, as well as the contrast between syllabic synchrony between all the vocal parts, which makes the text comprehensible, and counterpoint, in which music obscures our understanding of the text. Perhaps all these factors, traditional in choral writing, forced him to rethink the relationship between harmony and counterpoint, leading him to consider the idea of coherence more radically and deeply.

Nevertheless, the coherence that remained his central concern is largely achieved: not coherence in principle, but coherence in fact, which reduction to a small number of simple components made possible. In that, his approach is very similar to that of Kandinsky in the Bauhaus period, when the straight line, the square and the circle were used exclusively in pictorial construction. Mondrian, indeed, would deliberately shun anything other than straight lines. There is no doubt that in all works of this kind the world of form is distinctly impoverished; on the other hand, the idea of development in these forms, and their interrelationships, is completely obvious, and thereby harbours a certain secret, for one can relate the basic elements reasonably well to the work as a whole. According to Webern, the row 'came into existence when an idea occurred to us, linked with an intuitive vision of the work as a whole'.

What about form, though, that large form which the new method made possible again following the shrinkage caused by radical use of non-repetition? Does it follow directly from the system and the man-oeuvres it enables? In this domain we find ignorance of the problem, or a hiatus between plan and execution, or an ambiguity between the formal intention and how the system is used. The three approaches to the newly circulated method attenuated their inherent divergence with regard to the concept of form, modelled entirely on – not even derived from – the heritage of tradition, albeit with notable differences. In most of his strict works, Schoenberg integrally adopts, without real modifica-tion, the conventional schemes of sonata, rondo and so on. Berg follows those schemes in principle, though either the narrative requirements of concert music or the dramatic ones of opera made him deviate from the framework and pushed him to experiment with mingling those forms; the models are there, but distorted by citations, insertions and discon-tinuities. Forms as historical orientations become, in turn, the material for a new level of creativity, and their meaning is to do with narrative force and dramatic expression as much as architectural balance. As for Webern, what he achieved, as his technical ability made it possible, was fusion of the different classical forms. When explaining the formal structure of the Variations, op. 30, he ended up claiming that in practice everything is connected. Schoenberg had returned, in his op. 31, to the set of variations, each based on precise and distinct characteristics. Berg uses a similar principle for continuity. Webern, not stopping at temporal continuity, wished to integrate the various surfaces into a global form, in which the way the system is manipulated will be largely responsible for the musical events.

These variations are in fact an overture, he explained. The theme is the introduction, the first variation is really the theme, the second a tran-sition, the third a secondary theme, and the fourth leads to the reprise of the theme, for this is a song form; and so the analysis proceeds to the end of the piece. It is not difficult to see the deliberate confusion of these specific forms based in a single overarching form, in the same way that at the level of language the canonic writing exactly matches the row usage. Thus, the form itself refers to the system, but through the filter of trad-itional form. One could say that Berg ends by showing the impotence of the system through the fact that the themes forgo any abstract, detailed, mythically numerical preparation of its rows, whereas Webern tends to show the impotence of classical forms when it comes to responding adequately to the compositional method. Ambiguity stands as an act of obedience to history, but beyond that tribute the work can be regarded from a quite different point of view, more directly linked to the actual structure of its language; reference is abolished at a stroke. This work is at once real and ghostly: real in respect of the laws of its new language, ghostly in its reference to the old world. It is neither Schoenbergian validation nor Bergian nostalgia, but an illusion, a formal mirage.

✻ ✻ ✻

I have considered above all procedures of this Father, Son and Holy Ghost. They remain to this day the most remarkable, the most acute, the most thoughtful of the first half of the last century, although it is certainly true that other works of quality, or genius, appeared at the same time. But next to the stance of these composers, others seem to indicate the end of a journey rather than the birth of a new direction: their reflection on language is partial, sporadic, indeed inconsequential and vague. Their use of vocabulary and syntax hardly goes further than ideas that are borrowed or overdone. The excessive was in fact able to survive for a while, grafted onto functions that were losing their identity and, thus, their power, but the borrowed and the excessive could carry only the external appearance of novelty. When renewal does not go deep, the limitations of such ornament will show up very quickly. Certain characteristics that were little noticed by the Viennese, even set aside by them as disruptive of their fundamentally traditional hierarchy, appeared here and there among composers with a very different outlook: characteristics such as the noise–sound continuum, or questioning the make-up of intervals and scales, leading to the restoration of idiosyncratic pitch schemes, or widening concepts of duration or of the more general concept of time – all those characteristics designed to outstrip the limits within which the evolution of our tradition had contained us. Their potential for novelty is undeniable, but one could easily say that it was only brushed against, that intuition remained hit-and-miss, short-lived, that these efforts remained scattered, interrogating neither writing as such nor formal concepts. They were not even thought through as the elaboration of a *system*, in that systems, as we have seen, flourished; or if not systems, then different kinds of collections of coordinates codified more or less effectively to provide a sense of seriousness and security. Where there were no properly codified collections, there was a resort to rather grandiose ideas, aesthetic and philosophical blends bearing hardly any relationship to reality. In that way, for example, a lot of ground was covered on the noise–sound relationship, on the idea of continuity, and with fanatical enthusiasm: it was said that the Western tradition had eliminated noise to keep only phenomena that were pure, and had concentrated on sounds solely to force them into a hierarchy. And of course that was true: noise hinders the concept of hierarchy because it does not, and cannot, take part in a strongly constructed order other than as emphasis, articulation, reinforcement – in other words, as a secondary parameter. Is that any reason, though, to elevate noises to the equal of sounds, without bothering about their specific potential? In any case, the relationship of sound to noise mostly remained, in this period, superficial, pretty sterile, relying on partial, crude concepts and analyses.

Similarly, if we think of the famous idea of that *continuum* – which occupies the place in some musicians' minds that I imagine turning metal into gold has for alchemists, or the obsession with a utopia of perpetual motion – then, clearly, given that our tradition progressively favoured the equal-tempered semitone over all other imaginable theoretical solutions, such extreme and exclusive rationalisation would jar with those who dreamed of a richer, more flexible universe. People dreamed of reconstituting the primordial plasma to abolish this insufferable, unique partition; the continuum was to be regained, and thus the siren came into play, and glissandi – a slender pittance, considering the ambition of the departure point. Here, too, people did not think carefully about what is really represented by what was rather pompously called the sonic continuum. This continuum is a limited case, undifferentiated, the most general possible matrix, with highly limited qualities that lack any true characteristics as such – I do not want even to address the non-artistic connotations in the particular case of those famous sirens. Even if the connotations are weak, or indeed non-existent, as is the case with instrumental glissandi, lack of differentiation still remains the dominant factor. What makes a continuum interesting is its virtuality and its being extracted from an underlying, significant phenomenon. How you divide this continuum into more or less regular intervals, or how you reduplicate an initial model to cover the entire sonic space – those are the ideas that are interesting through being mobile, active, generating variable dimensions, compared with the continuum in its pristine state, which is, so to speak, inert, passive, unable to generate structure through any kind of order. To integrate the idea of a continuum in the material, in the form of variations in how it is segmented, would suggest thought that is deeper and more demanding than just the use of a glissando. Such thought, to sustain a utopia – to get rid of a hierarchy locked into rational constraint, in effect – was missing.

That makes me think of micro-intervals. Traditional and non-European music offer a multitude of examples; musical expression is not strictly limited to the semitone. In both vocal and instrumental music, the expressive power of music is strengthened by using more subtle or refined intervals to which we find ourselves attending more acutely, with greater discrimination. Quite a number of attempts have been made in this spirit, across various countries, to explore the world of the micro-interval. In this domain, however, there was a serious handicap to do with how instruments are made, although this was sometimes overcome. There was the quarter-tone piano, harmonium and clarinet, among others, but the results were limited and episodic. The semitone temperament was replaced by a different kind, simply by dividing by two. In fact, there were other, even smaller subdivisions that, to my knowledge, were always made with pianos – that is, the instrument least susceptible to pitch fluctuations and most capable of being prepared. We would need to give thought to the works written for these instruments, or for strings, which can in theory give you the entire universe of any intervals you might want, even if approximation is more evident than precise specification. These works clearly do not indicate exceptional imagination and are often of interest only for their unusual intervals; but if we pass over them, disregarding their lack of originality, the important thing once again is that this new material failed to stimulate genuine reflection on the very compositional practice it posited.

With intervals of that kind, you cannot settle for using the same laws of writing as were made for, or adapted to, a different universe. One also has to ask whether the timbre of our traditional instruments is suitable for such intervals. The very writing, in its many ramifications – size of intervals and, among others, the definition of texture and of polyphony, the richness or poverty of the timbre, matching register to the intervallic density – all of those would need to be completely reconceived, from basic components to how elements are combined. That is not really what we saw happening; rather, we observed a pretty routine use of the language in which only the intervals were different. It was then evident that a satisfactory transformation of the vocabulary was not to be expected, and for that reason works written in this manner were inadequate in many ways.

To complete my account, I will add that the uses of duration came from a 'mechanist' impulse (rightly called 'motorisch' in German), and this rhythmic vitality merely exaggerated some features of the traditional way of doing things. Even a strong, coherent language, such as that of the best Stravinsky, quickly degenerated into a catalogue of mannerisms that amounted to displacements of traditional metre, made through irregularities, contractions and expansions, of no significance beyond the moment. Most importantly, these rhythmic processes were not integrated into the language in any way, but tacked on as very superficial decoration.

What is missing in all the domains of compositional utopia is the *coherence* so dear to the three Viennese. I would say that aesthetic reflection – or rather, aesthetic desire and decisiveness – was not in phase with the exploration of potential techniques. It is not unusual to see these displacements and mismatches, especially since the twentieth century, and it is common knowledge that progress is not, and cannot be, purely linear, but sometimes the lack of coherence is striking. Perhaps this derives from the individualism that marked the whole nineteenth century. Everybody took note of their tradition and placed themselves accordingly in a national framework or, indeed, local context, and individuality could not multiply the consequences of a certain choice or situation. The language used always tends to be both in harness with and independent from aesthetic choices. A radical new aesthetic will bring a certain type of vocabulary, but not necessarily a fundamentally innovative one. An aesthetic and a language are not necessarily connected, in the strict sense of the word. The question remains: Is coherence of that kind necessary?

It seemed to be, as I have said, at the time when the Viennese joined in. This coherence did not seem all that coherent to their successors, because despite it being questioned the Viennese took a close interest in only one part of the musical vocabulary (doubtless the most important part), and because the other compositional dimensions unfolded in a kind of strict automatism, or through the more or less fortunate application of free choice. There was certainly a logic in the way that durations, timbres and dynamics were used; they were meaningful, yet their organisation lay far outside the system, which was so rigorous, narrow even, regarding pitch as such. So what was to be done, other than unify the system and give equal importance to all the components of the sound? It meant a heavy increase in constraint, but equally it gave reassurance, albeit superficial, as to the absolute necessity of writing in a disciplined way. How comforting in the face of the uncertainties of choice to be able to tell oneself that a bundle of pre-compositional structures, a network of organisation derived from a unique model, would give you, through a strictly organised synthesis, the right, inevitable note – the solution that eliminated chance, the solution that by virtue of its objectivity would have to be correct! For it really was utopia that drove integral serialism. Beyond a desire to unify the system, to justify components that had previously been neglected, to rehabilitate them, no less strong was the belief in the infallibility of *order*. There was an almost superstitious faith in its mystical virtues, which while not completely substituting for the composer's personality, and bringing the disadvantage of a certain anonymity, nevertheless provided robust support in the struggle against uncertainty.

Some works from this very brief period of dogma remind one of the brief period of cubism proper, because of the systematisation and conformity it involved: personality defers to order, and the individual urge to express oneself gives way to an urge, presumably collective, for the rigour of everything being in its place. The law that composers invented to subjugate personality protects them from the disorder of the moment; it acts as the revelation of something *true* that they would otherwise not be able to detect, let alone reveal.

'Revealing order' is in fact an exact summary, with hindsight, of what that obstinate attempt to reduce discourse to total alignment entailed. The previous generation had aimed for objectivity, especially in neo-classicism. Expression was supposed to be ideally captured by formal perfection and beauty. Order and objectivity were the goals pursued by an 'Apollonian' manifestation of beauty, as opposed to the 'Dionysian' excesses of Romanticism. To the next generation, such order and object-ivity seemed derisory, above all in its wish to be instantly historical. The order was niggardly, and the objectivity uninteresting.

So all domains were to be organised by the same rule. All parameters would undergo the same methods of pre-compositional classification, their proliferation controlled by the same processes. The interplay of those parameters seemed enough to construct a work. This idea was not as myopic as it might at first seem. It had the advantage – and it is indeed an advantage – of eliminating reference to classical forms inherited from tradition, in which the contradiction between form and system, or at best, the ambiguity in their relationship, had become clear. Now, the ways in which the system was used directly determined the form. What is more, the dream was realised – the nightmare perhaps – of a 'work' that went beyond the individual, beyond happenstance, a work in which the composer had carefully prepared the underlying material, and little more was needed than to set into motion the mechanism that had been prepared and let it do its work. The composer was writing at the behest of a combinatorial power, ultimately intervening only to ascertain that the realisation was accurate, that the machine did not get carried away and produce nonsensical results; so sure of the system as no longer to need to bother with problems of perception – to which, frankly, little attention was paid in any case, as they were considered secondary to the requirement that the system should work properly. Perception would work as long as the mechanics worked. The composer would soon see that in reality the problems were less simple than had been imagined, in the enthusiasm to follow a superior order that, contrary to what was hoped, would not validate a number of neglected components, whether within the construction of the object itself or in how it was perceived. The system took into account the most elementary part of the language, but did so formally in a very superficial way, overlooking the particularities of each of the domains it was organising.

Looking at pitch, the twelve notes may in reality be considered to be completely equal. None of them will attract more attention than any other, whether or not they are heard in order, and in whatever permutation they are placed. For that we need to refer to criteria of proximity and repetition, which are certainly latent in the row but have to be highlighted to be perceived; initially, without any higher operation, there is equality. That is not true of serialised rhythmic values, for a value of 12 (that is, the equivalent of twelve units) is not perceived as equal to the unit itself (a value of 1). Values that are mathematically higher will take more time, in whatever order they are played; as a result, the raw series of values will be perceived as fundamentally unequal, whereas the series of pitches, in isolation, lacks orientation. As regards duration, if we want to set up a certain equality of beats, then we have to implement a higher-order operation, such as deliberately dividing each value by the same unit and also using dynamic or harmonic accentuation to emphasise the original values that have been divided. I do not emphasise dynamics here – the most ephemeral dimension – where being literal has a poor chance of coming over integrally, given our fragile and fuzzy way of measuring it, and also given that it is linked to a steady musical gesture, in which discontinuity stresses the exception and implies dislocation. As for instrumental timbre, it is very difficult to apply a true scale of values to it: we cannot set up absolute categories without the risk of writing nonsense. At best, some kinds of dynamics and register enable us to create an analogy to the continuity that can be imposed on a sequence of vowels, one that is abruptly disturbed and disrupted when consonants interfere. One can hardly do more than apply numbers to vocal and instrumental timbre, and even dynamics, and while this is convenient, it hardly corresponds with reality. Even with synthesised

335

timbre, which allows areas of transition and interpolation, classification proves to be essentially subjective, context remaining indispensable as a criterion of judgement. Although the classification of some parameters remains highly questionable, some kind of automation in the unfolding and combination of qualities is useful, if greatly restrained and restricted to having no beginning or end, but instead being designed to contrast with determinate, goal-directed processes.

We shall return to these formal and informal relationships, which yield a system that is conceived globally and very flexibly, but I will first focus on the deficiencies of rigid methods and their inability to resolve some central compositional problems. I shall certainly not cover everything, but I would like to address some that are especially important, through the nature of the answers, in exploring the validity of every system.

It is well known that some of the tension at the very heart of musical expression comes from the struggle between figure and system. Just one example, which with the passage of time has become academic, is fugue. A subject is given in the tonic, then in the dominant the interval of a fifth changes to a fourth; it is impossible in principle to keep the subject as it was, but other than in exceptional cases it is subjected to what is called a *tonal* answer. The system counts more than does the interval; in order for the fugue subject to be able to work within the tonal system, it is essential that it be distorted, its inner make-up changed. It is, nevertheless, perfectly recognisable, not only because it keeps all its other features, but because the system preserves its integrity thanks to the functions it assigns to it. When the interval seeks to be stronger, the system is dangerously challenged, and the autonomy of the intervals becomes less and less reducible to the system. One of the most striking examples of that situation is in the development from the fugue of Beethoven's op. 106, which is in effect limited to the interval of a tenth, where the harmonic system is seriously shaken by the preponderance of this interval saturating the texture. (It should be added that this tenth, the head of the fugue subject, is sometimes major in its original form, and sometimes minor, depending on the requirements of the harmonic system.)

With the arrival of the tone row, however, a different question arose regarding the relationship of figure and interval to the system. Interval became an abstract matrix that could generate a number of real intervals; I can manipulate that original interval as I please, changing its register, or indeed its identity, by retrograding it. Do not these extensions, retrogrades, transpositions indeed, make recognition of the original interval impossible? Does not the character acquired by manipulation of that kind destroy, by its very existence, all reference to the model, all trace of a relationship that exists in principle, but which in fact the operation has effaced? Again we see figure in conflict with system. Which is stronger in the relationship between two figures: pitch retention regardless of context, or is it rather a question of contour, direction – that is, an actual relationship? Is not an ascending major third closer to an ascending minor third than to a descending minor sixth? The formal nature of a constellation of intervals is less apparent than the contour of those intervals, there being a difference between the strength of what is real and the potential of what is virtual. Obviously, a figure has other characteristics – its rhythmic structure in particular, which gives its true profile – but they have to be all the more crude and persistent if the intervallic structure is truly going to vary, even when the original features were identical.

The question is, what are the limits to how the original figure will keep its identity, above all when its polyphonic setting makes it hard to perceive? The partition of its elements by rests, or the confusion caused by extremes of register, and the intersection of different figures over the entire registral space – all of that makes identity and, by the same token, identification highly problematic. Now, among those differences sufficient elements of repetition from memory and perception must be activated in order for us to recognise the original object in its different versions. A figure's *envelope*, so to speak, is therefore as important as its constituent intervals; it is exactly in that way that the system of intervals comes into conflict with the reality of an idea. Polyphony itself, along with the relationship between density and perception, is problematic for the perception of individual figures, not so much because of the tension between figure and interval, but as a result of accumulation and layering. When there are no real harmonic laws, and beyond a certain density, voices will no longer be perceived as individual lines, but rather as a statistical whole. It follows that one precise interval or another will not matter in hearing such cumulative polyphony, where precision of reference is no longer the most important factor. A particular register is filled – or less crudely, analysed, scored by lines that are not strongly controlled by any intervallic hierarchy, but rather guided by a more flexible principle: complementarity, parallelism, individuality of some lines with respect to others. The system will be much too rigid and restrictive for a context of polyphonic intersection requiring a more fluid approach that is less signifying, more pliable, viewed more statistically.

This leads me to address the rigidity of the system with respect to what I will call adjacent phenomena, by which I mean devices of writing grafted onto the main phenomena and enriching their expressive strength. The appoggiatura, the delay, the anticipation – those are also adjacent phenomena, but in the tonal system; they are not purely ornamental like a mordant or turn, their importance stemming from their direct link with harmonic function, lending it more tension than a chord or a chord progression could ever hope to give. One is neglecting very fertile ground by wanting to limit everything to one central kind of unity, where the resulting lines have to match the model with no possible derivation. That would be to work with a system of equality where in principle there are neither weaker nor stronger elements. But connecting things in that way is abolished. There is a sense in which it denies to sound and line the chance of carrying any *aura*.

In fact, a sound can be regarded as a centre around which satellites can be placed to enrich it, to lend it importance that in itself it could not have. This aura might be a linear ornamentation, but it can just as well arise in the form of a vertical aggregate, temporarily grafted onto the sound without being integrated with the structure to which the sound belongs. Similarly, heterophony is in some sense the aura of a melodic line. No rigorous rule is needed to construct it; on the contrary, the swirls around the main line are derived from it freely and unpredictably, enriching its presentation by not changing its structure. Writing for orchestra benefits enormously from this extra creative dimension, the auras around the structural lines creating an illusion based on different distances, contrasts of outline, a build-up in perspectives. In this way, you can establish a genuine instrumental acoustic, which I feel is more rewarding than the mere use of acoustic proportions.

These last can often be disappointing for two different reasons: firstly, their unsuitability for forming figures that are anything other than transcribed portions of the resonance; and secondly, such transcription will often not really embrace timbre as actual fusion. What is being reproduced is definitely not the phenomenon itself, but an abstract relationship to it, which sidelines how these elements fluctuate in relation to each other. The most rudimentary cases result in the dominant seventh and ninth chords, which carry very strong stylistic connotations, even when incomplete, diverting our attention towards the idea of style and the match between that style and the work's harmonic content; whereas in the most refined cases, given the need to use micro-intervals to which our instruments can approximate only pretty randomly, interesting collections of sound arise that have little to do with true deductions from acoustic phenomena. The weakness of this kind of acoustic reference lies above all in its fixing the discourse in an excess of verticality, thus depriving it of considerable dynamic potential; it produces composition that is like an unfolding frieze, for although such a system can produce happy results acoustically, the work's figuration remains so dominated by them as to seem far too weakened. I would say that the acoustic dimension, real or illusory, belongs in essence to the category of adjacent phenomena, which are indispensable in enriching the central phenomenon but incapable of living separately. Earlier, this potential symbiosis was overly neglected because, with the laudable aim of contributing all their significance to harmonic perception, adjacent phenomena were made responsible for something they were unable to accomplish, which did not correspond with their real meaning. I believe that what I call aura is a good way to resist a system's inflexibility and narrowness, but that it can be only a strength held in reserve. It is disruptive at the same time as needing a clear framework of application in which to appear, which it can enrich by means of its expressive power to emphasise and contradict.

Conflicts of system and figure happen in an orbit that has directionality, or form. But idea can use system with a very different purpose, to create something amorphous, be it for phases of transition or to create schemes of a different kind. We conceive the finished work, a closed form, a known trajectory, meaning lying in a closed structure, hence its construction from precisely defined figures transformed over the course of a work, their metamorphosis being the very substance of development and determining its limits.

Athematicism was already mentioned by Webern, discussing the row. Indeed, the Variations for Piano, op. 27, for example, are not variations on an organised, recognisable theme as such, as with Schoenberg's Variations for Orchestra, op. 31; we find instead variations on a virtual theme created in different places by properties of the row, as well as by some figures of various kinds. The concept of a virtual theme, which appears so distinctly in this work, indeed shows how far the radical use of the row contradicts that other concept: finite choice. The row, from the beginning, introduced the principle of equality of all its members, of infinite possibilities of permutation that were all equally valid; on the contrary, the theme or figures imply a predetermination of how the music unfolds, of the relationship with other parameters, of expressive character – all things that, though they can be varied, and manipulated with great flexibility in the articulation, are nevertheless the opposite of what can be called virtual: very real objects offering no choice.

The virtual object has its own dimension containing concepts of permutation, interpolation, random structure, sieves, recursion, mapping and rules of writing, all suggesting the open ground of development. This dimension is seen in elements, the informal, as much as in their combination – but is not 'informal' in the sense that Adorno intended. It is the continuum of pitches defined by their extraction, by some temporary scale, happening randomly; or rhythmic structure rewritten through a number of rules; or a criterion for density that depends on the type of intervals used – categories that are able indefinitely to generate ever-new material within a given field, more or less determined depending on whether the rules controlling them are more or less restrictive. The overall trajectory becomes more important than each of its moments. It is undifferentiated, implying no arrow of time pointing to the end, somehow assuming incompleteness, and expecting sporadic listening.

Listening to a work based on the mechanics of the tone row and its permutations, one may indeed have the impression of hearing an arbitrary fragment of a tangle that had no beginning and can finish only through spoiling a much bigger collection of combinations. It is as if the composer instinctively knows that our attention will not be held beyond the moment when we unconsciously take in the constructive principle, for there is now hardly any discourse. The composer can stop the mechanism after having turned all the right cogs, or the ones thought to be right, but what was discarded as superfluous remains an unuttered, ghostly presence. Between the two extreme positions of the idea controlling the system and the system controlling the idea, many interactions can be imagined, assuming the relationship of system to idea is used for what it really can do: in one case, bringing transformation and form; in the other, creating the amorphously informal. This is the dialectic I used from my earliest compositions (especially the *Sonatine* for flute and piano), when I set in contrast thematic and athematic development. In a rudimentary way, and still strongly connected with thematic concepts – figure, cell, interval – it was about that fundamental relationship of strict and free writing. Later, some of Klee's pictures and his Bauhaus teaching helped me to define those categories more precisely and make them generally symbiotic, but we need only a very simple observation from nature to show the relationship of the formal to the informal: clouds offer us the perfect example of an informal trajectory against actual events in time seen simultaneously. One could believe that such a use of system would be like improvisation. Improvisation relies on a precise rule for varying the presentation of the musical events it generates – chord progressions, melodic variation – but leaves a relatively flexible space for ornamentation according to given formulas. Those formulas, though, are already part of the fixtures and fittings, in principle if not in actuality, and are not stimulating true proliferations because they are generally connected to a kind of trajectory, to a route that is relaxed enough to allow them to be inserted but clear enough to preserve surface coherence. This is the phenomenon of transition between fixed and indeterminate form. As for recent incarnations of improvisation, it would be hard to say that they are productive, other than in instrumental experimentation that is free to develop and discover techniques and modes of playing to which an overly strict and precise practice would not have led. But since their style has been basically abandoned – so that if not quite a distant memory, it is merely the more or less involuntary citation of older works – it is difficult to see any value in them except as individual psychological case studies, or indeed a collective ritual participated in by practitioners of a particular cult. The thought involved and the practice itself are too perfunctory to be productive.

There has been wild talk about *deconstruction*. In effect, what this has meant is 'deconstructuration', but in the sense that the improviser tried in vain to be disconnected from the models stored in his memory. In fact, scraps of encountered and remembered works criss-crossed in the attempt to create the 'informal'. The result, far from what was intended, was the inevitable formal monotony of the inexhaustible repetition of a tension–relaxation sequence. It is a kind of contract that has been very useful, but only when formulated more subtly. With this kind of improvisation, a merely perfunctory formulation leaves little hope for really discovering anything.

The same goes for that confidence in the value of graphics, which, at a particular time, involved some fetishes of which we can say only that they represented either great naivety or useless cunning – as if this kind of premonition, this preparatory stage could replace actual realisation through compositional practice, regardless, moreover, of the chosen method. Graphics are a system that leads everywhere, relevant to anything in any way, able to provide only crude indications that lack the fundamentals, properly speaking, of musical language. You can put any idea you want into them, which is most convenient, but far from convincing. I am happy to appreciate the desire for something new that topples the old ways, but I am much less happy about the amateurism of the result. In truth, writing is at the heart of all evolution in musical thought, and can be dispensed with only at the cost of instability and obsolescence.

✧ ✧ ✧

At the extremes of the scale of possibilities, there are two ways of writing music: *absolute* writing, whose components are dictated by a strict system of deduction and duty; and *relative* writing, in which very general criteria of coherence permit a wide margin of freedom. Is it necessary, in order to conserve the work's unity in either case, to go back, possibly irreversibly, through distortions that were not controlled in the preparation, to a pivotal system on which creativity completely depends? Like Schoenberg, Webern believed in the existence of the row as an intuition that informed everything, and that once this hierarchy was set up, all that remained was to write the work, like a sort of divine dictation. This is to see creativity through the lens of Genesis and to liken composition a little too eagerly to divine powers, not taking stock of the accidental. Obviously, finishing a composition ends the happenstance that preceded it, or that seems to end it, but is that happenstance not included instead in the reality of the work? Is the composer there just to fill up the compartments of a completely predefined and preprogrammed structure? The central role played by creative renewal implies a strong measure of the unforeseeable that leads us from one derivation to the next in relation to the initial idea, estimating at its true value the vital importance of each moment. And creativity relies on all its intuitive short-circuits to find a solution that meets all the needs of the moment. Whereas a fully resolved deduction will have offered us infinite solutions, where we are spoiled for choice with valid outcomes, intuition lets us reject everything superfluous and leads us to *the* solution – which may be provisional, to be remodelled later, but remains essentially unique. When we are confined by a collection of rigid systems, the inevitable note will be deduced – inevitable at least in relation to all the surrounding parameters. It seems inevitable because it results from a calculation, and so exhibits objective truth beyond personal choice. Yet if our aesthetic instinct tells us that this solution is not the right one, then what? Should the composer correct the system, relying on free choice, on creative powers that supervene the systems he has made, knowing better than them what should be written? That comes down to regarding the system as an aide, a crutch, a stimulant for the imagination, which otherwise would not really be able to conceive of the world that has been dreamed of. I choose, therefore

I am; I invented the system only to give me a certain kind of material, for me to eliminate or distort later on, in the name of what I judge to be correct, beautiful, necessary.

One could certainly be more scrupulous, arguing that since the system has not truly provided these discounted results, the answer is to go back to the source, rebuild how things are organised, reconsider the interface with the parameters and look forward to more satisfying solutions from these rearrangements. That would imply a lot of patience and a certain lack of self-confidence, if also courage and obduracy. Do not be so ready to disobey the structure in order to find the right response! In one case, one accepts that the exception, the irregularity or licence are better, more valuable than what pure deduction has provided. In the other, one imagines that engaging with the short-circuits of the imagination, above all in quitting the system, points to superficiality, indeed some laziness in the exercise of logic. There is a third case, obviously, which is not to choose, and in fact many works that are called aleatoric fall into this category. Several solutions will have arisen in response to a particular development: the composer has already made many choices, and discarded many figures, before arriving at images that are thought to be the most representative; yet at this moment of the work they can all claim the same degree of validity. After that, why eliminate further? Why not offer all these images? There are sufficiently few to make it unnecessary to give in to an unrealistic utopia by offering them all the right to populate the score; they belong to the same phenomenon, and so within the overall form, they can easily substitute for one another, making a sort of virtual variation that would be comprehensible only if there were multiple performances relying each time on the performer's different choices. Provided that the work is the sum of the fragments chosen each time from a field of potential variations, there is a global, unexpressed variation, both written into the work by the very nature of the fragments, and also written from the work in that it can never be understood in itself. The innumerable possible choices make a literal repetition impossible if one follows through the premeditated, multiple rule for choosing, or makes a choice that is not premeditated and is, therefore, inevitably multiple.

The work is a virtual model from which one can draw out real examples at will. System and idea relate to each other by teetering between the finite and the infinite. It is not chance, but a refusal to eradicate chance. An idea is grasped and fixed in music, but uncertainty in how it is handled remains; free will is in play up to the last moment, even if is controlled somewhat, reduced to a subordinate role. Moreover, where can intuition really lead us? Or does it serve to create the illusion that our free will is better? But one should not forget to submit this intuition to the discipline of a system, for intuition makes us believe in creative freedom, even when that threatens to be a plaything we have picked up in our work or from our memory – the memory of ourselves being even more dangerous than our memory of others! Intuitive detachment through purely technical work, through the constraints of thinking about the tenets of a language, can be a big help to creativity, enabling it to come up with solutions that it could not have achieved on its own before being stripped of its customary perspective. In future we can be very far removed from bureaucratic centralism, from the theocratic hier-archy held up by a generation as the absolute ideal, which is in fact not an absolute evil but merely a useless, harmful and paralysing form of control. But to make up for the vacuum, do we have to resort to local bureaucracy? That would be to parcel out the problem without really changing it. But then how are we to consolidate variation and coherence, universal vision and passing chance, with no fortuitousness but sustained free will, prizing order above all and yet not just following rules?

Is that an unreasonable hope, to reconcile the irreconcilable?

To write music is to encounter – very often, if not always – the prob-lem of correctly and freely making micro- and macrostructure interact, referring to each other at every point, as well as overall; which is to say that local organisation derives either directly or step by step from a very generalised and mouldable idea, a source to which there is absolutely no obligation always to refer. Thus, when direct contact with the source is lost, the chain of derivation will be composed powerfully and visibly enough, and the 'genealogical tree' will be like a watermark as the work develops. The idea must directly transcribe the system, the system being sought and found in terms of the idea. There is no longer any unilateral hierarchy between one and the other but an exchange, a deep duality – like twin stars, to offer an analogy. Moreover, the system embraces some very different operations, worth examining in more detail. Without really wanting to categorise them strictly, two kinds can be identified: those applying to preparation, to the raw material; and those used on the worked material once the music has been realised – systems of formation and application, therefore. Systems of formation themselves function either on the work or within its structure. As something external, the system is a potential resource, not applied directly, as, for example, with the choice of scales, the make-up of an interval collection or the registral placement of pitches; and this is equally true of scales themselves, or abstract durational relationships that precede real values or, of course, any actual tempo.

Systems clearly fall into these two categories, especially the first. They precede implementation, controlling it virtually, and are, rather, the resource through which implementation can occur. This means a very general, uncontained rule, except that it applies to only one work; an inert rule, latent, as it were, offering only general constraints, such as very small intervals yielding a narrower tessitura, for example, or a slow tempo, or relatively thin polyphony. Such a system will directly influence the writing by imposing reciprocity. For example, when larger intervals are chosen, then the tessitura in particular may stretch, not to speak of further consequences for tempo and texture. Yet I would still say we are before implementation. Prior to that, but always close to it, the system of formation is to be used within the work if rules are made for the relationship between two or more parameters, and at that point thought will be given to how durations may be organised in relation to pitch, to deductions and derivations one may create, to the harmonic fields that can be decided based on interpolations or permutations that have been selected – in short, to everything that can be imagined that characterises the appearance of the structures by working on the potential for proliferation and manipulation that those structures will produce.

That is the moment, if you feel you need it, for real invention or sketching to play a vital role, thinking through the consequences, trying to push them to the limit of quality and quantity, grouping them in families, even if there is no intention to use them all. These sketches mean familiarisation, limbering up for the work itself. Perhaps there is always the risk of something gratuitous and sterile. These attempts sometimes seem to lead to results that cannot be used, or only in small part; but if another sketch is sometimes more valuable, the prior exploration may have confirmed some procedure, or steered some new workings towards sound outcomes. Although it may seem meaningless and abstract, exercise of this kind must not be neglected as a source of inspiration. At the very least, it has the advantage of deflecting us from our habits and making us think about the original premises of the language, and it can also lead to original solutions when routine may have produced banality, or when we have ground to a halt through having focused too much on the composition's outcome, or on a particular stage. Isolating a difficulty from its surroundings, focusing on it creatively, stepping aside from contextual burdens and restrictions – this indeed can prove a source of inspiration, not just a laborious mode of exploration that kills spontaneity; on the contrary, it fuels our intuition by focusing it on particular data.

Thus, raw material is prepared both externally and internally. What now remains is to mould this material through an application system. That term does not imply that formulas are ready and waiting, and that all that is needed is to apply them in order to realise the score. That will, of course, work at this initial level – as mentioned earlier – if the intention is to create something undifferentiated, an *amorphous* realisation, almost anonymous, one might say. The fields of application of the various systems of formation have to be defined and must be free to proliferate through interaction when they are set in motion. For example, I will allocate, to each system, intervals, textures, durations, rests, accents and various periodicities – these last will work together to create constantly evolving, family-related objects that I allow to emerge on their own. As already mentioned, such an amorphous, omnidirectional structure does not need active, sustained listening because it equates to itself throughout, and strictly speaking it has no inherent sense of development; I therefore use it for what it is, equally good as a continuous background for directional structures or used intermittently when directional structures make it appear or disappear. By creating a situation suitable for it

I will therefore have given it a reason for being there, making it perceptible in a way that it suggests. However, in contrast to that *amorphous*,
undifferentiated realisation, application systems are used to shape the
raw material, in isolation or in context, which directly influences form.
At the level of the element, this concerns shaping *figures*, the thematic
content that will feed and structure development, and materialising –
that is, incorporating the original material and making it audible through
an 'abstract' prototype, which is irrelevant to the perception and understanding of the finished work. This is the stage at which one needs to
include those features, crucial to freedom of choice and flexibility in
deployment, that will eliminate the deadly rigidity of overly literal relationships. Above all, it is a matter of description and of aura.

What is freedom of description? Take a block of sound made up of a
number of pitches that are your raw material. You mould these pitches
by separating them according to interval, which for convenience can be
arranged vertically – this visual order also being a sign of omnidirection-
ality, though clearly showing the harmonic field, too. This object can
be written horizontally in what seems in context to be the best order;
for instance, because it relates to a similar object. The melodic similarity between these objects having thus been described, a contour will
have appeared, endowing the strongest meaning to the link, which was
possible only from being free to ensure the closest match. But for this
possibility of being adjusted to context, the two juxtaposed contours
would not support each other and the meaning would be less, or nothing
at all. Freedom can also matter within the sound object itself, unconnected with another object. In this way, I may think of it differently
and let it play out its different aspects. Thus, I am able to select a focal
pitch in this object and make the others depend on it, underlining this
relationship through an appropriate rhythmic setting, the polar note
having a distinctly longer rhythmic value, while the others appear very
quickly in extremely short values as a cluster. I can emphasise that with
a special dynamic, if I want, the long note being louder than the short
ones; or again, if the short notes lead to the long one, I can show this
with a crescendo. In summary, I am describing this object through contour and different gestures, and I can enhance it by placing its various

appearances in a temporal and textural perspective. This work on a single object, this freedom to describe it, lets me compose with ready-made material and, vitally, shape it to do what I want in order to acquire the expressive force necessary for its particular place in the work I am contemplating. There is no limit to what I can decide, to my free will, in describing an individual object, while the nature of the objects described is determined by a deeper relationship. Freedom to manoeuvre does not threaten or mask coherence, but brings it out in such varied ways that its dependency seems secondary to showing it in a new light. Description also enables its rhythm to be linked to the very nature of the objects and their complexity, durations reflecting the object and enhancing the internal relationships one is able to find in it. Description can even become a thematic element if, for instance, it applies the same contour to all the objects being used. It is easy to see that this is not just superficial (albeit sophisticated) manipulation, but a concept that, although it may remain purely ornamental, can easily direct and even organise the compositional process.

I have already mentioned what I understand by *aura* – something comparable to the appoggiatura, for example – but emphasised that I did not wish to go back to old values, thinking rather about what they represented and being inspired by them to create equivalent values in a differently constituted language. My earlier example was a sound object presented in as many different ways as there are components. These objects have the disadvantage – if such it is, for example, when I want to present them side by side – of containing the same number of notes and, therefore, a profile that is too literally repetitive. So I may introduce length into a group of short notes by inserting extra notes to change the duration and importance of the group. There are two ways of doing this. One is amorphous, inserting chromatic complements within an interval, following the principle of the acciaccatura literally by putting the complementary notes somewhere in the same register as the group – filling in the intervallic space or placing them more freely. The other is morphological, inserting into the whole group or part of it intervals deduced by transposition, interpolation or permutations, like grafting onto a structure a derivative of it. The group of rapid notes thus gains a different profile and duration each time, and I can distinguish the original notes from their adjacent ones by writing differentiated dynamics. Using timbral differentiation, when there are several instruments, I can superimpose the various derivatives on the original group through this principle of aura, each time creating a new object so that the description of the original object is based on a more complex aggregate, but nevertheless playing a completely recognisable generative role. I can perform the same operation just as well on the long note, giving it a different density every time it appears, here, too, playing with the amorphous chromatic complements, or aggregates derived, say, from the relationships of this long note to the others at the point where it appears: before the other notes it will take account of them, whereas after them it will not, or vice versa.

Aura can be expressed in infinite ways. It can arise in descriptions, where its deployment sheds light on compositional needs that moments later no longer exist and do not call for the same kind of invention. Needless to say, aura is the home ground of acoustically derived relationships. Being sometimes too weak to support a work's structure, and given their thematic limitations (intervallic relationships necessarily depending on their own rules), their potential as adjacent phenomena is, on the contrary, highly contingent, which corresponds to their true nature.

At the level of elements, system can always be either based on similarity (figure by definition controlling the intervals) or generative (the interval giving rise to, and characterising, the figure). Here is a very simple example of this relationship between figure and interval: I select four notes from a scale to make a chord, and this chord will contain three intervals, depending on the layout of the notes. If I take the top note of the chord and place it higher up the scale without changing the interval structure of the chord, the three other notes will no longer correspond with the scale of the top note, so the chord figure is controlling the intervallic scale. On the other hand, if I regard the four notes of the chord as four scale degrees and displace each one by the values of that scale, the chord will then be a different one because the four displacements are not strictly parallel, so now the intervallic scale is controlling the chord figure. For scale and figure to equate, the scale has to be composed of equal intervals, in which case whatever the transposition, the chords will always match and the scale is always reproduced intact. That is one of the most simple cases, but one can say more generally, with regard to the figure/interval relationship, that maintaining the profile means imposing directionality on the intervals, or that intervals considered as a matrix able to generate a collection of similar intervals will distort the profile and render the original figure unrecognisable. In the first case, the figure prevails through its identity, which is how it is recognised; in the second, despite the identical original configuration, if varied in presentation by register and intervallic inversion, the identity of the figure can dissolve to the point of being lost altogether. Identical origins come nowhere near to supporting perception without the powerful mediation of the figure, the gestalt.

Material moulded at the level of the element is then dealt with at the level of the whole. Based on elements – cells, figures – created in reality or virtually, various kinds of appearance and transformation are deduced to exploit those resources. Structures are made to interact, and we see what they are made of, we show one design through another. This sequence of deductions – not necessarily continuous but perhaps including breaks – is configured by means of what I call *envelopes*, their articulation marked by *signals*.

An envelope is a global feature, a parameter which may operate either within a language or externally. By an external parameter I mean, for example, register, which makes little or no intervention in actual writing. Obviously, a consistently low register will not call upon the same intervallic configuration or the same textural density as a consistently high register; but in the middle register writing does not have to conform to particular types. Perceiving such an envelope depends on very succinct but very effective standards of evaluation that orient the listener even before any content is apparent; listening again, and having located the envelope, one can concentrate on more deeply effective details. Thus, the envelope can be an external quality such as a register, a unique timbre or established blend of timbres, a favoured dynamic or a speed. And yet the envelope may impinge directly on the writing itself, as a pitch filter dictating that a certain collection will be used to the exclusion of all others, or a constant rhythm which means that all durations have the same common factor and can be identified in performance only by dynamic accentuation. It may also be a compositional type – homophony, heterophony, polyphony.

In short, the envelope is what individuates a process and lends it a particular profile as the work unfolds. Further, an envelope is not tied inevitably to one kind of process, which may well be individuated by a different envelope at a later stage – and envelopes can replace each other imperceptibly. Take, for example, a rhythmic envelope of regular, quick semiquavers, and progressively introduce a short note between them – very occasionally at first, then at ever-closer distances. In due course the short notes will no longer be separate but will increasingly intervene as groups, which thus completely disrupts the regularity of the semiquavers and slows them down considerably. At the end of a process of that kind, the semiquaver envelope will have been completely erased by the envelope of short, irregular notes; what was primary has become incidental, and vice versa, while the tempo has been totally changed, slowed down step by step as one envelope has replaced another.

With a global envelope, the signal, of course, punctuates it, indicating articulation points where the form changes direction, the meaning alters, the flow encounters points of modulation or climax. In the most succinct cases, a signal will be one note, a chord of irregular length or a rest prolonged beyond what can be immediately expected from the context, but it does not have to be an event in itself, anticipating further developments. When envelopes are registral, for example, an abrupt shift in register – which therefore does not alter the envelope's intrinsic character – will serve at once as a signal directing attention towards some new kind of envelope. The signal is not necessarily isolated, since if the form is changing shape fairly often, the signal can refer to a succession of similar signals from the same family. It goes without saying that the signal can use any feature, and that they can be planned, defining notable points of a process without having to be involved in it; so they appear like foreign bodies, their singularity immediately obvious and marking them out from the prevailing texture, which is what makes us rightly perceive them as articulation points. In this way, the use of a phrase that is the initial basis of one process can later articulate a different one, where these are segmented.

It is highly productive to use such systems: they meet local goals, they are deployable very flexibly, they offer the advantage of a completely fluid hierarchy, and they are equally able to appear within the fabric or to dominate only its surface. Their use takes account, too, of the various perceptual levels we are playing with, and enhances the primary role of memory in judging identity through the appreciation of similarity or difference, as well as in recognising the work's direction and the vectors that cause that. As mentioned, there is a perception that is global – perhaps synoptic, intuitive, almost a reflex action – which grasps the envelope and its signal straight away without fully taking in the content; and there is also more acute perception – analytical, attentive to the relationships that bind together the interior of the musical discourse. The first type of listening is almost passive, when one experiences the big trends rather than knowing what they are, their presence and impact registering below the level of attention; whereas the second type, in contrast, is active and implies attention and engagement. Both types of hearing contribute to helping us follow the successive stages of a work. Yet without memory we would be at a loss to take in that journey, hence the role of signals. We can play with them by making some hidden structures evident, or occluding the evident ones. With a rhythmic structure, when we do not first offer orientation through overall periodicity, then orientation by grouping, finally stating the rhythm clearly, the orientation through general periodicity will seem incomprehensible – the result of chance, separate from any organised structure, highly sporadic and irregular. However, orientation by grouping lets one sense relationships without knowing their precise meaning, and the clearly stated rhythm will be immediately perceptible. Memory will then work retrospectively – not reconstructing the precise way in which the stated rhythm has been prepared, but making us understand the perceptual tightening that brings about the moment when we switch our focus to grasping the whole. Conversely, there must be a moment of distillation, when all we are offered are points of general periodicity, and we surrender our assimilation of the stated rhythms despite their familiarity; memory is not strong enough to retain their relevance when they are only hinted at. It is the same with pitch. Take a figure that repeats the same number of notes each time but in a different order. Apply to these figures – which are perfectly coherent and which you perceive accordingly – a pitch filter that excludes first one, then two, then successively all but one. Your initial, perfectly managed perception will certainly not prevent you from losing your grasp of these increasingly sporadic figures that are reducing to an intermittently repeated single note. The reverse procedure is just as revealing: you will understand nothing, not even suspecting that there could be organised figures, until a certain number of notes have appeared and you suddenly become aware of a defective figure offering you nothing but the need for completion. Perception and memory hand each other the lead: memory can defeat perception, just as perception can make memory aware, little by little, of the impressions it is being fed.

✦ ✦ ✦

I have described very different approaches to organisation, using systems on different levels and with very different capabilities. I have described them according to a hierarchy that concerns raw material, moulded material and the organisation of this material into a meaningful form. This hierarchy was needed to explain what kinds of relationships can be set up in composing a work, or part of one. In reality, these operations cannot be separated: they interact continually, always in dialogue, referring to each other. Thus, the system relates to the idea, which transforms the system, which recreates the idea, and so on, endlessly, in the spiral of the musical process. This pairing implies infinite evolution, and points to the analogy of the expanding universe. There is a cycle of exchange, which, if not unpredictable, is nevertheless not entirely predictable – a dialectic of rule and chance.

A musical universe without rules cannot exist. This is another way to express the coherence so beloved of Webern. But rules alone do not allow for chance, and thus deprive music of the most spontaneous aspect of its expressive means. Can we do without that in the name of dogmatic discipline, which has no real historical basis, even among composers who have pushed academicism to an extreme? We cannot give in to such disfiguring of creativity. Chance has to be continually incorporated by rules, while the rules must be endlessly renewed by chance. Neither of these two poles of writing can safely be neglected, and so we have to preserve both for continual use. The dialectic of system and idea equally embraces the distinctive and the amorphous, points that are centred and moments of suspension, thereby extending to defining within a work the categories of time I have previously described: striated and smooth, which entirely correspond with the sense of direction or lack of orientation in a section of a work.

Although I am going back to the analogy of the expanding universe, we could just as well refer to infinite form in the way that Wagner spoke of infinite melody, form in constant transformation, with no need of the old prototypes. I believe that to be one of the most important phenomena of that era. Gradually, references to classical models faded and died out, rendered entirely inappropriate by the evolution of the system/idea duality, literally meaningless in the new emerging context. Infinite form implies continual transformation of aims and perspective, which only a sufficiently rich and evolutionary technique could attain. One might well say that rigid dogmatism can be a necessary evil, especially in times of 'eternal damnation', although in art as in music that surely produced relatively feeble works; indeed, the creators of those works sought approval and wanted to recover something through an anxiety and nostalgia that are all too easy to understand.

To fend off anxiety and nostalgia, which were no more appropriate in different circumstances, dogmatism, an even more radical dogmatism, prevailed for a time, which is common enough: there was a need to reformulate the language, and nothing would have been achieved without a radical approach. Dogmatism has its limits, though, and creativity is its worst casualty, as was quickly and routinely proven. After that, it became a matter not of recovering tried and tested methods – not validation, not recuperation – but of finding tools to integrate freedom in a universe that was otherwise considered and organised. Every work inspires its own form, requires its own methods, implies a particular way of working. Clearly, there is no question of reinventing everything every time, from the most basic vocabulary right up to the grammar. The very general principles of writing keep their worth from one work to the next; what changes is the way they are applied, which is renewed while the substance of the work emerges.

Utopias often guide us towards reality. The spiral work, the labyrinthine work – these are the images that reflect the complexity and infinity of the relationship between system and idea. Chance is abolished by the work at the same time as being resurrected to make it possible.

1　An earlier and shorter version of this essay was published as 'Le Système et l'idée', *InHarmonique*, no. 1 (Dec. 1986), pp. 62–104.
2　For Boulez's harmonic term 'vague' we are using here Schoenberg's 'roving'. See, for example, Arnold Schoenberg, *Structural Functions of Harmony* (New York: W. W. Norton and Company, 1954), pp. 164–5.
3　Arnold Schoenberg, 'Composition with Twelve Tones', in *Style and Idea*, ed. Leonard Stein, trans. Leo Black (Berkeley, Los Angeles: University of California Press, 1984), pp. 219, 223 and 224 respectively.
4　Ibid., p. 245.
5　See above, p. 94.
6　Anton Webern, *The Path to the New Music*, ed. Willi Reich (Bryn Mawr, PA: Theodore Presser, 1963), p. 51.
7　Ibid., p. 52.
8　Ibid., p. 53.
9　Ibid., p. 54.
10　Ibid., p. 53.
11　Ibid., p. 54.
12　Ibid.
13　Ibid., p. 55.
14　See above, p. 322.
15　See above, p. 321.

11

Between Order and Chaos[1]

(1987–88)

Of professional musicians' abilities about which the amateur may ask, one immediately thinks of their being able to imagine, purely from reading a score, the sound of the result. How do they mentally transcribe the written code and fully understand not only what it means, but also what it represents? Are they so secure in this mental representation as to be able to access it without any possible mistake, without reality intruding to spoil some detail or even confound everything? When beginning to study solfège, one learns to listen analytically in order to be able to transcribe the musical object brought to our attention. What we have is a copy of the real thing, rather like in a basic drawing lesson: melodic intervals or chords are reproduced in the same way that one reproduces a cup or a spoon; the code for transcribing will work differently, but this is the same kind of operation. Later, when one studies composition – harmony, counterpoint, fugue – the first recommendation, if not requirement, is to avoid relying on the sounding object itself: as they say, 'Do not use the help of the piano or you will never learn to hear'; in other words, you have to suppress any direct form of reference. *Hearing*, however, is not captured just by that negative command. It implies much more than imagining the target musical object: it implies conceiving the precise network of satisfying relationships between any given data and their implications, which have to be identified and absorbed correctly. If you are offered a melodic line, you have to find a harmonic accompaniment to realise the functions implied by this melodic line. When these functions are simple, it is relatively easy to crack the code they are following, and of which they are the outcome; when they are more ambiguous and complex, there may be various solutions which have to be created and which must be clearly hearable. The writing being taught may be vocal, but in fact these exercises take place in a kind of sonic vacuum, and they are checked cursorily by the teacher at the piano, who will reward you with a 'not heard', an ignominious scribble to make you aware of how little your internal hearing has to do with reality. You have heard neither the object nor the relationship between objects; your only way to check it is through sonic realisation. After study of that kind, rigorous about the virtual representation of an object, you will certainly be inclined to believe Mallarmé's idea of the 'ideal flower absent from all bouquets', which for the musician can mean the note absent from all objects.

Such teaching can seem absurd in denying something that is more essential among the musician's gifts: knowing how to deal with material in sound, the required, abstract task seeming not to lead as directly as possible to this inevitable encounter. And yet behind this teaching there lies the ambivalence that will be the composer's lot for life: that of trying to write in a coded language which refers to an inclusive and fully assimilated reality. When writing is not marked by absolute precision of sonic relationships, you can tell that a composer's perception is, for one reason or another, deficient somewhere, a deficiency that may lie in incorrect judgement of the objects themselves or in a false assessment of their relationships. In any case, imagined perception has not worked. One therefore has to increase one's experience and realise what caused this failure, so that the imagination can coincide fully with reality by means of accurate perceptual projection. Then again, we are not talking here about completely controlled acoustic relationships at this stage of learning, for hearing is completely dominated by the codes of the language, and no component that can disturb that strict organisation is allowed. Musical dictation uses known, recognisable objects through a perfectly regulated sonic device that happens to be the piano. The ear becomes used to hearing through a particular prism, and it can be thrown, misled, even completely fooled if presented with objects that do not allow it to be oriented by its usual coordinates. Indeed, if you move from analysing a chord played on the piano to a multiphonic sound played on a wind instrument, or a sound produced on some percussion instrument, you will have a problem adapting to the very nature of these objects. The one belongs to a relatively assimilated category in which the medium plays less of a role in relation to the code, whereas the other tends to lie outside any system because of the very exceptional nature of its components, the medium being stronger than, or at least tending to dominate, the hierarchy. There is a huge difference between abstract and concrete relationships.

I call relationships abstract when they can be truly *dematerialised*, and concrete when they are, strictly speaking, inseparable from the material. Can we say that the former conform to a hierarchy, and the latter do not? The problem is sometimes as simple as that. A triad played on the piano is the most obvious example of an easily grasped musical object, instantly dematerialised, immediately attached to a hierarchy, a collection of functions. Neither the hierarchy nor the collection of functions needs to be expressed: they are latent, stimulating in us many affective as well as theoretical resonances, in a proportion that depends on a person's education, as well as on the powers of imagination. Although this test object comes to me in the timbre of the piano, it is heard in isolation, and it is not its timbre that I care about but what it is made of. Either I perceive the chord in its entirety or I analyse it without taking account of how it is presented. At most, I might be troubled by some defect in the sounding instrument, so that if the piano is out of tune, the difference between the real and the immaterial object might be experienced as impeding the perception of the ideal object within its hierarchy, and if my ear is sufficiently tutored, I could name the exact defect that is misrepresenting what I imagined; the perceived reality can be thought of as a deviation in substance compared with the hierarchically perfect. That deviation can also have affective connotations, and the out-of-tune piano just mentioned stands for a long possible list – and incidentally, its rather perverse charm has actually been used, by Berg in *Wozzeck*, among others. But let us return to the perfect piano and the no less perfect chord it has provided, which I have instantly dematerialised. Now, I take some kind of tam-tam, preferably deep. Striking it with some force, I will produce a sound of a complexity that will surely be entirely perceived but is infinitely harder to analyse. Returning to the triad, I am aware of the stability of its elements, allowing me to make a quick, thorough analysis, but with the tam-tam the analysis is difficult to complete and it is even harder to do it quickly, for the sound is made of harmonics of varied prominence, which seem too unstable for me to fix mentally, and its internal hierarchy resists any simple categorisation. The sound of the piano certainly has these acoustic phenomena also, but its classification as an object overrides these individual acoustic properties; on the contrary, it is a challenge to track the strictly acoustic character of such a chord, whereas its perception as an element of vocabulary is instant. I have no idea on first hearing in what way and into which category I can fix the sound of the tam-tam as an element of a vocabulary. Its acoustic properties strike me first and are an almost insurmountable obstacle to identifying it as an element of vocabulary other than one superimposed on a hierarchy to reinforce, decorate or obscure clearer elements – in short, an associated function. I could analyse the sonic elements of this tam-tam patiently and closely, but they are so individual, so individually grouped and blended, that I can only take note of this individuality, which inevitably undermines any generalisation; and not only does that make me think about the perceptual problems of more or less complex objects, it is also what leads me to note the disparity between, indeed incompatibility of, the most recent sonic objects. The abstract relationships we are taught to consider will be confronted by concrete relationships that are anything but simple; they are fluid, and it is difficult to find any configuration, let alone hierarchy, for them.

✿ ✿ ✿

So far I have discussed isolated objects in terms of the extremes of two perceptual barriers, deliberately leaving aside all the intermediate territory in which writing and codes will play such a primary role. But before addressing the function, or rather the many functions, of writing, I want to address the perception of a sonic object in isolation as presented by an orchestra, which is obviously the simplest and rarest case, writing implying movement above all, the change from one state to another, whether slow or quick. A slow change leaves analytical perception more room for manoeuvre, whereas a quick one very obviously favours overall perception. The perception of isolated objects may not occur often when listening to an orchestra, but it does happen, at the final chord, or a pedal point, or by repetition sustained enough to isolate the chord from its context. Those are emblematic cases, but I could easily find many others. It seems that study of the musical literature on how very distinct instrumental groups are integrated orchestrally offers limitless models, of which the overall development could be described as being from pure timbre, through the mixture of timbres within recognisable families, to the fusion of different instrumental components into a unique, complex colour in which the ear basks, as it is supposed to. At the end of a symphonic movement for string orchestra, when we hear the perfect triad of some tonality, we recognise it first of all as a perfect triad, only then noticing its configuration, thrust into the high register, or the low, spread across the whole range, and so on; then, already tuned in by the writing to this kind of acoustic relationship, we will notice the dynamic, or the various dynamic relationships shaping the chord, basically as a result of the writing or of expressive intention; only finally, if we have any analytical energy left, do we turn our attention to the strictly acoustic property of this chord. Perception, in order to appreciate things, goes through a number of phases, stops to linger over some of them, goes back, does some zigzags. Even in a language where some of the elements are thoroughly familiar and coded, the same theoretical musical object can stimulate perceptions that are pretty different, distinct or irreconcilable.

The A major chord with which the *Lohengrin* Prelude begins, in the high register, using harmonics and held for a long time, lets us take in all its detail. It is undoubtedly an A major chord, but it is also high strings, harmonics, long notes – which gives it all its expressivity, but an expressivity in which the acoustic features play a central role, as we have still heard neither melody nor harmonic progression. Wagner would enlarge enormously on this kind of harmonic stasis sustained by an acoustic feature in the *Rheingold* Prelude. Instead of a few bars we have several pages, in which the writing is much more complex than in *Lohengrin*. What was in the earlier work merely the establishment of a key becomes a vast suspended passage in which motion is mixed in with immobility, and the melodic shape and sustained chord confirm uncertainty, as it were. The chord emerges from a single line, the lines proliferate this initial lone image, leading to the vertical and horizontal fusing, and whereas perception is simple and direct when the line is alone, it becomes confused, split, when there are more lines; thus, starting from an object that was acoustically discrete, we have arrived at a complex one in which the thematic and the acoustic can no longer be distinguished.

On the other hand, looking at the presentation of the *idée fixe* in the *Symphonie fantastique*, this theme is in C major and uses the relevant harmonies. But how does Berlioz dramatise this presentation? First, he rhythmicises the chords by transcribing heartbeats into music, in a figure that is deliberately unconnected to the melody itself, giving these chords to double basses divided into four, glued to the low register – against all the textbook rules. These demand 'good intentions': higher means tighter, and lower means spread out, which is how the harmonic series works. What does Berlioz mean, or what, at least, do we suppose his intention was? He wanted to produce something like noise, a kind of indistinct, dull sound, and for that he needed sounds that would be contradictory, in that a tight configuration in this low register would go against clarity. We perceive that less as a chord which is also a sound, but a sound which is also a chord, acoustics here taking precedence over the function of being an element of the vocabulary. Berlioz was one of the first to use such strictly acoustic criteria so deliberately, though he was always on the watch for this in his predecessors' scores. You have only to read his treatise on orchestration, his analyses of dramatic effects in Gluck in particular, to realise that the specific, real object was no less important to him than general functioning in the language. When emphasising a chord with stopped, *cuivré* horns, he is more concerned with the sonority produced in relation to the dramatic situation than he is with emphasising in this way a particular scale degree, or a dissonance. I suspect that every musician experiences this dichotomy between the general functions of language and acoustic objects that are created because of, or in spite of, them. They experience it for good or bad according not only to what they have learned or focused on, but also to their gift for the *practicalities* of instrumental writing. One might even say that this power to imagine the object does not necessarily go hand in hand with musical imagination and can create problems in the language itself, as is sometimes the case with Berlioz.

In case it is not enough to compare a triad in Berlioz with one in Wagner to see how far perception of the musical object depends on its acoustic properties, I will consider a less classically oriented example of vocabulary – two excerpts in fact, one by Stravinsky and one by Schoenberg – where a lone chord plays a fundamental if not exclusive role. The Stravinsky example is the 'Augurs of Spring', immediately following the Introduction of *The Rite of Spring*. The chord, repeated in a regular rhythm in the strings, has irregular accents doubled by the horns. We identify this chord immediately for its unique timbre, and for its rhythmicisation, which is also due to a unique timbre. In this case, the timbre helps us to perceive a rhythmic dimension that would otherwise remain at too low a level. Although this case is more complex than those discussed above, identification is easy and meets its target spot-on. On the other hand, in the third of Schoenberg's Five Pieces for Orchestra, op. 16, 'Farben', you can hear a five-note chord clothed in two, regularly alternating timbres. Perceiving Schoenberg's chord is as simple in principle as in the Stravinsky: it is just as stable and offers no more internal complexity; although it changes as the music develops, this is note by note, element after element, and that, too, presents us with no difficulty. But how come we are still a little puzzled analytically? The five notes in Schoenberg's chord are given to five different instruments, the alternation needing ten. For the first chord, we are rather in the situation of the tam-tam sound as described above: five different instruments mean a different 'regime' for each note, different dynamics, so a variable relationship. We are back to every kind of acoustic vagary. The object in itself would not have been problematic if its acoustic constitution were not in the foreground of our response. That is totally different from the Stravinsky example, in which the acoustic constitution is a coefficient, supporting and clarifying; with the Schoenberg, it is a cause of instability and doubt.

The proportions of certainty and doubt can be tweaked according to how much of the object's brevity or permanence one intends to be heard. In this respect, I can mention my own *Éclat*, which is sometimes based exclusively on these absolutely unrefined features of how material is perceived. This work is scored for a collection of resonating instruments, from the loudest and longest lasting, the piano, to the weakest and shortest, the mandolin, via intermediate stages such as the vibraphone, harp, cimbalom and so on. How long they resonate depends on both register and dynamics. When a chord is played by a collection of these instruments and allowed to resonate, the listener will be able to recognise which ones resonate longer as they die away one after another. The shortest might not be heard, might be masked by the others, given their brevity and relative sonic weakness. Thus, there is a way retrospectively to analyse the initial timbre, given this decay in resonance. But if the same chord is played very briefly by the same instruments, there is little opportunity to pursue the analysis, unless, unfortunately, one instrument predominates by playing too loudly; and I refer here, too, to the Berlioz example just mentioned, for even though we may no longer be in the world of C major, the acoustic phenomenon remains basically the same even if it is deliberately highlighted.

I have chosen to give examples of isolated chords only where perception can be separated in some way from its context, or where writing is what matters internally, or where perception can be considered a key factor in the configuration of the acoustic object. Clearly, I will be returning to perception as the link between more general phenomena within a given context, but I feel that even taken in isolation, musical objects provide us with plenty of opportunity to ponder their nature and the way they are perceived. We are dealing once more here with an instrumental medium teeming with references. Every chord written in the abstract, without instrumentation, takes on a meaning for us, as a relationship between pitches. We will be much less certain what it is intended to mean if we modify it in some way with an instrumental coefficient. When this instrumental coefficient uses dimensions not very susceptible to manipulation, such as multiphonics, we are no longer certain what we will be hearing, to the point where we have to listen to the object itself to check the writing, which seems paradoxical, confirming the weakness of written realisation in relation to its original.

Arriving at the world of the synthesiser, we are often even more thrown than we would like to admit to ourselves. This affects the instrumental realm even in its most radical advances, if no longer by virtue of a rather abstract approach to the different categories of sound, then at least by the practical characterisation to which the instrumentalist needs to conform. Our instruments being constructed for very precise purposes, their peripheral qualities can refer only to that core, which is to say that there is a limit to possible transgressions, and one can list those usages in short order. Our instrumental world is based on these divides, which can be likened to the rungs of a ladder going from current, standard usages to recently adopted transgressions. Utopia has always meant climbing those rungs in a kind of ideal continuum. Musicians have tended to do this instinctively by gathering up practical knowledge of instrumental relationships, from the most to the least familiar. Researchers have tried to determine a timbral map, which I have never found very convincing, at least up till now, because context is too readily ignored. From common experience we know that a timbre is not only an instrumental colour – or a collection of colours with a strong, shared character – but also a speed of articulation, a potential for phrasing, and much more besides. Regardless of its potential for blending and transformation, a timbre is a defined domain, virtually self-contained. Liaison can happen by layering, accumulation, *tuilage*, by limitless procedures all more or less to do with writing and implementation, not to speak of all the aesthetic and affective connotations with which our upbringing has endowed us. On the face of it, the synthesiser offers us nothing but a vast horizon in respect of this scale of values, where anything is possible, to the point where one is paralysed, with no idea where to begin. Of course, we can distinguish between overtones and mixture, and use frequency modulation, phasing and some other tools, but we will always be in the dark about timbral and pitch relationships and other features that render the musical object amenable and comprehensible to our musical perception.

The first response, as you can well imagine, was to work from what was relatively well known – instrumental and vocal sounds – before finding new areas. Which new areas? First, the voice and instruments were imitated relatively faithfully after being duly analysed. The second stage was, and still is, to contravene that reconstruction and, by extrapolation, move from timbre to timbre, definition to definition. This second stage also meant transforming instrumental sounds by technological means, extending their scope beyond recognition. And harmonics of a typical kind were synthesised – for example, bells – in a way that gave them extra dimensions – for instance, regarding duration. Fascinated by what extension and transgression could do, people often stuck to rich objects that were interesting in themselves but difficult to manipulate, being very complex and relatively autonomous. Perception accepted them on their own terms and found it utterly challenging to integrate them, to regard them as actually musical. This is probably the big question of the moment: how to integrate timbre and the musical object into a language. It is not simple. It has taken many centuries to find provisional answers in the instrumental world, and in the non-instrumental world today we anticipate that any useful progress will probably take as long. In both cases, writing has played, plays and will play a crucial role, if by writing we mean a kind of combining of objects in the broadest sense: bringing into play, relating, connecting objects with each other in a context made for that purpose. The nature of the object and the logic of succession are thus bound together by a practically limitless collection of strategies that are not necessarily drawn from any rational logic. It could even be said that the necessary strategies emerge from relating things in a 'step-by-step' process that has short-circuits, reversals and rejections, making it an extremely complex operation. Eventually, it will be able to be described in linear terms, after the event, because this does somehow have to be told, even if the narrative cannot truly and completely capture the operation itself.

＊　＊　＊

In my approach to the musical object, I have considered it only in respect of pitch. Given that the musical object is dynamic, as I have said, why isolate it from every other dimension? One could equally well ask the familiar pedagogical question of why one first learns to hear pitch, the pitch of objects that are, so to speak, dematerialised. Especially in recent decades, people have resisted this tyranny of pitch, this veneration our culture has accorded it, almost like a costume. Indeed, a musician who is said or shown to have absolute pitch is assumed to possess the unchallengeably highest of musical gifts, but could we say the same of other attributes? Do we ever say that someone has absolute rhythm, or absolute duration? If only from that simple, everyday judgement, it is clear that pitch is not really a category like others, but refers in at least some respects to categorical perceptual criteria. When it comes to relative pitch, listening to our usual instruments, whoever has this famous 'absolute pitch' cannot make a mistake. This is not just a phenomenon in our own culture, for we can perceive absolute pitch in any music which offers us some particular hierarchy. I cannot have any doubt about pitch when listening to a Chinese violin, an African balafon, a Balinese gamelan or an Indian flute, even if I judge the intervals by the well-tempered system I am used to. If I notice a stretched minor third or a squashed fourth, these definitions are merely points of comparison I need to hone my response. And if I should be in doubt, it is because of more complex phenomena: vocal techniques very close to speech, for example, in which pitch is transient and, indeed, secondary to other features. But I am going to have the same problem with similar phenomena in my own culture. That the domain of pitch has been enriched and widened to the limits of analytical perception, or beyond, does not prove that we have favoured this component, excessively and unduly, over others. It is just different, susceptible to some absolute quality, regardless of context. Thus, there is a raw, perceptual hierarchy comprising the absolute, of pitch, and the relative, of dynamics.

Our perception of time, duration and rhythm is highly variable. Whereas perception of pitch can be totally objective and becomes subjective only in complex or fleeting cases, perception of duration is basically subjective and approximate, depending on many external factors, though the perception of rhythmic relationships remains objective up to a certain level of complexity. When a rhythmic pattern is repeated in a regular metre, our memory focuses on the prototype and can judge different variations and deviations in relation to that model. However, given a duration as such, unconnected with any beat and, as it were, suspended in space with no points of orientation, we can barely begin to measure it out. We try to relate it to the beat with which we are most familiar – the one lasting a second – which we pin down more or less psychologically, more or less accurately; it can be longer or shorter than a true, chronological second. This is demonstrated by the compositional practice, when writing a duration outside the tempo, of not referring to an acoustic constraint, such as the resonating time of instruments, or a physical constraint, such as the breathing of a singer or a wind player, but notating the duration in seconds – which is a neutral, anonymous length, designed to show complete independence from the beat or the speed, and negating in due course the tempo prior to this suspended duration.

We can judge similar values fairly accurately, even in irregular metre, getting these values roughly right in a limited context by averaging the calibrated pulse, which may be only an implied one. However, we will not be able to hold onto those relationships once the durations lie outside a certain range: we would have a hard time knowing what 'thirty in the time of two' is, for instance – particularly, and obviously, if there were no common factor between the periodicity of the 'thirty' and the 'two'. Even when a pulse is clear, we have to count in order to make an estimate that is anything other than intuitive and encrypted. There is no symbolism here to help, such as we have in the domain of pitch, which we can express very accurately regardless of the registral separation between two points. If I hear a bottom C played on the cello's lowest open string followed by a high F sharp on the flute, I will have no hesitation, despite the big distance between them. I will not want to start talking about 65.4 and 1661.22 Hz! My ear tells me the symbol for these notes instantaneously. Pitch perception is absolute whatever the interval, whereas the perception of duration is relative, indeed highly relative. When it comes to separation, it can even be said that it is often more difficult to determine intervals smaller than the semitone than it is to identify larger ones within the semitone scale. Our ear is not sure of the precise value of these very small intervals because of the proximity of the notes, and we have to listen more closely. So judging duration seems to be the inverse of sensing pitch, where the narrower the scale, the greater the discrepancy.

Time is doubly hard to pin down, for whereas pitch can be inert, 'unrealised', context-free, time is a category of motion. We perceive it through numerical relationships, therefore – for example, between the different values of a rhythmic cell – and we perceive the speed produced by these numerical relationships; there is an abstract, numerical absolute that is turned into the relative values of a real, concrete tempo. The listener perceives this relationship as a whole, while other musical forces help to separate these two features. The interpreter, even if not sufficiently schooled to make a rapid synthesis of these two schemes, is working continually at both levels, and this is what allows him to vary the speed with accelerandos and ritenutos, while mentally maintaining the numerical value of the durations and their 'absolute' values. The realisation through notation of rhythmic values demonstrates, were it necessary, this relationship of speed to proportion, although composers are sometimes not sure of which temporal unit to choose to produce the *optical* version of their ideas. Webern's sketch of the second movement of the Cantata no. 2 is written in small values, while the final version is based on values four times longer, but given the character of the music there was certainly no change in his overall conception, the density of the musical events remaining exactly the same. But in that case – similar to the sketches of other composers – it was doubtless to do with legibility, or providing a psychological prompt for the benefit of performers. If we did not already know some of the repertoire and had to transcribe it purely by ear without having seen the score, our transcriptions – even of the most familiar works – would not necessarily match the original scores in their choice of metrical unit. I am not saying that this is proof that the speed/duration binary is purely relative, because this visual aspect of transcription in fact reflects the psychology of the composer, who manipulates the code of rhythmic notation to guide the performer's eye as much as to create what he thus means to be heard.

I have deliberately mentioned only the most rudimentary samples of pitch material, and as to duration the most contained possible combinations, temporal units having no meaning on their own compared with the autonomy of sound alone. Moving on to the domain of dynamics, nothing is clearer than the basic relationship that can be summarised in the binary soft/loud – that good old *piano/forte* used so often for centuries. Everything can be quantified numerically in this domain, of course, but however precisely we measure things, this does not take account of dynamics as gesture/envelope. Again, we have to distinguish between, on the one hand, both actual dynamics that can be gauged objectively and psychological dynamics that are evaluated subjectively, and on the other, dynamics that are external to the object, shaped by the context, as well as internal dynamics, measurable only in terms of the result and not perceptible in themselves. Unlike pitch and rhythm, dynamics cannot be measured on a scale, or at least if there are degrees of dynamics, such indications can be only approximate, showing an intention rather than actual output. And dynamics, like tempo, basically depend on some continuous gesture, or less commonly, they express an interruption. Our notation evidences all of that, however late it arose, and the history of notation reflects a hierarchy of perception, in neumes showing precise pitch, then proportional rhythmic notation, and some centuries later dynamic indications that were initially synoptic, showing contrast and sudden change, leading to the detail that we are used to nowadays. It is difficult to contemplate the dynamic interpretation of very antiquated music compared with current custom. There was no ready gestural guidance, although – thinking of Gregorian chant – there were certainly implied, collective conventions. Dynamics were not laid out like the oscillographs they have become. What were these contrasts, other than responsorial ones? What phrasing did they emphasise, what polyphonic clarification? Was there some other kind of affective gesture of which we have lost track? There has been an increase in the dynamic potential for instruments (with greater possibilities) and voices (compare Mozart with Wagner), but what went before this? This surplus in specification that we are now used to is a sign of the greater affective control the interpreter has over the musical text to give it meaning and expression on an acoustic scale; in particular, connective gestures, such as increasing or fading intensity, are key to animating the score. The attempt, through degrees of detailed dynamics, to put them on the same level as other elements was an aspect of the utopian urge, making them obey the same rules, standardising, homogenising; and yet, for both interpreter and listener, practice revealed the limits of this desire to contain the purely affective gesture of dynamics. What remained was a fixed, not entirely successful calibration, which made one have to think about the still-unexplored possibilities of this *gesture*, based on a meticulous resource that had to be used flexibly, but did have to be taken into account. Nevertheless, it worked against automatic habits and established, or tended to establish, a new practice. Discontinuity no longer remained an exceptional component of the dynamic gesture, but nevertheless it did not become a component as habitual and essential as the dynamic envelope. A dynamic can be roughly evaluated in isolation, but it has no actual meaning, implies no hierarchy, and relates only to the vaguest, least systematic categories of perception. Judgement depends on many 'outside' factors, such as the dimensions of the performing space, its acoustic characteristics and timbral qualities – in short, it is difficult to think of dynamics as a truly independent component, for we perceive it only as blended with other qualities of the musical object, and we estimate on a scale that varies depending on the musical objects themselves, as well as on the relationships we can establish between those musical objects.

Compared with the three characteristics I have offered here – which range from, as it were, the relatively absolute to the absolutely relative – the category of timbre presents us with a scale that is not a scale. The instrumental world provides us with timbres that can in the end be grouped in families, given that some of them have an affinity in their origin or in how they are produced, and yet they appear to be in essence separate domains, side by side, which we can perceive precisely by their integrity, by the impossibility of mistaking them for each other or of a continuous transition from one to the other. Timbre is in some sense a manifestation of discontinuity, and if we want to establish some kind of scale of values for it, that scale will vary and sort affinities in this or that way depending on the context. Naturally, we can reference categories, such as darker, lighter, rasping or smooth, but there is no limit to subjectivity in such evaluation, and what is more, an instrument that is dark in some registers may be light in another, or it can even be light or dark in the same register depending on the dynamic, on the context and on its interaction with various surrounding instruments. The scale by which we can judge a timbre in relationship to another is a variable one, unstable, very difficult to define other than comparatively and subjectively – even though it may be the very discontinuity of this scale that we find most striking when we are simply confronted by it. The whole evolution of what we call orchestration was directed towards a timbral space that could give the illusion of continuity and fusion; it was surely not a question of wanting to lose the individuality of these timbres, but of making them communicate their substance – almost distilling it – in a continuous dimension always available to project their specificity.

Vocality is another aspect of this discontinuity, but it is no different, though it is even more acute in that the voice is enriched by the production of vowel colour and inflection from consonants. Modern music used, even abused, that potential. Vowels offered a continuous diversity of timbre, but raised the more or less grave problem of vocal emission for this or that type of vowel, depending on register and dynamics. Closed vowels and open vocal production do not make good bedfellows! As for arranging vocal timbre on some recognisable scale of values, it is unthinkable: there are too many individual qualities for attempting a classification to make any sense. The only kind of organisation, rudimentary but effective, is registral, basically dividing the voice into four areas, with some overlapping or extending *fioratura*, enabling us to describe, hardly any more accurately, zones that are only very relatively distinct, and in any case not related to timbre in the strict sense of the word. Composers have worked with these crude categories, but each according to the vocal characteristics of the age and to individual approaches. Describing the instrumental corpus and what we might call the vocal corpus is an assemblage of register, articulation and dynamics, and it reveals that timbre as we perceive it is probably the most global category, the one least separable from its cultural and affective sonic context.

There are undoubtedly families, particularly with reference to the binary production/effect. First come resonating sounds and sustained sounds: sounds sustained by the breath, with the concomitant limitations, and sounds sustained by means of a tool such as a bow, again constrained by the characteristics of that tool. Among sounds sustained by the breath we distinguished between woodwind and brass . . . That, too, has implications for writing. It is not only virtuosity and register that make an instrument, but also its mode of sound production. Sustained sound enables longer and shorter held notes, while resonance *must* use figuration to give the illusion of being sustained. We could thus proceed to derivation upon derivation, but we do not necessarily perceive something in reality according to such subdivisions and further subdivisions: at the end of the first movement of *La Mer*, when we hear, twice, the melodic phrase played by cor anglais and cello, we are perfectly aware of the proximity of these two timbres in register, phrase type and tempo. We recognise how gratefully they can combine, and we may even suspect an unstable balance if we tend to privilege one sound over the other a little, but at the same time we have suppressed, in this very specific case, every previous classification of sound production and general characteristics; in particular circumstances, a strong connection has been established that would, given a different register, melody or kind of articulation, have failed. This is why attempts to establish a scale of timbres seem to me, in such a case, destined to be doubtful or simply defeated. The kind of scale needed, claiming proximity or demonstrating distance, exists only through a context, a virtual scale into which writing intervenes. It comes about not only from the unknown or the absolutely unforeseeable, but owes its existence to the circumstances, and if there are no such circumstances, then this particular scale of values cannot exist either. There are thousands of others like it, no less valid, no less substantial, and the richness of the orchestra stems from this interpenetration of multiple scales of value, changing according to the expressive flow.

For convenience, analytically, we may separate parameters from each other, but we can be certain nevertheless that no dimension is perceived in complete isolation. The phenomenon itself, the sonic object, is a unity, even if we may attend to one component rather than another, which is easier and more realistic in some cases compared with others. We need to recognise, too, any tendency to confuse the categories, if only through vocabulary. Thus, Liszt was already regarding accelerandos and ritardandos as temporal crescendos and diminuendos. Think, too, of Schoenberg's *Klangfarbenmelodie* and Messiaen's *Neumes rythmiques*. As I have mentioned before, it is a very familiar complaint that our Western musical culture may have exaggerated the importance of pitch, the hierarchy of pitches, compared with other sonic realms; if one wanted to take this further, first we would somehow need to re-establish a necessary balance with more or less neglected components and to assimilate a hierarchy of sound within the most general categories of noise, complex sound and raw sound. Nor do I forget to mention a kind of 'nihilistic' or 'egalitarian' tendency, which says that any noise, any sound, can be included, deliberately or not, into a work or a non-work. What we have there is a determined refusal to distinguish between truly musical material and material which is not, between organic and found material – anything and everything can be integrated, particularly in Cage's experiments.

This can definitely be seen in the development of the orchestra itself, prior to actual writing, if only from the nomenclature used as resources have accumulated. Percussion instruments that previously did not merit any mention and had, at most, the occasional job of providing colour took on vastly increased importance, not only to articulate, not only as tools for emphasising material assigned to more favoured, controllable instruments, but as a distinct category with its own meaning. Although I refer to instruments of 'indeterminate' sound, pianos also came into this category. Now, aside from anything to do with language and the appropriateness of how different resources are handled and blended, perception tells us the differences in kind between refined sounds, potentially distanced, as it were, from their actual origins, and more complex sounds that are indissolubly associated with the object from which they are produced. Cases that are completely ambiguous, in both respects, are what can bring together these two domains and identify the frontier between them. In the most general of cases, our perception offers a virtual analysis of sounds that are pure enough to seem hierarchical, whereas with more complex, global sounds perception, too, tends to remain global and synthetic.

The same applies to other components: virtual analysis easily identifies the degree of loudness, for example. Dynamics do not effectively change the content of a chord; at most, they can influence how it is presented, and thus its affective strength. If I want to focus on this chord, I will eliminate the dynamics of the sonic object, or attempt to do so, which will present no real difficulty unless the dynamics of each of its notes are so different that it is not easy to hear them in relation to each other, due to acoustic masking. Clearly, this is what happens when I try to analyse multiphonic flute or oboe sounds. Not only do the pitch elements deviate from semitonal hierarchy, but they have a different structure of dissimilar and unstable intensities – in which case I can tell the permanent from the contingent only with difficulty, those categories being practically inseparable. It is the same with timbre: the more that a sonic object is presented with varying components, particularly within a narrow range, the more we will fail correctly to distinguish its different pitches, the analysis of each impeding that of the others. In the most complex cases, one has to do that separately to be really sure, analytically speaking, of what one heard. I must also mention the effect of masking, of absorption, sometimes of acoustic illusion, which one encounters in certain combinations, even completely isolated from any context. Add to this, with sonic objects from the orchestra, the unwritten variable of space, the actual distance separating the instruments, as well as the effects of homogeneous groupings compared with solo instruments, and one may well suppose that perception is confronted by an extra challenge – not the least of the challenges either, given that these factors reinforce the acoustic effects of masking, absorption and illusion. The actual qualities of sound – its weight, its brilliance, combined with the contingencies of instrumentation and the acoustics of the venue – completely *reify* the sonic object and resist the analytical capacity of our perception.

We must also take account of the speed of progression, the similarity of, or difference between, objects, their function and how they appear to confirm or disrupt the components of the language. Thus, Debussy will vary chordal make-up slightly or use literally parallel chords in order to colour a melody; Messiaen will use modally derived chords varied according to often very simple rules; and in my *Improvisation sur Mallarmé III*[2] I used a family of chords all based on the same principle, in different presentations. Harmony thus complements melody. Schoenberg, too, played with chordal variability and flexible function.

We also have to consider polyphonic density, its rhythmic complexity, extremes and proximity of register, and the identification or blurring in how timbre is written. Polyphonic density can go so far as to make

voices indistinguishable, especially when the vertical results of polyphony no longer obey simple, strict rules. Rhythmic complexity increases
individualisation and the effect of separation, impeding us from grasping
the autonomy of a voice when it is drowning in a sea of similar auton-
omies. The entangling of nearby registers and crossing between remote
ones have the same effect, making the identification of the components
difficult, if not impossible. Timbre adds to these difficulties in exactly the
same way: too many timbres and nothing is clear, as they fragment and
spoil our overall perception.

It is easy to say that the more distant we are from a strongly coded
and hierarchical language, the more listeners' perception becomes torn
between the imagined and the real, and the more difficulty they will
have in relating the heard object to a concept, to a matrix. So there is
no choice but to exit the hierarchy and no longer worry about those
fluctuating, challenging relationships; and this is why people reach for
percussion instruments, which, in this respect, present no problem –
they may do so conceptually, but that is more the composer's business,
and in any case, writing for them cannot be relatively complex. Even
with lots of instruments, though their material is varied, relationships
between them have no complexity, each instrument keeping its own persona, which does not change according to context or by being in various
combinations. Hence the impression of profusion, but not complexity.

o   o   o

Let us come, then, to the composer, to the role of perception in the ability to imagine, to create sonic objects. Say that the composer is nimble
and aware enough to perceive past objects credibly, recent as well as
more distant ones; has learned to listen and knows why a specific timbre
linked to a pitch and dynamic, and expressed in a certain rhythm, makes
a particular sound; and not to mention individual factors – call them
accidents – that slightly modify the profile of that combination. Based
on proven experience of many particular cases, the combinations supposedly needed can be produced at will, or invented by extrapolation.
The tighter the hold on a network of knowledge, the more easily the

composer will be able to use it to deduce outcomes that preserve the link between the real and the imagined. This work cannot really start other than from a language, though one may seem to be thinking about objects in isolation and inventing and imagining this or that sound through sketches or some kind of notation. Of course, it is no use telling me that a language-free imagination does not exist – you have only to read the end of Berlioz's *Treatise*[3] for enlightenment on this topic. Berlioz imagines the many different possibilities of a giant orchestra (which he calls a festival orchestra). It is always his language, naturally, that supports how he uses his instrumental forces. In his work we find the ruins – or foundations, depending on your point of view – of this fantastical edifice. Nowadays, apart from the gigantism, it is surely the demarcation of instrumental groupings that we notice. Demarcation to such an extent is clearly impossible in a normal-sized orchestra. Yet it can be discerned even among realistic resources: for example, in Schoenberg's op. 22 songs.[4] Nevertheless, the straitjacket of an all-purpose norm is one that twentieth-century composers since Strauss and Stravinsky have donned, if sometimes very impatiently. Thus, extrapolation is the preserve of a composer who understands the resources available, offered by history. And actually, the challenge is a difficult one if the composer does not use those resources, for with the synthesiser or electronics more or less accurate hypotheses have to be tested out. You can no longer judge the timbre/dynamics/duration amalgam in terms of received cultural norms, but only quantitatively, hence the difficulty of deduction, with its lack of determinate evaluations and choices. Extrapolation, depending on which domain is at issue, does not necessarily go without saying, but has to be driven, resolving in its name particular cases that reference the language and its combinations. Writing will play a considerable role in forming those objects, in that it is about introducing items into a situation where they will have seemed to occur naturally; forming them, but also, and just as importantly, relating them to each other, making them evolve and participate in the composition. Writing, external to the objects, will also have to become interior to those very objects.

We may need to isolate an object in order to perceive it in all its detail, but we rightly know that musical discourse is not made up of the successive accumulation of musical objects ranged one after the other in time; and although a preliminary stage of writing will do for inventing the lone object, the relationships needed to form a language lie on a higher level that is about the energy of objects and the evolution of their relationships. In the domain of pitch, which is primary, there are various priorities, ranging from the basic unit – that is, the interval – to the form itself in compositional practice, via envelope qualities such as range, density and texture. I start with the interval because it is the foundation of all perception, all judgement, the basic reference point both horizontally and vertically. Changing a scale or other relationships between intervals amounts to changing our criteria for judgement and, therefore, our perception. This seemingly abstract assembly, which we are hardly ever offered in its raw state, nevertheless controls even the smallest detail of our behaviour. A piano will sound wrong only if it fails to map onto the precise scale that it is supposed to be delivering. If you have been brought up in our tempered system, you have only to listen to Balinese, Chinese or Japanese music to sense the great divergence of their intervallic systems from ours, for you will not be able to use our customary standards. We have to deal with our cultural norms on the one hand, and on the other, the fact that every instrumental corpus is tied by its very construction to its intervallic universe or to the way that universe is used. Despite being used in a completely different way, our string instruments are always tuned in a system of fifths and fourths – though *scordatura* may be used to deviate from that norm to form chords that would otherwise be difficult or impossible. The Japanese *koto* can be tuned to different modes according to where the bridge is positioned. The harp offers a similar example, with different kinds of moveability. One could point to many other examples showing why it is not easy to take instruments outside their cultures. It is not only an aesthetic question, but equally an issue of construction. The intervallic system, or at least the way those intervals are defined, will, moreover, influence the very nature of compositional practice. Dense polyphonic writing is not suitable for very narrow, ornamental intervals, such as in vocal melisma, and rapidity clouds our comprehension of such intervals even more: beyond a certain threshold, multiple complexities (in this case, the perceptual acuity required to distinguish between intervals) are self-defeating; we can see such writing as a borderline case. A related case is minimal variation among very large intervals: the ear endows them, by approximation, with a relationship that it can judge and which thus becomes a kind of favoured perception. With a smaller interval, the modification is perceived more as one of *quality* than of quantity. Thus, there are initial coordinates influencing the realisation of musical ideas, with the more or less conscious aim of making them perceptually valid; but intervals are only propositions, subject to the type of writing that will make us hear them as handled more or less in a certain way.

Let us briefly review the two basic aspects of writing music: that is, temporal concurrence and succession, or the vertical and horizontal, which more traditionally we can call harmony and counterpoint. These concepts have, of course, been transformed over the centuries, but they have remained foundational to the story both of composition and of perception; they lie at the heart of our polyphony. *Heterophony* offers a sense of surplus that can control harmony, counterpoint and, obviously, melody, as a kind of simultaneous variation, not literally creating the musical object but, rather, multiplying our images of it. A balance was reached when the vertical exercised continuous control over the horizontal, when every departure or deviation from the horizontal in relation to the vertical norm was conceived strictly as a function of that norm. Passing notes, delays and appoggiaturas would be temporary dislocations in moving from one normative point to the next. In the nineteenth-century version of this balance, the two kinds of musical hearing supported and depended on each other. Yet even in this state of the language of music, the balance was precarious: a highly contrapuntal texture, moving with very varied goals and internal configurations, with strongly independent voices, would require our closest perceptual attention to follow the voices, or at least the most functionally prominent one. In a fugue, the subject will seem more important to us than the countersubject, and even more important than the other voice, and is thus the focus of our attention, assuming the composer and the interpreter help us to make the necessary distinctions – the former by means of the disposition and characterisation of the voices, and the latter by means of particular kinds of articulation. How to clarify such writing? Through dynamics, timbre, articulation, imitation and contrast? Moving on from this self-evident distinction in a baroque fugue, where generic rules will clearly tell us the hierarchy, we arrive at the complex polyphony of Schoenberg or Berg, composers who, for the avoidance of doubt, lead us by the hand in naming the main and the secondary parts as *Haupt-* and *Nebenstimme*. Even in a universe where vertical control is, so to speak, taken for granted, our perception is fragmented, so that to follow the discourse, it needs to establish a hierarchy, picking out almost deliberately the voice that seems to be in the lead and leaving be the others that seem less in control, given that they are not actually contradicting the overall effect. We listen selectively to what we want to hear, to what can confirm the way a composition is regulated. In a universe such as Berg's or Schoenberg's we are not oriented by any rules: there are no a priori formal rules about the importance and role of various themes and figurations, no rules to coordinate the connections between voices according to defined vertical relationships. The latter, in fact, result from random collections within an undefined total chromatic, each voice tending to maintain complete autonomy, forcing our hearing to fragment and focus on alternating voices, assuming our background perception of some known or foreseeable vertical sense, at least within certain constraints. Add to that some complexity because of timbral variety or instrumental prominence or register, and it can be hard perceptually to make a decision, let alone the right one.

I am reminded of my reaction long ago to these ideas of principal and secondary parts, which bring to mind exactly the simplistic, pedagogical highlighting in Bach's *two-* and *three-part* Inventions that I found crude and useless, the product of a conception of composition too reliant on *revealing* something. It is telling that Webern, my preferred model, never experienced the need to signpost his scores in this way, unlike Schoenberg and Berg. '*En dehors*', as found in Debussy, or '*in rivielo*', in Bartók, have seemed to me mostly sufficient for those rare cases where dynamic balance could be an issue. Stravinsky's orchestral scores, much less polyphonic in style, or not at all so, also forgo such precautions.

My experience of conducting has certainly led me to realise that a hierarchy may be clarified if it risks not being understood. Characteristics

that are sometimes difficult to disentangle have to be made explicit –
when polyphonic writing that tends to give the same weight to all its
components takes over, or when it is difficult or impossible instantly
to decipher the harmony, or when there is a mismatch of instrumental dynamic with instrumental register. It is all too true that failure to
observe the hierarchy of the main voice, the secondary voice and the
polyphonic backdrop leads to serious impairment of a work's legibility,
to the point where its text becomes incomprehensible, listeners being
unable to distinguish between what is important and what is secondary –
which is what enables them to follow the formal plan of a work, drawing
their attention to how it is organised.

In particular, perception relates very differently to the main categories of musical writing. Harmony is perceived instantly, when chords are
expressing it directly, whereas counterpoint has to deal with time, relying
for that on memory, however fleeting. Before becoming disconnected at
the beginning of the last century, the vertical/horizontal axes came under
strong pressure in both senses: contrapuntal writing in late Beethoven,
relying so much on the identity of particular intervals, diverted vertical
listening from its regulatory role, focusing our perception on figures.
In Wagner, where harmonic relationships control voice-leading, chords
are related by the internal voices that tilt our vertical hearing towards
the horizontal perception of connecting lines. I can point again to a case
where it is not clear at what level our hearing operates: the Introduction
to the first part of *The Rite of Spring*. Polyphony – which in this case I
would prefer to call 'multiphony', given the intimate association of the
word 'polyphony' with the idea of counterpoint – advances through the
stacking of independent melodic lines that are linked only through their
positioning within what might be called the harmonic unfolding. Each
line merely repeats the same thematic motive, with rhythmic and ornamental variations – in its invariant register each is clearly perceptible
within its block; and it is identified texturally, assigned to one instrument
or a pair of them, such as alto flute, oboe and E-flat clarinet. The timbre
and strength of the instrument will directly determine its selection, for
given the register and sonic characteristics of each instrument, then obviously we will hear the E-flat clarinet more than the oboe, the oboe more

than the alto flute, and so on, in the hierarchy the composer chose for his three lines. We hear the ensemble, though, and we can focus on one or another of these lines because we are able, with some effort, to disregard the acoustic differences. The writing offers us some flexibility in hearing, since these phrases differ in length, shape and degree of ornamentation; they maintain their individuality and develop independently. In this respect, moreover, we will be wondering about the particulars of how our Western musical culture has evolved, about its perceptual assumptions, for it is surely not the only one that has wanted to bring together instrumental and vocal groupings. Plenty of other cultures have stuck to a monodic aspect elaborated more or less heterophonically, antiphonally and multiphonically, as I just described the Introduction to *The Rite of Spring*. Our culture, on the other hand, conceived and adopted the idea of polyphony early on, and it evolved very rapidly to a high degree of richness and refinement. The devices that evolved for writing this polyphony, whether in rhythmic structure or the domain of pitch, are so subtle that they often make us question our capacity to perceive what they entail. Even the idea of a *cantus firmus* crosses that line by temporal stretching that makes it impossible to remain aware of the original conception of the melodic line. Our tradition started out by transgressing perceptual limits. Thus, our culture has relied on overstepping the aural, incorporating into polyphony what can sometimes be a high degree of internal contradiction of the perceptible. I do not mean just complexity, or the mere accumulation of voices, because while there is polyphony in many voices that is difficult to grasp mainly through their sheer quantity, there is also four-voice polyphony, where the contrapuntal 'tricks' are also not likely to be assimilated, even if the sonic output, being consonant, is aurally unproblematic. Or one may say that the problem lies in that consonance, which has such power to amalgamate different elements into a unique entity, as we realise that we can barely make out the voice-leading and thus identify the voices: they are so difficult to distinguish because they have almost the same profile, the same weight; they are *equivalent* to each other. Literal imitation inevitably renders voices anonymous, unless (for example, in a two-voice imitation) their characteristics are made to *alternate*. That will clearly not be the case when, as in the Stravinsky, there is nevertheless some divergence, if not disambiguation; and it follows that there is a price to be paid for that, which is apparent in some degree of melodic impoverishment. The melodic line, constrained by writing which is so controlled, sometimes actually restricted, by the counterpoint, will most often have to be shorn of any tendency to ornamentation. Strict vertical control will eliminate some of the potential richness of infinite horizontal intervallic variety. Because of the kind of writing adopted, our intervallic system has shown a strong tendency to standardisation; and we have barely escaped from this standardisation, hardly taken a step forward, even under the influence of new technologies.

Intervals can be redefined and have new relationships, even though the rules of combination then have to change – and not only as regards criteria of density and *distance*. Evidence for this is the absurdity that arises when, in a given composition, novel intervals are used, but with the same old compositional premises.

There can be no doubt that proliferation of material will force us to reconsider the various relationships assumed compositionally, since the two go hand in hand: the polyphonic concept will have to acquire different qualities in order to absorb new materials. In particular, it will have to call upon much more flexible principles and rely on different kinds of perceptual organisation, depending on what kind of structure one is aiming for. This will possibly mean discovering greater continuity in transitions, in passing from one compositional moment to the next. In my view, there are two basic, and different, types of *realisation*, relying on highly distinct modes of perception.

One type of realisation depends on *real* writing, the generation and deduction of figures from each other, and organic transformation which creates, as it develops, the elements needed to elaborate a discourse. Those concern rules of grammar that can form a coherent language. I have mentioned, in this respect, thematic identity, which can infuse the musical discourse in part or completely. The rules may be more or less strict, but the figures will have a common root. So this is very much about real writing based on concrete elements.

Another type of realisation depends on virtual writing, the multiplication and modification of figures already created by the implementation of some acoustic illusion. Such figures are neither generated nor deduced, but rather are derived one from another. This is only about the multiplication of an image by distorting mirrors, in various dimensions of the writing such as intervals, durations or, more superficially, dynamics and timbre. Multiplying a basic image in this way depends on ideas of ornamentation, perspective, disguise, ambivalence.

Clearly, the favoured territory of *real* writing will be the ensemble, where each participant is immediately recognisable, limited only by their number. *Virtual* writing applies above all in collective music, where the individual is subsumed into the group, and one can play with a degree of ambiguity regarding recognition of the individual.

To put it another way, in instrumental music, the chamber and orchestral genres differ not only according to the quantity of means in play, but because quantity becomes a quality, in the relationship between writing and perception. Yet this distinction applies equally to non-instrumental writing. Current technology certainly provides us with very powerful ways to multiply a real image into derived ones, and also gives us the means to create an *illusion* that is all the stronger for being related to the initial image more closely and quickly, so that one can no longer distinguish this image from the derivations with which it merges completely. Infinitely mobile spatial disposition helps this illusory writing considerably, adding a dimension that is effectively off-limits to any instrumental medium. If a melodic line is derived, in real time, from itself, then we can no longer speak of melodic imitation, or exact canon, in the academic sense: we are not hearing two lines in which one reproduces the other precisely, within a suitable harmonic structure, but a single line reduplicated in time, as it were. In *Notations III*, for instance, each note is taken on by a different timbre pulsing two, three or four times. By the same token, a melodic line and its inversion will not be perceived as inverted counterpoint but as a simultaneous mirror image, where any sense of harmonic origin will similarly have disappeared. A certain kind of writing can reduplicate or multiply the image of a single melodic line without actually attaining the independence – true independence of the voices – needed for real polyphony; although our ear will perceive this sonic image as complex, it maintains an undeniable identity, as produced, for example, by all the resonant instruments and the violas. Perhaps, departing further from the original, one may combine the melodic line with one or several ornamental variations of itself, either simultaneously or slightly separated, and still we will perceive the unique identity of the group, though according to an interplay of more ambiguous perspectives, even if here, too, the voices will be not independent, instead simultaneously projecting an image and its reflection, making what can be called heterophony.

In this way, writing and perception are brought into play, ranging from the most direct, incontestably concrete reality to illusion manipulated as we wish. So far, there will have been only divergences from a single image, divergences that timing, for instance, can control, depending on whether the main image unfolds in regularly or irregularly beating time, and whether the image or images derived from it unfold in a free and independent time that is not periodic, or that is periodic in some different way – another tempo, other durational relationships – and, moreover, whether or not there is spatial separation. All the same, it is about aural divergence, as in *Répons*: we will perceive the same overall phenomenon, according to a system of different coordinates. Of course, there has to be a very strong unifying phenomenon if divergent factors are to be perceived. When tempo, space and timbre diverge, the indispensable cohesive factor has to be pitch, the envelope, the trajectory. The rhythmic images in *Répons* of a line reproduced on each note proliferate immediately through the system of dependency, which creates the arpeggiation of arpeggiations of arpeggiations. What I have said about a melodic line applies equally to polyphony assigned to a given group, while some other image of this polyphony is assigned to another group. Strict separation of timbres, as in my last version of *Le Visage nuptial*, will assist our comprehension. With the original polyphonic lines played on strings, unornamented, ornamental heterophony is played by the resonating instruments, even interspersed with features of the original polyphony – woven in, as it were, in a slightly different form, so that the texture seems to diverge, even though it is directly connected to the initial ideas.

Let me explore this notion of a web, an essential element of our comprehension, our perception of polyphony. Studying counterpoint, writing more or less canonically, more or less fugally – indeed, strict canons and textbook fugues – the highest priority, as I have said, is independence of the voices; secondly, one is advised to leave the general register of each voice only exceptionally; thirdly, resort to voice-crossing – that is, inverting voices compared with their normal relative positions – as little as possible, except when such crossing is enforced by some requirement of the writing or some expressive need. What do all these scholarly rules, as we described them, come down to, completely gratuitous and absurd as they seem to be? Simply, preserving the identity of each line, and enabling them to be identified in due course by the listener. The voices must be independent, for sure, but internally each one must have its carefully preserved and marked-out space. Going from this textbook counterpoint to the reality of composition there will be plenty of transgressions, but these rules of identity have remained so strong, so much in evidence, that they have become enshrined as a necessary quality of writing – the sacrifice was well justified by the comprehensibility. Yet comparing such classic writing with Webern's, particularly in the instrumental works – given that the vocal works cannot offer such registral flexibility because of how the sound is produced – one can see how much the interplay of writing and identity has evolved in Webern's writing. The Symphony, op. 21, for example, is based on the strictest possible academic principles, at least as far as the correspondence of horizontal intervals and rhythmic imitation are concerned, even if vertical control clearly does not work in the same way and traditional harmonic function has disappeared completely in favour of chromatic complementarity, with one proscribed interval, the octave – there are no doublings in Webern's polyphony. How does he handle the identity of the various melodic lines making up the polyphony, paired as they are in exact imitation? By doing everything that the textbooks recommend not doing. Thus, the voices have no exclusive range, but given their intervallic make-up they cross continually; the continuity of phrases is interrupted by rests separating the cells that form the phrases; and the timbre changes from one cell to the next, the word 'cell' being understood in its strictest sense, each one limited to one or two notes. Because of these various characteristics of the writing, identification is sometimes hardly possible, especially when the collection of pitches assigned to each voice is invariant, fixed in a consistent registral stratification, each voice expressing the same system – or what I could have called the same language – of pitches. In general, then, we no longer perceive Webern's polyphonic voices in the way that we perceive Bach's; our hearing is oriented initially towards the parallel timbres, such as horn and clarinet, towards the design and the rhythmic figuration – everything that makes an ensemble, severely limited in content, provisionally coherent. Identity arises, disappears, arises again, where previously loss of identity arose above all from accumulation and control so extensive that it absorbed everything. In vocal polyphony – *Das Augenlicht*, or the two Cantatas – he sometimes uses another kind of contrast, both in phase and in conflict with the counterpoint, by reducing the temporal dimension to zero and thus producing lines synchronised in parallel or symmetrically, overcoming a closely defined harmonic identity that is lost again when these lines are distributed by being offset temporally.

In the first book of my *Structures* for two pianos, I have myself played a lot with this pre-eminence of register in respect of the voices making up the polyphony. It is impossible to fail to identify a single voice, very obviously, despite continual registral leaps, which are no help at all to aural stability – any more than the constantly changing dynamics. This line is on the very edge of coherence because each of its elements has its own path; we understand it as a unity for the very reason that it is unique. When a voice is playing on each piano, the different sonic source, for all its unique timbre, nevertheless helps to make the difference between the voices, but when polyphony consists of five voices that are completely fixed and stratified as to register, as in Webern's op. 21, our hearing does not lean at all towards perceiving each voice individually, which is impossible; what we hear, then, within this clearly discernible stability is the notes that are soon repeated – those that because they are durationally close can be taken as a comprehensible rhythmic figure, and which do after all dominate those around them dynamically. This is to say that our more or less statistical perception has little to do with what the writing presents to us: what we hear could not have been achieved – in my view, at least – other than by the writing in question, but our perceptions derive from the writing only to a certain degree.

I could cite other cases, particularly from Webern (Variations, op. 30) or composers of the 1950s generation, where what we hear relies on criteria of perception that are not the same as those that would directly result from intentions in the writing. Relationships that we have thought through remain inescapably virtual, however we might know them and analyse them, while real relationships appear to occlude structural coherence. The commonest gestalt is the one we have encountered, not the one we have conceived. The most direct and salient relationships dominate internal, hidden ones by virtue of strength and proximity. Is this to do with perceptual weakness or a serious conceptual failure? Should a score be as readable as its structures are? When one focuses on speculation about duration, numerical relationships and complex combinations, one cannot help but ask what is left to hearing. The most instinctive, philistine response is an accusation of gratuitousness and uselessness: when a structure is not self-explanatory, then it is not only useless, but also incoherent and absurd.

Thinking more subtly about *evidence* as the primary criterion and justification of structure, it must be obvious that this criterion is not specially privileged, or at least not with respect to immediate evidence, even if we feel instinctively that this kind of evidence cannot be what the composition is ultimately about, that there can be meaningful slippage between writing and the output, and that this divergence is hard or even impossible to foresee and to judge. A simpler way of doing things, more direct, less considered, less calculated, would not have had the same result. Durational permutations such as one finds in Messiaen's *Chronochromie* are, for sure, the realisation of such intricate numerical planning that there is no point in wanting to try to perceive the plans themselves. As to our impression, however, of durations, completely independent of any metre, that nevertheless conform to a hidden law of contrast between long and short values that we take to be both uncertain and definitive – uncertain in principle but definitive in how it works – the composer could not have achieved that impression by any more direct route, without his imagination relying on an 'objective' method that vitiates every subjective factor – to some degree, in one domain. Certainly, there is the danger of deterministic, mechanical unfolding with this kind of structure; compositional creativity cannot come down to the discovery of some latent combination on which every musical event has depended. Yet even on the basis of such literal durational determination, there are still many features – the most audible ones – that are subject to the composer's free will, to less rigid laws, to spontaneous inventions – the selection of pitches, of chords, the timbres devised, the use of different means of sound production, and so on. Those are intended to be heard directly, unmediated, and support the more covert temporal structure, but without always revealing it as itself. As I see it, nothing is more justified than this interplay of the visible and the hidden, though I definitely do not ascribe any virtue to the arithmetically mysterious; rather, to the kind of exploration that stretches the imagination beyond its customary zone, the means it uses to realise a different kind of order concentrating our attention on some unusual domain where one senses rule rather than being in control of it. Think of the esoteric relationships in learned writing from the fifteenth to the eighteenth centuries, which are nothing other than this way of feeding our perception of an illusion: the way that they can so quickly produce a series of events, the speed at which events can follow each other, these too can create uncertainty. What you can hear perfectly clearly at a moderate speed – the stacking up of lines, chord progressions, timbral shifts – becomes at a faster speed not more complex or confusing, but a whole in which you can no longer distinguish the elements. This is how I proceeded in some parts of *Éclat/ Multiples*, where by means of speed I could achieve overall perception, even in a relatively simple texture, with contrasting articulation and lines that cross; at a quick tempo those two features will be enough to defeat any separation of the amalgam. Another way to trick perception while maintaining awareness of the rule is to produce hollowed-out structures, like certain paintings by Pollock and Vieira da Silva in which some surfaces have been 'effaced', painted over, so that one perceives only certain flashes of the original conception. In one of my *Notations* (no. II), for instance, I wrote the percussion parts by advancing from the articulation of phrases to cells and then to complete rhythmic motives. When only the beginning of each phrase is signalled by the interlocking of rhythmic layers, the ordering of these durations cannot be grasped, and one has the impression of randomness, although this randomness is presented so rapidly it is not perceived as completely 'accidental' so much as being steered, without one really being able to tell what the rule is: it is revealed gradually as the rhythmic cells become more defined, switching from the latent to the audible. A pitch filter enables our perception of the melodic lines to be veiled, making them seem incoherent, though the return of eliminated pitches – progressively or all at once – confirms or reconfirms the meaning. Thus, it is not only extreme, complex combinations that play with our perception; very simple procedures, acting on the reality of the sound objects by manipulation of this or that element, can achieve the same result just as effectively. These procedures clearly happen in two phases: first, the creation of a perceptible reality; then, by some method or other, making this reality uncertain, indeed immersing it in an obscure perceptual environment. Writing works on different levels, ranging from the construction of musical objects to their realisation in a variable context.

What unites these different ways of working with the reality of sound in order to engage or deflect perception – and the reason we may criticise them – is their essential basis in the idea of the superfluous. If lines coalesce indissolubly because of a rapid tempo, there are two kinds of superfluity: texture and speed. Eliminating pitches by filtering and simplifying rhythmic cells by offering only their incipits implies the superfluity of something that has been written and then erased; and durational combination also requires calculation that is superfluous in that it is not, in itself, heard.

But is anything really superfluous? Rather, it seems that there is a surplus of information from which our perception is not sure how to select; or rather, it selects according to the most relevant events, leaving aside those that are less clearly interrelated. When layers of duration indicated by the harmony are superimposed, as in some passages from Messiaen's *Chronochromie*, our first and lasting impression will obviously be of values written in a metre that we cannot judge at all in real time since it is too complex; we know instinctively that there is a beat that is not pulsing but is instead slippery, assuming we perceive closeness to, or distance from, the values in each layer. The key information – about the rules of permutation – is not provided clearly but is mediated by the interplay of duration, and submitting to the desire to explain its rules would remove the very kind of doubt that attracts us to this type of writing. We are dealing with an overall structure that is not superfluous, but which shows through when we subject it to excessive precision. Altering a duration, or a permutation, or indeed several of them, would probably change none of the meaning of this passage. Thus, to regard accuracy and precision of planning as primary qualities would be out of place; they are surplus information needed to form a field of action, their number, strictly speaking, merely an order of magnitude. The random enters into the very nature of this type of structure; the order of events in the above case is only a convenient transcription of what is in principle fortuitous, an order that will not be harmed in any way by being distorted or even explicitly contradicted.

What I have just stated about rhythmic structures applies equally to melodic heterophony: strict tempo is certainly not an essential condition for it to be perceived for what it is. What matters most is the idea of the mobile in relation to the fixed. When the main line, for example, is at a given tempo, completely audible via a regular pulse, the derivations can appear in free tempo, deviating somewhat through modification of either the speed or the durations. In order for them to be fully sensed as deviations controlled by a model, they have to be inserted in a harmonic field that is subtly anticipatory or reflective, with a core that is nevertheless sufficiently strong and focused to make its pull felt. This is what I did in *Répons*, where the soloists' heterophonies conform to that principle; spacing enables a supplementary separation to distinguish the model played by the instrumental group at the centre of the layout from the soloists on the periphery. Precise tempo, or fluctuations from it, thus has no importance since it is not a crucial perceptual factor, and the metronome mark is meant to indicate the limits within which deviation occurs. That is a very modest case of aleatorics, but much more important and decisive ones can be imagined. In that sense, the filters applied to the pitch systems must indeed reflect a well-defined harmonic structure, but the succession of pitches eliminated matters little to the effectiveness of the process; it is the way to achieve one kind of result, and a different order would produce a different kind that is also valid. Whether we are talking about a surplus of information or information withheld, at any given point those two conditions unite in uncertainty and randomness. Moreover, I feel that one should take account of that in works thus conceived, so that one aspect of interpretation is to allow uncertainty and imprecision as unavoidable, constitutive elements. The randomness regarding the external organisation of formal elements, which was at one time a major formal concern, appears here within the very resources that draw together simple, elemental objects. This is a minor kind of deviation, but it clearly shows the limits of what structure can signify.

o o o

We began with the musical object, with our capacity – because of its constitution – to *deconstruct* it, or not, which makes us perceive it as a fundamentally neutral entity. In the first case, it is ready to be integrated into an overall structure in which it takes on a personality as a result of its precise function in a given context; whereas in the second, its strong individuality will not let it be integrated into the whole, either through a general system of relationships or through contextual proximity. We went on to *writing*, which either organises these objects or provides the resources to relate them to each other. When writing is simple and clear, it will let us perceive via the object itself the structure behind the network; when the writing is about ambiguity, the result of the musical writing can be perceived without any direct connection to the network from which it arose, and it may stimulate some different impression, restructured in another way. Still to be considered is the least direct object of perception: musical unfolding, or form. Ultimately, every musical work should be understood as a whole – not only as a succession of independent moments, but as a coherent sum of events that respond to, and support, each other. Perceiving a form does not only mean being able to follow a particular organisational plan, but also understanding, perhaps intuitively, the relationship between the plans and the musical material, between structure and idea. This therefore concerns a basically abstract operation in which memory plays a vital role, since it alone is able to make us evaluate the relationships between what we have heard and what we are in the course of hearing; when we know the work, it helps us to foresee and forewarns us of what we are going to recognise. Because the role of memory is primary, it is understandable that form has tended to be codified according to certain established plans corresponding to certain types of unfolding, sometimes characterised with absolute precision.

The more temporally extended a form is, the harder it is as a result to grasp as a whole, and the more its plane will be presented as both structure and character. You have only to read the accounts of sonata form in composition treatises: they speak, of course, of exposition, development and recapitulation, the successive formal phases, but they stress the contrasts in character that are supposed to involve the main theme, transition and second theme. Memory is thus guided by what the plan anticipates, putting the elements that make up the form in order as each arrives. It should be noted that these classical plans were based on repetition, that is, recognition: after the phase where we absorb data presented according to a sufficiently precise hierarchy comes the period of their elaboration, moving away from what was offered initially, exploring less predetermined and predictable territory, and then the data will be presented again, with or without detailed changes. This alternation of presentation, distancing and return could be repeated more than once, as in rondo form; and it could be more flexible and less prescribed, as in variation form, where the similar plan of each component compensates for less predictability in their succession. So the dialectic between foreseen and unforeseen, known and unknown, happens with maximum efficacy because it provides a sophisticated tool: a well-stocked virtual memory placed at the service of perception.

The development of nineteenth- and twentieth-century music shows that the plans were overloaded and engorged before being actually transgressed and then abandoned. To simplify a rather complex process, I would say that narrative first dominated and then eliminated those plans: narrative implied non-reversibility, non-recurrence, and thus contradicted formal thinking, of which return and symmetry were the basic principles. By referring to non-recurrence I do not mean that nothing was repeated, that musical information, as it were, stopped being restated. On the contrary, the more form became complex by adding diversion upon diversion compared with the original plans, the more it relied on direct memory of the elements. Global challenges had to be compensated for by local immediacy. Thematic profiles, highly characterised, served as orientation, and these themes would increasingly become personas to guide one through less predictable constructions.

With the evolution of language to a point of extreme concentration and restatement – in Webern, for instance – these themes would lose that profile, that indicative function, or at least they had it at the highly reduced level of the motive and even the tiny cell; non-repetition became a literally respected constraint. As a result, form became short to the point where it was merely the presentation of data, in which recognition would have no influence. In Webern's Three Little Pieces for cello and piano, op. 11, this concentration reached an extreme where one could relate only figures of two or three notes, rarely more, and one is never quite sure because although there are similarities, there is always divergence strong enough to emphasise ambiguity as much as closeness. To analyse the form in that case is to assert a succession of events related by ambivalent links, of which the transformational rules are fluid, inexact, not goal-directed.

It is not possible – unlike with some musical objects – to *deconstruct* this form into a scheme that distils our perception into a few simple concepts; we cannot respond to it except by describing literally the events that form it, without being able to *reduce* them. A concept of this kind requires the listener to follow the form in order to take it in, and to do so a sufficient number of times at least to gain some foreseeability, if not completely memorising it. On what elements should the listener's perception rely in order to register the form? Aspects such as melodic contour and harmonic density can lead our sensitivity, but the relationship we determine between the more or less singular events cannot be 'absolute', destined as they are by their nature to remain more or less individual. No description could be truly abstracted, in the way that it could for the first movement of a Mozart sonata or a Chopin nocturne, say. This is why, having reached such an extreme, Webern turned again towards plans: first in his writing, by sticking firmly and narrowly to canonical rules; and then by adhering rather rigidly to established classical forms, even as he tried to fuse them in a hypothetical, transcendent unity. Form could be thought of once more as a plan detached from reality, which one could summarise in a reduced, verbal description, even if the reality of the musical events could not appear truly, completely in that description.

It seems that the perception of form may, in effect, be our capacity, or acquired capacity, mentally to reduce the succession of musical events we are hearing to a global scheme, be it intuitive or figured out, that is completely and immediately within our control. Our memory holds ready a kind of synthetic image that lets us judge what we are perceiving in relation to other moments, past and future. The listener's memory is not cultivated consciously and is therefore a rather unrefined means of judging, whereas the interpreter's memory allows, if only by means of repetition, a permanent zoom on the synthetic from the analytical – and I do not mean the advanced idea of memorisation, but knowledge deepened by study. The composer who wants merely to be followed cannot fail to take account of this ability to go from a particular event to a global plan, and the first reaction to this challenge is something we know only too well: that is, composing section by section, the most convenient and visible solution, but perhaps the least convincing. The form will seem necessary, segmented by focusing on an idea or a primary characteristic that dominates and absorbs all the others, and when the possibilities of this constrained domain have been provisionally exhausted, one moves on to the next.

And, of course, all we have is a succession of differently profiled sections, with recurrences, alternations and contrasts of one kind and another. Even though this kind of form is not enshrined in the established schemes, it remains easy to follow thanks to its temporal blocks, which are nicely differentiated and quickly recognisable. Such a sectional form becomes legitimate and interesting only when development intervenes – that is, when the arrangement and formal articulation are disturbed.

This is what Stravinsky did in Symphonies of Wind Instruments, and in a more complex way, Berg in *Lulu*; it is what I carried out in *Le Marteau sans maître*, and what Stockhausen ended up with in *Momente*. It requires autonomous, differentiated developments that perception can directly comprehend as such: all the individualistic characters have to take part in order fully to isolate one structure from the others – perhaps timbre, vertical and horizontal writing, register, or dynamics – because recognition of the structural category has to be immediate, and blending or ambiguity will lead only to hesitation and confusion. This does not stop each of these structures from evolving in its own field, so that the polyphony, for instance, may become more dense, or a polyrhythm more complex, but the basic characters remain unchanged. Writing the form thus becomes a superior kind of combination able to reach a fairly high level of complexity without disarming perception, since it will still be capable of apprehending the elements that constitute the form. Our memory will register the specific characters of each formal component with relative ease; it will recognise them and tell us about the formal development and elaboration. We will surely not be able to decipher the precise combination right away – that is not really important – but we will perceive the formal intention and be ready to recognise that intention throughout the unfolding.

The further this sectional idea is from the form – which is in fact a limit – the more difficult it will be to orient ourselves and recognise the formal trajectory. After all, we can easily say what is the polar limit – in other words, perpetual transition, or the continual transformation of an idea from one character to another without interruption, which is a kind of infinite form, corresponding to the Wagnerian ideal of endless melody. Differentiation will take place continuously, using neutral or temporarily neutralised elements that marshal the transition, avoiding formal articulation and interruption; the avoidance of provisional characterisation of two neighbouring moments; the substitution of one character by another; or a principal character becoming secondary and reciprocally differentiating. The subtler things are, the harder it is for perception to recognise them, for the idea of transition cannot sustain everything, and there must be a minimum of distinction between the stable and the unstable. I have said already, and can only repeat, that in order to be comprehensible, formal development must therefore make even greater use of external characteristics, such as envelopes and signals. These characteristics helps us to depersonalise form, paradoxical though that may seem, since it is by frustrating reality that one helps the listener grasp more easily such abstract notions as formal structures. A registral envelope, for instance, as crude as possible, will help us conceive of some part of a development as an entity and element of the form; it helps us to reduce it down from the collection of its more complex elements, isolate it, contrast it with other sections of the development, integrate it into a whole. A signal, too – perhaps a held chord that is unexpectedly long in context – will be perceived as a musical object, but we can also extract it from its reality to make it an orientation related to other orientations of the same kind; throughout the development these musical objects will be perceived as orientations as much as real objects.

Both perception and memory, then, need a certain capacity for abstraction linked to a reality that personifies it. The same mechanism links object to writing as links writing to form. The more that formal elements are somehow neutral, the more form that can be complex needs to be characterised by external criteria; the more these formal elements have a personality, a certain inherent and structural complexity, the more form itself needs to draw on formal articulation, interruption, related directly to the very nature of the elements in play. Complexity in formal combination develops in the encounter with the complexity of the elements; in other words, there cannot be complexity of the same kind and to the same extent at the level of elements and at the superior level of formal combination. Where there is too much information, our perception can no longer make sense of the chaos, but where information is too simple, our perception loses interest in a predictable order.

We continually navigate between order and chaos, from the constitution of objects themselves to their inclusion in the temporal continuity of a form. What matters profoundly in composing is the unstable balance between the foreseeable and the unforeseeable – between chance and necessity, to rehearse that famous binary. One can easily control the elements of that balance over a very short timescale, but over a long unfolding it is harder and inevitably more precarious to judge it, especially when there are no longer any formal codes to guide us. Facing some sort of need to establish form in the course of writing, unfolding may deviate from the initial trajectory one had in mind, or it may lead to the discovery of a trajectory made up of all its moments, and this means a review – calibrating the past in respect of the present – of the totality of moments so far, which is not easy to do. For this compositional task of continually alternating between present and past while also staking out the future (given that in this case the future, or the idea of it, perhaps already exists before the present realisation) is precisely the task our perception has when listening to the finished work: it constantly oscillates between premonition and established fact, validating what is currently needed through memory of what is past, projecting into the future certain kinds of relationships that have already been assimilated.

With an unknown work, projection can be only vague and hypothetical, and if the work is familiar, then projection can be precise in the expectation of some notable event. As I see it, completely satisfying this perceptual prediction is not always what matters; the composer should also – and not least, I think – create an illusion, which could be to satisfy, but could also be to deflect, prediction; or again, it could be taking steps that will make memory retrospectively grasp past events that have remained obscure because of deliberately withheld explication.

Perceiving a musical work implies confronting the local perception of structures with the global perception of form. The succession of local perceptions presupposes moments that are more or less linked – and more or less separated, too – by different characteristics. Hearing a work for the first time, or too rarely to remember it, the moment monopolises our attention, our ability to analyse, and we tend to perceive it in isolation; we can isolate it completely artificially, because we are attracted to certain characteristics that strike us more than others, and have perhaps grasped it in a way that contradicts its contextual meaning. The more these moments accumulate, the more we have to try to reduce them, at any particular time, to a sense of overall provisionality – rather like observing a scoreboard! Thus, we get nearer and nearer, from one reduction to the next. As much as codified schemes help us to carry out these successive reductions hierarchically in our mental representation, invented form leaves us, from this point of view, famished. We can reduce it to something, of course, but we are never sure whether the reduction we are doing is the right one, never sure of the wholes we are erecting, any more than we are of the formal articulations we are trying to establish. We have to make several passes through the work to be able simply to find out 'where we are'.

I should say that all of this still applies to a goal-oriented, closed form, but in an open form there may also be the impossibility of actual repetition of the text, and thus the impossibility of literally comparing two different readings. Then there is the perception of what one might call informal structures, derived automatically from data restated continually through some mechanism for proliferation, when we perceive a moment free of any finality and can perceive another moment from this infinite trajectory similarly, without having to refer to anything from the intervening path . . . Progressively, the fixed orientation is removed to highlight the overall mobility and flexibility of each moment in relation to any other, and thus one takes away from the realm of memory a safe area that could inform our perception about how the musical events are coordinated; but one lets it keep its ability to modulate this perception, depending on the precision or otherwise of the criteria in play. One modulates its rigour or disperses it in different fields of elements.

The perception of an object, a structure or a form is global, but one provides a particular functional context so that it becomes analytical; and if, for instance, the common factors between several objects are overlooked, then perception will opt for the parameter that functions as a yardstick for those objects. I will offer an example taken from percussion objects. If you strike a cymbal and a bongo successively, one's comparison will depend on the length or brevity of the vibration, or the relative richness of the timbre, and one will perceive the disparity between the sonic qualities of the instruments. If I want to equate them, it can be done purely with respect to the length of the perceived sound, the most immediate practical solution being a very dry cymbal stroke of the same duration as the sound of the bongo. I will have a quality in common that enables me to equate them and thus eliminate the other features that could inhibit that. With two cymbals, or two bongos, the divergence in timbre or resonance disappears, and I will be attending instead to what differentiates these two similar objects, focusing on pitch as a criterion. Even if the pitch characteristics are not easy to grasp, they are what I will retain, and they will eliminate all other differences. This means that I have deconstructed the common dimension and used it as the parameter for comparison. What one perceives at the level of the object is as valid, if more subtle and complex, as it is at the level of local structure or the global level of form. What allows us to connect one formal element with another is, at least, a common element – a kind of writing, an aspect of the texture, a rhythmic structure, a timbral combination or registral equivalence. With this common element strongly asserting its presence, our perception annuls, as much as it can, divergences among other elements that also hinder comparison. Moreover, a form does not consist only of elements placed side by side that immediate memory enables us to compare relatively comfortably; it might very well be that some formal structures recur only after a period during which development has led us to numerous distant derivations. To signal a return therefore requires the recurrence of very strong determining elements with which memory is forced to reckon, and thanks to which it will be able to locate in the past the structure and the musical objects closest to those it is currently absorbing, and which it can compare only virtually. It will be clear that in the absence of these strong elements, virtual comparison does not happen, and one takes the variation or transformation to be a new event, for our perception is lured always by how things appear, even with a parallel underlying structure.

Must we regard these perceptual uncertainties as a fault to be avoided? Messiaen, in a different context, spoke once of the charm of the impossible, and I am happy today to speak about the benefits of uncertainty. When a composer is asking fundamental questions in the most trivial way, we can offer by way of overall response the short maxim: excess is tedious. Perception tires and wanders when too much is foreseeable, just as when too much is unforeseeable, and too much of the same dimension, whether vertical or horizontal, becomes unendurable. I could easily say more along these lines. But then, when do you stop?

When there is no more pleasure, as Debussy sarcastically remarked? But it is not easy to gauge the limits of pleasure, or even of mere interest. What we know and have experienced a hundred times is that our perception seeks to be both enticed and reassured, for which there has to be a variety of points of interest, and evolution in how they are developed. Only the right kind of writing can create this constant plasticity, the interplay of reality and illusion, where we grasp an object that may well be a fantasy. For this, there must always be a network of perspectives in a musical event leading us from one object to the next, gradually distancing us from where we started, reaching conclusions that are both totally logical and totally unforeseeable, as in some of Kafka's short stories, which are particularly striking in this way – I think in particular of 'The Judgement'. The total certainty of a work unfolds through, and is validated in, the uncertainty of the moment. It is between order and chaos that there is room for the most unstable, volatile and rich zones of both imagination and perception.

1 An earlier version of this essay was originally published as 'Entre ordre et chaos', *InHarmonique*, no. 3, March 1988, pp. 104–36.
2 Fourth movement of Boulez's *Pli selon pli* (1958–63).
3 *Berlioz's Orchestration Treatise*, trans. Hugh Macdonald (Cambridge: Cambridge University Press, 2002).
4 Four Orchestral Songs.

PART 6: MEMORY, WRITING AND FORM

12

Memory and Creation

(1988–90)

Shall I once again sing the praises of amnesia?[1] One feels that in the midst of an era ever more imbued with memory, to forget becomes so urgent . . . And yet not only do we not forget, but we gild all the libraries in all the Alexandrias – reference being integral to discovery, and the source of the only kind of renewal still possible. The era of avant-gardes and exploration being definitively over, what follows is the era of perpetual return, consolidation, citation. An ideal or imaginary library provides us with a plethora of models, endless choices and means of exploitation. There are always intrepid conservatisms, of course, ready to renew their resistance to discovery, to endeavour, to experiment, never ceasing to appeal to eternal values, to universals, to the inexhaustibly tried and tested: 'mankind', humanity, which knows how to express itself only through the channels of wide public understanding.

It is all very wearing, be it endless consultation in our libraries of culture or resorting to an intangible past. Wearing and unimaginative. We wilt under the weight not only of models, but also of secondary sources that have become models in turn; and not content with the models bequeathed to us by a lazy, needy tradition, we also demand absolute authenticity, or whatever we imagine that is. Whether the monuments are visual or musical, they have to be contemplated in a strictly pristine state. With paintings, it is hard enough to clean them up confidently, and polemics abound about whether we are in fact ruining rather than restoring them. Where music is concerned, the idea of authenticity is at its most utopian, for we resort to a kind of reconstructive guesswork that changes with the passing of the years, through more encyclopedic discoveries. On the other hand, for less distant periods, it is not clear that one would really be pleasing the composer – assuming he could return from the valley of the shadow of death to hear such reconstructions – by re-establishing performance circumstances that could never have been entirely satisfactory. We smear our attitude of conservation and reconstruction over epochs and figures that possessed, above all, the virtue of moving forward; contradicting their whole approach to progress and discovery, we deck them out with a genetic paralysis that distorts the deep meaning of the work. Thus, the drive for authenticity brings us to a memory that is sterile.

What is authenticity anyway, and can it truly exist? The more we tire ourselves out searching for it, the more it escapes us. Minds that have not experienced the era of the works that are being reconstituted cannot possibly know their reality and produce a real reconstruction. All research into authenticity is devoted to the reconstruction of the past such as we conceive it nowadays – more or less idyllic, coloured by a golden age that never existed. The more we look into this hallowed authenticity, the more we distance a work from our understanding, forcing it into a framework removed from our reality, which drives it into the land of pure utopia, a utopia that endows historical performances of musical works with a value they never had, their chronological place being a seal of identity, not absolute value. The values of the model are displaced by the values of some secondary source. Until recently, performers' realisations – indeed, those of composers too – lived only in memory, in more or less fictional reports. Now, we have evidence, deliberate when it comes to prepared, rehearsed and approved recordings, and more or less fortuitous when it comes to instantaneous performance in concert, with all the risks inherent in any interpretation that cannot be corrected. To regard such sources, interesting in themselves, as sacred is empty fetishism. Is a tradition supposed to be securely anchored just because it has been recorded? This is to forget that there is no tradition, but only a series of individuals who have made use of either models or foils. Interpreters who relate to what has been done previously will either follow such examples or shun them, and given a strong personality, will always transform them more or less consciously, rebelliously or otherwise, away from imitation pure and simple. So we have a collection of images or snapshots, and we can see how the conception of a work or composer has evolved across the

generations. This is not like ancient Greece viewed in theatrical costume, but a collection of family portraits in which we can no longer
discern profession or social class, where the era provides the primary
data. This documentary memory can be useful only when it is viewed
for what it truly represents: an image of transition, among others. I am
well aware that there are composers, important ones, who have claimed
a right to their tradition, including Wagner and Stravinsky. They did
this in very different terms, living as they did in eras that did not benefit
from the resources we have available. Wagner wanted to establish a
school to start an authentic tradition of his interpretations; he failed, for
lack of funds, but his quite justified desire to provide interpreters with
the basis for understanding his works would be transformed, after his
death, into a rigid code of conduct, repeatedly shown to be sclerotic and
harmful. As for Stravinsky, he asserted the unique documentary value
of his own recordings and maintained that future interpreters should
study them and be obliged to refer to them. Unfortunately, though, his
precarious gifts as a performer, the circumstances and time pressures
under which the recordings were made and the quality of the forces at
his disposal do not let us regard this evidence as any sort of absolute
model. In any case, can there be such a thing? Every interpretation
conveys an essentially transitory truth. Theatre people know this better
and feel it more sincerely than musicians, who, if I may say so, always
believe that they should be dealing with something eternal.

This documentary memory has to be rather faint, and perhaps even
entail, like some modern industrial products, built-in obsolescence. But
what about the memory of the models themselves? The image of other
times, in our time, elicits everything and nothing, and in this our time
is no exception. One may pit oneself against those who recoup all the
works of the past, experiencing visible elation with respect to archival
quantity and profusion, the *tabula rasa* jockeys for whom the present has
no past. To parody Hamlet, one could ask: 'To know, or not to know? To
forget?' Indeed, but how does one forget, and forget what? Of course,
one may be born with some talent for sound, but does that make one a
musician? What will make us into musicians is a random or deliberate
confrontation, encountering fortuitously or intentionally what daily life

407

or culture may offer us. From nursery rhyme to masterpiece, we are exposed to individual or collective memory. Whether we like it or not, this memory that grows and becomes richer, little by little, stimulates reactions in us, provokes choice, forms our viewpoints, engenders our situation. Does free will really control this formation? Or are we rather, from the start, entirely conditioned by our environment and culture, with no hope of escape other than through rejection, an intentional disruption, an express denial? Do we have to know in order to reject, or do we reject without knowing? This is the dilemma for those who fear imprisonment in a life of endlessly accumulated treasures of knowledge.

Learning is important, but do we really have to revisit the whole of history, be aware of the entire trajectory? That would be neither useful nor profitable. Our character and individuality steer us towards choices that are in tune with our own song; choices that change, if not with the seasons, then at least according to our needs. Something that seemed important is, after a while, less urgent, and we will head for something else that means more to us in the moment. Far from being systematic, these 'elective affinities' depend on impulse and mood, and also need, or perhaps circumstances. It is surely reassuring to locate antecedents, but must one always be obsessed with justification, direct trajectories, perpetual legitimacy? That I exist is enough; rational explanations will appear in no time. In any event, precise analysis and rational explanations are merely a way of disguising the profound ignorance of which we ourselves are the actual embodiment, we who are harder to fathom, more ephemeral, ever changing. Learning what, and how? We cannot use some random tool, for just as we ourselves are musicians by virtue of our contact with objects, with musical events, so the technique and language of others show us our own language, if we have one. This encounter is a kind of detonation, impotent except when it affects our need, our possibly obscure and ill-defined desire, and the substantive, vague subject matter we find in composers and their works. Adjusting to them and figuring them out happens bit by bit, led by some kind of authoritarian attitude or by unexpected, fortuitous connection. Libraries exist as well as memory, but they take shape on the basis of need, or else they are merely obstructions. I do not see how history can be avoided unless by blind fate. It is not an important basic question, whether to deny it or embrace it in the abstract, but what does a model require of us, even if we shun its presence? Do we follow it, distort it, forget it, pursue it, reassess it? So: to remember, or to forget? The answer is neither one nor the other; it is to acknowledge a memory that is intractable, deceptive, treacherous, retrieving the ephemeral that it needs.

Yes to the library! But only when I need it. And let us repeat that it has to be continually, unpredictably ablaze, then elusively reborn from its ashes. Should we preserve and venerate the flame at the heart of this library in a forbidden temple, or always steal it, however unsettling that may be? It is the endless struggle between the Vestal Virgins and Prometheus, and both are punished by the people and the gods for their sins. The struggle between guards and thief endures, whipped up by memory and artistic creation.

*　*　*

I would like to connect those thoughts with Claudel, by quoting from *Le Soulier de satin*, when Rodrigo, as viceroy in Panama, thinks of Prouhèze: 'Who was talking of remembrance just now? I have a horror of the past! I have a horror of remembrance! The voice I thought I heard just now deep down in me, behind me, 'tis not behind, 'tis in front, it calls me on; if 'twere behind me it would have no such bitterness and no such sweet.'[2]

Is the idea that this 'past' impels the action – rather than passive, impotent nostalgia – not an expression of Claudel's own philosophy of literary invention, conveyed by a theatrical character? Similarly, in a scene between Alberich and Hagen, with the words 'Be true, Hagen, my son' Wagner seems to be suddenly telling us about the permanence of the work of art – just as Claudel so strikingly analyses the relationship between history and action, history and what we acquire that propels us into the future, history and the permanent reciprocity between memory and artistic creation.

One could say that every creative act is based on memory, rooted in it, at the same time as reshaping and reforming it according to its needs – the roots clearing away the stones, the organic overcoming the mineral.

Civilisations at different stages of development ask themselves this question in different ways, and we cannot hope to find a law general enough to apply to every scenario. The function of memory has always changed within a given culture or at a particular place; and the origins, constraints and functionality of artistic creation have sometimes been diametrically opposed.

Moreover, soon enough we shall have to distinguish between the memory of creators and that of listeners, readers, spectators. Memory will be more or less specialised, more or less engaged according to whether we are producing or receiving, which leads us into the domain of voluntary and involuntary memory.

Finally, the creators themselves have to contemplate the memory of others as well as their own. They have to ask what are the inalienable characteristics of a personality or a style of artistic realisation, regarding every sphere of creativity, not only artistic, but also scientific. Our influences and our present culture perhaps emphasise the latter more than artistic creation. In science, the logic of development and transmission seems to have a much more objective character, while artistic choice seems to rely almost exclusively on subjectivity.

At the moment, civilisation is obviously addressing this problem of the relationship between memory and artistic creation very narrowly. There is, of course, fashion, and the so-called 'postmodern' (which the Italians dress up as 'trans-avant-garde') has drawn attention to the end of avant-gardes, to using the known as an object taken out of context and shorn of necessity – isolated, decorative, even preposterous. Yet although neither musical nor architectural solutions may carry conviction, the reality of this difficult relationship between influence and creativity is acutely emphasised, indeed with unintended cruelty, by these movements that never stop putting history in brackets or quotation marks and keep trafficking citations.

Nevertheless, I find that the problem of the relationship between memory and artistic creation has been artificially inflated in order to find some justification for what is sometimes only creative exhaustion or mental laziness. To reformulate the relationship between memory and artistic creation, between past and future, seems to me to call for resources that are both simpler and more radical than trivial display.

※ ※ ※

Let us return to the place of memory in different cultures. Given where we are today, with our wealth of documentation, when one can refer quite easily to all sorts of evidence and information, we may not realise how difficult it was in past eras for memory to be preserved: it had to be sustained, like fire, and that was the price of identity itself, not only of cultural identity. When only an oral tradition was available, there was no room for doubt or divergence: fidelity to the transmitted material was the essential criterion. Some variation in transmission would be inevitable, some weak link in the chain of communication. Influence was a collective property, protected by the taboo of precision, critique forbidden. In music, particularly the sacred music of worship, transmission was especially strict and rigorous, the fruit of a long, supervised apprenticeship, often in secret. Melodies kept for religious ceremonies were a privilege granted to a caste. From a lay point of view, we could say that both the musical text and the way of interpreting it were transmitted at the same time. This involves interpreters as a means of transmission rather than a personality. They should have assimilated meaning, method and impact perfectly, and if they have shown an aptitude for this kind of apprenticeship, then they will be the ideal vehicle. This quality of 'memory' is so essentially non-individual that memory could be regarded as a kind of family resemblance – a family of magicians and priests – conveying both knowledge and memory genetically, as it were. Language that is transmitted through the esoteric rites of the initiated may lose its direct meaning entirely, for the listener as well as the performer, in which case it is reduced to a state of sacred onomatopoeia, of which the sound alone bears its cultural function. This is how in north Brazil ethnomusicology was able to reconstruct the trafficking routes of slaves between that country and Africa, based on the languages preserved from original dialects: transmission had remained literal enough, beyond the forgotten meaning, to reproduce sources from about two centuries earlier.

The same could be said of the Roman Catholic liturgy in Latin. For most believers, actually understanding this language is not possible, and they need a translation. Yet it has been clear from recent reactions to liturgical reform and the adoption of the vernacular how strongly connected people had been by their *initiation* in a dead language, and how far secular memory had represented their religious identity. Once Latin was abandoned, the basis for feeling Roman Catholic was gone; the tribe lost its main attribute, which was all the more arcane for being irrational.

We find examples in architecture – in Japan, for instance – of memory preserved as a key sign of cultural identity. Shrines are rebuilt ritually, identically, after a certain number of years, as they need to be maintained and renewed, even after centuries. If they are destroyed accidentally in a fire, or the wood can no longer cope with the humidity and bad weather, they will be reconstructed identically by following the original plans to the letter. This happened in European sites, too, after the destruction of the Second World War. When need and economics meant both rapid construction and sparse funding, there was little talk of reconstruction, even in cases where the previous urban patterns could have been taken into consideration, but when it came to symbolic towns and monuments, huge amounts were spent and infinite ingenuity used to reconstruct what had previously existed as exactly as possible, with more or less plausible results and sometimes an uncanny resemblance. Who knows whether after a few centuries these surviving reproductions will not have taken on the veneer of authenticity in their turn, and be regarded as a past truly remembered?

This search for an identity that is in danger of disappearing is brilliantly symbolised in Fellini's film *Roma*. Archaeologists visiting the works for Rome's underground railway uncover a location where Roman paintings have been miraculously preserved, but the longer they stay to explore the space, the more the paintings disappear, leaving only blank walls. This scene elaborates on exactly what happened in Lascaux: memories going back millennia were discovered, then the visitors' curiosity brought so much pollution that the paintings were threatened with damage and disappearance. Hence, the caves were closed, but so that this memory could continue to be displayed the original was reproduced near to the actual site in resistant material. True memory but false documentation: does that tell us what stage our civilisation has reached? That is not the only example. In villages and historical sites everywhere, statues and monuments that are regularly damaged are moved to protected locations, while copies are on display that can resist an environment increasingly hostile to certain kinds of material.

※ ※ ※

But what of music, you may ask, and I am coming to that, because even if music and architecture do not behave in exactly the same way, their motivations align: both involve a passionate search for cultural identity over centuries, at the price, I would say, of an acutely mistaken sense of authenticity. When it is impossible, in the world of sound, to realise this utopian dream beyond merely yearning for it, period documentation is relied on to imagine reality as it could have been. In architecture and sculpture the degree of conjecture is relatively low since we are often dealing with stone, the most durable material there is; colours and inlays might present a problem that is by no means negligible, but they do not affect the formal structure. With painting, we are presented with more acute difficulties. Recent debates and disagreements regarding the ceiling of the Sistine Chapel have been entirely about self-interest and national pride. Did we recover the colours and relationships of the original and restore Michelangelo's radicalism, or destroy forever how the original was imagined and realised? These discussions may be the most recent ones, but as long as there has been restoration they have never stopped, and they come down to this: Is it necessary to rediscover the original, and is this indeed the original? Is it not better to preserve, along with the picture, the patina that has accrued over time, even the dirt? To put it differently, and more starkly: Is dirty more authentic than clean?

Musical performance is neither dirty nor clean, but the dirty does seem to exist when we are happy to perform old works under today's conditions, on new instruments, taking over from our predecessors without addressing the problems. Bach on the piano, Beethoven with a large orchestra, Berlioz without the ophicleide or serpent (the instrument, that is) – this is what is dirty. And what is clean? Undoubtedly, recovering contemporaneous conditions, the baroque ensemble, string instruments using only catgut, natural brass, and so on. And in that respect one can say that some things are certain, while others are less so, and some not at all, being nothing but speculation based on factors whose interpretation is totally flexible.

The certain includes, clearly, the nomenclature and classification of instruments – so yes, one uses gut strings, a harpsichord as continuo, natural brass. Yet we are in fact playing on instruments built today and cannot refer to a sonic model that would remove all doubt. Who is going to inform us about precisely the kind of vibrato, the ensemble playing, the kind of intonation that is needed? We do not truly know, and very likely we shall never know for certain, how controlled individual intonation was in an ensemble and how it differed from ours. Were those interpretation marks, which nowadays seem to us essential factors in ensemble playing, as important previously, given the great sensitivity of the materials used to variations in temperature and humidity? And how about actual volume? The venues where people played were in general much smaller, and thus did not require as great a quantity of sound. The Salle du Conservatoire in Paris lets us see, if not hear, the dimensions of a hall where Beethoven and Berlioz were once played, and the volume is about a quarter of that in halls built today. It is difficult to imagine the precise relationship between an orchestra of the time and the architecture we still have, because the amount an instrument of the period would 'project' is something we know only from Berlioz's account, leaving much – indeed too much – to our own imagination. Taking on board ideas on style makes the problem even more complex. We roughly know the stylistic facts. They even allow us to grasp works more easily than do the comparable stylistic facts regarding contemporary music. There are conventions, codes, sometimes adopted generally, often locally. We are quite well aware of them for periods that are not too distant. Yet as we go back in time, even conventions do not make for a precise interpretation, and differences of opinion multiply among specialists. Memory is uncertain about the value of the evidence, and it will choose what seems to be right without complete conviction, particularly since the existence of common, agreed stylistic conventions implies much that was unstated when the scores themselves were produced. In today's scores the composer might seem excessively meticulous about notation, indicating everything – metronome mark, dynamics, rhythmic relationships and instrumental characteristics. (Right at this point of such fanatical precision composers had introduced the contrasting idea of total chance – which clearly simplified everything . . .) Conversely, it was the practice in other eras to allow complete freedom over some aspects of notation: no dynamics were specified, there was no tempo indication since the nature of the music itself showed that, and whatever instruments were available were used, depending on the place and time. There was also room for realisation of the basso continuo, ornamentation of vocal and instrumental lines, and variation in repeats to avoid them being exact copies. On the one hand, convention, and on the other, freedom – neither of which we are completely sure about. It means that it is utterly presumptuous to speak of memory in this context.

Here, too, we are on the trail of a cultural identity that turns out to be completely imaginary. This is why the term 'authentic' in our searching through the past is more pretext than reality. People often speak of authentic instruments, but they are copies; of authentic realisations, but these are mostly speculative conjecture. Some areas really are closed to us. Who can ever tell us the true speed, the exact tempo, not only of a baroque concerto or a Mozart aria, but particularly of a madrigal from the early seventeenth century, or of organum?

We are reduced to deciding what seems to be good, and that is down to our living contemporary culture. It is the same with phrasing. Exactly what length should a staccato have? What is a legato quality? How do we do that nowadays, while completely forgetting the scale of values that we attribute to staccato and legato in the repertoire available to us? It almost goes without saying that authenticity has the most severe and narrowest possible limits. One is tempted to cite Pascal on truth, error and the Pyrenees . . .[3]

415

Without a doubt, dealing with old repertoire is legitimated by a dose of precise reconstruction. It empowers us to ask how a work could have sounded to the ears of its composer, to what extent we can approach the reality that existed at that precise time. Nobody would think any more of crushing a Brandenburg Concerto under the weight of a continuo realised on a concert grand piano; and the huge Handelian choirs of the nineteenth century are obviously out of proportion for the eighteenth. But aside from the obvious examples of that kind, or more detailed and subtle evidence such as with regard to ornamentation, it has to be admitted that some of the concrete ideas indispensable to the life of a musical work are almost entirely unknown to us, the main ones being tempo, intonation, ensemble, volume, acoustic relativities and balance. Even the fiercest of authenticists never stops inventing and reinventing memory – above all, I would say, because the more problematic authenticity seems to be, the more they are driven to finding solutions. So much so that in the end it is the imaginary that pervades in their interpretation of the evidence, and I see in this a tribal obsession with preserving cultural identity at a time when it seems to be drowning under a universal levelling down.

What does textual authenticity mean anyway? Can it really exist? This is not only a musical issue; we can see the same situation arising in the area of theatre. There, too, there is a text, perhaps by Shakespeare or Racine, not to speak of going back to Greek tragedy. But what was the art of acting? How did the actor speak those verses, how were they paced, with what intonation? What exactly does staging mean, beyond the obvious exits and entrances? Certain barbs about actors, sometimes rather esoteric, as found in Shakespeare and Molière, can provide orientation, and one can compare Lully's recitatives with Racine's ideas, deducing what might be Champmeslé's way of declaiming. But we learn only a little from that, and the conjecture about Lully only leads to conjecture about Racine; thus, there is the impression that we are directly in touch with the glorious seventeenth century, have a true picture of those ancestors, can justify and reinforce in this way our main *raison d'être*: Versailles thought, therefore we are!

My view is that this kind of memory is in some way static, even if it can ferret out evidence and use it directly for better knowledge of some era and the *circumstances* that gave birth to the works that are its best testimony. This is quite different from dynamic, creative memory. First of all, I am not sure that it can be used advisedly and does not reduce just those dynamic characteristics of creativity to certain one-off practices. I certainly see these attempts at reconstruction as partially convincing, but they are also hugely deceptive when it comes to the meaning of works and their creators. *Fixed* ideas are emphasised, rather than mobile. I cannot be the precise judge of the thinking of composers from eras long gone, but I do maintain that in our Western tradition there has often been a polemic between *ancient* and modern. This was true of the *ars nova* that Monteverdi prolonged. Such disputes were virulent in the eighteenth century, not only in the theatre of Gluck or Piccinni, but in the much more fundamental disagreements between Rameau and the Encyclopaedists. Conservatives and progressives were often opposed in the nineteenth century, such as Mendelssohn and Liszt, or Brahms and Wagner, among other polarisations around which opinion crystallised. Debate did not soften in the twentieth century – quite the opposite. It seems, then, that composers, while accepting contemporaneous circumstances from which they sometimes benefited, have felt themselves or even wished to be part of a movement. In the instrumental field, and from what we can know about the eighteenth and nineteenth centuries, they never opposed the evolution of their tools, but on the contrary were quick to adopt new practices suggested to them by makers. In interpretation, they often struggled against stylistic habits that were merely the degenerate remnants of a bygone age. Thus, exact reconstruction would mean reminding composers, if reincarnated, of memories they would much rather forget. The attitude of conservation and reconstruction is smeared over an era and people who possessed above all mobility, even if they did not campaign for it but regarded it as indisputably necessary. We therefore attribute to them a genetic paralysis that misrepresents the deep meaning of their works and deeds. It is reminiscent of the candles still placed on tables at ceremonies, candles that are *signs* of olden days, decorative and impractical, just like real fires, given that we have means of lighting and heating to make them obsolete. This kind of recourse to authenticity reveals above all our reliance on socially conventional, reassuring *signs* – symbols of our 'inalienable legacy', or at least what we like to think of as our legacy.

It seems to me that aside from being of rather passing interest, this leads us to sterile memory that is content with cultural appearance, that is not at all grounded in reality. Could that reality perhaps be different from what we imagine it to have been? And is it what helps us today to be what we are?

This is how we can pin down the probability involved in all reconstruction. For this I would like to turn to the example of theatrical costume. Greek tragedy, or plays that I would say are based on Greek mythology, has needed costumes created on the evidence – completely authentic in itself – of Greek statuary. We have more than two centuries' worth of abundant visual evidence regarding these costumes, in engravings and photographs, depending on the era. Beyond the imitations of Greek costume, we see inscribed the period that gave rise to these copies – in hairstyles, accessories, materials – revealing everywhere the place of the craft that created these faithful reconstructions. Thus, it is always Greek–1830 costume, Greek–1920, and so on. The costume drama is inviting us less to ancient Greece than to Cinecittà or Hollywood – that trivial avatar of authenticity in our musical reconstructions.

That perverse term pretends to bring back a long-gone reality: let us see it and hear it 'as if we were there' – all in all, the ideal of perfect voyeurism. Through surviving documentation we are offered the magical keyhole that lets us surprise the intimacies of past centuries; and in that way we are supposed to be worthy of our influence, to have restored to our tradition the sheen of its freshness, resuscitated the life of the past, ensnared the work's truth, uncovered exactly what it was at the very moment it first appeared.

Even assuming that the interpretation of the evidence used for this kind of reconstruction is not exasperatingly flawed, biased or arbitrary, is using it even desirable, other than to verify the practice of an era, or is it everyday contingency? For sure, musical creativity is conditioned by models provided, day to day, but also by what performers can achieve and by the possibilities of the 'tools' at their disposal. The musical text is therefore intimately linked to contingency, imagination being triggered by what it can find around it and by what can be projected into what does not yet exist, sometimes exceeding current possibilities. Without wanting to suggest that the composer's imagination is never happy with the various 'tools' available, it will nonetheless seize any opportunity it has to try new ways of doing things. Sometimes thought will empower these new tools, development carrying on in fertile collaboration; but usually these experiments will quickly fade away, be forgotten – you have only to visit a museum of instruments to learn what a cemetery of abandoned ideas looks like.

However much documentary interest may lie in the instrumental and stylistic contingencies of a given era, we should take even more note of the importance of the musical text that resides in the immanence of being written down. Writing – to the extent that we can confidently decipher it, which can be problematic, at least with very old texts – transcends that contingency to some extent, attaining the status of direct representation. In that sense we may very precisely assert the weakness of the superficial, fallacious idea of *authenticity*. In a way, it threatens transcendence by irresistibly linking the meaning of a text to its original, or supposedly original, sonic transcription. But what is the deepest attraction of a text? Its relative, contingent value, or its absolute, immanent value? Perhaps in music, as in the theatre, 'presentation' blends with content in a very complex way, to the extent that many listeners without any background in musical notation have only its presentation through which to know the content of a score, and sonic realisation of the score is always vital. Nevertheless, the score remains a mentally realisable resource, safe from any other form of dissemination. There can be a certain kind of degradation, particularly concerning timbre, a loss of some surplus meaning, some mutilation even. Looking, for instance, at 'Farben', the third piece of Schoenberg's op. 16, a piano reduction or chamber orchestra version will negate the structure of the timbre and its governing role, to the point of taking away a vital aspect of the piece's rationale – but that is an extreme case. Anyway, the hierarchy of value and precision underpinning musical language and perception arises again here. A transcription that retains pitches and rhythm can offer us a large part of the meaning; depending on the conception behind the work, dynamics may be more or less crucial to perceiving 'affect' and articulation; and in many cases timbre makes for extra meaning, part of a work's overall effect. Transcribing pitch itself may, though, be inadequate or impossible for a given medium: transcribing a percussion work such as Varèse's *Ionisation* for piano would be a nonsense. But we are nowhere near that with older repertoire in which the writing contains not raw sound but something approaching acoustic phenomena. There are many historical examples of cheerfully transcribing music from one medium to another, or to a different family of instruments, with such alterations as are necessary depending on circumstances. The acoustic nature of a work matters – power, resonance, capacity – but it was not always specified in the score, which remains independent from the means of realisation. What mattered was a particular technique, such as lute variations using more notes than the vocal lines they 'parodied', or in later periods a symbolic meaning, as with trumpets and timpani. Moreover, the different capacities of instrumental families (such as brass compared with strings) would mean them appearing as either the main instruments or incidental ones. And all that, of course, is reflected at the heart of the writing, but it has nothing to do with our concentration on the concatenation of timbre and of musical material, particularly since the start of the twentieth century – a concentration that is reflected, oddly enough, and no doubt unconsciously, in the desire, or obsession, of musicologists and early-music performers to rediscover original timbres in order to render a score authentically. Although this was certainly not their intention, they brought to old music a contemporary preoccupation that was pretty much unrelated to their beloved historical fidelity.

✿ ✿ ✿

I have already mentioned the inability of many musical amateurs to refer to the immanent musical text, in that they cannot read a score, and in their consequent reliance on the evidence of the work in performance. The evolution of recordings widened this gap and greatly amplified the dominance of contingency. What people remember is not the work but some version of it, the work being totally absorbed as that version, which remains the object of choice in their minds. At best, there is a kind of triangulation of the sonic landscape: people listen to two or three recordings, and by comparing them figure out what the actual score was. Naturally enough, unable to grasp the ultimate reality of the text directly, regardless of its interpretation, they try to locate its actuality relativistically. This is why prestigious performers are preferred and regarded as models. With the mania for collecting that exists in music just as in philately, people then hunt for the rare version, venerated and unusual, which can represent a work all the better for symbolising some magically acquired tradition. The childishness of these wonders, and the inflation of some event beyond its real value, show in fact a disturbing loss of mental acuity. This totemic worship hides an overly superficial grasp of the meaning of a musical text. This version, a cult object rather than a cultural one, fails to deal with representing the work itself.

When there is no period documentation – for a period more or less distant from the age of reproduction – people try to make it up, in the belief that they are constructing something authentic. But we need to be careful with what we call evidence. I would like to cite two cases showing the limits of authenticity regarding the transmission of evidence based directly on the authority of composers. They are from Wagner and Stravinsky, and I have chosen them because the one happened by means of posthumous oral tradition, after the composer's death, while the other arose from unmediated reproduction of the evidence, which occurred while the composer was alive. In truth, the only irrefutable evidence we have about interpretation during Wagner's lifetime, direct and quantified, is the timings of the premieres of the *Ring* and *Parsifal* duly noted in the documentation at Bayreuth. This is a most precise indication, chronologically, although it tells us nothing really specific about the actual tempi adopted and their overall relationships; and reading, in Cosima's diary, Wagner's complaint about Richter's tempi at the original *Ring* in 1876, it is not so clear whether we can completely rely on this historic record of interpretation. Otherwise, we have scraps of more subjective evidence in the notes taken by the choral conductors and assistants, recorded in some vocal scores. Some of these indications are positive, but many seem to be corrections of errors noted in

rehearsal, things to avoid rather than rules to be followed, and thus associated with the first performance itself rather than being stand-alone
indications. We know how passionately Wagner wanted to create his own
school of interpretation (to my knowledge, he never spoke of a school of
composition), how much he wanted to found a firm vocal as well as theatrical tradition for the interpretation of his works. He never found the
resources needed, so there was no actual school, but there was a seemingly strict posthumous adherence to what he himself had done through
curating the exemplary productions – even though, in the cases of the
Ring and *Parsifal*, he was rather dissatisfied with them. This obstinately
maintained Bayreuth 'tradition' quickly became a straitjacket, sclerosis
setting in just when interpretations such as Mahler's refreshed the performance of the works by referring not to a model that had supposedly
been handed down, but to the real one – the score. Wagner's justified
wish to see his music drama properly interpreted degenerated into a
kind of sterile evidencing that was devoid of the original meaning.

More recently, and using contemporaneous resources, Stravinsky,
finding himself betrayed by most of his interpreters, wanted to establish
a tradition of authentic execution. The word 'interpretation' was banned
at the time for being excessively subjective, implying the addition of
individual distortions to the meaning of the work as defined for all time
by the composer. This thirst for definitive textual authenticity did not
come, as in Wagner, from any wish to lead and educate, but was a sign
of the composer's own aesthetic. 'I will provide the work,' he seemed to
be saying. 'I don't need your interference. I am giving you the complete
model, and in order to play it how I intend it to be played, all you have
to do is comply.'

This brings us to the notorious objectivity of works and performers
that was a panacea in the 1920s, driving the era's neoclassicism. We do
have documentation for almost the entire oeuvre of Stravinsky. And
yet these recordings do not have the same authority as the scores, but
are subject to contingencies of the most trivial kind. For anyone who
saw Stravinsky conduct, it is no secret that he did not have the professional qualities of a great conductor, either in personality or technique.
Technical problems are only too apparent, in proportion to the difficulty

of the works performed, and apparently threaten such basic aspects of Stravinsky's music as strict tempo and rhythmic precision. Lack of technique accentuated certain weaknesses in the very nature of the musical text. It is equally clear that the economic backing of the recordings mattered, for the forces available or the time allowed for recording could be negative factors. In this way, the documentation that was supposed to be the model in our memory merely emphasised its contingency and undermined its purpose.

I am not saying that all secondary evidence is to be rejected as a more or less involuntary falsification of the only documentation – the text – in which one may have complete faith, but it can be regarded only as the product of its circumstances – privileged perhaps, but ephemeral all the same. Our memory of that documentation should be faint, with the aim even of forgetting it.

If we were able to create really 'authentic' documentation from the past, and if these objects were uncontroversial, does that mean they would be desirable? Would this really give us the strongest, most solid access to a work? It seems that, on the contrary, the more one tries to get to the original, the further one enters into a diminishing historical *aura*, or gets cut off completely. Historical, or rather historiographical, illusion situates the work, necessarily, in a particular setting, makes it totally artificial, forcing us to reckon with the great distance between it and ourselves. That distance is symbolised first by the instrumental group itself, which is going to look so different from our own environment, and by the instrumental practices, which will very obviously differ from those of today. This kind of gap, between our daily habits and those that appear as much before our eyes as our ears, creates not only distance, but in fact a distancing, in Brecht's sense of *Verfremdung*, although his purposes were not the same. We find ourselves in a time machine, creating a certain euphoria for some golden age. (Sometimes this is corroborated by the illusion of clothing and setting – bewigged musicians playing by candlelight amid baroque decor.) In this sense, all historical reconstructions, musical or otherwise, tend to give us the illusion of the divine power of immortality: we straddle the centuries and see mankind at various stages of development. This is how we would experience both today's events and those of yesterday and yesteryear, exactly as they did. If necessary, we can overcome the uncertainty, deception and mis-understandings of today through the necessities of yore, making firm decisions, safe from any unsettling dithering. Surely this is the triumph of fantasy, this artificial memory, recreated to protect us from having to interrogate the present. Such memory is formed to resist and avoid action: the destructive memory of a civilisation which can self-identify only in delectable rumination,[4] as Claudel might have said.

Being fixated on a fantasised past in this way also misses what a culture is essentially doing at any given time: that is to say, it misses the relationships, settled or otherwise, between society, or some of society, and the artist who puts a mirror up to it. All reconstructions, however meticulous, dissipate this crucial dimension in favour of a euphoric, insubstantial and meaningless consensus. The very structure of current society, its forms of communication, today's entire reality, rule out true authenticity, reducing it to meagre, artificial ideals that, far from being historical in the living, active sense of the word, exist outside time, in an imagination where reconstruction is destined above all to recirculate people's typical frustration with modernity, to provide some feeling of security to specialists living in a protected zone. To reconstruct truly, even assuming this were an interesting thing to do, one would first of all have to forget, to destroy who we are in favour of an open society which we can do no more than intuit, perhaps evoking some of its characteristics. From these precepts, the path towards an unknown goal is much less clear than its zealots think, so absurd that to 'stage' anything historically is actually detrimental to the work, to its meaning. We could do full justice to a work if the composer's original utopia were assimilated into general practice, sometimes after the composer's death, but practice develops and moves on inexorably from its origin, creating new utopias. Overly exact reconstructions destroy the composer's utopia with no trouble at all, restoring the situation that would have smothered it and thus falsifying the initial intuition, reducing it to unrepresentative contingencies. As one gets further and further from the composer's utopia, does the work not really become a *proposition*, a device ready to reveal its manipulators to themselves? One of the most harmful characteristics of a historicising attitude in fact is to see works as *objects* produced at a certain time, whose manufacturing processes guarantee their existence, if not their quality. This fetishising of the object eliminates the strong subject relationships through which the work continually offers us its vitality. That does not mean that we may act in a completely arbitrary way – a different kind of arbitrariness from reconstruction. We cannot respond wilfully to what the work is asking of us, act on it regardless of its structures, contrary to its organic make-up. Yet can we conclusively and definitively decide what it once meant, when we are barely able to know what it means for us at the present time?

Beyond, or despite, celebration, exaltation, authenticity and tradition, what validates a canonical work, beyond mere survival? It is mainly its stimulation of something else, its power to create, the way it shuns stasis, its potential to ripen. A masterpiece certainly closes some doors, as I have described, by breeding unrest and a desire to erase the model by breaking away from it. What seems to me the peak of authenticity is wanting to fix the masterpiece by chaining it to its era, almost making a prison or tomb out of that era. Figuring out the era becomes a substitute for value judgement, and so a generic category has displaced aesthetic response.

In fact, you can see the devastating effects of this displacement in the rediscovery of minor composers. For several reasons, a certain creative anonymity is prized, as is the abundance of anonymous creativity. The principle here is to take comfort in something other than today's individualism. This kind of memory offers safety and protection. Standardised language, possibly involving some specialised but nevertheless limited technique, yields a landscape of the habitual, in which routine practices are peppered by the search for what is unique, or rare, in individual practice. Musical schemes are much simpler, hence the interchangeability and fluency of a prolific literature – prolific because it is interchangeable and handy for satisfying a greedy appetite.

That approach is no longer something worth remembering, but just a stocking-up of an excessively trivial culture that we pretend to glorify through the twin optics of time and costume. What could be more reassuring in the narrowly circumscribed, carefully staked-out world of conservatism than history sanitised by kitsch, delivered up for pointless consumption by being systematically, fundamentally 'cosmeticised'? No more risky decisions, no more bold inquiry, no more links with today, no more challenge, no more questions! A brick wall between pleasant, comfortable surroundings and interrogating our experience. In place of normal uncertainty, a parchment on which any semblance of vitality has been eradicated by specialist discussion of the dotted i's and crossed t's; a comforting and intangible legacy, a protective inheritance, where handed-down rites let us belong to the tribe of insiders, the chosen ones. Even though this so-called respect, this misplaced veneration for mundane objects whose colours have been deftly revamped may be the surest sign of cultural infirmity and deterioration, revealing its weariness and disturbing weakness, it nevertheless does not seem to disturb the worshippers, who, on the contrary, indulge in the idyllic vision of something permanent, an artificially reconstructed culture, symbolised by a changeless fixed point, like a dead star.

The danger lies less in this sterile adoration, which brings a tacit rejection of new creation while it corrodes, but more in the contamination of creativity itself by historicism. The relationship between contemporary composers and the past is complex; some time ago it was already not simple, but the question of influence was not posed in the same way. Going back a generation, I can already see very different attitudes. For the Second Viennese composers, and particularly Schoenberg, who in this respect completely led the others, history is a single, absolute trajectory generating one composer after another. They aspired to be at the provisional end of this chain stretching from Bach to Schoenberg, believing that a successor would have to follow, and so on through the centuries. Memory generated creation through the process of transmission in some kind of perpetual transition: there was no break, but a long continuity, stretching back into what we know are the mists of time. And oddly enough, it was Schoenberg, creature of the break with the past, who most valued this idea of continuity – passionately even. I say 'creature of the break' advisedly, for it was he who abandoned codes of musical language and whom we can clearly see distancing himself from his predecessors; however logical this step was meant to be, it involved basic conflicts with what he had known and used as motivation. Yet for

him there was one, and only one, historical truth, to which he felt completely wedded. For Stravinsky, of the same time but a different culture,
history was both nearer and further away. It was nearer in the sense
that his early works were the outcome of his contact with what came
immediately beforehand – earlier music having clearly not concerned
him at that time. Deliberately or not, he did not join a long tradition, but
expressed himself through his immediate environment; the medium he
chose for his principal works, ballet, only emphasised his detachment
from the central German tradition to which Schoenberg adhered. Only
after this spontaneous first period did Stravinsky discover the virtues
and vices of that tradition and embarked, not on continuity, but on a
new kind of break, during which he neither explored nor carried on, but
discovered old cultural objects and manipulated them to make contemporary ones that were also stamped with the past. It is a difficult ploy to
turn from short-term to long-term memory. Thinking back a little, reading Debussy's writings we see him basically defining himself in relation
to his immediate forebear, Wagner. Others are not secondary but more
sporadic. He loved some of the composers of whom he spoke, others
annoyed him, but there was only one predecessor to whom he reacted. It
is quite something to see how dazzled he was by earlier composers whom
he considered 'primitive', always praising them for their innocence and
ingenuity. This idea of *primitives*, which was also widely true of painters, involves those who are now most distant from us, whether dazzling
or not. Thus, there were those who sparked his interest, influencing
his decisions and choices, and on the other hand there were remote
primitives, dizzy with lost ingenuity, a distant paradise. Going back even
further, to judge by their writings, Wagner and Berlioz relied on near, or
fairly near, predecessors. Gluck, Mozart, Weber and Beethoven are the
main references; they hardly mention Bach and Handel, while valuing
Mozart, Beethoven and Mendelssohn. The further we go back in time,
the more distant influence fades compared with direct influence, with
memories that were more recent and more vital and indispensable.

Nevertheless, is our memory longer nowadays? For sure, a more
extensive heritage is available to us; even when we do not use it directly,
it is available, and the idea of primitives, marvels or not, disappeared long

ago. We no longer think of the lineage as unique, since non-European civilisations, previously considered as primitive or barbaric, have taken their place in our collective memory. Yet perhaps we should distinguish between real memories of actual evidence, and the virtual memory of lessons we have learned from such evidence, which are very often distinct from the things themselves. This more or less amounts to distinguishing between the (direct) memory of the work and the (acquired) memory of its techniques.

o o o

When we learn to write music in conservatoires, a striking gap opens up between exercise and work. A large part of pedagogy is based on learning the most basic grammar, obeying, or not contravening, a certain number of rules: no parallel octaves or fifths, no unauthorised chromatic false relations, good and bad harmony, and so on. It is the same as learning how to write without learning etymology, grammatical agreement or conjugations, without reference to actual works of literature. There is a collective memory of the language that one learns apart from any real context. Then again, instrumentalists dealing with actual repertoire do not learn these rules formally, but experience them in the very act of playing: writing, writing's memory, is learned instinctively rather than rationally through analysis, or at least with a minimum of rationality by comparison with their favoured means of intuition.

The eventual composer thus begins by learning the basic rules of language, but also learns about development, because the vocabulary and rules in play have clearly evolved; and despite scholarly efforts to determine grammar in the abstract, referring to works has never been dispensed with.

The longer we learn, the more we have to deepen our study of the elements of the language and reckon with the reality of works, for the evolution of explicit and implicit rules is intimately connected to the vocabulary and syntax of a given composer at a specific time. These rules, originally so abstract, stripped of reality, we find enshrined more concretely in works, to the point where they seem to belong to us and are perishable. The more we progress, the more rules and works are made to coincide, until rules will seem to be only what they really are: the elements, indeed basic characteristics, of a style. This is how the student composer can walk in the footsteps of the most illustrious predecessors, hoping to be empowered to imitate the main features of models. The composer uses skill to assimilate the characteristics of a given style and to implement them, and in summary you can say that memory is helping the composer become a sort of forger. This is after learning how to write a four-voice chorale in the style of Bach, to compose an accompanied melody in the manner of Schumann, and so on through Debussy or Ravel. These exercises are supposed to provide not only fluent writing, but also a knowledge of styles, so that one may distinguish between the stable and the contingent. Thus, through abstract memories, fundamental ingredients, some exact memory can be summoned to move on to a new abstract memory that is a principle for writing, though animated by actual works. If one is intimidated by the weight of this memory – assuming one is already responding actively to this kind of learning, not simply being paralysed by the example of the 'masters' – one has to draw one's own conclusions, which means that once all the issues of writing have been absorbed, analysis must transcend passive memory in favour of the active, embracing new discoveries. I will discuss later this most important activity, analysis, which is about self-discovery as much as about study.

First, though, I want to consider how the interpreter is remembering, and to what aspect of a work this applies, because the interpreter, whether playing by heart or not, which is not the underlying factor, must draw on several kinds of memory. For the instrumentalist, there is obviously strictly mechanical memory, of the fingers, or more generally of everything involved in making the instrument speak – handling a keyboard or keys, breathing or bow hold – just as for the conductor the geometry of gesture will help to maintain the beat, subdivisions and rhythmic patterns. There is also a memory of vocabulary, subject to known codes, easy to take in and supported by the essential ability to understand and remember. The more irregular and complex the rules, the harder it is for memory to absorb and use them; from the interpreter's point of view, the language's coherence will be harder to understand and thus to convey. Fingers alone cannot record a vocabulary, and even the most intuitive of performers have a practical grasp of the language to inform their gestures more or less consciously. Then there is the higher level, form, essential for taking in and understanding a work, and for letting it be taken in and understood. This sense of form is often discussed in relation to interpretation, particularly with instrumental or theatrical Romantic repertoire, where works can be long and have to be kept coherent and fluid, without losing detail. The Germans have a special term to express a fully achieved trajectory: *der grosse Bogen*, the overall arc of a work. We can say that memory – of a kind, though difficult to formulate – plays a key role. We have to remember, on the spot, what is past and what will come, how important different moments are, how intimately connected, or how distinct or separate. When the formal plan is very clear, based on repetition, form is, as it were, easy to digest. Even for those who are not aware in principle of the plans and constraints of sonata form or rondo, it is simple to navigate works that use the most basic of such plans. It is simple to connect the corresponding elements mentally, and so to be able to equate them. So long as they are repeated closely enough in kind or in time, so long as the common features are more apparent than variations or differences, memory has no trouble making the connections that interpretation needs to incorporate, and as in interpretation, in being able to recognise these connections or adjust to them. The work's trajectory lies in these formal markers or, more precisely, between one marker and another; if they are easy to make, then they will be easy to follow.

If, however, the connections are either more complex or more difficult to make in any given context, the interpreter will come adrift, with what is secondary being mistaken for what is primary, and thus memory risks being dislocated, of being only a series of events retained without regard to relationship and sequence; memory will not work globally as it ought to, but will resort almost entirely to the local scheme, to adjacency. There might be some choice events, grasped in all their vividness and coherence, but in moving from one to the next we will not sense any certainty or inevitability, so there will be neither transition nor contrast, but an undefined moment. With complex works, memory *learns* – and again, not that misleading 'by heart' memorising, which is itself subject to the dichotomy between the mechanical and the conceptualised. How does it learn? Both conceptually and intuitively. Orientation is basic study for complex trajectories: marking the markers – to use a pleonasm; apprehending transitions and contrasts; identifying the pace of development and its real progression in relation to all the material – that is essentially the necessary preparation. What truly matters is this phase of observation, whether such work is done rationally or more pragmatically; and then putting it into practice involves instinct and technique. Instinct means discovering whether what is predicted proves to be right or not, and there will be times when one's judgement has to be modified, when one has to respond to a particular kind of sound. The hierarchies we think we have deciphered in the score are not always correct, and we have to alter or change them so that our memory can find the genuine connections on which to rely. Technique will be all the more important when it speeds up our ability to locate mistaken predictions and the means of correcting them. Once this initial work is over, instinct can absorb these rational features – perhaps quite quickly, meaning that they will become part of our memory; perhaps unconsciously; perhaps long-term, sufficiently for us not to have to summon the features consciously, but enabling them to appear when we want them. This is the way in which, without quite knowing how, we toggle between voluntary and instinctive memory. Personally, I believe that interpretation is valid only when the musical text has become a trigger for our reflexes, a kind of script for conveying things sensitively. And beware: I would not want anyone to think that this is about Pavlovian conditioning; although some of memory's guidance – especially learning 'by heart' – is certainly Pavlovian, that is definitely not enough to determine, let alone devise, an interpretation, but merely backup. What I have called toggling, between what is more or less rational and instinctive immersion, is very hard to grasp, but it comes incrementally, depending on the quality or nature of the music. Gradually, things join up and embrace the most refractory moments, the ones that were least clearly defined or most ambiguous, and a whole emerges in which memory can roam at will. You notice this ability to locate a given moment in a work when you can select it, exactly and quickly, all at once from all the others, in isolation and yet knowing exactly where it comes. But we do not really need this analytical memory, swooping into a work, as it were, which is so useful in rehearsal, when actually interpreting or playing; not only do we not need it, but it can interfere when there is a particular need for total synthesis.

Rhythmic intensity and synthesis, which is the most indispensable part of actual interpretation, can be based only on an essentially global memory, and this is extremely difficult to attain. At the very moment of playing, there must be the memory of what has gone by, and particularly of everything closely connected in formal terms to the exact point where we are, as well as a memory that anticipates what is coming, which will be even more directly connected to what is being played now. So at the same time there is recall-memory and prediction-memory, as well as direct contact with the present, or monitoring-memory. We are involved in a mobile network, continually reconfigured, of which our immediate awareness controls what is happening. It cannot be a concrete memory of the past or the future, which would only impede the present, but it must corroborate the present and lend it its full impact. I would compare this memory to the angle of vision that is vital to our spatial perception of objects. Vision focuses in a particular direction to see an object, while one is aware of other directions that are seen indirectly rather than directly; without this peripheral vision we are confused about the relationship between what we see and what we are looking at, so we find it essential. The same seems to be true of our memory of a work's past and future in relation to its present.

As I have said, this memory is assimilated, the rational becoming intuitive, but we can shape our study of a score according to these conditions. There is no substitute, with an orchestra, for being aware of a score, and making the players aware of it, in an unbroken reading of the *whole*, with all its inevitable gaps, errors and weaknesses; but rhythm will be enshrined in this basic procedure, along with more prominent features that may be sketchy, and surely not unalterable, but will endure into the final picture of the work – the one that will largely attest to the initial impression, though emerging from the disarray of its first reading. Of course, some impressions will have been forgotten or contradicted, but the goal of this process is not so much precision as a grasp of the whole, however malleable. As to how to work after that, I prefer not to discuss the technical details which, depending on their difficulty, will characterise a given passage more or less permanently in our memory. Clearly, a passage carefully rehearsed for its 'technical' challenges will be inscribed in memory by virtue of the difficulty overcome, what kind it was and how long this took. And it may well be that when the difficulty seems to be or is extreme, it may impede memorisation of a certain passage: one may recall its place and overall formal function without having conquered the details. One knows where and how to place this moment, but one feels, recurrently in certain works, that some detailed deciphering remains to be done, in which case there seems to be a disconnect between substance and function. Going beyond those challenges, which may clearly impede memorisation, there is the delicate question of knowing how to let others assimilate a form one has assimilated oneself, which puts one's own way of doing things to the test. I suspect that depends on the nature of the music. Continuous works have to be rehearsed in the right order so that everyone is conscious of where what is being rehearsed comes in the temporal succession of events, which are clarified and explained one by one exactly because they follow on in this or that way. But in other music, where a kind of discontinuity is in play, it is vital to let that appear for what it is, and to help people see how the items are arranged like a puzzle, in which temporal succession is not basic to when they appear. They occur, that is, at a time when there is no logical constraint on their appearance, because it is much more about a series of contrasts and continuity. Oddly enough, in rehearsal it is vital to put one similar piece of the puzzle directly next to another, so that memory records them not in strict continuity but rather in a proximity that establishes their enduring character despite being varied. When the work is performed again in the same order, memory will have created instinctive recognition, which will be able to recognise appearances of the same motive and also the network they belong to. This way there will be an intermittent continuity related to the various layers of the work, beyond the contrast they make with each other during an actual performance.

This play of continuity and discontinuity is most apparent in works such as Stravinsky's Symphonies of Wind Instruments and Messiaen's *Chronochromie*. Stockhausen's *Gruppen* is a more complex case, more embroiled in this idea. Continuous works are clearly to be found in Wagner and Mahler (I think in particular of the Sixth Symphony), all the more so because in these two composers there are formal *signals* which it would be wrong to underestimate, compared with mere continuity. Some motivic transformations would not make the maximum possible sense in memory were it not for the experience of the proximity. Moreover, it is significant that Berg described the motives of his opera *Wozzeck* as *Erringerungsmotive*, reminiscence motives, rather than the term normally used by his contemporaries (and by Wagner, of course), *Leitmotive*. These motives lead the musical development and surely us too, but through the mediation of memory. There is a composer's memory in the work itself, for while there is the memory of the composer in respect of what we might call heritage that points or draws us to what was produced, a memory also, perhaps even chiefly, lives within the work, organising its form, a reminder to the composer, when creating, of what had already been written and planned, of the composer's own previous works, an individual heritage. This memory within the work during its composition is what enabled it to be calibrated and judged, and it is what provides interpreters with an orientation that they, in turn, will use to plan its trajectory. In a letter in which Berg talks about completing *Lulu*, he mentions that he would have to read it through again from beginning to end in order to be able to gauge this trajectory. That kind of judgement depends in most cases on assessing the continuity, as well as the strength of the references, signals and envelopes at the heart of the finished composition. Such judgements can be verified or rejected only by the individual experience of interpreters.

❉ ❉ ❉

I would like to address the theme of memory with respect to the problem of analysis. When I briefly taught composition and analysis, I came to think that it was not possible to teach composition in the literal sense of that word. I also came to think that nor was it possible to teach analysis; or, more modestly, that one could teach techniques of analysis by offering models, or rather examples of one's own analysis. This way of looking at other people's works seemed to me the only real stimulus, not to composing, but to learning how to compose; for analysis, apart from investigating existing works, is a revelation of the self. It creates an active memory out of passive memory of a work, obliging us to make our minds up, to choose according to ever more personal criteria. It is a fact that when we begin to contemplate works of the past, we approach them cautiously, respectfully, seeking to find out what the author wanted to do, how ideas were thought to be deployed within the form. Often one would begin with an external description of the work, trying to capture it in a kind of synopsis, a reduction easier to handle and to work with than the piece itself. It was then more of a snapshot than an account of the deep elements of composition. The further one went with that, the more one explored oneself, the more insightful the analysis would become, but also the more slanted, because the compositional view would become more and more exclusive, eliminating everything that had been superfluous to the composer's own future in favour of what could be used to develop and strengthen compositional originality. In this way, starting with a certain objectivity towards the work, the analysis would become ever more subjective, to the point where it was of real use only to the composer carrying it out.

Faced with the amount of literature available, what should one choose to analyse? Should one embrace the whole of Western music since the birth of polyphony, or concentrate only on the most recent tradition? Should one include the music of non-European cultures? One certainly does decide, and not purely randomly. First of all, the choice depends simply on the greater or lesser accessibility of texts and documents. The composer approaching our heritage to absorb it does not share the musicologist's intention, having no desire to specialise. But then the danger is of not daring to visit the landscapes that seem to belong more and more to specialists, and the result is compartmentalised knowledge, which when pursued to excess leads to the exclusion of some creators.

The idea of heritage refers more and more to an attachment to, and preservation of, the past; it indicates accumulation, abundance, even an

435

excess of it, and thus implies a division of zones and responsibilities, and increasing specialisation, first to catalogue and then to evaluate. Specialists proliferate and stick ever more exclusively to their specialism. Whether it is for establishing texts in themselves or modes of interpretation, there is some tendency towards very narrow knowledge within tight chronological limits and specific authors. This happens in literature and the plastic arts, so it is hard to see how music could miraculously escape this specialisation. Yet the consequences are pretty damaging, in the sense that information is confined to specialists, and also in that no wider views can fertilise these closely guarded areas. This gives birth to a rather constrained, indeed restrictive historical outlook spread over watertight little pigeonholes, about which the composer does not really know what to do, instinctively keeping at a distance from such strongly demarcated territory. Grand overviews, which would give meaning and life to this cluster of specialisms, are rarer and rarer, even though that is what would interest composers and help them to make real sense of the heritage they are not sure how to approach, and from which they feel excluded by scholarship they do not have nor wish to acquire at a professional level and in all its historical detail. To the composer, the more specialists lock themselves away in the narrow circle of their interests, the more they are freezing events in areas of 'still life' that cannot intersect with creative instinct – 'still life' that corresponds to the *tableau vivant*', the frieze offered by specialist performers.

Thus, the composer is not going to approach historical divisions with the scholar's keen concerns. Composers are never interested, dare I say it, in the establishment of a text of unchanging integrity. Painstaking discussions of some doubtful phrase, of this note or that chord, of a correction in dynamics or instrumentation, are seen as only minimally important with respect to the actual meaning of the text. Obviously, it is best to use a correct text, but with contemporary authors adjustments and modifications are trivial, rarely even relatively important. A score will inevitably include some mistakes, and the composer has no fear in accepting that margin of error and not bothering to locate every last critical edition, even the most trustworthy. Composers' real thinking begins beyond this level of orthographical glitches.

The first question to be asked concerns chronology, given the historical nature of the investigation. Should one follow the literal chronological order? Should one proceed more or less methodically, by school and affinity of influence? Or simply follow one's instinct and taste? In an academic course the teacher will provide guidance – in counterpoint and harmony teaching – using examples from what are called 'the great classics', across the ages. Going beyond the most elementary grammatical analysis, one soon arrives at the study of what pattern of continuity is formed by the works offered as models. One has to address the problem of analysis at two extremes: morphology and form, although morphology is usually studied locally – that is, isolated from its formal context – whereas form is seen as a sort of set of drawers suitable for setting out ideas classified according to where they are stored. This is so much the case that analysis often seems like a string of samplings and calibrations at first, and one wonders what can be gained from this, given the disconnect between the two extremes of vocabulary and form. But perhaps therein lies the real need for analysis: to connect the external description of a stretch of music to the internal logic of the vocabulary that drives it. It is relatively easy to make that connection when facilitated by knowledge of the codified rules that govern vocabulary on the one hand and form on the other. It is not the same, though, for eras both more distant from us and also nearer to us, when laws have developed to the point of rejecting the past, among specialists, or when those laws are in full development and resist, perhaps in principle, any codification beyond the specific.

Moving away, then, from a really well-known literature that is widely performed, we embark on exploring in both senses, according to our taste and mood, the more distant as well as the most recent past. Investigating in a zigzag, rather than chronologically, allows us instead to make connections that are not only unforeseen, but above all that enrich our imagination as we piece together from across the centuries mechanisms of discovery and shaping that one would not have thought of comparing, and which may say a lot about each other. To achieve this, is it necessary to explore a great deal? Here, there is our capacity to extrapolate from the limited data we have studied. This extrapolation from a certain number of examples confirms the ability we have developed with our models, and the moment comes when we no longer need to refer to specific models, for we take possession of them as musicians, fully assimilated, part of our own make-up. Then they can be referred to in order to see how, and how far, we have developed. These are the significant kinds of orientation, the minor ones having evaporated during our journey. The highly individual profile that our constructed memory stamps onto musical works is a test of whether analysis has become substantial.

Initially, one can leave it at describing how things happen, and as I have indicated, that helps us to review the work and grasp it as a whole, like a plan. Moreover, that is as true for composers as for the performer: we schematise the whole to integrate its parts, and their details. After this starting point, the thematic material remains to be analysed: its potential for development, its particular potential for deployment (a fugue subject does not have the same content as a sonata theme, having a completely different purpose) and the course of the harmony; the nature of the contrapuntal writing, formal relationships, what kind of variability they allow and how the transitions work. In an instrumental work we need to determine the relationship between the instrument and the writing, what reciprocal influences have emerged; in an orchestral work, how timbre confirms or opposes the various elements of the argument. Thus far, despite some individuality in how sharply we explore and how much insight there is in our parsing of the score according to its variables, the analysis has been objective, if not exactly 'objectifying'. You describe what is composed by analysing the resources that went into it. You pass from the darkness of first awareness to the light of objective analysis. The most difficult task remains, moving from this apparent illumination into the obscurity of 'why'. It is not about finding an objective 'why' and reproducing what may have been the composer's path, because in the end that is not what interests us; but rather discovering in what we are contemplating the sources of our own methods, discovering those things that make us define ourselves. It is really a process of self-discovery. And there is no need to work with masses of evidence: perhaps just one source is enough to find what really matters. If this discovery of the self has not happened, I will not say that analysis has been a waste of time, but it will not have uncovered its purpose. If our own personality cannot measure up to that of our models, objectively, then by default our analysis will have become completely and cockily subjective, because it cannot really be at the service of anything other than what made it and takes ownership of it. The composer's memory will therefore have become a creative repository of unrecognised material, though it could have been predicted; ideas plucked from analysis that do not need the original material, ignoring what mattered at the root of the writing, even contradicting its principles – it is a kind of cannibalism.

I can tell you about some cases that were important to my development. I will address them in no particular order, as I recall them, not even thinking again about these pieces but relying on what I remember about what I learned.

When I mention Webern's Second Cantata, it is the whole work that I remember, with the main features that characterise it: the disjunct and conjunct choral motion in different movements; the registral difference between the two soloists; the instrumentation supporting the voices with combined instrumental timbres, in contrast to the individual timbre of the voice being doubled and that which is independent, reinforcing or interjecting; strict canonic writing; almost literal musical illustration of the poetic text, including via instrumental features, and in esoteric narrative detail (the twelve strokes of midnight at 'Mitternacht' in the second movement). I could offer more reminiscence, things that I find more or less interesting, along with some which in themselves are of no interest to me at all, like the strict canonic writing. My memory provides them at will when I focus on this or that detail of the work, but they are always available in my image of it. When I recall the Second Cantata in relation to myself, however, there are two ideas to which I am indebted, and which you will not find literally spelled out by Webern but are implied by the way he writes. He superimposes, in one phrase, four rows, homophonically, providing the choir with exactly synchronised chords of conjunct intervals; the next phrase will unfold the rest of the row, but canonically in four voices, one voice in one vocal part and the other three instrumental, all four voices using strongly disjunct intervals. There is so much information in this example that I may have forgotten

439

or at least not thought about for a long time, but here I would mention the relationship between the conjunct intervals (I am interested in the disjunct intervals only in that they create contrast between the two successive phrases); I am also ignoring the homogeneity of the vocal parts in the first phrase, and the heterogeneity of vocal versus instrumental in the second (for the same reason: the timbrally explicit articulation of one phrase compared to the other); finally, I will ignore too the strict canonic writing, since I find it more of a relic than a step forward. So what is left? A much more generalised idea, the relationship between writing and time, a quantitative relationship that becomes a qualitative clarification. The vertical dimension of the writing – that is, synchronic, harmonic, perceptually simultaneous, synthesising writing – and its horizontal dimension – that is, individual, polyphonic writing, with rhythmically independent components temporally deployed in superimposition: the 'here is something more' kind of time that horizontal writing produces, in relation to the original object, becomes, in vertical writing, time reduced to zero. By such temporal reduction or expansion I can move from succession to simultaneity, changing the perceived dimension, and I can also create the intermediate, diagonal states entailed in those two dimensions, when a single object becomes parsed in successive time but without losing its identity. In Webern, remember, this idea was applied to four twelve-note rows, which, after being overlaid, then became successive in classical imitative counterpoint. What matters in my analysis is to have grasped the constructional principle of the two dimensions. The dodecaphonic morphology and the canonic syntax are seen as secondary, ways of organising a conception that could have been realised in an entirely different kind of writing; but here, the virtual polyphonic score has become homophonic intervallically and rhythmically.

What is more, I draw a completely different conclusion, from this example, about real and virtual time in musical space. A musical object does actually take up, in the horizontal dimension, the time with which it is endowed, and thus permits or even enables a precise perception of the time until the next 'object' or phrase enters. Now, condense this object so that it is vertical, simultaneous, and between this object and the next appears a void, which this very object would have filled if extended horizontally, and thus there is a virtual distance that cannot be directly perceived, but only estimated approximately. By moving from the real to the virtual dimension, the nature of temporal perception has been altered, although the identity is preserved: by expressing that, or not expressing it, one either displays or hides its cause. An idea that at first may have seemed overly formalist has been turned into a very strong poetic claim about impact, about the hidden virtues of the force field of musical meaning.

When I speak of a musical 'object', it is a concept that I also derived from the Second Cantata, in this case from the first movement. This movement is a pure and simple, chordally accompanied melody. At first sight, there is nothing too exciting in that utterly classical idea, which can be seen thousands of times in the vocal literature. This movement is, from an academic point of view, part of the arioso recitative tradition, melodic recitation punctuated by chords, and there is nothing exceptional about that. (I might perhaps give it more thought one day, if I need something for a future composition that might find its origins here, but to date I have been able to find in it only literal recitation, that is, accompanied recitative.) And yet these chords, the way they are made, have given me a great deal to think about. Why? Because they are always made up of six notes from a twelve-note series based on two particular transpositions in which, within a defined field of pitches, some notes remain invariant and others do not. More precisely, the transposed version will have four notes in common with the original six-note object and two that are different. From this I draw three conclusions:

(1) Instead of working by accumulation, stacking up sounds – that is, individual notes – to define a harmonic vocabulary in terms of its components, I can work from the opposite premise, the sonic object, vertically condensing some of the pitches, superimposing simple elements and deducing from them the harmonic consequences necessary for a coherent vocabulary. Using the diagonal or horizontal temporal analysis mentioned earlier, I am able to describe this object variously and to model its identity depending on how I need to use it in one context or another.

(2) I can construct a collection of musical objects, deduced by a single principle from one source, comprising invariant and moveable notes, thus creating fixed harmonic fields but with varied inflections, grafting the moveable notes onto the invariant ones. Going further, I can see these variants as borrowed by one object from another depending on the fixed materials that are the real object, these reciprocal borrowings being the link between objects: the objects inflect each other, and therefore the inflection will change if the same object is linked with a different one. The progression will influence how the objects themselves are perceived, and thus the invariant and moveable notes are there not only to create variety in presentation but also variety of progression.

(3) A dialectic is established between the actual components of an object – pitches still in the abstract – and the real nature of these 'absolute' pitches when assigned to a register. One may therefore vary the identity of an object by assigning the same notes to different registral relationships – either subtly or with complete contrast, which either facilitates or obscures the identification of their origin (as Webern does in the first movement of the Second Cantata); alternatively, one can highlight the objects' common origin by assigning them to the same register, helping to identify their similarity given the difference in their pitch content. We either play with the varied presentation of fixed features, or vary the features within a fixed presentation.

Of course, such explicit conclusions did not immediately leap off the page when I looked at the first movement of the Second Cantata, for I myself saw at first only an accompanied recitative, drawing no particular conclusions from it about the musical conception or form. It was only through tracing the model, the matrix of these chords, after observing how effective they are, by analysing their behaviour, as it were, that I found what I was looking for. My memory gradually assimilated these objects, was seized by the idea of focusing on a series of deductions over the years, when it cared to, until I no longer needed the source material in order to go on deducing. My memory had thus absorbed the data to the point of becoming able to create something. The referencing is there, as I can still demonstrate, and yet at the same time it has been gradually erased.

This example that I have explained at length concerns morphology, but assimilation by memory occurs equally in different areas, at all creative levels, thematically as well as formally. On the thematic level, I can offer the example of Berg, in his operas *Wozzeck* and *Lulu*. There are three kinds of thematicism in Berg; we could certainly find other classifications based on different criteria, but I am deliberately restricting this to the contained, specific perspective below. I call them intervallic thematicism, thematic signals and motivic thematicism (the last of which does actually concern themes).

(1) *Intervallic thematicism* is both active and passive: passive in the sense of being completely unvaried, as the most simple possible element, the ultimate in invariance; and active because it can seep into any context, even invade it, or proliferate to the point of 'saturating' everything. As an example I would cite how the child of Wozzeck and Marie is symbolised in *Wozzeck*, this character translated musically into the interval of a minor second. This interval attaches to any of the thematic figures and works harmonically, providing a particular colour, but that is its only value, as it fails to develop in any way and is always attached to these materials in the same way, neutrally.

(2) The *thematic signal* is found as much in *Wozzeck* as in *Lulu*. In *Wozzeck*, one can certainly point to the famous B symbolising the murder, while the bare fifth A–E symbolises Marie's death. The symbols will reappear in different ways but always at pitch, invariants designed to trigger a reflex. They contribute to the musical texture but do not disturb it, are not affected by any development, so remain ready for instant identification. Similarly, in *Lulu* the doorbell signal D flat–A flat, which becomes a symbol of imminent danger, is invariant throughout the opera on these two tremolo notes. We might think this to be intimately, even inevitably bound up with drama. To symbolise a scenario, character or event, the most direct way is to offer such signals, which are as directly meaningful as a verbal expression; and yet in the case of Berg, such signalling is used just as often in his non-dramatic works – in truth, all his music is more or less directly associated with a kind of theatrical expression, even as it responds to his internal theatre. In the Chamber Concerto, for example, I find the inexorable three As – the initials of Arnold, Anton and

Alban – translated into the musical note A. The rhythmic figure, though registrally displaced, is always on the note A, punctuating the thematic development, articulating it but never being part of it.

(3) Finally, we come to *motivic thematicism*, which is in some ways more traditional, even if one may discern big differences between an evolving theme that takes part in a continually evolving musical narrative and a static theme that refers to a context without being directly associated with it. The first case is based on multiple transformations that treat a theme as flexible, transformable material, whereas the second treats it in a fixed way as more signal-like, but more complex. It may also be that a theme that has been treated as developmental when directly linked to a particular kind of action becomes, in another scene, static, a reminiscence.

If wanting to discuss Berg's form, I would have no choice but to refer to the dialectic between the static and dynamic use of motives and themes, going right back to his earliest works, just as I would have to point to the mingling of stricter forms to make the overall form. By way of a brief summary, I would say that from Berg I have absorbed certain highly important processes: a network of motives across different movements, no single one being really isolated, but each influenced by the others; the static or dynamic use of themes depending on their potential for development or use as reminiscence; the combination of different, fixed forms through both motivic hierarchy and motivic flexibility; and the creation of forms that, if not truly open, nevertheless can have their immediate continuity interrupted by other forms – that is, they are subordinate for a while and are revived, taking on a new meaning, when the overall narrative requires it.

These few examples from Berg and Webern indicate how selective my memory is, and how much it serves both to filter and transform. It does not restrict itself to stylistic characteristics, or elements of the vocabulary or, more generally speaking, of the language. Analysis takes account of that: it has to in order to observe how in a particular work the various components are arranged, how they function in relation to each other, how they influence each other reciprocally. This is description connected as intimately as possible to the features of a work. On that basis, we can engage with the most important part of analysis, emerge from observation of the particular case and deduce, both intuitively and rationally, general conclusions that can apply to another phase of the vocabulary, to different stylistic elements, different formal features. Intuition is all-important for the resulting generalisation and metamorphosis, even if in what is, strictly speaking, analysis a certain routine will do, developing the spirit of observation and rationalisation of the available facts. It is not enough to be struck by certain phenomena and merely point out what they are, noting their principles, causes and effects – at best, that is the territory of sterile memory, or memory that is overly constrained and controlled by the works being studied – nor am I suggesting that we should be detached from them or forget them. The memory of a masterpiece is a permanent generalisation, and even if we have not engaged with it for a long time, it will have left a trace in our biological life; aside from detail that may indeed be forgotten, it stays within us, perhaps in a false perspective and out of proportion. We do not retain the entire work but more specifically what struck us as its very essence or, on the other hand, some highly significant detail. Our memory retains only that which has preoccupied us and which we recover at two ends of the scale, since it preserves both the whole and parts of it. If we plunge memory back into the work by rehearing it or studying it again, our transformation is confirmed; we assess the work differently, perhaps not in its general configuration, but at least in how it is planned and in some of its details, in which we find either conformation or displacement. Yet if the analysis was very deep, if it really drew us in or strongly shaped our own development, it is almost certain that that contemporaneous perspective will cover our previous one, which is how we can precisely locate our evolution. I rediscover a work in the way I used to see it, without hindsight, fully involved, and see it from the distance I have been able to put between it and myself by implementing the methods it inspired in me. I am re-encountering the origin of aspects of my procedures and then comparing the results with what stimulated and generated them.

Besides, the choices we were able to make, largely intuitive – instinct having played the biggest part – have been decisive. This is because our character, our individuality, directs us towards choices that match our own core, choices that change perhaps not with the seasons, but at least according to our needs: some experience that preoccupied us seems less urgent after a while; we head for some other one which in the moment will be able to offer us more.

❋ ❋ ❋

Creative memory does not fortify us in the illusory stasis of the past but launches us into the future, possibly bringing some bitter discomfort, but above all the lure of the unknown, 'How can we live without the unknown before us?' writes René Char.[5]

I spent time earlier on the memory of the performer and that of the listener. Why, given that the preoccupations of a composer seem far from either? The composer was a listener before discovering a true self, a more keen and insightful listener perhaps, but nevertheless a listener who references the music of our culture as well as, if of an inquiring mind, that of other cultures, either selected or encountered. The initial experience is not different in nature from that of other listeners, in the sense of drawing conclusions, or trying to, from what is heard; I do not mean only rational conclusions, but also intuitive perceptions leading to definition and awareness of one's own personality. That said, the composer is not necessarily sensitive in a discriminating way to everything heard; perception is shaped by needs. The performer, by contrast, listens much more narrowly, insofar as what is played inevitably has a memory that I would call manufactured by one's training. If only through learning to play an instrument, through technique, through digital processing, performers learn the memory of an instrument and, via that, all the history that celebrates it or weighs it down – depending on whether you are an optimist or a pessimist. A preoccupation with history has recently become so important as to lead to reconstruction and a search for authenticity, and whatever one may think of the validity and pertinence of reconstructions, they indicate a role for memory that is very different from its previous one. This role, apparent in the fields of execution and interpretation, is not without influence on the composer, who in some cases will also pursue the mirage of historical reconstruction.

446

Moving on to the composer more specifically, even strong individuality is born of a network of influences, some fortuitous, some sought after, and even the most independently minded autodidact will not escape that. Disputes between schools and individuals were not invented by the present day. Talk of schools implies an agreement to learn; continuity is the transmission of knowledge, submission to the discipline or doctrine of a particular grouping. We speak of founders of schools with some admiration, mixed with suspicion that they might be shackling personalities that are less strong by nature or too young to resist domination. The founder of the school will overload a disciple's memory and stop that person from cultivating original work. Moreover, influence is not exercised through actual teaching, through normal pedagogy, but through compositions, writings, by examples followed without personal contact, simply through the power of imitation. The disciple's memory, deliberately or otherwise, is so infused by the master that it is incapable of the initiative required for real creativity. As for the disciples, the 'followers', there are no words harsh enough for the accusations we make of letting themselves be subjugated. They lack originality, we say, and the burden of direct memories kills off the hints of inventiveness that they may initially have had. They have been too well taught, and in the end they know only how to imitate the model, copy the original, which is useless and of no interest; in the end, memory will have really destroyed them. In contrast, we celebrate the individual who has known how to struggle successfully against the temptations of regimentation or being in a school. While this celebration of liberty can be wise and uplifting, it is sometimes applied indiscriminately, with too many hymns of praise to the most obvious and painful amateurism, leading one to say that learning has been not only dangerous, but a mistake. Clumsiness is taken as a sign of genius; lack of professionalism – lack of culture in fact – as the very stamp of personality. At the beginning of the last century, people decried the Debussyists, even while acknowledging the worth of the supposed founder of the school, and preferred 'individual' composers, both the relatively clever and the relatively incompetent. While the Debussyists did not leave much of a trace, the 'individual' composers left hardly any more: one-way memory or free-flowing memory was perhaps not the question. All the same, the Schoenberg school, which has been accused of doing so much damage – one has only to leaf through Ansermet's recently republished wild ideas to be suitably amused – bequeathed two major composers, Berg and Webern, along with some names to be reckoned with and endless fallout, like dust. But with other schools things are hardly any more glorious, because just as much dust is spread, the great names are even rarer, and there are equally inconsequential honourable mentions.

It is nevertheless undeniable that 'eccentric' or 'marginal' composers introduce new ideas, original points of view, but often weakened by precarious means of transmission, when the writing, the musical language, is uncertain and amateurish.

Does useful memory therefore work through skills training, and how may memory and skill manifest an essential assimilation of creativity? It will be objected that many composers have learned the necessary skills without, for all that, being creative; that originality lacking discipline is better than discipline devoid of originality. Indeed, I cannot find fault with that objection, but the interdependency cannot be seen as an absolute criterion, since skill and originality can and must go hand in hand. If one wanted to adopt the kind of title enjoyed by the moralists of old, one would have to write a book called *On the Good Use of Memory*!

Perhaps the thing to do is to distinguish two phases: collective learning, which means professional drill, and individual learning, or self-discovery. These phases can be relatively distinct or, conversely, closely fused, depending above all on the age at which one studies. With the exception of very rare geniuses, by beginning very early one learns the skills before even seeking them, let alone finding them. At a later age the phases are tightly intertwined, to the point of impeding each other, eagerness for invention conflicting with learning a discipline.

Studying skills is in fact a somewhat impersonal kind of learning. Learning basic harmony – that is, chord content and progression – is a little like learning the alphabet or the rudiments of grammar. These are the phenomena that, although expressed in a style, are general enough to be applied to highly contrasting examples. When I specify 'tonic–subdominant–dominant–tonic', it is like saying 'subject–verb–object', entirely without special pleading. The more I engage with grammatical complexity, the more I shall have to refer to examples, to the historical development of a usage. Similarly, in music, perhaps even more so, to engage with the detail of harmonic language I shall have to refer to works where the language has been used, or rather, from which it is derived. At its most academic, this impersonal kind of learning has tended to eliminate actual memories. The vocabulary has become separated from musical works and trapped in a sort of 'no man's land' in which the chronological place cannot really be identified. It is in the very nature of academicism to sterilise memory, to slice it from its origins, to refer only to rules. And why these rules rather than others? Why are they set in stone, never to be broken? Academic pedagogy means non-evolution, historical stasis, laying down a fixed code based on what is permitted and protected, with no justification of any kind; hence the impatience that the student can experience in this frozen, sterile environment that is the antithesis of living memory.

Can that kind of memory play a role in learning the fundamental skills of what we are calling writing? It may seem impossible to base learning how to write on the musical work itself, because a work will seem too complex to be used as a model, and one really must begin with more basic tasks. Of course, just as learning solfège is the first stage and *sine qua non* of being able to read a score, and needs practice before being applied to works of music, so theoretical assimilation of basic concepts is indispensable to being able to identify the components of a work. In that regard there is absolutely no point in drowning the student in a score that offers so much information and leads to confusion about concepts that are initially rather simple. As I have observed, harmonic inversions, for example, or the hierarchy of scale degrees are concepts to be learnt separately from direct contact with compositional applications – you do not crack a walnut with a sledgehammer. Once such basic concepts have been assimilated, however, one ought to *let memory loose*, if I can put it that way. Then you have to refer to actual music, learning to analyse it, work with it, to take on the past. Admittedly, the practice of writing itself often remains significantly detached from musical reality in the course of academic study. One sidelines works in order to get comfortable in an impersonal place, referencing nothing in particular, in a sort of all-purpose pedagogical style, anonymous, in which there seems to be no necessity since it is so removed from real musical creativity. Creativity leaves a live trace in our memory, whereas these pseudo-models go unheeded and do not make us in the least creative. Far from providing imaginative stimulus, such learning sterilises what it is supposed to be conveying. We might want to say that the transmission of knowledge plays an important part in what I have called collective learning, and yet I doubt it for many reasons. Some of it is worthwhile, but some of it is infinitely less so.

One often encounters the following objection, certainly outside trad-itional circles: Given that language has changed radically during the twentieth century, must we concern ourselves with past languages, not necessarily defunct, but in historical stasis? The comparison of Latin and Greek is not quite precise, since we hear the legacy of these two languages all the time. Thus, we are familiar with this legacy, though it would be irrelevant to deepen our relationship with it: that would be of no immediate use, and could even be destructive, weighing down our memory. Such cargo in our memory would stop us from blooming, slow us down, prevent us from recognising our originality, from confi-dently pursuing our modernity. This line of thinking goes even further when it comes to music that is not written but computer-generated, using equipment that we handle entirely by ear, the output never going through a stage of actual writing, but at most being subject to some temporal control of events that are too complex to record with trad-itional notation, however we may update it. So what would be the point of studying something that has no direct link to our thinking, to the way we compose, even to how we transcribe things? Perhaps, then, collective memory has become altogether useless, even destructive, which seems a completely sound argument, assuming training is considered to be only the learning of fixed rules, rigidly devoid of context, as it so often tends to be – teaching without conclusions, unconnected with active memory that can derive, deduce, transgress. Learning rules for their own sake, with no possible contemporary relevance, is fundamentally pointless, a flagrant case of defunct memory, a burden on the spirit that offers it no progress and makes it doubt itself. This is garnered knowledge that is inert, unrelated to any kind of forward movement. In contrast, the fertile study of writing consists hardly at all in interrogating concepts from the past – given our distance from it, that kind of engagement or rejection has no purpose – but rather in seeing them as provisional and temporary. Instead of finding fixed and intangible rules, those aspects of writing have to be seen as contemporaneous solutions: we experience their validity, examine how they worked, what kinds of relationships they presupposed. We never know anything better than what we have ourselves handled, and this rediscovered, centuries-old experience frees you, if you are so inclined, from any urge to obey, passively to adopt how things were. You are ready to figure out what is contingent and what remains as an absolute requirement, outside time. You unknot a kind of writing from its direct links with the period when it flourished and see how it can be reused: then what matters is not exactly how a polyphony was organised but why it was organised in that way, what requirements it had to meet and what was at stake. In this way, one does not stand outside time by extracting fixed rules from a shifting reality, but on the contrary by combining the variable of time with our duty to make a new musical reality. What we remember is not inflexible but becomes supple and volatile, no longer setting up a masterpiece as an intangible model but as a temporary, and temporarily perfect, crystallisation of one state of a language. Studying writing should be a stimulus to forward movement, to transgression, not a useless code needed as a cultural reference. From this perspective, even the most materially experimental creativity needs the study of writing, otherwise it risks ending up as, and has all too often become, tinkering, inconsequential construction rather than thought. It matters little whether we are transcribing in a different way, necessarily so, in that we cannot be transcribing the same kinds of phenomena as in the past: new methods of transcription must certainly arise; notation itself must change. The sounds created do not correspond to the notation we have learned to handle with ease, but have to be transcribed by different kinds of symbols, connected differently to the sonic entities that they represent. The actual symbology does not matter; what counts is how we implement it to correspond to the sonic components, to connect one series of events to another, to make them interrelate, to know how to deduce them, and to derive them according to relevant criteria. That is how to make a new work – I do not yet say original, or personal, but at least one that is valid and consistent. For any kind of expression, however advanced and modern in technique, it is how one conceives the writing that is essential, how one configures the elements of the language. One has to have learned and absorbed the language, and one must see it as the source, producing motion, the driving force of progression and development. There is no end to the study that can happen through this fundamentally active memory, and in addition, it is exactly this that takes the risk of pushing you towards originality, to discovering your personality. This is about experiencing reality, to which in my opinion we have no choice but to bow.

As for individual learning, assuming collective learning has got you that far, bear in mind that the latter was supposed to teach you skills, even if too often it has led only to convictions, depending on objective choices, based on incontestable, unchallenged facts. In return, it will let you launch yourself on your personal adventure, in the course of which it may do little more for you, or even nothing at all. One may sometimes wonder why there are things called composition classes. At most they may stimulate composer-like behaviour. Analysis is handed on, learned, even though what is literally learned may be some kind of schematic or quantitative analysis, if I may call it that – schematic in the sense that it can be reduced to a simplified synopsis of the chain of unfolding events. By naming those, and ascribing functions to them, one may therefore have an overview of the chain of events in time and can instantaneously generalise this unfolding in symbolic terms. These symbolic reductions work best with music based on formal schemes: their poverty or impotence is exposed by more fluid, undefined, improvisatory forms. At best, one gets a symbolic description of a chain of events whose logical unfolding seems like happy coincidence. On the other hand, the logical fury of some analysts makes them see relationships all over the place that are nothing but hypothetical. Symphonic themes, however distant from each other, appear together in one matrix. It is obviously easy to find any kind of connection by referring to a 'fundamental' arpeggiation, the figures that are regarded as generative being so elementary that they can in fact generate anything. All you have to do is eliminate some notes, putting them in parentheses and registrally transposing others, and you can show fantastic genealogical trees proving above all the ingenuity of their authors. This type of work applies not only to themes, figures and intervallic motives, but also to form, and one sees plenty of the most unorthodox forms brought into the preconceived canon, everything having to correspond to sonata form, or older forms, or freer, more flexible forms (such as 'bar form' when we decide to apply it to Wagner). Harmonic relationships, too, are stripped of all their inflections and surprises, reducing them to skeletons determining the form. All these kinds of analysis seek to *reduce* the work in an excessively simple way to a conceptual model, to regard underlying logic as the only way to conceive of musical form.

So what should analysis be, other than this ability to reduce? It may be useful to relate how sections are distributed according to this or that principle, but it is easy to see why this labelling, this symbolic numbering cannot explain what I will not even call the *why* of a work, but merely the *how*. For that, analysis can no more be taught than composition, though it has more hope of being shown for what it really is: a means of inquiry, more fruitful when it is more individual. All the 'professors' can hope to show is how they themselves respond to a given work, encouraging their 'students' to do the same. Here, we are at the turning point between what I call collective and individual learning, and so I return to compositional behaviour. This is equally high-level teaching, with what seems to be a very modest goal, but one that I find not only acceptable, but in fact the sole one to be envisaged. And here is the problem: I have often said, and do so again, that a composer's analysis that is truly useful draws from the work being studied extremely personal conclusions that nobody else could discern; and I repeat that it does not matter if the analysis is literally 'wrong' in relation to that repertoire, for what matters is the conclusions that have been drawn from it. But you can see the ambiguity in that relationship, the very ambiguity between memory and creativity. Analysis becomes something about oneself. The precepts of this kind of analysis lie in the mind of the analyst, the work being only a propitious opportunity to draw conclusions. One could say that a composer needs this work, this exposure, for greater self-understanding. Such a work may play no further role, perhaps for the rest of one's life. This is without doubt egocentric behaviour, but the only kind that is truly productive or seminal. There is, however, a considerable challenge here. The imagination of the composer has to be strongly present so that analysis can be genuinely fertile, finding in an old work some field worth prospecting. If an apprentice composer's imagination is frenzied, more addicted to its surroundings than it will be later, the means of transcription will be missing: without imagination the composer is condemned to being utopian, to good intentions and the clumsy, inadequate realisation that ensues. The inquiries of a student composer who is largely deprived of individual tools cannot therefore be very original. Such composers can initially only copy what they want to do, their analysis thus remaining largely impersonal. For them to draw conclusions that will be useful in future work, the analysis has to become more and more individual. That can happen only through the assertion of personality, and this personality will show through only when it is able to cast an eye on the past.

This feat of balance, this referencing by the individual creator of everything that has gone before, seems to pose an impossible question, particularly in the relationship between teaching and what is taught, regarding not only the quality but also the quantity of works examined. Beginning with the latter, is it useful to know, if not everything, then at least what is most important from past centuries? The reply in our era of archivism would tend to be: Yes, how can we absorb the development of our tradition, how can we condense it enough to be able to grasp it, if one does not know at least the significant historical markers? But I would be inclined to say no; that accumulation, even partial accumulation, achieves nothing and will not really enrich the creative potential of a composer. It is better to allow certain, purely individual combinations of 'accident and design', perhaps surveying everything, but deliberately selecting what seems interesting, without thinking about *gaps*. One will somehow extrapolate from works either chosen or encountered in a way that may have little to do with historical truth or completeness, but that will constitute your individual history, a history that varies in lockstep with accident and design. A teacher can hardly influence that, but at the most can encourage the student to forge this entirely individual view of history. This is Gide's familiar advice: 'throw away my book' and write your own. This phase when memory has to be confronted will be only brief, a foretaste of what one is able to become. The brevity of this period of development also implies concentrating a great deal on quality. What I have just said about confronting memory with history in general applies also to a composer coming into contact with a musical work. There is absolutely no need to know everything, to analyse down to the last detail – in short, to abandon oneself to the lure of collecting. It is a thousand times better to dig deep once, and perhaps only very narrowly. Undoubtedly, for a given work, it is vital to form a view of the whole, not looking only at details. When one fills in the details of a picture without taking in the entire image, it produces a deformed, falsified view of the work, and isolated detail can even lead to conclusions that are in conflict with the work as a whole. Once an overall appreciation has been achieved, though, we have to see above all how events, even the most basic, are derived, deduced from each other, observing the deep rationality of those derivations and deductions, how they join up, how they connect to generate before us all aspects of the form. At this point our memory of the work becomes permanent, because we have taken possession of it, and at the same time it is not a burdensome memory but active, labile; it is released from its literal connection to the phenomenon being observed, allowing it to generate consequences that may be very distant from the original.

In studying a work we have to see it in such a way as to separate it from its immediate context, not to schematise it – which is as far as many analysts can go – but to *dematerialise* it, discerning its concept, the deep-seated necessity of a deduction. The more we deepen our own potential, the greater the value of that contact with the other – and I mean not only the past, but also in the present: there will be no more fear of being influenced, of becoming merely a follower. The relationship with the other will become so proprietorial, so individual, that everything we observe bends to this perspective. (One may even literally reuse another composer's solution, but with completely different elements, which means going back to the principle, rather than dealing only with the effect, with what had already been achieved.)

* * *

The discussion above explains why, whereas teaching analysis is merely a beginning or trigger, teaching composition can barely exist, or else it defaults to the teacher analysing the work presented by the student. There is no point in returning to 'precedents'. Nevertheless, given the work being looked at, and apart from noting clumsiness and errors, the teacher will at most be able to say, 'I would have done it differently', or 'I would have done it like this', enforcing this memory, or just general competence, on the work presented. This kind of encounter will obviously not educate or reveal a great deal. The teacher is confined to an exclusively personal position unfavourable to student development, and the student will at best become aware of the teacher's self-centredness, from which in these circumstances there is nothing really useful to be learned. I can confirm that I have found myself in that situation more than once, and naturally my reaction was basically determined by the quality of the work presented. I do not even speak of those cases where there is such a lack of skill and reflection that it is hardly fair even to summarise the problems, when encouraging or otherwise is not even the problem! But in cases where you encounter someone completely unknown, you find it important to come up with, if not an opinion, then at least a response, to put your reflexes on display. This is to say that, explicitly or not, you pit your own universe and its norms and habits against a universe sufficiently distinct that it makes you recognise the difference. What is the student composer expecting from such an encounter? Apart from relationships being somewhat strained by anxiety and distrust, he (let us say) is not expecting only technical advice on this or that aspect or detail of the writing. So you feel, as the responsible person, obliged to proceed towards deeper considerations, and you will disappoint him if you fail to formulate them. Given that you have had the time, and used it, to study the score with enough care to know it thoroughly, you can make your own analysis, emphasising whatever matches your thinking or departs from it. You examine the premises, the musical ideas, how well they are realised, whether the development of these ideas fulfils their potential, whether the proportions seem to you to correspond with developmental significance, whether the form is goal-directed and meaningful; you decide according to your own scale of values whether what was planned has been achieved. In any discussion based on that exploration you can bet that there will nearly always be a response to your criticisms, for this work has been written after all, it is the manifestation of an urge, and the apprentice, however gifted he might be, will not always perceive the difference between intention and realisation, or may not even have asked himself how valid his intention was. The question is how to take on board this 'good faith' of the young composer without failing to take it for what it is, by overestimating it! All I can hope for is to make him aware of an issue that his realisation has not resolved. The act of composition is a big undertaking, implying a host of intentions, diffuse and of all sizes and types. It is vital to go back to the source if one seeks a worthwhile exchange between teacher and student, which is not always easy, for many reasons. The young composer may hesitate to return to the source or disclose it to you, thinking no doubt that he cannot reveal himself with impunity and must keep the origin of his actions to himself. It may be that the impulse cannot be expressed in words, and one is faced with obscure circumlocution that does nothing to reveal to you his intentions or motivation. Sometimes you can only go back to the starting point, step by step.

Instead of proceeding from my own analysis of the submitted work to stimulate, bit by bit, the composer's response to criticism, sometimes I work in another way, though I would not go so far as to call it a method. You ask this composer to make his own analysis of his work, to show you what he did, to enter into the detail of the realisation. As long as he is not struck with voluntary amnesia and does not resort to a completely externalised description, he will help you grasp how the work developed, in the big picture and in detail; he knows how to retrace his path for you, more or less skilfully. He is going to recollect in front of you what he created, which is not particularly pleasant, and is certainly not necessary outside this particular pedagogical situation; but it is vital, if in the face of a blockage or dissatisfaction one is going to improve

457

the work, which means putting oneself in the position of both teacher and student! Although that sort of 'interior monologue' implies above all instinct, and a short-circuit, in dialogue between two personalities with different experiences, many things have to be expressed quite explicitly. Thus, one will start a discussion of the validity and effectiveness of concepts alongside the qualities of the realisation or what is missing from it. Doubtless the moment will arrive when what strikes you as an error, as something concrete that is unfulfilled, will be described to you as intended and completely deliberate; and if this counter-argument is not just a facade, then you will certainly have nothing left to criticise and will come to the end of the dialogue. On his own ground, the young composer is surely right, and if not, he will have to find out for himself, on his own terms, why he is not convincing. Anyway, it is unusual for a composer, even a real professional, to seem absolutely convincing in every respect to another composer. The two will not have drawn the same conclusions from a slightly different history absorbed at different times, and even when they have absorbed the same history simultaneously, different temperaments will not produce the same consequences.

I do not want to return to that catch-all of incommunicability, but between composers there is a feeling of strangeness, which is in fact a good thing in terms of preserving and stimulating individuality, though it always makes teaching difficult. Even if the feeling of strangeness is less obvious, less strong, less ingrained during apprenticeship, when there is more of a wish to communicate experience, to pit it against someone else's – to learn and to test out – it nevertheless lies at the basis of all teaching. That is why, beyond a limited, rudimentary apprenticeship, composition is learned alone. You cannot do without this solitary school that vacillates between study of a model and realisation. Gradually, the very image of the model will become superfluous, or intermittent, and the composition will become a completely autonomous phenomenon that will basically develop by itself.

Before this final state of autonomy there is a period of 'autodidactism', in which concepts will be clarified and realisation will improve to become adequate for the ideas. That will be the real compositional apprenticeship. Not surprisingly, it is infinitely harder to describe this

apprenticeship in general terms because it is about individual experience: you would perhaps need to ask every composer to write a diary
reporting daily on what is going on, what approach has been adopted,
what solutions have been discovered. There would probably be as many
procedures as there are personalities. Some personalities appear very
quickly and very early on; others are much more cautious and take
longer to flower. Some will immediately have an original voice and hardly
need to adjust their personality, while others, in contrast, show hesitation, diversions or ambiguity, which are harder to follow. Compositional
apprenticeship is, in truth, the development and affirmation of personality – of what in the end we call 'originality'.

✣ ✣ ✣

Whether they admit it or not, and whether consciously or trusting to
instinct, all composers want to be 'original'. Of course, there are many
ways of wanting (or not wanting) that, in which pride or false modesty
will figure. All kinds of originality are a reaction to history, and thus a
very active function of memory. Either you slip into a comfort zone or
you feel dissociated: those are the two extremes that have been seen
everywhere since the start of the twentieth century. From the other
point of view, that of the observer, it is too easily assumed that originality
either is or isn't there, that it cannot be acquired because it is an innate
gift. Almost mechanistically, originality can be seen as coming from an
exceptional ability of the memory to grind down historical data to create
a new expressive situation whose antecedents have become an invisible
source of novelty. On the other hand, lack of originality comes from
some deficiency of the memory, making it unable really to assimilate
recent historical data, and as a result incapable of making new, distinctive data. The very fact that there are personalities that appear more or
less quickly should alert us to the complexity of a composer's development and the differences that occur within the process, not to mention
the circumstances that will be more or less propitious for an awareness
of one's own potential. The composer does not live in isolation from surrounding events, and the environment may be more or less helpful for

459

self-discovery. Assimilating recent history, which will in the end be crucial for development of the personality, may happen all at once, or may be much slower, and how people react in such different cases will clearly vary considerably. These are matters of conditioning which may defer, impede or obstruct. There have been very convincing cases recently: you can isolate a country from the flow of contemporary culture, so that its individuals are put in an uncultivated landscape and acquire only a partial, deficient memory, and they remain at a stage of knowledge that will stop them from taking part in today's developments, impoverishing their creativity and restricting its usefulness. If the landscape of knowledge is indispensable, personality is no less so, whether its potential for enquiry is rapid or not, strong or otherwise.

Originality of ideas and impetus are much more common than one may think. There is no lack of individuals who can launch seductive utopias, even if they generally launch them in the darkness of impracticality or impossibility. I think of what Mallarmé is supposed to have said to Degas: 'You can't make a poem with ideas . . . *You make it with words.*'[6] Music history is in fact full of such utopian originality, sometimes giving birth to worthwhile works, sometimes works that go back into libraries, coming out again decades later, only to be quickly returned. Recall, too, in passing some paramusical utopias, such as the direct connection between sound and colour, forever reappearing, from Père Castel's ocular harpsichord to Scriabin and Kandinsky. I would also mention micro-intervals of various kinds, talked about since Huygens and realised in more or less tiny divisions of the tone on instruments that did not catch on. But there are also utopias that are more closely linked to writing, to how writing looks, where aural perception is clearly not at a premium. Thus, there is no lack of 'ideas', and sometimes one may even have the impression that they are more interesting, radical and extreme than those realisations we regard as masterpieces. Perhaps, not having been realised, they leave us dreaming of something, whereas with an actual masterpiece it is not so easy to give in to vague reveries, in that they force us to reckon with them so much more concretely. A masterpiece confronts us directly, and we have to respond specifically through targeted thoughts and deductions. The utopia of ideas in general, as opposed to those that are pinned down or ill-conceived, can be discerned by our individuality only approximately and partially, and we cannot do anything with them or respond to their stimulus, whereas with a masterpiece our individuality has to push back by coming up with actual solutions, derived from or resisting what has been observed. I am talking here about two extremes: the non-work and the masterpiece. For sure, there is much middle ground in between, stretching all the way from the amateur composer (who may or may not be a genius) to the ivory-tower theorist.

Apart from that, does originality of ideas have to be there from the start to demonstrate individuality – is it a precondition or only a result? Is it possible to have original, individual ideas that are not directly connected to the musical material? What are the real hallmarks of originality? Rereading Paul Dukas's musical writings I found one that is specifically called 'Music and Originality', published in September 1895. It could be interesting to examine his perspective to see whether our opinions about this have changed since then or not. This article is certainly strongly imprinted by the presence of Wagner, who influenced all musical life at the time. Debussy had recently completed his String Quartet, in May 1894, which Dukas reviewed highly favourably, but this was some time before the *Nocturnes* and *Pelléas et Mélisande* (1901–2), which would be the visible sign of a liberated and adept succession to Wagner. Dukas wanted to try to 'define what real musical originality is, by looking at how it is apparent nowadays', and set himself the task of finding out 'whether it is really as rare as the malicious critics say, after having tried to identify the fundamental origins of this rarity'.

With regard to that last phrase, it appears that not much has changed over a century or so, that originality remains a rare commodity, that more or less benevolent observers of musical life continue to complain constantly about this rarity, and that they will always point to models from the past as precedents. And so as we go back through the centuries we will find that originality has always been the exception, which is hardly surprising! Reviewing the progress of those centuries, one might ask when the idea of originality became current, and in particular when it was that people conceived of the intention to be original. Opinion varies. The most common one, held to this day, is that the desire to be

original dates from the French Revolution. The social liberation movement freed the individual from the grip of hierarchy and tradition, so
that one could stand alone. Historically speaking, the first composer who
never ceases to be mentioned is obviously Beethoven. His works celebrate the individual, increasingly standing against the society around
him, which he found fundamentally incomprehensible. After that initial manifestation of independence and rebellion there has been no lack
of further examples of originality, which came as regular surprises or
shocks to societies that were pretty much unable to cope with them.
Wagner and Debussy naturally come to mind, but there are few composers who had a real impact on society and enjoyed success without stirring
up conflict. Verdi and Strauss are surely the most obvious examples, yet
we are talking about individuals whose style was completely bound up
with their personality. Other successful musicians who stood out from
their era were subject in general to less forgiving judgement, if they
were not totally forgotten. The rift between the individual and society
was confirmed only at the beginning of the twentieth century, especially
with Schoenberg and the Second Viennese School. Even today people
will not fail to mention that it is from that period, and that composer in
particular, that the irrevocable divorce between creator and intended
public stems, this offence being attributed to a quest for originality at
any price. Schoenberg is supposed to have deviated from supposedly
natural and thus unbreakable laws, and in doing so committed a mortal
sin that made his music permanently unsuitable for consumption, if I
may put it that way. Originality meant the sin of pride, the sin of an individual who believed himself to be exonerated from any duty to society.
At the beginning of the 1950s, this was a topic for debate as absurd as
it was passionate, not only in music, but also the visual arts, poetry and
literature. Originality must not be excessive or it would cut off communication and become elitist, no longer meeting the aspirations of the
people. This was Zhdanov's thesis: that language, including music, must
be instantly understood, thus relying on known, preconceived elements
and personal reflection, and outlawing the quest for originality. In the
West, this gave rise to trivial polemics and recantations, the state not
being directly involved in discussions and pronouncements – at most

this would be done by officials who could encourage one side or the other through subsidies. But where a dictator ruled over a state and its functionaries, people were reduced to silence, even by the suppression, where necessary, of 'individualism'. Individuality had to submit to the service of the state, and then there was no question of originality.

Aside from political debate, originality has always remained a highly controversial topic. When a composer cannot be understood, the first accusation that appears is of originality *at any price*. You are supposed somehow to be original in a completely natural way, without trying; to be yourself while being instantly recognisable. This debate has been fuelled, moreover, by composers themselves, including the most illustrious. For originality at any price is also found in another kind of discussion, about whether to be a revolutionary or not. It is true that the two composers of the twentieth century who were regarded from the start as incendiary revolutionaries – I speak of Stravinsky and Schoenberg – endlessly rebelled against that designation, which they categorically rejected. Both of them, the latter more than the former, were called revolutionaries, and both swore in their writings that they were not. Stravinsky praised imitation, and for a long time never stopped being its militant exponent. As for Schoenberg, he was happy to claim that he had never sought revolution but had merely drawn what he saw as the inevitable consequences from his predecessors. So these two icons of originality did not seek it in any way, but almost fled from it, one might say, by referring all the time to revered models. Yet Stravinsky, dealing with historically fixed models, could not help but breathe some of his personality into them, while Schoenberg, amplifying the implications of their language, seized them to make them his own. Originality appeared in some way *despite* themselves.

While Stravinsky and Schoenberg were on a higher plane, the troops on the ground argued in a more down-to-earth way. In seeking to distinguish originality at any price from acceptable individuality, they had never seen any difference other than that between the surprising or shocking and the charming or seductive. They could deal with the latter with minimum effort, with the minimum of surprise involved in resurrecting the well-known with a slight veneer of modernisation. As for the former, they could not keep up easily, put off by one kind of expression or another, formal or in the vocabulary. In the end, what could not be instantly assimilated was originality at any price, whereas acceptable originality based on respect and recognition, in all senses, meant no disorientation. Whether to respect models or take them as a starting point is ultimately a difference only of degree, not of kind. Neoclassicism and postmodernism use many such references and make for a cultural game almost comparable to Monopoly. To disrespect and make fun of a Greek column is, after all, to embrace it as a point of cultural reference. To disrespect some unknown cultural icon would have little significance, since one is not referring to any communal knowledge. This is why in music, too, one sees play, reference and appropriation applied to known, recognised musical objects. Is it innocent originality or applied originality, innate or assumed?

We will certainly need to differentiate between three kinds of originality that use explicit imitation, three approaches that are so deliberate as to be taken together, even if the degree of volition and originality in relation to the model may be rather different:

(1) Direct imitation because of lack of individuality, drawing directly on models, whether the indebtedness is acknowledged or not.

(2) Adopting a model while using a different characteristic vocabulary from the original. This can be called transforming, or reshaping, where the reference to a creator or underlying style is explicit enough to be recognised, but at the same time the reshaping is individual enough that we recognise how it has come about.

(3) Direct appropriation of pieces or movements, pasted into a new context neutral enough for an affinity, with an interplay of contrast and differences. In this case, if there is a style, it lies in how the collage is assembled.

In the first case of directly drawing on models without really rethinking them, listeners now can detect reasonable originality in the reflection's boldness and innovation – of a kind that can be produced only by originality at any price, an extreme originality. I can refer again to Paul Dukas, talking about his followers: 'They revel in previous eras and follow in the footsteps of their chosen leader. It seems that there are so many of them as to demonstrate that artistic intention, the morally superior quality, has nothing to do with the output, but on the contrary, all the power of originality *resides in the unconscious*. For if the tenacity needed to carry out a big idea is essential to giving birth to it, nobody can know how to father it, and the genius of patience differs from the patience of genius as much as the genius of desire does from the desire for genius.' Looking at the examples around him, he continues: 'Wagner imitation, confined to more or less servile reproduction of the external features of the master's music, which we observe to be the primary preoccupation of today's music, appears to amount to simply adopting a *formula*. It would be incorrect to regard this adoption as the essential condition for complete musical freedom. On the contrary, in our view real originality, even if it cannot free itself from this burden which wants to rest indiscriminately on everyone's shoulders, would at least be able to carry it without weakening and being restrained. It is precisely because all want to be in the Wagner school that most of the music written at the moment is like schoolboy composition, schoolboys who are often masters of the material aspects of their art, but lacking freedom from authority and the prize of personal ownership which is the mark of true creativity.' He concludes: 'For what is disastrous and damaging about all second-hand music is precisely such intolerable dilution of thinking, of which only the material expression has been appropriated. From this point of view nothing is more fatal to the work of a master than servile imitation . . . The internal necessity of this or that material effect and the spontaneous impulse of the creative mind are missing in the work of a disciple, who succeeds in evoking only a relatively perfect body lacking the spark of life. Despite everything, the master is always the master. Whatever harm is done by the dissemination of the master's procedures, his most original originality, as it were, remains inviolable all the same.'

Nothing needs to be changed in that analysis, which can be applied just as well to today as to the past. In fact, lack of originality stems less from servile, deliberate copying as from the inability truly to invent, so that one is led to *reproduce* the model, even if only unconsciously, if one thinks it has been assimilated when all one has done is stored its image.

There is even more danger when the vocabulary is based on rules to be followed. Both the success and failure of the Second Viennese School, for instance, lay in a set of rules that were relatively easy to absorb, in return for which one had a handy way of working available that guaranteed some apparent coherence and supported a particular style. Excessive, reductive systematisation could yield only the semblance of works, certainly containing the characteristics of the era, and yet lacking any individual stamp. The vocabulary was borrowed; the *gestures* of the model composer were copied; but the genuine motivation had disappeared, and all that remained was mannerism, nothing else. In the case of the Viennese School, there remained rules of musical construction and a rhetoric for implementing them, whereas in other cases there was even less to inherit – merely spasms of vocabulary.

The second case is about wanting to adopt and use a model by imposing on it constraints alien to its nature. Originality as such is shunned, because it is superfluous or damaging. Thus, originality will mean not self-discovery but the discovery of others through oneself. This is completely conscious, and its motivation is actually difficult to identify. If we take Stravinsky as the most illustrious case of this way of thinking and acting, we might ask why he went from completely individual and original expression to the frank appropriation of other means, if not other forms, of expression; why in some way he abandoned his own path for the continual seeking-out of objects to work with and to change. Merely wondering at the power of renewal of a genius offers an explanation that is too simple, and too idealistic. This renewal was apparent, in truth, only in the musical landscape he contemplated and tackled, whereas his processes of transformation and distortion hardly changed. His two main recipes for appropriation were rhythmic displacement and compression, and harmonic experiment and distortion, serious development remaining rather foreign to this sort of *reorganisation*. Was this kind of originality of approach enough, given that it was a conception needing no originality of resources, the only requirement being knowing how to copy well? All the pronouncements of interwar neoclassicism glorify originality as a means of appropriation. Yet should these declarations of victory be taken literally? It seems to me that with Stravinsky, there was a deeper issue of originality. Within a limited and strong cultural context the originality of his thinking was immediately obvious, but when this cultural context was exhausted, or diluted from a wider perspective, his originality would lose its grip, and from then on his thinking had to seek external justification here and there in order to settle on some kind of well-formed organisation. The musicologist Leo Schrade once compared this to a life of parody, literally, in which creativity could not be fired up except by a model. It is not about hiding the original but about openly recognising it and knowing adequately how to transform it to make a connection between origin and transformation. So this was a superior kind of interaction, culturally affirming, demonstrating clear originality in the context of that culture. Less deferentially, one might speak of cultural parasitism, in the biological sense, in the same way that we talk of grafting plants. You may find this theory disappointing, if you believe in originality that does not seek to be original although it is; but it remains my view that the scaffolding was erected only to conceal a distinct absence of originality.

Even there, uncertainty tried to disguise itself, to change into something positive. One wonders what to say, then, about my third category, the more recent one of textual manipulation, with true or deceptive texts based on direct imitation of a model. This begins with the convenient claim that modernism is exhausted, that every form of expression has been tried to the limit, that there is nothing more one can do with it in itself. The only kind of creativity that remains will be a certain combination of historical elements, which is, in short, the originality of the flea market. This pursuit of the found object inserted into a work has existed for a long time, especially in visual art, and the found object thus takes on a new meaning: remaining what it was, since it has been preserved, it has become something other by association. Generally, this was not a cultural found object, but something selected from everyday life precisely because it had no immediate cultural identity. Of course, it did indeed belong to culture, if you like, since it came from some sector of society, but it had no developed cultural meaning. Yet particularly in architecture there appeared a trend for cultural reference related to the original, and moreover people in that field worked intentionally on the heterogeneity of these borrowed items to play them off against each other and use them as weapons against modernity. The same was true in music, with the same intentions and virtually the same results. Originality lay in hotness, as it could be called at the time – incongruity and contrast were 'hot'. The story told by these clashes became the reason for doing them, and the more unlikely the story, the more original it would seem. There was no longer any real creativity in the sense of any clear and somehow compelling style, but stylistic *collage* instead. The extra-cultural found object that worked very well in the visual arts tended to resist the integration that musicians wanted to impose on it. It would be systematically referential at some cultural level: as an anonymous or popular object it would always refer to some folklore, as it were; as an isolated object – cited literally or imitating some work of art – it would be redolent of the author cited or evoked. To avoid this problem by pretending that it does not exist is clearly no solution, but merely means the assemblage of sundry citations, real or imaginary.

✿ ✿ ✿

Although we can say that such solutions are wrong, we still need to define what we mean by genuine, authentic originality that is blessed by History – to define it a little pompously. First, though, we need to see what artistic expression means and how it arises. I found the apposite phrase in Saint-Saëns – believe it or not! – even though it comes from a long review of the premiere of the *Ring* in Bayreuth in 1876, explaining the hostility, indeed outrage, provoked by Wagner: 'Every work of art depends on a *convention*.' A convention, he explains, 'continues for a certain time, after which the convention loses its prestige, the mirage vanishes, and a new convention becomes necessary. The art changes its ground . . . a simple change without which the life of art would become impossible' – words you would not have expected from that pen. And the next paragraph says it even more clearly: 'Great artists, being gifted with powerfully active imaginations, quickly use up their tools, like tough workmen: they have soon worn through the convention they employ to express their ideas; they then create another one for their uses and move their art to a different place, before the public, for its part, feels the need for it. There ensues a furious resistance.'[7]

Musical expression, even more than poetic expression, is tied to the state of the language used to convey it. Basically, this language is based on sonic as well as grammatical conventions that we consider to be natural, but which are so only because we are used to them. You have only to compare different cultures to see how different the conventions used are, involving listening habits that vary enormously from one to the other, and this is without considering people's attitude towards them, of respect or impatience, as well as how they are conveyed, by oral tradition or secret religious rite or in writing.

These conventions are themselves the product of works, just as much as they produce them. They may well dominate the grammatical material itself as much as they do expression or form. The way we conceive of the world of sound has long tended towards standardisation of all its phenomena, at whatever level of pertinence they operate. The exclusion of all scales other than major and minor modes, and the establishment of equal temperament, was motivated by the most stringent standardisation, allowing only a limited number of relationships within a given set of functions. Our instrumental world has tended towards purity of sound, according to one or another timbre, reducible to an abstract idea that can be easily embodied in a previously established pitch hierarchy. All adjacent phenomena are either simply rejected as inappropriate – which they indeed are in such a strict hierarchy – or assigned to the peripheral, adjacent, inferior category merely as colours (in the way that percussion was marginalised for a long time). This universe of convention was not limited to sound alone, which was only the first sign of a kind of organisation that would progressively cover everything: rules of harmonic progression, rules of counterpoint including interval treatment, proportion of formal phrases and the features in its development and structure, and definitions of form in its various schemes and patterns of construction based on the structure of the language itself. Nothing, even including the families of instruments in the orchestra, has failed to move in the direction of conventional, standardised definition. Here, in our tradition, convention experienced its most powerful moment.

Although it left room for individual freedom in implementation, there was nevertheless a passion for codification in music as in the other arts. Think of the rule of dramatic unities, or the rules controlling the sonnet and versification, and it is clear that music was not the only case of such organisation.

One might ask how originality could appear amid such requirements, and even whether we can nowadays imagine such a situation other than by comparing it with the point in our studies when we dutifully submitted to stylistic pastiche. Those duties, though, sticking to the conventions of a period, made no pretence to be original; rather, we know that conventions to which we bow for the moment as a school exercise are largely defunct, and we see them more as the rules of a temporary game that was once for real. And yet we have to try very hard to imagine that that really was the originality of former times. The more that past recedes, the harder it is to tell one individual from another, the distance amplifying similarity rather than difference, and so that becomes the business of the specialist able to reconstruct an inner picture of period detail, increasing discrimination but not offering complete protection from errors of judgement. This is all too familiar in painting, where such errors are responsible for significantly diverse judgements. This is not about telling truth from falsehood, about identifying a forger, which relies entirely on the degree of empowerment with which the imitation can come close to the model, but is much more – and more challengingly – about what counts as genius and what distinguishes it from talent. One might object that this is a matter of intuition, that the answer is plain to the ear, but it is evident only if we are familiar with the central works in music history and use specifically those as criteria for judgement. It is in relation to them that we judge the other, so-called minor works of a period, to the extent that we are aware of them. However, for all the books and treatises, and all the comparative analyses, I am hard put to find what makes, say, Mozart original, other than flights of descriptive fancy or analytical hyperbole. In the former, we are embroidering the impressionistic, and in the latter knitting with grammar, but in both cases the problem of originality is left untouched. It is hard to demonstrate purely through grammatical arguments that a series of intervals in a certain rhythm is more charming, more powerful or more effective. At best, one can prove that it is richer, more developed, more varied or contrasting, but here is the thing: descriptions of that kind are more to do with the quality of certainty, if one may put it that way, and elude the problem of the inherent originality of a melodic shape in terms of, or despite all reference to, contemporaneous convention.

Does this mean that originality is undefined, and undefinable? That would be a very negative conclusion. We can try to compensate for this lack by invoking proportion, formal relationships or the quality of the musical ideas. Proportions and formal relationships can seem to be relatively quantifiable, even though we know some masterpieces that are very obviously ill-proportioned, as well as more minor works where the proportions are, no less obviously, in better balance. A certain harmony in the proportions, a match between material and form, and well-articulated ideas – these are not enough to be seen as original. Maybe what we see as that nowadays stops us from discerning it more clearly in what came before. The main argument of conservatives or reactionaries is to say that in those days people were not seeking originality but accepted the conventions of the era, and had no other wish than to conform to them – apart from someone of exceptional individuality, a genius, who simply *was* original. Naturally, this argument is used to reject the contemporary idea of no longer being original but wanting to be, which is the very definition of the non-genius. This argument has been used for many years, always worn like a talisman.

Has not the idea of originality, though, itself been sidelined, alongside the conventions of musical language? Are we any better placed to identify originality today than in the past, when it could be defined only through acknowledging genius? But then, there are different originalities: the profound and central kind, and the kind that is eccentric, if not superficial. What allows me to assert this distinction, which many would surely repudiate and seek to silence?

There are a number of fairly recent cases where one can directly compare composers who were contemporaries and who worked in similar ways, but not truly at the same level. In France, I would name Debussy and Satie; in Austria, Schoenberg and Hauer. In both cases there were many debates about the precedence of discoveries: whether Satie anticipated Debussy, who, without him, could not have forged his own language; whether Hauer pointed the way to Schoenberg, who could not have formulated the principle of the twelve-note row before seeing his colleague's work. After many years, debate seems futile, for we can see all the differences between Debussy's work and Satie's, and Schoenberg's and Hauer's. Even for dogged defenders of Satie and Hauer, it is difficult not to acknowledge that the influence and importance of Debussy and Schoenberg are infinitely greater than those of their contemporaries, and so it is more than precedence – the question of who 'invented' first – that is in dispute. It is almost like a matter of certification, and certainly reflects a current notion of originality, which cites chronology – what is more, a hypothetical chronology – as a guarantee of quality. It may well be that in fact Satie used parallel harmonies and similar elements of vocabulary before Debussy, and it is equally possible that Hauer used twelve-note sequences or modes before Schoenberg codified his use of the twelve-note series. Yet, that being so, one could go back to Wagner to find augmented chords related to the complete whole-tone scales so dear to Debussy (and not to Satie), and to Bach and Mozart to find examples of twelve-note sequences (which people have never stopped doing by way of justification and apology – not very convincingly, in my opinion!). Originality is not, therefore, about precedence in using this or that local, partial, limited procedure. Satie and Hauer were what would nowadays be called 'originals', and far be it from me to write them out of music history, but we must also recognise their limitations. It would be wrong of me to call them eccentric rather than marginalised. They did have some powers of invention, but the strength of their imagination went only so far, and their language suffered not from being simple, to be sure, but from being simplistic. When you think of the richness in Debussy or Schoenberg, where so many elements combine or conflict, you can state only that these were central, crucial phenomena in the development of musical language, in the historical revolution that Saint-Saëns announced and in which he took such little part . . .

Originals like Satie, Hauer, Cage and Ives were very useful in forcing others to ask themselves questions, to interrogate their language and their poetics. Within their means, they had their place, and were a little like musical pataphysicians – a term I do not use disparagingly, because pataphysicians will always be more valuable and indispensable to me than scholars.

Nevertheless, we cannot rest content with this overly anecdotal definition of originality, and however uncomfortable the undertaking may be, we must continue to uncover what it is and is not. Is originality what we *do* as well as *do not* seek? As to seeking it, yes, because one's own individuality is what the composer aims to discover, which is not possible without assiduous application, either intentional or instinctive. As to not seeking it, one has to ask what the composer can be seeking if there is no individuality. It may take some time to find it, if it is initially poorly defined, badly situated, if it is not thriving in sufficiently propitious circumstances. So one could briefly say that originality consists in finding out what one is in oneself, which could be a useful or futile search, depending on each case and how it is done.

Let us return to Saint-Saëns: 'A convention continues for a certain time, after which the convention loses its prestige . . . and a new convention becomes necessary.' Is it only a question of convention and, thus, of the era? And most importantly, must the convention be collective, or can it be purely individual? Should the individual stay away from the collective, not only to avoid conflict, but bearing in mind also the need to communicate? To take the argument for originality to its logical conclusion: if any code or convention is defined purely by the artist or composer, without taking account of their historical or geographical situation, then they risk communicating only with themselves, which is absurd. The convention that forms a language is thus a code that should be set up in relation to certain givens that have been inherited at a particular time. Besides that, says Saint-Saëns, still talking in his particular way about the *Ring*, Wagner earned the right to change convention – to displace art, as Saint-Saëns puts it. Why? Because Wagner is immersed in tradition: knows it, changes its conventions knowingly, not through ignorance. By contrast, Saint-Saëns accuses 'modern' musicians of *not* knowing tradition, and hence denies them the right to change convention – because they do it, he says, in ignorant anarchy. Obviously, this argument, which may at first appear so pertinent, is dangerous if handled without caution, because it comes down to justifying or dismissing somebody's originality according to one's own concept of what is called tradition. Everyone does in fact recognise the mainstays of this tradition. Some may be considered more important than others, but there is a kind of general consensus, at least concerning that part of history which is close enough to us, hardly more than two centuries. But surely a creator's originality lies precisely in an individual take on that long lineage, noting one chapter rather than another, one individual rather than another. The more distant the period, the more general our consensus. For more recent periods, though, there is more divergence and the perspective becomes more and more personalised, because history itself is characterised by more and more individual phenomena. Where does that leave convention?

The development of Western music shows an obvious urge to value the individual character of creativity. Codes have been abolished or have fallen into disuse. Current thinking does not seem to put up with any kind of preconceived form or agreed convention. People all think they have their own type of expression generating individual characteristics of vocabulary, form and, more generally, idiom. Even the series as defined in the Second Viennese repertoire could ensure only a basic coherence in the writing, being only a slender and fleeting convention. Since then no general convention has arisen, even of that limited kind, to cover any ground other than that of the individual. Perhaps there were instinctive, unspoken, unwritten conventions to which everyone could conform, if only to be comprehensible, quite literally. One could even ask whether, given the frank individuality of an individual, there could be *absolute* or only *relative* originality, in that many compositional elements were defined more by the era than by the individual. Could it be that our era, the time when we enter the musical world, forces us to regard our inheritance in one way rather than another; and what role does the zeitgeist play, for which music is obviously important, though it is defined by many other ingredients? To put it another way: however individual one may wish to be, as a composer is one not at least partly conditioned by era and environment, taking part willingly or otherwise in a whole that shapes

474

attitudes? For sure, the composer is facing the *whole* of history, but is it really in such a comprehensive way? Naturally, education, the way one is shaped, involves studying some of the classics, in relation to which there is both familiarity and a keeping of one's distance: *familiarity* in the sense that these are the works that will have shaped one's youth, become part of us, a heritage that will even have shaped our judgement and taste; but at a *distance* too, in that those works are no longer of central interest, no longer questioned as a legacy, not directly relevant because they are part of previous conventions. Composers have trouble in taking on their immediate predecessors, who evoke strong feelings, much more than they do with their general heritage – where there may be preferences, regrets and neglect, but rarely instant passion that affects their own creativity. Past conventions are accepted, for they are only generally and vaguely decisive; the most recent conventions will constrain composers most, forcing them to take a stand. Those are the elements to be chosen or rejected, and they will determine one's approach, hence the passionate terms, positive or negative, in which those choices are considered. You rarely encounter a neutral vocabulary, a passive attitude, in relation to important forebears, but on the contrary, a committed, militant positioning, since this is a decisive point in the definition of individuality and originality. It is easy to find in composers' writings since the beginning of the twentieth century the signs of sometimes strident campaigning to support their views. Think only of Debussy's and Schoenberg's self-revelation expressed in search of individual principles.

How, then, may one define these individual principles, or originality, which are the goal of any self-respecting composer, even if not declared overtly? As Schoenberg said, 'I must confess that I belonged to those who did not care much about originality, other than taking pleasure in it and preferring it to its absence.'[8] Does the power of originality lie in the unconscious? I merely ask the question. But this is what Paul Dukas claims in 'Music and Originality', using the following argument: 'To define musical originality one could call it "the result of an as-yet-unexperienced auditory impression". Undoubtedly, to create such an impression in the listener, ingenious combinations and their more or less fortunate effect are of no use if they fail to respond to inner necessity as a vivid feeling completely free of external influence and imitation.' Not content with this definition limited to strictly musical talent, he adds a perspective that he regards as essential: 'One of the features of great musical individuality is that it corresponds closely with the sensitivity and morality of its possessor. It is the immediate expression of individual personality shown in the special ability coming from artistic aptitude.' Using the example of Beethoven, he feels that 'in a sonata like this we possess more than a successful work of art: here the content exceeds the form, and the deeper sense of such a conception surpasses its musical meaning.' This goes far beyond simply avoiding convention, although only in principle, for is it not really the composer's sensitivity and morality that lead to 'displacing art'?[9]

How does a young composer react on discovering immediate predecessors? That discovery is in reality self-discovery. The composer exists essentially by and through them: they represent above all, at that moment, an urge for realisation, even if the compositional journey has already begun, producing work that is at the most evidence of talent, but which for now remains only relatively necessary. The predecessors important for the composer to discover are attractive because they provide those 'as-yet-unexperienced auditory impressions' mentioned by Dukas, which actually go far beyond the auditory. They call into question the composer's familiar world, enriching it but also destabilising it. The composer intuitively perceives this displacement and even the killing off of conventions that had seemed to be the very basis of the language. This is attractive, but equally the composer wants to understand what has changed, look more closely into the cause of that change and analyse its characteristics, duty-bound to come to terms fully with the work, to scrutinise it critically to see what can be made one's own and what cannot be assimilated. This elementary filtering is itself the beginning of compositional self-discovery, and the way in which it works will be a first and highly indicative pointer to individuality and possible originality through progressive appropriation, rejection, choice and modification. These influences transform composers into their real selves, in which one can see kinship and parentage, but also independence from all precedent. Their characteristics become more marked as the legacy is increasingly assimilated, individuality asserting itself in an instantly recognisable way.

It is always extremely interesting to look at juvenilia, because in light of the works that ensue you can spot the features that will become strongly characteristic. You spot them in an inchoate, febrile, vacillating state, and can even imagine that such indecision could only have led to something unremarkable had their nature not been suddenly and very strongly clarified in the next work. Such is the mystery of individuality forged both continuously and in fits and starts, in the foreseeable and the unforeseeable, by chance as well as through creative necessity. Of course, there is hard work, proliferation and development, but at the same time there is something magical in how individuality that defies any kind of literal description is captured.

Nevertheless, we can analyse works in retrospect and clearly see the characteristic features. Naturally, there are many types of reaction and development, and we can tell slow and continuous development from the abrupt and discontinuous. Some composers go ever deeper, imperceptibly following a path to more and more complex kinds of creativity, whereas others stumble around, if I can say that, temporarily occupying one territory before going on to explore another in what can seem a disconcertingly disorganised way. And that is not to speak of the peaks and troughs of the imagination, which are not as consistent as one may wish. Some composers are very open to what is around them, to the currents and shocks of their era, whereas others remain quite isolated and stick doggedly to the path they feel they have to follow (as Gide says, 'Follow one's inclination, provided it leads uphill'![10]). These different attitudes clearly influence one's view of musical convention, and thus of what we can call, in its widest sense, tradition. There is a fundamental difference between composers who take part in continuous development, or think they do, and those who select their prey based on desire and need, almost or entirely regardless of continuity.

What can we in fact study when we contemplate an immediate forebear, examining the works bequeathed to us? First of all, we see a model that has caught our attention, filling us with enthusiasm, and we want to know how the composer achieved this outcome. We know that the composer's thinking involved certain kinds of development, and these are what we want to recognise – in other words, the work's world of convention. We believe, quite rightly, that knowing how the work was made will certainly not mean unveiling its 'secret', but we will have isolated some characteristics that are vital for discerning what stage of development it represents. Then, analysis. This will probably inform us on two important points: connections with the past and original features. We do not use it to try to quantify the novelty, which would be both naive and absurd, but to understand how the composer's thinking relies on the past and by what means it is distinct from that or renews it. How does that thinking realise this relationship while maintaining individuality? If one takes an example as variable and adaptable as Stravinsky, compared with one as stable and unyielding as Webern, one will have an internal gauge of where the extremes of creative musical development lie.

Taking only four of Stravinsky's most important works, *The Firebird*, *Petrushka*, *The Rite of Spring* and *Les Noces*, you can see the composer's originality being displaced by each subject that is tackled. It is very hard to perceive them using the same criteria. As we know, they are ballets, designed to tell a story, and as a result the music itself strives to makes this narrative visible and audible, hence the stylistic adaptation of each. You cannot tell a fairy story using music suitable for accompanying a pagan rite, or portray a puppet show in the same way that one embodies a wedding ceremony. That said, and given the different kinds of *illustration* needed for these topics, you can see the melodic and rhythmic vocabulary emerging progressively across the huge differences between the four works. This is really what makes for a deep connection between them: Stravinsky's true originality, beyond surface variety, is in the way his rhythmic language is constituted, very differently from previous Western music, yet grounded in a certain popular tradition. We can easily see how this originality appeared, and did so in particular domains, while other areas were neglected or even abandoned because they were regarded as less important or figured less immediately in the composer's temperament. Particularly in the first three works, we do not find much by way of formal preoccupation, these works being the accumulation of separate moments, linked of course to the discourse to which they are attached, but having no formal connection other than the pattern formed by variety and contrast. Why this originality arose would be infinitely more difficult to say. It might be called a matter of temperament. Stravinsky's innate creative talent took him towards the rhythmic world rather than any other means of musical expression. That is clear, but it is not saying much, and it remains a complete mystery what attracted him to this great commotion he made about rhythm – a commotion that was almost unprecedented.

With Webern, the continuity in his inspiration and technique, in his way of conceiving musical creativity, is self-evident. He joined in with his tradition passionately, declared it faithfully, took on the mantle as obediently and humbly as possible, while being maximally innovative and radical. He dealt with the language and all its implications with regard to rigour and the results of deduction. From the outset he sought extremely powerful unity, which for him was provided by a precisely controlled relationship between elements. Techniques culled from past centuries gave him the means to do that – techniques that had fallen into disfavour or disuse, which he resurrected. Strict writing such as the passacaglia and canonic composition had been effectively abandoned in the middle of the nineteenth century, for they shackled the freedom of deduction and inspiration that was so dear to ubiquitous individualism. Mobility and specificity in musical ideas and development contradict the idea of rigorous writing; disorder among and conflict between *moments* somehow contradict the order and hierarchy that reign over strict formal elaboration. And yet Webern makes the exact opposite happen, combining in an unforeseeable and unforeseen way the fragility and variety of moments with the ever more comprehensive control of stringently controlled deduction. Hence, from his earliest works, the recourse to old forms of writing, renovated but still marked by the past; then more fluid writing in which discipline is flexible and subtle and deduction works with more suppleness, making step-by-step derivations. Finally came the need for extreme rigour, which, based on previous experience, was no longer satisfied by adopting historical techniques directly but would change their meaning by infusing them with ambiguity. Webern's writing changed as it evolved, becoming more innovative and radical the more deeply it grounded itself in tradition. Yet at the same time there was no break, no visible fault, no contradiction; it pursued a smooth, continuous trajectory. One could apply T. S. Eliot's idea to this exemplary case: 'Tradition . . . cannot be inherited, and if you want it you must obtain it by great labour.'[11]

Eliot formulated this relationship of the past to the present with infinite perspicacity. He describes our 'perception . . . not only of the *pastness* of the past, but of its presence . . . a sense of the timeless as well as of the temporal and of the timeless and of the temporal together'.[12] Eliot's formulation there can seem strange at first, especially when it is conceived so decisively, but this idea of past–present interaction reflects with great precision the relationships necessarily established between memory and creativity, whatever may be the apparent disruption or continuity. In the essay from 1917 entitled 'Tradition and the Individual Talent' (of which I am aware only of these comments relevant to the thorny question of authenticity and the interpretation of ancient music), Eliot also states this: 'What happens when a new work of art is created is something that happens simultaneously to all the works of art which preceded it. The existing monuments form an ideal order among themselves, which is modified by the introduction of the new (the really new) work of art among them. The existing order is complete before the new work arrives; for order to persist after the supervention of novelty, the *whole* existing order must be, if ever so slightly, altered; and so the relations, proportions, values of each work of art toward the whole are readjusted; and this is conformity between the old and the new.'[13]

Without being preoccupied or obsessed with the need to conform, even without an urgent desire to join in with *the* continuity, or any continuity, composers are nonetheless more or less dependent on the fact of their birth. Yet their position in history does not have to impose to the point of making them obedient or servile towards their predecessors. Eliot says this better than I can: 'If the only form of tradition, of handing down, consisted in following the ways of the immediate generation before us in a blind or timid adherence to its successes, "tradition" should positively be discouraged. We have seen many such simple currents soon lost in the sand; and novelty is better than repetition.'[14] In short, what is interesting in a new work is not that it renovates the past, reflects a particular culture, or that it can be related to a trend or tradition. That is a passive, inert, inconsequential view. What matters is that this work changes how we see history, forces us to view it, to conceive it differently, provides a different perspective. It is for this reason that the words 'tradition' and 'authenticity' are very far from meaning what one too often wishes them to mean. History is readjusted every day, as it were, even if few works force us into radical reassessment. But Eliot remembers to stress how each genuinely new work, even if of little importance, imposes a readjustment, however minimal, however localised. And it hardly matters how the readjustment is done: it happens in very different ways, sometimes posthumously. During a composer's life, if nothing seemed to change, the work was misunderstood and held to be negligible; still, once it is discovered it forces us to reconsider the erstwhile disposition of history – as with Webern, and also as with certain painters in the second half of the nineteenth century. But the readjustment can also happen as a disruption, in the present, when something sudden strikes like lightning – very obviously in the case of some of Stravinsky's masterpieces. And so the reordering, the rereading of our cultural heritage can happen in different, contradictory ways, but the more or less short-term consequences are always the same: readjustment.

We could add to Eliot's ideas by emphasising how this readjustment, inevitable though it may be, will always be coloured by individuality – and moreover, here things become more complex. One's reading of history, despite many common factors, remains individual. The stronger the personality that individuals reveal, the more irreducible features you will find in their work. Paradoxically, individuality on the cusp will seem commonplace and hardly differ from what others can do. During apprenticeship, the milestones of a trajectory will be spotted and selected, and the more a personality appears, so will the choices that have determined it. The individual's take on history will change by becoming more and more personalised, to the point where one's *own* history is created – conditioned, moreover, not only by temperament, but also by inherited culture. So I do not conceive of history as linear, as Schoenberg and

Webern described it, for instance. In their case, it is possible to think of a unique sequence of events which their works altered by joining it, avoiding any other direction. In some ways, their culture was the opposite of an encyclopedic one, fundamentally foreign to eclecticism. Next to the great Germanic tradition all the rest could be regarded as secondary, or inessential anyway.

Perhaps we are currently less certain about what counts. We have to admit that masterpieces – if you wish to avoid that term, then call them 'essential works' – thrive more within a tradition, but equally all overly rigid and exclusive classification is misleading and results in false or artificial conclusions. Today, we probably take a view that is opposite to the unilateral one that the Second Viennese School adopted with such a clear conscience and so candidly. We clearly tend, on the contrary, to accumulate knowledge, however sterile. We thesaurise documents, both those that concern us directly and those that are more distant in time and space. The danger of such bingeing is that the relationships formed tend to be superficial; we are inclined to become tourists through history, or geography. This tourism itself tends to develop a taste for exoticism, and here I return briefly to the *authenticity* of the past, which is both an interesting and a futile search, for then we tend to isolate this past in a historically reconstructed truth. But the reconstruction is illusory, being based on conjecture, and changing conjecture at that. This means that there is nothing strongly authentic about the so-called authenticity of reconstructions, but mainly a kind of suppression of historical implications. Trying to rediscover the authenticity of evidence from the past – a laudable curiosity as limited in its ends as in its means – is a completely anti-historical attempt to destroy Eliot's readjustment. Moreover, this vision corresponds fairly precisely with a certain tendency to corner composers not in a duty to readjust, but as *rearrangers*. The composer is accused of historicism that is professionally credible but not fundamentally innovative. Thus, in the mania for rearrangement we find strange bedfellows: the most ferocious partisans of historical authenticity alongside adherents of postmodern eclecticism, linked as they are by a non-evolutionary concept of history – though 'concept' may not be the right word for what is in reality a showcasing of history. History becomes *merchandise* in fact, which does not need to be classified at all but requires labels and stickers of some kind to indicate dates and prices. In both cases they need a shop rather than a museum; there is no longer any guidance regarding what to choose. All the components of history are left floating in weightlessness. Any kind of guidance would be an enemy, impeding freedom of choice, forcing us to make value judgements, to impose a hierarchy, even temporary, an order, even provisional.

When you put it that way, the composer's position seems hopeless, lying as it does between two equally unfortunate illusions. Is there an ideal solution, which would be to know how to choose one's history, to be sufficiently individual to know how to carry out oneself the readjustment mentioned by Eliot, and as a consequence force others to carry out this readjustment your way – that is, in light of your works? That would not be the desire of an enlarged ego, for all composers seem to have the ambition to change others' vision according to their own, if only for a moment. To express, to express oneself, is in very general terms a desire for memory to take account of creativity, perhaps be modified by it. That said, it is not a purely rational process, in which actually to do it would be to succeed. As Paul Dukas wrote, 'Artistic intention, the morally superior quality, has nothing to do with the output, but on the contrary all the power of originality *resides in the unconscious.*' And yet he adds: 'One of the features of great musical individuality is that it corresponds closely with the sensitivity and morality of its possessor. It is the immediate expression of individual personality shown in the special ability coming from artistic aptitude.' The attitude of composers and artists in general towards the past, to which they are inextricably tied, turns out to be extremely complex.

I began this discussion by quoting Claudel's *Le Soulier de satin*, when Rodrigo, as viceroy in Panama, thinks of Prouhèze: 'Who was talking of remembrance just now? I have a horror of the past! The voice I thought I heard just now deep down in me, behind me, 'tis not behind, 'tis in front, it calls me on; if 'twere behind me it would have no such bitterness and no such sweet.' That highlights a scene which ends in an even more acute and peremptory way: 'Thrill my heart with that unknown voice, with that song that never was! . . . With that voice that tries to impart the unknown and does not manage to say orderly what it wants; but what it does not want is pleasant to me too!'[15]

Thus, the composer, vessel through which life incessantly replenishes history, makes sense of memory through new creativity.

1 A reference to Boulez's earlier essay subtitled 'In Praise of Amnesia'. Pierre Boulez, 'Style ou Idée? Éloge de l'amnésie' (1971), in *Point de repères*, ed. Jean-Jacques Nattiez (Paris: Bourgois, 1981), pp. 312–22. English translation: 'Stravinsky: Style or Idea? In Praise of Amnesia', *Orientations*, pp. 349–59.

2 Paul Claudel, *The Satin Slipper, or the Worst is Not the Surest*, trans. John O'Connor (New York: Sheed and Ward, 1945), p. 184.

3 '. . . each should follow the customs of his own country . . . Truth on this side of the Pyrenees, error on the other side': Blaise Pascal, *Thoughts* (New York: P. F. Collier & Son, 1909–14), p. 48, Part 1, §294.

4 This is probably a pun on Claudel's phrase 'delectable enumeration', in the first of his *Five Great Odes*, where Claudel expresses how every word of poetry is in fact a repetition of something. See Paul Claudel, *Five Great Odes* (London: Rapp & Carroll, 1967; originally published in 1913 in French as *Cinq grands odes*).

5 Preface to *Le poème pulvérisé* (Paris: Fontaine, 1947).

6 Paul Valéry, *Degas, Manet, Morisot* (Princeton: Princeton University Press, 1960), p. 62; emphasis in original.

7 Quoted in *Camille Saint-Saëns on Music and Musicians*, ed. Roger Nichols (Oxford: Oxford University Press, 2008), p. 105.

8 Arnold Schoenberg, *Style and Idea*, ed. Leonard Stein, trans. Leo Black (Berkeley, Los Angeles: University of California Press, 1984), p. 126.

9 *Les écrits de Paul Dukas sur la musique* (Paris: S.Λ.E.P., 1948), p. 288.

10 André Gide, *The Counterfeiters: A Novel* (New York: Vintage Books, 1973), p. 354.

11 T. S. Eliot, 'Tradition and the Individual Talent', *Perspecta* 19 (1982), pp. 36–42, 37.

12 Ibid.

13 Ibid.

14 Ibid.

15 Claudel, *The Satin Slipper*, p. 185.

13

The Concept of Writing

(1990–91)

Why focus on writing, and why attempt to define it as a *concept*? My immediate response is that if I have an opinion about a score, a composer, such a concept is the essential criterion behind that opinion. A composer either knows or does not know how to write. This manifests itself to me in well-nigh decisive ways. If I'm asked the question, 'Can you even make such a distinction about the most recent scores?' I reply, 'Yes' at once! Even with the most radical style, the most innovative, the least familiar, I can detect or distinguish this phenomenon of *writing*. (Naturally, the eye grasps various longer-term parameters more immediately than the ear. Yet performance, if it is competent, guarantees instant recognition of the compositional adequacy of both writing and hearing.) With a work that shuns traditional means, and that can be represented on paper only by way of roughly diagrammatic equivalents of sounding elements, a work of a kind for which presentation on paper has not previously been attempted, can we nevertheless still employ this concept of writing? Again, my answer is 'Yes', basing my decision on a 'document' for which transcription on paper is not crucial: the unfolding, conjunction, validity of the sounding entity guarantee the quality of the *writing*. Indeed, these categories are far from absolutely separate, but it is by way of such criteria that the failure, the inadequacy of a work's writing may be determined.

This may appear arrogant, and the questions will arise: How can you be so sure, and on what basis can you declare that a work is composed or not? Now my response becomes less confident. I rely entirely on intuition, habit, experience, all short-circuiting logical expression. But if I try to establish the source of such intuition, to discover exact criteria, I will have difficulty, not knowing if I can give an adequate account. I know that I believe in the concept of writing, but the idea remains highly elusive, extremely vague. In the end, I fall back on notions of connection, continuity, development. Applied to works of different character, from different epochs, the word 'writing' cannot have exactly the same meaning, or be used in exactly the same way. For one thing, it refers to many different aspects, from the specifics of instrumental writing to the manipulation of linguistic elements. In fact, it is a term that gets applied precisely or imprecisely to any particular repertoire, a term one nevertheless uses constantly, and even for the least significant examples. We also refer to 'pictorial writing', 'architectural writing' – no areas of creativity escape the predations of a concept that means everything and nothing. It can be thought of as a 'keyword', and equally as the most banal of clichés: a keyword able to connect the most diverse modes of expression, however different each is from the others; a cliché because it cannot deal with the specifics of any particular work. This concept of writing, however precise and specific it appears at first glance, becomes harder and harder to pin down the more attention we give to it.

If we nevertheless keep referring to writing, however ineptly, it is because such a concept must be central to the working-out, the realisation of imaginative and inventive creativity. Perhaps above all it provides the only means available to us for the written transcription of imaginative ideas and intentions, in whatever medium we employ. But we acknowledge the sense we have that writing as composition is not simply a way of decoding thought, an essentially neutral process that has no influence on thinking or imagination, something that plays no part in creativity but simply transmits a message, transcribes information. The most superficial thought shows that writing and thinking are not disconnected, but are inextricably linked through signification: what one says is inseparable from how one says it, and the same is even more true of music, where the nature of language and power of expression intersect. To find a neutral quality, with no signification, it would be necessary to home in on a single note, its pitch abstractly conceived, removed from any actual vocal or instrumental sound, and with none of the signification that a sounding context provides.

We would still need to agree on the meaning of a single, neutral sound prior to it being variously contextualised. A rapid glance at various musical civilisations reveals radically different ideas in this area. I would like to recall what I have said in the past about the reality and neutrality of a sound. An isolated sounding phenomenon derives its richness or poverty from a collection of specific properties. Is it solely in terms of such richness or poverty that one determines its suitability for placement in a specific context? Yes, in the sense that the more a sound has distinctive individual qualities, the less conformable to other sounding phenomena it will be, to the extent that it will tend to preserve its own special profile. The richer a sound, the less it can be 'deconstructed' to achieve an ideal position within a broader context. It will tend to *perforate* the context in which one attempts to insert it; at best, it might mark a special moment, non-recurrent, or, at least, recurring only in a different way. By contrast, a neutral sound, deprived of all inherent properties, could be realised in various vocal or instrumental ways, and be inserted in any possible context, since its neutrality allows it to adapt itself to any context. Such a neutral sound actually acquires its identity through its closeness to other neutral sounds, the myriad of combinations in which it can participate. However, since we refer to 'combinations of sounds', the term 'writing' also arises, for is writing not simply an extremely elaborate instance of such combination?

Before reaching this conclusion, or rather this deduction, we should attempt to reflect on what writing stands for in music, to what necessity it corresponds. First, we should affirm, paradoxically, that writing is not simply that which is physically *written*. I also include unnotated musical traditions in the concept of musical writing, which, even if they are not written down by individuals, follow known principles of development, of the relations between elements. Moreover, it is often the case that such music can be accurately transcribed, with sufficient precision to show us how it is put together. In studying such transcriptions, which have been made by a meticulous and demanding composer – by Bartók, for example – one becomes aware, without the shadow of a doubt, of the rules that underpin their structure. In this case, with multiple versions of the same melody collected here and there, a basic model for these diverse derivations can be established. Similarly, to move to the other extreme, with works that are entirely electroacoustic, and with no graphic transcription, however vague, one can evaluate the coherence of the material through reference to the combination of sound events, without speaking of a satisfactory formal design as such.

Initially, then, I think of writing as greatly exceeding the bounds of what is conventionally thought of as the written sign. However, I must immediately add that the material fact of 'writing' influences the more general, global phenomenon of writing. Where secular oral traditions are concerned, or the mechanical manipulation of sound objects, the combination of elements is not subject to the same constraints. The simple possibility of seeing what one has written brings with it a way of thinking that implies a different order, if not a higher level, of complexity. True, with traditional oral music, or – closer to our own time – baroque or jazz improvisation, the complexity of a soloist improvising an ornamented melody might turn out to be richer rhythmically than melodically, and difficult to transcribe exactly. That identifies the basic difference between music as played and music as read – music as played moving away from music as read. I can only repeat that the interpreter refers to categories that are quantifiable only with difficulty, but which are fundamental to his performance. A jazz improviser deviates more or less constantly from a regular pulsation; it is precisely this plethora of deviations that makes his playing interesting, and they sometimes compensate for the relative poverty of other compositional components, like the harmony.

In the case of Bartók's meticulously detailed transcriptions, you can see how determinedly he attempted to provide exact rhythmic values for inflections that are the result of instinct, impulse, spontaneous freedom. The contrast between this meticulous visual constriction and the freedom of the peasants he was recording shows the extent to which performed music can be rich in qualities that elude notated music. Notated music must root itself in a hierarchy of separate values, with respect to tempo, register and dynamics. Our notations can only embody continuity by way of useful but crude approximations: with pitch, the glissando; with tempo, accelerando or ritardando; with dynamics, crescendo or decrescendo. These notions are at once the most imprecise and the most rich, since they allow for legitimate deviation. With Western notation, we can say that the more precise that notation, the more exigent the instruction it conveys. The notation of ancient music lacks such signs of continuity, hence the imprecisions. Its practitioners might have had ways of ensuring a certain degree of continuity, but it is impossible to know for sure. Dynamic changes were the first to be notated, then changes of tempo, which brought to music this sense of floating in space that more precise notation resisted. Changes in pitch (that were not accidental) were accepted to the extent that they fitted into the overall harmonic context. Any musician belonging to an ensemble or orchestra will tell you that with respect to pitch, accuracy is relative, not absolute. It is clear that just as we talk of written music, we must accept the existence of essential categories beyond notation, whose interpretation supplements the written text by means of variants involving deviations reflecting the personalities of individuals, the acoustic conditions in which the performance takes place and other, even more general features, such as the different perceptions of style between the time of the performer and the time when the work was composed. An early-twentieth-century interpreter of early-eighteenth-century German baroque music would have had a different sense of style to an interpreter in our own time who aspires to *authenticity*. It is utterly pointless to try, in written notation, to pin down these imponderables, to eliminate the variants that enrich the reading of a musical text. Composers like Ravel and Stravinsky, seeking to counter the excesses of interpretative subjectivity and excessive inflections, praised interpretative objectivity, the strictly literal realisation of written notation. But we know, in the case of the pianola, of which Stravinsky was a passionate advocate for a while, that textual objectivity imposed severe limitations, to the point of freezing the text into uninteresting inertia: 'deviations' were sorely missed. Before initiating a discussion of what writing entails, it is worth recalling the limitations of written sources, which convey only a part of what has been created. Written accounts of music have a long history, but until we approach fairly recent times, it is difficult to reconstruct those interpretative qualities that alone can bring a text to life. With plainchant, or the music of the Middle Ages, we are reduced to conjecture: we refer to theoretical texts without any certainty as to their correct application, and the endless arguments among specialists make definitive conclusions difficult. New specialists challenge the conclusions of older ones, speculations changing shape as the years pass. One has to ask, given the weight of accumulated knowledge, whether we can ever be sure of authentically recreating a text, of understanding authenticity in relation to the occasional variants of the written hierarchy. Is it that after an optimum period in which interpretation and text are in phase there is no more need to link the written text to the performed one? As in oral traditions, does the written text not tend to transform itself as the years – the centuries – pass? In the end, is not the written work a delusion that the urge for authenticity can never return to its original truthfulness? In any case, does that original truth truly matter to us? Does the interest of a written work, in comparison to the oral tradition, reside not only in the variations it allows for, not only in its relation to individuals, but in its relation to the centuries? Are not variations in interpretation similar to Heisenberg's principle, which, simply put, states that observation distorts the observed object and prevents you from perceiving it with absolute objectivity?

Writing, Learning and Perception

We should start by defining the relationships of the composer and performer to musical writing. How do they learn it? How do they use it? How do they turn abstraction into reality? What connections emerge between creativity and musical writing? How do connections arise between sound and writing, between eye and ear? What part does abstract speculation play in the creation of a language, and what are its connections with acoustic events? Clearly, we are asking questions about the basics of compositional acts.

Let us begin with the years of study. Before any study of musical writing in itself, many conventions will already have been absorbed through theoretical and practical education. It has already been necessary to learn notation and its links with acoustical principles. Notation is grasped in the most abstract way possible, always at a distance from sounding objects; one learns to sing intervals according to a certain notion of time. This indicates a highly controlled and restricted learning process, dependent on a rudimentary grammar organised in terms of clear and constrained hierarchies. On the other hand, to the extent that one makes progress, one is able to perform more and more complex works, thus acquiring, through practice, a knowledge of the fundamental features of musical language: elements of vocabulary, grammatical rules, relations between these and musical objects, ideas about harmony, chord progressions, construction of melodic lines, etc. When one approaches various types of musical writing, one therefore has, in principle, a certain practical knowledge both of the language and its notational conventions; and thanks to exercises in dictation, you acquire an understanding of sound materials that is increasingly refined and analytical, which enables you to transcribe what you hear. Dictation teaches you to link the sound as heard to the analysis of its components, as successions of both pitches and durations. Perception of the actual techniques of transcription is the main element in an essential, unambiguous identification system. One connects the heard and the written in a two-way perceptual process: on the one hand, you realise the heard as writing; and you are also validating the written in the heard. This area of education is vital, decisive, since it facilitates the give-and-take of aural experience and its transcription, the aural prediction of what can be written down. Conventional linguistic constraints certainly affect acceptable transcription, since a well-ordered, selective reality produced by an instrument conforming to a very precise and restricted hierarchy is involved. One therefore sets aside more complex, even anarchic acoustical aspects, features difficult to transcribe without adding a plethora of additional signs to the notational conventions in use or switching to other more suitable conventions. However, one will have acquired a certain awareness that will enable one to approach musical writing as such, beyond any particular transcription.

Musical writing is approached through its two poles: harmony and counterpoint, extended in due course into fugue. Usually, harmony comes first: the nature of chords, root position and inversions, ways of building chordal progressions according to the language of tonality, the historical evolution of chord types and their connections. This learning of musical writing is wholly dominated by the state of the language in the nineteenth century – by the reality of works from the past, yet utterly divorced from that reality. To study musical writing is to accumulate a coherent set of codes that, in the end, do not actually belong to any particular individual or epoch. What is involved is an exercise in manipulation that is outside time and detached from those functions that make harmony such a powerful controller of form. In practice, this type of writing follows the conventions of a four-part transcription that has a certain *raison d'être* but is far too restrictive to represent the truth about works to which, after all, one refers, despite their abstract and allusive character, and which lack any specific historical context to underpin this pedagogy. In such exercises in harmonic writing, one learns voice-*leading* – the four constituents of a chord must be linked to others in a way that creates an individual entity subject to an overall coherence. One thereby emphasises a certain kind of autonomy for each component, always subject to rules of relationship. Above all, however, a style of writing that is essentially free and unconstrained is involved, where rules apply only flexibly. To learn harmony is not only to learn a style of writing of a predetermined kind, it is also to learn to imagine a complete text stemming from a given fragment, to know how to invent a solution with a partial text that has already had *its* solution. Beyond straightforward application of the rules of musical writing, one must know how to exercise one's analytical ability to achieve a complete realisation. Materials provided for students to work with have been much criticised, above all for their lack of style; there has also been justifiable doubt about their riddle-like character. In effect, by omitting parts of the complete text, giving just the melody and bass, for example, an exercise in academic writing is given the spice of an exercise in detection: find the correct answer. In many cases, such exercises might be seen in the same way as certain kinds of archaeological reconstruction, which are of no interest in themselves. There are certainly stylistic exercises to be found that are more worthwhile and more musical, because they stem from interesting models. But it is not my intention here to contemplate a reform in teaching, rather to imagine how the fledgling composer might be sensitised to harmony, in learning the rules of transcription and manipulation, able to imagine for himself the possible outcomes arising for a text given in fragmentary form. As a result, he will learn to channel his invention through harmony, and to control ideas with the help of relatively flexible laws of compositional writing.

In addition, whether at the same time or not, the apprentice composer will study counterpoint. Here, we change centuries. If the study of harmony is tied to the language of the nineteenth century, that of counterpoint fits with the first half of the eighteenth. Here, too, one often evolves within a sort of no-man's-land, aligned for sure with the baroque, but often avoiding direct references. In the writing of harmony, progressions can be devised with a degree of freedom; the study of counterpoint is more concerned with constraint. Here, writing is stricter, more hierarchical, with restrictions that can make progress extremely difficult, inventiveness paralysed by the rigour of the rules that must be obeyed. The more one progresses in the study of harmony, the freer one feels to be creative, and the more one benefits from the richness of means at one's disposal. As one progresses in the study of counterpoint, one can feel bound hand and foot by the salient rules, by their strictness, by their apparent absurdity. Imagination can be paralysed, an impulse to reject can arise, and such constraints can be reflected in the rapport that exists between the written and the heard. Considered simply as going through the motions, such exercises are either useless or irrelevant; considered as materials for reflection about the essential nature of musical writing, they perform a vital service. If harmony exercises lead you to realise or articulate given sonorities in the best possible way, they do not provoke an examination of the relationship between a given sonority and musical writing, because that relationship is instantaneous. Harmonic perception is all-embracing, occurring in the moment when the object is perceived. The relation of musical writing to counterpoint is much less direct, involving horizontal layers that can move in different time values, as with counterpoint by augmentation or diminution. In addition, the relation of line to line need not be consistently parallel, but can be symmetrical (involving reversal); it can use a feature that is much less directly audible, retrograde motion. In short, the more speculative aspects of counterpoint can create associations with palindromes and acrostics such as occur in poetics. An acrostic becomes visible through a typographical presentation that draws attention to it, but it is impossible to perceive it when hearing the text spoken, because it avoids verbal 'sense' in its collection of vowels and consonants. Counterpoint, on account of its layered, horizontal layout and the independence of its simultaneous constituent voices following stricter or freer rules, is the domain par excellence where musical writing can develop its visible speculations – however hard it is to reconcile these with the audible. How does perception work when it comes to counterpoint? It will attach itself to a leading voice and determine instantaneously if the other voices are subject to specific harmonic controls or not. Bach's counterpoint will not be perceived in the same way as Schoenberg's. Despite following the same principles of linear construction – intervals repeated exactly at a particular intervallic distance – the lines combine to very different effect. In the case of Bach, there is overall harmonic control determined by a repertory of specific functions; in the case of Schoenberg, alignments occur in the context of an anarchic chromaticism concerned only with avoiding the exact duplication of any particular pitch. But whatever the period of the composer determining the nature of contrapuntal writing, we must underline that it is with reference to that period that the separation between speculative writing and sounding realisation must be thought of. Why? Because while harmony is essentially the domain of simultaneity, counterpoint – especially in its most extreme forms – is the domain of succession. With vertical perception, synthesis is of the essence: the components aggregate to form a global entity, perceived instantaneously and often difficult to analyse if the progression of different elements is too rapid or if the internal relations of the elements are too complex. To analyse a harmonic entity of uncertain perceptibility, its succession of elements can be set out as an arpeggiation; and one increases its significance by rendering the analysis as an interesting descriptive illustration. This remains a kind of simultaneity, since each harmonic entity will be set out in a more or less sophisticated succession of its elements: an open or folded fan shape – to adopt the language of Mallarmé – such as befits the description of properly harmonic writing. From the first prelude of the '48' to the lieder of Schumann, from Berlioz to Debussy and Messiaen, the relationship of harmony to perception through the medium of writing has common features, over-riding differences of style and personality. Such a concept of 'vertical time' is replicated in the understanding of *'objets sonores'* and aesthetic rationales in civilisations distant from our own. Think of the sustained sounds of the mouth organ (*shō*) in Japanese *gagaku*. The sounds produced by different mouth organs are simultaneous, but in investigating them we can make use of microtonal deviations, comparable to dynamic variations, which distinguish this or that component. This is different from those identifications as arpeggiations or ornamental figures devised for music in the Western tradition, but we draw attention to a specific component in terms of the temporary deviation that one defines.

Whatever the identities assumed in harmonic analysis, these are always subject to global phenomena. It is clear that boldness and speculation in our tradition involve ways of progressing, of connecting one entity to another. The study of writing provides a certain number of routines for progression in terms of accepted logic, the consequences of grammatical laws that one has learned to understand and respect, at least as a first step. As study of the language of harmony progresses, its laws can appear subtler and more flexible: the objects one employs can possess different functions, different qualities; they can be folded into different contexts, not in fixed positions, or be relatively fixed according to precedent. The internal associations of a basic harmonic entity can change, but its external associations can be less variable, depending on a limited number of connections. The more complex the entities themselves are, the more the nature of progressions changes; the possibilities for progression proliferate, become ambivalent, the rules of grammar gradually relaxing their constraints. Harmonic writing turns speculative by way of surprising progressions – in innovative, individual, even unpredictable style. With the governing grammar weakened, a grammar of more local, less predictable associations takes over, which finishes up making for difficulties in perception. This is because once certain constraints on the recycling of progressions are exceeded, comprehension runs into difficulties, since one is unable to discern any overall logic to the harmonic successions; or because no such logic exists in any case, since one proceeds by way of immediate connections only; or it can be simply too difficult to detect the governing logic, whose laws are subtle and constantly changing. It follows that harmonic or vertical writing leads to speculation about language, invariably based on the instant identification of objects as the essence, and on the connection we can establish between them. Speculation is rooted in a succession of vertical simultaneities. Writing ceases to function if the instant is, so to speak, too weighty, or if the succession of these instances is too rich or lacks coherence. This is the case with different objects that progress from one to the next in a complex language. But if the single object is complex and the progression is straightforward, vertical writing quickly regains the power to be perceived. Let us consider three examples: stasis, parallelism and description.

(1) *Stasis*

When a vertical object is offered to perception in an extended form, or if the duration of the written event is prolonged on account of its complexity, and its immobility makes it possible to analyse the object (even with those minute variations of one of its components I've mentioned in connection with the *shō*), the construction of that object can be as complex as one wishes, and will be understood thanks to its defining duration. The object and the perception of the object are linked by the phenomenon of writing, through which one understands that it is not only the constituent pitches of the chord that matter: durational values are equally important. Because the internal pitch components of a chord can be gradually altered, writing gives life to the sounding object, and does not deprive it of its identity. Identifying the transformations it undergoes does not change one's unitary perception of the object. It goes without saying that the more refined the intervals, the more time is needed for the ear to adapt to them: microtones within a chord require the most careful definition in comparative terms, since the specific elements of both duration and pitch are inextricably bound together in the construction of such an object.

(2) *Parallelism*

When an object, however complex it might be, moves in parallel to a given horizontal or melodic line, it can be identified even before it is analysed. One might even say that there is no need to analyse it in order to understand it satisfactorily, because what focuses our attention is the fact that this object moves without changing. If a single line is not strictly parallel, this differentiates the progression, but a majority of lines moving parallel to a freely moving line is usually sufficient to preserve the initial identity of the basic harmonic entity that determines the rest. This harmonic entity changes its function with reference to those operating in the progression from chord to chord; its predominant function is to provide harmonic coloration by being grafted onto a melodic line. The chord's identity is sufficient unto itself; it does not need to be connected to a similar or contrasting chord in a progression to embody its function, but manifests it in another dimension – which is not so much that of duration, as before, but rather that of timbre, particularly blended timbre (matching or contrasting to a greater or lesser extent with natural harmonics). Debussy has shown extensively, with what at the time were called successions of parallel chords – sevenths, ninths, fourths and fifths – what could be made of a language in which functional harmony changed its character, and for which harmonic writing devised new laws.

(3) *Description*

I spoke a while back about the first Prelude of the '48', or the accompaniments to Schumann's lieder, among other things. Description involves detailing the components, one by one, of a sounding object – over a period sufficiently restricted to offer the immediate possibility of synthesis. For a complex object, this mode of writing proves to be a powerful aid in fixing the details of our perception. The simplest instance is the arpeggiation from top to bottom or bottom to top; but such a description is overly basic and not an authentic part of musical writing, since it is incapable of renewal, and the way of describing it, simply because it is so basic, ends up devouring all the objects and applying a uniformity that erases their differences. Description in terms of a style of writing presupposes some variation in the succession of pitches that comprise the essentially vertical object (the matrix), which analysis considers according to intervals, whether in the relations between individuals and the remainder – diatonic intervals of lesser tension relative to chromatic intervals of greater tension – and whether along the way they generate a more or less interesting melodic contour. A chord can be broken down horizontally in many different ways, and is scarcely any more acceptable for the lack of melodic interest in its sequence of pitches. (A close-position chord provides more focus for fragmented melodic lines than a widespread chord that gives supportive focus to, or else maintains distance from, a smoothly flowing line). One can certainly add a fluctuating metric structure to this: constant changes of speed, using accelerandos and ritardandos; small-scale features like arpeggiations, in which the writing is insufficiently structured to sustain the invention for very long; or proportional rhythmic relations highlighting with greater analytical precision the intervals and their relations at the heart of the object in question.

These are three ways in which one can see that the generative sound object, conceived vertically, can be employed or described in notated terms in order to be better understood, with richer repercussions. I would say that, in this case, it is a matter of virtual, *fictive* writing, because its usefulness is limited to its derivations, to its consequences: merely to manipulate the object and to present it, as it might be, in different lights, from different angles. Though the object might be enhanced by a description, through parallel usage, through fixed stability, referring to categories of tempo and timbre linked to that of pitch, it is clear that the object itself does not change or transform itself, but retains its identity, these ingenious tricks of musical writing simply facilitating its comprehension, grafting onto an essentially static object the potential for being integrated into a composition as a result of its more superficial elements.

Abstract speculation and difficulty of understanding, applied to the initial object, begin when writing hypothesises a family of objects by way of certain transformational principles, because – if the deductive principles are too severe – the initial object disappears for many reasons, and the ear can no longer connect these various members of a single family. In the classical style – and separate from their traditional functions within progressions – different types of objects can easily be detected, not just because they are simple or contain a limited number of components – in general, three or four – or because those components conform to the fundamental overtones of the harmonic series, but because, in any position or inversion, their connection to the basic, root position can be recognised. To use classical terminology, it is a matter of a chord and its inversions. But move away from this simple principle and one soon becomes disorientated in attempting to apply the same basic criteria to a source and its derivations. It can indeed be difficult – if importance is attached to the establishment of a connection or a transformation – to discount what represents a given interval when an interval assumed to be generative does not create (by simple displacement of registers) similar, if not identical, intervals. A major third will not easily be heard as close to a minor sixth at two or three octaves' distance, even if the same basic registers are involved; a minor third, however different its character, is closer to the basic major third than to a major third with all the inversions and changes of register that can be applied to it. There is a contradiction between an abstract theoretical identity and a less precise equivalence that can be experienced as much more meaningful.

We can consider two basic ways of creating harmonic objects, one of which is deduced from an abstract model, with components of no particular registral location, tempo or dynamic level. These are virtual materials, able to generate a multitude of forms of actual objects. The other involves connections deriving from the physical model of natural resonance, and pushing derivation to the limits of what is perceptible. I will now consider these two extreme positions in what I will call 'notation of the object'. Both stem from speculation about what the object represents in relation to language: the first stems from abstract consideration of an object's identity in a world of coordinates in which the fixed and the relative are understood to have equal importance; the second involves theoretical and analytical ideas about the spectral constitution of sounding objects and their projection, beyond the domain of acoustics, narrowly defined, into vertical structures built according to extremely precise acoustic values, extending (in some sense) the 'fundamentals' of Rameau and creating refinements that challenge conventional tunings and generate in all their richness sonorous objects justified by natural laws.

✳ ✳ ✳

499

The notation of the *absolute* object, if one chooses to describe it thus, belongs to an 'ideal' source, a collection of pitches without registers or any other specific qualities. An actual interval is in effect excluded from such a source because it can arise from two given elements in any registral position, at any distance, in any context or inversion. On the basis of this source, one can create any object without changing the pitch-class identity of its components by changing registers, and also having the possibility of changing placements by way of inversion. An object varied in this way can change not only its appearance, but also its properties. A constituent interval changed from a fourth to a fifth will not have the same weight or the same stability; a close-position chromatic interval will not have the same degree of tension as the same interval in more open position, the major seventh having a different intensity to the minor ninth; again, an interval placed in a high register will not have the same effect as the same interval in a low register. Finally, an interval that conforms to the harmonic series and one that deviates from it will not have the same function within the overall structure of the object. This shows again that the abstract basis of a sonorous object, its virtual notation, is only a starting point, but one that already has a number of properties latent within it that manifest themselves with smaller or greater variations. Clearly, the notional fourth or fifth acts differently to a notional major third/minor sixth: these are the concrete realisations of a virtual object. The components of the source contain thousands of possibilities, and the more such components there are, the more difficult it can be to identify the derivations, since the possible number of combinations approaches the infinite. While one can easily see that an object made up of two or three elements will remain identifiable in all of its transformations, with an object made up of five or six elements it is very difficult to distinguish one derivation from another, if all the elements are altered. An object with different elements whose actual intervals are closer to those in the source will be heard as having an identity closer to that source than a more distant derivation from the same object; the degree of proximity will be much more relevant than the nature of the derivation from the original source. But notation clarifies the functions of both the degree of proximity and the derivation from a given source, so that membership of the same family of given objects can be recognised. To choose a shared feature stronger than variation that controls the other elements, to vary the elements stage by stage until the object has been completely transformed, noting aspects of fixity relative to aspects of mobility – such are the many possibilities of which vertical writing can make use to derive one object or a whole family of objects from a single source. Once this family is established according to explicit principles, one can benefit from the absolute fixity of its components, and they can also be used as the basis for a more comprehensive writing scheme. One can transpose these objects, set them against each other in different contexts, use them for simple harmonic colouring – in short, use them within a language that represents a higher level of writing. The use of harmonic structuring following both local and larger-scale laws gives the language a homogeneity without which decisions would be made on a purely ad hoc basis.

As against an approach that starts with the *absolute* object and draws relative objects from it, we can consider the outcomes of taking a *relative* object and deriving another relative object from it, basically in terms of degrees of similarity, requiring transitional stages tracing the transformation of one entity into another. The relative object belongs essentially to the study of acoustic givens. Those that have been in common use until recent times derive from harmonic principles that have a simple arithmetical relation to a fundamental. The more distant from the fundamental, the more one exceeds the restrictions imposed by equal temperament; one can easily calculate frequencies digitally and then find acoustic equivalents by way of synthesised sound. The result will be precise, but raises the problem of finding a timbre that endows the synthesised sound with the extremely complex components necessary for such an exercise. On the other hand, it is extremely difficult, even impossible, to achieve precision with existing/conventional instruments, especially with the modes of playing commonly available. Either the necessary notational indicators are lacking, or they are excessively abundant; it is a matter of approximations, like the quarter-tones which, in allowing for deviations from semitonal norms, simply lead to overly vague degrees of definition in a tuning too small in its defining interval. In the end, to the extent that one thinks about it, there is a well-nigh unbridgeable gap between the direct perception of harmonics in a sounding body, such as can be derived from physical analysis, computed as necessary, and what one might attempt to 'reconstruct' by instrumental means. These have a particular spectrum, being simply neutral objects available for fusion. This fusion of sounds is a bit like a version of the old dream of the alchemists, resulting from a critical mass; that is to say, when there are enough sounds assembled within a complex collection for perception to founder and imagine a synthesis of one kind or another. This is more a matter of illusion than reality, in which the profusion of compositional choices, the sonic micro-events, plays an essential role. With more austere textures, when the number of parts is limited, it is as if each sounding element in a vertical construct can be heard independently, and since the whole can be broken down by an instant analysis, the phenomenon of fusion, of synthesis, no longer applies. Instead, it is the aspect of style that brings things together, more explicitly than purely acoustic phenomena. The initial object having been created, the connection with a consequent does not depend fundamentally on the manipulation or permutation of intervals. Objects created on the basis of such a physical model have structures relatively independent of each other, and it is possible to connect them more by notions of proximity than by deduction. I mean that each component of the initial object will be linked to corresponding constituents of the resulting object by definable trajectories, following a relatively rapid course. The more distant a component from its counterpart, the more attenuated the process, the larger the intervals between each element will be. They can be fixed, in sequence, or project a constant progression or diminution – it matters little, the overall span being so extended. These chordal families are easily identifiable if one hears them in sequence, because the close similarities function with maximum efficiency, assuming no breaks in the continuity; especially as one is not obliged to change the components of a vertical object all at once, transitions can be achieved in stages, one component changing at a time, while all the others stay the same, etc. It can already be a little more difficult to trace the evolution and hear it correctly if the continuity is broken and one moves in a kind of zigzag between the first object and the last. If the density remains unchanged, and if the replacement of components is at a regular rate, one can reconstruct more or less consciously the virtual connected trajectory. But if the objects are moved in a mobile notation – that is, transposed – and with altered registers, connections will certainly become less and less obvious: as the link through proximity is broken or concealed at the same time as the order of succession and displacement or 'translation' of register, continuity is difficult, even impossible to detect.

To these two ways of generating vertical objects, whether on the basis of an abstract source or a concrete model, both of which nevertheless imply a possibly theoretical way of conceiving intervals, a sense of system, however provisional, contributes to our response to those literal, actual objects that shun an essentially rational system, a marginal object that our systematic instruments *also* produce: marginal objects – peripheral, if you like – interesting and rich in their own right, but disruptive in terms of strict musical grammar. While they are not totally alien to the principles of writing, by way of certain approximations employed to bring them into line, they are still difficult to manipulate because of their highly distinctive character, clearly refusing to display that neutrality usually preferred in a simple component.

❃ ❃ ❃

Given these different ways of thinking and acting – in the choice of components, the notation of the object or its description – one has a huge palette at one's disposal for the formation of vertical entities. I therefore prefer to speak of musical writing that is not, strictly speaking, the 'realisation' of the composition but which can be the first stage, the pre-compositional state preparing a kind of raw material, already particular to the composer, bearing the mark of his personality, his inventiveness – but still only a preliminary stage. It is clear that language cannot exist save as something perceived, and which refers, among other things, to vertical categories. As I've already said, it is this comprehension of the vertical, this control of verticals that helps us to understand sounding objects in relation to each other, this capacity to control functioning instantaneously. It can therefore happen that a composer confronts different preoccupations in this class of ideas: to best realise control step by step through the links of proximity that function in a local context, or to refer to more general laws of generation and connection that will better promote coherence, but also shape the work on a larger scale. The writing, by whatever means it manifests its identity, implies a certain vertical coherence, even if that does not involve simultaneous elements, but it controls elements that evolve over time with a certain independence.

Organising this pre-material does not require strict rules of connection, context-free, applied with restrictions; on the contrary, if overall coherence is necessary, flexible processes and variable fields of application are essential, indispensable conditions. It is certainly not a matter of a predetermined process with no precise objectives; the pre-material already refers to a specific composition, even if it reaches beyond it and generates other deductions and deviations about which one has so far reached no conclusions. In its preliminary form, the material can nevertheless submit to specific constraints or directives; it thus moves towards the definitive state it will achieve in the work proper. It's worth pointing out that a vertical object can exist only in a context that lays down the minimum requirements for its realisation. I will give a very simple example of the rapport that can be created between object and context: a given chord moves through a sequence of intervals that do not necessarily comprise the notes of the chord; we can determine the different transpositions, the different *states*, of this chord according to the degree of the scale on which it will be placed. There are therefore two possible solutions:

(1) *The chord controls the scale* through which it moves; it will be transposed onto each degree of the scale, but its components strictly conform to the initial intervals, and therefore respect their rates of change. The identity of the chord remains unchanged, and can be immediately identified; this identity will be stronger than that of the scale, which is persistently undermined by the structure of the chord.

(2) *The scale controls the chord*. Rather than moving in parallel, the components of this chord move according to the scale. The scale does not necessarily contain the same pitches as the chord, each pitch moving in the same direction, but strict parallelism is abandoned, each line not

employing the same interval simultaneously. The chord is only slightly changed, its different forms resemble each other, but the identity of the scale will be stronger than that of the chord, which has a different structure, an internal rapport between slightly different intervals.

One is not creating unique vertical objects; to bring coherence to the musical discourse, we must think of groups of objects joined together by constants and variables. It is the interplay of these constants and variables that creates distance and proximity, implying that they work primarily through the power of intervals. Other elements like dynamics and timbre help to provide differentiations in the specific context of a composition. Constants and variables can function in relation to either absolute or relative values. By absolute value I mean that the pitch or interval is not yet fixed in register; by relative value I understand the specific registral placement of pitches and intervals. One can play with the rapports involving absolute and relative with respect to perception and its immediacy. For sure, in a language whose functions are clearly defined and accepted, obeying overall laws independent of registral placement or of the pitches with which they are associated, variability of register has no more importance than dynamic level in musical processes, but becomes essentially a matter of orientation. *Absolute laws* govern their *relative* context. In effect, it matters little, in the language of tonality, if the key is D major or F major, or if the register is medium or high: the functions of tonality and of chordal progressions remain in place whatever the circumstances. However, tonalities have the function of orientation with regard to form: for example, they mark the recapitulation in sonata form, the return of the refrain in a rondo. Tonality certainly has the character of a signal, but mainly as a global cue, since the connecting functions are recognised in any particular context. It is clear that this formal articulation by way of established tonal return was abandoned in the language of late Romanticism. In Mahler, for example, form is governed by narrative and the principle of non-literal return, as opposed to the principles that control the classical symphony: since certain movements or song settings never return to their initial tonality and end in a different key, the signal of returning to the initial tonality can only function as a contradiction of the narrative quality that governs the form. But in a language where the functions and relations of vertical objects are very precisely defined by the composer himself in the body of the work, the signalling function of pitch certainly needs to be given much more attention. If the relation between objects is not explicit to a more or less constant degree, that relation will be very difficult to perceive. The invariant feature that links two objects can be either internal or external to the object, or it can belong to both categories.

(1) The invariant will be exterior to the object when it is not involved in the structure of the object itself but, for example, determines all the components, whatever they are, in a clearly established position. One might therefore have a complete fixity of registers that constrains all the sounding events; moving away from this extreme, the degree of constraint can be reduced and the proportion of fixed registers to those that are not fixed can be varied. This constraint pays no attention to the structure of the object itself; it can even deconstruct or 'anonymise' all the objects by making them appear more similar than different.

(2) The invariant can be placed alongside the original object, according to a rule that generates its derivations. This constant will be reinforced by the inclusion of registral placement, which singles it out and gives it the quality of a signal.

(3) Finally, the invariant might be thought of as embodying the limits of an internal field within which derivations take place. Think of two boundary pitches, low and high, from which a chord cannot be generated. Successively, all the components of the initial chord will replace the boundary pitches at the top, while the others trace a circular descending motion, transposed into the lower register; this will create a family of chords with very diverse intervals, after applying transposition, but preserving the boundaries will confirm the similarity of the heard objects to the listener: the same densities, the same spans, but altered internally. The twin constants frame the variables.

Basically, the vertical pre-material donates its overall or local coherence to a language that has to discover and formulate its own laws. It comes down to very basic associations for easily located objects, as with Webern. It can be the first factor of a formal component, as with Berio or Ligeti. Even more it can be, as with Carter, a fundamental element not only of vocabulary, but of form. With Carter, the pre-material fixes many other features of the language, because it brings the specificity of intervals to bear (some more prominent in relation to others), as well as the registral placement of these intervals and their associates, and the density of objects; therefore, their virtual and actual functions become the foundational component of the work, and control a formal development brought naturally to bear on the other thematic processes.

❉ ❉ ❉

So far I've explored the role of the vertical in musical writing: how we can organise the specific sounding object, construct families of objects; how we can determine what role this pre-material plays in a composition; how, in consequence, it might be used to *characterise* different modes of expression; what cohesion a similar resource brings to musical writing, and what solutions it offers for fixing not only the immediate connections, but also the global connections between the successive events of a composition. Several times I've recalled that academic study separates the two disciplines of harmony and counterpoint; moreover, this opposition between vertical and horizontal writing usually underpins the assessments brought to bear on a composer's language or on a specific work. This opposition is less artificial than it might appear, the perception of one or another dimension having a very different rapport with tempo, for sure, but also with the ability to distinguish, to discriminate aurally in the case of superimposed strata that are not synchronised. I want now to return to the problem of perceiving vertical objects.

The hearing of vertical objects implies a kind of *frozen* time; even if the objects are described through listing their components successively – as arpeggiations or figurations – we synthesise the object and understand it as a unity, occupying a certain temporal space until it is replaced or gradually altered. The relation between a succession of vertical objects bound by a rhythmic pulsation will also be heard as a unity. Obviously, a monody will be heard as a succession; to understand it fully, to grasp its articulations, it is necessary to appreciate the 'present' of this monody in relation to its immediate past – readjustment, reappreciation becoming necessary as the monody unfolds; we hear while making reference to what has gone before, and at the end of the process we aim to globalise our hearing, and finally to sense the coherence in a sequence of separate events. We can be guided in this – even without the help of explicit or underlying harmony – by many factors that attach to the particular intervallic source: the primordial given involving curves, symmetries, repetitions or variations. But however meticulously constructed the intervals may be, these alone cannot determine our perception. Rhythmic structure plays the principal role, organising periodicity – and by this I mean regular, symmetrical periods just as much as irregular, asymmetrical ones, based on extension or curtailment. The use of a temporal structure, a subdivision, enables us to grasp intervallic profiles, to relate them to each other, and even gives us the power to memorise them for however brief a time. Other elements like dynamics can confirm this perceptual grasp, but are much less fundamental. In the case of a monody, our perception is therefore entirely absorbed by a single object. If another horizontal line is added, attention, and perception, must bifurcate. We should perhaps distinguish two instances symptomatic of different cultures that imply a specific mode of perception. Many cultures, Asian or African, have in fact used heterophony as a means of increasing the density of events. To put it very simply, heterophony is the same event presented simultaneously with rhythmic changes and added ornamentations, shifts in tempo and register; but the basic structure remains the same, and the lines are placed in parallel. The closer the similarity, at particular moments, the easier perception of the two lines as a unity becomes; the more marked the divergence – strong variations in tempo or richer ornamentation – the more perception is split, even though it is basically a matter of the same sounding event. In this case, timbre and dynamics have a major role in the comprehension of one line in relation to another, in terms of subordination or equality. The usual example instances a vocal line doubled by a monodic instrument: the voice, more varied in its phonemic inflections, moving more slowly and with less ornamentation, is superimposed on an instrumental line, inevitably more unified, more homogeneous in timbre, more decorated, the rapidity of these decorations contrasting with the greater breadth of the vocal sound – often weaker in dynamic level, and displaying a degree of freedom with respect to synchronisation.

There have been passionate debates between specialists to decide if it is necessary to consider this kind of heterophony as belonging to what we term 'polyphony'. Perception tends to be divided, since the heard events do not coincide; however, they stem from the same source and are recognisable as such. There is therefore no real transformation, no deduction, no path to individual independence; adherence to a single schema remains predominant and controls perception with respect to the superimposition of the same image in two states. The writing takes possession of this quality and takes it to the limits of perception of a common identity. How so? It is sufficient to grasp one changing feature with respect to the original and give sufficient importance to it to create a very clear divergence. Many means are at our disposal, the most obvious being ornamentation. Given a group of notes, without even changing their registers or their ordering, one inserts more rapid movement between them, then much more rapid movement, which creates a divergence in the prevailing tempo to which the temporal *values* no longer conform, being regularly disrupted by the intermediary values of the derived ornamentation; in addition, the importance of the principal notes will be reduced to the extent that they combine into groups and acquire a different meaning: in attaching themselves to the ornamental groups that erode their durations, they can no longer be heard as dominant. The perception of two lines associated in this way – a simple line and an ornamented line – works consistently with convergence and divergence, with the articulation of the ornamentation with respect to the model. Every temporal coincidence makes perception clearer, each divergence dissolves it. Another possibility is tempo oscillation in a heterophonic line relative to the model; this procedure will be more effective at a fast tempo at which perception, unable to distinguish the different values, is constantly deceived in its attempt to estimate difference. Difference, variable difference, will be perfectly perceptible as such, but it cannot be evaluated. It is not even that, in a complex context, a variable sense of forward motion suffices; for a temporal value in the model, a lesser value will correspond in what follows, then an equal value, then a higher value, etc. No need here to change the order of the notes: temporal oscillation suffices to make the two lines diverge; if one wishes to fix the notation of this oscillation, the use of a different timbre, or a different dynamic level establishing a different sound plane, will be absolutely necessary. But if one wishes to lead perception astray, inhibit the realisation of what the elements belonging to the oscillation are, one will retain the same timbre and dynamic levels for the two lines. There are plenty of other possibilities, such as those involving register and note order. The derived line might distance itself from the original line, or get closer to it, coincide with it; it can tend, the more the register deviates from the original, to acquire a certain autonomy, intensifying as the temporal deviation increases. But deviation that cannot be corrected, if I may put it in that way, begins as soon as one touches the notes of the original. Thus far, if the rhythmic values are changed, or insertions are introduced, the original order remains the crucial element in the perception of similarities. As soon as one touches that succession, the mode of recognition gradually loses its basic orientations, to the point of projecting two lines that are strangers to each other, in which any idea of connection, of common ancestry, will have disappeared. The intervallic profile will change as the displacement of the notes gradually leads to complete autonomy. To break down a strongly marked profile, more elements must be changed, but the final result will, in any case, be non-recognition.

Certainly, the types of writing I have described, one by one, dealing with ornamentation, rhythmic values or register, can be used simultaneously to create strata that do not, strictly speaking, belong to the category of vertical writing, or to horizontal writing, but rather to a kind of diagonal writing. Organising heterophonic layers that derive from an initial line requires conceiving them in terms of vertical principles. All the lines are placed in a harmonic field of action, perceptible overall as a vertical entity, even if synchronicity is not rigorously maintained. Accordingly, one or more of the layers can diverge to varying degrees from the original, using one of the procedures I have described; the individual displacements fit with each other through a vertical hierarchy heard globally as the outcome of two dimensions, diagonally integrating strata and divergencies.

Although this heterophonic writing implies different strata, perception works along global lines, the different horizontal elements being variants of a basic horizontal element. From the beginning we are a long way from the concept of counterpoint, even if those procedures, in terms of their growing complexity, tend to be heard in a similar way. Nevertheless, I would define heterophony as a simple derivation, with no creativity other than in the presentation, while counterpoint implies decisions that place different vertical objects in play which cannot be truly understood in global terms, but require attention to multiple centres of interest. Genuine polyphony, with the independent movement of voices, has always created the problems for the listener discussed in texts on the subject. One tries as often as possible to make the elements of polyphony explicit, to guide the listener as to what might be heard and how. Dynamic gradations are useful in this – something instruments of the period, harpsichord or organ (if we are speaking of polyphony from the first half of the eighteenth century), could not provide in an appropriately differentiated manner. One can point to the importance of a fugue subject relative to a counter-subject, one gives priority to the cells that organise an episode, one stresses – sometimes in an extremely emphatic way – themes in augmentation or diminution. In short, one tries as far as possible to inform the listener about the character of the polyphony; one *must* hear this, one *can* hear that. This understanding about what is audible lies behind Berg's notation, when he writes 'leading voice' (*Hauptstimme*) and 'secondary voice' (*Nebenstimme*) in the score and leaves the rest unlabelled. His notation implies a sounding perspective that orientates hearing along the lines of central and peripheral vision. What can be heard of the horizontal relations of polyphony is indeed much harder to analyse and explain than the perception of a vertical sounding object. It implies a separation into strata conditioned by temporal relations, which, whatever the common factors, allows for considerable difference in the constituent intervals. Are we genuinely able to grasp the horizontal components as separate entities? And how do we relate them to each other?

* * *

We should begin by asking ourselves about the specificity of properly horizontal writing. Counterpoint is simply an exercise in academic directedness, a more *reflective* way of conceiving writing than vertical construction, sometimes referring to highly refined thought processes concerning placement and similarity. Horizontal writing stimulates divided hearing, in that the ear can follow in reasonably independent fashion a number of voices which unfold according to relationships that might be strictly controlled or relatively anarchic and uncontrolled, if there are no rules to which the vertical coincidences in the different voices can be referred. The voices have different degrees of *intensity*, and I understand *intensity* not in terms of dynamic level, but in the way a more *intense* voice asserts its superiority over the other voices and subordinates them to its specific character. But the voices may tend to equality within the hierarchy, so that attention is not forced to give one priority over another. Both fixed and free relations are possible. Free relations become clear when two voices reflect no obligations towards each other apart from those laws which govern harmonic relations, those laws representing a convention, or personal laws established for a particular context. Strict relations are much more constraining, imposing something on the basis of what has already occurred, according to laws – intervallic relations, tempo considerations, direct or indirect – which greatly augment the difficulties in obtaining an acceptable result, to the point where the control of harmonic relations can become excessively difficult, if not impossible. However, the specificity of writing strictly understood plays a very important – indeed capital – role in polyphonic development. On its own this works by developing a principle of identity, identifying each component that refers to the same model. Yet since the deductive principles are neither strict nor literal, there are more blurred regions where one finds voices governed by imprecise imitations, moments of strictness alternating with moments of freedom. Polyphony has continued to extend its domain and to acquire both rigour and flexibility of execution. A certain number of qualities will ensure the cohesion of each line: duration, articulation, phrasing, those that project a specific profile in tempo, in register and, if necessary, in timbre.

How do we aurally grasp the superimposition of these lines? Do our ears have such powers of discrimination that they can follow different and complementary profiles at the same time? If the number of voices is limited, it is not so difficult. But as the number of components increases, the more difficult it is to distinguish one from the other. This is obviously because of the increasing complexity of their interactions, with more generalised and ambiguous associations; also because the vertical controls are especially constraining in the uniformity of the relations imposed, almost always the same, and leading at the same time to a certain 'anonymisation' as well as homogenisation of the constituent voices/parts – hence the impossibility of distinguishing them. But it is not only numerical complexity that makes it difficult to hear polyphony. Two other dimensions are at least as important: register and continuity, temporal or spatial. If the components, even when reduced in number, occupy the same registral space, endlessly crossing and intersecting with each other, it is hard to distinguish them, especially if they employ the same timbre; the ear may assign a particular pitch or sequence of pitches interchangeably, the identity of each component becoming utterly uncertain. When the lines cross from time to time, losing their identity temporarily, occasionally threatening to lose it only to recover it the next moment, the ambiguity is quickly resolved. Moreover, this phenomenon of registral separation applies just as well to a single component: if the intervals are very widely dispersed, with frequent registral leaps, the ear will establish another type of relation within the line it encounters, and will create, for instance, two privileged zones which, if the speed of progression is sufficiently rapid, will give the illusion of two separate lines. (This effect is called *streaming*.)

Temporal discontinuity is another characteristic that can serve to hinder the perception of polyphony. Any line whose elements are separated by silences, or whose elements are not linked with sufficient immediacy, risks not being understood as such, but heard only as a succession of discontinuous elements, without the connectivity that can give it logic and cohesion. Like the spatial discontinuity of intervals, temporal discontinuity makes elements come across as utterly disjointed by comparison to the logic that gave rise to them. I do not mean the secondary effects of certain techniques like the reversal of phrase direction compared to their initial presentation; nor do I mean secondary effects that involve an alternative profile or conflicting rhythmic values. But the more speculatively musical writing moves in the direction of intentionally confusing space with duration, the more necessary it is to have the conventions and methods to indicate the rationale.

In consequence, what becomes interesting is not that one directly perceives the relation between writing and the sounding object it generates, but that one appreciates the difference between the imagined object and the real object. The more one moves in effect into a certain speculative region of horizontal writing, the more one will understand that perception of the result moves forward from the source. The evolution of harmonic language, even when it is extremely unsystematic, is based essentially on immediate perception; the connections between chords, between musical objects more generally speaking, can become more ambiguous, more abrupt or linked more directly to the expression of the moment – as in the era of Viennese 'expressionism'; they are immediately grasped for what they are, because neither temporality nor memory play any role in the way our perception grasps these objects. The logic governing them, governing their progression, is more of a problem. In a harmonic vocabulary, ease or difficulty of orientation results almost always from two causes: the first involves a collection of objects conforming, or not, to a known convention, which makes them instantly familiar or unfamiliar; the second involves the predictability or unpredictability of their progression, due to its complexity or the speed of its articulation. But with such objects, the elements of a harmonic vocabulary will in effect be under the control of our perception. I do not mean that we will be able to identify the functions of these objects, to pass them through our analytical prism and ensure that our perception adopts them as accepted and evaluated components; we might have only an intuitive, fragmentary understanding, but it is completely explicit even in what it lacks. I believe, on the contrary, that with respect to speculation in the domain of horizontal writing, elements are infinitely less clear because, for one thing, the composer freely ventures into uncertain regions, and for another, the perception of certain categories exercises an immediate capacity to connect with the duration of phenomena that have essentially been conceived spatially, and the transcription of this space in time is nothing less than evident.

It is true that throughout the history of Western music, there is often speculation in the domain of horizontal writing leading to highly complex techniques where one finds symbolism, even esotericism, playing with difficulty, conceptual virtuosity, the cleverness of the expounder. What is it that leads the composer to speculate about methods of musical writing, to the point where perception is literally frustrated? What happens to perception in such a state of affairs? The composer's thought, or characterisation, is transmitted materially by a writing that uses the space on paper. The values inscribed thereon are therefore seen in terms of space, even if one is well aware that they are destined to be heard in temporal succession. Nevertheless, the eye that oversees the hand navigates this space, and perhaps tries to navigate in this space to judge to its satisfaction the connections between values that do not communicate directly through proximity. The eye *sees* these connections between values, effortlessly bridging the space that separates them, temporarily destroying the temporal quality that gives these values their real weight, their actual impact. The composer is drawn to such divergences between space and time by the material substance of the paper on which he creates; this silence, this world outside real time in which he constructs progresses towards a domain in which one *sees*, in immediate conjunction, events destined to be heard as successions. There is therefore a great temptation to counter the power of visual simultaneity – literally speaking – with the capacity to synthesise the hearing of succession in the same way. If one reads a score as one listens, one's simultaneous awareness of written space and its transcription in time helps one to grasp categories or characteristics which, at first hearing, may partially or totally escape us. At best, we can actually memorise this conformity between writing and hearing, but we need this writing–hearing rapport to be aware of the transmission in time of what is conceived in written space.

What therefore can drive the composer, in the distant past as much as in the present, to use techniques more *visual* than temporal, other than this immediate appeal of paper-space? Visual techniques based on symmetrical values, quantitative parallels, an architecture of number in the domain of register or duration; symbolising techniques can just as well use completely strange *signs* for sounding phenomena. We can cite ancient and recent instances. The esoteric significance of number symbolism has provided the framework for composition, ranging from the very simple to the highly complex. The symbol of the Trinity has given birth to innumerable utilisations of the number three: I will simply mention Bach's great organ fugue on three subjects in E flat major, and Messiaen's *Mystère de la Sainte Trinité*, written in strict three-part counterpoint. In the world of opera, there is *Die Zauberflöte*, with its triple symbolism connected to Masonic ceremony, or *Lulu*, in which the number five symbolises Death – in particular, the five revolver shots that kill Dr Schön. Throughout his life Berg was as obsessed by number symbolism as by the pitch transcription of German-language letters: *Wozzeck* uses the number seven from time to time; the *Lyric Suite* is riddled with numerical allusions; the Chamber Concerto is built entirely around the number three; and there are many other examples. The nature of number symbolism, from the *ars nova* to Obrecht, has given rise to innumerable speculations: when one reads musicological studies of this subject, one gets a similar impression as from books on Egyptology, in which the smallest unit becomes a number freighted with esoteric significance. Whatever the exaggeration in the use and exposition of such symbolism, it genuinely exists, and is difficult to conceive as an expressive category; symbolism certainly governs musical events in the sense that it provokes them, but the result is not received as clearly connected perceptually to this symbolism, save in the obvious instances of the ternary symbolism of the overture to *Die Zauberflöte*, where the three chords are detached from their surroundings as independent signs.

More profoundly, it seems that when the composer has recourse to such number symbolism, he will seek to override it as much as to affirm it. Whether it is a matter of complex structuring by number or of pitch symbolism, the composer assumes that it will not be heard as such, to the extent that it is submerged in his text and remains a secret between him and his score. He aims to justify himself in appealing, in an unstable and intensely individual expressive world, to categories he deems stable and immutable, in particular the category of number. For this reason, musical writing has concerned itself from time to time with arithmetical speculation or manipulation, with applications of, or parallels to, scientific laws, as a way of bypassing personal failings by reference to factual generalities that transcend the individual and legitimise his creative work. By this means the 'world order' is revealed to the composer, who does nothing more than transcribe it in some fashion, guaranteeing him value, power and permanence. The composer does not depend on sound as the sole arbiter; he becomes the intermediary of higher powers. His speculativeness thereby becomes completely justified, even if it cannot be directly perceived and understood. This hidden meaning will be unconsciously transmitted to the listener by that special power that transcends aural perception. Even when one moves away from this symbolic terrain – whether scientific or religious in nature, it relates in every way to that 'world order' which we imagine – it is clear that the composer is drawn to speculate about writing for relatively mundane reasons, directly connected to the coherence he seeks to bring to his work. If, starting from an initial idea, he aspires to develop and organise a kind of universe, however restricted or compact in extent, he needs to integrate the various components into a whole; with very good reason, when a very large ensemble is involved, the composer must submit the variety of moments that follow on from each other to laws that ensure a necessary unity, however flexible they may be, for the creation of connections between successive stages as much as on the larger scale. The variety of these connections and their *audibility* will guarantee both continuity and diversity.

One might often ask what remains, during listening, of the composer's speculations. So-called 'intellectual' composers are often accused of completely sidestepping matters of perception, and therefore of ending up speculating in the void. One might nevertheless recall Berg's advice: at the end of his lecture about *Wozzeck*, having analysed the work's themes and explained the formal construction of various scenes using sonata, fugue, invention, etc., he made a final recommendation before hearing the opera itself, a recommendation that can be summarised thus: 'Forget everything I've said, listen innocently!' All the knowledge and the multiple resources of writing have the single goal of promoting the most spontaneous kind of listening; none of the riches previously accumulated contributes *consciously* to perception. Both the esoteric and the naive are taken to extremes; and the advice is not without either cleverness or artifice, but it indicates, with or without frankness, the legitimate desire to be heard differently depending on the success of the various modes of writing and listening. Writing might be thought about in a certain way, but it is actually designed to be heard as the composer conceived it, and has he not also created, without specifically wishing it, other, more explicit categories with which the listener will connect when the work is presented to him? Contrarily, might not effects thought of as secondary control perception and lead to the forgetting of more basic schemas? In *Wozzeck*, it is significant that it is the 'inventions' in the third act that are most easily perceived, while the second act's sonata, fugue and rondo are much less so. One could say, however, that strict forms create the strongest orientations; in reality, and although their rapport with the dramatic action has been conceived coherently, their formal autonomy is in opposition to a much less 'formalistic' dramatic unfolding. On the other hand, it might be argued that the free forms of the third act are harder to evaluate, given the fluidity or, one might say, fragility of their formal design. From this point of view, they follow the dramatic text step by step and interpret it in the most direct and literal manner. But they have a very direct impact because they home in on a single quality that pervades the musical writing as a whole. With the inventions – on one note, on a chord, on an ostinato or on a rhythmic figure – cohesiveness has a direct effect throughout, because there is always a referential constant involved. That constant can be heard underpinning everything, organising and unifying our overall perception more strongly than more elaborate categories requiring a stronger memory and a more decisive capacity for abstraction. In this way, the paradox emerges of a flexible, informal structure having a more immediate impact than a much more stable formalised design.

But the secondary effects, the marginal effects of the writing are not only apparent through their formal outcomes; they emerge equally on the smallest scale. Webern's writing lends itself particularly well to this type of observation, since it involves a certain number of ambiguities, creating so many secondary effects. I will not claim decisively that these were intentional: they exist, and for that reason we can observe them today. In effect, Webern's polyphony employs all the categories that one could term 'negative' with respect to preferred classical procedures, and which I have already listed. I will consider particularly the instrumental works following on from the Symphony, op. 21, which almost exclusively make rigorously contrapuntal use of canon. Each voice is composed in such a way as to be difficult to disentangle from the other voices. Let us take the specific example of the beginning of the first movement of op. 21: a double canon with two pairs of voices, which can be thought of as two principal and two subordinate voices. The four voices use exactly the same registral distribution; their paths are constantly crossing, and it is difficult to distinguish one from the other, except through the group- ings of short related figures close together, where we can immediately hear the imitative relationship. In addition, there are constant rhythmic interruptions that divide the phrases into minuscule units, which can even reduce to just a single note; as a result, when heard within the over- all counterpoint, it is impossible to connect them to one of the canonic voices, given the absence of an overall profile. We can grasp the charac- teristic qualities of the two principal voices; as for the subordinate ones, it is virtually impossible to give them a clear definition. The most abiding quality, in our perception, is of the total fixity of register within which all the sounding events occur; this quality is sufficiently dominant to give the passage the character of an exposition. And it is this that we retain as the principal criterion, around which we anchor the others.

At times, indeed, the writing is heard in a manner totally opposed to the conception it transcribes. There is a striking example of this in one of Webern's Variations, op. 30.[1] The compositional principle in this variation is extremely simple: a strict canon at a very short distance, the shortest possible, with two voices, each one having equal density – pro- ducing chords of four notes. The constituent phrases have cells, often with just two notes, separated by silences, the silences appearing *inside* the cells to produce isolated chords. It is therefore extremely difficult to follow *one* of the voices, given that continuity in each voice is constantly interrupted, not least in timbre, passing from one instrument to another. The strongest link between the two voices is therefore the relationship of proximity created by such close canonic writing; the resulting rhythmic cells are clearly audible and eliminate from our perception connections between cells belonging to the same voice, which have more distant and weaker temporal connections. Paradoxically, we perceive only a secondary dimension – the distance between the two voices that activates the brief melodic cells, connected and regular in appearance – and not the main structure; we cannot tell the two voices apart, since they are indissolubly amalgamated. It is hard to know if Webern intended this variation to be heard in a way that differs fundamentally from its source, or if this effect is produced through the sheer force of the temporal proximity compared to the elusive structure of the individual voices. Memorising such a passage precisely confirms this way of hearing: to function most effectively, memory latches on to the most explicit gestalt, that which makes immediate sense, and to the extent that one gets the point that this is the real structure, the virtual structure implies it.

Another instance of what one knows to be intentionally ambiguous, creating a global mode of perception – fluctuating, statistical – is what Ligeti called *micropolyphony*. He used this to create sounding objects that are precise in their field of action and imprecise in their contours by confusing, or fusing, their components. In this case, one must contravene the compositional principles by which, by registral stratification, by the individuality or complementarity of voices in their melodic and rhythmic design, one can locate the particular profiles of these voices. We give each voice that contributes to the polyphony exactly the same ambitus, give them an 'anonymous' melodic profile, by way of permutations of the same pitch material, each having a similar density of activity, a similar rhythmic profile, while avoiding any articulatory emphasis. If one plays these voices one after the other, none of them will project a striking identity or appear very different from the others, confirming their anonymous character. These voices, confined to a homogeneous group of instruments – the strings, for example – form an indissoluble whole, each element in a voice similar to another; our perception will be governed by the impossibility of functioning analytically, and will finally be reduced to acknowledging the shared space of all the voices, defined by the limits within which they move. However, one will not identify the actual components of this texture, but rather the extremely unstable virtual texture that emerges, to the extent that the degrees of registral proximity between the various voices are established. One perceives the types of intrusions within the given field of activity, the closer connections between the pitches of each voice being more prominent than more distant connections. One can perhaps speak of a deliberate ambiguity creating a virtual texture clearly perceived in contrast to an actual texture that remains in the perceptual shadows.

Real and virtual writing are not perceptual states that remain rigidly fixed in relation to each other. They are not governed by see-sawing, by incompatibility. To pass imperceptibly between the real and the virtual, it suffices to accentuate to a greater or lesser extent the qualities that lead perception in one direction or the other.

Another mode of musical writing can be used for this purpose, which I call *implied* writing. By this I mean that when a passage is completely worked out and presented, the next stage is to *erase* an element of the writing to leave only certain markers; the more one eliminates the connecting aspects of the writing, the more difficult it will become to grasp the 'why' of what one is hearing. In the end, one cannot but sense an outcome that seems completely accidental, incoherent with reference to any logical principle of writing, whether to do with durations or intervals. The composer can progressively make the cohesion of the writing appear by gradually restoring the elements that control it. In retrospect, one will have the sense that the apparent incoherence at the outset was, in effect, a hidden logic, not directly accessible. Equally, one could adopt the reverse position of a clear, explicit structure moving towards an obscured, dismantled structure that cannot be pinned down: at any given moment, perception loses track, because there are not enough points of reference or things to latch on to, to constitute a whole. How to understand this? One approach would be just to write rhythmic cells grouped in phrases or periods for their entire length, then mark the start of each cell in order to reduce the density of the events that one renders strange by marking only the beginning of each period. In this case, one cannot connect the events one perceives as separate without some perceptible temporal phenomenon that is able to connect them. Depending on which direction one takes, perception will gain traction or lose its footing: one moves progressively from real to virtual writing, or vice versa.

* * *

Essentially, to the extent that I've inevitably been referring to instrumental writing, I've been talking about writing as a conceptual tool, but I am no less committed to the appropriate relation between the conceptual and the instrumental. It is certain that chamber music, if only because of the number of instruments involved, belongs above all to what I would term the transcription of the real, since the use of larger formations, up to the full orchestra, provides better opportunities for sustaining the writing of illusion, acoustic illusion in the sense of multiple ways of listening and uncertainty of understanding. Using a small chamber group, one is subject to the reality of each instrument, and because of the number it is not so easy to create deceptive schemes or perspectives, since each member of the instrumental group preserves its individuality too strongly for it to vanish inside a strictly limited group. In essence, the act of writing involves developing this distinctiveness relative to that of other instruments. Each sounding object, each line is given a timbral identity, according to the typical expressive characteristics of the chosen instrument. Different components can only rarely be fused, or circumstances arise in which an object presented by one instrument can occur at the same time, but in a different way, in another. One discovers different usages, different unfoldings of this type in some of Debussy's late works, like the Sonata for flute, viola and harp, and *En blanc et noir* for two pianos. The two or three instruments embody a single sonorous body projecting different interpretations of the same sounding material and superimposing them in one audible instance. The opposite effect creates a virtual polyphony, when an actual melody 'dislocates' the polyphony, rendering it successive rather than simultaneous as it should be. In certain movements of the solo violin sonatas by Bach, one finds this *streaming* effect that I've already mentioned, when a continuous succession of notes creates the illusion of two different voices through changes of register, the articulative character of the phrasing and the binding of intervals into motifs. This is not a matter of a purely acoustic effect resulting solely from rapid succession and the systematic divergence of registers; it is more to do with a conceptual tool based on writing itself, on the manipulation of motifs and the structuring of lines. Virtual polyphony, the basis of writing, which one can easily reconstruct, which one can transcribe as real polyphony, with separate voices, becomes layered and reduced to a single 'real' dimension which, nevertheless, one perceives as entirely present and dominant: it imposes the apparent qualities of a monody on implicitly real dimensions. Hence, this paradoxical exchange between the real in the virtual and the virtual in the real.

With a solo instrument within a small instrumental group, it is possible to work mainly in real writing, but with a change to virtual writing – and especially orchestral writing – one has the opportunity greatly to expand the field of action and to move freely from one state to another, with all imaginable degrees of transition.

I need rapidly to retrace the evolution of the orchestra and its use, because it is not simply a matter of changes in number or richness. The orchestra has undoubtedly brought in more and more musicians, gaining in sonorous weight; it has increasingly enriched the instrumental families. From the strings to the percussion, the groups have been constantly expanded and homogenised. Up to the baroque period, instrumental grouping was mainly a matter of individuality and specificity. Arias in Bach's Passions or the cantatas were orchestrated to give them a distinctive and unambiguously recognisable sound profile: with the viola da gamba, the oboe d'amore, the violino piccolo the overall atmosphere and symbolism of the piece were fixed by choosing one, two or more instruments exclusively for this purpose. Of course, there are pieces – chorales in particular – that require a fuller, less distinctive instrumentation. But this deliberate contrast in the instrumental writing, the instrumental *signature*, between the different movements of a work will be apparent. You still find traces of this instrumental signification in the concert arias and operas of Mozart. But as we move into the nineteenth and twentieth centuries, the more standardised the orchestra becomes, whatever the reasons – musical or sociological – for this evolution. It is simply symptomatic of the way in which the orchestral instruments have seen their roles evolve. They might still become soloists, developing such-and-such a principal melodic line, but they can just as well return to accompanimental anonymity, being used precisely because of their value in contributing to a collective effect. Their role varies, and only very rarely will a symphonic movement be characterised in terms of its instrumentation. The orchestra thereby becomes a conglomerate of instruments whose roles can vary in importance, and which function according to type – individually, collectively, anonymously. It is at this stage that 'orchestration' begins to be spoken of as a specific type of musical writing, the writing of timbre; Berlioz wrote his *Traité d'orchestration* which, as much as a technical manual, is a manifesto of musical writing. Also from this time instruments became more and more standardised and many of the members of the families found in baroque music were abandoned. To simplify a little, each family corresponded to a particular register; an instrument that expanded the register continued to be used in particular contexts, like the cor anglais or the E-flat clarinet in the *Symphonie fantastique*. In general, however, it was less a matter of particular, irreducible timbres than of combinations of similar timbres. At this moment illusionistic writing begins, of which to my mind Wagner was the most brilliant exponent. Illusion could be founded in different kinds of writing. The beginning of the Prelude to *Das Rheingold* uses a family of horns to unfold a simple arpeggio; as these arpeggios gradually accumulate, one cannot decide whether to focus on the horizontal dimension that generates them or the vertical dimension which is the result of these multiple superimpositions. At the end of the third act of *Die Walküre*, the multiple arpeggiations of the wind chords and the contrary motion in the strings create an oscillation of tone-colours almost literally matching the visual flickering of the flames. The wind chords outline a smooth object, the strings a striated one; superimposing these two elements creates the illusion of rapid movement grafted onto slower movement, an illusion effected by spectral changes in the highly coloured chords. As the orchestra evolved, and its families of instruments were enlarged and enriched, it became possible to *divide* the orchestra according to the needs of the moment, and for it to adopt all sorts of internal configurations without the need to change its layout. Debussy, especially in *Jeux*, and above all Schoenberg in Five Pieces for Orchestra, op. 16, and *Erwartung*, among other works, showed the way towards a particularly malleable and transformational kind of orchestral writing. The best models of such writing are those in which timbre is used to transform dull, monochrome ideas into events with many perspectives, stimulating multivalent hearing. For me, orchestral writing is virtually an analytical tool that highlights musical ideas and gives them resonance and profile. I don't mean 'analysis' in a didactic sense, but as communication, as signal. I aim to reinforce the connections between things that have an implicit affinity and to draw attention to this affinity; I aim to emphasise that each stage of a work belongs to a different level from the preceding stage; I draw multiple images around the same 'fact', which I present in various ways; on the other hand, I expose the scaffolding around which an ornamental line is built. All this, indeed, is achieved by way of timbre; but timbre is put in play by way of writing, to enrich the content. This is because orchestral writing is nothing more than a recostuming of the idea, yet also a development of it. Perception of sounding events is thus completely transformed because, as the functions of the orchestral instruments evolve in importance and in their ability to converge or diverge, so one's perception of this evolving writing is mobile, in constant flux: it does not fix itself into one mode of presentation but has the capacity to follow the appropriate path, just as perspective allows us to penetrate to the interior of the painting. I've said that orchestral writing is a powerful means of analysis, and in consequence, of connecting, clarifying. But while it can establish a visible reservoir of connections that, up to a point, remain latent, it makes the situation more complex and less directly audible. Put another way, this writing of virtual potentialities underlines what the real writing has shown; but at the same time, it sometimes overloads reality to the point of rendering it virtual and becoming, in itself, the writing of a hyper-reality.

1 Variation 2, bars 56–73.

14

Notation, Transcription, Invention
(1991–92)

I have no intention of providing a history of notational graphics, but I would like to consider what it is that graphic inscriptions communicate, and how that communication works. First of all, codes have been developed in different places by the specific communities familiar with their use. Gradually, these codes become unified – even, in due course, effectively standardised. Allowing for certain variants, an entire musical community will recognise them; not only will the eyes have adopted these norms, but musical intelligence will recognise the conventions in use for tempi, ornamentation – in brief, for practical music. This works well for the notation of a number of characteristics, or details, conveyed in instructions, forming part of a collective practice. But the constraints created by these notions cannot do justice to the ways in which the musical text becomes increasingly individualised in expression. A large number of shared and generally accepted ideas will remain, but the nature of works and their elaboration and the individuality of their style demand an increasingly individualised presentation. Individual attributes will tend to prevail over collective significations. To the extent that composers tend to acquire a personal vocabulary, they collapse into confusion when the actual notational signs become properly individual; one individual's signs are different from another's, and indeed can completely contradict one another. There is accumulation, divergence, the proliferation of signs, and the constraints on meaning that come with notation, as in transcription itself, present great difficulties. For instance, if transcription involves unfamiliar and highly individualised objects – special effects for which acoustic definition is difficult, variable or impossible – cases arise where even detailed and precise explications, backed up by samples, will give you only an approximation or an equivalent of what one should be hearing.

Such an evolution in writing has not facilitated decoding and the manipulation of the transcribed elements, and one might say, at certain points, that all conventions other than those of the individual have been abolished. At this point it becomes difficult, even impossible to establish a process of communication, something that acknowledges a tradition. The risks of loss accumulate, and such works, when transcribed, risk being seen as deformed; or worse, being forgotten. Should one therefore adopt more reductive transcriptional codes, whose communicativeness can be relied on, at least for a certain time, or should one accept the risk of not being understood in the short term, if one believes that one's musical creativity cannot be reduced to today's most robust codes? Or, when I invent a code, should I seek to ensure that it has universal potentialities, deriving these from its usage? At what point should an accepted code be employed if the transcription of musical objects is of such complexity that one has the greatest difficulty in realising them? To put it another way, from a certain threshold, should a code of possible actions rather than of results be used?

Let us take two examples of musical objects commonly found today. There are two ways of notating multiphonics, intervals different from traditional tuning with unstable and variable ratios. One can struggle to analyse these sounds precisely and to invent signs that define their pitch in relation to the tempered scale. Many signs have been devised for this purpose, with arrows, double sharps, double flats, etc. An approximation of pitch results, but when timbre brings a perspective to the ensemble that includes dynamic proportions, usually very unstable, such a transcription is only relatively satisfying, because if one has never heard the sound or sounds in question, it is hard to imagine them exactly. These are real objects described as well as possible, but lacking a dimension essential for them to be absolutely fixed. To repeat a term I've already used, one does not 'deconstruct' the object or produce an analysis that makes it possible for any performer to reproduce it under any circumstances. The object and its representation do not exactly coincide; transmission remains aleatoric. For example, if instead of notating the sounding result one notates the fingering an instrumentalist needs to produce it, one risks the circumstance that with a differently constructed instrument, that outcome will be different or impossible. To be completely certain, a double notation is needed: *action* – exact notation referring to a system; *result*, approximate notation but sufficiently indicative. The closer one gets to complex objects, which are not covered by a general, abstract grammar, but which, by contrast, exploit the sounding body in something like real terms, the more one risks an over-elaborate notation, which, through its irritating over-elaboration, invites scepticism.

My other example is the transformation of a sound by means of computer technology. One changes timbre and pitch; one generates rhythmic sequences, chance procedures. Should one notate the result with all the deviations implied in relation to the original sounds? One would end up with a multiplicity of signs whose decipherment would be illusory. In the domain of pitch, all the intervals are non-tempered, and to force them to conform to a tempered scale makes no sense when precision is the objective; but this can only serve as a single point of reference, and approximation is most useful. In the field of duration, where there is no pulsation, it makes no sense to try to notate figuration in all its complexity. In this case, equally, a 'notation for action' is the most useful. One indicates whatever means will diversify a sequence, and the result can be guaranteed. The simplification of notation is not reductive; and if it does not in itself provide a written representation of the resulting sound, it faithfully outlines the facts that make such an outcome possible.

This notion of action notation might seem to have both a new and casual relationship to reality. One has only to think of the notation of transposing instruments to understand how, on a very simple level, the action reflects the resulting sound only through a visual trick. When a clarinet plays a written C, I hear a B flat. I correct through transposition, using a different key to the one I see, and I harmonise the image of what I see with the reality of what I hear. It is the same with all instruments using tablature. A 'notation for action' is therefore in no way strange or uncommon. However, in the most recent instances this idea has acquired unprecedented prominence, and has even become part of the realisation of what is conceived, inseparable from creativity itself, where previously it was only something ancillary, facilitating instrumental practice.

I have already spoken of precisely quantifiable parameters and non-quantifiable parameters that fall outside the grid without always being foreign to it. Here, it is mainly a matter of quantifiable parameters, even if the quantities in question belong to aleatoric categories. It is no longer a matter of manipulating codes, but simply of the resultants which current notation cannot deal with, yet which the ear is perfectly able to detect. I am not happy with the assumption that complex sonic phenomena cannot be aurally discerned if they cannot be notated simply. We should perhaps distinguish two kinds of perception: that of a single object, and that of a sequence of objects or structures.

It is well understood that our musical language survives through placing constraints on the natural resources it gives us. All the labour of instrument-makers down the ages has been guided by the desire to prune away all that is parasitical, to attain sounds as pure as possible across the different families, possessing a basic vocabulary but avoiding particular obstacles. Hence, equally, a purified notation, avoiding particular anomalies, acoustic detritus, a restricted notation for a restricted instrumentation. It is this, truth be told, that guarantees a language. A coherent language cannot evolve without this necessary, indispensable sacrifice, otherwise you risk having only a collection of borborygmic rumbling noises and onomatopoeics. Writing takes account of this reductive tendency and faithfully reflects it, transcribing a purified system, applicable in a general way. When the musical world of composers has needed to include more complex elements, which cannot be made to conform to the restrictions of such a rigid notational system, the difficulties are plain; we hear these complexities perfectly well, but their notation proves elusive. Notation has none of the manipulative subtleties that the performer can introduce, but the greatest differentiation of sounding sources that evade systematic logic and reductiveness. The difficulty for the composer is to integrate complex objects, with their autonomous tendencies, into a disciplined context, at moments when a different compositional level is involved, bypassing what in the end are the relatively straightforward problems of notation.

Besides, is the notation always meant to be taken literally, even when implying a certain degree of freedom? In most cases notation is effectively 'imperative', and allows no freedoms save within very precise limits. But there is also what might be called a 'launching notation', which is above all an invitation to the imagination, the starting point for improvisation. This kind of notation was much in use from the eighteenth to the middle of the nineteenth century; since composers have become so tyrannical in their individuality that there has been less and less room for performers' personal initiatives, other kinds of music – jazz, above all – have seized the baton and satisfied this need for freedom and improvisation. How can notation avoid a high degree of arbitrariness while retaining enough internal logic to support such individual improvisatory arbitrariness? Notation relies on the framework; it simplifies; the rules one is bound by are much simpler, and the routines required by the code allow plenty of elbow room. In jazz, like the stylistically very different baroque music, the text is regarded as an ensemble of conventions in which phrases and chords are regulated, but within the music's structure, which is at once fixed and flexible, performers are able to introduce a decorative, personal quality. Clearly, this can work only at this stage of invention: enriching a certain number of conventions with personal additions must always remain within the boundaries of those conventions. The constraints of this genre are quickly understood – or, in any case, what seem to be constraints as much as incentives. The convention is accepted and leaves a limited but definite space for *interpretation*. As I have often said, it is here that memory is more operative than creativity; more exactly, creativity operates on the remembered materials and gives them new qualities. Paradoxically, the more habit and craft are included in the manipulation of conventions, the more genuine spontaneity will fade within this framework. In effect, one feels literally closed in and free to display one's own fantasy within this frame.

* * *

This raises some more general questions. As it is transcribed, does writing in any way obscure the idea, or on the contrary, at what stage might the idea appear more at home at the heart of a framework it no longer needs to occupy? How many composers have uttered this confession: 'My ideas are too complex to be truly and efficiently notated. I therefore have to simplify the notation in order to be understood, and this – naturally – is to the detriment of my ideas'? Other composers take the opposite view and act accordingly. They move to the very limits of their ideals, and are only marginally concerned with the attempt to find a scrupulously precise notation. In other words, is transcription of the idea compatible with an efficacious realisation? How might transcription influence the idea? Can the idea contradict the transcription?

It is not simply effectiveness, as I've termed it. The issue of effectiveness is certainly legitimate, especially if it is linked to the essential function of the musical gesture, which can be either supported or destroyed by failings in the notation. But beyond finding the most practical solution, we should ask if notation influences the idea, and how it does so. As a result, it is necessary to find different means from those one has inherited. Clearly, education has a role to play in giving us experience of certain conjunctions between thinking and writing, between the idea and the notation. The reservoir of codes that we have inherited is useful: polished by use, if I may put it that way, it is a practical tool and corresponds, especially in the early stages of our work, to the world of our imagination. Since, to no small degree, the desire to compose comes from the contact we have with our musical heritage, our imagination naturally – necessarily – fits itself into regions defined by the lessons we have had. We think by way of them, thanks to them; and these ideas will conform to traditional kinds of notation. Yet new methods are vital when reflection intensifies our awareness of the differences between our heritage and ourselves. Using smooth time, in the realm of duration, where pulsation is no longer evident, or any point of reference to unity, and none of the multiple units of value such unity embodies, implies that we seek out either a spatial distribution that visually represents the temporal distribution we are imagining or an approximate correspondence of values for which an exact numerical correspondence is impossible. Only rarely is it necessary to invent a new notation. Most of the time we can remain content with received devices, because one can quickly fall into notational routines that appear original but which are not, strictly speaking, necessary. The one vital practical feature to keep in mind is to appreciate the different analytical categories separately inscribed into the musical idea on the way to an instant synthesis; to aim to aggregate these different levels in synthesised symbols that reveal all their characteristics goes against not only the basic organisation of the idea itself, but also the way in which we understand it. Such notation creates more problems than it solves because it makes the understanding of ideas more difficult. I know we automatically tend to prefer what we already know and what we want as directly as possible. However, to repeat, instances in which transcribing an idea genuinely requires original forms of notation are rare indeed.

✿ ✿ ✿

In the case of known, familiar objects, which belong to an accepted acoustic code, with universal conventions, transcription is a simple matter, but runs the risk of influencing ideas to ensure that they can be included in a familiar mould without special problems. With new objects, the result of exploration, of new methods of research into the means of production, whose codes are presently uncertain, even non-existent, transcription becomes difficult, imprecise, exaggeratedly complex – complex to the point of uselessness – because one no longer knows how to connect an over-elaborate notation to the object in question. The problem lies in the attention required by the signs defining the object that one wants to communicate – quantitative or qualitative. Familiar signs, newly invented signs, super-elaborate signs, deceptive signs – a large number of solutions are available to the *inventor* who might, in time, become a composer.

The habitual signs need not so much explanation as reflection on their consequences as we understand them. I will not embark on an irrational, unreflective eulogy to these signs, because the retort can be made, even when I've scarcely begun, that I am eulogising habit and routine. This becomes a paraphrase of 'regrets about my old dressing gown', and adapting Diderot to reliably solid traditional notation, I will ask, 'Why not keep it? It was made for me; I was made for it.' But I might add: 'It fits around all the folds of my body without causing discomfort,' adding the explanation that 'poverty is nearly always unofficial'; or I could better reply that traditional writing is a 'rather strict, starchy, stuffy' idea. However, before buckling down to an expansion of methods of transcription, a clear understanding of the purpose of notation and how it operates is needed, in the way it leads us to transcribe what we see into gestures. Historically speaking, notation grew richer at the same time as certain developments in the musical language degenerated, but always to assist practical readability and visual discernment, in the physiological sense of the term, and our capacity for visual analysis. Many fabulous, simplifying reforms aiming to make music more accessible have failed for the simple reason that the eye cannot discriminate between them. For example, in a language where, in principle, the twelve tones are equal and no longer depend on a tonal hierarchy, one dispenses with the whole idea of accidentals – sharp, flat or natural – and each of these twelve sounds takes its place within an expanded field. One thereby clashes with the fact that there is an immense expansion of visible space, and that if one increases the number of lines in one stave from five to seven or eight, the eye gets lost; one difficulty, to do with accidentals, which our hearing easily copes with by way of a mental category of perception, is replaced with another, greater difficulty because it involves a more specific, essentially physical kind of perception. Traditional notation involves different categories of signs which refer to different types of perception, resulting in a global synthesis. Take the phenomenon of pitch: we place graphic signs in a restricted *symmetrical* space – which is extremely important, because this reduces what is read and creates a central line around which everything is polarised; the graphic signs are distributed either side of the axis of symmetry, two times two, or two times three. Spatial discrimination is maximally facilitated by this symmetry, the small number of signs and the two categories to which they refer: on the lines, between the lines. Nothing could be simpler or more effective. Does the system grow more complex and demanding, between the gaps? One adds other signs, which do not change the visual space they are squeezed into, but individually modify in coded fashion, according to general usage, the symbols already employed. Hence the need for those flats and sharps, which fill the requisite interstices. One can equally well use the symbols for quarter-tones, the reading of which need not be so difficult, because it conforms to the same basic principle. Accidentals are read differently, not being part of the vertical space (top to bottom, bottom to top) but part of the horizontal space, being placed before the note; this is perceived rather as a 'notional' modification of a physical placement, and retains that signification whatever the position of the modified sign in the space range. One can further verify the acuteness and limits of the visual by the use of supplementary lines. These lines are not added to the initial range, but solely to the note they define; they do not therefore refer to the overall space, but define an individual space that is strongly connected to structure and distance. Beyond the five supplementary lines, discrimination becomes very difficult. Why? Because the five lines exactly encompass the content of the original span; there is an exact duplication. A sixth line destroys this reproductive precision, and in consequence prevents the faithful reproduction of the basic model.

Each aspect of traditional notation can be analysed in the same way. So it is with the arsenal of durational values that straightforwardly cover the entire repertory of pulsed music and encompass a sufficiently wide territory to cope with anything one could imagine needing to notate. Here, too, by way of some examples, one can see how with the help of simple components one has an infinite combinatorial process at one's disposal, whether by multiplication or by division. An immediate comparison that comes to mind is between duration and money. The point is not the need to multiply the elements, but rather to choose the best elements in order – above or below a standard mean – to deploy the largest as well as the smallest values. Here, too, it is necessary to know the uses one is bringing to bear and at which precise point the eye needs or does not need to analyse them, or if, to a certain degree, instinct can be relied on. In the highly decorated adagios of Beethoven, there is a profusion of demisemiquavers, even hemidemisemiquavers; but if we know, say, the quarter-note pulse, we will know instinctively if there will be sixteen or thirty-two regular subdivisions, and we will also be helped by the melodic and harmonic structure. If, in recent music, pulsation seems absent, and the material using those demisemiquavers is irregular, comprising duple or triplet values, there are two reasons why we

534

might stumble: the eye hesitates to divide the tied groups – into five and three – and has to initiate and convey an analysis of different values for one compared to the other; reading is therefore more uncertain. But in the Romantic piano literature – Liszt or Chopin, for example – where the lines are flexible and the numbers of notes are not forced into regular hierarchical subdivisions (four, eight, twelve, sixteen, etc.), one simply adds a number beneath the signature – eleven or twenty-three – and, always with the help of the harmonic structure, appreciation of the rhythmic figuration is immediate, spontaneous: we have acknowledged the time values without simply taking them literally. All durational problems are thus resolved by a reading on several levels: the profile, whether clearly notated or not, attaching a dimension emphasised to some degree (here again the number five appears to be the limit), is used so that each element contributes, in a different way, towards the description that leads to the synthesis of an object in all its dimensions. As for dynamics, they make use of letters that we read in a different way, to determine degrees and to indicate the distances between these degrees by graphic signs (increasing or decreasing) totally different to all the other signs in use, through their oblique disposition with respect to both the horizontal extent and the vertical boundaries.

Why, when this system seems so perfect, seek an alternative? Because of an instinctive rebelliousness against a system that can seem limited by its historical role, but equally through naivety, a lack of analysis, and also a lack of confidence (in the system?) and a certain degree of reluctance to preserve a system from evolving through expansion. As I have said, wanting to change notation without reflecting on the why and wherefore easily turned into a leap in the dark, and attempts at reform were soon forgotten because they were impracticable or unable to bring real bene-fits. However, from the notation of action, normally, to the notation of result, one could establish a number of links helping to embody musical objects and events in as fitting a way as possible. Clearly, I am refer-ring to quantitative ideas and elements, well aware that this easily turns into the vain pursuit of definitively determining the qualitative aspect of notation. The relentless pursuit of objectivity is shown to be an utter illu-sion, and if truth be told, now seems to us simply a reaction against those subjective exaggerations which, at a certain moment, led their advocates to distorted choices.

* * *

I have spoken at length about habitual signs, and why they have become habitual through supporting and obeying the visible perception of graphic signs, and of the flexibility that reading them allows for. To deal with various recent areas – with that of so-called aleatoric music – I refer mainly to individual choice within a certain field of limitations, like that of a 'floating' music without pulsation, but also with non-tempered intervals, where certain local notational features must be devised.

I am not forgetting what belongs to ensemble music, to the very idea of ensemble, and what will function for a small or much larger group. More and more, our music has been conceived and written to achieve ideal synchronisation or coordination. In effect, forces have expanded – have in every case had the space to expand, to proliferate – at the same time as the language has become, in some respects, more complex. From the moment relations between the diverse written elements (in the most general sense of the term) became tighter, more restrictive, simultaneous superimpositions needed to become more precise, in horizontal as much as in vertical domains. Moreover, when acoustic components are brought to bear on this type of constraint, with some degree of equilibrium, the weight of instruments becomes an essential factor in the creation of a mobile or static sonorous object, and the need for synchronisation appears yet more urgent. If a degree of liberty remains for the interpreter, it is a liberty strictly controlled at the heart of a restricted framework; one has to deal with a decoration, a kind of arabesque, that is basically rather strict; even if the work has a certain pliability, it is a collective pliability, if these two words do not seem excessively opposed. The discipline of the group prevails over the freedom of the individual. But if one wants to relax this constraint from time to time, paying particular attention to all that is individual, and to leave a sufficient margin for individual freedom – coordinated, nevertheless, sufficiently to avoid chaos – then we encounter a novel situation, and the signs do not help us to control it. For example, how to strictly coordinate a collection of players, then give them a degree of freedom, then bring them together again, or rather give them a degree of individual freedom without their losing sight of a collective pulsation? Those are the kinds of novel situations for which it is vital to find a solution. As a result, it is necessary to devise a notation that suits the individual part as well as the collective text.

＊ ＊ ＊

I now come back to the sequence of signs – arbitrary, for sure, but not as much as they appear at first glance. In any case, the name given to them matters less than the function assigned to them.

From familiar signs we went on to *altered* signs and *overloaded* signs, in order to arrive at *invented* signs. Odd terminology, you might think; why not move directly from the well-established to the newly invented? My response is that in the majority of cases, radical innovation is not required, and that one sometimes 'innovates' because one misunderstands the true power of signs, the possibility of extending them or playfully seeking a unique, individual graphic identity. How can one, in effect, imagine the possibilities that present themselves, when the entire notational arsenal is unable to do justice to a given situation? The relevant range of registers must be considered, and use made of both extremes of that potential range. One needs ways of transcribing the vaguest or, on the contrary, most precise notions, creating, as it were, a 'behind' and a 'beyond' for the actual notation. With this aim, one needs signs either less or more filled with meaning.

It is especially in the realm of duration that one finds the former (ones less filled with meaning), and in the realm of pitch that one finds the second (ones more filled with meaning). Quite often the composer will want to use a rhythmic notation that is not strictly metrical but refers to a background pulsation. To notate this, the normal values appear far too restrictive, and whether on account of their familiarity or the connotations they imply, they drive interpretation in a particular direction. It is necessary to find the mediating levels between the strictly metred and the metreless. In contrast to arithmetical notation, we will choose a more abstract notation, a spatial distancing on the paper, to be interpreted optically. In such a case there are two ways of being 'imprecise'; or rather, one leaves the interpreter to choose the distances subjectively in a completely free temporal environment, with no indications of tempo. Here, the eye – a rather primitive means of investigation when it comes to the determination of numerical values – provides a completely free reading, based on an impetus that could be considerably modified by the sonic phenomena it manipulates – their density, their dynamics, their texture – because these durational equivalences can be applied to individual objects (notes, chords) or textures (ostinatos, figures of various kinds). What is already a very approximate visual assessment will become even more awkward and distorted by the musical object as situated in time: this 'sub-notation' of time will therefore be very useful in cases where one wishes performers to *lose* themselves in time to some extent, or at least where tempo will in effect be controlled by another dimension. The alternative consists in providing a scale of tempi, globally or chronometrically calibrated. Globally: a particular passage is measured in a number of seconds; a space comprising a certain number of events corresponds to a specific duration, fixed in time. Chronometrically: a scale of tempi is provided for the events, the unity – that is, the spatial unity – determining the speed at which they are performed. The relation becomes more precise if at that moment you refer to a fixed or variable metronomic beat, not necessarily tied to a particular number of beats per second, as determined by a metronome. In individual performance one notes that 'sub-notation' of duration allows a departure from perfectly precise arithmetical transcription to general indications that are as vague and subjective as possible. For a general location within temporal space it is enough to rely on another element – for example, acoustic, as with the duration of resonance – for any idea of *pulsation* to disappear in favour of the idea of *drive/energy*. Again, I am speaking here only of individual performance. With group performance, whether or not controlled by a 'coordinator', there are many other possibilities: from the confrontation between various diversely controlled free tempi to the subordination of a free tempo through contrast with a regularly rhythmic tempo.

In this case, the length of a free sequence played by one performer might depend on a rhythmic sequence played by another performer or by a conducted group of performers, with the tempo modifications always implied by the performers; as a result, this rhythmic sequence will impose constraints on the free sequence. One readily appreciates what I hardly need to insist on: rhythmic 'sub-notation' facilitates the use of extremely variable tempi, greatly enriching the expressive character in this respect. This becomes possible through the degeneration of familiar signs, removing their numerical symbolism in some way, provided that this does not contradict other symbolic signs, or that one does not use signs already endowed with a different function and a different meaning. It suffices to write notes without stems, to extend them with features of varying length to indicate short or long sounds, and the 'sub-notation' is perfectly convenient for the performer. Perfectly? With a certain familiarity, which will help him to feel, to experience tempo differently; the initial reaction in a similar context/area is to make fairly substantial mistakes in the overall estimation of tempo. If it is hedged about with constraints – other players using a chronometric tempo – one notes that the musician's reaction is almost always to pile up all the events he is allotted to play in the shortest possible time, usually much shorter than has been provided. Correction takes place bit by bit; quite quickly he learns to take his bearings in an unmeasured time – perhaps in a unity – but in which he intuitively feels the fluctuations, an intuition that comes with experience.

We are dealing here with signs *altered* by restricting their meaning. One has not changed them greatly in a visual sense, and yet one has distinctly destabilised the whole subject of musical tempo. That said, one could equally well work with the idea of tempo by making it non-directional, if I can say that, through more traditional means. This means using them in an oblique manner, to contradict the need for precision that brought them into being. There are two ways to achieve this goal. We can provide values without an order: for pitches that are not given precise durations, one provides a collection of values to be used randomly. This collection needs to be large enough to ensure that choice undermines connection, directedness. If the pitches appear in written order, relations are relatively simple; but when connecting a collection of pitches to a collection of durations, relations will be more complex and will naturally have a non-directional tendency. In this case, it is enough to locate traditional objects in a new context to obtain a totally different result. Even more simply, there is no need to use a parallel dichotomy. When one uses values very different from each other, that do not easily reduce to a regular pulsation when juxtaposed, the performer will not, *cannot* employ such a pulsation: different values – irreducible to some degree – ensure this, unless referring to a unity too small to count for anything. The notation has been deconstructed in meaning and function; it has acquired other qualities, for the purpose of which the very essence of the graphics is changed.

❀ ❀ ❀

I have spent much time on *signs* and notation – familiar signs, signs deprived of their original function, newly created signs – because they bear witness to this ambiguous and uneasy relation between intention, creativity and the variety of codes. In a certain sense, creativity is conditioned by codes that are already available and of an appealing convenience. At a certain stage in composers' evolution – even if they find these signs insufficient, overly constraining – they might turn their minds towards well-tried solutions, without adaptation or originality. That is why, at any given moment, one observes the flourishing of various signs that suggest more an immediate utopianism than the deepening of an idea, and which have therefore rarely survived because they are virtually unique to that individual requirement. Often, they have emerged from an incomplete reflection. The interpretation – the perception and analysis – of a sign is subject to specific laws; not to take account of this, consciously or unconsciously, makes the reading of the sign both difficult and illogical; it will be quickly rejected and forgotten. Nevertheless, the composer is often drawn to traditional notation, however suspiciously, to which he can apply, here and there, those so-called 'cosmetic' adjustments that enlarge the sense of the sign while continuing to refer to its normal meaning. Is this an admission of defeat?

540

To what, in essence, does the composer aspire? To write down the unheard. There are clearly two planes on which his imaginative activity can be observed; firstly, knowing how to project his imagination through 'ideal' sound objects according to 'ideal' sonic equivalents, separated from reality, as it were, but nevertheless regarded as sounding entities; the second plane is this sonic reality itself, with the solidity of its use of instruments, their timbre, their possibilities, generally speaking, and also, in more recent terms, the possibilities of technology. There are therefore two kinds of preliminary hearing: one abstract, the other actual. Given that the sounding reality is the objective, which is the synthesis of these two modes of hearing, I think that these two levels of notation, as invention rather than simple transcription, are most often kept separate because developing them at the same time seems too complex, belonging to a different kind of creativity. By this I mean that even when the process of transcription appears to be simultaneous, it takes place, in our imagination, on two levels that refer to different kinds of inventiveness.

We are engaged in creating within an *abstract* universe where, strictly speaking, concretely inscribed sounding objects – written in real time at a given tempo, with associated dynamic markings – no longer exist. If we use traditional pitch notation with, if needed, the elaborations necessary to move beyond the restrictions of equal temperament, writing involves knowing how to judge the connections between intervals within a particular object, to hear them even if they exist only in the imagination. It also involves imagining progressions of these objects, with reference to their construction and also to their spatial dispositions. It is the knowledge of how to arrange superimpositions on various horizontal levels. Notation at this stage is about understanding how to project, in *absolute* terms, the connections possible between *abstract* phenomena, from individual to individual, or from group to group. Naturally, these connections occur at a single moment for separate objects, or successively for linked groupings, but this time is also an abstract time, not connected to a specific tempo for moving forward, but progressing, even if we foresee specific categories – a slow tempo or rapid progression – with definitions that are broad enough to be subject to more elaborate processes later on. It might be objected that we are obliged to proceed differently with percussion instruments, because during our provisional internalised hearing we cannot refer to an *abstract* pitch within a fixed referential system. In effect, since the dialectic of sound in this domain is not the same, the sounding objects provided avoid a predetermined hierarchy, and our expectation cannot function in a similar way. We still think in terms of families, of connections related to register, to short or long durations – of dry or resonant sounding objects; briefly, we think in terms of the most concrete categories, but sufficiently detached from sounding reality as such to be manipulated apart from sonic and durational actualities. So, too, with sounds, invented objects: as our imagination accumulates them, we project their reality through a kind of reductive image and are thereby able to manipulate them and relate them to one another. Within whatever sound world we work, we apply a reduction to the elements we are disposed to put in play and imagine deductions, confrontations, superimpositions and everything that suggests development of the idea. This expectation of a reality extending beyond any concrete object, but dependent on our ability to reproduce it, is one of the composer's most indispensable attributes. His writing will have a much reduced validity if the evolution of connections between abstract sounding objects – potential sounding objects, as it were – is not properly worked out. This internalised hearing is not necessarily instinctive: it can be learned; it demands a very particular kind of imagination. You can quickly tell, when reading a score, if the relationships have been heard internally at the time of writing or if they have simply been devised by the eye, speculatively, without being linked to a definite outcome. One sometimes speaks of compositional virtuosity. For my own part, I believe that this virtuosity can be defined by the fluency with which prediction and manipulation are linked: vertical or horizontal relations, rhythmic notation, judgements about density and texture – all the dimensions of the compositional process will have been properly evaluated, and if the instrumental or technical writing is adequate, creativity and writing will interact in a completely satisfying manner. There will be no difference between expectation and reality.

❖ ❖ ❖

I have been speaking about instrumental or technological notation. In practice, the second level of writing is found here. I have separated them for convenience, but it is clear that writing as abstract and writing as actual can combine, even if they do not always belong to the same creative moment. In works for a soloist or a small group, I would say that not a single gesture, even thought, at the time of writing can realise abstract ideas for instant application. In a preliminary phase, when the composer is essentially concerned with the material he intends to exploit and first devises outline pre-material that is not yet fully coherent, he is not concerned with an instrument save in terms of broadly general categories concerning register or possible simultaneities. But at this relatively simple stage, when expectation is involved, the distance between abstract writing and actual writing is reduced to a minimum. It is different with orchestral writing, which involves other aspects of invention, more autonomous than in the past. Such group writing does not imply an immediate and direct correspondence between image and reality, the equivalence of one with the other, as is generally the case with solo compositions.

Group or collective writing is a writing of illusion, because it can take account of acoustic phenomena on many sonic levels, of timbral combinations, heterophonic rhythms, with which one avoids clear individual identities in favour of an ambiguous, changing collective identity. Identifying components becomes more difficult and less necessary, and that is because with this writing, illusion is the perceptual category that is accorded privileged status. Clearly, invention moves from preliminary dispositions onto a completely different level. It is not simply a matter of orchestration, of instrumentation, but of devising a kind of transformation from a simplified reality into a more far-reaching, more diverse reality. It involves creating frameworks, figures, for dissolving a primordial sonic reality through the prism of multiplicity and difference from the instrumental origins. Given the complexity and variability of textures, it is very rare that one can achieve creative conjunction between domains that are so different yet so mutually interdependent. One might say that establishing a text is creative, while its orchestral disposition is super-creative, an invention on an invention. There is a great difference since, in the first case, the concern is with the construction of objects and their relations, their progression – and to take this further, with the development of ideas, their large-scale organisation, all the fundamental problems of composition. In the process of orchestration, writing involves the presentation of objects, their relative positions, with the composition of textures. As I have said, it is about a notation of illusion; to create this illusion, one needs all the resources available for notation of the real – variable lines, the addition of an acoustic dimension, variable rhythms, schemes that unfold in different ways, images proliferating, etc. How relevant are the expectations of the composer at this stage? Is it like the inner hearing we thought appropriate to musical writing's own domain? Clearly not. It is a matter of completely pragmatic expectations, dependent on education and experience alike. Certainly, it is a craft made from fluency and familiarity, but it is also a matter of imagination and drawing conclusions in relation to what one has heard. There are instrumental constants from which one cannot escape, and despite evolving instrumental techniques, qualities of weight and speed of articulation change little. One needs to develop interactions between groups, the blending of dissimilar components, the interruption of one group by another, the effects of disguise, the use of statistical textures. But I repeat: it is by means of diversified and customised modes of writing that one will be able to create illusions that involve identification.

As to the more recent sound sources, these have to be organised according to the same principles of texture, perspective and illusion. However, these principles are of such generality that you retain considerable freedom of choice as to the manner and extent of their application. If the routines of orchestration are the most familiar, we can easily transfer those principles and concepts into regions where they can be applied, subject to certain transpositions. Masking effects, textural parallelisms, statistical grouping – all are equally realisable thanks to current technology. We can even apply techniques that are practically impossible for instruments, the same resources one applies to different elements, whether in the realm of pitch (intervals chosen with flexible connections, using different scales) or in the realm of durations (changing rhythmic connections, modified tempo); musical objects of which one systematically changes the timbral components by addition or sub-traction, and so on. This is doubtless a less straightforward operation, because the extrapolation we can devise takes place in an area where we are less certain, an experimental terrain where one nevertheless still needs to control and verify the extrapolation. This difference apart, it is no less important that the objectives can be similar between the instru-mental and non-instrumental worlds than it is essential to connect them in a homogeneous and logical manner. Naturally, the methods employed are different, since they apply to different areas of the realisation, but a given work must always display a unity of thought. I insist that in the two worlds, it is writing and its principles that give genuine validity and mean-ing to the sonic reality. So, too, in realisations that are non-instrumental or not exclusively instrumental, one soon recognises products where writing has played little or no part, judging by the reductive quality of excessively linear temporal schemes. Like durations, pitches are not placed in an essential, indispensable dimension. This is not something 'written', or even properly 'thought': we are left with a collection with-out reaching the work. Certainly, a schema of linear successions is not a form. A sequence of events, even if it seems to acknowledge a kind of alternation, or if it is stratified, has nothing organic to enable it to achieve a formal synthesis. I will return later to this relationship between writing and form.

＊　＊　＊

I have already said that the legitimate desire of every composer is, through the medium of writing, to invent the unheard. True, this 'unheard' can be imagined just as well through the rapport established between the objects as within the objects themselves. There are probably two kinds of imagination that do not forcibly coincide in the same composer, but above all there should be no attempt to establish a hierarchical order between these two kinds of invention – one more utopian, the other more pragmatic. Virtuosity of writing in the instrumental domain, for a soloist or an orchestra, is a much clearer phenomenon than the vir-tuosity of writing I have just been discussing. Virtuosity of writing, strictly speaking, is a more specifically conceptual notion that can be properly appreciated only by those who have considered the problem sufficiently to be able to judge it. We can appreciate the richness of the writing because we can grasp it through the abundance of components, the reservoir of interrelations it places before us. But virtuosity of writing, which involves solving a problem with flair, is less explicit; up to a point its character is more esoteric without involving a literal awareness. Though the virtuosity of both instrumental and non-instrumental writing is immediately perceptible, it attracts through richness of texture, by renovating sounding phenomena and by clarifying, one might even say explicating, the musical text.

I believe in fact that good instrumental writing is a kind of *explication de texte*. One understands the basic text better if it is presented to us in terms of a texture (instrumental or not) that helps us to hear articulations, single events, and to understand its phrases, phases and subdivisions through the simple fact that they are expounded in an adequate, convincing, (even) seductive manner. If, by contrast, the textures are unclear, poorly articulated, hesitant, we cannot grasp the text and are unable to follow it; there is a disparity between what we should be hearing and what we actually hear. Naturally, an overly simple didactic explanation will be inadequate for a richly endowed work. It might work with clarification or ambiguity, attract or divert the attention, promote direct comprehension or reinforce uncertainty.

There is no hierarchy within these different types of writing. There is no ineluctable ordering during the process of creation. I've already suggested at what point the two types of invention coincide in solo writing.

The kind of imagination that will determine all the characteristics of the writing can be *abstract*, drawing reality from abstract objects, or *concrete*, starting from acoustic properties that stem from a kind of abstract writing but seek to find an appropriate place in a contextualising ensemble. I have already described the situation, perhaps the most relevant, where abstract invention precedes pragmatic realisation, where the instruments involved – whether conceived abstractly or circumstantially determined – inspire fully realised writing. The qualities of the chosen instrument or group will steer the imagination towards a certain kind of invention, a field delimited by the writing that best realises these qualities. The sonic profile, resonance and rapidity of articulation of the instruments will determine the kind of writing and also the kind of invention. We should not assume that each instrument has so distinctive a profile as to require a very specific kind of writing that ideally emerges to fit it. Instruments have common features; for a long time, writing could be less specific, with timbre playing a less important role, and more interchangeable – its identity was stable, and stability prevailed within timbre itself, one solution among others. One could provide transcriptions, composers adapting their works for other groupings, not to mention distributional transcriptions, where the objective was the dissemination of works that otherwise one would not be able to get to know. These common instrumental features were made possible by an undifferentiated writing, with attention given above all to register, as well as to tension, volume, weight. But beyond these shared characteristics, each family has distinctive qualities demanding a different type of writing, with agility, resonance, sustaining power among the more obvious features.

❋ ❋ ❋

To summarise, the composer's actions can operate in one of two ways: starting from a chosen sonority, drawing appropriate consequences in terms of the writing, which is to say to *abstract* this material in order to subject it to notation; or else to devise a reservoir of relations drawn by the writing from *abstracted* materials and adapt that to an actual situation, creating whatever real circumstances are the best available. This implies, in these two extreme cases, deduction and adaptation; hence the importance of the 'materialisation' of the active agent that is writing.

When starting from a real situation, choosing an instrument or group of instruments – it matters little whether the choice is free or imposed – immediately implies a number of features and constraints that invention, and therefore writing, must take into account. What are these conditions? The most immediate is that of duration linked to sound production. Some sounds are naturally short: string pizzicato, percussion with wood or skin. To fill out time for a given pitch, it is necessary to devise a repeating figure like a trill or tremolo, a repetition in time that compensates for the natural brevity of the basic sound, otherwise one might make use of organised figures that occupy a certain period of time. With percussion instruments producing dry, short sounds, the alternative is clear: one either employs a span of time that is amorphous and undifferentiated, in which case an amorphous figure like a roll will suffice to compensate for the brevity of the sound; or one fills the time span in a more dynamic and differentiated way, presenting a rhythmic profile, continuous or discontinuous, perhaps with features like a dynamic curve, with regular or irregular accents. But in these instances, amorphous or shaped ways of filling out a block of time, the writing has to compensate for what the material itself does not provide. Even in the simplest case, the composition must acknowledge and take advantage of the kind of material it is using. To do this it must appeal, in more or less sophisticated ways, to the concept of writing.

At the other end of the scale, one deals with material that has extended or extremely long resonance. This involves instruments like the piano, harp, vibraphone, etc., and also includes metal percussion, like cymbals and tam-tams. Yet however extended the resonance, it inevitably decreases, at various rates, depending on the nature of the instrument and its registral range. There are two possibilities: either to allow the resonance to continue for its natural span, or to prolong it. In the first case, one strikes a note, or a chord, and waits passively for it to disappear. But what does this have to do with writing? Once no more pulsation is possible – if, in order to initiate a new event, you wait for the ending of the first, when it passes the threshold of audibility – you are following an idea of duration that defines the writing as that of non-pulsed time, controlled purely by the acoustic phenomenon. To counter this and take control of duration, even if non-pulsed, use must be made of an interactive element: writing a figure, for example, however undifferentiated in itself, perhaps a tremolo or a trill once again. This admittedly embryonic example of writing introduces an intentional, purposeful use of time. The material itself leads us to write in such-and-such a way depending on the use we wish to make of it. It is not a matter of the complete, absolute definition of musical ideas, but of the *envelope* they can be placed in: speed, density, ways of extending the sound, resonance, etc. Starting from these very general criteria, there are many possibilities to do with choice of intervals, rhythmic or dynamic profiles; in brief, everything that characterises the essential individuality of a musical idea.

At the other extreme, it might appear that the musical material need not be taken into account at the moment of creation, and even less as the composer prepares and formulates his raw material, separate from the sounding reality. What matters most are issues of generation, intervallic relations, densities, textures, which are created with decisions bearing no *direct* relation to a given *corps sonore*. A text is created that will need to be actualised in many different ways, as the composer chooses. Will he write long sustained chords, as the sonic source for mobile lines? The three familiar families of sounds are at his disposal – wind, brass, strings; just these, since he cannot employ resonant instruments that require a figure like a trill, as already pointed out. Choice of timbre will therefore depend on the character timbre gives to the chord and also its dynamic weight, subject to breathing and bowing – that is, its mode of expression. Does one require a timbrally homogenous chord, or else a mixture of timbres to underline the chord's internal architecture? Should one individualise the components by giving them different dynamic profiles? Should these profiles be located in similar regions, or present strong dynamic contrasts among the components? There are multiple choices, and one must latch onto the idea, once it has actually been devised, and enrich it with many aspects not present at the beginning. Against the situation in which the material imposes a form of writing to be used in such-and-such a context, one notes the opposite circumstance: to create, on the basis of writing, material that develops the idea. Certainly, exploring this coincidence between the idea and the material necessitates reflection about writing itself, but this can become much more to do with aspects of form.

A form can emerge from confrontations between different types of notation. Take the case of vocal writing in relation to setting a text to music: one might privilege syllabic writing, where each note corresponds to a syllable of text; or one adopts melismatic writing, which gives the vocal line priority over the dissected text, one syllable set to a larger or smaller number of notes. The consequences of these types of writing rapidly emerge – in respect of the text, first of all. Syllabic writing – whether slower or faster – promotes comprehension of the text, but it also favours rhythmic pulsation. Melismatic writing, especially when it spreads out the enunciation of the syllables with a proliferation of notes, can inhibit the immediate comprehension of the text, but promotes a richer poetic aura. The writing of vocal polyphony intensifies this phenomenon and can provide it with an extremely secure foundation. Syllabic writing involves homophonic – vertical, simultaneous – writing; melismatic writing implies contrapuntal writing, in various ways. Renaissance madrigals, thinking especially of Monteverdi and Gesualdo, systematically employ this contrast and often use it in conjunction with chromaticism and diatonicism, polyphonic passages being essentially diatonic and homophony being reserved for chromatic progressions. A form is thereby created from these two types of writing.

In my 'Deuxième Improvisation sur Mallarmé' I linked the sonnet form to a kind of vocal writing. The first quatrain uses melismatic writing, the second syllabic – not insistent, however, but very slow: the meaning of the words dissolves to the extent that each syllable is separated from its successor by an increasing temporal distance. For the tercets, their melismatic or syllabic character is determined by the alternations of the rhyme structure. That the musical form derives directly from the poetic form is shown in the most visible way by the kind of vocal writing employed. The instrumental writing follows this alternation and this evolution, but leads almost to the opposite. The melismatic line is accompanied by chords, which highlight the vertical dimension; the syllabic articulation is accompanied by separate features, highlighting polyphonic, linear listening. In this case, the writing creates the form. The syllabic and melismatic concepts are capacious and abstract enough to generate an infinite number of musical ideas, but they are also sufficiently concrete and potent to create an organic development. They are focused, for sure, but in terms of constraints; and they provide the writing with sufficient material – motives for variation – to make it possible to organise a form.

❖ ❖ ❖

But how is it when one confronts non-instrumental technology, or technology that impinges on the world of instruments? Is writing still possible? If it exists, can it extend, complement, elaborate instrumental writing? Certainly, at the outset, using machines deprived of their original purpose, 'bricolage' – in the true sense of the word – reigned supreme. One manipulated a groove in a disc, one worked with a tape recorder and gradually built up a sequence of sound 'events' – if they can be called that – to arrive at a rosary whose beads had practically nothing to do with each other. You were echoing the collages devised by the cubists or surrealists. In the first case, there was from the outset a strong formal logic into which fragments of reality were inserted, reimposing a flexible organisation: material and form reinforced each other thanks to a certain process of selection. In the second case, the poetic quality of convergence, unintended or incongruous, that could be established between the aligned fragments, and the meaning this alignment created – all this contributed to the perception of the whole. If this fundamental cohesion was absent, all that was left was a superficial and arbitrary contact that – once the initial surprise had passed, and it did so quickly – was insufficient to accrue genuine value. This explains the inherent limitations of products based exclusively on agglomeration, where the basic idea of writing was missing. The technique might have been strongly controlled, but the *making* was anything but. And even with technical control, electronic compositions brought to bear a reflection on the rapport between sound, idea and composition. Inevitably, they show their age today, though as compositions they retain their validity. At least, with appropriately unconventional graphic realisation – sometimes entirely symbolic – one can very precisely take account of and study the writing that is essential to them: deduction, articulation, connectedness and coherence.

Today's technology improves on bricolage, but no more or no less than in the instrumental world, where amateurism can prosper perfectly well. On the other hand, given its incredibly rapid evolution, technology offers much richer possibilities for writing; it makes possible writing – the realisation of concepts, that is – no less versatile or flexible than in instrumental writing. The possibilities accumulate according to the speed and suppleness of the means available to the technician and the composer. If those means are difficult to manipulate, restricted in their field of application, the composer feels too hedged in by a mechanical rigidity that fatally impacts on processes that are generally cumbersome and crude; hence the disillusion arising from the fact that if one can devise basically interesting material, the dialectic of its development cannot be placed on the same level of organisation and manipulation as material that is not only simpler, more ordinary, but more flexible. If the two worlds confront one another in the same work, the difference becomes clear, and is more negative and annoying than the bearer of useful antagonisms. If one can work in real time, it is clear that the conjunction between the two worlds, rudimentary of necessity, becomes possible without being to the detriment of either of the two components. Speaking of real time speaks also of restrictions in the domain of timbre, an interesting synthesis requiring time for preparation irreducible beyond certain limits. Nevertheless, the possibilities are enormous.

Two regions are available to composers: what I might call sonic writing; and a writing of *text* and *context* within which the sound is inserted, and to which it gives a meaning. Put another way, this is a notation of instrumentation, of structure, of compositional process in the true sense. Naturally, the one cannot function without the other, but these two notations operate at a different level from that of creativity.

Where the establishment of a sound as such is concerned, there are two main branches of writing: the internal structure of the sound, and the hierarchy according to which the sound will function. By internal structure I mean the disposition of partials, their dynamic profile, the temporal embodiment of their components. It follows that the identity of these objects will be understood as chords whose components preserve their individuality, or on the contrary, as actual sounds to the extent that the components blend into a single entity. Above all, this type of writing is pragmatic, referring to essentially acoustical properties. The more one refines these properties, the closer they get to fusion; the more one distances oneself, the more one approaches accord. It can be rewarding to explore this range of possibilities during the process of composition, playing with the identities of components or with the impossibility of identifying them except with a high degree of uncertainty. One is creating classes of objects more or less close to, more or less distant from, fusion; and one thereby moves from harmonic to timbral language. Starting with this writing, one is creating collections through the progressive transformation of one or several components.

So, too, for durations, where two fields of activity exist: arithmetical rapport between values, and the speed at which this rapport is conveyed. Similarly with registers, there will be correspondences between the internal partials of the object and the scale of intervals that gives them their mobility. The choice of the object and of the scale within which it is located will be determined by the overall writing, the final stage of the compositional disposition. The suppleness and richness of such resources are virtually limitless; the challenge is to find ways of devising individual profiles, of creating distinct categories, of establishing a hierarchy not given by the instruments within a completely predetermined universe.

If one uses an instrument and modifies it with amplification (in a very general sense), one already benefits from a sonic profile, a gesture, as communicated by the instrumentalist, the interpreter. Two possibilities exist, which need not explore the same type of writing: one, more acoustical, is confined to modifying the sound; the other, more structural, extends or develops it. In the first case, one seizes the instrument's sound and elaborates its density or its timbre: one elaborates it by means of a given harmonic complex, fixed or variable, working on its internal components and adding to, or subtracting from, one or several frequencies, the relations of the partials being modified accordingly. But since these operations imply a treatment unit by unit, the result can occur simultaneously with the emission of the sound. There are no changes to the overall structures, and one is merely enriching the sonorous content of each element. In the second case, one seizes a sound or a sequence of sounds and effects a temporal extension by means of a rhythmic structuring and a range of intervals. Each sound in a sequence gives rise to an extension, a sequence deducible from the original and providing a multiplication of the image, as in a hall of mirrors. The strictness of an extension in which the given values do not vary at all impinges on the flexibility of the sequence heard; the extension augments the original, but also enters into conflict with it. And if the extensions are tightly knit, temporally compact, they are able to destabilise the original to the point where one ceases to recognise it, hearing only the consequences it has provoked. One can also inhibit the recognition of the original by way of rhythmic similarities: if the extensions have exactly the same rhythmic character as the original, all the images project themselves exactly according to this particular pulsation, and one cannot distinguish the derived sounds from the originals. Everything I have described applies to transformations, extensions occurring during performance. But one can also appeal to memory. One memorises a performed sequence in order to recall it later in response to a given signal, marking, for example, the return of certain means of expression. This recall need not be literal; it can be transformed, fragmented, by way of variations in presentation that take account of the context that triggers the recall.

If one thinks about associations between the instrumental and non-instrumental domains, one delimits the specificity of each and the nature of the means employed to give them significance. There is no doubt that in an instrumental context, the presence of an interpreter triggers what I would term a *notation of events*, just as the writing best suited to a non-instrumental context would be a *notation of process*; one could also talk of the difference between *gesture* and *state*, when 'gesture' corresponds to the interpreter's decision, and 'state' indicates a stage in the evolutionary process.

For the performer, notation can only be deterministic, creating precise events connected together by a developmental logic that arranges them according to rules of proximity or contrast, of continuity or rupture. The text sequences the events, and the interpreter must give life to that sequence, showing its soundness, its coherence, its necessity. Even when the writing does not attempt to determine a *unique* sequence of events, and allows for some freedom of choice, this does not affect the decision of the interpreter: there is a choice between different trajectories, and events can proceed in one way or another, even with modifications to the profile or characteristics of presentation. On the

other hand, one could say that in cases where the performer provisionally decides on the immediate sequence of events, from within multiple
trajectories, his role is a double one: to decide about succession, and to
present events. Whatever approach is adopted to create musical events,
completely predetermined or completely random, it is the interpreter's
choice what to make available to the listener. The attention, the percep-
tiveness of the listener will – should! – be captured from one end of the
trajectory to the other, an 'integral' hearing, one might say, integrating
the trajectory's events presented in sequence, and where it is necessary
to have heard one to understand the other; a hearing that begins and
ends, and which implies an initiation and a completion. For sure, there
are non-directional moments in the recent instrumental literature, areas
of arrest, more often in works for groups than in solo compositions.
Such moments will be embedded in directional events, even if these are
superimposed as accompaniments. They are, to some degree, *ostinatos*,
freer than ostinatos usually are, more imaginative and diverse; but they
are, in effect, provisional or accompanimental structures, subordinate to
the principal events. One refers to a repertory of ideas sufficiently basic
to be assembled in different ways. In deciding to combine or disperse
them, the interpreter follows certain instructions. One quickly appreciates the variational limits of such ostinatos, not only with respect to
the interpretative abilities of the performer, but also on account of the
rather primitive characteristics of the process. When one tackles more
elaborate methods, one should have recourse sooner or later to a higher
level of writing, and then one returns to the event.

By contrast, non-instrumental writing can rely on process, whether in
the sense that it involves the memory of a machine that can marshal a
large number of elements, or in its ways of treating those elements. The
difference to an interpreter used to working with materials of a similar
kind is that there is no intention, no gesturing, but a purely combinatory
activity. Once set in train, no accident can disrupt this process, whose
only finality is its own. The memory for materials is vast and faultless; it
never loses sight of the goal of generated events whose progress, when
there is an interpreter, can be diverted in a particular, determined direction. This non-instrumental world is highly susceptible to the production

of unique trajectories, specific events in a completely fixed environment. Here, there can be a disadvantage for the interpreter, when the text that is articulated can never be transformed by a gesture. It might have all the properties of a trajectory, but the distortion and accidents that bring the structure to life are missing, or are there only in embryonic form, as the result of simple manipulations of the dynamics of transmission or the distribution in space. Up to a point, these superficial modifications give the impression of an interpretation, but the basic elements of the realisation are not modified at all. On the contrary, if one employs the essential characteristics of the technology proper to the non-instrumental realm, one acknowledges that this is, par excellence, the region of *infinite* processes. With a repertory of materials that can be both immense and multifarious, one can make use of a reservoir of transformations for materials as well as structures, either precisely and definitely or in aleatoric fashion. In this latter case, the consequence of cross-references between the different evolutionary processes will be formally amorphous, if this term can be applied, or in any event, lacking a fixed form. These structures are not meant to be registered in their own right, following a certain trajectory or sequence of events with a beginning and a necessary ending; rather they are blocks of time, understood as without beginning or ending, appearing, disappearing, constantly on the move towards a different state, in a slow progression, indifferent to any idea of forward development, the states not literally identical but with a quality of basic similarity – blank sheets of unfocused, uneventful sounds. One can equally well conceive of rapid amorphous sounds, aleatoric, a kind of flickering sonority where perception is entirely statistical, orientated by the textural density, changes in register, etc. A given kind of structure can be transformed into another by the modification of chosen parameters, as long as there is no modification of the absence of focus from which these structures derive. To realise such musical phenomena, the writing must be very specific; it implies choices from among the various relevant parameters, as well as choices concerning the kind of evolution applied to each collection of parameters. But it does not imply choosing particular resultant events themselves; these emerge from within a particular course of action, but their order of succession, like their individual characteristics, emerges solely from their particular conjunctions. This implies that the choice of parameters and the areas of conjunction should be employed with the greatest possible care, to avoid absurdity or impossibility; the area containing the operations of the various components is crucial to the formation of wider expectations. One is dealing with a kind of *sub-structure*, making self-contained objects, for want of a better term, available to the writing.

Are the two kinds of writing compatible? Does amorphousness exclude fixity by definition, or does it confront it? The two kinds of invention, gesture and state, can indeed confront one another, corroborate each other, respond, be superimposed, in any instrumental or non-instrumental domain. They can be manipulated in such ways, but one should not forget that *gesture*, with all this implies regarding freedom and unpredictability, remains above all the concern of the interpreter, while *state* is the special domain of the machine able to realise it in better, richer and more satisfying ways. The two notations can thereby interact with each other, provided one takes care to derive correspondences from compatible aspects of the given materials. For example, imagine that one wishes to superimpose instrumental writing consisting of successions slowly evolving from a basic sonority – adjacent sound-fields – onto materials presented by the instruments. Obviously, the solution lies in the harmonic field from which both kinds of music emerge. Both fields can be entirely static, no problem; the two worlds can be superimposed without needing to synchronise. If the two harmonic fields evolve slowly, problems of synchronisation can be avoided by organising areas of transition involving common elements between the two fields, these areas having a sufficiently flexible extent. If the instrumental harmonic field changes quickly, it will suffice to give the non-instrumental dimension a field that complements the changes in the instrumental material, to the point where no pitches are held in common and the problem of synchronisation is again resolved. It will be noted that I have had to introduce the issue of duration: to connect gesture and state, duration is indispensable – both properly musical, subjective time, and objective, chronometric time. In one case, duration involves striated pulsation; in another, it involves the smooth, unpulsed evolution of material. If superimposed, the two modes do not interact, and remain in this respect indifferent to each other. But realisations are possible in which interactions are desired and provoked, where the interpreter's gesture is repeated and transformed by the suitably programmed machine. What in this essentially irrational gesture is transformed? Temporal and dynamic relations, and – definitely – pitch relations. These last are the most predictable and the least predicted, and simply require that the other dimensions are recorded and digitised, to give birth to derived structures which retain the personal stamp of the interpreter. These sources will serve to generate circumscribed and determined consequences – progressive modifications of initial rhythmic relationships by equalisation or disequalisation, for example, generating infinitely malleable structures, to the point where another gestural event acts as moderator, suppressing or replacing them. A dialogue is thus initiated between gesture and state, the one depending on the other, the one instructing the other, the two types of writing opposing and interacting with each other.

One must also consider a required notation for virtual writing to render materials visible, without actually fully notating those materials, since they will be different for each presentation of the given structures: the possibility of objects rather than actual objects from moment to moment, under such-and-such conditions, even if the field is precisely fixed. Instrumental writing, in aiming to embrace the aleatoric, and being content to present the basic outlines of sonic events that the instrumentalist will determine at the point of performance, will have recourse to some unusual kinds of notation: reservoirs of pitches, durations or dynamics, which the player can use freely; placements on the page that allow for different routes; the absence of strictly limiting elements, like register (notes suspended in space) or temporal values (replaced by relative distances on the paper). These devices, and many others, have been used in the attempt to escape not only from the constraints and specifications of traditional notation, but also from the reflexes imprinted on the performer by his education. In most cases, one employs a notation of action, not of outcome; this is logical, since if one desires an outcome that changes every time, it would be absurd to notate one outcome and impossible to notate all outcomes. The only adequate strategy is to describe how one is to act in terms of what materials to use; hence the dichotomy, in the notation, between the elements to be used and their mode of use. It is the same with certain types of non-instrumental writing, where one seeks endlessly changing outcomes from encounters with materials. On the one hand, one assembles the sonic elements one wishes to use, with their different characteristics; on the other, one specifies ways of using them, with the necessary information describing and delimiting the field of action. With the notation of complex sound objects, one does not describe them in detail, but transcribes their manner of production, which is easier to read, even if it must then be validated by the ear. Similarly, with virtual textures, one cannot transcribe the outcomes, since this would go against their essentially mobile identity, but one notates the manner of sound production, later verifying the sonic reality, if required, in order to grasp its content. Notation is thus used in a way that goes against tradition, one that prioritises outcomes and leaves the mode of use to be supplied by experience. By contrast, with a notation of method, of action, one cannot be sure about the sonic reality until one has heard the result.

15

Writing and Idea
(1992–93)

How are writing and idea connected? How can the idea construct or transform the writing, not only in the way it is written, but in its priorities, its hierarchies? To what extent and in what way are writing and formal structures connected to creativity? How, in the final analysis, do we recognise, by way of writing, a composer's individual profile, and from what basis, what level of experience, with what degree of distortion can we become more familiar with a composer's tics and mannerisms? What makes it possible for us to identify a particular language in relation to certain general features of an epoch, however individual these might be? In addition, what are the common features in our time, and can these truly exist, in a latent state, uncodified, or be adaptable in the form of a diluted code? All these questions are currently being posed, and they may receive no completely satisfactory responses. Perhaps they do not require definitive answers. Yet it is still interesting to ask them, since they touch on what is probably the most intangible aspect of personality.

What one can assert, at the start, is that shared codes have a growing tendency to dissolve in favour of personal codes to which the qualifier *shared* would be difficult to apply. The last attempt at a shared code had an astonishing but brief flourishing. Twelve-tone serialism appeared as the only effective cure for an alarming anarchy; it made a *serious* claim on the *future* (I insist on those two words) in the face of the short-sighted concoctions of a system on the verge of extinction, ad hoc efforts that succeeded only in flaunting a certain *past* while reducing its identifying markers to an absurd degree through routines deprived of necessity. In the face of deficient memory, laziness and facileness, the attempt to restore sense and vigour to the laws that governed the language seemed a perfectly judged solution. Sadly, this solution bypassed many problems, mostly without trying to deal with them adequately, either ignoring them or appealing to ancient laws in order to prop up and justify new ones. After noting the lacunae in such systems – combining excessive prescriptiveness with lack of control – one concludes that the deep unity of a work does not wholly depend on a unifying principle that is too vague and yet also too strict. One vital dimension is hard to find in such a system: harmonic control not simply as a control by numbers, but acquiring justification through the perception of actual objects, and also by the relationships that govern them. This demanding reality has to be borne in mind. Two reactions are possible: either rehabilitate the old system while laying waste to its internal logic and preserving only disconnected aspects; or pay close attention to acoustic phenomena without oversimplification, and without close conformity to the relations that made the erection of the structures and hierarchies of the tonal system possible. In either the longer or shorter term one turns eagerly to individual systems, without claiming to create universal laws. True, in the second case – that based on the analysis of acoustic phenomena – one has noted similarities between sounding universes. But these do not set up a collection of generally viable procedures/codes. The problem remains comprehensive, and presents itself immediately to a composer when he begins to *imagine*.

In effect, a musical idea – of whatever sort – never emerges context-free. It proceeds, even in its most elementary guise, in the form of a language. In practice, however, this language does *not* exist. Intervals exist, a world of intervals that no pre-existing rules can organise. If this world is organised, it owes this to our memory – our memory of other models, or of particular models. It is only partly true to say that a reservoir of intervals is not directed to the moment of its use, because we rely on a whole system of references that allows us to orient ourselves, even if we do not do this consciously. To speak only of pitches, it is certainly the case that the more we distance ourselves from an existing collection by, say, a semitone in synthesised complexes (the most worked on but the least familiar), the more difficulty we have in composing spontaneously; as orientations become more and more elusive, the idea remains inchoate, an ideal, utopian entity, and we do not know how to manipulate the tools capable of realising it. As a result, the idea depends on the intuitions we are able to derive from the material. The better the material is understood – the raw material, that is – the more rapidly the idea, the scheme of relations, however primitive it is, will reveal the means whereby we can experience this material. With familiar assimilated material the idea still depends – from the outset – on the functions and extensions one decides to apply to it. To take an example that is purely classical, a fugue subject will have neither the profile nor the character of a sonata-form first subject; and the further one moves from models or stereotypes, the greater the divergence in modes of construction between musical ideas destined for different functions.

But I will revert to the gradual elimination of generalising codes that have made the musical idea's writing a contributor to the establishment of a musical language. Without attempting to summarise our entire musical history, it appears that the most prominent general feature is the increasing individualisation of thematic material. The further back in time we go, the less apparent individual attributes are – or perhaps it is that, because of distancing, we are unable to discern them in the way contemporaries would have done. As it is, we are usually aware of anonymous shapes, formulaic outlines and even highlighted episodes that are indistinguishable between one composer and another. As time passes, one becomes more aware of strongly defined ideas, devised specifically to be retained in the memory. In Wagner, this tendency reaches a seismic extreme: when he uses detached segments of those ideas, one might revert to a confusing anonymity – we note again the risks of fracturing, of the primacy of one interval in the development of ideas. The individualisation of musical ideas in the true sense – motives, themes – remains the most brilliant feature of the twentieth century, until the radicalisation that came with serialism, because for a relatively brief moment there was no genuine difference between the essential idea and the structure that had brought it forth. Early in the twentieth century, especially with the Second Viennese School, a kind of constant proliferation of musical thought led to a certain anonymisation of ideas. No idea was more prominent than any other; at best, one might observe preponderant *phases* in ways of 'speaking', and therefore of writing, in relation to others. It should be remembered that such works were often extremely brief. (Works from ancient times were also generally short; longer duration required stronger points of orientation, evidently.) Nevertheless, there was the risk of an evenness in the compositional continuity, which could be countered only by two external characteristics, two envelopes: density and timbre, in association with a third, dynamics.

During serialism's most radical phase, sometimes called 'total' serialism, it is clear that the musical idea was simply the *working out* of the underlying structure. Creativity as such was found more at the heart of the sub-structure than at the heart of the musical idea itself. This did not come about by accident or default: the aim from the start was to eliminate thematicism and to have entities imbued with all the requisite characteristics from the different and arbitrarily separated fields of action of sound (pitch, duration, dynamics, contour) develop mechanistically. Where is the domain of the musical idea? Nowhere, because it is deliberately avoided. What remains, as already said, is the *working out* of a *plan of action*: the application of completely organised structures, defining a profile and establishing a trajectory by means of an arbitrarily superimposed array. Clearly, the primary criterion of this active process is register: low, high, medium; wide or narrow, fixed or mobile – things that clearly leave considerable room for freedom of choice. The second criterion is density: one of many serial layers will determine the form of the piece, and that too is entirely independent of the composer's choice. Therefore, there is in such a work (like 'Structure 1a' from Book 1 of my *Structures* for two pianos) a stratification completely free of choice or non-choice. The musical idea does not exist, because the succession of twelve notes is entirely the result of a similar succession of durations, dynamics and textural profile, which are imposed – superimposed – on it; a completely different superimposition could be used without loss of meaning, since meaning is solely the outcome of this mechanical combination. If the elements of the musical idea are rooted in total anonymity, they recur in the trajectory established by register and density!

This is an example of a negation that can exist only as an extreme instance. Subsequently, I have sought to include free spontaneity, the power to make decisions, at the heart of the design from the outset, so as to be able to shape the idea with maximum flexibility, and also to achieve an organic connection between the structure (the potential elements of a language) and the idea itself.

First, however, one must consider the nature of the musical idea, how to work creatively. Does one immediately need some kind of vocabulary at one's disposal to bring an idea into being, and can this vocabulary emerge without the support of an entire grammar? I like to distinguish between virtual idea and real idea – between projecting a generalised idea containing the means of its realisation and a fully realised, restricted idea that can proliferate, expanding into a generalised concept. I see these two categories as equally valid, since the idea can run its full course in either case: from the local to the global, the totality to the cell. The global idea, in virtual form, has no need of a precise vocabulary; it can be the idea of a trajectory, the evolution of an envelope, the sequence of transitions necessary to pass from one type of musical material to another. In this case, the vocabulary can be what one finally finds in its functioning details, because to make an actual transcription of a trajectory from one state/type to another, one needs a very specific tool. But the opposite is also true: if a musical idea is rich in potentialities, it might be worked on in the opposite way; developing its different potential germs, one needs to discover an overall profile by which to order them, and the form must appear as the outcome of a process of expansion and proliferation. In this latter case, the idea needs to be placed in the frame of an adequately explicit musical language; without this, the development of potentials runs the risk of being chaotic and incoherent.

I will therefore begin with this particular instance, in which the musical language needs to be put in place to lead to the formation of the musical idea. Also, this establishment of a vocabulary can occur without a clear sense of how it might explore the idea's potential: that separation seems essential if one wants to retain an indispensable degree of freedom. That might appear paradoxical, since one can no longer rely on well-established and accepted systems or codes to seek out a collection of materials that makes it possible to proceed in a more certain and secured manner. Naturally, the method that involves the consistent development of a system securing the coordinates to channel creativity and ensure its sustainability is not so simple. One falls back on the certainty assured by the series, which is supposed to produce an entire system more or less rooted in numbers, along with transposition, permutation or interpolation. It is not essential to construct an entire system before entering the field of application known as writing; to do this could even be a handicap, since the idea might easily lead one to abandon a system that proves too narrow, too unilateral. The balancing act between the rejection of speculation and the application of the idea as such, extended by systematisation of certain consequences, turns out to be the most engaging and rewarding method, permitting accidents and opposing the false unity imposed by an obsessively singular system.

But speculation about what I might call, to simplify it, the system might help, even encourage one to devise musical ideas that might not have occurred to one without this provocation. It certainly counters the most obvious mechanistic tendencies of systematisation, and also encourages caution with respect to those inbuilt automatisms that would tend to appear were it not for the intervention of what we might term a foreign body, requiring consideration of other non-spontaneous and unexplored possibilities.

Why erect, at whatever level of sophistication, a kind of array of co-ordinates? To make the birth of the idea possible, placing it in space and time, giving it the possibility of developing within a given *context*. This context need not be goal-directed, since it can be reduced to a simple slice of a sounding continuum defining a fixed succession of intervals; the power of this pre-organisation will be more or less constraining depending on the degree of precision given to the coordinates. If I start from the division of the continuum by intervals conforming to a specified structure, like Messiaen's modes of limited transposition, the melodic ideas that use such modes will be composed within a precise framework; harmonic relations will also be clearly defined. In this way, the idea can be sewn into a network of connections that can be applied to it in order to develop it, relations that can be used to set up a collection of functionalities. This is a concrete embodiment of the idea free from temporal specifics. Two dimensions remain to be provided: that of time – numerical, proportional relations of duration or rhythm – and placement in real time according to decisions about tempo. Two options arise: either a dimension is kept free, unconstrained, or else it is fixed. When free, placement in time involves following spontaneous divisions, either with or without an underlying pulsation. When fixed, the relations between durations are drawn from an array of time values, devised separately, which give definitive signification to a succession of intervals. Those same intervals can acquire a very different expressive power if they are projected through such-and-such a rhythmic structure, at such-and-such a tempo. But it must be emphasised that the musical idea does not necessarily come into being in a form where synthesis will necessarily operate between these two essential factors – pitch and duration. The two networks can be conceived and prepared at different stages, by different methods, and come together as the musical idea takes precise shape, when they then contribute to other such indispensable elements as contour, dynamics, timbre, etc.

The network generates the idea, or at least furnishes more general aspects of identity than a simple slicing of the continuum by a given value. This array already suggests constructive elements enabling the idea to evolve in a context of well-established potentialities. In this respect, the example of Elliott Carter seems to me very representative, because the source materials he chose range from a single focused interval to an interval collection of limited size whose varied combinations can provide a considerable number of similar objects. I use the word 'object' intentionally, since no aspect is as yet privileged; I might also use 'aggregate'. These can be read vertically, with just one presentation in a given register; in that same register, there can be other ways of reading this intervallic construction, the *distribution* of these aggregates, as I like to call it, providing freedom of choice within the overall constraint of the source collection. Naturally, variation is also possible with respect to registers; that is, with the notation of real intervals that at first have not been subject to any particular constraints. With regard to aggregates, one notes that the established array is rich and strong, and that the idea is, as it were, *preconditioned*; its meaning depends on other qualities – free or fixed – that can be added, but it is conditioned by the array of coordinates pertaining to the idea. With Carter, as well as source collections one also finds less constrained ideas, with preponderant intervals or with missing intervals. For example, in the vocal line of 'O Breath' (*A Mirror on Which to Dwell*, movement no. 6) all the intervals are used except the perfect fifth and the minor seventh, while – by contrast – the instruments emphasise these two intervals. As a result, the musical idea – in the most general sense – uses a sufficiently generalised strategy to avoid inhibiting creativity, yet sufficiently strict to lead in the direction of characteristic regions. Durational constraints are added, and used consistently; also, more exceptionally, the determination of rhythmic values in relation to speed. It is in this way that temporal relationships parallel such durational features as three in the time of two or five in the time of three, etc. Stravinsky showed the way in *Les Noces*, where many of the musical ideas equate to a precise initial pulsation. Carter sets up his array of metronome marks in a more complex way, and the entire musical idea is necessarily subject to a similar array. Here, too, one can observe that the constraints are both strong and loose: every thought and every development of a thought is subject to a given tempo, but the relationship with duration, the rhythmic structure, is completely free. With Carter one usually finds that with the conception of the idea the range of conditions – some precise and constraining, others more general and non-restrictive – that presides over the elaboration of a richly interactive process, and allows the idea to evolve within a dedicated space, helps it to be perceived.

I would add that while these resources obviously have the potential to proliferate endlessly, the composition uses only a small proportion, with characteristics that provide clearly stated points of orientation. Born of the coordinates, these functions do not involve a disorderly proliferation, an uncontrollable multiplication of possibilities. On the contrary, the more one has foreseen the array's possibilities, the more circumspection is brought to their use, employing criteria of audibility and perceptibility. Before continuing my investigation into the origins of the musical idea, I want to underline how one is more and more concerned to integrate the problem of orientation. We have seen that privileged intervals might be used, and also privileged orderings of intervals; the greater the variety of objects, and of aggregates used, the more attention can be given to their location, and to the features they need to display. This means that one rediscovers stability and fluidity as permanent criteria. Contexts in which registers are fixed are easily spotted: memory latches on to them, noting many of their characteristics and keeping them in mind. If one perceives another period of stability, a moment of immobility, the first aspect recalled as the basis for comparison is indeed stability; and so these two stable passages, though separated in time, have common features – a note, a chord – which are quickly remembered; memory makes the connection, especially if one uses the same frequency, which can act like a reflex. In episodes that are less stable, perception loses its props, as it were, becoming mobile and uneasy until some means of orientation is provided. Is this not exactly what the world of tonality provides, this increasingly forceful alternation between stability and instability, in language as much as in form?

It therefore seems to me that the essential question is not which grammar one employs, but rather the way in which one organises stability and instability. For the perception of form, this can involve the use of perceptual orientations, as I have just said; with the use of objects as such, the elementary vocabulary and grammar, it is the acoustic rapport that should play the main role. Since the Second Viennese School, one has often heard of the emancipation of the dissonance, and one has treated consonance and dissonance, traditionally set in opposition, in the same way. Indeed, it has even been exaggeratedly argued that there are dissonances that are more attractive, more seductive than consonances. This supposes that one can separate oneself, intentionally or not, from basic acoustic relationships, or at least that one can rely almost exclusively on instinct or the desire for order. Acoustic relations remain the essential basis of perception, to which many familiar enculturations can be added or superimposed. Intervals not fixed by temperament, and of which we have no regular experience, can appear to deviate painfully from the norm. Similarly, we might be struck by certain Asian examples of the use of intervals for precise purposes, making distinctions that, in our culture, are not considered precise. These enculturations are not admitted, but accepted as such, contributing to our 'deformation', and it should be asked if the rapports might promote the clearer definition of the objects employed, and their properties, so that they can be integrated, with suitable flexibility, in one's vocabulary and grammar. If the total integration of sounds whose acoustic properties we can analyse today is a utopian dream, because our instruments cannot realise them, it is still useful to take note of the degrees of tension that govern intervals, and to consider carefully the registers in which these intervals are presented, since rapport among the frequencies in question is essential to activate those greater or lesser tensions at the heart of a sonic aggregate. From simple diatonic relations to the most extended chromatic associations, from the closer or further placement of intervals in the natural harmonic series, one can determine the degrees of tension or balance that can be defined as dissonant or consonant, if one removes from these terms the functional associations they formerly possessed. But even if these characteristics cannot serve to determine a complete linguistic hierarchy – because of exaggeratedly simplified workings – it is undeniable that this category of very specific musical objects must be taken into consideration. It will help to ensure a better definition of the place and potential of the musical idea.

I will briefly repeat the necessary distinction between horizontal and vertical writing, types of writing long set in opposition to each other. It is true that over the centuries a kind of give-and-take has been established between the two types, the one coming into prominence as the other recedes. To some extent harmonic complexity engenders a horizontal anonymity governed more or less by laws of smooth progression – 'good voice-leading', as academic language puts it. Even with extreme complexity strict counterpoint involves a certain harmonic anonymisation, restricted – if codified and managed – to summarising and repetitive rapports. For sure, today there is no shortage of accumulations of horizontal lines whose superimpositions are uncontrolled; it is no longer a matter of counterpoint, where the lines are *responsible* to each other, but of accumulations whose conjunctions are subject only to chance. With no satisfactory interaction, they evade the issue, except with static superimpositions; in such cases, one's perception establishes an exact rapport between the components of the different melodic shapes. Since the stability of these rapports is reinforced by the fixity of each layer, the *distribution* (of external character) can be as mobile as one wishes, and will be grasped without difficulty: this is the kind of superimposition of ostinatos and their intrinsic rapport we find at the beginning of Stravinsky's *The Rite of Spring*.

But there is more. Recall that the grand utopianism of the Second Viennese School, and Schoenberg in particular, was absolutely explicit about regarding vertical and horizontal as different projections of a single dimension, organised according to the same generating principle. Comparisons have often been made with painting, and especially with the transformation of objects in cubism: no more high and low, front and back, no more perspective in the normal sense, but a synthesis of these points of view in an object analysed and reconstituted from several simultaneous angles of vision. This *integrity* of the object applied to the musical language, or at least placed in parallel with it, has the ability to seduce; and even if the cubist enterprise and the promulgation of the series have literally nothing in common, one can appreciate that Schoenberg's big idea was to free the musical object from the weighted-down rootedness of traditional harmonic perspectives. A certain degree of mysticism was associated with this liberation, as found with Swedenborg and Balzac's *Séraphîta*: musical space shrugged off all the constraints of the dimensions that had thus far been imposed on it. A law regarding the unity of musical space was also formulated: 'The unity of musical space demands an absolute and unitary perception.' To clarify, Schoenberg goes on: 'In this space, as in Swedenborg's heaven (described in Balzac's *Séraphîta*) there is no absolute down, no right or left, forward or backward. Every musical configuration, every movement of tones has to be comprehended primarily as a mutual relation of sounds, of oscillatory vibrations, appearing at different places and times. To the imaginative and creative faculty, relations in the material sphere are as independent from directions or planes as material objects are, in their sphere, to our perceptive faculties. Just as our mind always recognises, for instance, a knife, a bottle or a watch, regardless of its position, and can reproduce it in the imagination in every possible position, so a musical creator's mind can operate subconsciously with a row of tones, regardless of their direction, regardless of the way in which a mirror might show the mutual relations, which remain a given quality.'[1]

It is not, therefore, a matter of anarchy in the accumulations I have spoken of, but one must seek out an underlying, unique order, like that which governs the universe. Here, it seems to me, there is more religion than acoustics, faith than critique, yet the idea of a profound linguistic unity can be intensely seductive! Even if one considers this innovation from an entirely rational point of view, it is certain that the spirit can be satisfied only by the desire to reunify by the same logic the two fundamental aspects of musical language. Utopianism apart, the unitary method brings order to what otherwise might seem a precipitous flight into chaos. All that was once empirical and small-scale; and to some degree the models were not lacking, having already explored how to unify musical textures by the use of a virtually permanent thematicism: the German tradition from Mozart to Wagner and Mahler, and not forgetting Beethoven, is rich in such examples. (It is worth noting that such works, or such moments in works, occur almost always during late creative periods.) After the Second Viennese School, one seized with enthusiasm, and perhaps insufficient reflection, on this myth of unity, so that it appeared to have as much seductiveness as falsity. If in some instances one moves from horizontal writing to vertical writing by way of a kind of diagonal motion, a kind of shaping unfolded over the span of the musical object; if one can work with a certain extension or contraction of time in connection with the object (from zero time – simultaneity – to a period of time); if one can also give a melodic line a kind of latent harmonic identity (such as one finds in some of Bach's solo violin sonatas, for example); and if – in the opposite way – one can deploy a harmony preserving its intervals, while challenging the placement of those intervals as such, a serious problem emerges. One must accept that if identifying a transformation becomes impossible, this could be a minor fault, if this was not the intended expressive goal of the shift from one dimension to the other; but one should also be aware that in contradictory instances where the modes of writing need to control each other, the myth goes by default, because the apparently rigorous unity reveals its basic failings. If the writing is essentially horizontal, the vertical relations that result are utterly anarchic; if the writing sets a melodic line and vertical support in opposition, this can work only by way of that complementation of total chromaticism that has no basis in acoustic logic; if, finally, the same aggregate moves from one style of writing to the other, as from vertical to horizontal, and if the intervals are not rigidly preserved, as in an abstract matrix, the functions become entirely different and the intervals become incompatible, to the extent that they belong to one or other style of writing. It is in this latter case that the concept of unity ceases to be pertinent.

Empirically, one might seek for specific points of orientation on the basis of aural experience as well as acoustic analysis. I do not believe, as far as I can formulate this, that there are genuine laws by which vertical and horizontal writing can achieve a new symbiosis. But the control of vertical relations has become a topic of increasing concern. The danger remains of their being entirely self-referential, or of being placed at the first level of language. While in the harmonic language of classicism, types of chord and the rules governing their progressions played a crucial role in the structure of the language itself; there were many examples of transition, conflict and ornament that brought interest to this language, gave it great potential for renewal and great expressive power. By this I mean what one calls suspensions, anticipations, passing notes, etc. All this has enriched acoustic relationships with phenomena foreign to – or distant from – pure acoustic structuring. To me, the most interesting language is that which takes account of the acoustic foundations of the sounding objects we employ, but which resists and obstructs those foundations, foreign bodies that fine down, infiltrate and are absorbed into the acoustic components. The tension between horizontal and vertical writing must be preserved; without it, one would end up writing nothing but arpeggios, such as one sees in lesser works with accompanied melodies, particularly in the late nineteenth century. One notes the absurd absence of tension and interest in those insipid and repetitive arpeggiated shapes; the harmony as such can indeed be adequate, as interesting and well conceived as in Fauré. But the presentation – the *shaping* – is inert and thus devoid of interest. Returning to our present-day problems, if we have a mind to refer to source materials where the sound is less 'pure' than in what we call the 'classical' tradition – if we call on synthesised sounds that are natural or complex – harmonic control will not be the same, and might lose all sense, given that the material cannot be controlled in this way. To tell the truth, if one tackles this complex material, with its self-referential tendency and resistance to becoming subject to a context, one can ask if the concepts of vertical and horizontal writing still make sense, and if it is not preferable to speak of relationships in terms of proximity or distance. Given that these are different by nature, control itself should change its nature, discover other criteria, other methods. In works that use such materials, and separately from the value of intuitions as such, it is striking to consider how often these materials have difficulty in becoming part of a dialectic, remaining prisoners of an elementary juxtaposition, and how the composition resists them. It is difficult, even impossible, to unearth the elements these different objects hold in common. If one superimposes or combines such objects with more classical features – instrumental, for example – one can fully appreciate the difficulty of fusing such elements, of bringing them into meaningful conjunction. This is not just a matter of the quality of the objects as such, and of the quality of their diffusion or elaboration; there is also a fundamental issue with the heterogeneity of the writing.

The truth is that the greater the distance from classifiable, what I call 'de-realisable' objects, the less applicable are categories of writing from past times, which defined the musical objects of our Western tradition. Even at their most extended, these notions ended up having no connection with what they professed to control. A new kind of writing was bound to emerge to suit our demand for stability, not to mention logic. But to connect two unclassified objects, as embarrassing for their individuality as for their heterogeneity, requires something other than simply clearing the decks by pretending that pitch is no longer the prime carrier of meaning it was once heard as. The emphasis will be placed on other kinds of connection, temporal structures in particular, and external formal processes like stabilisation or repetition. This is to pursue the problem, not solve it. Perhaps one should address the writing of objects as such and attempt to find the solutions guaranteeing both the nature of the objects and their sources. When I spoke of establishing a network of coordinates, the basic acoustical problem prevented the establishment of a coherent organisation, because it concerned ideal

573

objects, abstracted from reality, just as in geometry one talks of a point, a line, a scheme without precise identities. Category is the only characteristic of these objects, and they can be realised within many different acoustic contexts. With objects that are not easily reducible, or when one creates, through synthesis, complex objects whose structure cannot be contained in a simple ideogram, and whose individuality resists tidy classification as words like 'hierarchy' or 'transition' lose their meaning, is it possible to establish a framework of coordinates? Does writing acquire a totally different signification? Since the establishment of rapports, except for hierarchies in the traditional sense – because the objects are distinctive, even when placed side by side – suggests connections or ruptures according to particular characteristics, it is necessary to introduce acoustic writing, something completely absent in the case of 'ideal', 'de-realised' musical objects. Everything subsequent – profile, dynamics, components – needs to be included from the outset. The networks apply to a more developed level of writing and have freedom in relations between objects only to the extent that one can create a minimum of correspondences between the complexes. This remains difficult to evaluate, given the difficulty, even impossibility, of establishing audible and convincing connections. It should not be forgotten that comparable phenomena, more or less unclassifiable and as a result unable to be used in the same way as elements in a traditional hierarchy, can nevertheless function from other perspectives like moments of articulation, points of division and other exceptional events. At this moment they are uniquely detached from their normal function and become part of another design with a different type of writing, playing a punctuating, explicatory role. They are integrated in such a way that they can preserve their distinctiveness without damage, if that distinctiveness justifies their presence in an alien context. In this way, the two types of writing can refer to each other, reinforce one another, while preserving their natural opposition – one based on hierarchy and connectedness, the other on separateness and exceptionality.

✻ ✻ ✻

Reverting to the notion of the musical idea's preliminary framework, I am explaining – after dividing the continuum according to modes and the use of specific aggregates that can even be reduced to a single interval – the challenge of creating order through the series, and also the now-historical phase of the twelve-tone method. This did not just provide a resource that was sufficiently precise and sufficiently vague to allow the musical idea to emerge. The Schoenbergian series was born from thematicism, and implied thematicism; as I have already said, it was both an infratheme and a supertheme. All other dimensions, accordingly, were subordinate. This was the general position for Schoenberg, and also for Berg, though he used it with more freedom, even casualness. Webern's position was to reduce this excessively cumbersome 'theme' to small, self-replicating cellular fragments from within the total chromatic, creating prototypes easily manipulated by the musical idea. This idea then became, in many cases, completely synonymous with the structure of the fragment. If one retreats from such clarity, it is in order to rediscover an even greater clarity, a move comparable to distant modulations preceding the return of the principal tonality. The structure becomes the idea's essential foundation. This is because one uses maximum simplification to ensure complete memorability.

Today, it is facile to criticise and reject a process that might seem excessively reductive and that – intentionally or unintentionally – takes no account of certain crucial phenomena that reference the dominant utopianism of the proposal: horizontal = vertical. One could equally well observe that any array as strict as the twelve-tone series merits the same critiques: Scriabin's mystic chord, for example, creates equally unilateral and restrictive consequences, obstructing free spontaneity by providing no exit strategies and requiring exaggerated and unviable contortions to restore some freedom of movement. At the same time, many of the features of writing – the more mechanistic as well as the more intuitive – were involved in the search for genuinely intuitive ways of using mechanistic processes. All this is clear today, after years of experience and polemics; but for too long this pragmatism was opposed only by generally feeble models, and what Adorno called 'restorers'. The problem was how to escape from this state of affairs, and not to slide back into it.

Various lessons can be learned from the Second Viennese School – less to do with the first level of writing, which specifies the setting up of an array of coordinates prior to actual composition, more a matter of the organisation of texture, of 'text'. For sure, contradictions arise between the desire for variation and a fixed point of reference – such as archaic forms like strict canon with exact imitations whose use now seems ambiguous. Nevertheless, the essential point is this: secure linguistic coherence with the constant application of clearly defined processes. Undeniably, the results are of uneven stylistic quality; the definition of coordinates and the ways in which they are used are not enough to define a style, and this is the fate of a total system of coordinates that is simply a condition, nothing more. With the strengths and weaknesses of particular compositional realisations, it is the principles that need reasserting in order to study usage, develop a course of action, create a rapport between hierarchy and spontaneous freedom that can be included in the actual array of coordinates. If one finishes by disentangling the constraints of total determination, compositional resources will be multiplied and references to archaic writing become superfluous.

Loosening the grip of determinism and taking refuge in the most convenient shelter, knowing that *everything* is acceptable, everything can be a source, that there is no valid distinction between what is organised, what can be organised, and that which is not or remains resistant to, estranged from, devoid of all hierarchy – is this extremism? No sign can be accepted as a written representation unless it belongs to a specific grammar. The fact that one uses a written sign to stand more or less for what one wishes to indicate at the moment of use, and the fact that the sign does not have the same realisation according to its user, should in principle endlessly extend the field of application of a writing considered as a collection of graphic signs whose fraught origin – drawn from models having nothing to do with either an acoustic or a grammatical phenomenon – cannot be regarded as an essential factor in decision-making. One deflects representations from their meaning in order to apply them, arbitrarily, to a sounding transcription; it is enough to create a transcriptional code of some kind to establish a field of action. These signs of graphic notation can refer to all kinds of sources that have a certain reality – a map of the stars, for example[2] – or that refer to geometrical curves. Perfectly legitimately, like all sources and all stimuli stemming from a foreign world stimulating invention by analogy, the image of a constellation can suggest locations in space of different sounding objects, while a curve can inspire some kind of monodic trajectory, or bunch of trajectories. The problem lies in the apparent logic in the transcription of signs that are artificially obliged to stand for something other than what they are: the absurdity of literal rapport. A related sign has a very precise source for signification, transcription, geometrical or cosmological, and can stand for something else without fetishism or even impotence. I would say that the true problem has not been confronted if one approaches it sketchily by way of a superficial logic that has nothing in common with one domain or the other. The solution is more complicated, and one cannot be sure of having found a way to free the writing of its traditional laboriousness, thanks not only to a subversion of meaning, but also to a contradiction of the sign. This type of subterfuge being what it is, one can also commit to a convenient postulate about the material, and decide that all materials will be concerned not with function but only with appearance: everything is equal, and everything can be used without hierarchical differentiation, with an egalitarian enthusiasm based on distinctly vague philosophical ideas about contemplation and marvelling before what plays the largest part in what surrounds us, without much perspicacity or critical judgement. So it is that the freeing of writing is hard to root in such simplistic criteria. Does this need emphasising? A musical object exists through rapport with a language: either it conforms to a language, because a language has formed it; or it resists or contradicts language, whether it encounters that language in an accidental or organised manner. In other words, the musical object in itself, or a sound in itself, exists only as the spontaneous component of a language. This sounding object can be beautiful, interesting, ugly, inert, with acoustic properties of a particular kind; it can be appreciated for itself, in isolation, but it can only make an effect in terms of its possibilities, which access the index of a language. For a long time this has seemed to me to be an abdication, a total misunderstanding of what a sound stands for, as an object in itself and, in other words, as something to be respected as the basis of a work. In all the compositions from a relatively distant past that are rooted in this fixation – the sounding object (I will not say *musical* object) regarded as the basis of an imagined solfège – I find only amateurish juxtapositions, revealing a basic misunderstanding of the essential functions of writing. Only in relation to a language – whether individual or collective – can the object make sense. Without this, we have only a collection of illustrations, anecdotal or not; these are not mechanistic manipulations conveying meaning, but at most changes of appearance. The only structure remaining in operation is, in literal terms, the structure of nonsense. There is only the functioning of total chance if you attempt to parcel up the incongruous encounters of disparate objects; and so, by analogy, when listening one brings a momentary order to the successions, at the moment of succession. This may be a worthwhile educational technique, though it rather resembles a Rorschach test.

The musical object does not have the special possibility of being put together from elements of a vocabulary, and of therefore being located within an array, with a dialectic available for its use. At best, it can be *encountered*, a found object, unclassifiable, with strong individual properties, charged with connotations. At the time of its presentation, this is not a neutral object: it has the potential to integrate or resist, and it is in this way that it should be used. It can eventually be used according to considerations that are not strictly, narrowly musical, but which share a different logic – theatrical, dramatic. It is then no longer inert, but an active agent of dissociation, non-reducible, a sample brought out from a background to which it then returns.

These freedoms, whether applied to signs or materials, are only a simulacrum of freedom, based on deficient reasoning, incomplete or superficial. The deceptiveness is a measure of the expectation: if one does not wish to be content with this reach-me-down patching together, one must persist in the search for a resource that will provide multiple varied objects and also the means for using them in many well-varied ways. To revert to my basic criticism of the twelve-tone method, it constantly addresses single notes, unitary objects. To begin to create a diverse musical entity, one has to combine these isolated units using a strict discipline deriving from the initial ordering. There are two constraints, two *invariants*: the ordering and the elemental unit. In retrospect one can see that there were also two ways to satisfy the need for liberation. One involved employing a collection of pitches distributed statistically; the other preferred to create successions of objects with different densities and exploit the possibility of distributing them differently.

Let me take the second solution first, as that is closest to me. Devising regions, harmonic divisions, is a basic concern in trying to differentiate vertical rapports that, if no law pertains, rapidly descend into undifferentiated inertia. One produces harmonic fields by privileging certain combinations, transposing them, deriving them from a matrix. But the most important thing is to create rapports between these different strata, associating the properties of one block with those of another. One thereby creates an ensemble of sound blocks, of variable density, using a certain number of common intervals. Finally, one escapes from the monotony of uniquely composed objects and has at one's disposal a great variety of sonic devices that can be flexibly organised. But it is also necessary to introduce the idea of *distribution*, which is to abandon any idea of a fixed order. *Distribution* means freedom of movement; it regards the sounding object as a whole, capable of being analysed as time passes, according to an order chosen freely at the moment of decision, according to expressive imperatives. By the phrase 'as time passes' I imply a rhythmic structure – regular, irregular – that gives equal meaning to intervals and to contours. One therefore has freedom on two fronts: that of the variety of objects, and that of varied distribution. Many additional or subordinate phenomena can be added that enrich the objects with notes borrowed from preceding or succeeding objects, and which may belong to a complementary structure.

Thinking of these sounding blocks in horizontal terms implies a relatively 'thick' use of time, highlighting common pitches that, when repeated at a relatively short distance, can indicate their degree of commonality and eventually expose their point of origin. In this way, it is possible to reveal the latent harmony of a melodic line and, if desirable, also realise it in a subordinate structure. After all, variations in presentation, in the horizontal layout, are practically infinite. One therefore needs only very restricted and identifiable basic material in order to organise far-reaching processes. Such properties of sound blocks particularly lend themselves to heterophony, encouraging exploration in terms of different temporal structures: melodic processes can involve reorderings, restorations, parallelisms, shifts of phase, without losing the identity of each component or the identities that connect them.

Vertical relations are equally rich and supple. I will discuss three specific cases: multiplying intervals as a form of continuity; chromatic complementations; and borrowed adjacencies.

(1) Imagine a sound block disposed vertically with a given arrangement of its intervals, over a wide or narrow span. Each of these intervals, according to the space separating its two component sounds, has the possibility of organic filling-out. One defines an 'anonymous' continuum without any particular connection to the sound block itself, within a pre-determined frame, and one links the extremes of the interval by means of this limited and temporary scale, a scale that can be modified for each component of the sound block. (It can keep the same proportions and therefore use non-tempered intervals that technology can easily calculate and synthesise.) But in other cases this multiplication can be linked to the structure of the sound block itself, and can reproduce, in reduced form, its basic design, as an image of itself.

(2) For an interval of the sound block we can make correspondences from a kind of passive multiplication – a regular line of semitones, for example – and move its component notes into different registers, while remaining aware of acoustic relations. The initial block is thereby enriched by a kind of resonance that makes it appear in a different acoustic light. Depending on the interval one has chosen to create these acoustic complementarities, the same block, with the same presentation of its original components, can be subject to variations of resonance that change the way we hear it while preserving its identity.

(3) Shared proximities between blocks involve preceding or succeeding blocks: one selects a note or two from an adjacent block to influence a given block, making a point of harmonic association and modifying its profile. In sound blocks that have the same structure, a similar sharing creates the possibilities of variation and cohesion. In all three cases,

the idea of a foreign body has been introduced into an initial structure, to which it is nevertheless organically related, while also increasing the potential for its use and integration into the discourse: it is what I term the *accident* of its appearance that makes a more articulated, more diverse discourse possible, charged with expressive possibilities linked to the moments where these accidents appear.

The idea of decision has been introduced from the outset into the generation and manipulation of the initial structures; one has, in consequence, an infinitely more flexible field of action, while at the same time one can control characteristics like harmonic design more effectively. This freedom has also introduced, in a more directed and restricted way, the idea of directly relating musical material to a statistical field of writing. It involves the charting of a given space by way of scanning simultaneous lines that are not heard as separate entities but as a statistical whole, the individual profile of each component less important than its participation in a global entity. One can thus foresee a succession of fields linked to one another by particular properties – different structures, expanding, shrinking, coordinates of different types – and *define* them by submitting them to other criteria: melodic lines, rhythmic patterns, ostinatos, etc.

✿ ✿ ✿

There is no shortage of methods for the creation of materials. While I am not saying that composers each create their own, it is clear that resorting to a certain number of types provides connections through deduction or proximity, or through combining with each other. But these resources are difficult to regard as purely intuitive, and in general, to present itself clearly the musical idea needs source material that embodies it but does not restrict it. Is the musical idea therefore equivalent to the exploitation of the initial source material? For a moment this was the danger. Every effort, or something like it, was devoted to the creation of the source materials, the symmetrical characteristics, the more or less special properties. Yet with poor, defective or overblown usage, the properties of the source do not actually appear in the realisation of musical ideas themselves. These qualities seem to have been devised for their own purposes and are not translated into reality with sufficient directness for a strong and clear connection to be perceived. How to move beyond the first stage of writing, with all its advantages in respect of visible invention, if I can put it thus? First, one needs to decide if one is the prisoner of an initial source that oppressively predetermines everything. As we have seen, the concept of source has become more flexible; it allows for modification or specific use, according to the needs of the moment. One therefore no longer needs to worry about an inflexible rigidity, which has disappeared. All the same, the connection exists and it is good to exploit it in a manner that avoids falling into incoherence. The difficulty indeed is to move from a basic grammatical structure that requires an effort of the imagination, but in a restricted area, as yet deprived of expressive power, to a dynamic musical idea, not simply justifying that basic grammar, but giving it its meaning and necessity. Nothing, if I may say so, is irreparable when creating an array of source materials; everything depends on the invention of the musical idea as such.

The invention of the musical idea is an essentially intuitive process that nevertheless implies a powerful internal logic. The idea is a *gamble* – a bet on validity, expressive character, potential for development; in short, on certain well-known quantities, and on others that are completely unknown. The idea is a gamble in the sense that it links a certain number of elements without certainty that those elements are effective save at that particular moment, or if they are at risk, as they evolve in relation to each other, of setting up multiple outcomes. Clearly, the gamble involves givens of a certain potential that one can evaluate only to a limited extent, and only direct experience of actual manipulation will show if the gamble was worthwhile or if it fails to fulfil its promise.

As I have said, the musical idea depends on a network; since the level of detail of the possibilities of this network is variable and can sometimes be no more than minimal substructure, the musical idea might not have clear potential at first, or might immediately reveal the outcomes one can draw from it. The idea might connect pitches and durations, along with other more precise and detailed features. Undeniably, a particular profile, a dynamic, an expressive trajectory can be part of this initial apprehension of the idea, but these features are essentially intuitive and not dependent on a system to introduce and distribute them. To be experienced, tension or relaxation, contrasts or similarities need only to be embodied in real objects. They are latent, ready to shape living materials; expressive power is a kind of magnetic field that exists virtually, but which, to become reality, must be organised by way of writing. At first, this expressive power has extremely limited objectives and can manifest itself intuitively only through very imprecise notions that are hard to transcribe in terms of writing. For example, in the case of the expressive power of resonance, my first vague desire would be to compare resonances – to juxtapose, superimpose, *process* them, in the sense that I could let them ring or, at the other extreme, interrupt them in a more-or-less abrupt fashion. While not yet writing, this is already writing. Because starting with this idea of resonance, I move to the idea of register – register that gives me a resonance of a particular length; then to the idea of interval – narrow or widely spaced, in a relation of proximity or distance to natural resonance; and mixed into these two notions, the idea of timbral distribution – providing resonances variably rich in harmonics, in textures of variable length; and finally that of dynamics – which, depending on degrees of loudness or softness, produce rich, long or short, weak resonances, and all this within the domain of a single timbre. Thanks entirely to expressive intuition, I have at my disposal the hearing of resonances, letting the sound evolve in the listener (myself, initially, internally, abstractly), giving the impression of fluctuating in time without being manipulated. I have a large reservoir of qualities at my disposal, which I can transform in definable quantities: intervals, registers, dynamics, timbres. It will be noted that I do not need a specific array of durations, because when expressive power is vested in audible resonance, it is the acoustic span, as well as the trajectory of that resonance, that provides a sense of duration. Naturally, as I develop the idea I do not necessarily remain reliant on the inert trajectory of the resonance; if I allow that trajectory to diminish progressively until it disappears, and different registers do not suggest significantly different durations to me, the profile will remain the same. I need to create a process, to work with that trajectory – contradicting it, suppressing it, superimposing or juxtaposing different ways of using it, placed in parallel or as contrast. Starting from this simple notion, I begin to work entirely from intuition – and that means above all an expressive intuition. At best, I have only a sporadic understanding of how precisely to interrupt the resonances, of what interactions I will employ. Preliminary essays in writing will certainly be required to determine the values to be adopted in the actual writing.

❊   ❊   ❊

The musical idea is, therefore, an 'unreal' and intuitive combination of imprecise parameters conceived from the position of a weakly defined expressive power. The idea will employ a number of arrays, intuitive or organised, in order to be literally realised – incarnated – in reality; in the case of an orchestral group, reality requires a further level of invention, more specifically timbral or acoustic. It is well understood that these levels of invention constantly interact; it is not a matter of expressive power, source materials or timbral characterisation on their own. Expressive intensity can exist prior to any source materials – and sometimes it can remain as an internal sketch that is not realised as an idea or in a work – but one cannot ignore the impulse given to the idea by the source. As I have already mentioned, and need to emphasise, in some cases the 'abstract' and 'arbitrary' study of a source's possibilities – for pitch, durations or particular combinations – can trigger an idea that expressive intuition alone could not have birthed, leading to an expressive charge of which one had not been consciously aware. The source can stimulate the idea, just as the idea can create the source. The evolution and implications of the idea can – should – suggest more localised, more individualised sources, for this or that segmentation. It is a matter of short-term as well as long-term thinking. Paradoxical though it might appear, the short term is indispensable: rather than undermining coherence, it promotes greater richness of development, while constant recourse to a central authority can easily become an inhibiting obstacle. This raises one of the most important questions that a composer must face: can one invent an idea (spontaneously or systematically) in full awareness of all the possibilities that are hidden within it? Through analysis, the only way we have to begin to understand and penetrate earlier or more recent works, we habitually think of the musical idea in terms of its consequences rather than its origins. We observe it as it progressively deploys and unfolds all its possibilities; the more able and imaginative the composer, the more we observe him devise a theme, a motif, a way of creating consequences that we find not only logical, but clearly and permanently embedded in the original idea. Is this truly so? This theocratic idea – the god-composer perhaps needs at least six days, but he is all-knowing, all-powerful from the outset – was created by fantasy, turning into myth because it is so convenient to refer to, complacently incorporated into biographies, even by composers themselves in their more 'cooperative' moments. But does this idea hold up when one subjects it to a more intensive investigation, involving examination of manuscripts and surviving sketches, and even a deeper study of the score?

It is convenient to refer to a work as being like a cascade of miraculous deductions, the product of a vision that constantly deepens as the work proceeds. From the outside, no other approach might seem possible, since the work is turned in on itself, with all stages of its evolution burned for ever into our memories. However, sketches show us that even if intuition is strong at certain points, and engenders the steadily evolving compositional process, there are other moments when the nature of the idea demands passages of rather less precision – superficial, even – en route to a definitive realisation. I have not studied many sketches, but those I have seen – directly or by way of sketch studies – make me very cautious about my own reactions. We bring our memories to these sketches; the 'definitive' form of certain works will have been part of our upbringing, an integral part of ourselves. We have inside us a referential or preferential reflex that is hard to escape. We see a rejected possibility with minimal differences – a displaced accent, a longer rhythmic value, a change of harmonic context – or much more fundamental upheavals – the suppression or insertion of a transition, a complete change of tempo – and, used as we are to the final version, this sketch disturbs us; and because we are disturbed, it seems inferior, unsuccessful. Inevitably, logical and rational arguments counter our disarray and dissatisfaction, noting the justification for the more polished, more expressive correction. But quite often these rationalisations can have the opposite effect: the rhythm that one found superior in the more extended final version might now seem stronger and more powerful in its shorter version; the first sketch of a phrase, simpler than the more elaborate and subtle final version, can appear more directly expressive, less mannered. If the composer leaves us in doubt about his final intentions, there will be endless arguments about which solution to adopt, proving only the extreme subjectivity of our judgements. What can be more troubling when we examine the actual processes of composition is the disorder, even the chaos in which ideas destined to follow on from one another, or to be connected through a particular process, are presented. Our analysis imposes an order, often chronological, on a conception full of short-circuits and round trips, of gaps filled in at a later stage. Analysing a completed work leads us to exaggerate the logic of succession, to empha-sise deductions, even those which probably did not exist at the time. This is best illustrated by the example of a composer studying his own work and *reading* all the processes and internal relations that can be found among the different ideas. Schoenberg gave an example from his First Chamber Symphony of thirty years earlier in his 1941 essay on twelve-tone composition. He described how two of the symphony's principal themes occurred to him spontaneously; having completed the work, he saw these themes as totally unrelated. Full of remorse about this appar-ent lack of coherence, he was preparing to rework the themes when, once more, his instinct urged him to leave them as they were. Many years later, studying the score again – perhaps in order to explain it to pupils (he did not say) – he discovered the source for the two themes, the second being a simplified inversion of the first. After the dates of composition and examination, it is clear that the Schoenberg who, in 1909, composed this symphony was at an intuitive stage very different from the Schoenberg of 1929, the recent inventor of the twelve-tone method, who was now in a phase of extremely logical deduction. In 1941, he described this with a certain good-humoured detachment. This nevertheless remains for me a typical example of what is put into a work and what is not, whatever one adds to it or can say of the intervals, which, like numbers, can be combined in different ways, flexible and capable of being manipulated in any way at all. The notorious dictum 'all is in all' can sometimes apply to a certain kind of hyperanalytic vision of a work.

❋ ❋ ❋

I spoke earlier of the disorder that can give birth to works. It is both surprising and reassuring, proof that the representation of a work as an entity – as if, in some ways, recopied by way of writing – is more legend than reality. Is the work not discontinuous in advance of its true existence, before being organised? It is as if in referring to certain encounters between idea, source material, grammar and writing certain notions emerge quite quickly, but do not thrive, temporarily or permanently. They are waiting, held for a provisional period, at the edge of a shadowy and unexplored realm. Others emerge without direct links, as invention jumps from one point to another, without seeking connections – all the more so when there are no pre-established forms and the ideas are not destined to be inserted in a given moment, according to a privileged character. They bob about in an absence of narrative, or unfolding, without direction, without any foreseeable function. They wait to discover their potential for development, their potential usefulness, and gradually they are able to create a geography.

One might still ask at what point does writing create an actual idea. Twenty years ago, the concept – and practice – of 'intuitive music' emerged, based entirely on the performer throwing himself into intuitive improvisation, individual or collective, on the basis of uniquely 'poetic' ideas: that is, written suggestions re-emerging in another style of writing.[3] It was soon clear that the musical ideas suggested in this way were clichés, whether as reminders of specific works or of the general stylistic qualities of a particular period. Could it have been otherwise? I start with this as an absurdly extreme example of the impossibility of renouncing notation in the concretisation of musical ideas. But we must go further if we are to understand how one moves from source materials to a fully formed musical idea and its projection.

In chronological order, it is clear that an idea can emerge independently from a particular collection of coordinates. It appears in isolation, born

587

from a vague acoustic gesture, or a more elaborate gesture, with more detailed components, but of short range; a brief gesture whose consequences are not insisted on, not fully understood; an intuitive gesture, linked to a direct expression, a momentary pulsation, able to crystallise only in a small space, from all points of view. This intuitive, spontaneous gesture can generate a chord or a melodic sequence, or a figure that is rhythmically well characterised. Let us say that this 'primitive' figure, which exists in isolation, has occurred to you, or seems to have done. It is certainly the product of thought, of an underlying progression, a more or less conscious reaction in conjunction with acquired antecedents of yours which have not been explored in earlier work, or in conjunction with particular characteristics of unfamiliar works that have struck you, on however casual a basis. This discovery, this trigger can just as well be the beginning of a deliberate process as of an unexpected short cut: a gift from one's intuition is never completely free. Whatever the nature of this initial object, what is to be done, how should one proceed? Should one immediately disperse it into a solid collection of deductions, or allow it to proliferate anarchically? How might writing take possession of it and reveal its potential?

Upon initial examination, the musical object inspired by intuition can be exploited at once. For example, there might be a rhythmic sequence that quickly provides the basics for both fixity and variation, easy to deduce and to put in order – one can quickly see the consequences, since the grammar for such an operation is relatively simple and the methods are direct. If the initial musical object is more complex, on a higher grammatical level, it proves more necessary to see how this isolated object can be placed within a collection that stems from the object, a collection that could lead to modification of the object, since some of the object's most basic features are not included in the source materials. These deductions emerge thick and fast, and do not necessarily retain contact with the original object. One therefore takes longer to find solutions and other objects that were completely unexpected at the start. The deductions require a certain logic, but they also owe their position to chance, to local conditions. As one begins to see the multiple possibilities of a unique intuition, and one sees a still limited number of usages and deductions, can one already contemplate an overall form? In certain cases, this is possible; in others, it is not, and this is not always desirable. If one intends to explore a development by gradual expansion or contraction, or one intends from the start to place two very different types of material in opposition, this implies a form of consistently increasing or diminishing density, or else a regular alternation of these two characteristics. In both these cases, the form fits with either alternation or continuation, as a direct consequence. However, it is clear that there are also forms where invention is the outcome of momentary activity or provisional solutions found along the way; such a form cannot be foreseen or deduced from something on a larger scale. Inventiveness gradually reveals it; and as the consequence of invention it cannot exist in advance, as happens when creativity conforms to more linear principles. Moreover, even in the case of linear principles, creativity applies itself to those aspects of linearity that spark its interest and are not totally foreseeable. If there is an increase of density, for example, fluctuations of tempo could ensure that this textural density can be perceived only globally, provided that one's hearing is adequately analytical. In any case, the form of a work cannot be a foreseeable unfolding of possibilities that one uses up on the basis of given restrictions; nor can it be a succession of moments without perceptible connections. This is the problem of writing, properly understood: coherence and diversity.

✻ ✻ ✻

In a more immediate and spontaneous manner, encountering non-cultural objects not clearly connected to the worlds of sound or noise can promote, through analysis, the conception of a musical idea that requires writing in order to be realised. Much has been said about nature as a source of inspiration for poets and musicians, especially during the Romantic period. But studying Paul Klee's drawings from nature, taken from his courses at the Bauhaus, clearly shows how the visual transcription of elements or motions inspires and pervades his invention, his graphic writing. This individual graphology, as writing, stems from the elaboration of sources in nature. If the musical transcription of such external phenomena risks being merely imitative, it is nevertheless possible to regard them in a much more interesting way, as transformed elaboration – symbolic, direct or indirectly metaphorical.

Few sources for writing are unavailable to the musician willing to work at this elaboration. Whether the sources belong to regions we term cultural or non-cultural, to properly musical fields or other means of expression, the work emerges from the contact between what is written and what can be written. In one case, I would say that this is a matter of transliteration – one changes the alphabet without fundamentally changing the writing; in the other, transcription is involved – one must adapt the material to a given system of writing.

As I have often said, a work can be inspired by extreme points of view. It can be born out of an orderly instinct or out of chaos. Writing can, from the outset, be a basic component of this inspiration, or it can result from an elaborate search for ways of finding a convincing packaging for the idea. The composer's memory is a kind of reservoir: in his earliest years, memory is mainly the depository of the writing of others; as he moves forward, it becomes his own depository, and despite his complaints and his attempts at renewal, he is confronted by his own genetic inheritance, one that he has steadily created and for which he is responsible. Through mechanisms that only appear paradoxical, the more the composer believes himself to be spontaneous, the more risk he runs of sinking back – however unconsciously – into his inheritance. Those skills in writing that he has gradually acquired through his previous experiences allow him to formulate a 'spontaneous' idea with more aptitude than a strange idea, which he cannot truly understand without writing rooted in his unconscious.

Nevertheless, instead of evolving from a concrete or rapidly concretised idea or group of ideas that can be blended into a coherent whole, a work can be designed from the outset like architecture, like a large structure whose trajectory and evolution are foreseen, and where one imagines phases and even more precise characteristics, but whose actual components have not yet been invented. Musical ideas must emerge in order to validate this structure; sometimes ideas that have remained unexplored, latent within a kind of imaginary catalogue, suddenly find a suitable outlet for their development. Most of the time, such encounters are unforeseeable; they follow a subterranean route that one can barely understand oneself; they appear and disappear on the way to finding outlets in reality. One can observe that if writing inevitably generates form, then form in turn can create the writing it needs.

When one speaks of form, one can hypothesise that ideas will emerge in a particular order of importance, a hierarchical temporal order enforced by deduction. But it must be recognised that ideas can emerge, on the contrary, in total confusion, transcribed with an appearance of simplicity very different from what they will eventually become. The transformations of the idea one observes – in studying the pages of a fully finished work – between the first and final versions prove that the primitive idea is usually arrived at without context, and without indicating what the context might be. Hence, this maladjustment that one has to remedy. The writing is as yet rudimentary, devised to suit an initial approach; the more the work adapts to the idea, detecting its consequences, the more refined the writing, with richer possibilities for development. The intuition of the composer reaches ahead and into the unknown, thanks to the proliferation by way of the writing.

One can appreciate that the work can emerge from a 'plan' with no real substance – although the inventor, at the moment he conceives this plan, is already working on the material, or is able to construct a global structure on the basis of a few concentrated ideas deriving from an extremely localised aspect of the writing. Whatever the trajectories and the sources of creativity, it is always writing that fertilises that creativity.

---

1 Arnold Schoenberg, 'Composition with Twelve Tones', in *Style and Idea*, ed. Leonard Stein, trans. Leo Black (Berkeley, Los Angeles: University of California Press, 1984), p. 223.
2 Probably a reference to John Cage's *Atlas Eclipticalis* (1961–2).
3 So-called intuitive music was proposed by Karlheinz Stockhausen in his 1968 text-based improvisation score *Aus den sieben Tagen* (1968).

16

The Work: Whole or Fragment?
(1994–95)

The problem I tackle here, one that I feel to be particularly personal, involves the very foundations of the work, its *raison d'être*. Is the work as we know it a genuine totality, or is it rather the restricted fragment of a much larger project, without boundaries, but without which this fragment could not exist or give the illusion of wholeness? Has one any basis for thinking of oneself as the creator of a single work? In the nineteenth century, in particular, there was no shortage of ambitious creators who focused on a single substantial project. Balzac, Zola and Proust are instances of a relatively spontaneous, relatively fabricated determination that inveigled these authors into creating huge, even gigantic sequences, or more constrained and concentrated collections within a more circumscribed domain. However, the constituent elements of the collections can be separated from each other, read singly without their coherence being compromised. So, a genuine entity or a chain of detachable fragments? Is a book itself a book or an album? Album: a collection of separate leaves (as with Schumann's German title *Albumblätter* and its many less illustrious successors), grouped by affinities or by contrasts between the items, but lacking connecting continuities. In Mallarmé's thinking, this leads to links between the Book and the Album: a Book, with a capital 'B', where the album leaves can change appearance and meaning, while still being linked at a higher level. Utopia was never attained, but we have the sublime 'fragment' of 'Un coup de dés', however far removed from its initial objective.

In the realm of music, the one inescapable example – probably the only one of such size – is Wagner's *Ring*, a project pursued over many long years, with a unity of conception deployed with tenacity.

The history of its genesis reveals a kind of inverse trajectory to that given in actual performance. *Siegfried's Tod* generated the remainder of the cycle, the music following chronological order, thereby moving in contrary motion: for the most 'operatic' plot in conventional terms, the most complex music; for the most innovative dramatic ideas, a music still in the process of finding itself. But here, too, experience has shown, the segments are detachable from the whole: *Die Walküre* is performed more frequently than the other panels, as completely self-contained – though one knows that it is part of a sequence. Wagner well understood that, and for one reason or another retold the background to the story within each separate episode. There is therefore a certain contradiction between entities tending to autonomy and the synthesis of the whole. This is why, even in this case, one can speak of a divergence between the whole and the fragment.

Of course, we are dealing here with opera, with theatre, not with pure forms, but because of this dialectic of whole and fragment one finds within operas 'detachable' arias, recitatives and ensembles, to such an extent – and Mozart is not exempt – that one can replace one aria with another, as the singer wishes, without the chain of fragments suffering irreparable damage. The theatrical link can be sufficiently strong to assert the continuity and coherence of the whole.

What is the situation in pure music? During the classical period, the dialectic of whole and fragment is found – and constantly used – in the most common forms: sonata, concerto, symphony. The work is assembled from autonomous fragments linked by an overall structure based on contrasts that are usually clearly coded. In the earlier baroque period, the links were looser but had exactly the same function: to bring a semblance of wholeness to an ensemble of fragments, however disparate and interchangeable. Replacing a gigue in a Bach suite with another will not disrupt our listening habits, for if the rules of tonality are observed, there will be no fundamental incoherence of style, form or generic character. This is how Mahler proceeded when selecting movements from two Bach suites and 'reordering' them in a suite he arranged himself and then performed, in New York and elsewhere. Given our present obsession with historical authenticity, we find this mildly scandalous, though Bach himself didn't shrink from including old pieces in new contexts, as the Brandenburg Concertos and cantatas attest. And when we note with incredulity those nineteenth-century programmes where single movements of concertos were played, or the movements of a symphony were separated by concert arias, we can appreciate that a practice that now seems absurd and destructive to us poses a genuine problem: can the succession that implies the whole be interrupted and isolated by actual fragments, as autonomous compositions? Today, we often profess exaggerated respect for the integrity and 'integrality' of the whole. In the case of the *Christmas Oratorio*, all the parts must be performed, and in order; with the Mass in B minor one reacts with horror if only one section is done. I could mention other anecdotal and futile examples, like the tendency to regard applause between movements as a manifestation of boorishness, of disrespect for the work. Does applause really destroy that which knits the fragments/movements of a symphony into a whole? Isn't its interruption simply the most superficial manifestation of a presumed comprehension? Except when the author has written a transition specifically to make a connection, what does a pause interrupt? Can't one play a fugue without its prelude? Must an entire collection always be performed, as one often finds with Brahms's Intermezzos, for example? We have evidently become very respectful of the letter, but what about the spirit?

Clearly, there is a world of difference between the movements (*Sätze*) of a sonata, symphony or concerto and the pieces (*Stücke*) in an album, whatever the overall title – Nocturnes, Ballades, *Estampes*, *Miroirs*, character pieces (*Charakterstücke*). The titles Symphony, Concerto or Sonata stand for a given order, a specific contrast, and in some cases a rhythmic schema, metre, even a duration. Minuet or Scherzo signify triple time, repeated figures and other constraints that restrict the length. True, such forms were later treated in freer ways – by Mahler, for example. However, earlier on, and in classical times especially, the sequence was sonata form, song form, minuet or scherzo and rondo. I am simplifying, because especially in works called Sonata much greater freedom was possible: between the two movements of op. 111 and the seven movements of the C sharp minor Quartet, op. 131 (both late works, it should be noted), Beethoven didn't hesitate to change the limits on mobility. But can one still speak of movements in the C sharp minor Quartet? It is more a matter of contrasts between fragments and movements proper. If such movements as the fugue, the finale, the variations and the scherzo are well developed, the third can be thought of only as a brief transition; even the sixth (adagio) is adumbrated rather than genuinely developed. One senses the composer's very direct desire to place the various movements and fragments in a fixed order that is very carefully considered. There is no question of fragments being interchangeable; the work is far from a sequence of coded movement types, but a whole strictly followed through from beginning to end.

Strangely, the fusion Beethoven was seeking – rejecting all ordering conventions, the mere assembling of separate pieces – finds its fulfilment at a distance, in the Wagnerian music drama. Romanticism, as a reaction to classicism, promotes the album as a collection of separate pieces that no longer need to follow the usual rules of succession. When they do use the classical conventions, the Romantics treat them as a sacred, inviolable inheritance, or in a deliberately naive and literal manner. The musical ideas are often very fine, but they sometimes fit awkwardly into a form to which they are not best suited. There has often been talk of 'heavenly length' in Schubert, of laboured and redundant developments in Schumann, the sole exception favouring the whole being the B minor Piano Sonata of Liszt, who devised a continuous single-movement form, utterly divorced from classical models, even if these are occasionally hinted at. The essence of Romanticism is not simply to invent fragments, but to give them a strong *raison d'être*. This was the era of collections, albums, single pieces that prioritise the instant, the moment – as in Schubert's *Moments musicaux*. The form is often simple, symmetrical. The fragment is certainly complete in itself, but it is also open to everything and nothing; it does not need preparation or consequence, but exists separately, and its value depends on no formal correspondences. It is there as an aphorism of whatever length, independent, but with the possibility of being associated in due course with other aphorisms of a similar kind. All that can be sacrificed, especially with pieces for piano – the instrument par excellence of the strolling single person's reverie – but also with certain chamber compositions, including the well-nigh sacrosanct genre of the string quartet. After

Romanticism, sonatas are relatively rare, as with the younger Debussy and Ravel, though they returned to the genre in their later years. On the other hand, one finds albums – Debussy's *Images* and *Estampes*, Ravel's *Miroirs* and *Gaspard de la nuit* – or else suites – *Suite bergamasque*, *Tombeau de Couperin* – all at some distance from the very idea of the whole. We are dealing instead with a collection of fragments conceived as such, and entirely separate. Faithfulness to the text means that one invariably plays *Estampes*, *Images* and *Miroirs* in the printed order; but there is no reason not to choose a different order as long as certain contrasts of character are maintained.

At the dawn of the twentieth century, the ultimate in such fragmentation was reached and pieces gave the impression of being sketchy notations from an intimate journal. With both Stravinsky and Webern, the miniature was reduced to the inscription of an instant, totally opposed to the very idea of development. The idea has total concentration; in this way, it involves a brief fragment of time and is completely turned in on itself. This is particularly prominent in Webern: one might protest that all his works are short, but most of them employ the concept of development, though this is highly condensed. The pieces I am referring to – in particular those for cello and piano (op. 11), op. 10 for ensemble, the Bagatelles for string quartet (op. 9) – completely resist this idea of development. The idea is set out, the fragment is shown in a special light, the moment of hearing passes by. The obsession with non-repetition – with the fragment as entirely unique, and uniquely entire – was described by Webern himself as an extreme condensation of thought that imprisoned him, and from which he had to escape in order to continue composing.

We also find this culture of the fragment in Stravinsky and Berg, but as a model reduced from a larger projection in other works. All Stravinsky's Russian miniatures of the years 1914–17 – *Pribaoutki*, *Berceuses du chat*, *Russian Peasant Songs* ('Saucers') – are small-scale satellites of the much larger *Les Noces*. In contrast to these earlier compositional fragments, *Les Noces* presents a synthesis of fragments strongly linked together by the idea of a core tempo, completely unchanging across the different rates attached to it. Sometimes Stravinsky's fragments remain fragments: the *Lyriques japonaises* and *Le roi des étoiles* are two brief fragments, the latter especially enigmatic in character. These are not satellites, but rather objects lost in a world that would completely forget them. As for Berg, apart from his songs, the pieces for clarinet and piano (op. 4) could be considered sketches for the theatrical enterprise of *Wozzeck*, which would soon absorb him entirely. Here, one finds that antinomy between the restricted form and the much more expansive theatrical gesture. One almost thinks of them as a fragment of a work, the rest of which we do not know, or which has been erased by its author. The dialectic between fragment and whole is fully deployed in the form-plan of *Wozzeck*, a sequence of closed forms, interconnected by a complex reservoir of motifs and signals of various kinds.

And what of Schoenberg? Having begun with forms building on late-Romantic traditions, especially in *Verklärte Nacht* and *Pelleas und Melisande*, he came to write *Pierrot lunaire*, destined to be regarded by the public as his most significant work. *Pierrot lunaire* is a collection of twenty-one very short pieces – twenty-one fragments, as it were – assembled into three groups of seven, but fragments nevertheless, as independent of each other in texture as in thematic material. Indeed, it is the brevity of these successive fragments that in large part created public resistance: early reviews emphasise this constant renewal of moments, which impedes aural continuity and inhibits the perception of the work as a coherent whole. Yet fragmented vocal works, composed from short fragments, were not unusual before *Pierrot lunaire*. I have mainly song cycles in mind, by Schubert, Schumann and Brahms in particular. *Dichterliebe* and *Frauenliebe und -leben* are genuine cycles of very short pieces. But they are *narrative* cycles, which is not really the case for *Winterreise* nor even for *Die schöne Müllerin*. As far as narrative is concerned, these resemble fragments arranged into a sequence according to a certain agogic design. There is none of this in *Pierrot lunaire*: nothing is narrated; each fragment benefits from an undeniable poetic autonomy, even though the poems relate to a single persona and share a common atmosphere. True, the cycles are essentially poetic, tragic or nostalgic in character, but there is no governing continuity. We connect these fragments to one another thanks, in part, to the composer, who meticulously guides us in their linkings – whether with direct transitions or by marking

a longer or shorter interval between the pieces. The three parts are separated by longer pauses to help us to recognise them as such; and the
specific orderings organise the various fragments into an organic unity
despite the absence of a predetermined framework. The work has its own
integrative quality, which must be experienced in order to be understood,
and experienced many times to become familiar and avert disorientation.

Pierrot lunaire consists of a series of short, even very short pieces, and
my own *Marteau sans maître* makes conscious reference to this principle,
though the individual movements are relatively long: the three cycles
that constitute the whole are not separate but are interleaved with each
other, precisely to avoid separation and also to avoid grouping fragments
of the same type together. With luck, during hearing, one reconstitutes
from memory the cycles involving the same principles stemming from
the single text that has given rise to each. One deduces the underlying
cycles from the actual sequence of movements, despite their continuity
being broken, and as a result one detects a different dialectic between
whole and fragment.

* * *

An emphasis on fragments that have a tendency to get separated out
from the whole, an instantaneous instant, happens with increasingly
powerful hostility to the idea of unity, when fragments are inserted
with no separation into a forceful and restrictive continuity, which tests
memory and perception to their limits. Romanticism had created two
opposite tendencies: the fragment freed from the whole, and the fragment dominated by the whole. Strauss and Mahler come particularly
to mind – Mahler probably more than Strauss. Certain movements in
Mahler symphonies are much longer than normal, and contain many
episodes, often of a theatrical character, highlighting a solo instrument
or solo group – a solo trombone, a group of cellos, a post horn, two
horns. These episodes have a clear tendency to detach themselves from
the whole, and they acquire a virtual autonomy by means of extrava-
gant gestures, but at the same time their true meaning is the result of
the context in which they occur. They are fragments isolated by their

signification and, to some extent, their distinct sonorities, but they are also strongly linked to the whole: a virtual fragment that is inseparable from the whole.

These examples of separate fragments in a Mahler movement give the strongest evidence of a theatrical character. There are also frequent examples of fragments integrated into a development that unifies the most diverse elements. In a symphonic movement one therefore finds a very variable notion of the relation between fragment and totality, due in large part to the *narrative* character imposed by Mahler on the concept of 'movement'. Inserting episodes or fragments into a whole is not a purely formal affair, but connects with a narrative that is not explicit but 'speaks' through variably dramatic gestures. Episodes or fragments were thought of by Mahler as scenes in an imaginary drama, in which fragmentation demands continuity. Nevertheless, there is no pictorial storyline, as with Strauss's symphonic poems in the tradition of Liszt and Berlioz. Here, there is straightforward description of real events, domestic or Alpine. This kind of episodic construction requires a clear narrative to connect the sections with each other, a narrative without which they lose their *raison d'être*.

How did the divergence of these two tendencies come about – towards large-scale design dominated by unity on the one hand, and towards small-scale atomisation, with the extremely brief demanding radical autonomy, on the other? The most basic element, and also the most striking, is clearly duration. And what is duration conditioned by if not linguistic structures? It is there that we must seek the reasons for greater or lesser fragmentation, greater or lesser integration.

Considering our Western tradition, we understand that the overriding aim is a *completed* work, in which the presence of polyphony has severely limited any tendency to improvisation. Other cultures – India, sub-Saharan Africa – do not have this circumscribed notion of time; they make use of techniques – repetitive rhythmic patterns, melodic formulas or (more precisely) matrices – that allow for extension in time, accumulating and connecting episodes that are as much fragmentations of time, time that does not function as it does in our own society. Possibilities remain open – with limits, for sure, for it is not a matter of infinity, of time without any control – for fragments added to other fragments, so as to create a mood and a character to be integrated into a whole that defines itself as one listens. There is nothing comparable in our written tradition. Perhaps the structure of polyphony explains the impossibility of such a character. Polyphony requires restrictions that can function only within a closed and limited circuit. Since the earliest organum, we have understood musical duration as limited, and technique – rhythmic, in particular – has refined itself, to the point of becoming overly complex, as compositions have been compacted, condensed. Until the nineteenth century, all works concerned especially with time involved fragmentation. Composers of baroque operas, oratorios, cantatas, Passions – all vocal works employing religious or mythological texts – have available a limited duration and a fixed field of action. These are large forms, undoubtedly, but closed off, organised in panels, building on contrasts of weightiness and density, each panel rarely exceeding a moderate duration, and in a sense calibrated in similar, if not identical, ways. The baroque had tended towards a standardisation of timings, which from the beginning of the nineteenth century was fundamentally disturbed. As the nineteenth century proceeded, time spans would again observe certain conventions, as much in strict forms as in freer ones, but these conventions were increasingly challenged or ignored by innovative thinkers who did not follow their precepts.

Why these conventions, and why were they set aside? The explanation can be found in the language itself and its structures. As long as the functions of language were not standardised, and thus possessed a formalising potential sufficient to control the different components of a composition, duration could be satisfactorily applied to parameters only in the short term, not the longer term. The more functions were clarified, the more authority they acquired, the more they could contribute to making larger forms possible, and comprehensible. The functions of tonality, as they were strengthened and clarified, could control not only the generation of basic vocabulary, but also the entire form-plan. Once the fundamental functions of tonic, dominant and subdominant, etc., had been defined, a hierarchy was created, to which episodes and also aspects of writing were subordinated. It can be applied in relatively strict contexts to certain formal archetypes like fugue and passacaglia, or in freer contexts with, nevertheless, a fixed trajectory. The duration appropriate for such a structure grows as a function of its flexibility. Clearly, a fugue, in the strict sense, cannot have the trajectory of a sonata or a set of variations – this last, in particular, having recourse to considerable freedom or procedure, in the way compartmentalisation can serve formal continuity. As usual, there are exceptions in late Beethoven, with the fugue in the Piano Sonata, op. 106, or the *Grosse Fuge* for string quartet completely overturning the conventions of the academic fugue, greatly extending its duration by introducing the principle of variation, the essential tool for diversity in unity.

This tonal language with clearly defined hierarchies also implies precise thematicism and, in consequence, a constrained combinatory capacity. Developmental aspects will, of course, vary, depending on composers and compositions, but there will usually be a hierarchy between the exposition or repetition of themes and development in various episodes. The hierarchy that organises the unfolding of a movement allows relative importance to different episodes, different fragments of the form as we hear them in time, helping us to connect them together into a synthesis and perceive the whole. But even a very powerful hierarchy, such as controls a large amount of music in the classical period, is not so rigid as to determine every successive detail. Considerable variety in proportions is possible: the exposition of themes can be more or less extended, the development sometimes condensed, sometimes enlarged. But the formal constituents will always be distinguishable; and just as formal design allows only for work on the particular material that has been stated, and development cannot enter completely uncharted territory, they work within the limits imposed on them by the thematic material. Broadly speaking, classical-period sonatas by Haydn, Mozart and Beethoven observe similar temporal proportions. Standardisation of components is matched by standardisation of durations, something already more flexible than during the baroque period, when sonatas by Scarlatti and concertos by Vivaldi had almost exactly the same durations.

With emancipation of language came emancipation of duration, on both the larger and smaller scales. Tonal relations loosened up, acquiring unprecedented flexibility and a versatility that made them better able to adjust instantaneously. The richness of modulations, the freedom to bring more distant, unrelated chords closer together, made possible an expressive intensification that impinged on the perception of duration. In one sense, one risked anarchy, because lack of control over basic linguistic elements brought disorder, with loss of continuity. Hence the need for stronger thematic associations than formerly applied if one wished to organise the flow of time – as with the celebrated Wagnerian leitmotivs, which made orientations possible in what might otherwise seem to be a chaotic jungle of modulations. But this liberty worked even better on the small scale. Here, there was no more need for thematic contrasts validated by the structure, no more need for a hierarchy between principal themes and developments: the hierarchy between fragments could be abolished and the whole constituted differently. But building a whole from fragments without hierarchy was specifically a matter of duration.

To organise fragments or episodes into a form, a hierarchy is required to create order. Chronological order is not enough. A process of developmental logic is needed. This logic is first found in what might be called the word-for-word, the basic vocabulary. Since these words are organised according to evident logic, accepted instantly, without thought, or accepted after being thought about, the fragment is constructed with terms that are or rapidly become adopted. When the terms as such – the elements of the vocabulary, strongly individualised – avoid any overall organisation and their relations either do not exist or cannot be directly perceived, it is clear that connection will be more difficult to establish and that each entity will have the tendency to refer only to itself, to be self-contained. The higher-level logic that governs these elements will be that much more difficult to establish if they are strongly individualised. Hence the great difficulty, through the refusal to establish a palpable hierarchy, in making connections between one object and another at this most basic level. Repetitions will familiarise you with the chronological order, but the fragmentation remains. That fragmentation will be acceptable for a limited period of time, but the more it is extended, the greater the difficulty in connecting successive fragments, in hearing their relatedness, not just as direct successions, but within an overall span suggesting temporal synthesis.

◊ ◊ ◊

One of the strongest causes both of a work's fragmentary perception by a listener and of the composer's reduction of the work to a relatively brief span of time resides in the grasp of the instant as such, the complete non-repetition of whatever character it possesses. If, to take this to an absurd extreme – with respect to perception rather than to constructional logic – no interval, no rhythm, no timbre, no figure of a given number of notes and durations is repeated, the fragment cannot continue for long, since the possibilities for total non-repetition are extremely limited. Such a totally non-repeating fragment was briefly an obsession of Webern's, comparable to the pure squares of Malevich. This crisis of the absolute having been overcome, there was no further attempt at non-repetition as the determining feature of a composition. If a certain duration was to be sustained, it was also necessary not just to repeat textures to embody fluency within limits – a simple return to the past – but to acknowledge analogous situations, however different in their actual materials. It was necessary to set up a repertory of evolving materials, sufficiently characterised to invite recognition, in order to connect the different fragments as well as to differentiate them. This process could apply to all linguistic elements on a scale of greater or lesser extent. The micro-form would as a result be gradually defined, while the macro-structure results from the collection of micro-forms, its evolution resulting from the interactive interplay of the different elements. The fragments thereby constituted are unified by an organic development enabling the listener to recognise them through the similarity of the audible situations in which they are placed.

The conjunction between the fragment and the whole is certainly the hardest to establish, and for both composer and listener the fragment – despite all the precautions one might take – has the tendency to autonomy, to separate itself in time from others. Yet just as there is no such thing as an absolute fragment, there is no such thing as absolute continuity, particularly on the largest scale. Memory, especially in a work being heard for the first time, or one that is relatively unfamiliar, seizes on fragments, and sometimes not at all in the way the composer has conceived and executed them, when characteristics of sound – more strongly than characteristics of writing – interpose themselves between the work as conceived and the work as perceived. To reconnect the fragments that memory has grasped then temporarily forgotten in order to grasp them freshly, the process of synthesis is retrospective: one can never be sure that one has mentally reconstituted the actual whole. This is especially true of non-repetitive music, with relatively complex textures, but it is also true for older forms of writing that cannot be instantly grasped: I am thinking of certain kinds of strict canonic writing, whose legitimacy is determined more by the eye than the ear. There are certain tests for the recognition of the form of a piece as one understands it after one or several hearings, and these exist for listeners lacking specific knowledge of the music or piece, as well as listeners with refined professional understanding. If form is the dialectic globally uniting the fragmentary components of the episodes, these tests have proved very revealing of the deep impulse we feel to connect fragments grasped in an instant into a whole that the memory cannot reconstitute in its entirety. The first hearing reveals only the most striking fragments, those that stand out on account of their uniquely arresting profile, and which will be the first fragments to be isolated and recalled. As for the rest, they cannot be grasped straightforwardly, as memory goes in search of very typical profiles that they gradually accumulate. First impressions are therefore of a sporadic fragmentation separated by completely undifferentiated areas; the first perception of form will be discontinuous, and one attempts to connect these little islands as best one can, seeking out what links or divides them. With repeated hearings, the most striking fragments that one has initially latched on to, out of context, will increasingly be located within a whole, and attention focuses on the fragments that are more difficult to absorb, as their complexity creates confusion or a dispersal of their trajectory; or they are ambiguously constructed, hard to connect directly to one criterion or another. As I have said, separate fragments might not be heard in the way the composer conceived and intended them; there might be ancillary effects – of dynamics or density – that are stronger than the written structure and which lead perception down paths more truthful, from this perspective, than those of the composer. I've called these 'envelopes' or 'signals', thus giving the impression of an insistent basis for understanding; quite primitive criteria, in truth, but with major importance for defining the essence of the fragment one is grasping, and also its rapport with other fragments. One therefore builds up a hierarchy of fragments, usually quite small, where one quickly determines the profile and characteristics that memory quite rapidly assimilates – very rapidly, if they are particularly striking; but also those that one perceives to be more vague, as interspersed moments, transitions whose components and trajectory are not clearly grasped but are accepted as less precise moments among those that are more clearly defined. These investigations into form from the perspective of relations between fragments and wholes are a way of detecting not only whatever the general problem might be, but the particular manner in which this rapport is grasped. I would not go as far as to say that the numbers of descriptions will equal the number of describers, because they agree to some extent on the most salient points; but where these elementary contours are concerned, descriptions of form can diverge greatly and only vaguely coincide, if at all, with the objective description of the work, given by the composer or an analyst of the written score. There will be different degrees of exactitude in the approach, depending on whether the listener is more or less persuaded, more or less educated, and has heard the work a number of times. The narrative-creating ability of a listener with respect to a particular piece of music is in one way reassuring. Frequently, given a number of fragments that his memory has grasped, he will construct a personal narrative of the work's form, confirming his ownership of the work. There may indeed be occasions – when the language remains unfamiliar or he resists the aesthetic aura – when his memory will be unable to grasp and retain the slightest fragment; everything seems chaotic, and he has no desire to persist with listening because he feels absolutely no need to construct connections between sensations other than those that are instantaneous. Very quickly, he senses only incoherence and vacuity, because all that gives value to a language and meaning to what is heard seems utterly lacking. I would add that if the composer has not allowed for these crucial criteria in his work, it is abundantly clear that the listener will not be able to hear them, whatever the chosen language; the inconsistencies of an amateur composer, whether he tries to imitate Beethoven, Chopin or Debussy, remain incoherent, or skate over the surface of the language's most superficial aspects. On the other hand, the profound unity of a complex work will emerge if one discovers ways of coming to terms with its repetitions. Coherence and the relation between fragments and whole are not matters of style, but rather a question of contextualising different elements that converge and diverge.

With relations between fragment and whole, I would like to refer to a very particular aspect of contemporary painting of which I've become aware. The museum director Pontus Hultén has drawn my attention to a phenomenon in painting that I had never thought of, never even considered. He has spoken of the prominence of reproductions of paintings as a result of the enormous increase in art books, comparable to the dissemination of music on disc. But discs provide a faithful reproduction of a work, similar to what can be heard in live performance, except when special effects are used; recording techniques do not 'adulterate' the work's balance, at most clarifying the balances that are difficult to realise in performance. The art book, on the other hand, has manipulated space in a way that recording has never dared. In art books, practically without exception, there are many details – a hand, a cloud, a corner of the landscape – alongside reproductions of the complete painting, which give a very different perspective on the original. One therefore dissects the painting as a whole into a series of fragments, made completely unreal through enlargement. Hultén claims that this culture of the fragment has greatly influenced the thinking of certain painters, their understanding of painting. This kind of disproportioning and isolation from context in which the fragment becomes a whole is detached from the canvas or, more broadly, from the easel. Has this happened, can it happen, in music, other than by way of extremely distorted sonic balances, like those found in pop music?

When one reaches the domain of electroacoustics and the computer, I have no doubt that the comparison can be made between the enlarged details in a painting serving to launch a new idea and the transformation of an acoustic sound by various manipulations, creating certain types of structure that stretch real time beyond all reality, fragmenting space into trajectories that are virtually impossible for traditional instruments. I would also observe that a machine can realise what I might term the 'infinite fragment'. This is not in fact a whole, but frames the unending fragment in such a way that it seems like a whole, conceived as such: an aleatoric fragment designed so that the only possible ending seems arbitrary. There is actually no need for a computer to realise such a concept; one can do so, in reduced form, with sufficiently reduced materials that suppress the individual characteristics of the composer as fully as possible. This is what happened, more or less intentionally, during the 1950s, with the systematic permutations of given materials. The starting point being already arbitrary, deriving from the same logical choice as the others, the subsequent choices owed their existence less to aesthetic decisions than to the automatic outcomes of the process. With the right kind of initial materials the deductions could be multiple, even endless, with no hierarchy involved: everything is equal in importance, in weight, like raw material. In truth, composing was not composing but juxta-posing a fixed number of outcomes, ending when one decided to end, arbitrarily and without excluding all possibility of a more important con-tinuation. In allowing the parameters to operate autonomously, one did not actually create a whole, but defined a fragment in time that necessar-ily remained in the state of a fragment from a whole. One was incapable of perceiving this in its entirety, given its endlessness: the permutations and other manipulations could have continued indefinitely if one did not decide to stop them at a certain point. Of this infinite fragment, one finds examples created manually, inspired by Messiaen's 'Mode de valeurs et d'intensités', a relatively short piece but setting out the problem in the most direct and striking fashion. Pieces that followed on fairly directly from this, like Stockhausen's *Kreuzspiel* and the first section of my *Structures* for two pianos, brought into play this ambivalence about the structuring of time, which did not involve real choices but decisions con-sequent on the fact that an absence of profile cannot generate a strong and convincing form, and certainly does not support an extended time span. In the works of this period, 'combinatorial' thought, which meant the permutation of parameters, became so insistent as to give rise to an infinite number of possibilities, between which one refused to choose. Since the basic materials were sufficiently neutral and anonymous, one arrived at their indiscriminate, systematic utilisation by suppressing the personality of the composer as strongly as possible. The initial choices – of parameters or functions – being arbitrary (the musical idea not genuinely determining the selection of components that brought it into being), the resulting deductions were literally infinite, with no hierarchy, no consequence or necessary order of succession, but each as important, as weighty, as the other. One therefore decided to carve out a tract of time from this infinite potential, a fragment of the whole that one would be unable to imagine in its completeness.

With such automatism, such an absence of decision, this fragment offers no orientated listening, leaving perception afloat in a gravity-free ocean: the concept of *whole* is by definition inimical to it. But it seems clear to me that this is an aspect of perception (disorientation, absence of directedness) whose use can be justified, as a kind of non-gesture, anti-gesture, provided one knows precisely what nature and functions one can attribute to it. Hence the challenge for composers at this time, stemming from similar grammatical materials, of finding meaning and directedness in the deductions derived from a model or a matrix, and to combat (through unique and finalised solutions) the indeterminacy and open-endedness of the fragment, its anonymity and arbitrariness, its literally formless structure, by means of a usage totally alien to this kind of writing, and to rethink the notion of a hierarchised whole.

✳ ✳ ✳

The hierarchy of choice was shattered because, in the face of a certain number of deductions, one felt no need to choose, everything being equal in character and value. The direct result was to call the work 'open', a concept that did not arise from thinking about form, but from the multiple possibilities existing at a more elementary linguistic level. Why this solution rather than others, if they are all equally valid? The joining of fragments itself became a problematic issue, given the range of possible options. How to choose between these, when the composer can find no reason to decide, or the interpreter who is provided with materials, and who makes his selection, brings his own arbitrariness to link fragments into a necessarily provisional, personal whole? Completely different choices can be made by a different interpreter, even if he has decided, for another performance, to create a different whole. What is essential for the open work is not spontaneity of choice regarding the fragments or the proposed ordering, this spontaneity having no influence on the final result, and genuine spontaneity being impossible the more familiar one becomes with the suggestions of the composer; what remains essential is the practically limitless possibility of reconstituting different wholes from the fragments supplied. One has enhanced the problem of choice at the heart of form and meaning, rather than limiting it to the realms of the basic structures. Clearly, the concept of the open work can promote the realisation on more or less general levels, or within a very localised, very controlled field of action. Choices can be made at the moment of execution or be the object of systematic preparation. One might therefore often speak of open moments rather than an open work: quite brief moments introducing an audible difference with respect to the fragment itself or the sequence of certain fragments. Here, however, the imprint of the composer is indispensable, in anticipating the ordering of fragments, or at least the fields of action, the eventual or probable trajectory that arranges them into a whole. We again find in this compositional situation the utopia of Mallarmé and his *Livre*. Even with more modest ambitions, and if one does not go so far as to conceive the musical Work as the unique deciphering of a world, a genuinely multiple, comprehensive work is inconceivable without a number of rules affecting the making of choices, the bases for decision becoming more important than the decisions themselves and leading to useless diversity. The utopia of the open work has left certain traces and introduced a new dimension at the heart of the fragment, as well as in relation to the possible connections between fragments. The practicalities of interpretation have revealed their strengths, but also their limitations.

There is, nevertheless, another area of application for the notion of 'automatic' generation, without the intervention of 'gesture'. The computer is perfectly capable – using multiple materials and rules of organisation – of generating this fragment of the infinite that I mentioned earlier. Though incapable of characterising the composition, the machine offers infinite combinations of parameters that have been submitted to it and weaves the fragment of the infinite in a richer, more varied manner if one has provided complex or flexible rules. But such a fragment is clearly not intended for attentive and connected hearing, as one might hear a succession of characterised fragments such as an interpreter might present you with. A different rapport is therefore established between the large, uncharacterised fragment and a whole composed of a multiplicity of gestures. The interaction of two worlds requiring a common criterion – duration or dynamics, for instance – creates a multivalent aural response, equivalent in the visual arts (Klee, for example) to undefined bases that can be worked with according to very detailed specifications, from which specific pictorial processes will stem. Here again, two approaches confront one another, not simply of segmentation, but also of perception in time of sounding objects that do not follow the same logic of generation and choice.

Alongside the direct relevance to works following a given technique, I would like to offer some reflections on the closed work and the open work, in relation to the concept of the fragment and to assumptions about the opposed relationship between the formed and the unformed.

The open work is seen as an exemplar of deliberate incompletion, which at first glance has nothing to do with the *fragment* as such. Why deliberate incompletion? Because one requires the interpreter or interpreters to do more than follow a prescribed, predetermined route, imposed on the imagination. Given that in our tradition the slightest trace of the improvisatory has been banished, except for the most superficial kinds of ornamentation, the performer has been confronted by the strictness of the given text, loaded – supercharged, even – with a superfluous wealth of notational details: of rhythm, for sure, but also of dynamics, along with modifications of tempo and countless other details. Strict conformity to this plethora of signs reveals its inanity, inhibiting characterful performance. Reacting against all this leads to pure chance, the deliverance from an intolerable tyranny by anarchy posing as a principle, as a rule of conduct. This reaction, aspiring to reinstate spontaneity as essential to a 'reading' – if that word can be applied to elements vague enough, remote enough from any concept of grammar, or any realisation of anything but a purely graphic idea – cannot be taken too far. Pure spontaneity and even a minimum of permanence do not necessarily fit well together. It is too simple a solution to counter the tension it creates; it relies more and more on the anecdotal, in the material as much as in the way it is offered, a reliance that has decisively degraded it.

But the germ of spontaneous freedom is there, of a decision not imposed from without but which restores the possibility, not of real improvisation – the grammar does not allow for this, not being rooted in established and accepted procedures – but rather of a certain flexibility of choice: choice of direction, the elements decisive in determining the overall form; choice in the least constraining aspects of the notation, like dynamics, mode of attack or ways of sustaining sounds, ways of describing sonic aggregates – the determination of pitches being barely affected by this flexibility, requiring transposition, change of register, much more complex elaborations, so that constraint re-establishes its presence in a more radical manner than before.

If one wishes to ensure that performers do not produce something beyond every basic linguistic principle, their participation in the unfolding of an intentionally 'incomplete' structure can be confined above all to those essentially *non-quantitative* aspects of the language and the formal trajectory. These variations are not purely superficial, as perhaps with ornamentation. They impinge on expression itself in modifying the agogics of a phrase, its dynamic profile, its accentuation, its shape; all expressive power depends in essence on speed and dynamics – which, in turn, allow or disallow a certain kind of rhythmic or polyphonic writing, for example. A succession of regular rhythmic values will acquire its character from a certain degree of speediness or slowness; dense polyphony will not make any sense if the speed at which it must be read exceeds certain limits. The text to which such modifications are applied is not neutral; it must be composed in harmony with the requirements imposed by one's chosen variables. A certain significatory polyvalence will be essential if one wants the text to function on different levels and acquire a signification that is slightly or profoundly different. The sounding object is directly implicated: on a resonant instrument (piano, harp, vibraphone, etc.), the liberal use of that resonance requires a slow or very slow tempo. With 'dry' instruments, it is clear that the silence separating the events will, as far as *tempo* is concerned, be perceived in a much more disjointed manner, the ear having nothing to analyse or perceive between two events, but being uniquely expectant of the event to come. In this case, the resonance, the perception, engages with a transitional present created by the preceding event, and allows itself to be surprised by the succeeding one; when resonance is absent, and the memory is not engaged by an instantly graspable sonic object, perception is essentially anticipating a future event. It is not just a matter of a filling-out or an emptiness between one event and its successor, but rather of a radical opposition between attention to the pastness of one part and the prospect of another: the temporal category is completely reversed.

We used to be greatly entranced by modifications of a musical text by a performer – at first, through the shock of the intrusion of pure chance through the notion of spontaneity. For myself, I have never been inclined to encourage this course of action. What is involved in the manipulation and the flexibility of a text? Is it truly the shock of an encounter that is constantly renewed? Yes, if the rules for performance are simple, if someone chooses them for you, and you are required, without immediate preparation, to conform to them. The interpreter who decides on his own is not truly free in making that decision: he will already have brought the text under control and his decisions, whether he intends this or not, will be dependent on the habits triggered by that text. All his decisions are determined by these underlying features. The categories he prioritises are the most superficial, which is not to say that they are the least immediately expressive. On the contrary, the more the modifications are determined by the immediate power of expression, the more they bring out the simple agogics that one imposes on phrases, or more generally on musical phenomena. If one relies on someone else – whether this be a partner (as in music for two pianos) or a conductor

– for ideas to which one reacts, to establish a sonic balance in a trajectory imposed by another, or if one conforms to an order of succession that is imposed at the last minute, this brings a kind of tension to the performance that is unattainable in other ways.

Nevertheless, the field of action of this spontaneity is very limited and partly justifies the imposition of a variable dimension of the text. For more profound results, we must see deeper levels of reflection. And this is essentially the task not of a group, but of an individual. To study a text, to see in what way one approach or another might be employed, does not require spontaneity but repeated exercises around the variability of certain parameters. The interpreter can write down his own variants because he has the option of privileging a particular trajectory, a particular rhythmic character, a particular acoustic profile: a polyvalent text permits him to establish a personal association with a particular aspect of that text. Yet as already stated, the composer must prepare a text embodying that polyvalence; the strongest characteristics of envelope and trajectory are necessary attributes to ensure the success and conviction of a parallel strategy. Clearly, this is a long way from the shock of recognition, which usually comes down to a rather banal instance of the famous encounter between the sewing machine and the umbrella on the dissection table. The study of an *absolute* musical text that is open to an *absolute* amount of transformation is clearly utopian. Is it even *absolutely* desirable? It involves nothing less than the multiple significations of a text, going well beyond purely emotional comprehension, to find very deep foundations in a grammar that privileges the relative and the multiple. Perhaps this is the ultimate manifestation, or the latest, at any rate, of the principle of variation . . .

✽ ✽ ✽

To return to the opposition of formed and unformed, in parallel with the open work and the completed work, one might say that the unformed connects directly with completely open structures, endless and endlessly renewing, and however deprived of finitude, of individual personality, while the formed connects directly with the completed work, closed in on itself by a finite trajectory. In other words, while the unformed validates the fragment by its incompletion, the formed acknowledges the fragment as it freely defines a segment of time. But is it not rather the opposite? As already noted, the unformed implies a certain endlessness of transformations, without personality or directedness, rapidly draining interest from perception and finding itself confronted by an amorphous temporality where foresight, however vague, is not disturbed by any individual event. The fragment is thus the sole means for the exercise of its real power. If it is the principal text, a limited time will show a sufficiency of possibilities for isolating this fragment and for perception to remain alert, not having lost the capacity for foresight; the fragment thwarts curiosity and it can re-establish its presence at the heart of a directed, determined form, for non-directional moments. The concept of the fragment, the cut-out, is essential for the use of a parallel developmental technique. The concept of an 'unformed' musical structure applies to a *subtext*, something subordinate in the hierarchy of musical events, which can evolve from an audible continuity to a constant exchange between audible and inaudible following the trajectory of a characterised, structured text. The unformed appears or disappears according to how one controls the formed. The concept of fragment therefore does not always connect to a notion of excision or discontinuity, but it could well involve apparent or absent continuity, fluctuating according to a law imposed by the formal design. This can easily be realised by a computer that one has provided with a number of materials and processes; but it can also be realised purely instrumentally, if enough instruments are available and are used not on account of their potential for mass effects, but to provide a statistical collection whose individual materials are not perceived, but present a synthesis whose sounding envelope can be varied practically without limit. The writing changes accordingly: since individual components are not perceived as such, it is necessary to avoid events that stand out from a line compared to others; all the events must be as similar as possible with respect to the frequency of their appearance, their importance and their density. The mode of playing and timbral shades can be added, and varied in ways small enough not to stand out as such; the more the anonymous lines comprising this texture cross and get confusingly mixed up, the less any individual qualities can be attributed to them, and the more they approach an unanalysable statistical effect. The whole must nevertheless be governed by harmonic criteria. This is not to say that one must be able to refer to chords; statistical harmony must progress indistinctly, from a dense superimposition of intervals where perception is lost to a precise chord defined in statistical fashion. It seems clear that the 'unformed' has many possibilities, which have been little exploited in Western traditions.

Why should the 'formed' have been so privileged? As our traditions have developed, the work has been considered as a process, but a fractured one, in which the ordering of fragments is progressively codified in more and more rigid ways to deter individual freedom of choice in matters of ordering. Above all, one must appreciate that form, and the pursuit of forms, is allied to language and its structural characteristics: this makes it possible to sustain and articulate one's invention, to establish it in time – and time is the most significant factor in the evolution of form. For this very reason, one can speak exactly of fragments, because the most classical kind of work is an accumulation, whether in a predetermined order or not, of different fragments preserving a certain autonomy. Form is ineluctably connected to time and language: the rapport between them justifies the form, in various ways. The more numerous the variants and deductions from the initial material become, following a sufficiently flexible and wide-ranging logic, the more capable the form will be of expanding and accommodating elaborate developments. The main problem therefore becomes that of continuity in respect of the fragment, because while the fragment remains the fundamental source of any concept of composition, its integration into a whole – without which form as such cannot exist – remains the main tactical preoccupation of the composer. To establish itself in time, a form will be based on both evolution and rupture, continuity and discontinuity, similarity and contrast. As it gained strength, the concept of form established a hierarchy of successions and contrasts, which in the nineteenth century culminated in codified models, capable of variation – a hierarchy increasingly enfeebled as the language evolved to include ever more unstable principles of progression. The relation between different formal fragments depended increasingly on instinct rather than codes. Form was freed from a constriction that had become too rigid to be useful, yet this created the danger of the non-integrated fragment, of heterogeneous components, of a fragmentation of discourse that inhibited perceptibility, assimilation and comprehension. Between Mahler and Webern, who might stand for the two extremes of thinking about formal design, one notes the gulf that could appear between the integration of the fragment into a larger continuity and the identity of the fragment as a special (separate) moment. These two extremes created problems of perception. With the very brief fragment, and the complete abolition of repetition, grasping the whole was undermined by the brevity and constant change. Perception could not rely on orientation; surprised by novelty, it could not refer to a past, the piece having eliminated the function of memory. Hence the difficulty of listening to these pieces, not so much on account of their materials, or the novelty of their actual vocabulary, as for their resistance to memory through the radical qualities of the fragments: brevity, condensed time, time abolished. At the opposite extreme, the long movements of Mahler's symphonies present an accumulation and a succession of developments, involving a renewal of musical events, which the memory strains to grasp. Segments more strongly characterised than others stand out as separate entities, but perception often lacks the acuity necessary to join them together. The diversity and extent of a movement tends to ensure that for a long time it resists integration and is heard as a succession of separate fragments. That is true for the listener, and also for the performer; if he has not managed (analytically, consciously, or else pragmatically, literally) to appreciate the integration of the segments into a whole, he is not fully able to do justice to the work's overall trajectory. What is relevant to one symphonic movement could certainly apply to the different movements in a symphony. Even if they were written at different stages and without intentional connections, they belong together in the order the composer has finally determined. For sure, there are dissimilarities, but in presenting contrasts and similarities they still belong together. The integration of these larger fragments into a coherent whole – even though it allows for inconsequence and incoherence, because these contribute to a higher coherence – remains the ultimate objective of composer, interpreter and listener. It is not only after the end of the nineteenth century that the coherence of a large-scale whole became a problem; this is already very evident in a work like Beethoven's *Missa Solemnis*. Comparing Beethoven's treatment of the same Latin text from the standpoint of form rather than of style with Bach's approach in his Mass in B minor, one sees how different the relation between large form and fragment can be. As a text, the 'Credo' is the most difficult to set to music, containing as it does a challenging conjunction between narrative and dogma. Bach treats it as a succession of separate forms, which disentangles the mixture of genres. He separates the pictorial from the abstract, and thereby avoids the cliff over which Beethoven tumbles. Rather than transcend feeling in formality, Beethoven opts for multiple episodes and accentuates their theatricality, underlining their diversity. The integration of these fragments, which have a natural tendency to assert their autonomy, remains difficult to pull off: large form and fragment remain opposed within a continuity constantly placed in question.

The opposition between fragment and whole intensified as the nineteenth century progressed, ending – as I have already mentioned – with the deep chasm between Mahler and Webern. This followed the evolution of the musical language; increasingly, the more that language was thought of not so much in terms of established conventions, but rather as something to be determined individually or in the course of a work on its own terms, the more pressing became the problem of opposition between large form and small form, and of how to integrate the fragment into the whole. This was the case whatever the musical language involved in supporting the large form. There was an evident accommodation between language and form. We can observe this throughout history. The demands of certain kinds of strict writing are inimical to extended processes. Fugue or canon impose such constraints that the combinatorial properties of certain materials are notably restricted. By contrast, variation imposes no checks on formal invention: the more freedom it has, the easier it is for it to extend the initial materials. No rigorous formal constraints are involved, unlike other forms of writing.

How, then, does musical language appear today? In respect of form, what different possibilities exist, and how are the fragment and the whole affected? The absence of comprehensive codes and conventions has encouraged diffusion: diffusion of ideas, structures, processes. More specifically, the desire to avoid exact repetition tends to isolate separate successive events, each of which focuses on a distinctive quality. The resultant risk is an absence of cohesion and the impossibility of following the connections between a series of events when these connections remain obscure. Such step-by-step processes reinforce the fragmentary character to the point of disjunction. How, then, to avoid this constant risk of breakdown in the temporal unfolding? That is indeed the problem: how to arrive at a situation where the foreseeable and the unforeseeable interact to keep the perception alert, but without disorientating it. To achieve this it is necessary radically to rethink the idea of form. Inherited schemas, even when pushed to their extremes, cannot provide an adequate answer. It seems to me that it is necessary to integrate the fragment, so that the hierarchy takes a different form in relation to the principles of writing.

What fundamental changes have the most adventurous twentieth-century composers brought about? It is not just a matter of musical language, where the reference points have become individual, fleeting, adapted to this or that situation. It is above all the nature of the musical idea as such. One need not simply link the evolution of Western music to the evolution of the idea of the theme, but it is certain that the increasingly specific individualisation and characterisation of what we call 'theme' has been a basic tendency. We can now say that musical forms should be determined according to precise references to an idea exactly determined in all its components, in comparison to much vaguer references to general schemas relating to a common and less individualised background. While certain aspects correspond to relatively anonymous formulas, others very precisely reflect highly individualised characteristics. This depends on the chosen form, and at its heart, those moments that it implies. In baroque music, for example, the prelude often fits with descriptions of arpeggiated successions of chords, without particular thematic content, and following a course of fairly conventional progressions; at a higher level, and in a more symbolic vein, this references the first,

C major Prelude from Bach's *Wohltemperierte Klavier*. The arpeggiated presentation of each chord is highly repetitive, functioning as a consistent unifying principle; and at the same time it is difficult to think of it as a theme, for it has a rhythmic profile reduced to the simplest expression of a regular unity. With no power of transformation, it is nevertheless perfectly suited to adaptation. The only deviation serves to signal – or rather underline – the closing of the harmonic sequence provided by the chordal cadence. This final event signals that the trajectory has reached its conclusion, that this temporally unified fragment is complete. In the fugue, by contrast, there is the manifestation of a *subject*, found – or rather defined – through the manner of its use: organised according to strict principles of writing to perform multiple functions, yet also fashioned sufficiently clearly for a range of less complex procedures. There are, therefore, passages of strict writing and passages of freer, more supple writing. The strict passages connect directly to the formulation of the idea; the supple passages employ elements loosely drawn from the idea, in skeleton form, transitional. In this way, the fragments of a parallel process are linked with one another in this relatively supple way, at varying distances from the initial idea. It must be emphasised that these are organised – consciously, in the most challenging instances – from the perspective of a parallel dialectic.

✻ ✻ ✻

The musical idea has evolved as a function of the form it has created, at the same time as that form, especially with respect to length, has required a musical idea capable of functioning appropriately. Here, too, however, one can argue that the model has adapted itself to very different situations and usages. The thematic model as expounded has the potential for all treatments, from the simplest overall reconstitution to reduction to its simplest individual elements: single intervals or rhythmic cells. One can, for sure, recount the dangers of making over-explicit use of simple constituent elements. In Wagner's *Tristan*, increasing chromaticism has strong symbolic functions, and heard in another opera, a different context, the association is strongly established and asserts itself beyond any

619

organic connection. The danger of extreme fragmentation in relation to the original musical idea is of skeletal processes whose precise function one cannot determine: the coherence of the fragments is put at risk, the point of reference for some of them being clear, but not for others.

This is certainly true with developments in musical language since the Second Viennese School – after Wagner – where the overview, however fragmentary, has become increasingly problematic. At the other extreme of the landscape, there is Stravinsky's repetitive technique. *Les Noces* is the most striking example: the basic idea does not have a completely defined identity; its traits are sufficiently definite – intervallically, rhythmically – to be memorisable, and sufficiently indefinite to be subject to variation – rhythmic, especially – and thus lend themselves to necessary extension. Here, too, the idea comes into being as having potential for development, and it is with this kind of development that one comes closer to the fragmentation of the work: because it involves successive ostinatos (to simplify), one moves endlessly from one fragment to another, each one different. If one believes that, at its most adventurous, the Second Viennese School basically moved towards a kind of perpetual transition in which the fragments were linked in a continuous development, Stravinsky, at his most adventurous, emphasised rupture, finding his most potent and accomplished manner in the Symphonies of Wind Instruments.

I have mentioned the risks of perpetual transition, in the sense that the relation of fragments to wholes is too generalised and too drawn-out; one can also note the dangers of disruptive fragmentation, where the components never comprise a unity, remaining strangers to each other, and even stranger the more often one hears them, since they embody an autonomy that isolates them whatever the context in which they occur. This is the quality of some of Messiaen's most obstinately segmented forms, whose continuity remains elusive because each formal unit, even if subject to notable transformations – extension, elongation – is confined to its own inviolable space: of texture, timbre, register, dynamics. Even if it aids memory, that space isolates each fragment and prevents it from participating in genuine confrontation; one is left with a succession, where perception notes above all the principle of fragmentation.

It is from reflecting on these experiences that one can attempt to imagine how the collection or integration of fragments could comprise a form. As I have said, a form is connected to what it presents, to its musical idea. How can this be conceived today? An early concern – since my *Sonatine* for flute and piano from 1946 – was to establish a distinction between thematicism and athematicism. Of course, this idea was not mine alone: it arose from the contradiction noted at the heart of the Second Viennese School between series and theme. A succession of pitches – whether all twelve chromatic notes or some other number or character – could be the source of a shaped or amorphous structure. With the amorphous, one can draw from the initial series a restricted or limitless number of other successions, imposing on the original ordering the simple deductions of transposition and permutation, successions determined by an aleatoric process. Registers are not fixed, nor the actual intervals, any more than the durations, rhythmic schemes, dynamics or densities. These notes float in weightless space, which merely indicates their order. One can therefore relate them to quite different matrices on paper, for they have no musical character and imply no directedness. I began with a series of pitches that can be written down in different ways; but the preliminary material could equally well be a collection of durations or dynamics – whatever. What is vital is that this material is not slanted initially in any direction, not subject to any criteria, and has no thematic *obligation* to speak of. It is not that the initial amorphous material cannot provide a trajectory, an envelope: it can evolve according to the matrix in question by expanding textural density, then reducing to return to the starting point, or by fixing actual registers and dynamics – all characteristics that give the material direction and character, specific expression, but which are not directly connected to an initial *figure*, with all its particular descriptive qualities. One returns here to the idea of figure in outline, which I connected to certain transitions in baroque or classical music. These are comparable to what I call, by analogy, the 'interstitial tissue' that helps to bring coherence to fragments, without actually being part of them. In my *Sonatine*, there is just such transition-like material between the different movements of the single-span sonata form. To oppose this kind of process, I use procedures derived from themes, figures or motifs with strongly marked characteristics: groups of intervals connected in a rhythmic profile with a given dynamic; a group with a strongly expressive character. This thematic entity can provide segments, short motifs that run through the development without losing their identity: they remain recognisable, even when broken up; they have a repetitive role despite the variations and transformations applied to them. Permanent perceptibility is the principal characteristic of this thematic material: whatever aspect is developed, the fragment is unambiguously identifiable. In opposition to development is what I call 'athematicism', the outcome of treating matrices as unordered collections. 'Thematic' development focuses on clear, recognisable figures – using the matrix in fixed order. Listening is organised very differently, depending on the degree of liberty or constraint in question.

The type of writing is capable of generating form, proposing fragments of different kinds, whether linked into continuity or proceeding by separation. One can favour the integration of a given fragment into the whole by making it contribute to the unconscious evolution of developmental criteria; equally, one might prefer to valorise the fragment, as not conformable to the one that precedes it or the one that follows. Depending on the musical idea to which it refers, development can therefore take very different forms, setting up structures specifically designed with that objective. Does this leave us with individual forms that cannot be placed within broader categories? True, for a long time the problem of form was acute, and presented genuine challenges. It is no accident that the most successful works that attain a certain expansiveness suggest a compartmentalised form, or have a brevity underlining the fragmentary character of the structure. The two most notable works from the early twentieth century – *The Rite of Spring* and *Pierrot lunaire* – have become veritable symbols of modernity in representing the extremes of their epoch and in both consisting of juxtaposed fragments. *Pierrot lunaire* involves a succession of short or very short pieces that have no thematic materials in common, beyond the varied, truncated reprise of No. 7 ('Der kranke Mond') at the end of No. 13 ('Enthauptung'); and even this might be thought of as a quotation, a foreign body rather than a development, reinforcing the idea of the fragment in not promoting the continuity of an extension. In *The Rite,* meanwhile, the order and grouping of the pieces clearly involve variety and contrast, with a succession of dances or episodes, each of relatively short duration based on a limited number of elements; certain figures or themes pass between one segment and another, which preserve their identities and change in importance rather than function because they do not fully decompartmentalise the forms, remaining separate and self-referential entities. As in *Pierrot lunaire,* the juxtapositions are planned in terms of carefully handled contrasts, which are not helpful to an accessible integration. To rediscover a truly integrated developmental form, the two composers returned with mixed results to classical schemas, like the sonata, variations and the pre-classical suite, all schemas with well-defined procedural codes. There is a certain difficulty in thinking of musical language and form together, with their recourse to techniques of aggregation and integration from another epoch. The connection between fragment and whole had to be fundamentally rethought.

Not to beat about the bush, this remains a major problem. If we refuse to accept pre-existing schemas that are 'applied' to a reality that does not call for them, we have to approach the problem on a different basis. There are many ways of considering the integration of the fragment into the whole, even from the beginning. Allowing the fragment itself to proliferate might generate a form, as the outcome of criteria applied to the development of the musical idea: for instance, the convergence of one characteristic in relation to another, the gradual intrusion of one typology in relation to another, might create segments whose profile will change imperceptibly; the succession of segments will employ criteria of difference dominated by unifying factors, but will be strong and effective enough for the modifications to be perceptible. Here, in effect, the evolution of the parameters will determine the form; continuity induces change, the fragments will be more strongly integrated into the whole. But the opposite could just as easily occur, knowing that within a certain category of action, ways of assembling the fragments must be found to justify and realise a particular juxtaposition.

❋ ❋ ❋

How to think of integration and juxtaposition, how to insert the fragment into a form, remains an essential preoccupation of composition, even *the* essential preoccupation. With no justification for insertion, the fragment remains autonomous, and the form does not properly exist. Before addressing this problem directly, I will speak about the material itself, because it is this that suggests essential solutions affecting fundamental features, principles of connected continuation. Earlier, I proposed an opposition between thematic and athematic processes, the one based on ordered and characterised materials, the other on matrices. This opposition between specific attributes and general contours remains useful as the basis for generalisation. Precision of criteria and parameters is the necessary condition, in effect. With what is extremely precise and constrained, one approaches the idea of the figure, the theme; with greater generality one accesses only unordered collections. Depending on the kind of process one wishes to use, one must define the degree of constraint to be applied to parameters and criteria; the more extendable they are, the closer one gets to the 'unformed', as discussed above. Conceiving material restrictively or open-enddedly will determine the nature of the developmental process, characterising the fragment. These ideas and procedures are more flexible than those implying a theme, but less vague than those for a series of sounds that has no implied consequences, even with respect to intervals. I spoke of parameters and criteria: needless to say, these terms apply to quite different materials – pitches, durations, etc., that is, to specific materials. These materials can be specific, but they might also be more generalised and fluctuating, like texture, density, register, evolution, etc.

In these terms I can describe the possible types of integration or juxtaposition of fragments within a whole. For me, this implies various ways of conceiving that integration: first, thinking of it as finite or infinite; second, regarding it in relation to continuity or discontinuity; finally, considering it as a function of succession in time – or not. These are three very broad criteria, but they give a key to all the ways of integrating fragments into wholes, and might even involve thinking of the fragment as an ideal whole or, the opposite, that fragments can exist while the whole is impossible.

Regarding integration as a rounded model, the consequences of the material must be limited, or one will be able to use only its proximate effects, so that with strong constraints, such as a total absence of repetition, one consciously restricts the musical idea's field of activity – in this way, the fragment displays its restrictions, as it were. A form of much larger dimensions has the capacity to juxtapose completed fragments, to situate them through affinity, or through contrast, to create an overall process of connection or disconnection. The formal trajectory consists of the regular or irregular alternation of completed fragments, which can belong to different families, strongly characterised by external features that are instantly recognisable, such as timbre, register or density (in time or in sound-space), fragments not reducible to the same source or, by contrast, linked by many common factors. One therefore obtains a mixture of the static – the nature, the very character of the fragments – and the mobile, their ordered presentation due to other considerations, such as frequency of appearance or regularity. Such a form takes no account of the order in which fragments from the same family appear; the length of development plays no role in their appearance, or in their degree of complexity. Time matters at the moment of their appearance, but takes an independent course, unfolding on its own terms. However, the presence of strongly defined common elements makes it possible to identify them, singling them out whatever the context. A compartmentalised mosaic form can be the result of this arrangement of fragments according to their character.

I've proposed finite and infinite categories to represent the nature of a procedure. If the chosen categories are highly constrained, a certain arrangement of parameters arises – and I understand that this is not simply exchanges or permutations, but that the parameters increase their productivity at higher levels in the hierarchy of musical ideas, an arrangement that ends after a particular number of statements, after which there can be only restatements, textual repetitions cancelling the value of the fragment as such, and also its value in respect of what constitutes a directed grouping. If, on the other hand, the criteria are strongly projected, with a potentially limitless number of outcomes, the fragment paradoxically becomes an element opposed to integration within a *fully finished* form; one senses that it can continue to evolve indefinitely, leading the form towards an absence of clear-cut definitions, into necessary formal incompletion. This is an actual example of open form: not because one has decided not to worry about establishing the specific logic required for such an outcome, but because the idea, the material cannot create a restricted ensemble or a closed form.

Is this form *directed* or not? With directed form, the fragments, the segments of a larger whole follow a particular chronological order, and they must be heard in a given sequence, and not otherwise. Suppose, in effect, that a given fragment implies, in one way or another, integration with the preceding fragment or fragments, the last being the total of all the preceding ones – a total that can appear as a simple accumulation, or a superimposition, or some more subtle arrangement than these two elementary operations. The need to perceive these fragments as more and more extended imposes an apparent chronology – if they are to be heard as they really are. Any alternative will make sense only a posteriori, since it confounds the evolutionary process. In any case one is not obliged to prefer a chronological order in a composition that is merely an accumulation; that accumulation might indeed occur in the work, as a succession of subtractions leading the listener to grasp less and less of the initial fragment that alone represents the entire process. But there is a completely different way of understanding the fragment as a component of a whole. Fragments do not depend on an order of appearance, since they are all of equal weight and of similar design – if not of exactly the same length. A fragment might be more extended, more energetic, louder; the fact remains that it plays the same role as another fragment, and its temporal location cannot affect understanding of what it represents, the role it plays. It is a matter of a *non-directed*, floating form, which will eventually be subject to choices 'improvised' by the interpreter, justifying the intrusion of aleatoric procedures into the form. I use the word 'improvised' only on the understanding that this choice occurs within a fixed structural context, implying acute awareness of the multiple possibilities available to the performer. Here, as always, it is a matter of a spontaneity belonging to whoever has learned how to manipulate the different fragments. Whatever the immediate decision, the overall trajectory will always project a sense of the close or distant connection established between the fragments through the different envelopes that characterise them. But, I repeat, thanks to the structural equivalence of these various fragments, the order of succession matters only to the extent that it establishes the moment-to-moment trajectory that gives them a provisional meaning. In this way, chance is both celebrated and denied: all chance in the work must be subject to necessity, however obsolete.

The word 'fragment' solely implies, in the immediate sense, an idea of segmentation, of discontinuity. This is one possibility in the conception of the work as fragment. The form can be thought of as a mosaic of elements: more or less foreseeable, because they stem from a single network of ideas, elements distinguished by family having given the collection its identity; yet a succession that is not unforeseeable but which uses a different logic belonging to different collections will give birth to its own suitable fragments. There is a dialectic of rupture and discontinuity within such a plan of action, though at the same time there is a profound continuity in the organisation of each collection. The continuity is latent rather than obvious, constantly contradicted by unpredictable events; there are continuities linked by dotted lines on different levels making only sporadic appearances. Similar formal conceptions do not necessarily imply a completed trajectory: this depends essentially on the potential richness of each stratum, and on the number of strata involved. With a very targeted 'scanning' of the strata – treating each one in turn, or when a maximum turns to a minimum and in turn becomes a maximum, etc. – one creates a closed, directed form from the initial mosaic of fragments. But if each stratum has a kind of limitless arrangement, one returns to what I've called the 'unformed', where closure is an unknown quantity. Paradoxically, it is the 'unformedness' that gives the whole its fragmentary character, in contrast to an imagined and in some ways 'in-finite' whole, since limited potentialities bring to a fragment that is reduced in length a *finite* moment that is an absolute, restricted whole. The interplay of the two organisms turns out to be interesting with regard to perception: the *finite* having been conceived as a whole, the *in-finite* can be grasped only as a fragment. In one case, the boundaries and the trajectory play crucial roles in defining the scope of what is heard; in the other, perception has no need of continuity and can be only intermittent. One can call listening either event-governed or non-event-governed: event-governed means that the fragment is like a whole, attracting attention at every stage; non-event-governed means that the whole is like a fragment, needing moment-to-moment listening, constantly cut short.

A mosaic form, where discontinuity in the succession of elements is the basic principle, is opposed to a spiral form, based on the continuity of events where elements are constantly renewed in the same order, while being enriched by variants that absorb or renew the texture of the previous state. The principle of this trajectory is extremely simple, constantly implying a connection to the rate of development. If the order of events is fixed, one's entire interest is absorbed by the complex intersections of the process, as well as by the accumulation within a developmental process, in terms of the permanent features of certain foundational resources like texture, rhythmic sequences and the mobility of other materials such as register and dynamics. Just as in the mosaic form revision of the order of events is tied to a discontinuous sense of time, so in the spiral form the presence of a fixed succession of elements promotes not only a perception of time as continuous, but also a kind of temporal comparison: since the *present* time of a segment is, to a degree, foreseeable, it can refer to the *past* time of a segment from the same family (similar but not identical, whose ease of recognition will depend on the degree of distance or closeness), and similarly prepares the *future* time of its next appearance. There is the constant presence of features that resist immediate and mechanical recognition: first, the degree of variation between a segment and its predecessor and successor; second, the progress of the process of development. In effect, the segments grow longer and longer through the simple process of absorbing their predecessors, the result being a doubling. Segments from different families succeed one another at wider and wider intervals, the sense of proximity that was very strong at the outset weakening through temporal distancing, each segment tending more and more towards autonomy. From a partial whole that is relatively simple to perceive because of being constructed from short fragments easily fitting into the whole, one progresses to another partial whole that is more and more difficult to hear as such, since perception has more difficulty in integrating the collection of fragments into a unity that one can barely grasp in its entirety, the memory losing its capacity to synthesise. With such a very ramified whole, the expanding work risks becoming a succession of separate fragments, more and more developed, however precisely orientated. Such a form is, essentially, a fragment of a potentially infinite whole. To be heard as a finite form – or provisionally finite – no matter the number of stages involved, each stage will be perceived as generating an autonomous structure. How to 'arrest' this process that might appear unsatisfactory on the grounds of this quality of incompletion? No need to mark the beginning with a special signal, as one immediately begins the process of gradual unwinding; clearly, one can use such a signal to attract attention to what in due course will prove an indispensable signal of completion. With a sequence that always has the potential to connect with the following sequence, it is vital to set a *limit* to the eventual linking proximity. Naturally, like the material it uses, the imagination has limits – the material itself imposes limits on the imagination. One cannot speak glibly of infinite form without falling into conceptual absurdity. It is nevertheless interesting to observe that even a finite form can be presented in fragmentary fashion, provided that the final phase cuts off the evolutionary process, reuniting the final phase to the opening phase, if there is one, eventually reuniting transitional phases that signal the appearance of a new sequence. In comparison to the closed forms that are the essence of our tradition, it is interesting to contemplate forms that are unlimited in principle. It is in this sense that one can conceive of a work as part of a whole that it is not necessary to realise, that might indeed be impossible to realise, that leaves the listener or reader with the illusion of a continuation for which he alone is responsible. This is how, for me, the open work becomes a reality. While necessarily closed in respect of any particular realisation, it remains open to an infinite number of other interpretations.

In this survey of forms using the fragment/whole dialectic, I would like to include a scheme whose formal principles impinge on each other, intersect and interlock, a kind of extension of the concept known as *Durchführung*, no longer applied to themes but to formal principles. This might extend from simple accretion to a veritable disintegration: not so much imposing order or disorder on fragments and sequences, but instead producing an interaction by multiplying the basic elements by each other to produce transformations by reciprocal actions. In a more complex and ultimately irreversible way, fragment becomes whole; fragment grafts itself onto fragment and thus turns into an indissoluble whole. In his *Lyric Suite*, Berg showed how this technique can give new meaning to traditional forms: a fragment of one movement appears in another, not as a quotation remaining striking out of context, but as an integral part of a context different from that in which it had previously been heard. In this way, all the movements of the *Lyric Suite* are connected by a kind of 'passing the baton'.

❊ ❊ ❊

Ultimately, what concerns me is to resolve the conflict between the virtual and the real, between the closed and the open, between the whole and the fragment. Can a work, to the extent that it is unified – in the past as much as in the present – be considered as anything other than a succession of fragments, with their individual qualities and functions? A more or less flexible, more or less rich musical language can provide these fragments with a larger dimension, a stronger facility to interconnect without countering the power of their separate specifics, according to the characteristics giving them unique and irreplaceable profiles. It is typical that in the analysis of works, one constantly uses the word 'section', based on materials related to the exploitation of musical ideas or an arrangement of those ideas. According to the relevant genres, such sectionings will be more or less precise, more or less fluid, facile or hard to detect, tied to specifically instrumental ideas or to poetic or dramatic subject matter, as has always been the case. But the sense of the whole has been more dominant than that of the fragment. The whole is what justifies the existence and location of the fragment. Since traditional forms have gradually lost their dominance, the fragment has become essential in itself, standing for something not abjectly subordinate to the whole. In the extreme instances – Webern, especially in the very short pieces of the years 1910–14 – one can conceive of the whole only as a fragment, the work as a succession of fragments that remain unintegrated into a whole, not as a totality. This is what Mallarmé called an Album as distinct from a Book: detachable pages resisting connectedness and a single ordering.

One can now, after all one's experiences of the twentieth century, arrive at this completely provisional and doubt-filled conclusion: the work can be only a fragment of an imaginary whole. The work thought of as a whole is never more than a convenient illusion, but as with light through a prism, it deconstructs into fragmentary components, which when given a temporal continuity regain the appearance of a whole. But as with the uncertain, inconclusive endings of certain novels by Kafka, the work as such – disowning long-cherished narrative functions of language – can only seem unfinished, a fragment of an unreal, hypothetical whole. With language freed of constraints and conventions of closure, any *ending* can only artificially truncate a whole that entirely rejects the concept of finality, of completion.

In other words, and provisionally to complete my remarks: having no reality but the fragment, the whole is nothing but an endlessly renewed, endlessly sought-after illusion.

Index

absolute, desire for the, 114

absolute music, 174, 222, 613

academicism, 173, 204, 206, 210, 297, 355, 449

accelerando, 176, 180, 369, 373, 488, 498

accent displacement, 145

accentuation, 80, 145, 611; and dynamics, 142, 335, 352; harmonic, 335; and perception, 74; percussion, 44

acciaccatura, 349

accident: and chance, 58; and composition, 24, 45, 63, 64, 76, 104, 106, 107, 115, 116, 119–20, 131–2, 247, 250, 273–5, 277–8, 343, 376, 390, 521, 555, 556, 563, 565, 577, 581; and design, 454–5; *see also* chance; language, musical

accidentals, 123, 489, 533–4

accompaniment, 104, 128, 162, 214, 357, 497, 524, 555

acoustic complementarities, 580

acoustics, 282, 290, 302, 339, 360–4, 368, 370, 382, 416, 420, 490, 491, 499, 501, 526, 529, 536, 538, 544, 553, 571–4, 583, 584, 588, 607, 613; absorption, 375; code, 532; effect, 523; environmental, 267; illusion, 375, 384, 522; instrumental, 339; masking, 375; notation, 126; phenomena, 61, 339, 360, 364, 420, 502, 543, 548, 561; properties, 81, 291, 292, 361, 363, 371, 546, 552, 569, 577; psychoacoustics, xix, xxii n. 34, 72; rapport, 568; relationships, 350, 358, 361, 568, 572, 580; research, xi; structure, 14; terminology, 142; of venue, 375, 489

acrostics, 493

adagio, 156, 194, 200, 534, 595

Adorno, Theodor, 159, 203, 313, 340, 575

aesthetics, vii–viii, x, xv–xvi, xix, 11, 16, 82, 97, 114, 187, 201, 203, 282, 290, 292, 295, 296, 300, 306, 310, 330, 332, 333, 425

affect, 370, 372, 374, 420

African culture, 293, 367, 508, 599

agglomeration, 551

aggregates/aggregation, 38, 338, 350, 494, 532, 566–9, 572, 575, 611, 623; chromatic, 293; tonal, 211

aleatorics/aleatoricism, xvi, 49, 276, 344, 391, 529, 556, 558; elements, 37; forms, 97; fragments, 607; indeterminacy, 50; layering, 256; and Nature, 169; notation, 536; process/procedure, 621, 626; transmission, 527; works, vii, 344; *see also* chance

alla turca style, 127

alternation, 38, 48, 98, 144, 179, 220, 324, 363, 393, 395, 545, 550, 589; and fragments, 625; stability/instability, 568

amateurism/amateurs, 42–4, 149, 172, 182, 285, 342, 357, 420, 447, 448, 461, 551, 578, 606

ambiguity, 103, 128, 134, 145, 154, 172, 190, 194, 200, 203, 205, 229, 230, 257, 282, 283, 290, 292, 321, 324, 328, 329, 334, 384, 392, 394, 396, 453, 459, 479, 513, 521, 546

ambivalence, 172, 263, 358, 384, 394, 495, 607

amplifiers, 11

analysis, 21–30, 33, 34, 38, 50, 51, 56, 67, 72–3, 75, 80, 186–7, 194, 290–1, 322, 328, 330, 408, 435, 437–8, 441–2, 444–5, 452, 453–7, 478, 585–6,

630; as communication, 525; of form, 437; morphology, 437, 440, 443; and notation, 527; numerical, 171–2; objective, 438; and reduction, 453; schematic, 452; and self-discovery, 429, 435, 438; spectral, 282; and subjectivity, 435, 439; virtual, 374; visual, 533

anarchic procedures, 5, 127, 130, 131

anarchy, 149, 208, 288, 294–7, 307, 473, 560, 571, 602; as principle, 611

ancient Greek music, 103

anonymity, 167, 213, 246, 248, 264, 347, 368, 382, 468, 520, 524, 562, 569, 580, 608, 614, 618; anonymisation, 506, 513, 562, 569; and collectivity, 76; of composer, 58, 138, 333; and creativity, 425; and individuality, 58; of instrument, 102; of performer, 58; of style, 450

Ansermet, Ernest, 448

anticipation, 338, 572

antiphony, 113, 179, 257, 260, 382

applause, 594

appoggiatura, 132, 338, 349, 379

apprenticeship: for composers, 25, 33, 52, 454, 457–9, 481, 493; in oral tradition, 411; see also education, musical

appropriation, 34, 187, 188, 207, 220, 464–6, 476; misappropriation, 188; see also borrowing

arbitrariness, 23, 63, 68, 137, 156, 158, 164, 170, 204, 223, 243, 245, 248, 262, 266, 295, 341, 418, 425, 530, 537, 551, 563, 576, 584, 507, 607–9

archaism, 59, 77, 94, 154, 292–3, 576

archetypes, 144, 173, 188, 197, 198, 217–19, 259, 601

architecture: and cultural identity, 412, 467–8; performance spaces, 414; reconstruction, 412

archivism, 454

arpeggio/arpeggiation, 50, 385, 494, 495, 497–8, 507, 524, 572; arpeggiated, 163, 618–19; compound, 211, 311; fundamental, 452

arrhythmia, 48

ars nova, 106, 417, 516

art song, 154

articulation, 34, 64, 67, 80, 127, 132, 137, 140, 142, 151–4, 157, 164, 167, 177, 180, 185, 189, 195, 197, 208, 227, 228, 241, 253–4, 269, 287, 324, 330, 340, 351, 365, 372, 373, 374, 379, 380, 389, 420, 444, 471, 493, 512, 514, 546, 574, 581, 615; emphasis, 520; formal, 137, 176, 182, 203, 267, 395–7, 399, 505, 507; freedom of, 266; instrumental, 547; means of, 132; melodic, 214; of motives, 163; of ornamentation, 509; phrasing, 523; points of, 180, 244, 253, 295, 352–3; speed of, 544; syllabic, 550; and text, 159, 556; of timbre, 164, 440; vocal, 129–30, 372; writing, 551

Asian musics, 103, 207, 508, 568

assemblage, 224, 372, 468

athematicism, 96, 166, 222–78, 340, 341, 621, 622, 624; and development, 266; and techniques, 237; see also thematicism

audibility, 190, 254, 315, 348, 389–91, 478, 493, 494, 511, 517, 520, 522, 525, 548, 567, 574, 583, 603, 609, 614

audience participation, 271

augmentation, 93, 199, 231, 302, 493, 511

aura, 207, 338–9, 348–50, 550, 605; historical, 423

Austrian music, 471

authenticity, xvii, xxiv, 53, 207, 284–5, 312, 405–7, 412–26, 446, 480–2, 490, 593; documentary evidence, 407, 411, 413, 418, 419, 422–3; instrumentation, 414, 416; period style, 414, 489; and reconstruction, 411–12, 416–18, 423–6, 446, 482; textual, 416; writing, 419, 497

autodidactism, 447, 458

automatic writing, 66

automatism, 119–46, 333, 565, 608

avant-gardes, vii, 405, 410

Bach, Johann Sebastian, 29, 103, 108, 188–9, 200, 220, 253, 387, 414, 426, 427, 429, 472, 494, 523; The Art of Fugue (Die Kunst der Fuge), 92; Brandenburg Concertos, 219, 416,

593; canons, 106; cantatas, 523; choral works, 200; chorales, 523; *Christmas Oratorio*, 594; Fugue in E flat, 516; fugues, 22; inventions, 380; Mass in B minor, 594, 617; *The Musical Offering*, 189; Passions, 523; solo violin sonatas, 522, 571; suites, 593; *The Well-Tempered Klavier* (the '48'), 494, 497, 619

Bacon, Francis, 118 n. 3

balafon, 367

Balinese music, 378; *see also* gamelan

ballet, 222, 260, 427, 478; *see also* individual works

Balzac, Honoré de, 307, 592; *Séraphîta*, 307, 570

baroque music, xxiv, 214, 220, 277, 291, 321, 380, 414, 415, 488, 489, 493, 523, 524, 530, 593, 600, 601, 618, 621

Bartók, Béla, 207, 213, 220–1, 259–60, 296; and folk music, 207, 213, 221; free/strict techniques, 220; and pizzicato, 73, 132; rhythmic practice, 232; scores, 380; thematicism, 220–1; tonality, 296; transcriptions, 213, 486, 488

WORKS: *The Miraculous Mandarin*, 221; *Music for Strings, Percussion and Celesta*, 132, 219–21; Piano Concerto No. 2, 220; Sonata for Two Pianos and Percussion, 221; string quartets, 34, 132

Bauhaus, 112, 327, 341, 589

Bayreuth, 421–2, 468

BBC Symphony Orchestra, ix

Beaumarchais, Pierre de, 118 n. 3

Beethoven, Ludwig van, 27, 95, 108, 161, 185, 188–9, 194, 195, 198, 202, 294, 414, 427, 462, 476, 571, 594–5, 606, 617

WORKS: adagios, 534; Diabelli Variations, 188–9; *Grosse Fuge*, 601; late quartets, 28, 155; late works, 31, 381, 594, 601; *Missa Solemnis*, 617; Piano Sonata in B flat ('Hammerklavier'), op. 106, 194, 235–6, 336, 601; Piano Sonata in C minor, op. 111, 594; piano sonatas, 28, 601; String Quartet in C sharp minor, op. 131, 594–5; symphonies,

202; Symphony No. 3 in E flat (*Eroica*), 304; variations, 100–1

bells, 122, 366; *see also* sleigh bells

Berg, Alban, 31, 113, 155–61, 165, 174, 188–90, 194, 203, 218–20, 226, 231–2, 301, 303–4, 312–17, 319–20, 323–5, 328–9, 396, 434, 443–4, 448, 516, 517–19, 575, 596, 596; codes, use of, 91, 106, 158–9; and constraint, 311, 316–17, 333; and deduction, 314–15, 323; and *Erinnerungsmotiv*, 155, 434; and folk sources, 174; and form, 444; and harmonic language, 303–4; *Hauptrhythmus*, 231; *Hauptstimme/Nebenstimme*, 511; incorporation, 323; *Monoritmica*, 50, 231; motives, 444; nostalgia, 329; notation, 511; and numbers, 160, 165, 314–15, 323–5, 516; scores, 380; and serialism, 313–17, 319–20, 323, 325, 575; sub-thematic procedures, 158; symbolism, 106, 159–60, 314, 443, 516; symmetries, 95; technique, 313–14; and texts, 153, 155–60; thematicism, 220, 315, 323, 443–4; tonality, 304, 313, 316; and tradition, 309; and twelve-tone row, 220, 316

WORKS: *Altenberglieder*, op. 4, 155, 161, 597; Chamber Concerto, 106, 157, 443–4, 516; lieder, 260; *Lulu*, 91, 113, 158, 160–1, 165, 174, 188–9, 314, 316, 324, 396, 434, 443, 516; *Lyric Suite*, 34, 91, 106, 157, 165, 220, 314, 316, 319, 516, 630; Violin Concerto, 304, 316, 317; *Der Wein*, 316; *Wozzeck*, 31, 34, 113, 155, 157–61, 174, 190, 218–19, 303, 311, 313, 359, 434, 443, 516, 517–19, 597

Berio, Luciano, vii, viii, 123, 127, 506; *Circles*, xi, 123

Berlioz, Hector, xvii, 154, 195, 202, 294, 362, 363–4, 377, 414, 427, 494, 599; and *idée fixe*, 150, 362; orchestration, 362, 377, 401 n. 3; sonority and drama, 362

WORKS: *Lélio*, 294; *Roméo et Juliette*, 294; *Symphonie fantastique*, 294, 362, 524

WRITINGS: *Traité d'orchestration*, 524

blending, 365, 396, 544

bongos, 400

borrowing, 27, 218, 277, 292, 324, 466, 579; adjacencies, 580; forms, 227; material, 135, 188, 191, 199, 206–7, 209, 240, 329, 442; thematicism, 220; *see also* appropriation

Boulez, Pierre: compositional techniques, 233, 236–58, 263–4, 275, 341, 344, 348–50, 363–4, 366, 375, 384, 385, 387, 389–91, 396, 525, 550, 563, 583, 598, 621–2; as conductor, vii, ix, 380–1; education, xvii, 439; literary style, xvii, xviii, xxv; and modes, 242; as pianist, 221; as teacher, 434–5, 456–8
WORKS: *Anthèmes 1*, xvi, xxiii; *Anthèmes 2*, xvi, xxiii; *Cummings ist der Dichter*, 113; *Dérive 1*, xvi, xxiii; *Dérive 2*, xv, xxiii; *Dialogue de l'ombre double*, xviii; *Éclat*, xxv, 97, 258, 363–4; *Éclat/Multiples*, xviii, 254, 257, 389; . . . *explosante-fixe* . . . , xvi, xxiii, 18 n. 4; First Piano Sonata, 237; *Le Marteau sans maître*, 251, 396, 598; *Mémoriale (. . . explosante-fixe . . . Originel)*, xvi; *Messagesquisse*, xv; *Notations* for orchestra, xxiii, 258, 384, 389–90; Piano Sonata No. 2, xxv; *Pli selon pli*, 113, 263, 278 n. 3, 375, 401 n. 2, 550; *Répons*, xv, xvi, xxiii, xxv, 256, 278 n. 2, 385, 391; *Rituel*, xv; *Sonatine* for flute and piano, 96, 166, 233–8, 240, 256, 341, 621–2; *Structures* for two pianos, xiii, xvi, 33, 97, 117, 191, 240–1, 244–6, 251, 387, 563, 607; *Sur Incises*, xv, 146 n. 1; Third Piano Sonata, xvi, 38, 97, 278 n. 2; *Le Visage nuptial*, 385
WRITINGS: 'Aesthetics and the Fetishists', 56 n. 1; 'Alea', viii; 'At the Edge of Fertile Land (Paul Klee)' ('À la limite du pays fertile'; 'An der Grenzen des Fruchtlandes'), 56 n. 5, 83 n. 4; 'Athematicism, Identity and Variation' ('The Thematic Challenge'), xiii, xvii, **222–78**; 'Automatism and Decision', xi, xii, xvi, xxiv, 119–46; 'Between Order and Chaos', xiii, xvii, xxv,

357–401, 401 n. 1; 'Composition and Its Various Gestures', xii, xvii, xxiv, 87–118; 'Concept of Writing, The', xiii, xvii, 485–525; 'Corruption in the Censers', viii; 'Current Investigations', viii; 'Idea, Realisation, Craft' ('Musical Invention I: Origins and Antecedents'), xii, xviii, 21–56; 'Invention/Research', xii, xvi, 8–18; 'Invention, Technique and Language', xii, xvi, 3–7; *Jalons (pour une décennie)*, xii, xiii, xxiii, xxv; 'Language, Material and Structure' ('Musical Invention II: Dimensions and Codes'), xii, 57–83; *Leçons de musique: Points de repère III*, xii, xiii, xx, xxiii, xxv; 'Memory and Creation', xiii, xvii, xviii, xxiv, 405–84; 'Necessity of an Aesthetic Orientation, The', viii; 'Notation, Transcription, Invention' ('The Concept of Writing'), xiii, xvii, 526–59; 'Notion of Theme and Its Evolution, The', xiii, xvii, 149–81; *Orientations*, xvi, xxiii, 484 n. 1; 'Periform', ix; *Points de repère*, viii, xxiii, 484 n. 1; 'Possibly' ('Éventuellement'), 278 n. 4; 'Research and Creation', xiii; 'Schoenberg Is Dead', x; *Stocktakings from an Apprenticeship*, 56 n. 5, 278 n. 4; 'Stravinsky: Style or Idea? In Praise of Amnesia' ('Style ou Idée? Éloge de l'amnésie'), 484 n. 1; 'System and the Idea, The', xiii, xvii, xxiv–xxv, 281–356, 356 n. 1; 'Theme, Variations and Form' ('The Thematic Challenge'), xiii, xvii, xxv, 182–221; 'To "Think" Music Today' (*Penser la musique aujourd'hui*), vii–viii; 'Work: Whole or Fragment?, The', xiii, xvi, xvii, 592–631; 'Writing and Idea' ('The Concept of Writing'), xiii, xvii, 560–91; agendas, xiii–xv; correspondence, viii, xvi

Bourdieu, Pierre, xi

bow/bowing, 429, 549

bracelets, 130

Brahms, Johannes, 161, 189, 195–6, 198, 202, 417; Intermezzos, 594; symphonies, 202; *Variations and*

Fugue on a Theme by Handel, 189; *Variations on a Theme by Haydn*, 189

brass instruments, 150, 372, 420, 549; natural brass, 414; *see also* individual instruments

breath/breathing, 133, 368, 372, 429, 549

Brecht, Bertolt, 288, 423

Breton, André, 18 nn. 3, 4, 40, 56 n. 4; *Contes bizarres d'Achim von Arnim*, 56 n. 4

bricolage, 551

broadcasting, 11

Brown, Earle, xi, 83 n. 2

Bruckner, Anton, 202; symphonies, 202

Bussotti, Sylvano, xi

cadence, 151, 173, 208, 619

caesura, 24, 208, 275, 276

Cage, John, vii, xvi, 374, 472; *Atlas Eclipticalis*, 591 n. 2; *Music of Changes*, xi

canon, 50, 106, 168, 169, 172, 199, 237, 320–1, 384, 386, 395, 425, 453, 617; double/quadruple, 172, 321; forms, 37, 163; imitation, 193; strict, 317, 318, 320, 576; techniques, 37, 228–31, 297, 439, 519–20; writing, 144, 169, 229, 328, 439, 440, 479, 520, 604

cantata, 154, 593, 600

cantus firmus, 37, 64, 102, 189, 192, 223, 382

Caplet, André, 221 n. 2

caricature, xviii, 103, 116, 144, 173, 174, 204, 206, 218, 289

Carter, Elliott, vii, viii, 177, 178, 506–7, 566–7; metrical modulation, 177, 180 WORKS: *Eight Pieces for Four Timpani*, 177, 181 n. 5; *A Mirror on Which to Dwell*, 567; Third String Quartet, 178

Castel, Père Louis-Bertrand, 460

cello, 368, 373, 598

Cézanne, Paul, 110

Chabrier, Emmanuel, 278 n. 4

chamber ensemble, 101, 419, 522

chamber music, 175, 291, 293, 294, 384, 522, 595

Champmeslé, Marie, 416

chance, xi, xvi, xxiii, 12, 14, 32, 33, 40, 45, 68, 70, 96, 97, 98, 106, 119, 120, 131, 136, 138–9, 141, 183, 209, 264, 265, 268, 276–7, 326, 345, 353–5, 397, 415, 528, 569, 578, 611, 612, 627; abolished chance, 58, 68, 265, 356; aleatoric elements, 37; coordinated, 112; and determination/determinacy/determinism, 119, 121, 133, 135–6, 264; elimination of, 119, 333; as entertainment, 136; manipulation of, 17, 29; and premeditation, 134; *see also* accident; aleatorics/aleatoricism; determinacy/indeterminacy; material, musical

chaos, 45, 119, 300, 536, 571, 586, 590; fear of, 300; formal, 160; and order, 102, 320, 357–401

Char, René, 32, 446; *Le poème pulvérisé*, 484 n. 5; 'Song of the Sorgue', 56 n. 2

Chinese music, 378

Chinese violin, 367

Chopin, Fryderyk, 195, 211, 311, 535, 606; nocturnes, 395

chorale, 135, 217, 429, 523

chords: acoustic property, 361, 362; ambiguous, 290, 296; arpeggiated, 163, 618–19; augmented, 472; built on fourths, 303; cadence, 619; complex, 73, 299; emotional power, 151; families, 152, 227, 250, 375, 506; inversions, 99, 499; major/minor, 149, 159; modally derived, 375; multi-directional, 292; non-cadential, 173; non-standard, 212; parallel, 208, 299, 375, 497; progressions, 152, 292, 338, 341, 389, 491, 505; and resonance, 364; and scales, 350–1, 504–5; sequences, 162; and serialism, 307; structure, 137, 255, 298, 504, 549; succession, 245, 618; triadic, 290; types, 137, 173, 491

chromaticism, 73, 94, 103, 152, 212, 282, 290, 292–3, 296–7, 303, 313, 494, 550, 569, 572, 619; chromatic continuum, 249; complementarity, 162, 227, 292, 296, 302, 307, 319, 349, 350, 386, 580

Cimarosa, Domenico, 285

cimbalom, 217, 364

clarinet, 331, 381, 387, 524, 528

classical tradition, 196, 277, 572, 593, 601, 621

classicism, 5, 31, 288, 317, 595

Claudel, Paul, 409, 424, 483–4, 484 n. 4; *Five Great Odes*, 484 n. 4; *Le Soulier de satin*, 409, 483–4, 484 n. 2, 484 n. 15

cluster, 348

collage, 133, 134, 468

collectivity, 17, 31, 53, 58, 60, 61, 76, 103, 115, 117, 128, 283, 288, 334, 342, 370, 384, 411, 473, 524, 526, 537; evolution of, 289; identity, 543; individuality, xviii, 18, 41, 58, 283, 473, 578, 587; language, 267; learning, 448, 450, 452, 453; memory, 408, 428, 450; performance, 143; style, 29; writing, 543

Collège de France, ix–xv, xvii–xix, xxiii

Combarieu, Jules, ix

combinatoriality, 135, 165, 167, 211, 224, 241, 307, 315, 316, 334, 534, 555, 601, 608, 617

composer: analysis, 453; communication, 515; hearing/ reading, 515; imagination, 454, 477, 541–2, 545–6, 561; individuality/ personality, 447, 452, 454, 458–60, 461–3, 473, 476–8, 481, 503, 530, 560, 608, 692–3; influences/models, 110–11, 447, 455, 476–7; juvenilia, 477; mannerisms, 560; memory, 590; and musical history, 475, 480–3; originality, 459–62, 465–6, 468; self-discovery/understanding, 454, 460, 466, 476

composition: agogics, 597, 611, 612; anonymity, 138; automatic, 246, 610; automatism/decision, 119–46; centre–periphery binary, 131; and choice, 14, 16, 25, 27, 37, 41, 55, 60, 61, 63, 65–7, 70, 89, 93, 97–8, 106, 112, 119, 137, 141, 170, 237, 243, 247, 292–3, 309, 344, 502, 615; closed/formed, 610, 613, 615; coherence, 300, 333, 345, 349, 517; complexity, 530–1; continuity, 298, 426–7, 433–4, 447, 480, 502,

517, 563, 614, 622, 623, 624, 627; convention, 468, 475; deduction, 87, 110, 137, 170, 173, 174, 182, 185–6, 223, 274–5, 344, 346, 455, 502, 504, 585, 586, 588–9; deflected prediction, 398; density, 563; derivations, 346, 350, 400, 455, 500, 501; differentiation, 505; discipline, 174, 333, 354; discontinuity, 433–4, 614, 624, 627–8; disorder, 587; economy, 182–4; evolution, 590; and external forces, 109–15; finite/ infinite, 624–5, 627, 629; form, 87, 236, 270; fragment/whole, 592–631; free/strict, 137, 142–6, 168, 211, 236–7, 247, 298, 309, 314, 341; genesis, 587–8; improvisation, 90, 117; incompletion/incompleteness, 266, 340, 610–11, 614, 626, 629; infinite possibility, 608–9; memory, 430, 455; models, 451, 458, 461, 464–6, 470; and musical history, 446, 481; number symbolism, 516; open/ unformed, 608–10, 613–15, 624, 627, 629; ordering, 242, 615, 621, 626; reduction, 110, 399; renewal, 272, 466; sketches, 91, 183, 184, 346–7, 585–6; succession, 139, 141–2, 144, 586; symbolism, 517; technology, 89, 117; trajectory, 184, 243, 254, 264, 266, 272, 274, 340, 341, 385, 396, 398, 399, 430–1, 434, 502, 503, 563, 564, 583, 590, 601, 604, 605, 609, 611, 613, 616, 621, 625, 627–8; transgression, 109–10, 386, 393; unity, 170, 194, 273, 545, 561; validation/validity, 182, 273, 300, 309–10, 335, 344, 355, 545; virtuosity, 89, 117, 542; visual techniques, 515–16; *see also* accident; aleatorics/aleatoricism; language, musical; material, musical; writing

computer-generated music, 11–12, 15, 242, 606, 610, 614; chance, 119; choice, 97; deduction, 97–8; notation, 126, 450, 528

concerto form, 593, 594

conducting, 380–1, 421, 422, 429, 539, 612

consonance, 382; and dissonance, 568; parallel, 144

constructivism, 114

continuity, 31, 51, 80, 111, 164, 173, 176, 237, 253–6, 330, 426–7, 277, 292, 295, 297–9, 309, 328, 330, 335, 372, 383, 386, 426, 427, 433–4, 437, 444, 447, 477, 479, 480, 486, 488, 489, 502, 503, 513, 517, 519, 554, 563, 580, 593, 598, 599, 602, 604, 614–17, 620, 622, 623, 628, 631; aural, 597; and discontinuity, 274, 275, 434, 614, 615, 624, 627, 628; formal, 601; historical, 309, 312; temporal, 275, 299, 328, 397

continuo, 414–16

contour, 41, 210, 266, 274, 286, 299, 305, 313, 314, 337, 348, 349, 520, 563, 566, 579, 605, 624; melodic, 394, 498

convention, 12, 36, 43, 58, 99, 151, 153, 155–7, 281, 290, 414, 415, 468–71, 473–8, 490–2, 512, 514, 526, 527, 530, 532, 593, 595, 600, 617–18, 631; collective, 370, 473; forces, 217, 501; form, 156, 157, 179, 214, 294, 328, 601; individual, 473; notation, 126, 491; sounds, 131; structure, 157; style, 415; transcription, 126; tuning, 499

cor anglais, 373, 524

counterpoint, 31, 35, 39, 47, 100, 144, 152, 162, 163, 193, 257, 297, 302, 303, 321, 326, 383–5, 387, 469, 494, 511–12; augmentation, 493; diminution, 493; and harmony, 327, 379, 507; imitative, 199, 440; retrograde motion, 493; strict, 37, 211, 223, 307, 310, 569; succession, 494

crescendo, 348, 373, 488

crotales, 217

cubism, 307, 333, 551, 570

cymbals, 127, 217, 399–400; resonance, 548

Dahlhaus, Carl, xviii, 83 n. 2

dance, 90, 128, 214, 217, 219, 221, 623; *see also* ballet; individual entries

Darmstadt International Summer

Courses for New Music, viii, 3, 83 n. 2

Davies, Peter Maxwell, vii

Debussy, Claude, xxv, 31–2, 110, 114, 151, 170, 179, 199, 203–12, 215, 292–5, 375, 401, 427, 429, 461, 462, 471–2, 475, 494, 497, 522, 606; clarity, 206; constraint, 311; disorder, 208; economy, 204; moderation, 206; originality, 206; the picturesque, 207; and the Romantics, 205; scores, 380; subversion, 212; thematicism, 206, 209–12; tonality, 211, 293; transition, 210; whole-tone scale, 282

WORKS: *En blanc et noir*, 221 n. 3, 522; *Estampes*, 204, 594, 596; *Études*, 31, 34, 204–5, 211–12, 294, 311; *Images*, 204, 206, 210, 596; *Jeux*, 206, 209, 210, 212, 294–5, 525; late works, 23, 522; *La Mer*, 204, 206, 209, 294, 373; *Nocturnes*, 204, 206, 209, 461; *Pelléas et Mélisande*, 154, 209, 461; 'Pour les accords', 212; 'Pour les arpèges composés', 212; *Pour le piano*, 204; 'Pour les quartes', 211; *Prélude à l'après-midi d'un faune*, 199, 206, 209, 210; *Préludes*, 204; 'Rondes de printemps', 206; Sonata for flute, viola and harp, 522; sonatas, 204, 294; songs, 154; String Quartet, 204, 461; *Suite bergamasque*, 204

WRITINGS: correspondence, 221 n. 2

Debussyists, 447

deconstruction, 342, 392, 394, 400, 487, 506, 527, 540, 631

decrescendo, 488

deduction, xvi, xxiv, 30, 34, 39–41, 45, 51, 67, 87, 104, 105, 108, 110, 137, 144, 149, 152, 162, 163, 165, 166, 168, 170, 171, 173, 174, 179, 182, 183, 185, 186, 189, 194, 196, 201, 202, 224, 227, 239, 250, 264, 274–5, 292, 293, 296, 297, 304, 306, 308, 310, 322–4, 343, 344, 346, 351, 377, 383, 442, 455, 460, 479, 487, 502, 504, 509, 542, 547, 551, 581, 585, 586, 588–9, 591, 607, 608, 615, 621; and acoustic phenomena, 339; constraint/freedom, 98–102;

directional/non-directional, 97; electronic music, 46, 377; and idea, 89, 94–8, 104, 110, 274; numerical, 160; principles, 94, 512; procedures, 144, 162, 168, 171; and serialism, 314–15, 317–18; strict, 158, 163; thematic, 153, 195, 303; *see also* composition; form

Degas, Edgar, 460

Delacroix, Eugène, 285

delay, 338, 379

Deleuze, Gilles, 99

Deliège, Célestin, xviii

density, 34, 55, 64, 73, 126, 146, 160, 174, 235, 242, 245, 246, 248–50, 255, 269, 337, 340, 350, 369, 378, 383, 503, 508, 519–21, 538, 549, 553, 563, 579, 589, 600, 605, 614, 624, 625; harmonic, 394; intervallic, 332; and perception, 337; polyphonic, 375; registral, 229; temporal, 216, 235; textural, 267, 351, 542, 556, 589, 621

Descartes, René, viii, ix, 278, 278 n. 4

determinacy/indeterminacy, 119–46, 211, 266; *see also* indeterminacy

determination, xi, 96, 98, 119, 137, 186, 212, 225, 336, 538, 567, 576, 592, 611; durational, 389; multiple, 141; non-determination, 143; over-determination, 79, 134

determinism, 14, 17, 49, 50, 68, 136, 137, 169, 201, 248, 264, 265, 273, 276, 287, 389, 554, 576

detonation, 25, 27, 408

deviation, 122, 176, 178–9, 240, 273, 325, 359, 367, 379, 391, 392, 488, 489, 495, 501, 504, 510, 528, 619

diatonicism, 152, 212, 292–3, 296, 550; white-key/black-key, 165

Diderot, Denis, 532–3

diminuendo, 373

diminution, 93, 199, 231, 302, 493, 502, 511

discontinuity, 52, 80, 254, 274, 275, 335, 371, 372, 433, 434, 614, 615, 624, 627, 628; spatial, 513; temporal, 513

disorientation, 314, 464, 598, 608

dissolution, 199, 203, 205

dissonance, 362, 568

distortion, 135, 173, 187, 192, 289, 343, 422, 466, 556, 560

distribution, 252, 317, 547, 569, 579; aggregates, 566; formal, 187; horizontal/vertical, 108; intervals, 38; material, 66; pitch, 230; pulsation, 258; registral, 519; sounds, 108; spatial, 531, 556; statistical, 246; temporal, 531; timbral, 583

Domaine Musical concerts, xi

doubling, 137, 200, 296, 386, 628; octave, 230

drums, 77; bass, 217; pitch, 122–3; snare, 122–3, 217

Dukas, Paul, 464–5, 475–6, 483; 'Music and Originality', 461, 475–6, 484 n. 9

duration, x, 29, 50, 90, 93, 109, 117, 125, 166, 169, 191, 192, 199–201, 223, 225, 228, 231, 232, 235, 240–2, 244–5, 246, 254, 255, 273, 302, 312, 314, 329, 332, 333, 335, 346, 347, 349–50, 352, 366–9, 377, 384, 385, 387–91, 399, 491, 496, 497, 509, 512, 514, 516, 521, 528, 531, 534, 535, 537–40, 542, 545, 547, 548, 553, 557, 558, 563, 565–7, 582–4, 594, 599–603, 610, 621, 623, 624; absolute, 367, 369; cell, 228; constraints, 567; electroacoustics, 48; equivalences, 538; and form, 50, 104, 214; notation, 6, 124, 368–9; outside tempo, 368; permutation, 388, 391; and pitch, 232, 235, 237; and pulse, 145, 240; resonance, 538; rhythmic, 268, 281; and serialism, 244, 335; and speculation, 109; speed, 553; speed/duration binary, 369; standardisation, 601; structure, 46, 48; sub-notation, 538; suspended, 368; synchronisation, 557; and system, 281; time spans, 600; unequal, 145

Durchführung, 630

dynamics, 6, 47, 50, 64, 122, 124–6, 133, 140–2, 152, 160, 162, 174, 178, 191, 239–42, 245, 246, 255, 262, 264, 267–9, 302, 333, 335, 350, 363, 364, 367, 369–72, 374, 377, 380, 384, 387, 396, 415, 420, 436, 488, 505, 508, 535, 538, 556, 558, 563, 566,

574, 583, 605, 610, 611, 620, 621, 628; accentuation, 80, 145, 611; and affect, 420; external/internal, 370; extreme, 268; and indeterminacy, 122; notation, 124, 369–70, 489, 535; *piano/forte* binary, 369; and serialism, 241, 245; *see also* notation

ear–eye relationship, 106–7
early music, xxiv, 420
economic determinants, *see* market forces
education, musical, 10, 15, 35–6, 47, 75, 80, 358, 408, 428–9, 434–8, 445, 447–50, 452–8, 475, 490–1, 493, 531; collective, 448, 450, 452–3; conventions, 490; exercises, 429, 492, 493; harmony, 492, 493, 495; individual, 448, 452–3; and models, 429, 438–9; musical language, 491; notation, 490; and schools, 447; self-discovery, 448; skills training, 448, 452; and style, 429; teacher–student relationship, 456–8; *see also* apprenticeship
elaboration, ix, 96, 126, 153, 167, 169, 171, 184–6, 188, 192, 193, 197, 202, 209, 222, 228, 265, 281, 286, 299, 324, 330, 393, 396, 479, 526, 528, 541, 567, 573, 589, 590, 611
electric organ, 76
electroacoustic music, 4–6, 44, 48, 54–5, 606; and creativity, 80; inertia of material, 269; obsolescence, 77–8; without performers, 267; scores, 83 n. 3; and timbre, 102; and transcription, 61, 486; and validity, 44, 79
electronic music, 4, 42–3, 45–7, 269, 551; and accident, 132
electronics, 15, 377; constraints, 87–8
Eliot, T. S., xviii, 480–3; 'Tradition and the Individual Talent', xviii, 480, 484 n. 11
enculturation, 568
Encyclopedists, 417
ensemble, 291, 384, 387, 536; baroque, 414; coordination, 536–8; intonation, 414; pitch, 489; synchronisation, 536

Ensemble InterContemporain, xi
equal temperament, 73, 330, 469, 501, 541
esotericism, xxiv, 91, 160, 389, 411, 416, 439, 515–16, 518, 546
ethnomusicology, 411
exoticism, 43, 207, 292–3, 482
exposition, 93, 159, 172, 190, 194, 196, 197, 200, 203, 229, 287, 320, 321, 325, 393, 519, 601
expression, xvii, xviii, 4, 17, 34–5, 55–6, 58, 59–61, 63, 80, 88–9, 91, 92, 96, 102, 108–10, 120, 130, 149, 151, 155, 156, 170, 177, 197–9, 206, 214, 227, 229, 231, 236, 251, 254, 266, 270, 271, 277, 284, 287, 295, 300, 301, 304, 306, 314, 328, 331, 334, 336, 370, 443, 452, 465–9, 474, 476, 479, 483, 485, 486, 507, 514, 526, 549, 554, 588, 590, 611, 612, 619; *see also* non-expression
expressionism, 514
expressiveness, xviii, 26, 54, 61, 62, 89, 91, 101–7, 129, 133, 150, 152, 155, 176, 177, 192, 193, 195, 196, 202, 206, 231, 238, 269, 294, 299, 314, 315, 317, 331, 338–40, 349, 354, 361, 373, 386, 459, 516, 522, 539, 566, 571, 572, 579, 581–6, 602, 611, 612, 621, 622
external forces, 109–15

facility, 30, 31, 630
fashion, 59, 410
Fauré, Gabriel, 572
Fellini, Federico, 412
fermata, 253
Ferneyhough, Brian: *Time and Motion Study II*, xi
figuration, 31, 198, 507, 528, 535; rhythmic, 141, 192, 225, 339, 373, 380, 387
figure: appropriation, 187–8; deduction, 189, 297; and form, 193–4; identity, 337, 351; and interval, 337, 350, 351; ornamentation, 211; and perception, 258; and posterity, 185; potential, 185, 195; and register, 256; and rhythm, 337; and scale, 350; and structure, 189–90, 325; and

system, 336–7, 339, 354; as thematic element, 255

filter/filtering, 33, 49, 255, 267, 444, 476; pitch, 351, 354, 390, 391

fioratura, 372

Flemish music, 317

flute, 368, 374, 381–2

folk music, 129, 173; eastern European, 179; sub-Saharan African, 179

folk sources, 174, 202, 206, 213–15, 217, 219, 221

form, 182–221; appropriation, 187; archetypes, 259–60; canonical, 37, 163; and chance, 98, 264; classical, 105, 198, 395; closed, 121, 244, 261, 265–6, 399, 626, 627, 629; combination, 397; constraint, 174, 244; continuous/discontinuous, 275; conventional, 179; and correspondence, 224; and creativity, 227; and data, 394; deconstruction, 394; and deduction, 179, 274–5, 292–3, 322–3, 455; deformation, 269; depersonalisation, 397; derivation, 322, 455; determined/indeterminate, 266; and development, 156, 179, 255, 268, 275, 305, 397; directed/non-directed, 626, 627; directional, 159; dramatic, 156, 159; and duration, 104; elaboration, 193; envelope, 264, 322, 397; and evolution, 160, 260, 265, 270, 287, 295; and expression, 102–7; and figure, 193; fixed/indeterminate, 341; and fragments, 621, 624, 625; free/strict, 144, 230; gesture, 266, 274–6; and harmony, 492; and hierarchy, 292; hybrid, 194; and idea, 93, 152, 292–3, 619; improvisatory, 452; incompleteness, 266; infinite, 355; and invention, 261; and inventories, 171; kaleidoscopic, 179; and language, 615, 617; large-scale, xvii, 67, 81, 89, 93, 95, 155, 179, 187, 195, 204, 256, 259, 275, 327, 600, 617; mechanisation of, 261; mobility, 142–3; and models, 236; mosaic, 625, 627, 628; and musical language, 194, 231, 270; and narrative, 293, 328, 505, 617; non-evolving, 159; open, xvi, 121, 243–4, 261–6, 399, 626; operatic, 158; organisation, 245, 392; and performance, 430; and permutation, 175, 275; and plan, 395; realisation, 268; reduction, 394; renewal, 272; and repetition/variation, 175, 259, 296, 394; and reprise, 293; sectional, 395, 396; and serialism, 308; signals, 397; small-scale, 89, 93, 617; spiral, 275–6, 356, 628; and stability/instability, 568; standardisation, 99–100; strict, 31, 144, 156, 159, 287, 294; subversion, 203; and symmetry, 96, 293, 394; and texture, 255; and thematicism, 194–5, 210; and theme, 150, 157, 159, 191, 194, 197, 222; and time, 277, 615; and tonality, 505; and tradition, 328; trajectory, 247, 262, 264, 274; transformation, 203; two-theme, 193; and unity, 270; and writing, 591, 622; *see also* analysis; articulation; micro-form; and individual genres

formalisation, 46, 87, 93, 94, 104, 216, 311

formalism, 26, 100, 159, 206, 294, 302, 310, 311, 441, 518

formant, 50

Foucault, Michel, ix, xii

found material, 46, 65, 374

found objects, xi, 130, 133–5, 174, 312, 467–8, 578

fragments/fragmentation, xvi, 68, 124, 134, 135, 140–2, 164, 172, 275, 301, 341, 344, 492, 551, 575, 592–631; and autonomy, 603, 620, 624; coherence, 620, 621; computer-generated, 607; disjunction/disruption, 618, 620; and form, 616, 621, 624, 625; hierarchy, 605; identity, 616; integration, 616, 617, 618, 622–6, 629; juxtaposition, 622–5; and memory, 604, 605; and repetition, 616, 625; sequence, 626; *see also* aleatorics/aleatoricism; alternation

Franck, César, 204

freedom, 6, 63, 142–3, 157–8, 169, 174, 204, 247, 248, 251, 253, 262, 265, 270, 271, 276, 295, 298, 309, 343, 345, 348, 349, 355, 415, 465, 470,

479, 483, 488, 493, 512, 529, 530, 536–7, 544, 554, 557, 563, 564, 566, 574–6, 578, 579, 581, 594, 601–2, 611, 615, 617; and athematicism, 237; and constraint, 81, 89, 98–102, 237; and notation, 529–30; and performance, 116, 266; and synchronisation, 509; from tradition, 172

French music, 207, 471

French Revolution, 462

frequency, 47–9, 568; modulation, 365

fugue, 22, 31, 47, 93–4, 99, 144, 150, 156, 157, 192–4, 220, 221, 235, 237, 286–7, 325, 336, 357, 379–80, 386, 438, 491, 511, 516–18, 562, 594, 595, 601, 617, 619; augmentation, 511; complexity, 193; diminution, 511; evolution, 194; *see also* prelude and fugue

gagaku, 495

gamelan, 367

Germanic tradition, 170, 172, 175, 482

Gerzso, Andrew, xi

gestalt, 109, 178, 234, 351, 388, 520

Gesualdo, Carlo, 152, 550

Gide, André, 455, 477; *The Counterfeiters: A Novel*, 484 n. 10

Giugno, Giuseppe di, xi

glissando, 114, 330, 331, 488

Gluck, Christoph Willibald, 362, 417, 427

Goethe, Johann Wolfgang von: *The Metamorphosis of Plants*, 165

Goeyvaerts, Karel, vii

Goldman, Jonathan, xxiii, xxvi

Gounod, Charles, 278 n. 4

grace notes, 252, 257

graphic scores, xi, 342

Greek mythology, 418

Greek tragedy, 111, 416, 418

Gregorian chant/tradition, 124, 283, 370

handclaps, 127, 214

Handel, George Frideric, 29, 189, 416, 427

harmonic fields, 39, 106, 249, 282, 346, 348, 391, 442, 510, 557, 579

harmonic progression, 151, 154, 188, 193, 208, 290, 291, 361, 469, 493, 495; and affinity, 208

harmonic series, 499, 500, 569

harmonics: synthesised, 366

harmonium, 76, 217, 331

harmony; anonymisation, 569; and counterpoint, 327, 379, 507; coloration, 497, 501; density, 394; and form, 492; function, 338; hierarchy, 210, 211, 224; and idea, 151; identity, 571; language, 303, 323; latent, 579; and melody, 227, 307, 375; relationships, 453, 512; reprise, 145; roving, 292; sequencing, 195; and serialism, 326–7; and simultaneity, 494; statistical, 615; traditional, 570; and variation form, 100–1

harp, 364, 378; resonance, 548, 612

harpsichord, 414, 511; ocular, 460

Hauer, Josef Matthias, 471–2

Hauptstimme, 380, 511

Haydn, Joseph, 189; sonatas, 601

hearing, 357–8, 393; abstract/actual, 541–2; and analysis, 359–61, 364, 375; complexity, 529; connected, 610; divided, 512; and form, 604; and innocence, 518; integral, 555; memorising, 520; multivalent, 525; and timbres, 387; and writing, 382, 491, 493, 515, 518

Heisenberg's principle, 490

heritage, 11, 213, 288, 328, 427, 434–6, 475, 481, 531

heterophony, 180, 338, 352, 379, 382, 385, 391, 508–11, 580

historicism/historicity, 9–10, 12, 309, 312, 426, 482

history, musical, ix, 4, 5, 12, 24, 26–7, 32, 34, 37, 43, 322, 408, 436, 454–5, 459–60, 470, 480–3; archetypes, 259; chronology, 437; and composition, 238, 426–7, 515; in eighteenth century, 100, 389, 416, 417, 489, 493, 511, 530; in fifteenth century, 389; and idea, 90, 91, 151; and kitsch, 425; learned music, 134, 179; and memory, 459–60; as merchandise, 482–3; of the Middle Ages, 489; and musical language, 62, 64, 79,

284; in nineteenth century, 95, 100, 150, 222, 283, 288–9, 293, 295, 300, 379, 393, 416, 417, 479, 492, 493, 523–4, 530, 572, 594, 600, 615, 617; and perception, 75; in seventeenth century, 389, 415; in sixteenth century, 129, 389; in twentieth century, 94, 105, 265, 282, 288–9, 291, 293, 295, 393, 417, 420, 450, 459, 462, 463, 475, 489, 524, 562, 596, 618, 622, 631; writing, 451

Holliger, Heinz; *Cardiophonie*, xi; *Psaume*, xi

homophony, 152, 352, 439–40

horizontal–vertical relationship, 37, 39, 46, 80, 102, 106, 108, 144, 154, 163, 230, 246–7, 250, 255, 307, 325–7, 348, 361, 378–9, 381, 383, 386, 396, 400, 440, 507, 542, 569–73, 575

horn, 362, 387, 524, 598; *cuivré*, 362

Hörpartitur, 83 n. 3

Hultén, Pontus, 606

Huygens, Christiaan, 460

hyperlogic, 143

hyperthematicism, 222, 224, 227, 229–30

hypertheme, 222–3

idea, 281–356, 560–91; adaptation, 92; anonymisation, 562; association, 91; avoidance of, 563; and codes, 91, 92, 151; constraints, 91; context, 565; and creativity, 171; and deduction, 89, 93–8, 274; development, 151–3, 162, 184; and duration, 90, 582; elaboration, 202, 281, 286, 324; finite/non-finite, 96; and form, 286, 619; and formalisation, 87, 92, 93; and framework, 93–4; genesis of, 88–93; and harmony, 151; and hierarchy, 91, 298, 625; individualisation, 562; individuality, 549; influences on, 90–1; and language, 286, 561, 564; local/global, 564; and material, 66, 68–9, 95–6, 549, 562, 630; and melody, 151; and memory, 562; and notation, 531–2; and pitch, 90, 302, 582; real, 564; and reduction, 168; and scales, 90; sequence, 205; spontaneity, 286;

and structure, 91, 151, 563–4; and system, 281–356; and tempo, 90; transcription, 532; transformation, 92, 98, 286, 396; transition, 396; and unity, 167; virtual, 95–6, 564; and writing, 560–91

ideogram, 125, 574

imitation, 16, 29, 32, 41, 285, 300, 382, 406, 418, 447, 464, 465, 467, 470, 476; of battles, 129; of birds, 129; and forgery, 470

imitation (device), 152, 300, 380, 382, 463; canonical, 193; imprecise, 512; melodic, 384; and neoclassicism, 300; rhythmic, 386; strict, 251, 297, 320, 576

improvisation, 70–1, 90, 115–17, 266, 271, 341–2, 452, 530, 599, 610, 611, 626; and freedom, 271; Indian ragas, 96; and intuition, 119, 587; jazz, 488; and memory, 116, 342; *see also* jazz improvisation; performance

inaudibility, 290, 614

incantation, 129

incidental music, 150

indeterminacy, xi, xvi, 50, 81, 98, 106, 119–46, 211, 266, 341, 374, 608; directionality, 121; notation, 123; *see also* aleatorics/aleatoricism; determinacy/indeterminacy

Indian flute, 367

Indian music, 96, 599

individual/collective, xviii, 18, 29, 41, 58–61, 283

individualisation, 61, 185, 248, 264, 376, 562, 618

individualism, 59, 80, 283, 297, 299, 332, 425, 463, 479; political suppression, 463

individuality, 5, 6, 58–60, 98, 103, 220, 249, 267, 300, 321, 333, 338, 360, 372, 382, 392, 408, 438, 445, 447, 458, 461, 463, 464, 471, 473–8, 481, 483, 520, 522, 523, 526, 530, 549, 552, 573, 574; and anonymity, 58; *see also* collectivity

infrathematicism, 222–6, 241–3, 246; and hierarchy, 225; and series, 225

infratheme, 222–3, 575

inharmonic sounds, 282

InHarmonique, 356 n. 1, 401 n. 1
innovation, xii, 10, 78, 173, 212, 291, 293, 295, 299–300, 464, 537, 571
instability, 113, 132, 215, 236, 342, 363, 568
instinct, viii, 45, 69, 82, 159, 170, 177, 205, 208, 296, 298, 302, 306, 310, 317, 326, 327, 341, 343, 365, 388, 390, 428, 431, 433, 436, 437, 445, 458, 459, 473, 474, 488, 534, 535, 542, 568, 586, 590, 616
instrument-makers, 529
instrumentation, 31, 210, 216–17, 364, 375, 436, 439, 523, 524, 529, 543, 552
instruments, musical: amplification, 553; and authenticity, 414–15, 417; and bow, 372, 549; and breath, 372, 549; centre–periphery binary, 131–2; characteristics, 547; combination, 373, 375; and creativity, 149; dark/light, 371; determinacy/indeterminacy, 131; dynamic potential, 370; experimentation, 341; fingering, 527; found objects, 73, 130; hierarchy, 131; history of, 75–6, 419; and improvisation, 90; keyboard, 77, 122; and mechanical memory, 429, 431; obsolescence, 75–6; playability, 77; precision, 501; qualities, 77, 87, 399; range, 77; register, 371, 372, 524; resonance, 372, 400, 547, 549; selection, 381; and signification, 523; sound production, 372–3; standardisation, 121–2, 524; synthesised, 365; technique, 446; timbre, 332, 335, 365, 373, 381, 439, 469, 547, 549, 553; and transcription, 419–20; transposing, 528; virtuosity, 115, 372; and writing, 438; *see also* acoustics; individual instruments and families
integration, 5, 15, 44, 63, 65, 73, 132, 134, 135, 150, 152, 222, 243, 468, 569, 581, 599, 615–17, 621–6, 630
integration/disintegration, 135
interpolation, 216, 218, 336, 340, 346, 349, 565
interpreter/interpretation: approximation, 125; and authenticity, 407, 417; and

education, 558; and form, 430; freedom, 536–7; and memory, 429, 432; modes of, 436; and models, 406; and personality, 411; and reflexes, 431; and transmission, 411; and written text, 490; *see also* performance
interruption, 370, 396, 397, 519, 544
intervals: amorphous, 228; and chords, 504; and codes, 91; collections, 346; configuration, 215; conjunct, 439–40; connotations, 103; consecutive fifths, 208; contextualisation, 305; and contour, 299, 305, 337; decorative, 212; density, 383; determining, 212; directionality, 351; disjunct, 440; distance, 383; emotional power, 151; families, 224; and figure, 337, 350, 351; hierarchy, 211, 212, 338; identity, 303, 305, 499; intervallic density, 332; intervallic inversion, 351; intervallic relationships, 136–7, 163, 165, 211, 350, 512; intervallic scale, 250; intervallic space, 249; intervallic systems, 378, 383; inversion, 500; multiplication, 580; percussion, 123; and pitch, 348, 378, 505; placement, 571; and register, 500, 507; and rhythm, 234, 305; and series, 223–5, 237, 305; standardisation, 383; subsets, 224–5; and symmetry, 324; and tempo, 346; and texture, 346; transpositions, 172, 224; and unity, 224; *see also* micro-intervals; multiphonics
intonation, 73, 414, 416
intuition, 11, 13, 15, 26–8, 39, 54–6, 57, 119, 183, 187, 228, 231, 232, 329, 343, 345, 347, 424, 428, 445, 470, 485, 539, 562, 573, 583–5, 588, 591; and memory, 345; and rationality, 232
invariants, 131, 156, 167, 211, 218, 304, 381, 387, 441–3, 489, 506, 579
IRCAM (Institut de Recherche et Coordination Acoustique/Musique), xi, xii, xvii–xix
Ives, Charles, 172–4, 472; as amateur, 172; incoherence, 172; thematicism, 172, 174

Japanese culture, 293, 412
Japanese music, 378
jazz improvisation, 488, 530
Joyce, James, 63
juxtaposition, 38, 573, 578, 623–4; of
    strict and free writing, 144, 236

Kafka, Franz, 401, 631; 'The
    Judgement', 401
Kagel, Mauricio: *Acustica*, xi; *Exotica*, xi
Kandinsky, Wassily, 111, 297, 327, 460
key, 47, 152, 205, 290, 304, 307, 311,
    361, 505, 528; symbolism, 159
keyboard instruments, 77, 122, 429
kitsch, 425
Klangfarbenmelodie, 164
Klee, Paul, 112, 341, 589, 610;
    *Monument am Grenzen des
    Fruchtlands*, 83 n. 4; *Pedagogical
    Sketchbooks (Pädagogisches
    Skizzenbuch)*, 118, n. 4
koto, 378

labour songs, 128–9, 214; repetition,
    214
Ländler, 173, 198
language, literary, 63
language, musical: accident, 58; and
    aesthetics, 333; and choice, 121;
    and codes/codification, 61, 137, 151,
    153, 284, 358, 376, 426; coherence,
    283, 333, 506, 529; collective,
    267, 578; comprehensibility, 462;
    consistency, 98, 99; constraints,
    88, 529; and convention, 469, 471,
    476; and creativity, 183, 282; and
    deduction, 94; and discovery, 173,
    174; duration, 281; and education,
    428, 430; elaboration of, 265; and
    electroacoustics, 61; elements of,
    57; emancipation of, 601; evolution
    of, 169–70, 193, 222, 226, 288, 290,
    292, 394, 450, 514, 533, 617, 620;
    and expression, 61–3, 300, 469; and
    extra-musical motivation, 135; and
    form, 231, 270, 286, 615, 617; and
    frameworks, 61, 93; and graphics,
    342; harmonic, 152, 203, 292, 449,
    514; and hierarchy, 57, 72, 74, 82,
    211, 212, 376, 419; historical, 58–60,

71; and idea, 151–3, 175, 286, 561,
    564; and impulse, 271; individual,
    578; and intervallic structure,
    161, 172, 332; issues with, 71–2;
    liturgical, 58–9; manipulation, 58;
    and material, 62, 65–6, 70, 79–81,
    106, 122, 128, 133, 143, 175; modal,
    149; morphic/amorphic, 98; and
    musical object, 63, 65–6, 69, 130,
    366; and narrative, 631; and noise,
    127; non-tonal, 149; and notation,
    61, 70; organisation of, 57; and
    performance, 430; and pitch, 281,
    302; rejection of functions of,
    293; renewal, 272; and repetition,
    168; and rhythm, 176, 231; and
    rigid application of, 137; rules,
    283–4; scientific, 113–15; and
    sensibility, 109; and serialism, 240,
    308–9; and stability/instability, 568;
    standardisation, 102, 425, 600; and
    structure, 324; style, 57; and system,
    282, 335; and techniques, 205; and
    text, 155; and thematicism, 194; and
    theme, 197, 199; timbre, 281, 366;
    tonal, 149; transmutation, 115; unity,
    277–8, 571; universality, 62; and
    validity, 38, 57, 65, 68, 72; vectors,
    172; in Western culture, 152
Lascaux, 412–13
Lautréamont, Comte de: *Les Chants de
    Maldoror*, 18 n. 3
Le Roy Ladurie, Emmanuel, ix–x, xvii
learned culture/tradition, 213–14, 216,
    221
learned music, 106, 134, 179, 283
legato, 258, 415
Léger, Fernand, 111
leitmotiv, xxiv, 150, 155, 161, 253, 434,
    602
lieder, 104, 163–4, 260, 494, 497; *see
    also* art song
Ligeti, György, vii, xii–xiii, 33, 114, 506,
    520; *Artikulation*, 83 n. 3
listener/listening, *see* perception
Liszt, Ferencz, 195, 198, 202, 211, 294,
    373, 417, 535, 599; Piano Sonata in B
    minor, 595
litany, 175, 178
literature: correspondence with music,

111, 133, 284, 294; *see also* music
drama; poetry; text; theatre
liturgical music, 103, 129; Latin text,
412; *see also* sacred music
Loriod, Yvonne, 221 n. 3
lullaby, 158
Lully, Jean-Baptiste, 416
lute, 420
luthéal, 76

McAdams, Stephen, xix
McCreless, Patrick, xvii
Machaut, Guillaume de, 38
macro-structure, 157, 305, 603
madrigal/madrigalists, 151, 152, 415,
550
Mahler, Gustav, xxv, 105, 154, 161,
173, 174, 198, 200–2, 204, 206,
207, 292, 294, 306, 434, 571, 593,
594, 598–9, 616, 617; as conductor,
422; continuous development, 201,
203; critics, 202; and folklore, 202,
207; form, 198, 203, 505; narrative,
201, 203, 206, 294, 505, 599; slow
movements, 200; thematicism, 198,
201–3; variations, 199
WORKS: late works, 199; *Das Lied
von der Erde*, 198; symphonies, 198,
201–3, 598, 616; Symphony No. 5,
199, 201; Symphony No. 6, 203, 434;
Symphony No. 7, 203; Symphony No.
8, 198; Symphony No. 9, 199–200
Malevich, Kazimir, 603; *White on
White*, 318
Mallarmé, Stéphane, 28, 68, 108, 168,
205, 250, 284, 326, 358, 460, 494,
592, 609; Album/Book, 592, 631
WRITINGS: 'Un coup de dés',
28, 83 n. 1, 592; 'Le demon de
l'analogie', 118 n. 1; *Igitur ou la folie
d'Elbehnon*, 278 n. 1; *Livre*, 112, 118
n. 5, 609
mandolin, 364
Manet, Édouard, 285
manipulation, 43, 44, 100, 218, 223,
232, 243, 264, 267, 269, 271, 337,
346, 349, 364, 390, 492, 517, 552,
556, 578, 582, 607; and accident, 58;
of chance, 17; of conventions, 530;
electroacoustic, 44; of intervals, 502;

of material, 87, 133; of motifs, 523;
serial, 316; of sound objects, 488;
of structures, 581; textual, 467, 486,
612; thematic, 233, 237; of time, 196,
199; of transcribed elements, 527; *see
also* language, musical
mannerism, 26, 35, 332, 466, 560
mapping, 340
march, 158, 173, 217–19
market forces, 10–11, 77
material, musical: absolute, 242;
abstract relationships, 359–60;
accidental object, 120; alteration,
187; amorphous, 226, 246; and
analysis, 23, 67, 187; and articulation,
228; borrowed, 188, 191, 207; and
chance, 70; and codes, 66, 230;
concrete relationships, 359–60;
constraints, 88; and deduction,
228, 581; dematerialisation, 359;
and density, 174; and development,
223, 431; and duration, 228;
elaboration, 82, 228; evolution of,
8–10, 16, 230, 261; evolving, 603;
familiarisation, 78; fixed/non-fixed,
139–42; flexibility, 247; and form,
36, 40, 230, 274; found, 46, 65, 374;
generation of, 191; hierarchy, 291,
354; and idea, 549; inadequacy of,
3–4; individualisation, 562; and
instrumentation, 43–4; inventories,
68–9; limitations on, 10; and musical
language, 5, 30, 37, 57, 61, 62, 65–6,
80, 81, 122, 128, 133; naivety, 135;
non-development, 167; notation, 126;
novelty, 78; order/sequence, 139,
141–2; organisation of, 44–7, 61–71,
74, 82, 87, 91, 92, 105, 116–17,
121, 137–8, 170–1, 243, 246, 252,
293, 309, 313, 348, 351, 354, 383,
552, 573, 581, 589; and pitch, 228;
pre-compositional, 225–6, 503–4,
506–7; preparation, 346–8, 503; and
realisation, 52, 69, 71; reduction
of, 110; relative, 242; and stylistic
integrity, 17; and symbols, 66–7; and
systems, 65; and technique, 4–5,
30, 32, 41–2, 46; and technology,
11–13, 42–4, 48; and tension, 174;
and timbre, 54, 228; and time, 48;

transformation, 556; trickery, 135; variability, 145; virtual, 499; *see also* chance

Matisse, Henri, 111

matrix/matrices, 252, 253, 296, 302, 304, 305, 307, 315, 323, 330, 337, 351, 376, 442, 452, 497, 572, 579, 599, 608, 621, 622, 624

Mattheson, Johann: *Das neu-eröffnete Orchestre*, xvii

Méfano, Paul: *Périple(s) à 1*, xi

melody: configurations, 154; development, 162; and harmony, 227, 307, 375; and idea, 95, 151; melodic contour, 394; ornamentation, 488; transformations, 100–1

memory: abstract, 429; active, 435, 452; analytical, 432, 434; collective, 408, 411, 428, 450; as constraint, 91; and creativity, 405–84, 530; deficient, 460; documentary, 407; and fragments, 604; and idea, 562; and identity, 411; immediate, 28; and improvisation, 116; individual, 408; instinctive, 431; and interpretation, 432; and intuition, 345; latent, 28; learning by heart, 429, 431; mechanical, 429; and models, 91, 231; monitoring-, 432; passive, 435; prediction-, 432; recall-, 432; reductive, 271; references, 231; sporadic, 28; and stability, 568; and sterility, 449; of techniques, 428; virtual, 428; voluntary/involuntary, 410, 431; *see also* perception

Mendelssohn, Felix, 417, 427

Messiaen, Olivier, 33, 50, 191, 375, 400, 494, 620; modes of limited transposition, 565

WORKS: *Chronochromie*, 388, 390, 434; 'Mode de valeurs et d'intensités', 108–9, 191, 240–1, 245, 607; *Mystère de la Sainte Trinité*, 516; *Neumes rhythmiques*, 373

metre, 145, 146, 176, 281, 367, 388, 390, 594; classical, 73; irregular, 218, 237, 368; metreless, 538; notation, 145; traditional, 332

metronome, 538; markings, 176, 314, 391, 415, 567

Michelangelo Buonarroti, 108, 413

micro-form, 167, 603

micro-intervals, 73, 256, 331–2, 339, 368, 460

micropolyphony, 520

microtones, 496

miniature, vii, 209, 596

minimalism, 178, 180

minuet, 90, 214, 594

modernism, vii, xix, 467–8

modes, 152, 213, 235, 242, 247, 281, 292, 296, 472, 558, 565; major/minor, 469

modulation, 151, 159, 352, 602; metrical, 177; rhythmic, 177

Molière, 416

Mondrian, Piet, 110–11, 327

monody, 382, 507–8, 523, 577

Monteverdi, Claudio, 151, 417, 550

mordant, 338

moto perpetuo, 157

movements as separate units, 594–5

Mozart, Wolfgang Amadeus, 28–9, 38, 156, 194, 370, 415, 427, 470, 472, 571; concert arias, 523; operas, 523, 593; sonatas, 395, 601; *Die Zauberflöte*, 516

multiphonics, 132, 358, 364, 375, 382, 527

music drama, 105, 422, 595

musical education, *see* education, musical

musical history, *see* history, musical

musical instruments, *see* instruments, musical

musical language, *see* language, musical

musical material, *see* material, musical

musical/non-musical, *see* perception

musicology, xvii, xviii, 32, 58, 103, 317, 420, 435, 467, 516; and performance practice, 58

musique concrète, 269

Mussorgsky, Modest, 292; *Zhenitba*, 154

mysticism, 314, 315, 570

naivety, 135, 150, 342, 535

Nancarrow, Conlon, 177

narrative, 24, 87, 197, 198, 200, 201, 203, 206, 287, 293–5, 328, 366, 393,

439, 444, 478, 505, 587, 597, 599, 605, 617, 631

nationalism, 207, 214

Nattiez, Jean-Jacques, ix, x, xii, xviii, xx

Nebenstimme, 380, 511

neoclassicism, xxiii, 81, 95, 134, 144, 219–20, 260, 288–9, 300–1, 334, 422, 464, 466; and parody, 134, 289

neo-expressionism, vii

neo-Romanticism, xxiv, 289, 301

neumes, 124, 152, 370

neutrality, 77, 132, 136, 140, 163, 185, 188, 234, 236, 249, 486–7, 503

New York Philharmonic Orchestra, ix

noise, 127, 132–3, 152, 362, 374, 529, 589; noise–sound continuum, 329–30; *see also* sound

non-European culture, 428, 435

non-European music, 58–9, 103, 331

non-evolution, 449

non-expression, 288

non-recurrence, 230, 393–4, 487

non-repetition, 94, 105, 163, 168, 178, 223, 293, 297, 304, 318, 320, 328, 394, 596, 603

Nono, Luigi, vii

nostalgia, 95, 114, 136, 144, 304, 313, 316, 329, 355, 409, 597

notation, 526–59; absolute, 136; abstract, 127, 538; accidentals, 123, 533–4; of action, 528, 558–9; aleatoric music, 536; amplitude, 125; and analysis, 6, 21; of ancient music, 489; approximation, 124; arithmetical, 538; and authenticity, 419; chance procedures, 528; and codes, 61, 526, 527, 529, 531, 532; collective practice, 526, 537; communication, 526–7, 532; complexity, 530, 532; computer-generated, 126; of computer-generated music, 450, 528; concrete, 127; continuity, 488–9; conventions, 491, 527, 530; density, 126; difference, 145; duration, 124, 125, 368–9, 533–5, 537–8, 558; dynamics, 124–6, 369–70, 489, 535, 558; effectiveness, 531; of events, 554; evolution of, 451, 527, 533; fidelity to, 267–9; graphic signs, 535–40, 576; and hierarchies, 126,

370, 488; historic, 59, 415; and the idea, 531, 532; and imagination, 530, 531; imperative, 529; imprecision, 489, 532, 538; and improvisation, 530; and indeterminacy, 123–4; individual expression, 6, 60–1, 537; individualised objects, 526; launching, 530; margin of error, 124, 125; multiphonics, 527; new methods, 531; of object, 499–500; ornamentation, 526; oscillation, 510; of outcome, 558–9; over-elaboration, 528, 532; pitch, 124, 125, 368, 489, 527, 528, 533, 541, 558; placement, 558; precision, 415, 539; of process, 554; proportional, 149, 152, 370; reform, 535; register, 124, 503, 537, 558; result, 528; rhythm, 369, 528, 537; of sound objects, 559; speed, 538; standardisation, 526; stave, 123; synoptic, 370; and technology, 6, 36; tempo, 124, 177, 489, 526, 538–9; tied groups, 535; timbre, 528; traditional, 42, 527, 531, 533–4, 540, 541, 559; and transcription, 491, 526–8, 531–3, 541, 576; transposition, 503, 528; virtual, 500, 558; Western, 488; *see also* acoustics; analysis; ideogram; writing

Notation in New Music (Darmstadt, 1964), 83 n. 2

Nouvelle revue française, La (NRF), viii

object, *see* found objects; instruments, musical: found objects; language, musical; material, musical; notation; perception; rhythm; Stravinsky, Igor; virtual object; writing

objectivity, 25, 33, 268, 333–4, 489

oboe, 375, 381

oboe d'amore, 523

Obrecht, Jacob, 516

Oliveros, Pauline, vii

ondes Martenot, 76

onirism, 66

onomatopoeia, 129

opera, 113, 158, 222, 328, 593; libretto, 113, 157; *see also* music drama; theatre works

ophicleide, 414

oral tradition, 58, 213, 283, 411, 421, 469, 488, 490

oratorio, 600

orchestra, 291, 373, 375, 384, 469, 522, 584; divided, 525; evolution of, 523–4; pitch, 489; rehearsal, 432; size, 377, 414; timbre, 291, 372, 438, 584

orchestration, 14, 30, 372, 377; continuity, 372; development of, 374

order–disorder/chaos dialectic, 65, 256, 357–401

ordering, 62, 150, 153, 224, 242, 256, 270, 275, 390, 509, 546, 567, 579, 595, 598, 609, 615, 621, 631

organ, 511

organicism, xvii

organum, 415, 600

orientation, xv, xxiv, 28, 75, 105, 335, 353, 355, 367, 394, 397, 399, 416, 431, 434, 438, 505, 510, 514, 518, 561, 563, 567, 568, 572, 602, 616; harmonic, 304; historical, 328; *see also* disorientation

originality, 12, 27, 32, 60, 73, 75, 102, 175, 218, 230, 331, 435, 447, 448, 450, 452, 459–68, 470–6, 478, 479, 483, 540; absolute, 474; and chronology, 472; relative, 474; and tradition, 474

ornamentation, 38, 100, 144, 178, 187, 189, 199, 200, 211, 212, 252, 254, 257, 323, 338, 341, 349, 378, 381–5, 415, 416, 495, 508–10, 525, 526, 610, 611; historic, 415, 416; improvisatory, 610; *see also* articulation

oscillators, 11

oscillogram, 104

oscillograph, 370

oscilloscope, 115

ostinato, 50, 158, 218, 233, 518, 538, 555, 570, 581, 620; durational, 231

overture, 168, 190, 214, 230, 328, 516

Paganini, Niccolò, 189

painting, *see* visual arts

palindromes, 493

Paris: Salle du Conservatoire, 414; Théâtre des Champs-Élysées, ix

parody, 17, 134–6, 227, 277, 289, 313, 467

Pascal, Blaise, 415; *Thoughts*, 484 n. 3

passacaglia, 94, 156, 158, 159, 161, 189, 231, 297, 479, 601

passing note, 132, 144, 379, 572

Passions, 523, 600

pastiche, 470

pataphysics, 473

pedagogy, 4, 10, 283, 428, 447, 449–50, 492

perception: absence of directedness, 608; and absence/presence, 259; accentuation, 74; and acoustic relationships, 568; and active listening, 298, 347, 353; and ambiguity, 256, 514; and analogy, 182; analytical, 353, 359–67, 374, 398, 399, 520; barriers to, 72–3; and codes, 106, 291; coherence, 508; of complexity, 145, 180, 382, 396; concrete, 127; continuity, 164, 277, 513, 614, 628; convergence/divergence, 509–10, 606; counterpoint, 381, 494; and deduction, 99; density, 337, 605; differentiation, 396, 511; discernibility, 247; discrimination, 374; disorientation, 608; displacement, 510; duration, 367–8, 602; dynamics, 367, 370–1, 508, 605; and emphasis, 245; envelope, 351; event-governed/non-event-governed, 628; evolution of, 73–4; familiarisation, 96, 298; figures, 381; of form, 392, 394–5, 398, 604; of fragments/fragmentation, 380, 603–5, 608, 610, 612, 614, 629; frustration of, 515; global, 353; of harmonics, 502; harmony, 381, 508; heterophony, 509–10; horizontal elements, 511; and idea, 98; illusion, 389, 629; and imagination, 107, 376; imagined, 358–9; imagined/real, 376–7; and innocence, 186, 210; and innovation, 295; and insecurity, 163; interest, 401; internal contradiction, 382; of intervals, 305, 368, 378–9, 508, 513; and intuition, 88, 446; and invention, 259; of irregularity, 145–6; levels of, 353; and memory, 100, 152–5, 159, 186, 231, 246, 253–4, 258–9,

291, 299, 337, 353–4, 381, 393–8, 400, 446, 508, 612, 616, 629; of the musical/the non-musical, 74–7, 79–82; narrative, 605; of orchestra, 360–1; of order, 244; and ordering principle, 224; orientation, 246, 353, 616; passive, 353; pitch, 367–8, 400, 513; pleasure, 401; polyphony, 511–13; prediction, 398; problems of, 334–5; projection, 358, 398; recognition, 224–5, 232, 295, 297, 396, 510, 521–2; and reflex, 253; register, 513; and repetition, 167, 259, 337; of rhythm, 74, 177, 178, 367; selectivity, 380; sequence of objects, 529; and serialism, 160, 324, 325; silence, 513, 612; and simplicity, 180; single object, 529; and specification, 146; and speculation, 106–7, 109; spontaneous response, 298, 518; and stability, 568; statistical, 387, 556; subjectivity, 367; synthesised sound, 366; and taste, 75, 437; of technique, 108; of tempo, 369; temporal discontinuity, 513; of timbre, 371; of time, 73–4, 201, 367, 441; and understanding, 88, 89, 163, 168, 182, 283–4, 298–300, 324, 354, 381, 386, 397, 514, 521–2, 532; unexpected, the, 97, 99, 101–2, 134, 136, 296, 393; of unity, 272–3, 629; of vertical objects, 507, 511; voice, 367; and writing, 381, 385, 387–8; *see also* hearing

percussion, 258, 358, 376, 389, 399, 542, 548; accentuation, 44; anarchic procedures, 130; functions, 129; hierarchy, 122; history of, 43–4, 77, 374, 469, 523; indeterminacy, 122, 127; pitched/unpitched, 122, 217; resonance, 548; timbre, 122, 399; time-filling, 548; and transcription, 420; *see also* individual instruments

performance: approximation, 123, 125, 137–8; and chance, 265, 611–12; and choice, 139–40, 243, 261–2, 265, 271, 344, 554–5; collective, 143, 384; and complexity, 268; extensions, 554; and familiarity with score, 262, 268; and form, 430; and freedom, 270–1, 554;

gesture, 115, 268, 270; group, 538; imperfection, 269; improvisation, 115–16, 266, 271, 626; and impulse, 262; individual, 538; individuality, 123; initiative, 530; instinct, 431; and memory, 116, 446, 554; as model, 421, 423; objectivity, 136, 137–8; pathway selection, 121, 139, 141, 143; precision, 138; and style, 489; technique, 431; and technology, 115; tension, 611, 613; trajectory, 554–6; transformation, 554; as transmission, 136; virtuosity, 115; without performer, 269, 276

performance practice, historical, 58–9

periodicity, 152, 180, 216, 218, 353, 368, 508

permutation, 63, 68, 72, 99, 160, 163, 171, 175, 187, 241, 262, 263, 265, 275, 316, 323, 335, 340–1, 346, 349, 391, 565, 607–8; *see also* variation

phasing, 180, 365, 523

phrase/phrasing, 33, 80, 81, 151, 163, 164, 166, 178, 208, 209, 215, 226, 233, 235, 239, 253, 258, 267, 287, 352, 365, 370, 373, 382, 386, 389, 390, 415, 436, 439, 440, 461, 469, 512, 519, 521, 523, 530, 546, 586, 611, 612; and authenticity, 415; construction, 152; direction, 513; marks, 38; melodic, 81, 215, 218, 373; and respiration, 215; rhythmic, 74, 213

piano, 217, 258, 331, 364, 374, 378, 387, 414, 416; literature, 535, 595–6; out of tune, 359; prepared, 331; quarter-tone, 331; reduction, 419; resonance, 548, 612; transcription, 420

pianola, 489

Picasso, Pablo, 111, 285, 297

Piccinni, Niccolò, 417

Pirro, André, 103

pitch: absolute, 366–7, 489; and acoustic conditions, 489; dematerialised, 366; and determinacy/indeterminacy, xi, 121–3, 132; deviation, 489; dominance of, 366–7; and duration, 166, 232, 237, 346, 539–40, 566; elimination, 390; field of pitches, 326; filter, 351,

354, 390, 391; fluctuations, 331; and grid, 230; hierarchy, 90, 125, 142, 373, 375, 469; and idea, 90, 102, 302; intensity, 375; and intervals, 348, 378, 505; irregularity, 145–6; and modes, 281; multiplications, 250; and musical material, 174, 225; notation, 368, 370, 489, 528, 533, 541; organisation, 152; precision, 267; register, 94, 505; relative, 367, 489; retention, 337; and scales, 281, 527; schemes, 329; and serialism, 94, 225, 230, 240–1, 335, 563; signal, 506; similarity/difference, 225; and style, 489; substructure, 250; and transcription, 420; *see also* notation

pizzicato, 547

placement, 141, 235, 255, 264, 269, 487, 500, 505, 512, 534, 558, 565, 566, 569, 571; registral, 200, 346, 505–7

plainchant, 58–9, 489

playability/unplayability, 76, 77, 142

player piano, 177, 217

poetics, xxiv, 64, 195, 473, 493

poetry, 222, 284, 462; *see also* text

Pollock, Jackson, 389

polyphony, 64, 111, 144, 168, 192–3, 199, 201, 229, 230, 253, 256, 260, 306, 326, 332, 337–8, 346, 352, 375, 378–87, 396, 435, 451, 509, 511, 519, 599, 600, 611; accumulation, 337; density, 375–6; four-voice, 382; layering, 337; virtual, 522–3; vocal, 550; writing, 440; *see also* micropolyphony

polyrhythm, 396

polyvalence, 612, 613

pop music, 10, 606

popular music, 47, 128, 134, 283

post horn, 598

postmodernism, xxiv, 410, 464; eclecticism, 482

Pousseur, Henri, vii, viii; *Mobile*, xi

prelude and fugue, 144, 237, 594

primitives/primitivism, 179, 427

programme music, 105, 197

Proust, Marcel, 59, 88, 184, 592; *Jean Santeuil*, 182, 221 n. 1

provocation, 133, 565

proximity/distance, 100, 221, 335, 368, 375, 388, 392, 433, 434, 500, 502–5, 515, 520, 521, 554, 581, 628, 629; and distance, 96, 373, 573, 583

psalmody, 178

psychoacoustics, *see* acoustics

pulse/pulsation, 47, 55, 145–6, 176–8, 180, 218, 237, 240, 258, 268, 277, 368, 384, 390, 391, 488, 507, 528, 531, 534, 536–8, 540, 548, 550, 554, 557, 566, 567, 588; derivatives, 176; deviation, 488; and duration, 240; striated, 557

quarter-tones, 533

quotation, 134–6, 174, 218, 221, 277, 294

Racine, Jean, 416

radicalisation, 260, 562

ragas, 96

ragtime, 217

rallentando, 176, 180

Rameau, Jean-Philippe, 282, 417, 499

randomness, 29, 64, 66, 135, 138, 143, 243, 244, 258, 270, 304, 313, 339, 340, 380, 390–2, 407, 408, 435, 539, 555

Ravel, Maurice, 111, 136, 429, 489; and luthéal, 76

WORKS: *Gaspard de la nuit*, 596; *Miroirs*, 594, 596; *Suite bergamasque*, 596; *Le Tombeau de Couperin*, 596

rebellion/rebelliousness, 129, 174, 288, 462, 535; *see also* subversion; transgression

recapitulation, 159, 194, 196, 197, 200, 203, 325, 393, 505

recitative, 153, 155; and harmonic progression, 151; *recitativo arioso*, 151; *recitativo secco*, 151

recordings, xii, xiii, 11, 123, 406, 407, 420–3, 488, 606

register/registration, 13, 15, 34, 39, 94, 101, 124, 141, 142, 163, 165, 169, 172, 174, 200, 216, 229, 235, 242, 245, 253–6, 264, 267, 268, 298, 302, 304, 320, 321, 325, 326, 332, 335, 337, 338, 346, 349, 351–3, 361, 362, 364, 368, 371–3, 375, 376, 380, 381,

386, 387, 394, 396, 397, 400, 439, 442, 444, 453, 488–500, 503, 505–10, 512, 513, 516, 519–21, 523, 524, 537, 542, 543, 547, 548, 553, 556, 558, 563, 566, 568, 569, 580, 583, 611, 620, 621, 624, 625, 628; density, 229, 332; envelope, 264, 351, 352, 397; equivalence, 400; extremes of, 337, 375; fixed, 506, 519; as gel, 325; and intervals, 505, 507; nodes/antinodes, 142; and pitch, 505

rehearsal, 421, 432–3

relationality, 137–8, 140

religious music, *see* liturgical music

repertoire, 9, 204, 284, 291, 294, 369, 420, 428, 453, 474, 486; and authenticity, 414–16; durability, 76–7; familiarisation, 78; novelty, 78; replacement, 9; Romantic, 430

repetition, 27, 78, 90, 94, 99, 101, 102, 127, 131, 135, 140, 145, 153, 154, 156, 159, 163, 167, 168, 175, 178, 179, 195, 199, 214–16, 222, 223, 231, 234, 238, 249, 250, 258, 259, 293, 295–7, 320, 322, 335, 337, 342, 344, 361, 393, 395, 399, 430, 480, 508, 548, 573, 601, 602, 606, 616, 618, 625; *see also* non-repetition

reprise, 105, 145, 154, 156, 172, 195–7, 203, 205, 208, 215, 222, 293–5, 297, 328, 622

resonance, 145, 257–8, 339, 359, 364, 372–3, 385, 400, 420, 499, 525, 538, 547–9, 580, 583–4; and silence, 612

respiration, 215, 217

responsory, 260

rhapsody, 158

rhythm: articulation, 267; augmentation, 231; and codification, 90; complexity, 178, 375–6; compression, 466; density, 141; and determinacy/ indeterminacy, 122, 132; diminution, 231; displacement, 466; and duration, 240, 268; envelope, 352; equalisation/ disequalisation, 558; fixed/mobile, 218; and found objects, 130; handclapping, 127; and hierarchy, 152; and idea, 95, 102; imitation, 386; instability, 215; and intervals, 234,

239; irregularity, 145; and labour/ work, 127–8; notation, 369, 370, 528; phrasing, 74, 267; physiological, 130; and pitch, 239; processes, 332; repetition, 127, 231; and speed, 267; sub-notation, 539; symmetry, 127; synchronisation, 128; techniques, 600; and texture, 267

Richter, Hans, 421

Rimbaud, Arthur, 28; *Une Saison en enfer*, 18 n. 2

ritardando, 373, 488, 498

ritenuto, 369

Roma (film), 412

Romanticism/Romantics, 104, 144, 195–6, 204–5, 277, 288, 289, 303, 306, 334, 430, 505, 535, 589, 595–7, 598

rondo, 150, 156, 157, 168, 194, 230, 325, 328, 393, 430, 505, 594

row, twelve-note, 164–6, 169, 171–2, 229–30, 239, 244, 316, 319–21, 323, 325, 327–9, 336–7, 340–1, 440, 472; and hierarchy, 172, 343; and intuition, 343; subsets, 229; and theme, 165–6, 323; transpositions, 230; and unity, 166, 272; and variation, 238; *see also* serialism; twelve-tone technique

rubato, 176, 269

sacred musics, 411; *see also* liturgical music

Saint-Saëns, Camille, 468, 472–3, 484 n. 7

Satie, Erik, 471–2

saxophone, 76

scales, 46, 50, 90, 128, 165, 166, 208, 213, 215, 226, 255, 281, 329, 340, 346, 350, 351, 371, 373, 378, 469, 538, 544, 553; acoustic, 370; and chords, 350, 504–5; chromatic, 318; degrees, 165–6, 208; diatonic, 165; exclusion of, 469; hierarchy, 226, 287, 449; intervallic, 350; major/ minor, 208; pentatonic, 207, 208; semitone, 368; and series, 226; and steel pans, 128; virtual, 373; well-tempered, 292, 527, 528; whole-tone, 208, 282, 303, 472

Scarlatti, Domenico: sonatas, 601
Scherer, Jacques, 112
scherzo, 156, 198, 214, 294, 594, 595
Schloezer, Boris de, 34
Schnebel, Dieter: *Maulwerke*, xi
Schoenberg, Arnold, x, 23, 31, 40,
    60, 81, 92, 94–5, 100–1, 105, 108,
    111, 113, 151, 166, 183, 185,
    188–9, 194, 226–7, 231, 238, 241,
    260, 272, 288, 292, 297, 301–9,
    312–14, 316, 318–20, 323, 328–9,
    363, 375, 426–7, 462, 463, 471–2,
    475, 481–2, 494, 570, 575, 586,
    597; and constraint, 311–12, 333;
    counterpoint, 494; and deduction,
    306, 308; and harmonic language,
    303–4, 307–8, 313, 323, 494; and
    harmonium, 76; incorporation, 323;
    Klangfarbenmelodie, 373; models,
    463; notation, 123, 124; originality,
    463; and the past, 426–7; 'roving',
    356 n. 2; school of, 448; scores, 380;
    and serialism, 223, 233, 305–9, 318–
    19, 323, 472, 570, 575; *Sprechgesang*,
    123; and sub-theme/super-theme,
    302; and subversion, 127; and texts,
    153–5, 260; and tonality, 303, 313;
    and tradition, 309, 312–13; and the
    twelve-note row, 165, 241, 272, 302–
    3, 318, 320, 323, 343, 586; and unity,
    272, 302–3, 306
    WORKS: Five Pieces, op. 23, 108;
    Das Buch der hängenden Gärten,
    303; *Erwartung*, 23, 80–1, 95,
    113, 153, 154, 227, 525; First
    Chamber Symphony, 233, 586; Four
    Orchestral Songs, op. 22, 377, 401 n.
    4; Five Pieces for Orchestra, op. 16,
    304, 363, 419, 525; *Die glückliche
    Hand*, 113, 154; *Gurrelieder*, 31;
    Moses und Aron, 113, 155; *Ode to
    Napoleon*, 123, 304; *Pelleas und
    Melisande*, 597; *Pierrot lunaire*,
    123, 153–4, 200, 304, 597–8, 622–3;
    Suite, op. 29, 188–9; Variations for
    Orchestra, op. 31, 23, 31, 96, 100–1,
    328, 340; *Verklärte Nacht*, 29, 31,
    597; *Von Heute auf Morgen*, 80–1;
    Wind Quintet, op. 25, 308
    WRITINGS: 'Composition with

Twelve Tones', 356 n. 3, 591 n. 1;
    Structural Functions of Harmony,
    356 n. 2; *Style and Idea*, 256 n. 3, 484
    n. 8, 591 n. 1; *Theory of Harmony*,
    303
Schopenhauer, Arthur, 111
Schrade, Leo, 467
Schubert, Franz, 154, 195, 595;
    Die schöne Müllerin, 597; *Die
    Winterreise*, 597
Schumann, Robert, 195, 196, 429, 595;
    Albumblätter, 592; *Dichterliebe*, 597;
    Frauenliebe und -leben, 597; lieder,
    494, 497; *Moments musicaux*, 595
scordatura, 378
Scriabin, Alexander, 460; mystic chord,
    575
Second Viennese School, *see* Viennese
    School
sectionalisation, 100, 227
segmentation, 101, 114, 165, 167, 215,
    234, 244, 325, 331, 584, 610, 627
self-expression, 60
serialism, xvi, xxiii, 31, 81, 94, 101, 105,
    160, 227–30, 240–8, 264, 278 n. 4,
    305–8, 313, 315–18, 335, 472, 560,
    562, 563, 565, 570, 575; absolute,
    264; and choice, 248; and deduction,
    224, 230, 308; density, 245–6; and
    development, 229, 245; duration,
    563; dynamics, 245–6, 563; flexibility,
    248; and form, 308; and inequality,
    248–9; integral, 240–1, 243, 246, 333;
    and intervallic relationships, 223–5,
    230; and neutrality, 249; and order,
    333–4; and perception, 224–5, 229;
    pitch, 225, 245, 563; profile (playing
    style), 245; and referencing, 248, 305;
    and repetition, 223, 249; rhythm,
    335; techniques, 239; and theme,
    233, 240; and timbre, 246; total, 563;
    see also row, twelve-note; twelve-tone
    technique
serpent, 414
sieves, 340
Shakespeare, William, 111, 416;
    Hamlet, 407
shō, 495, 496
signification, 284, 486, 523, 526, 534,
    566, 574, 577, 599, 612, 613

signs, 537–40; altered, 537, 539; degeneration, 539; invented, 537; overloaded, 537

silence, 321, 513, 515, 519, 612

simultaneity, 88, 97, 106, 112, 124, 180, 215, 224, 225, 249, 250, 254, 305, 315, 341, 379, 384, 385, 440, 458, 494–6, 504, 505, 508, 510, 515, 522, 536, 541, 543, 550, 553, 570, 571, 581

sirens, 73, 330

Sistine Chapel, 413

sketches, *see* composition

sleigh bells, 130

solfège, 357, 449, 578

sonata/sonata form, 90, 150, 156, 157, 159, 168, 190, 194, 195, 205, 230, 287, 308, 324–5, 328, 393, 430, 438, 453, 505, 562, 593, 594, 601, 621, 623

song cycle, 597

sonic continuum, 330–1

sonorities, 599; opposed, 211

sound: brilliance, 375; in combination, 486, 487; complex, 374; contextualisation, 486; deconstruction, 486; frequency, 553; hierarchy, 552; identity, 486; internal structure, 552, 553; mass, 170; partials, 553; poverty, 487; production, 559; raw, 374, 420; reproduction, 11, 27; richness, 487; synthesised, 501; weight, 375; *see also* noise

sound blocks, 245, 249–52, 348, 579–80; deductions, 250; density, 250

Spanish music and culture, 207

specialisation, 70, 436–7

speed, 28, 124, 142, 146, 160, 176–8, 180, 197, 200, 212, 216, 242, 255, 267, 351, 365, 368, 369, 375, 389–91, 415, 498, 513, 514, 538, 544, 549, 552, 553, 567, 611; absolute, 6; relative, 6, 235

speed/duration binary, 369

spontaneity, 14, 23, 25, 31, 48, 49, 71, 74, 90–2, 109, 116, 119, 128, 130, 139, 141, 143, 144, 181, 194–6, 207, 208, 226, 262–4, 281–3, 286, 295, 298, 306, 316, 347, 354, 389, 427, 465, 488, 518, 530, 535, 561, 563, 566, 575–7, 584, 586, 588–90, 592, 609, 611–13, 626

stability, 59, 304, 310, 359, 387, 498, 500, 547, 568, 569, 573; *see also* instability

staccato, 141, 258, 415

stasis, 273, 283, 326, 425, 496; harmonic, 361; historical, 446, 449, 450

stasis/movement, 58, 143, 167, 175, 179, 326, 361

stave, 123, 124, 533

steel pans, 128, 146 n. 1

sterility, 35, 80, 109, 248, 267, 270, 281, 288–9, 294, 306, 309, 312, 330, 347, 406, 418, 422, 426, 449

Stockhausen, Karlheinz, vii, viii, 33, 177, 396, 591; *Aus den Sieben Tagen*, 591 n. 3; *Gruppen*, 177, 434; *Klavierstück XI*, xi; *Kreuzspiel*, 607; *Momente*, 396; *Texte zur Musik* ('Texts about Music'), viii

Strauss, Richard, 156, 159–61, 202, 306, 377, 462, 598; symphonic poems, 599

Stravinsky, Igor, xxv, 31, 56 n. 1, 105, 111, 134, 136, 154, 172–5, 177–9, 207, 213–20, 259–60, 288, 292–3, 296, 297, 312–13, 332, 363, 377, 396, 407, 421–3, 427, 463, 466–7, 478–9, 481, 596, 620; abstraction, 217; and authentic interpretations, 407, 421–3, 489; ballet, 427, 478; as conductor, 422–3; and conventional form, 179; detachment, 174; folk sources, 213, 215, 219; and found objects, 312; humour, 174; immobility/variance, 215–16; models, 218, 220, 463, 466–7; neoclassicism, 219–20; originality, 175, 463, 467, 478; and parody, 313; and the past, 427, 466; as performer, 407; and pianola, 489; recordings, 407; referencing, 217, 220, 313; rhythmic practice, 232–3, 479; rubato, 176; and rupture, 620; 'Russian' period, 215; scores, 380; thematicism, 172, 173, 213, 215–20; tonality, 296; and tradition, 312, 427 WORKS: *Berceuses du chat*, 596; *Dumbarton Oaks*, 219; early works, 427; *The Firebird*, 29, 478; *L'Histoire du soldat*, 173, 215, 217–19; *Lyriques japonaises*, 596; *Les*

Noces, 105, 175–9, 207, 215–17, 221
n. 3, 478, 567, 596, 620; *Petrushka*,
478; *Pribaoutki*, 596; *Pulcinella*,
220, 285; *Ragtime*, 173; *Renard*,
217; *The Rite of Spring* (*Le Sacre
du printemps*), ix, 33, 215–16, 218,
292–3, 363, 381–3, 478, 570, 622–3;
Le roi des étoiles, 596–7; *Russian
Peasant Songs*, 596; Symphonies
of Wind Instruments, 175, 178–80,
215–16, 396, 434, 620; *Three
Japanese Lyrics*, 215; *Zvezdoliki*
(*The King of the Stars*), 215
streaming, 513, 522
stretto, 192, 235
string instruments, 331, 385, 420, 523;
catgut, 414; tuning, 378
string quartet, 595
structure: amorphous, 266, 347–8;
archetypes, 197; and chance, 277;
closed, 340; coherence/incoherence,
388; complexity, 397; and duration,
601; and event, 63; evidence,
388; and external forces, 113; and
figure, 189–90, 325; fixed, 48–9;
harmonic, 187; and hierarchy, 90,
131; hollowed-out, 389; and idea, 91,
151, 563–4; incorporation, 322–5;
informal, 399; interaction, 351; and
intervals, 161; and language, 324;
and material, 63, 74, 82, 116–17;
mobility, 48–9, 142; partial, 140;
random, 340; and repetition,
156; rhythmic, 353, 508, 579;
and text, 157; and thematicism,
160; transformation, 556; *see also*
acoustics; macro-structure
stylising, 134
subjectivity, 23, 25, 33, 80, 97, 336, 367,
370, 371, 389, 410, 421, 422, 435,
439, 489, 536, 538, 557, 586
sub-theme, 302
subversion, 17, 127, 128, 202–4, 208,
211, 212, 577
succession, 38, 39, 62, 97, 98, 101, 141,
142, 144, 171, 204, 205, 225, 228,
233, 242, 245, 248–51, 255, 273, 276,
352, 366, 379, 392–5, 398, 440, 461,
491, 494, 496, 497, 503, 507, 510,
513, 515, 523, 545, 555–7, 563, 565,

566, 578, 579, 581, 586, 589, 594,
595, 603, 608, 610, 611, 613, 615–18,
620–4, 626–31; harmonic, 495;
temporal, 48, 62, 139, 225, 433, 515
suite, 204, 308, 593, 596, 623
superimposition, 180, 225–7, 230,
246, 440, 509, 512, 536, 541, 542,
563, 569–70, 626; of figures, 144; of
hierarchies, 243; of intervals, 615;
multiple, 524; of ostinatos, 233, 570;
of periodicities, 180; or resonances,
583–4; of transpositions, 245
super-theme, 302, 575
suppression, political, 463
surrealism, 18 n. 3, 63, 551; and
randomness, 66
suspension, 121, 132, 254, 572;
and memory, 254; temporal, 55;
trajectory, 254
Swedenborg, Emanuel, 307, 570
symbolism, 23, 106, 150, 159–60, 196,
314, 368, 443, 515, 516, 523, 539
symbols: formal, 150; intervallic,
150; and musical material, 66–7;
numerical, 106, 150, 160, 165, 314–
15, 516, 539
symmetry, 5, 81, 95–6, 100, 127, 165,
167–9, 215, 225, 228–9, 253, 293,
295, 319, 322, 323–5, 394, 493, 508;
and asymmetry, 325; distorted, 215;
intervallic, 324; numerical, 229
symphonic form, 105, 156, 195, 196,
198, 201–4, 210, 287, 293–5, 505,
593, 594
symphonic poem, 105, 599
symphonic tradition, 214
synchronisation, 128, 508–10, 536, 557
syncopation, 145
synthesis, 16, 27, 90, 164, 203, 255, 270,
333, 369, 432, 494, 497, 502, 532,
533, 535, 541, 545, 552, 566, 570,
574, 593, 596, 601, 603, 604, 614; and
memory, 629; retrospective, 604
synthesiser, 364–5, 377

tablature, 528
tam-tam, 122, 359–60, 363; resonance,
548
taste, *see* perception
technology, xii, xviii, 9–16, 36, 62, 78,

89, 115, 117, 217, 384, 528, 541, 544, 551, 556, 580; evolution, 551; impact of developments in, 78; and intervals, 383; and multiplication, 384; and performance, 115; sound transformation, 365–6; and writing, 551

tempo, 90, 122, 142, 145, 176–8, 180, 181, 200, 237, 242, 257, 346, 352, 368–70, 373, 385, 389–91, 415, 416, 423, 488, 489, 498, 499, 507–9, 512, 538, 539, 541, 544, 565–7, 585, 589, 596, 610, 612; alteration, 142; and characterisation, 160; chronometric, 538–9; complexity, 145; evolution, 180; fluctuations, 391; global, 538; and idea, 6, 90; and indeterminacy, 122; non-directional, 539; non-tempo, 146; notation, 489, 538–9; oscillation, 509–10; playability/ unplayability, 142; relationships, 145; unity, 176; see also notation; pulse/ pulsation; speed

tessitura, 142, 152, 346

text, 260, 439, 461; imagery, 112; mythological, 600; religious, 600; setting, 89, 91, 94–5, 110, 113, 153–5, 164, 549–50; spoken, 494; as stimulus, 105, 112–13; strophic structure, 112; unity, 164; see also articulation

texture, 73, 81, 101, 104, 141, 142, 145, 151, 152, 156, 160, 176, 199, 200, 212, 254, 255, 257, 267, 269, 306, 319, 332, 336, 346, 347, 352, 378, 379, 385, 389, 390, 400, 443, 502, 521, 538, 542–4, 546, 549, 559, 571, 576, 583, 597, 603, 604, 614, 620, 624, 628; and characterisation, 160; complex, 604; contrapuntal, 379; and form, 255; harmonic, 104, 151; organisation of, 156, 576; polyphonic, 199; statistical, 544; thematic, 104; undifferentiated, 73; unifying, 104; virtual, 521, 559

theatre, 110, 135, 150, 222, 407, 416, 417, 419, 593; costume, 418; imaginary, 135, 197, 294

theatre works, 89, 91, 110, 135, 196–7, 293–5, 597; and integration/ disintegration, 135; and structure, 157; see also theatre: imaginary; incidental music; music drama

thematic processes, xvi–xvii, 178, 231, 244, 254, 266–7, 277, 294, 303–4, 394, 438, 619; and tempo, 178, 181; virtual, 247

thematicism, xxiv, 157, 160–1, 170, 172, 174–5, 182–221, 232–4, 322–3, 341, 575, 601; analogy/difference, 182; and athematicism, 233–4, 237, 621, 624; and creativity, 220; distortion, 192; elaboration, 184–6, 188, 192; elimination of, 563; evolution, 194; and form, 195, 210, 217; found/ reformulated, 173; and inspiration, 183; intervallic, 443; motivic, 443, 444; and musical language, 192, 194; phrasing, 215; repetition, 201; rhythmic, 180, 215, 232; signals, 443–4; structural, 190; techniques, 210, 237–8; and variation, 238; see also athematicism; hyperthematicism; infrathematicism; ultrathematicism

theme, 33, 54, 90, 92, 96, 99–101, 104, 119, 144, 149–181, 182–221, 222–78, 281, 286, 287, 306–8, 311–13, 315, 318, 322–4, 328, 340, 362, 380, 393, 394, 438, 443, 444, 452, 453, 511, 517, 562, 575, 585, 586, 601, 602, 618, 619, 621–4, 630; all-theme, 242; borrowed, 188, 191, 207, 209; combination, 171; concentration/ fragmentation, 172; and creativity, 227, 229; deduction, 194–5, 201; and development, 90, 104, 150, 175, 185, 222, 601; economy, 202; elaboration, 188; evolution, 149–81; exposition, 601; and form, 150, 191, 194, 197, 222; function, 191–2, 202; generation, 227, 228; and hierarchy, 104, 167, 601, 602; and history, 186; identity, 187–9, 222–78, 383; and language, 197; main, 202, 210; non-theme, 242; ornamentation, 187, 189, 212; potential, 195; principal, 194; repetition, 201; and rhythm, 226, 232; and row, 165; secondary, 202, 210; serialism, 233; significance, 191; static/dynamic, 444; sub-theme/

super-theme, 302; subordinate, 194; and symbolism, 159; symphonic, 452; transitional, 194, 202, 210; and unity, 149, 151, 153, 162–3, 165, 167, 176, 234; and variation(s), 100–1, 150; virtual, 340; *see also* hypertheme; infratheme; leitmotiv

timbre, x, xi, 6, 31, 34, 40, 46–50, 55, 64, 65, 102, 110, 114, 121, 122, 130, 131, 152, 163, 164, 174, 178, 179, 217, 228, 229, 239, 242, 255, 258, 281, 291, 302, 332, 333, 335, 336, 339, 351, 359, 361, 363–6, 371–3, 375, 376, 377, 380, 381, 384–7, 389, 396, 399, 400, 419, 420, 438, 439, 469, 497, 498, 501, 505, 508, 510, 512, 513, 520, 524, 525, 527, 528, 541, 547, 549, 552, 553, 563, 566, 583, 603, 620, 625; and authenticity, 410; blurring, 375; categorisation, 371; combination, 375–6; differentiated, 350; discontinuity, 371; and electroacoustics, 102; envelope, 351, 563; fusion, 361; and idea, 152; identification, 375; identity, 522, 547; and indeterminacy, xi, 121–2, 131; instrumental, 102, 439; logic, 333; and musical material, 174, 178, 239–40; notation, 371, 528; and serialism, 241; simplification of, 110; and system, 281; and transcription, 420; *see also* articulation

time: chronometric, 145, 242, 557; and duration, 565; extension in, 599; hierarchy, 131; non-directional, 145; non-periodic, 385; non-pulsed, 548; notation, 125; pulsed, 277; real/ virtual, 440–1; and rhythm, 565; segment/slice of, 68, 120, 139, 614; smooth, 240, 277, 355, 531; striated, 240, 277, 355; structuring of, 607; subjective, 557; sub-notation, 538; unmeasured, 539; and writing, 440

time-distance, 125

time–pitch coordinates, 126

timpani, 122, 127, 177, 216, 217, 420; pitch relationship, 127

tonality, 3, 46, 60, 153, 160, 211, 282, 292, 303, 308, 313, 316, 318, 361, 491, 505, 568, 575, 593, 600; breakdown of, 60; chromatic, 282, 313; close/remote, 160; connotations, 103; elimination of, 153; enlarged, 211; establishment of, 292; and form, 505; and harmonic function, 338; and hierarchy, 93, 561, 600, 601; language of, 491; longevity of, 3; and pitch, 4, 282; and serialism, 316, 318; signal, 505; standardisation, 99; suspension of, 303; tonic–dominant relationship, 160, 218

totality, 25, 38, 105, 398, 564, 592, 599, 631

tradition, xvii, 4, 5, 29, 46–8, 58, 64, 75, 80, 101, 130, 143, 150, 154, 155, 158, 160–3, 172, 175, 179, 181, 186, 198, 199, 202, 204, 207, 213, 217, 224, 226, 259, 260, 283, 288, 289, 307, 309, 312, 315, 322, 328, 329–32, 334, 382, 405–7, 418, 421, 422, 425, 427, 435, 441, 454, 462, 469, 473, 474, 477–82, 495, 498, 527, 539, 540, 559, 599, 600, 610, 615, 629; chants, 128; choral music, 327; classical, 196, 572; dance, 128; dissolution of, 205; European, 5, 170, 172, 175, 194, 427, 482, 571; folk, 215; form, 328, 630; Gregorian, 283; harmonic, 208, 379, 386, 570; hierarchy, 75, 329, 574; instruments, 332, 607; late-Romantic, 597; learned, 221; metre, 332; musical material, 80, 213; national, 207; non-European, 58, 59, 293, 331; notation, 6, 36, 450, 487, 531–4, 540, 541, 558; oral music, 488; popular, 478; rejection of, 42; scales, 128; stylistic, 9; symphonic, 196, 202, 214, 233; tuning, 527; writing, 321, 533; *see also* oral tradition; Western musical tradition

traditional musics, 331; transcription, 213–14

transcription, 6, 36, 41, 54, 61, 104, 106, 113, 114, 123, 125–8, 130, 169, 213, 214, 339, 369, 391, 419, 451, 454, 485–8, 491, 492, 515, 516, 522, 526–59, 564, 576, 577, 589, 590; and authenticity, 420; and electroacoustic music, 61, 486; four-part, 492; graphic, 487–8; idiomatic,

127; lexical, 127; means of, 454; new methods of, 451

transgression, 8, 31, 41, 45–6, 50, 109–10, 288, 316, 365, 366, 382, 386, 393, 450, 451; conventions, 126; and liberation, 109; and system, 288

transition, 31, 111, 159, 167, 170, 175–7, 190, 206, 210, 227, 232, 234, 235, 237, 256, 273–6, 294, 328, 336, 340, 341, 371, 383, 393, 396, 407, 430, 431, 438, 501, 502, 523, 557, 564, 572, 574, 585, 594, 595, 597, 605, 612, 619–21, 629; athematic, 166; coherence, 199; and harmonic progressions, 193; perpetual, 210, 396, 426, 620; and theme, 194, 202, 210

transition–caesura dialectic, 275–6

transmission, xvii, 9, 32, 52, 57, 58, 88, 115, 117, 130, 136, 149, 207, 244, 410, 411, 421, 426, 448, 515, 527, 556; and oral tradition, 411

transposition, 99, 101, 172, 224, 230, 241, 245, 249, 264, 285, 291, 305, 307, 308, 337, 349, 351, 441, 504, 506, 528, 544, 565, 611, 621

tremolo, 548

trickery, 135

trill, 548, 549

trombone, 598

trope, xvii, xxv

trumpet, 420

tuning: conventional, 499

turn, 338

twelve-tone technique, x, 22, 81, 94–5, 108, 160, 165, 171, 190, 228–9, 318, 322, 335, 575, 578, 586; deduction, 95, 322; derivation, 322–3; exemplification, 95; and identification, 224; see also row, twelve-note; serialism

ultrathematicism, 223, 231

uncertainty, 32, 68–70, 145, 185, 209, 210, 219, 313, 333, 345, 361, 389, 392, 400, 401, 424, 426, 467, 522, 546, 553

unfolding, 67, 203, 326, 327, 336, 381, 389, 392, 396, 398, 452, 485

unity, 5, 23, 38, 46, 101, 129, 134, 135, 149, 151, 153, 161–7, 170, 172, 173, 176, 194, 201, 223, 224, 230, 232, 234, 255, 259, 269, 270, 272–3, 276–8, 288, 297, 302–4, 306, 315, 318, 322, 338, 343, 373, 387, 395, 479, 507, 508, 517, 531, 538–40, 545, 561, 570–2, 592, 598, 599, 601, 606, 619, 620, 629; deductive, 318; and diversity, 306, 601; false, 565; hostility to, 598; thematic, 303

utopianism, 35, 540, 570, 571, 575, 613

Valéry, Paul, 183; *Degas, Manet, Morisot*, 484 n. 6

Varèse, Edgard, xxv, 111, 127, 172, 174–5, 292–3; deduction, 174; musical material, 175; rebellion, 174; and sirens, 73; and subversion, 127; thematicism, 172, 174–5; titles, 113–14

WORKS: *Amériques*, 175; *Arcana*, 175; *Hyperprisme*, 114; *Intégrales*, 114; *Ionisation*, xi, 122, 123, 420

variables/variability, 49, 55, 82, 122, 131, 132, 145, 163, 171, 194, 216, 230–3, 251, 254, 263, 269, 270, 309, 323, 324, 331, 363, 367, 371, 375, 390, 438, 478, 495, 496, 504–6, 509, 526, 527, 538, 539, 543, 544, 553, 579, 582, 583, 596, 599, 612, 613

variants, 104, 156, 442, 489, 490, 511, 526, 613, 615, 628

variation, 30, 31, 66, 90, 96, 100–1, 121, 125, 131, 140–2, 144, 150, 154, 156–9, 165–8, 172, 175, 182–221, 222–78, 287, 293, 297, 308, 311, 318, 320, 323, 328, 331, 340, 341, 344, 345, 367, 379, 381, 385, 388, 400, 411, 415, 420, 430, 490, 495–7, 500, 501, 508, 519, 520, 550, 554, 555, 566, 576, 579, 580, 588, 595, 601, 611, 613, 615, 617, 620, 622, 623, 628; absolute, 241–2; and aleatoric works, 344; and deduction, 95, 144; form, 177, 187–9, 191–2, 194, 199, 308, 328, 340, 601, 623; harmonic progression, 188, 193; and memory, 100; ornamentation, 100; permutation, 187; principle of, 297; and serialism, 248, 320; techniques, 140–1, 175

Velázquez, Diego, 285
Verdi, Giuseppe, 462
Verfremdung, 288, 423
verse–response pairing, 175
vibraphone, 76, 364; resonance, 548, 612
vibration, 62, 570; duration, 399
vibrato, 414
Vieira da Silva, Maria Helena, 389
Viennese School, 31, 60, 71, 105, 153, 170, 171, 194, 288, 292, 296–7, 299, 301, 305–6, 309–10, 329, 332, 462, 466, 474, 482, 514, 562, 570, 571, 576, 620–1; coherence, 332, 333; dissonance, 568; expressionism, 514; and form, 259; and the past, 426; rhythmic organisation, 231–2; series v. theme, 621; and system, 301; and texts, 299; texture, 576; and tradition, 309, 329; unity, 571; utopianism, 570; *see also* Berg, Alban; Schoenberg, Arnold; Webern, Anton
viola, 257
viola da gamba, 523
violin piccolo, 523
virtual object, 225, 340, 500
virtuosity, 29–31, 47, 89, 115, 117, 192, 284, 300, 317, 372, 515, 542, 545, 546
visual arts, 427, 462, 470, 481, 606; correspondence with music, 111–12, 114–15, 133, 285–6, 355, 389, 413, 467, 468, 525, 570, 606–7
Vivaldi, Antonio: sonatas, 601
vocabulary, *see* language, musical
vocal music, 91, 123, 127, 128–9, 152; affinity/contrast with instruments, 129, 164; coloration, 130; discontinuity, 372; expressiveness, 129, 152; folk music, 129; and hierarchy, 129; incantation, 129; labour songs, 129; melisma, 378; and respiration, 216, 217; syllabic synchrony, 327; and text, 129; timbre, 130; *see also* performance; *Sprechgesang*
voice: articulation, 129–30, 372; breath, 372; consonants, 372; dynamics, 370, 372; phonemic inflection, 508; register, 372; speech, 367;

synthesised, 365; timbre, 372, 439; vowels, 372
voice-crossing, 386
voice-leading, 192, 381, 382, 492, 569
volume, 414, 416, 547; excessive, 73

Wagner, Cosima, 155, 198, 421
Wagner, Richard, 23–4, 88, 95, 103, 111, 150, 152, 155–6, 160, 161, 185, 195–200, 203, 209, 210, 253, 292–4, 355, 361, 363, 370, 381, 396, 407, 409, 417, 421–2, 427, 434, 461, 462, 465, 468, 472, 473, 524, 562, 571, 593, 595, 620; and authentic interpretations, 407, 421–2; bar form, 453; dramatic development, 201; harmonic language, 303, 472; leitmotivs, 150, 155, 253, 434, 602; narrative, 200; school of, 465; sketchbooks, 185; symbolism, 196; and tradition, 473; transition, 210, 294
WORKS: *Lohengrin* Prelude, 361; *Parsifal*, 177, 209, 293, 421–2; *Rheingold* Prelude, 361, 524; *The Ring*, 421–2, 468, 473, 592–3; *Siegfried's Tod*, 592–3; *Tristan und Isolde*, 290, 293, 295, 619; *Die Walküre*, 524, 593
Weber, Carl Maria von, 427
Webern, Anton, 22, 31, 37, 38, 92, 94–5, 110–11, 151, 161–9, 176, 185, 189–90, 194, 226–30, 232, 301, 303, 312, 317–29, 340, 386–7, 394, 439–41, 444, 448, 478, 479, 481–2, 506, 519–20, 575, 596, 616, 617, 631; and coherence, 317–18, 327, 332, 354; and deduction, 162–3, 165, 166, 168, 317–18, 322–3, 479; and duty, 317; and harmonic language, 303–4, 323; and harmonium, 76; Idea and Image, 168–9; and incorporation, 322–3; and intervallic structure, 161–2; Order, 169, 318; plans, 395; and repetition/non-repetition, 163, 168, 318, 320, 322, 394, 603; scores, 380; and serialism, 228, 232, 249, 318–22, 325, 440–1, 575; temporal folding/unfolding, 327; and texts, 153, 163–4; and thematicism, 161–2,

164, 166, 169, 190, 322–3; and tradition/history, 309, 322, 479; and transcendence, 144; and the twelve-note technique, 164, 167–9, 176, 190, 228, 318–19, 321–2, 324–5, 327, 343; and unity, 322, 479; and the voice, 164
WORKS: Four Songs, op. 13, 23, 303; Five Movements for string quartet, op. 5, 162, 304, 326; Five Pieces for Orchestra, op. 10, 162, 596; Five Sacred Songs, op. 15, 23; Six Pieces for Orchestra, op. 6, 162; Six Songs, op. 14, 23; *Das Augenlicht*, 387; Bagatelles for string quartet, op. 9, 162, 168, 596; Cantata no. 1, 326–7, 387; Cantata no. 2, op. 31, 304, 326–7, 369, 387, 439–42; cantatas, 164; Concerto for Nine Instruments, op. 24, 319, 321, 324, 325; lieder, 163–4, 260; *Passacaglia*, op. 1, 29, 190; Quartet, op. 22, 109; Second Cantata, 176; String Quartet, 33; String Trio, op. 20, 304, 319; Symphony, op. 21, 172, 194, 304, 319, 320–1, 325, 386, 387, 519; Three Little Pieces for cello and piano, op. 11, 394, 596; Two Songs, op. 19, 319; Variations for Orchestra, op. 30, 96, 109, 190, 232, 304, 328, 388, 519–20; Variations for Piano, op. 27, 96, 168–9, 190, 323, 340
WRITINGS: correspondence, 168; *The Path to the New Music*, xvii, 94, 118 n. 2, 181 n. 1, 318, 356 n. 6
Wehinger, Rainer, 83 n. 3
Wessel, David, xi, xix
Western musical culture/tradition, 35–6, 47, 58–60, 96, 101, 103, 127, 128, 136, 152, 181, 215, 216, 267, 283, 292, 297, 330, 373, 382, 417, 462, 469, 474, 495, 573, 615, 618
wind instruments, 73, 123; breath, 372; key clicks, 133; multiphonic sound, 358; unpitched breathing, 133; woodwind, 372
word setting, *see* text setting
work, *see* composition
work songs, *see* labour songs
writing, 560–91; absolute/relative,

342–3, 505; abstract/actual, 543; acoustic, 574; amorphousness/fixity, 557; and arithmetical speculation, 517; articulation, 551; aural experience, 491; and authenticity, 419; canonical, 144, 169, 229, 328, 439, 440, 479, 520, 604; chord types, 491; clarity, 381; codes, 358, 360, 492, 560; coherence, 310, 342, 474, 504–6, 551, 589; cohesion, 521; and composer, 490; as concept, 485–525; concrete elements, 383, 385; connection/connectedness, 486, 551, 574; constants/variables, 505–6; constraint, 311, 346, 617; continuity, 486; convergence, 551; counterpoint, 491, 493, 494; and creativity, 490, 542, 560, 591; deduction, 342, 551, 591; description, 496, 497–8; development, 486; diversity, 589; duty, 342; dynamics, 583; exceptionality, 574; extrapolation, 377; fictive, 498; and form, 396–8, 550, 560, 591, 622; freedom, 342, 577, 581; fugue, 491; for groups, 543–4; harmony, 144, 491, 493, 495; and hearing, 382, 491, 493, 515, 518; heterogeneity, 573; heterophony, 511; hierarchy, 490, 493, 552, 560, 574, 618; horizontal elements, 511–12, 514–15; hyper-reality, 525; and idea, 560–91; and identity, 386, 504, 544; illusion, 384, 385, 401, 524, 543–4; implied, 521; instrumental, 438, 543, 550–2, 557–8; interval, 583; intuition, 575, 583; learned, 389; meaning, 310; mechanistic, 575; melismatic, 549–50; and melodic line, 383; and memory, 429; methods of, 515; and multiplication, 384; and musical history, 451; narrative, 366; non-instrumental, 555–7, 559; for orchestra, 338–9, 525, 543; orchestration, 524, 543–4; ornamentation, 510; parallelism, 496–7, 504; and perception, 385, 387–8; for percussion, 548; and performer, 490; plasticity, 401; precision, 358; principles, 310, 356; real, 383–4, 521, 523, 525, 544; reality, 310, 401;

reciprocity, 346; register, 510, 583; resonance, 548; rhythm, 510; and science, 517; separateness, 574; signification, 574, 613; sonic, 490, 493, 514, 552; stasis, 496; statistical, 581; study of, 451; sub-structure, 557; succession, 379; superimposition, 557; syllabic, 549–50; and technology, 551; temporal concurrence, 379; texture, 546; and thinking, 531; timbre, 524–5, 552, 583; and time, 440; tonality, 491; transcription, 491–2, 529, 530, 589–90; and transgression, 451; and the unconscious, 590; undifferentiated, 547–8; vertical objects, 494–9, 501–7, 511–13; virtual, 383–4, 498, 521–3, 525, 558; virtuosity, 545–6; for voice, 549–50; *see also* composition

Xenakis, Iannis, vii, 114
xylophone, 77, 217

zeitgeist, 207, 474
Zhdanov, Andrei, 462
Zola, Émile, 592